Saturday's Child

Saturday's Child

A MEMOIR

Robin Morgan

W. W. NORTON & COMPANY
NEW YORK LONDON

For information about permission to reproduce selections from this book, write to
Permissions, W. W. Norton & Company, Inc., 500 Fifth Avenue, New York, NY 10110

The text of this book is composed in Fairfield Light
Composition by Sue Carlson
Manufacturing by Maple-Vail Book Manufacturing
Book design by Lovedog Studio

Library of Congress Cataloging-in-Publication Data
Morgan, Robin.
Saturday's child : a memoir / by Robin Morgan.
p.   cm.
Includes bibliographical references and index.
ISBN 0-393-05015-7
1. Morgan, Robin. 2. Authors, American—20th century—Biography.
3. Feminists—United States—Biography. I. Title.
PS3563.O87148 Z477 2000
818'.5409—dc21

[B]   00-055445

W. W. Norton & Company, Inc., 500 Fifth Avenue, New York, N.Y. 10110
www.wwnorton.com

W. W. Norton & Company, Ltd., 10 Coptic Street, London WC1A 1PU
1 2 3 4 5 6 7 8 9 0

For those of you who turned immediately
to the index of this book.

But really for Blake Morgan.

Monday's child is fair of face,
Tuesday's child is full of grace,
Wednesday's child is full of woe,
Thursday's child has far to go,
Friday's child is loving and giving,
Saturday's child has to work for a living,
But a child that's born on the Sabbath day
Is fair and wise and good and gay.

—Anonymous

Contents

Part One

Part Two

Acknowledgments

This is a brave book—which is not to imply that its author is courageous. On the contrary, *Saturday's Child* got itself written despite quite a few obstacles, including my own resistances to writing it. This is the first book of mine that was not my own idea (and the last). Mary Cunnane, my previous editor at W. W. Norton, urged me years ago to do a memoir, believing that the somewhat bizarre life I've led would make for fascinating reading. I declined. There were other books I was working on, and still others I had planned. Furthermore, I felt that memoir writing as a genre had in contemporary times largely declined to an exercise in self-promotion by people who are not now, never have been, and never will be *writers*. Over the years Mary wore me down. Then, once I finally began the book, she blithely quit New York publishing and moved to Australia, reconstituting herself as a literary agent. As her friend I wished her well. As her author I wished a koala bear would tumble from a eucalyptus tree onto her head. Now, having completed the book, I thank her for the idea and for her pursuit of it. This is all her fault.

Fortune has blessed me with my current editor, Angela von der Lippe, whose dedication to literary excellence is equaled by a subtle sense of humor and a sophisticated grasp of politics. It's rare to find any editor whose sensibility you can trust with poetry as well as both fiction and nonfiction prose; Angela is such a one. I'm grateful for her editing and her friendship.

The members of the Sisterhood Is Global Institute, and my friends Jessica Neuwirth and Pamela Shifman of Equality Now, deserve special acknowledgment for having given me the excuse to interrupt this book at every possible opportunity because of some crisis in the national or international Women's Movement. Without the aid of these activists, I'd have missed a bit of fun and the manuscript would have been finished eight months earlier.

Thanks also are due to certain people without whose help the memoir would never have been finished at all.

In 1997, while a visiting scholar at the University of Denver for three months, I had all the files for the book—including old journals, clipping files, scrapbooks, and early chapter drafts—shipped to Colorado in a huge carton via Federal Express: I planned to work on the memoir between teaching duties and political-organizing shenanigans. FedEx *lost* the carton. This is a writer's nightmare. Almost a year and a half later, some of the contents were finally located, fire- and water-damaged, in one of FedEx's "Overgoods Centers"—a euphemism for what I learned are its many enormous warehouses crammed with packages it has misplaced. During the intervening months, my murderous impulses were kept in check by my attorney, Loni Adler, whose innovative legal maneuvers to get FedEx's attention were matched only by her refusal to give up. Watching this five-foot-tall woman confront the arrogant corporate power of Federal Express would have been a treat even if we hadn't won, which we did.

I'm also grateful to various friends who lent me their recollections. Somewhere in your fifties, you come to rely increasingly on collective memory: it can take five intelligent women at dinner fifteen minutes of working in tandem to piece together a single name—which then bursts out in a hallelujah of communal triumph. In this regard, appreciation is due to the usual suspects, the friends who've been there for me and for my work over the years, especially Andrea Dworkin, Theresa Funiciello,

Edite Kroll, Suzanne Braun Levine, Isel Rivero, Lois Sasson, and Gloria Steinem, all of whom let me "interview" them regarding periods in our interwoven lives. Mary Thom and Joanne Edgar were generous with specifics of our mutual years at *Ms.*, and Susan Brownmiller was helpful jogging my recollections about portions of the late 1960s and early 1970s. It's impossible to interview oneself, but I recalled how perceptive Maria Nadotti's questions had been in the taped book-length interview she'd done with me in 1995 (published in Italian as *Cassandra non abita più qui: Maria Nadotti intervista Robin Morgan,* by La Tartaruga edizioni, in Milan, 1996); her questions had addressed certain aspects of my life I'd not engaged before, and had elicited startling answers. So I'm thankful that Maria, with the help of her sons Paolo and Emiliano Benzi and the transcriber Diana Cook-Turano, went to some lengths to track down the long-lost original English-language transcript of the interview; it served this memoir well.

In the category of General Survival, appreciation is due to Jacqueline Lapa for her valuable advice during the early 1980s, and particularly to Carol Drexler, whose compassionate, wise counsel was of such importance during the bleak period described in Chapter 18. Deborah Ann Light's friendship and support continue to be expressed in multiple ways warranting multiple celebratory gratitudes. Alida Brill has lovingly offered a wide repertoire of sustenance, including taking time from her own writing to read parts of this manuscript.

Blake Morgan has done pretty much all of the above, while juggling the tribulations of his own life, writing terrific songs, and making me laugh. Those are only four of the thirteen hundred reasons this book is dedicated to him.

As for literary influences, I owe thanks to Wallace Stevens and Luigi Pirandello for, respectively, the poem and play that inspired the titles and formats of this book's Prologue and Epilogue. I'm also indebted to myself. For decades, earlier me's have drafted my experiences as subject matter into the service of (hopefully good) writing and politics. Writers do this sort of thing. But having already exposed so many aspects of my life—in poetry, fiction, and nonfiction—made the writing of this memoir both more difficult and easier. The difficulty involved refusing merely to repeat myself but trying to dig deeper beneath material I had previously used in order to reach what I hadn't dared approach before. In some cases, though, if a specific experience had already been depicted as well and fully as it ever would be, it was easier and more honest to resort to plagiarism. (After all, if you can't steal from yourself, whom *can* you steal from?) I wouldn't want some future doctoral candidates to think they'd stumbled across a scandal in spying a similarity now and then, so let me say that I've here recycled certain phrases or the occasional paragraph from earlier books of mine, as well as reclaimed certain incidents previously rendered. Reality in this case tells a better story than invention.

It's been quite a challenge, finding a style capable of carrying off the truth.

Robin Morgan
April 2000
New York City

Thirteen Ways of Looking at a Memoir

1.

Rummaging through storage, you come across a single roller skate. And find yourself staring, following it into that space where its broken mate and long-lost key still exist; find yourself standing motionless except for the finger flick that absently spins one of the pitted wheels. Around you, a sense of speed is reconstructing itself—subtle adjustments of balance, sting of wind-rush in your eyes, the peripheral blur of cityscape passing, one particular gold-leafed October afternoon, an entire autumnal season.

Memory, the original virtual reality, operates doubly like a hologram or a synecdoche: it's vividly unreal, and the enlargeable whole is nested in each of its fragments.

A memory is the cousin of a dream.

2.

Memories have nothing to do with fact.

When the content of a memory can be collectively agreed upon by a sufficient number of people—or by a few people with the power to encode their version of reality—the memory gets passed on, in a kind of Darwinian selection, until it acquires the patina of history. But time and successive waves of interpretation scar the surface and erode the substance. As details gradually crumble, the best—sometimes the only—fixative is invention, however much that might be denied by those who care more about facts than about truths.

Memory is the reason rhyme was conceived, writing was invented, painting, sculpture, musical scoring, and choreographic labanotation were devised. The great library at Alexandria was a skull housing the memories of the ancient world, lost forever to Caesar's flames.

Memory is why writers, artists, and musicians create.

Vintage memory always mellows into fiction. Even into myth.

3.

Lavender, a ghostly fragrance even when fresh, rubbed on the wrists of a dying aunt. A lover's way of frowning. The message, even if you can't understand the words, in a voice dropping to a whisper. The features of a lost, dreamt, parent's face. Taffeta's slink against an ankle. The stored taste that distinguishes an orange from a tangerine from a grapefruit.

Memory moves as a process of accumulation, shards of experience floating toward each other along mysterious currents beyond their control, then lodging together the way a reef amasses itself from living coral bodies and dead coral corpses. (There's that memory you're alone with, that moment only you remember. . . .) At the same time, memory moves in a process of increasing *dis*order—of entropy, as our individual recollections, along with our individual consciousnesses, flicker, flare brilliantly, then wink out and vanish into the black holes of a universe indifferent as any Alzheimer's-sequined brain resembling it. (There's that anecdote in someone else's summary of you, your whole life encapsulated into a moment you yourself have completely forgotten. . . .)

But always—whether rough or precise, partial or expansive, vivid or vague, acknowledged or denied—memory is art.

It may be good art or bad art; it may even be kitsch. But art it is, the remembered subject having been elevated to a prominence beyond mere artifice not by ethical virtue and not always with craft, but simply through choices decided in lateral leaps by the unconscious.

The question is: how to make it good art?

4.

I dreamed I kicked the door shut behind me, dropped my keys, shuffled the mail, and left it scattered across my desk. Then I hit the playback button and half listened to phone messages while drifting through the rooms like a sleepwalker, undressing, fixing a bite to eat. . . . I can't remember at what point I flopped down across the bed, diagonally, only for a moment, just to stretch out—but fell asleep and . . . dreamed I sat at my desk, writing a recollection of having slept so realistically it might have been a form of waking: it had an almost discernible meaning—as if a key were turning in the lock, a door opening . . .

So I kicked the door shut behind me, dropped my keys, shuffled the mail, and left it scattered across my desk. . . .

5.

"Paths delude us into thinking we're not lost."

I wrote that years ago, and thought it was a pretty good line. Now I think it was a touching sign of youth that I imagined I saw paths at all.

Now I know that any honest writer has to acknowledge wandering the terrain of a memoir like an archaeologist in Laos roaming the Plain of Jars, able only to speculate about what really took place: whether this was a burying ground, a religious-ritual site, a storage area; why one stone jar is ten feet tall and others tiny enough to be held in one palm, why there are hundreds of jars, empty jars, broken jars, perfectly intact jars, jars filled with centuries-old silt, and jars filled with recent as-yet-unevaporated rain.

There are differing theories, but the real story eludes everyone.

So it's no use asking, because there's no one to answer.

6.

Maybe it's better to think of memory as a garden, a work simultaneously in progress and in retrospect. I like this metaphor, since I came late but passionately to gardening. Then again, as garden writer Robin Chotzinoff has noticed, "There are no child prodigy gardeners," and lateness is subjective. When I was in my existentialist teens, the phrase "Dirty Hands" meant to me not soiled fingers but the Jean-Paul Sartre play by that title. Though I still love the play, today its title first brings to mind weeding, deadheading, spreading compost, planting bulbs. Today I understand how memory, like a garden, has at least eight dimensions: width, length, height, depth, temperature, time, moisture/aridity, and chiaroscuro—the play of light and shade. Furthermore, just because the gardener has planned and toiled for certain results is no guarantee things will grow that way—water, mulch, or fertilize as she will.

Gardens and memories are useful cures for hubris.

7.

By the time anyone has earned enough years to write a memoir, aging has bestowed a bemusingly selective memory that seems to kick in (or rather out) starting around one's late forties. It's a mild disability, but one that nevertheless can escalate memoir writing into more of a Grail-quest challenge than it might be if one were young enough not to have had the experiences one is now old enough to share but not always recall.

As for objectivity, well really. How is that possible? Even quantum physicists no longer believe in the existence of objectivity. On the other hand, though memory lives along a slippery incline, there have to be some limits, at least some *traction,* to the slippage. If honesty means daring to trust the politics of the subjective, it also means admitting, in my case, a personal dread of sliding over the edge, damning myself to circles of Lillian Hellishmania.

Thank god memoir is by definition a reasonably subjective genre— unlike autobiography, which bolsters its pretense to objectivity by flaunting footnotes.

In essence, nothing is more subjective than memory.[1]

8.

Bracing advice to Reluctant Memoirist (RM) self:

"Look, dear. Friends, acquaintances, readers, strangers, and your publisher all seem to think you've led an unusually interesting life. You might think so too, if you hadn't been there every moment. You know how it looks: baby model/child actor/teen TV star, grows up to be a poet and marry another poet who's also a founder of the Gay Liberation Front, has a child by him and stays married for twenty years; a mother, a political activist for three decades, a feminist theorist, a novelist, playwright, journalist, editor, organizer, divorcee; and the lover of two different women in substantive physical and emotional relationships, all before turning fifty. What others think of your life is hilariously romantic, exotic, even perverse: Show-biz kid! TV's little sweetheart! Bloomsbury lifestyle bohemian! Drugs/sex/rock 'n' roll Sixties Yippie! Civil-rights worker, militant revolutionary, temporary terrorist! Jailbird! Passionate poet! Wild-eyed radical feminist! Broom-riding world traveler! Bra burner/radical mother/lesbian orgiast!"

Little do they know how tame and wholesome it's been.

Little do they know that, looking back, it all dissolves before what remains as the sole consistent reality. day after year after decade of hunching at various desks, trying to wrestle nouns toward precision, intensify verbs, and cut, cut, cut adjectives.

9.

And trying to invoke the descent of exact metaphor as if it were grace—that mysterious visitation for which you must always be in an attentive state of readiness, but which, no matter how you try (and try you must), you can never earn.

What is a sense memory, anyway, but a vivid metaphor?

[1] Except amnesia.

The nap of that sapphire-blue crushed-velvet princess dress with satin frog buttons my five-year-old self loved so—which wound up being donated by my mother to the Franciscan priest who requested it.

The nervous, almost sexual tension of waiting, in full costume and makeup, for my entrance cue, standing behind the set: that smell . . . plaster dust! That basketweave grey canvas backing of the painted brick "wall." The chalky rub of white shoe-polish smears on my eight-year-old hands.

The warm scent of my mother's terrycloth bathrobe, a dark bronze cinnamon musk laced with faint almond and not-quite-turned cream.

They say the oldest sense is olfactory, lodged in the remaining corner of what was once our reptilian brain.

If so, perhaps a snake thinks in metaphor.

10.

OK. No more procrastinating. Ways of organizing a memoir:

Chronologically: "The first thing I remember are crib-slat shadows striped by sunlight, like the bars of a—" (Oh, who gives a damn. Besides, it would take forever.)

By dramatic events: "I was four when the old man first felt me up." Or: "I opened it—an acceptance note for what would be my first published poem." Or: "Reader, I married him." Or: "Reader, I divorced him." (Lethal. A new genre: Soap Memoir.)

By central characters: "The Mother and Aunts," "Teachers," "Lovers," "Friends, Sisters, Colleagues." (Limited, but has potential in shifting the focus to others and away from the self. Still, risks sounding like the *Reader's Digest*'s moronic "Most Unforgettable Character I've Met.")

By time periods: "Childhood," "The Teenage Years," "Young Wifehood," "In Jail and Out." (Artificial, pompous, too like the chronology above. A fatuous pretense that living is linear.)

By subject matter: "Sex," "Poetry," "Feminism," "Mothering." (Gross. Sounds like sections in a women's magazine.)

All of the above: Deliberately eclectic, sometimes contiguous, sometimes fragmented. (Surprising, at least. Risky. More like existence itself. Has possibilities. . . .)

But which voice? The personal, philosophical, literary, political? Which style? That of a journalist, diarist, satirist, epistoler, historian, critic, essayist, novelist? *All* of the above? But two genres should be prohibited: polemics (too banal, been there lifelong, done that to death) and poetry (too profound, see elsewhere: six books of poems). Otherwise, what the hell. *Risk* it. *All* of the above—*the genre called "life."*

11.

Bracing advice to Reluctant Memoirist (RM) #2:

Reluctance be damned. You still wear the curses of your sex and your generation: wanting to be *liked*. Forget it. A memoir is an exercise in narcissism no matter what you do or other memoirists claim. So stop moaning, distill your literary angst to the humble essence of a TV sneaker commercial, and Just Do It. After all, you have two major motivations, probably shared by every memoirist (though you may be the first one dense enough to confess them).

See where they dangle, like promised beta-carotene rewards:

(1) You get to set the record straight (or crooked) yourself. If you don't, others will. In fact, they will anyway. But this way your version is at least a contender.

(2) By the time you finish the thing, it will have grown on you the way every book you write does, and you will feel a certain fond loyalty to it. Besides, you can then live on the balance of the advance while you get back to writing poetry and fiction—because in poems and novels you can continue to *really* tell the truth. For that matter, in poems and novels (and certain essays and many unpublished letters) you've *already* written this memoir. But the genre wasn't formally "memoir," so nobody believed you.

12.

Elders among the indigenous Hopi people ask a floundering seeker to answer three clarifying questions.

What are the goals?

To tell emotional truths as well as literal ones. To see as clearly as possible, with a merciless eye. To describe as fairly as possible, with a compassionate voice. To move backward and forward in time guided by an ethically charged compass.

What are the obstacles?

Memoir flirting as an act of flattery, manipulation, score-settling; memoir as the brandishing of a polemical tambourine. And most of the hyphenate "selfs" (except self-restraint): the whine of self-pity, the huff of self-justification, the bray of self-aggrandizement, the mumble of self-censorship. Fear.

What are the tools?

Love of language, of irony, of humor. Some experience navigating the rapids of imagination and obsession, as well as commuting those trade routes between received truth and experienced truth, related truth and deciphered truth. A lifelong tendency of choosing to speak out from fear rather than stay silent from fear.

13.

What else but memory has taught us most of what, when, how, and even why we feel?

The amygdala, a tiny section of the brain, stores all emotional memory, even when conscious memory of how it got there has been repressed— usually through physical or emotional trauma. We gain access to repressed memory, if at all, from clues dropped by the amygdala.

Erase memory, that most intimate of tutors, and all emotive associations are cut loose from their moorings, adrift in helpless automimicry of those basic feelings already hardwired at birth: excitement, fear, desire, pain, rage, pleasure.

So memory is the scaffold, the skeleton of our emotions. If sometimes that skeleton is all that remains of what was once electric, living content, the memoirist's job is to revive or at least approximate that flesh, cartilage, skin, those joints and muscles and veins, that pulse.

This is autopsy in reverse: an attempt to discover the time and cause of life.

Erase memory, and all but the rawest primal knowledge vanishes.

Erase memory, and all means of self-identification disappear.

I remember, therefore I am.

Part One

Matrilineal Descent

Nothing ever wipes out childhood.

—SIMONE DE BEAUVOIR

Every ancestry begins with the mother, but mine ends there, too.

I never met any of my grandparents. The maternal pair had emigrated from that permeable-membrane part of Eastern Europe that was one day Polish, another Russian, a third Prussian. My grandfather Reuben, for whom I was named, had been a rabbi in his village. According to family lore, he was a gentle, scholarly man with a sense of humor, an idealistic outlook, and a passion for softly scrambled eggs. However, his wife, Rose, was, according to all three of her daughters, a matriarch straight from the tales of the Brothers Grimm: fierce, strict, loud, a bully to her husband and children. She certainly looks formidable in the one picture I have of her and my grandfather: Reuben Teitlebaum, slouching, regards the camera with a slightly amused expression, just short of a smile, but Rose wears her frown like semaphore signaling a storm, and her posture is as rigid as the corset encasing her bulk.

Then again, she had reason to frown. Life had uprooted and disappointed her sorely. She had made a real "catch"—a man of prestige, a *rebbe*—married him, and started a family, only to be hauled away from her village into a strange new world where he couldn't find a synagogue to hire him, so had to clerk in a hardware store. She, who was to have lived her life as a *rebbitzen,* a rabbi's wife, the most respected woman in the village, became a nobody—poor, without prominence, burying three infants in childbirth and raising the two sons and three daughters who survived in an immigrant Jewish community based in, of all places, Atlanta, Georgia. He consoled himself with books, Caruso's phonograph records, and scrambled eggs. She consoled herself with rage.

The sons, naturally, were the hope of the family. My memories of Uncle Aham and Uncle Samuel are so hazy they might as well be cut from gauze; I was barely a toddler the few times (I'm told) I met them. By then my mother, Faith, was already in flight from what remained of her family, except for her two older sisters, Sally and Sophie.

These three women shared a lifelong bond: resentment. They co-cherished indignation as if it were a family heirloom, and their lives provided them with ample justification, as in the case of their brothers: the boys had been sent to college, but the two older daughters were flatly denied higher education, while my mother was permitted to sample it but was yanked out after one tantalizing year. My uncles and what families they eventually had accordingly vanished into a category that, had it been acknowledged, would have been labeled "Don't-discuss-around-the-child-unless-absolutely-necessary-and-then-only-in-Yiddish."

Both aunts, on the other hand, were vivid presences throughout my childhood. Much as each of the three sisters considered herself unique, they all shared the same body type (short and overweight), and they all exhibited certain similar characteristics. Among these was an excessive reverence for perceived authority: bus drivers and waiters were addressed as "Sir"—but this was definitely not out of any courtesy or respect for the working class; in Georgia, they *were* working class, yet under my grandmother's tutelage they carried themselves instead as Daughters of a Rabbi. More likely, such obsequiousness was rooted in first-generation-immigrant anxiety, or further back, in the periodic pogroms that would terrorize their native village. In any event, whatever rebellious energy the sisters possessed they reserved for use at the kinship level, to be expressed through continual railing against existence—in the guise of blood relatives.

They also shared a capacity for exaggeration that rocketed past puny art into stratospheric lie. No doctor could be merely good; to warrant confidence, he (and it *was* "he" then) had to be "the top in his field," "the best in the world," the medicine-magician "sheiks journeyed from Arabia to see." (I kept trying to figure out why he chose to practice out of a two-room office in Yonkers.) A low- or mid-level theatrical agent or a would-be producer became "the most powerful man in show business." Even a plastic necklace cleverly molded into fake coral spikelets was once vigorously defended as "rare coral, imported direct from the Great Barrier Reef." Since the sisters' own individual and collective histories were also prime subject matter for their exaggerative talent, they frequently reinvented themselves, their present, and their past. But they rarely did so in concert, which meant screaming matches over whose version was true. Sometimes I had a French great-grandmother named Yvonne who was "wildly popular at the court of the tsar"—and sometimes I didn't; sometimes the family had a branch of "great scholars among the Sephardic Jews back to the Middle Ages"—and sometimes it didn't. Consequently, I learned two lessons the hard way but early: that understatement was ineffective for making oneself heard at home, and that reality was decidedly relative. I grew up witnessing truth as the tennis ball in a match between Dionysus and Lao Tzu.

But however ectoplasmic facts may have been to these women, emotion was real—utterly, suffocatingly real. All three of them Drama Queens of Ashkenazic Family Theater, my mother and aunts performed their lives in operatic fashion and at decibels aimed for the fifth balcony's back rows. Each preferred arias, but they often went at it in duets, and their periodic trios were memorable.

The middle sister, Sophie, led the closest to what in those days was considered a "normal" life: she married (a distant cousin with the same surname, Teitlebaum), bore a son and a daughter, and seemed content to become an obsessive housekeeper and a wonderful cook. I can still remember the pungency of her cooking smells, their promise beckoning from far down the hall outside her apartment door: comforting chicken soups bobbing with *kreplach,* crisp noodle *kügles,* pot roasts with garlicky dumplings—and the heavenly, moist, almond-flour cakes she would bake in special molds the shape of lambs, then decorate with vanilla frosting and shaved-coconut curls, raisin eyes, and a maraschino-cherry mouth.

Unfortunately, I also remember the yelling, tearful fights she waged with my cousins, her son Jerry and daughter Dorothy, both already teenagers when I hadn't yet started school. Jerry fled to enlist in the navy and was based at Pensacola, Florida (to my child's ear and logic, this became Pepsi Cola, Florida, named after a product as was Hershey, Pennsylvania, which I knew about since I had once appeared there in a fashion show). Dorothy's revolt took the form of as many boyfriends as could be crammed into a given day—a tendency that had persisted, until I lost track of her, through three marriages and three more live-in relationships.

Still, Aunt Sophie cossetted me, let me help with cutting out cookies and decorating the "lambie cakes," told me stories, and, unlike Aunt Sally, seemed to care more about my schoolwork than about my fan clubs. Her husband, Uncle Harry, a retired semi-invalid with a colostomy, made me nervous: he rarely said anything while shuffling through their apartment en route from bedroom to bathroom and back. Sophie could also unnerve me on occasion, as when she enjoyed removing her false teeth and snapping them in my face or chasing me around with her vacuum cleaner, an upright with a roaring motor and a single light glaring from its forehead like a robotic cyclops. Scaring young children is considered by many adults to be an act of good-natured fun, but it's always struck me as a sadistic display of grown-up power thinly disguised as "teasing." The small-bodied people—children—get the message on all levels, and learn to respond with manic laughter signaling not so much humor as submission.

Aunt Sally was very different from Aunt Sophie. For one thing, she lived with Mommie and me. For another, her approach to cooking was to boil all vegetables a uniform grey color the consistency of mush and fry chops until they were so well-done they bounced on your plate when you tried to cut them. If in my childhood archetypes Mommie was cast as the Good Mother, Sally was the Evil Aunt.

The oldest of what in my adolescence I would come to name the Weird Sisters, Sally had been born in the Old Country—Russia? Poland? it depended on who was telling the story—and claimed to remember the boat trip to the New World, a journey she nonetheless refused to discuss. It would take me decades finally to see Sally for the poignant figure she was. In her youth, she'd apparently had a glorious voice (all three of them actually agreed on this), and had longed to be an opera singer. But for a woman in that era and in the conservative European Jewish culture of her family, a life on the wicked stage was regarded as one lewd flounce away from prostitution. So her music was denied her. Then, so the story went, she fell in love with a Christian who cared enough to convert to Judaism in order to marry her. Rose, horrified at her daughter's defilement of the family by such a marriage, decided conversion was insufficient; she demanded that her new son-in-law be circumcised, a barbarous enough ritual when inflicted on a newborn and a particularly savage procedure when carried out on an adult. Still, Sally and her husband were, briefly, happy. Then she gave birth to stillborn twin sons, and, soon after, their father died in a car accident. My grandmother celebrated both tragedies as punishments from Yahweh, her jealous god's revenge on Sally for having loved a "goy." Sally, left a childless widow, shifted her grieving attentions to her youngest sister—and eventually to her youngest sister's child.

I now realize that Sally suspected I only pretended to love her, while most of the time I detested her. She was the hands-on operator of my childhood career as first a model and then an actor, so she functioned in my mind as the blameworthy stage mother. I've often suspected that the idea of putting the baby me to work as a professional model in the first place originated with Sally's seeing in my infant prettiness and toddler precocity her own second chance, albeit vicarious, at a stage career. To make matters worse, she'd adopted her mother's dictatorial style. My mother, on the other hand, had a wider repertoire, choosing confrontation only when manipulation failed (except in certain circumstances against which you could never prepare yourself for the shock of her full frontal attack). Poor Sally. In style and substance, she came to represent in my mind everything crude.

When I think of her, what comes to mind are the cast-and-crew jokes about her thick body's profile blocking everyone's view of the set monitor, and her sycophantic apologies before sidling up to it again. In one of those so unfairly preserved moments of perfect recollection, etched deep by the acid of embarrassment, I will never forget one particular Saturday. We were at home, in the little third-floor walk-up apartment she, Mommie, and I shared, when my teacher dropped in unexpectedly. Mommie was out, but Aunt Sally didn't tell me to entertain Miss Wetter while she made herself presentable. No, whether in a state of innocence, indifference, or defiance, she received the visitor just as she was, without flinching. Her hair stood in peaks stiff with peroxide bleach foam, reeking of ammonia that dripped onto the frayed towel around her shoulders. She sat large-bodied at the kitchen table in brazen undress: the heavily boned bra, pendant from the weight of her large breasts, hung from soiled straps that cut dark pink grooves deep into her shoulders; the batwing flesh rippled and hung from her bare arms; the huge underpants showed their outline under her faded pink half-slip. And all the while, she continued busily squashing the bright orange "Flavor Dot" into a brick of white oleomargarine—oleo for short—and kneading it with her bare hands through the oily blob until the whole pound marbled into one pale yellow. Miss Wetter managed to carry the moment off, but soon recalled another appointment and rushed away. I wanted to die. I swore silently with the intensity of a nine-year-old to *will* myself into forgetting the moment ever happened—which is doubtless why it remains so crystalline almost half a century later. Time may have lent me some insight into my childish snobbery and some understanding of the class context in this moment, but neither time nor understanding has quite erased the mortification.

As a child, I had a lively imagination, but like most children's it was centered on myself and the worlds I created in my mind; an imagination singularly lacking in the generosity that might extend it toward other people in real life—especially those who had power over me. So I couldn't imagine Sally young, slender, or talented; couldn't visualize her, face contorted with grief, bending over the empty crib that might have cradled her lost twins, or slowly folding her dead husband's shirts one last time before giving them away. I thought her grotesque. I loathed her coarse features, her facial moles that sprouted tiny hairs, her jowls, her neck wattle, her guttural Yiddish, her peasant ways. I blamed her for everything I could, and she obligingly fed me a glut of behavioral details to fatten my dislike. No matter how I struggled against it, she would spit on a hankie or tissue to clean my face—and the memory of her sharp spit smell can even now raise my gorge to nausea. I knew she was engaged in a guerrilla war with my mother for possession of me, and I reveled in the knowledge that my genteel, perfumed, delicately featured, porcelain-skinned mother would, if pressed, turn tigress to wrest control of her daughter's life from this interloper. (She would do the same to wrest control of it from her daughter, too—an insight I was mercifully spared at the time.)

The worst memory I have of Sally is of the one real beating, a spanking, I ever received. I was seven years old. It was a test of wills about a particular cotton dress I hated, which Aunt Sally insisted I wear two days running. With the powerless fury of a child, I screamed at her that I would never *never* forgive her for hitting me when my mother had forbidden it, that I hated her with all my heart, that I hoped she would die. Later that night, and nights after for weeks, instead of secretly reading by flashlight under the bedcovers as usual, I prayed for her death or disappearance with an intensity I recognize today on the faces of anti-choice picketers outside abortion clinics: that fanaticism able to bridge devout hatred with devout faith in a god merciful enough to answer one's prayer to destroy others.

My one tender memory of Sally goes back to my being four years old. We had been out getting groceries while Mommie was at work clerking lingerie in the Lerner store, and in one of the shops a radio bulletin had announced the death of President Franklin D. Roosevelt. The grown-ups were all shocked and saddened, but I was indifferent until we got outside and Aunt Sally did something I'd never seen her—or anyone else   do. She took a few steps, stopped still in the middle of the street, and burst into tears. Mumbling about how "he cared, that man cared about little people," she dropped her shopping bags and sank to her knees on the sidewalk, hunched over with weeping. I stood watching her, awed. She was unrecognizable. I actually felt sorry for her, so I knew something major had happened.

When I turned eleven, the power struggle between Faith and Sally broke into the open. Sally lost. She was exiled to Florida, to a bungalow that, Faith announced between clenched teeth, "We bought for her, to set her up like an empress." Sally went bitterly, my mother quit her job to work full-time on my career, and she and I moved into Manhattan, just the two of us. Sally and Faith barely spoke for a while and never reconciled fully, not even when Sally lay dying of a cancer that, left ignored as a breast lump, colonized her spine. By then, she was deep into Christian Science, but her attempt to "pray away" the cancer was notably unsuccessful. In retrospect, though, that may not have been its real purpose: one final self-punishing gesture of revenge, instead, aimed at her mother's conservative Judaism.

Sally's guilt trip of choice was a refrain borrowed from her idol Sophie Tucker: "You'll be sorry when I'm gone; you're gonna' miss me then." She repeated this frequently, in her own variation of Tucker's delivery. Unfortunately for her, it was not a self-fulfilling prophecy. When she was dying years later, I went—a grown, married woman—to Florida to visit her. She was being tended by loyal Sophie, by then widowed and relocated there as well. It was a hideous week, one of those entries into virtual childhood when the adult personality finds itself astonishingly shrunk, rendered powerless by old patterns, choked, cramped, and wild with frustration. But although I can now grieve for the emptiness of Sally's life and try to remember her as a woman who mourned the New Deal, the truth is that I was not sorry when she was gone, and I haven't missed her since. (Admitting this was a lesson in how self-deluded predictions that "history will absolve me" can be.)

I forgot Sally most of the time, but I never forgave her, even when my mother took over the stage-mothering, thus overturning my assumption that everything would change for the better if *only* Aunt Sally could be got out of the picture and if *only* Mommie took charge. Possibly the dirty little secret is that I never forgave Sally for removing, however reluctantly, her convenient, scapegoat self—because after her departure I soon was forced to see Mommie plain, the Infanta without the court dwarf to make her appear fairer by contrast.

Mommie. Traces of her influence run like dark threads through even the brightest patches of my life; sometimes I think her influence *is* the fabric, and only the cut is of my devising; sometimes I feel I'm the material, but she's the cutter and the pattern is of her devising. Her effect remains stronger than I can always notice or acknowledge. And when I was a child, her power over my life was as unquestionable as my centrality was to hers.

Unlike Sally's stage yearnings, Faith's sole lifelong desire, she claimed, was to have a daughter just like me. (No pressure *there*.) It wasn't until I was an adult, going through chaotic shoebox "files" of hers after final-stage Parkinson's disease confined her to a hospital, that I discovered the notebook. She'd kept it during her two semesters at college—before she'd been hauled home to care for her mother after her father died, since the sisters were married at the time and the brothers were, well, brothers. The little notebook is touchingly filled with grammar basics and "tips for writers," such as explaining what a cliché is and why it should be avoided. She'd wanted to *write,* I realized, and then I was distracted by hearing someone murmur "Oh god, oh god" over and over—until I recognized my own voice. I'd been so certain my love of writing not only was independent of her but was the route to liberation away from her. It *was* the latter— but independent of her it apparently was not.

Suddenly I remembered my favorite photograph of Faith, taken when she was seventeen, in Mexico City, during the one real vacation of her life. She is radiant in it. It was the sole free time she'd ever know, on a trip won as a student prize, when she could stand in front of the burnt-orange murals of Orozco, the Kahlo alizarin-splashed canvases, when she could break away from the Victorian shadows of the rabbinical home and pose in a bleach of lemon sunlight surrounded by trumpets of crimson hibiscus and toss back her hair and laugh into the warm breeze.

But in time I became the only one who remembered that long-dead seventeen-year-old, the sole repository of an existence she'd had to bury and forget, too busy becoming the living testament to her concocted image of me, the perfect child, smiling and curtseying. So we lived, each of us haunted by the girlhood of the other.

Faith had left college after that one euphoric year, forced to return home, seething to find herself again under her mother's constraints. Then Sally's triple tragedies hit, and, as a means to support herself in her childless widowhood, Sally opened a small corset and lingerie shop near Stuyvesant Town in New York City, where she and her husband had been living. A few years later, when my grandmother died, Faith moved north to New York, joining her sister to work at the shop and sharing Sally's apartment in Stuyvesant Town, one of the lower-middle-income "projects" in Manhattan.

By then it was 1940, and the war preoccupied everyone. Horror stories about the existence of concentration camps had begun to leak out to the world. Various American Jewish organizations set up programs under which Jewish refugees from Europe could emigrate to the United States, but each exile needed the sponsorship of a U.S. citizen. My mother, the first "full real born-here American" in her family and newly a proud career girl in the big city, decided to sponsor a refugee.

When she mentioned my father, which she rarely did, Faith would talk about this period. How he had walked off the boat from Europe and she'd fallen for him on the spot, standing on the windy Manhattan pier, anxiously making small talk while his papers were being checked; how she'd stared at this tall, handsome Austrian Jew with wavy blond hair, hazel eyes "that penetrated your soul," a wry smile, and "the devil's cleft in his chin." He spoke excellent English—and French, and of course German. He was educated, sophisticated, European. And he was a *doctor*.

By the time he was temporarily ensconced on the rollout cot in Faith and Sally's living room, my mother was, as she later put it, "a goner." Details of the paternal saga get vague at this point, but the overall plot goes like this:

Mates (Hebrew for Mattheus or Matthew) Morgan had been a young surgeon in Vienna when Austria welcomed the Nazis, and he had lost his entire family—my paternal grandparents, his siblings, aunts, uncles, cousins—to the camps. He himself had managed to escape from not just one but two concentration camps, relying on his wits to wend his way across Europe in an underground flight to survival, barely making it out of one country after another as they successively fell to Hitler's storm troopers. Although he'd already had a successful practice in Vienna, he still had to take his U.S. medical-board examinations in order to be certified here; this meant months of refresher study plus acquainting himself with U.S. medical procedures, which in turn meant he was unable to earn sufficient money to strike out on his own. So he stayed with Sally and Faith. My parents-to-be fell in love, had a whirlwind courtship, and got married. Somewhere in all this, Mates acquired U.S. citizenship, enlisted in the army, and was sent back overseas as a medical doctor with the rank of major. But it turned out my mother was pregnant, so she and Sally moved to Florida, to get away from the bombing target New York was feared to be. There, in the small town of Lake Worth, near West Palm Beach, on January 29, 1942, I was born. When I was less than two years old, my father was killed in action while giving medical aid to wounded soldiers at the front. I knew only his photograph.

Sally, experienced in the ways of widowhood, wrapped her life around my mother and me like a mourning veil. The sisters closed ranks. To be in closer proximity with Sophie, Sally and Faith moved themselves and me back north to Mount Vernon, a lower-working-class suburb of Manhattan, where Aunt Sophie and her family lived. Today, Mount Vernon is almost exclusively a poor, African-American enclave. During the years we lived there—the heart of my childhood, from the time I was two or three until I turned twelve—it was racially mixed but always notches lower on the social scale than whiter working-class Yonkers or much whiter middle-class Bronxville, its neighbors. White Plains and Westchester were where the rich people lived (actually the upper middle class, but to us they seemed rich). The "millionaire types" lived farther away, in exotic places named Tarrytown, Scarsdale, or even Connecticut.

At first, Aunt Sophie took care of me days, while Aunt Sally and Mommie got jobs working in the lingerie department of Lerner's, a small department store in Mount Vernon. Thirty years later, during one of Bella Abzug's political campaigns, one of her supporters, Judy Lerner—wife of the owner of Lerner's—actually remembered me as a child with golden ringlets, big brown eyes, a precocious intelligence, and a nonstop tongue. These assets didn't go unnoticed by others, because at some point during this period I was put up for modeling assignments and rather quickly became a successful tot model, both for photography sessions and for runway work in fashion shows. Aunt Sally convinced my mother that work was the best thing for a heart crushed by loss, so in an odd switch Faith kept her job at Lerner's, while Sally quit to look after me and my growing "career."

Still, Faith claimed that motherhood was the hub of her existence, and I was never allowed to forget it. In fact, her two favorite stories were revealing as propaganda.

The first was the story of Cornelia's jewels. Cornelia, a second-century B.C.E. Roman matron, was the mother of the revolutionary Gracchi brothers, who led Rome's democratic faction. (Politically, at least, my mother was unwittingly prescient.) Cornelia became famous for her response to a visitor who asked to see a display of her jewels: "My children," she answered proudly, "are the only jewels I need."

The other story, which I can't recall Mommie's ever telling without brimming eyes, was the Greco-Roman myth of the mother-daughter goddesses Demeter and Persephone. Persephone, sometimes called Kore ("slim ankled" Persephone, as Homer characterized her), is Demeter's beloved only child. Persephone's abduction by Hades—variously god of the underworld, the dead, or hell—devastates Demeter, who wanders the earth in search of her lost child and whose grief is so great that she, goddess of agriculture, curses and withers all growing things, inventing winter. Hermes, the gods' messenger, persuades Hades to free Persephone, who has meanwhile become transformed into Hecate, queen of the dead. But the release will hold only if she has eaten nothing in the underworld. Since Persephone has swallowed three pomegranate seeds, she is permitted to return aboveground only temporarily—but must redescend to Hades for three months each year. When she reemerges onto the earth, Demeter permits the world to wake and bloom again. Thus, the myth goes, did the seasons come about, a cycle perpetuated as Persephone redescends to become Hades' queen, then resurfaces as Demeter's daughter.

It wasn't a coincidence that the first serious poem I wrote began, "Go, rage, winter the world with despair," phrased in the voice of Persephone rejecting Demeter, invoking some powerfully demonic Hades to sweep me up, abduct me to a darkly passionate hell, and free me from the bright glare of my mother's love.

I'm at one with my most of my generation in this: it was a given that my mother never understood me. How could she have, when she'd been kept from understanding herself? But at least I never doubted that she loved me. Much of the time, in fact, I longed for her to have mercy and love me a little less. But with hindsight—having known certain friends and lovers who grew up shuddering in a chill of unexpressed parental affection—I now can afford gratitude for the warmth, the intense heat even, with which her love radiated. Granted, some middle way would have been nice. But Faith was ignorant of moderation, though she did know how to display her love in myriad ways.

She was an artist with needle and thread. Never one for knitting or crocheting, she sewed her artistic creations without using a pattern. Such attention to detail! Exquisitely embroidered butterflies with silver-ribbon wings that lifted and folded back, resting as if newly alit on the handmade organdy pinafore to which they were stitched! Her vocabulary may not have been terribly sophisticated, but she knew words like "baste" and "bias," "peplum" and "rickrack," "princess line" and "bolero jacket"—and of course "ensemble," as in "matching ensemble." When we shopped, it would be Best & Co. for me and Peck & Peck for her; well, at least that was the longed-for ideal. The more common reality was Klein's Bargains on 14th Street for her and the homemade frocks for me. But there she didn't stint. Her chosen fabrics, acquired on trips to discount fabric stores in Orchard Street—the Ashkenazic immigrant section of Manhattan's Lower East Side—were velvet and velveteen, organdy, taffeta, and linen. The hours, the fine stitching, the ironing all this required! From about age three until ten, I rarely sat down free from guilt: at creasing the organdy too soon—before the photograph, public appearance, or audition.

My mother was a beautiful woman. But she fought weight all her life, and even at her slimmest tended toward plumpness, which she hid by the convenient fashions of the period, including longish full skirts and waists cinched by torturous one-piece corset-bras called Merry Widows. Her finely boned face, her long, slender neck, her clavicle and shoulders were the best features, and she knew how to use them to her advantage. The unblemished skin was a classic alabaster—creamy pale, with a faint natural glow. The eyes were large, sable brown, and expressive; the nose small and delicate; the mouth full, sensual. She had perfect teeth—white, even, sharp—and adored crunching things between them. Peanut brittle was ground to powder in those percussive jaws, ice cubes were fragmented, and chicken bones gave up their marrow to her loud crackle and suck. But when I was small, she was the loveliest woman in the world.

Yet she could embarrass me thoroughly (though never as much as Aunt Sally had), as when she'd flirt with headwaiters or coo seductively over the phone to her stockbroker. By adolescence, I felt ashamed of her yet ashamed at *being* ashamed of her, felt pity for her and disgust for her, and mostly felt mortified at her making of herself such a spectacle. All teenagers go through this, but in my case, you'd think I might've recognized misplaced rage at her making of *me* such a spectacle.

A spectacle I was, too—having segued from modeling into "fashion commentary," where my memory and verbal facility served me well ("I'm sporting a pastel pink sleeveless cotton piqué pinafore, buttoned down the back, with duckling design along the double hem and matching pink

Capezio shoes . . ."). Then there was my own radio show at age four, being a Juvenile Jury radio and TV panelist and, by age seven, becoming a TV fixture in the homes of America, as Dagmar, the youngest daughter of the popular TV series *Mama*.

It's impossible for me to remember a time when I was not already a consciously serious professional, aware of my responsibilities. The message was that our family—Mommie and Aunt Sally—depended on me for survival. The lesson at the core of the message, however, was that perfection was not only attainable but imperative. Furthermore, only the elect, of which I was one, were fit to accomplish it. Therefore, failure to do so, from sloth, self-doubt, or sloppiness, was perhaps the only sin. "You can do anything you set your mind to," Mommie said and said, adding, *"there is nothing you cannot be."*

By age four, I'd already experienced the ambivalence of being in charge while lacking any authority; of being considered abler, more privileged, talented, blessed—but therefore *owing:* owing luck or god, owing society, owing Mommie and Aunt Sally. Still, it has to be acknowledged that my envy of other kids' freedom was all mixed up with my secret glee at *their* envy of *me*—and a growing sense of what I couldn't yet name I felt about all these tangled envyings: irony.

To this day, despite my intellectual certainty and experience to the contrary, I remain haunted by the myth that I must be the most capable person in any given vicinity in any given circumstance and so must rise to the occasion. To some degree all women carry this spectral load, since we're raised to be caregivers. But I've taken the basic problem and run with it, as if it were my special role to find out whatever's wrong and somehow— by invention, self-sacrifice, or sheer will—make it right, heal it ("co- dependent with the whole world," as one friend puts it). This can strike people as enviable self-confidence, which is even sometimes actually real. At other times, it's alloyed with a sternly self-righteous arrogance, a near- contempt of others for their perceived weakness or low standards (as com- pared to my lofty ones), and a martyr's resentful seethe at not being regarded with an intensity equal to that I've lavished on *them*.

Perfectionism and the accompanying severity carry a dubious benefit: one is less prone to self-pity (except in the secret depths of the soul). But that's only because one is so busy denying being any sort of victim whatsoever; to do otherwise would contradict too dangerously the omnipotence inherent in being so capable and caring an Earth Mother.

Mommie taught me never to say, "I can't," never to say, "No." I was in my thirties before I dared put up a small handwritten sign beside the phone, reading simply "Learn to say *No*." And I was in my early fifties before the canny words of a therapist friend, Carol Drexler, struck me with the full force of their implication: "How can anyone trust the 'yes' of someone who can't say 'no'?"

But you couldn't say No to Faith, the manipulator with the eyes of god. You couldn't say No because she was Demeter, the life bringer, the opposite of death or hell—although you suspected she was all three (another reason you didn't say No). You didn't say No because you sensed that disobedience is evolution and you'd learned to be afraid of whatever lay beyond the vastness of her distant boundaries, much as you longed to go there. You didn't say No because she established herself as the epicenter of your child's universe, as your first and basic preoccupation, as the beloved for whom you would nurse a lifelong passion, staggering under its burden, sometimes of bitterness or fear but mostly of merciless love.

A lifetime of fleeing her, being caught by her, escaping her, reclaiming her; supporting her emotionally, financially, and physically; organizing her liberation, dancing and singing or speechifying and organizing hundreds of thousands of women who were her and never her, all to win her love. Small wonder that to this day I adore eating pomegranates.

Suffer the Little Children

Of course you appropriated me. But too much.
— WOLFGANG AMADEUS MOZART,
IN A LETTER TO HIS FATHER, LEOPOLD

$\mathcal{N}$o child is an island. My childhood, like everyone else's, was experienced in numerous overlapping contexts, among them culture, place, historical time, and that other unique time/space dimension of *being* a child. It's important to glance at some of these contexts, even if we need to pause for a moment in the personal story in order to do so.

For starters, it's crucial to understand that childhood is a new invention. That is, regarding childhood as a distinct phase of life is a fairly recent event in Western culture. The historian Philippe Ariés, in his pioneering work *Centuries of Childhood: A Social History of Family Life*,[1] argues that until the close of the Middle Ages, the child, almost from the moment of weaning, was regarded as a small adult who mingled, competed, worked, and played with full adults. Such demographic changes as

---

[1] Originally published in France as *L'Enfant et la vie familiale sous l'ancien régime* (Paris: Librairie Plon, 1960); English edition, Jonathan Cape, 1962; U.S. paperback edition, Vintage Books.

the lengthening life span, the shift in social emphasis from the community to the family (and eventually, in the twentieth century, to the nuclear family), and the spreading concept of formal education as a necessity all influenced the birth of the idea of childhood.

In many, perhaps most, parts of the world today, childhood still is only a vaguely accepted idea, and adolescence a nonexistent one, although the spread of Western practices, largely through entertainment media and multinational corporate culture, is changing that (distinct "age groups" yield more targetable markets). Adolescence can be particularly absent for girls: when you can be betrothed in infancy, married by age nine, and a mother at fourteen, where *does* adult womanhood begin? One of the priorities of the Nepalese Women's Movement, for example, has been the plight of cloistered child widows in that Hindu-fundamentalist society— girl children as young as eight who, having been married off to men in their seventies, are then widowed but not permitted to leave or remarry, spending their lives as perpetual mourners and human property, serving their husbands' families.

Our own culture, claiming to cherish children, worships youth, which is altogether different. But it *sentimentalizes* children: all that cloying rhetoric from politicians about "the nation's future" and "for the sake of our young"; all the rants from the Christian Right preaching "the sanctity of our pre-born children" while opposing welfare rights, head-start programs, gun control, or the teaching of evolution and sex education in school.[2] This, in the United States, a country so rich that children are considered a major consumer market—while one in every four of them goes to sleep hungry each night; a country so reverently observant of "family values" that one in every three women and one in every seven men has survived some form of childhood sexual, physical, or emotional abuse.

Unfortunately, the United States isn't unique in its hypocrisy. Every nation trots out tots to curtsey, smile, and offer bouquets to visiting dignitaries (this is the unthreatening aspect of a welcome ceremony; troop review, planes streaking in formation, and cannon salutes constitute the

---

[2]The late Simone de Beauvoir summed up this position most succinctly in writing that the Roman Catholic Church "reserves its most uncompromising concern for child welfare to the child in fetal form."

threatening aspect). East European countries became notorious for pluck-
ing their youngest athletes and dancers early on, then training them with
a rigor tantamount to boot camp for marines, with a few steroids thrown
in for good measure. China's idea of impressive spectacle invariably
involves thousands of children in some square or stadium—berouged, lip-
sticked, pigtailed, and regimented in rows, singing, dancing, and twirling
ribbons or flags. "Cultural relativism" is usually the defense for these practices—that same handy justification once employed for pogroms, slavery,
polygamy, purdah, foot binding, and other quaint customs. In this case,
though, since the children are smiling, they must be loving it—so where's
the harm? Besides, they're so *cute*! Most adults seem willing to perish
from diabetic shock brought on by megadoses of cuteness. Perhaps they
never knew or conveniently forgot the etymology of "cute": the word is a
shortened version of "acute," its original meaning having more to do with
intelligence than with treacle.

If children are "our tomorrows," then we're warping the future in the
image of the present. Even a quick scan of the United Nations Convention on the Rights of the Child is alarmingly educative, because there's
never a need to articulate rights unless they've already been ignored or vio-
lated. Everywhere, children lack basic civil and political rights: free
speech, free assembly, privacy, suffrage, and the right not to be categorized
in many legal systems along with convicted felons, the mentally ill, slaves,
animals, and inanimate property. Children, together with women, constitute 90 percent of all refugee populations on the planet as well as the vast
majority of those living in absolute poverty; the "feminization of poverty"
means that children are poor, too, since most parenting is done by mothers. In both the so-called developing and developed worlds, little girls are
tortured and maimed by genital-mutilation and genital-amputation procedures rationalized by religious or customary "law," while little boys are circumcised—a less severe form of mutilation, but mutilation
nonetheless—with the same excuse. Child prostitution, child pornography, and the trafficking of children for sexual-exploitation purposes are all
growth industries on the rise, and children are the preferred prostitutes in
much of Asia, and parts of Africa and Latin America. Child marriage is still
prevalent in many cultures, with the tiny bride sent off to her husband's
family as early as age two, to live in servitude for the rest of her life (unless

she dies for lack of sufficient dowry in one of those suspicious kitchen accidents more accurately termed "bride burnings"). Meanwhile, in Northern Ireland, in parts of Central America, in theocratic Iran, and during the recent attempted genocide in Rwanda, little boys as young as eight have been recruited for missions ranging from errand running (with live munitions) to mine clearing (they walk ahead of the army and get blown up since they're regarded as dispensable) to outright assassination. Modern, lightweight weapons have expanded the involvement of children: many "seasoned" Khmer Rouge soldiers in Cambodia were all of fourteen years old; recent civil wars in Uganda and Sudan kidnapped and armed ten- and twelve-year-old boys for their militias. *There are approximately 250 million children in the world's labor force,* primarily in developing countries in Asia and Africa—and this is *without* counting (just as it's not counted for women) bonded labor, prostitution, pornography, domestic servitude, subsistence farming, child-rearing (of younger siblings), water hauling, fuel gathering, animal husbandry, and hidden-economy sweatshop labor. Tuberculosis, body lesions, malnutrition, and venereal disease are rife among the world's 80 million homeless street children—an estimated 30 million of whom roam in packs through the midnight streets of Brazilian cities alone.[3]

---

[3]*Action for Children*, vol. 1, no. 3. See also Robin Morgan, *The Demon Lover: On the Sexuality of Terrorism* (W. W. Norton, 1989) and *The Anatomy of Freedom: Feminism in Four Dimensions*, 2d ed. (W. W. Norton, 1994). In June 1999, the International Labour Organization (ILO) finally adopted a treaty intended to abolish the most hazardous forms of child labor. Under pressure from the United States, the United Kingdom, Germany, and the Netherlands, however, the ILO compromised, not prohibiting people under age eighteen from *enlisting* in the military, although the treaty bars "forced or compulsory recruitment of children for use in armed conflict." As trade unions, most human-rights organizations, and such countries as Canada, Denmark, and Norway note, military service *is* hazardous, whether the participant has gone compulsorily or voluntarily. The United Nations Children's Fund (UNICEF) estimates that more than 300,000 children under age eighteen are serving as regular soldiers, guerrillas, spies, cooks, sexual slaves, and suicide commandos in current conflicts in approximately fifty countries. By trying to raise the recruitment age to eighteen, UNICEF is attempting to change the 1989 UN Convention on the Rights of the Child, which set fifteen as the minimum age for military recruitment at the insistence of the United States and the United Kingdom, both of which wanted to continue recruiting high-school graduates. In January 2000, the United States finally dropped its opposition: the Pentagon retained the right to *recruit* seventeen-year-olds but agreed to keep them out of direct combat until age eighteen.

Not surprisingly, there's a gender differential. In some societies a female child is more likely to be denied food in favor of a male child; she must eat last if at all, and fish, eggs, meat, and other protein foods may be considered taboo for her. She joins her mother as part of the female two-thirds of all illiterates on the planet, and is more likely to be denied education as well as most forms of basic safety and health care. She often carries or births a child while still a child herself. She risks not surviving infancy in China, where female infanticide is still epidemic, because of the government's one-child-per-family policy and its failure to educate the rural populace against a preference for sons, or in India, where amniocentesis misapplied for sex selection has now created a serious imbalance in the birthrates of male and female infants. Because she is female, a little girl can suffer doubly, from sexism *and* from being a child. Sometimes the work she's forced to do links the two oppressions neatly and appallingly. In 1984, on the resort island of Phuket, Thailand, there was a fire in one of the many brothels patronized by international visitors, primarily though not exclusively from Japan. The charred skeletons of six female humans were found, chained to their beds for fear they might escape from what its defenders outrageously claim is valid, voluntary "sex work." They were all between the ages of ten and twelve.

Male children are exploited sexually, too, although their labor is more often of a different sort. Not long ago, a twelve-year-old boy riding his bike on a bright April day was gunned down in his village near Lahore, Pakistan. His name was Iqbal Masih. In a six-paragraph story buried on a back page, the *New York Times* reported his murder as described by activists with the Bonded Labor Liberation Front (BLLF), a Pakistani organization opposing child labor. Iqbal, who had worked as a carpet weaver under horrifying circumstances for half his brief life, had dared to speak out about the conditions child workers face. Because he was brave, smart, articulate, and lucky enough to get heard by sympathizers, Iqbal was freed. The BLLF brought him to speak at an international labor conference in Sweden, Brandeis University offered him a full scholarship when he was ready for college, and Reebok awarded him its Youth in Action Prize (U.S.$15,000—relative to the profits of their sweatshop factories in Asia a pittance, but one slickly transformed into a public-relations gesture). Iqbal's dream was to use the money to get an education, then become a lawyer when he grew up, to continue his fight for children's rights. Although he was the target of numerous death threats from people in the carpet industry who were angered at his visibility and volubility, he persisted in his campaign. So did they. Now both the little boy and his dream are buried. He had been sold by his parents at age four, and had been shackled to a carpet loom for six years. When he was freed, he still owed his boss 13,000 rupees. Iqbal had earned one rupee a day.

These children are not abstract statistics to me. I've talked with them and listened to them. I've seen the fourteen-year-olds pouring out of factories run by international corporations in the "free-trade" zones of Central America and South Asia, where women and children are the preferred labor: cheap, marginal, desperate, nonviolent. Or the migrant-worker kids in the agribusiness-owned fields of the United States, their fingers flashing as they pick fruit for growers who don't care that their pint-sized labor force has seen the inside of a school for an average of only five years. Or the four-foot-tall child laborer in South Africa's KwaZulu-Natal, carrying six bricks in a sack on her head and a baby brother slung on her hip. Or the ten-year-old bar girls in the former R & R towns of the Philippines that once catered to the U.S. Navy—flat-chested little girls wearing push-up bras stuffed with rags, neon-red lipstick outlining their fixed grins. Or the "pre-teen" prostitutes sold by their villages in Laos or Cambodia to brothel keepers in India or Thailand—sent back home, HIV-infected, to die before their thirteenth birthday. Or the six-year-old peddlar boy, one of many who accost your every step in Giza, Egypt, offering to sell anything: sight-seeing maps in different languages, dirty postcards, drugs, camel rides, his sister—"A virgin, I promise!"—and, with a wink, himself.

I've seen these children.

Such a sight forever changes the way one looks at childhood.

The way I look at childhood had been perforce skewed since well before I encountered such children. Yet I cannot conscience this book existing without acknowledging their shadowy presence, although I know that the inclusion of the above-mentioned statistics risks heightening the contrast between such children's situations and anything approximating what was my own. I can hear a reader gasp, "How can you possibly compare . . . ," and indeed, I am not comparing. It's always a failure of ethical nerve to settle for compare-and-contrast-oppression competitions. Instead, the challenge is to use one's own suffering as a skeleton key to gain access to the suffering borne by others. This does *not* mean arrogantly assuming one *understands* anyone else's pain; it simply means acknowledging it, with empathy and respect—not pity—*and* offering active support toward trying to heal it.

At first glance—certainly as measured against the hideous situation of a child worker in, say, the carpet factories of Nepal—a child performer in Europe or the United States can appear incredibly privileged, to herself/himself as well as to others. After all, the basics—water, food, shelter, clothing, medical care, education—are firmly in place; in addition, sometimes there's wealth, fame, adulation. Yet these promised or actual privileges make any idea of revolt more indefensible, in turn making the distress and anger more bewildering. The wounds are different, the scars less visible.

Although the hardships of child labor can differ dramatically in *degree*, they are intimately related in *kind*. The premature violation of innocence is the same, as is the loss—lifelong—of truly comprehending what "play" is. Accelerated maturation, inflicted responsibility, imposed discipline: the same. The boil of emotions confusing the child—fear, rage, sadness, and an odd, indomitable pride—is the same, and so is the deeply embedded ignorance of how to be idle. The fantasies of rebellion are the same, as is the guilt at entertaining such thoughts, because rebellion would violate the trust and respect adults have bestowed on you by giving you such responsibility: you learn to mistake their requisitioning of your labor as "trust" and "respect" for your sanity's sake—denial as a survival tool.

Interestingly, whether in a hill village in South Asia, a London music conservatory, a Russian athletic gymnasium, or a Hollywood film set, *the adults' justifications are also the same,* giving a new meaning to the term "labor relations." Their repertoire includes the following:

You're lucky. I never had the chance to improve my family's life, but you do.

(Or, conversely:) *I was working at your age. Why shouldn't you?*
How can you be so selfish? Do it for me/us.

Look what I've/we've sacrificed for your sake; you owe us.

It's the way out, don't you see? (Out: of poverty, the village, the working class, the projects, the ghetto . . .)

You should be honored to be given so much responsibility at your age.

You have a God-given talent/gift/skill/opportunity, and it would be a sin to throw it away.

The child reels at the clutter of such multiple messages, because the child hears all at once how the justifications range (and overlap) from the hypocritical (*You* have *to love doing this or you couldn't be so good at it!*) to the brutally frank (*It's not a choice; we need the money*).

A child contributing financial support to her/his family is in a very different situation from a child doing household "chores," which is in turn distinct from a child helping out on the family farm or in the family store (albeit too often with little or no wages and little or no respect). Being a breadwinner child is qualitatively as well as quantitatively different. Being the *sole* breadwinner is a terrifying assignment—because under all the adult propaganda runs a core message:

Without your labor, the family will starve. Then who will care for you?

You are literally fighting for their lives—and thus for your own. This realization invests every action with inappropriate significance. Having such power while simultaneously knowing yourself to be powerless creates a vertigo about capacity. Furthermore, if your family depends on you, you're trapped. Escape is impossible, so, like the prisoner of war, kidnap victim, or battered woman, you come to identify with your captor: Stockholm Syndrome. It's crucial to make that captor your friend; if that captor is *not* your friend, your death is likely. But *if* you can believe you're on the same side (and these are your *parents,* after all, this is your *family*), then love *must* prevail: your love for them (*See how obedient and good I am? See what I've accomplished?*), and their gratitude, expressed as love, for you. This means you get to stay alive—contingent on their approval, of course.

The illogical logic of such a universe is hermetically sealed, a tautology. And this belief system was devised by people with the power to enforce it, people who are larger-bodied than you—who literally loom over you, who can pick up your entire self or knock you down, lock you places, hurt you, exercise control over your body, daily life, and perceptions of them, the world, yourself.

Moreover, *this is the only life you know*. You might hear of or witness children living in other ways, but you have no experiential grounds for comparison. So while intellectually you might realize yours is an unusual way to live, what you *feel* is normalcy—the normalcy of existing in a state of emotional tuberculosis, where your spirit can never quite draw one deep breath.

Is this a state of privilege?

~ ~ ~

All the clichés about child performers who grow into neurotic (or worse) adults have been sadly validated for too long by too many survivors—and by quite a few who didn't survive.

Midori, the violinist who made her debut with the New York Philharmonic at age ten, had severe "digestive problems" as a child, and is rumored still to suffer eating disorders as an adult. Eugene Fodor, another child-prodigy violinist, was arrested for heroin possession as a grown man. Ruth Slenczynska, a child-prodigy pianist, suffered a total breakdown and reclaimed her adult career only after years of refusing to perform publicly. There are others. . . .

Child athletes and young dancers face a shorter career span than musicians, so the race is on: gymnasts trying to stunt their growth, skaters who fight weight with anorexia, teen ballplayers plucked from schoolwork to earn billions for a franchise owner (and millions for themselves, to be lost on booze, drugs, and fees for criminal lawyers defending them against rape, assault, or murder . . .). There's a gender differential here, too, as Joan Ryan noted in her prize-winning book, *Little Girls in Pretty Boxes: The Making and Breaking of Elite Gymnasts and Figure Skaters* (Doubleday, 1995; Warner Books, 1996); girls must race the clock against puberty, but boys peak athletically *after* puberty, when their muscles strengthen. For girls, agility, lightness, and pliability (emotional and physical) are paramount. Olga Korbut, the former Soviet gymnast and Olympic gold medalist, began smoking at age ten to keep her weight down, and has openly accused her trainer of physical and sexual abuse, claiming that many female gymnasts were treated like "sexual slaves as well as sports machines" by their trainers.[4] Young tennis stars like Jennifer Capriati have discussed the damage caused by relentless pressure to succeed. Finally, in 1996, the Women's Tennis Association ruled anyone age fourteen or under ineligible to play professionally at any level; as of the same year, Olympic gymnasts have been required to be at least sixteen years old.

Child actors usually fare even worse, since cuteness, as much as if not more than thespian skill, tends to be their prime commodity, so they face "has-been" status more often than, for instance, the small musicians. There *are* the legendary ones who managed the transition to adult stardom—but not without paying the price of shattered lives: Judy Garland, Mickey Rooney, Elizabeth Taylor, Jackie Cooper, Margaret O'Brien, Roddy Mc-Dowall, Natalie Wood. Of course, there's always the exception to those who became substance abusers, batterers or kleptomaniacs, serial marriers and multiple divorcees, skid-row bums, felons, or suicides: Shirley Temple, perhaps the most famous child star of all time, did not become dysfunctional. She became a right-wing Republican. The choice gives one pause.

In more recent times, it's become a frequent headline: the latest young TV star or movie idol sentenced to prison, rehab, or community service for using or dealing hard drugs. Patty Duke survived alcoholism and a disastrous marriage before having to resurrect her acting as an adult because she knew no other skill. Mary McDonough of *The Waltons* has suffered alcoholism, eating disorders, and nostalgia conventions. Paul Peterson of *The Mickey Mouse Club* and *The Donna Reed Show* was driven to drugs by age twenty. Dana Plato, from the sitcom *Diff'rent Strokes,* died in 1999 of an overdose of painkillers and Valium, after years of drug use and arrests for robbery and parole violations. Her co-star, Gary Coleman, has lived a comparably chaotic life, exacerbated by his being African American and suffering renal disease and stunted growth as a result of immunosuppressants administered during two failed kidney transplants: he sued his family for allegedly misappropriating $18 million of his childhood earnings, has been sued over a punching incident, had to attend court-ordered anger-management classes, and declared bankruptcy in 1999.

[4]Interview in *Komsomolskaya Pravda,* the Moscow newspaper, quoted in the *Daily Telegraph* (London), June 25, 1999.

Dr. Lisa Rapport, a clinical psychologist at Wayne State University in Detroit, has done a study of the subject, noting that former child actors endure a drug-and-alcohol-abuse rate three times the general average (that's not counting those who become codependents and enablers—after a childhood in training on both counts). The study was done for A Minor Consideration, the group Paul Peterson founded in 1990 to counsel young actors and their parents and push for legislation to protect the work lives of such professional children. The group works with the Screen Actors Guild, and has made its most impressive gains in California—where five thousand of the country's seven thousand child actors work—and where, in 1997, state, industry, and union representatives finally agreed on regulations to raise educational standards for studio teachers, the traditional guardians of minors on the set.

According to a September 2, 1997, *New York Times* article, A Minor Consideration has also campaigned about such issues as "children's working conditions," the "arrests and drug and alcohol problems of young stars," overlooked safety precautions—"the killing of two children in a helicopter accident on the set of *Twilight Zone: The Movie*"—the recruiting of premature infants to portray newborns, and the vulnerability of "teenagers involved in romantic entanglements with adult stars."

The organization also addresses the need for tougher laws governing requirements that some of the money earned by child actors be set aside for their future. Children in entertainment were exempted from national child labor laws in 1938. To this day, state laws are outdated, vary widely, and are unevenly enforced. In my childhood, there was no Coogan Law[5] in New York State, so when I left home I moved to a sixth-floor walk-up apartment and worked as a secretary in a literary agency while my mother bought a co-op on Fifth Avenue and played the stock market. In my day, the sole watchdog agency was the Society for the Prevention of Cruelty to Children (SPCC)—yes, it was related to the one for animals—whose representatives on the set looked you over for any visible bruises (but didn't asked you to undress in case there were hidden ones), then went on their way. In my day, for New York kid actors in television or on Broadway, the

---

[5]Named after the former child star Jackie Coogan, who, after a lucrative movie career, grew up into poverty, then sued his parents for misuse of monies he had never seen.

Professional Children's School was thought to be the solution to bother-some education requirements. The PCS was most obliging: it overlooked undone homework and absentee attendance, and bestowed passing grades despite an abysmal scholastic reality. Fortunately for me, my mother and aunts shared an Ashkenazic reverence for education, so they scorned the PCS in favor of a small, serious private school and, when I got older, tutors (and therein lies a tale, about which more later).[6]

I wish Paul Peterson and his group all the best. They're doing much-needed work. But the experienced political activist in me knows that bet-ter legislation, while a crucial component of any battle for progressive social change, doesn't solve oppression. The strands are too varied, the knots too tightly woven to be unraveled quickly or simply—and it takes a long time to saw through them. Whenever habitual denial is threatened, it feels to the denier as if the world were about to explode. Though often unacknowledged, it feels this way to the *powerless* as well as to those who wield power over them. This is true of adults and even more so of chil-dren. Thanks to the research of such psychologists as Alice Miller and Jennifer Freyd, we now know a bit more about how deep the influence of early imprint really goes.

Having responsibility but lacking authority is a fatiguing, contradictory kind of power, and the child performer lives a fatiguing, contradictory real-ity. Seduced into collaborating with one's own commercial salability while ignorant of one's own human value, proud of the talents and skills one has while mortified at the use they're put to, unable to break free of the shame-pride-guilt-responsibility dynamic, an intelligent child develops a sophisticated sense of irony so keen it teeters on the edge of self-disgust.

That's when it's time for the perks and rewards to kick in.

Like the dolls.

---

[6]Education or the lack of it plays a central role in a child performer's chances of sur-viving into a sane adulthood. I think it's no coincidence that two child actors whose adult lives seem to be conducted with dignity and purpose have had decent educa-tions: Jodie Foster, who manages to act in, direct, and produce films with quiet integrity; and Sheila Kuehl, formerly of the TV sitcom *Dobie Gillis,* now a member of the California State Assembly (D., Santa Monica), sponsoring progressive legislation for women's, children's, and lesbian/gay rights.

On Air

Show me my face before I was born.

— ZEN KOAN

It's a rare little girl who gets to play with a doll of herself.

There was a Robin Morgan doll. There also was a Dagmar doll, named after the character I played for seven years on TV. The Dagmar doll was a large, cloth-stuffed-with-cotton, floppy, genial creature, attired in 1910-era period clothes, the navy-blue "sailor suit" middy blouse and skirt with long black stockings that constituted Dagmar's costume (wardrobe permitted me variations for festive occasions). Her yarn hair was done up in the braids I'd made famous at the cost of a scalp so tight I had a permanent, mild headache I no longer noticed.

Sent off with Aunt Sally on a ten-city tour to hype the Dagmar doll's sales in department-store toy areas, I cheerfully sat in costume, signing photographs for tongue-tied kids and their gushing mothers, all of us surrounded by eerie, smiling, life-size, stuffed versions of myself.

But the Robin Morgan doll was even spookier. It was manufactured in a limited number, as an elite doll—that strange commercial category known as "a collector's item"—although I was allowed to keep one for promotion purposes. A plaster cast was made of my six-year-old face—a claustrophobic experience where you breathe through straws placed in your nostrils—and then the cast was re-created in hard rubber. This doll also wore her hair in pigtails, but the wig was from human hair almost identical in color to my own, and she had tiny eyelashes fashioned of fine gold wire. Her fifteen-inch-tall body was also made of hard rubber. Her clothing could be taken off—real buttons and buttonholes, real hooks and eyes on real patent-leather shoes—and she even had a petticoat and underpants that came on and off, showing a smooth sexless body (which I examined the second I was alone with her) with hinged limbs and detailed hands complete with fingers and nails. It's just as well I hadn't yet heard of voodoo, or I might've felt even uneasier gazing at this creature than I already did.

She lost her limbs one by one over time. Finally, a few years ago, burrowing through Scrabble boxes and chess sets gathering dust on a closet shelf, I came across her head—disembodied but smiling brightly, the wire eyelashes only a bit tarnished and bent out of shape. I think I must have saved her (or at least her head) less out of fondness than some inchoate self-preservative impulse that was discomfited at the possibility of such a graven image falling into anyone else's hands.

But then there was the Doll Collection.

The doll collection began well enough, in the for-play category. But it wound up in the good-peg-for-press-interview category. Over a period of years, the doll population grew into the hundreds: wee dolls and dolls the size of a three-year-old child, baby dolls and grown-up dolls, cloth dolls, antiques with porcelain heads, and a subcategory of "exotics" from other countries, the kind you see displayed in tourist shops sporting national dress. The elite line of Madame Alexander dolls found its way into the collection one by one, usually as gifts from agents and producers: the Queen Elizabeth II in her coronation robes, the Prima Ballerina, the Cinderella, the Sleeping Beauty, the Little Women set—Meg/Jo/Amy/Beth (Beth arrived cross-eyed, but I wouldn't send her back) and Marmee—and naturally there was the Bride Doll. A doll was dutifully carried for photo shoots and public appearances, making me the object of bilious envy for most other little girls—who didn't know that these dolls were considered too expensive to *play* with. Nor did they know that the one thing I really wanted, a dollhouse, was "out of the question": it would take up too much space, and it wasn't portable, meaning it had no function for publicity purposes.

When I grew a little older and an omnipresent doll was less required for my adorability factor, it became more permissible for me to have some fun with the dolls. I dressed them in creations of my own making from scraps of cloth, washcloths, an old chiffon scarf of my mother's. I wrote plays for my miniature repertory company, with multiple heroines (there were no boy dolls back then, no Kens or GI Joes). I rearranged everybody, putting Queen Elizabeth's crown on Beth, switching the Ballerina's toe shoes with Cinderella's glass slippers. I threw them a pajama party—an act of invention on my part, since I'd never been to such a party and none of them had doll pajamas anyway.

Still, only one doll ever claimed my heart. She was a plain Raggedy Ann with shoe-button eyes, a stitched-on grin, and a printed heart that declared *I love you*. She sat on my bed all day and slept in it all night, got packed in suitcases when we traveled for location taping or promotional shots, got frayed, torn, restitched, and lumpy. But, like Faulkner's Delsey, she endured. Of all the characters in the doll collection—donated with fanfare publicity to a children's hospital when I was fifteen—she's the only one I still have. Any average little girl, any *real* little girl, could have had a Raggedy Ann, you see.

I know nothing about the type of rewards working kid actors today ostensibly enjoy. Swimming pools, it seems. Porsches, coke snorts, and sex by age fourteen, perhaps. Vacations at Cannes or Palm Springs. I suspect it's far less glam than it sounds. For my part, I worked more in radio and television than in theater or films; this meant a New York, not California, base—something beneficent in the universe about *that*. But it meant that the money, though steadier, was less lavish. I was also the daughter and niece of women who apparently had stored in their emotional genes a vigilance that at any given moment Doom might arrive or the Cossacks thunder in *(Who knows?)*—and so were highly suspicious of swimming pools *(Careful! You could drown or catch polio!)*, cars *(Why would you want to learn to drive, anyway? Someday you'll have a chauffeur! Besides, buses don't exist?)*, any kind of drugs, even medicinal *(You don't want an aspirin; it'll make you groggy for days)*, sex *(What?)*, and certainly "vacations."

I can remember only two vacations from my childhood. The first, when

I was very little, maybe three years old, is part memory and part inherited story from my mother and aunts. It was while we still lived in Lake Worth, Florida, where I was born, before the move back north to Mount Vernon. My mother and Aunt Sally had taken me to the Everglades, for, they told me, a family vacation. It just happened that the papers had been filled for weeks with the news that a major Hollywood movie was being filmed there, *The Yearling*, starring Gregory Peck and Jane Wyman, and introducing a young boy in his first acting role, Claude Jarman Jr. Hindsight focuses the motives for my mother's and aunt's choice of vacation site: I might be "discovered." Indeed, every day they brought me to watch the filming along with the other gawkers. Apparently, however, something I'd eaten disagreed with me and caused me to lose my big chance at baby stardom; what's more, it covered us all with shame and me with something more specific. The first memory of disgrace dates from this time, when I recall Mommie kneeling beside me in the ladies' room, cleaning my legs with wet paper towels, and crying while she did it. I couldn't have helped it, yet I knew I'd let her down.

But there was a *good* vacation, too.

I must have been no more than four when I was taken for a holiday in North Carolina. The particulars of how and why we went there are hazy— something about Uncle Aham's having rented a house for the summer— but the sense of that holiday is anything but hazy.

Whatever magic North Carolina and the Great Smoky Mountains must have worked on us, I remember only happy moments from that trip, at least until its ending. Was it a week? A month? An entire summer? I'll never know, because those who could tell me are dead, and what I retain is a child's sense of time, which is to say a sense of timelessness. Whenever I hear Samuel Barber's poignant setting of James Agee's "Knoxville," especially the version recorded by Eleanor Steber, it throws me back in nostalgic yearning to that vacation, as if it were a memory of my whole childhood, not one unusual occurrence.

There were early yellow mornings and long violet twilights, and in between the days were hot and slow and smelled like oranges and nobody shouted. When the dusk blued into night, I was allowed to stay up and see the stars—the first time I ever met them—and I was introduced to the Big Dipper.

My lifelong love of gardening began on this trip. That love would remain abstract until my twenties and then, for the next thirty years, be confined to window boxes, potted plants, and city-rooftop planters until it could nestle into my own real earth garden at last, only a few years ago. It was my mother who unwittingly began this gentle obsession, by sharing with me what I now realize was her sole experience with nurturing plant life, one her mother had taught *her*. On discovering that one of the sweet potatoes she'd bought at the market had already sprouted "eyes," she showed me how to prop it with toothpicks in a glass jar half-filled with water and promised that "sweet-potato ivy" would sprout and grow. She hadn't anticipated that I'd promptly sit down to watch it happen, refusing to budge in case I might miss the moment of sprout. The sweet-potato jar of necessity became portable; otherwise, she would never have got me to the lakeside, or even out on the porch. And sprout it did, eventually. But only after we were back home, by then in Mount Vernon—and the ivy, grown long and lush, twined up and around the living-room window and remained such a delight to me that every windowsill in the small apartment held rows of differently shaped jars and glasses containing sweet potatoes in varying stages of ivyhood development.

But that vacation was also the time of the puppy—one of a neighbor's dog's litter given to me. Oh, he was a classic: a golden, silky, loose-limbed, floppy-eared, eight-week-old cocker spaniel with enormous liquid brown-amber eyes that blinked at me worshipfully. I named him Happy, which he made me very. I carried him everywhere, slept with him, talked, played, and planned with him, and knew I'd made a friend for life.

It wasn't until the neighbor was helping Mommie pack the car to leave that the two of them told me I couldn't take him with us. Mommie said we were too busy to care for him, and they both burbled the usual adult inanities that he'd be well cared for and they'd never thought I'd grow so attached to him in such a short time when all they'd meant was for me to enjoy having a pet for a while. He was pulled him out of my arms and passed to the neighbor, as both he and I howled our mutual loss.

I've never forgiven the well-meaning cruelty of that temporary gift, the unspoken lie that it was for keeps. A few years later, when I was working steadily in television, Mommie and Aunt Sally announced I could have a pet. I requested a Happy—but was informed that walking a dog was a time-consuming nuisance, and that I wasn't old enough to have such responsibility (the irony of this was not lost on me). Instead, Aunt Sally came home one day with a small aquarium and three miniature turtles— the kind whose tiny shells some pet stores hideously painted with patterns or faces, a practice now fortunately as illegal as dyeing chicks pastel colors for sale around Easter. I had been reading about the Round Table myths in the Junior Classics series, so I named the turtles Arthur, Guinevere, and Lancelot. But turtles were unsatisfying; you couldn't cuddle a turtle, and gazing into its beady eyes only served to remind you it was a cold-blooded creature, a reptile.

I resented the turtles, who gave little pleasure but required work to demonstrate (again) my responsibility. Their smelly water had to be changed, and their little shells scrubbed lightly with a nail brush to remove accumulated slime. They had to be fed their turtle food plus shreds of lettuce on a regular schedule. They showed no affection in return, of course. "Their God is not my God," D. H. Lawrence wrote of fish, which fairly describes my attitude toward those turtles, an attitude only intensified on finding, one day, that owing to my having been remiss about feeding them twice in a row, Lancelot had become impatient and eaten Arthur. Because he was so thorough, this sad fact wasn't revealed until a week or so later, during which time we searched the apartment for a theoretically escaped Arthur, to no avail. It was only when I horribly repeated my carelessness about feeding them that the awful truth emerged—because Guinevere devoured Lancelot, but daintily left part of a tiny claw and some shell shard as a clue to why she seemed so sluggish but content.

I felt like a murderer, aware for the first time how thin the tissue is that separates the power to help from the power to harm. I did care for Guinevere solicitously until the day of her death, which was of apparently natural causes. I declined the offer of replacement reptiles, and was again denied a dog. So I gave up on pets, at least as a child.

Only as a grown woman did I discover the glory of cats.

~ ~ ~

There is something missing here, in this telling of perks and rewards, however limited.

It's not the sense that one is "special"—because that can vanish pretty quickly, plummeting one's emotions to the nether side of unworthiness. I don't know if the particular reward I'm groping toward describing is a reward at all, and I don't know if it's been experienced by all or even most child actors. Somehow, I'm afraid not, or their lives might've turned out a bit saner and more fulfilling. Ultimately, I can speak only for myself. But to do so honestly means admitting the recognition (with hindsight) that there *was* one beneficent legacy—a more accurate term than reward— bequeathed me by my working childhood.

It was the idea that work could be something one loved doing.

I don't mean by this that I loved performing. Sometimes I enjoyed it, sometimes I detested it, mostly it was just a given. But I did like being *good* at what I did—anybody does—and I was repeatedly *told* by others how good a child actor I was, and how that must mean I loved what I was doing. I would smile politely and ponder this in my little heart. Meanwhile, the notion that it was possible to love one's work lodged somewhere in me and excited me tremendously. Gradually it dawned on me that what *I* loved, in fact what I'd most loved doing as far back as I could recall— making up stories and poems, playing with the magic of words—could be a life's work.

I knew how passionately I would *love* that. And I wasn't wrong. Chosen, meaningful work has been the consistent exercise, luxury, pleasure, challenge, and regimen of my life.

Later, other legacies would surface, but not until I was ready to claim them as my own and apply them for my own purposes. A sense of self-discipline (handy for a freelance writer working mostly at home). A sense of professionalism (practical for a freelance editor). A respect for drama and for humor, a sense of timing, and a well-modulated voice with the knowledge of how to project it (valuable for poetry readings and advantageous for political speeches). Ease with reporters, microphones, cameras, and audiences (convenient for political organizing and useful for book tours).

But the process of learning that such skills were in a sense value-free was difficult. At first I refused to avail myself of any of them. To my mind, they'd been inflicted without or against my choice, so they were painful, cheapening reminders of what felt like years in unwitting servitude.

It wasn't until I discovered that I was also infatuated with making social change—infatuation being markedly different from love but damned potent in its own right—that these skills reappeared in a more flattering light. Politics had to wait, however, until I connected with the concept of rebellion itself. For someone who never went through "the terrible two's," because she was already busy modeling tot fashions, making that connection took time.

But once it happened, and *that* energy became linked to the love of writing, I never looked back. In this I've been extraordinarily fortunate. Finishing a poem that I know is strong and moving has been for me that high only achievable for many of my child-actor contemporaries by other, more destructive means. Helping to inoculate others with the healing virus of resistance to injustice has been for me the outlet for rebellion those colleagues could express only in car crashes and substance abuse.

Not too long ago, I found myself remembering when my defiance first broke the surface.

I had forgotten that defining moment until 1994, when I saw Robert Redford's movie *Quiz Show*, based on the TV program *The $64,000 Question*. That 1950s show—notorious in broadcasting history for its fixed answers and corruption of contestants—had been presented by Barry and Enright Productions.

Those names brought back more than a few memories. Dan Enright (in the 1940s, pre-name change, it had been Ehrenreich) had produced and directed my half-hour weekly national radio show, *Little Robin Morgan*, on WOR for two years (age four to six). "Pop Goes the Weasel" was my theme song, and I played records, told stories I'd made up, chattered on about my "adventures," and sometimes interviewed "children from other lands," tapping into the resource of United Nations publicists (and, friends now joke, presaging my later involvement with the global Women's Movement). I apparently did *not* appreciate being referred to as "the world's youngest disk jockey," because a *Chicago Tribune* clipping quotes me as firmly correcting the reporter: "I am the world's youngest *story-teller*."

I loathed "Mr. Ehrenreich," whose body odor, nicotine-stained fingers, and whinnying laugh seemed to be all over my life. He also produced *Juvenile Jury,* and his business partner Jack Barry (pre-nose job) was the moderator. That show, for its first year on radio, for its second on both radio and television, was the competitor of *The Quiz Kids,* and was staged before a live audience. Like that of other Barry Ehrenreich Productions (and Barry Enright Productions to come), its spontaneity was an illusion; the questions and answers were fixed beforehand.

We were a group of children ranging in age from four (I was the youngest) through eight or nine (Dickie Orlan, overplump and always hungry, Charlie Hankenson, who squeaked rather sweetly) to age fourteen (Peggy Bruder, a ladylike almost-adult with long blond corkscrew curls I coveted). We sat on studio folding chairs—my feet unable to reach the floor—behind a long counter equipped with table mikes and glasses of water. Our job was to "counsel" other children, who wrote us letters asking for advice on such matters as "My best friend's family is moving away; can we still be friends long-distance?" Some of the questions were drawn from actual letters sent in by real children, but most were devised by Barry, Ehrenreich, and their team of hack writers.

We were assembled before showtime, told what questions Mr. Barry would read on the show, and assigned our answers. Ehrenreich was shrewd enough to permit us to phrase our replies in our own words for a more natural effect, but it was clear that no one should even *think* about diverging from the substance of an assigned answer. And no one did. Ehrenreich, who always patrolled the stage behind us while we were on air, had a habit of grasping an errant child—someone who rambled on too long or talked over audience laughter—sharply by the shoulder. He had developed a singularly effective method of communicating his displeasure by digging his fingers in between the shoulder and collarbone, while his thumb gouged at the shoulder blade—a sort of Vulcan neck pinch long before Mr. Spock.

I was perhaps all of five years old when I turned insubordinate. One of the questions, we'd been told, was from a child complaining that when he was naughty, his mother reported it to his father, who then spanked him

too hard; what did the Juvenile Jurors think the child should do? We had
been duly assigned our replies. One Juror had been told to advise the letter writer, "Just don't be naughty anymore" (certain to evoke a laugh from
the studio audience); another was told to counsel him to beg his mother
to do the spanking instead, on the assumption she would wield a more
compassionate hand; still another answer was that he should ask if his
mother and father could take turns doing the spanking. My assigned reply
was that he should beg his father very nicely please maybe not to spank so
hard (sure to get another laugh) or else to sneak some padding under his
pants (*big* laugh). Not one of the assigned answers challenged the concept
of corporal punishment.

But once we were live on air and my turn came, I said something
different.

I don't know why. I can't remember the thought processes or emotional
valences that kindled this act, although I do remember the fear and what
I now know was the adrenaline surge that overrode the fear. I leaned forward toward my table mike and said it out loud.

"I don't think you should be spanked at all."

Instantly, I felt the Ehrenreich vise on my right shoulder.

I went on. "I don't think it's good that children get hit."

He clamped down harder. I could feel his fingernails through my
starched organdy dress.

But I went on—about how maybe if the letter writer asked his parents
to make up some other punishments for him when he was naughty, they
might.

Ehrenreich reached in front of me and turned my mike around, facing
it away from me.

On I recklessly went, giddy with it now, suggesting alternate punishments—". . . like losing a privilege, maybe, or being sent to your room
without supper." That, I admitted, was what happened to me when I was
bad, because my mother didn't think I should be hit.

Finally, so enraged that I could feel his bodily anger through his grip,
Ehrenreich clapped his free hand (the other one was still embedded in my
shoulder) in a muzzle over my mouth. Behind his sweaty fingers that stank
of the nonfiltered Camels he was never without, I mumbled on intrepidly.

That got a laugh. And we went rapidly to a commercial.

Afterward, both Ehrenreich and Barry administered a stinging verbal dressing-down in front of all the other kids and their mothers, meant to humiliate me and serve as a warning to anyone else so inspired. Although I can't recall any previous revolts on my part, there must have been at least one other, because Ehrenreich shouted that this wasn't the first time I'd disobeyed on air but it had goddamned well better be the last. Aunt Sally was crying, her mascara all runny. She was stuttering, reassuring him, whereas I was engaged in a serious examination of the suddenly fascinating toe-tips on my black patent-leather Mary Janes. I was scared, but somehow intuited even at that age that I was too valuable a commodity to be dismissed. While that didn't translate into any sense of personal power or security, it did feel vaguely protective, and the idea settled into my ego like an oysterous grain of sand. I knew, narcissistically, my worth in their terms—but not in my own. I knew I was the only Juvenile Juror with her own show on the side, and the one who received the most fan mail. I'd paid sufficiently for both by enduring gibes, pranks, and pinches from the other Jurors. I wished that Aunt Sally had stood up for me and said as much about my value, there, in front of everybody, and I wondered what reply Barry or Ehrenreich might have made if she had. I was confused by the lack of support from her and, later, from my mother, because after all I'd learned my position about no hitting from them, so shouldn't they be proud of me? I didn't understand that their rejection of corporal punishment, while partly a matter of principle, was also based on anxiety about my ever appearing bruised or being in any way incapacitated for work.

But Aunt Sally's groveling to Ehreneich and silence in defending me didn't alter my own perceptions. Nor were they changed by the fear I'd experienced while rebelling, the physical pain (my shoulder turned black-and-blue), or the subsequent public embarrassment in front of the whole group, enabling the other kids to giggle with pleasure and their mothers to beam with satisfaction. I distinctly recall that I was busy feeling something utterly new, something fragile but strong enough to weigh in at a balance with all the negative results of my insurrection.

It was something akin to feeling proud of myself—but it was a new kind of pride. It was not a reflective pride, because no one else had praised me. It was from someplace inside *me*. I knew I was right. I knew kids shouldn't get hit. I'd got that *said,* aloud, live and on air, and I'd refused to let them stop me.

My vocabulary was large, even for a precocious five-year-old, but not so large as to embrace such words or concepts as righteous action or self-determination. Learning those would take years. And it would be decades until the memory of that mutinous act would be resurrected by an unwitting Robert Redford, to whom I'm grateful. But from the moment I remembered it, I realized that I loved and respected that child who fought back in what was the first political act I recall ever daring to make.

How intensely she longed to speak in her real voice, that child!

How I wish there were a way of giving her back her own voice, her own truths, even if only by some literary conceit.

She did keep a diary, on and off, for years.

Let her speak for herself, then.

FOUR

. . . .

Possession Game

. . . that wild, unknown being, the child,
who is both bottomless pit and impregnable fortress . . .
— COLETTE

*D*ear Diary,

These are the first words I'll ever write in a diary. Mommie gave you to me, the best of all the presents I got on yesterday, my 8th birthday. I will never have another 8th birthday in my life. Mommie and me had lunch just us two at the Plaza Hotel and we were given tickets to go to the opera last night to see Carmen who had a rose between her teeth and got killed.

But you are best of all, Diary, because I wanted you and Mommie knew that and here you are. I love your shiny blue leather cover with the strip that has a lock in it and the tiny golden key that can shut you. Mommie is going to keep the key because she says I'll just lose it and also she wants to check and be sure I write in you every single day and also so she can correct my spelling mistakes. Because she says a person never knows who else might look. I'm a pretty good speller and I think nobody would look if I had the key but then you never know and they could always just cut the strip I guess. It's a wonderful feeling to write in you because your paper is smooth and slippery and the color of the cream I lick off the milk bottle's round cardboard top. You are very important to me even if anybody else can look into you because a person never knows.

Your friend,
with love,
Robin Morgan

Dear Diary,

Mommie says she is glad I wrote down all the good things we did on my birthday. She says it will be a treasure for me to look back on when I grow up and remember how happy these years were. I'm sure Mommie is right because otherwise a person might forget these things when they get old.

Today we got up and had breakfast. Mommie always has coffee and a muffin which is also one of her names for me, Muffin not coffee. So our joke is Mommie always has coffee and me for breakfast. Aunt Sally loves bagels a *lot*. I had hot cereal that I always hate. I hate cold cereal too. Anyway, then we got dressed and I wore the pink organdy with white butterflies aplikayed (spelling? Help Mommie!) on it that Mommie sewed for me (Mommie makes all my clothes, Diary, and she's wonderful at it) and my black patenleather (spelling?) maryjane shoes with the straps I hate. Then Aunt Sally and me took the train into New York City (we live in Mount Vernon, Diary, which is called a suburb sort of) and went to rehearsal and then I had an interview which is why the pink organdy today and then we took the train back. Then there was school and afterwards ballet and tap classes with Mrs. Liccione and then I did my homework and practiced piano and studied my lines for tomorrow's rehearsal. I should write more but I'm too sleepy. I almost didn't write in you tonight but I want to every single night so I did.

Your friend,
with love,
Robin Morgan

Dear Diary,

I'll tell you about me. I'll tell it the way I'm supposed to in an interview.

I started talking when I was only four months old and really got to talking when I was eight months old and Aunt Sally says then I never stopped. I won the All American baby medal when I was six months old and was Miss Baby Palm Beach Florida when I was two. I had my own radio program when I was four and also I was on *Juvenile Jury* for two years. Before that I was a model and sometimes I sang and danced and recited, like Portia's speech about mercy from Shakespeare. I like Shakespeare. I do not like singing. But people liked it and clapped when I sang "Mairzy Doats" and "Cement Mixer" and "Alexander's Ragtime Band." The only song *I* liked to sing was "You Are My Sunshine" because it's Mommie's favorite along with "Besame Mucho" but that's in Spanish and I don't know how to sing in that. Also I acted in a movie called *Citizen Saint* when I was almost seven. I played Mother Cabrini as a child. She became a nun before she got to be a Mother which means a boss of nuns not a Mommie and then she got to be a saint, the first one ever from America. The movie had a big opening at the Bijou Theater on 45th Street and Broadway with lots of publicity and priests. And I also did guest shots on radio shows like *We The People* with Art Linkletter and *Arthur Godfrey's Hour* and once I was a talent judge on Ted Mack's show *Amateur Hour*.

Anyhow, now I'm on television every week in *Mama* (that's the name of the program) and I play a little girl named Dagmar. Our show comes from a book that was called *Mama's Bank Account* by Kathryn Forbes who is the first *real book writer* I ever met! Also there was a play and a movie called *I Remember Mama* from that same book. We wear old-fashioned clothes because we are supposed to be living around 1910 in San Francisco on Steiner Street. Our set is this oldtime house with a parlor and a player piano and stuff that's very awethentik (spelling?) because Mr. Jac Venza who is our set designer cares about things being just perfect. In the cast, there's Mama and Papa who came to America from Norway and there's Nels (my show brother) and Katrin (my show sister) and me. Our show is very popular and has won awards and I am famous I think. But I am not just famous. Mr. Ralph Nelson who is our director says I am a serious actress because I can be anything anyone wants me to be.

Anyway, I live with my Aunt Sally, who takes me to rehearsal and stuff, and my mother, whose name is Faith Morgan and it fits her because she always says she *never* loses faith. We live at 50 South Second Avenue in apartment 3-A, on the third floor (we don't have an elevator but Mommie thinks someday when I make enough money we can move into the City and live in a fancy elevator building). Aunt Sally sleeps on the livingroom rollout sofabed that is covered by a blanket Mommie bought a long time ago in Mexico. Mommie and I sleep on twin beds in the bedroom. Our building is only one block from the railroad station which is good because we go into the City for rehearsals and shows and stuff every day but not on weekends and sometimes I do a fashion show even on a weekend day (I'm still a model, Diary, but not so much as when I was young).

What is not so good about our apartment house is that on one side of us is a Greek Orthodocks church where on Greek Easter (which is different from ordinary Easter), the priests march around the church carrying a coffin which is scary to look out the window and see, and they sing loud. Mommie says the coffin is empty and not to be scared. What is also not so good about our apartment house is that (on the other side) it is right next door to a place everybody says they should tear down and make into something clean like a parking lot because it has lots of little funny wooden buildings on it, sort of leaning like they could fall down. A lot of Negro people live there and some of the houses don't have electric light and everybody says they are a fire hazard. They are a fire hazard because the Negro people have to use candles to see by and have wood stoves everybody says. But I don't know how you're supposed to see in the dark or keep warm if you don't have electric plugs. They are very poor, Mommie says, and always on Thanksgiving and sometimes on other holidays (but not Jewish holidays because Mommie says none of the Negro people would ever be Jewish) Mommie and I go over to the houses with shopping bags. We bring cans of food we buy at the A&P on special and oranges you can get in sort of wiry bags. And we put some of my clothes I get too big for in the shopping bags. But we never put the organdies in there even when I get too big for them. Mommie thinks we should save them so I can treasure them when I grow up and also she says where would the little girls next door wear such things?

There is one little girl next door who is pretty much the same age as me and her name is Roberta which is sort of like Robin and I think she would look beautiful in one of the organdy dresses because she has a nice smile and seems friendly but Aunt Sally told me it would be an insult to give her one of the organdy dresses and I would never want to insult Roberta. I'd like to go play with her sometimes but Aunt Sally and I talked about that. She told me everybody was exactly the same and Negroes were just as good as white people and poor people as good as rich ones. But life wasn't perfect, Aunt Sally said, and you had to face facts. Facts was that if Roberta came to 3-A to play she would only get jealous of all the dolls and pretty dresses and how lucky I was. And if I went over to Roberta's house to play first it was too small and we would have to play outside and we shouldn't play outside because the ground over there has broken glass and bottle tops and rusty metal things and I might fall and hurt myself or even bust up my face. And Mommie also explained that wanting to play with Roberta was a nice idea but it wouldn't work because Roberta and I had nothing in common and Roberta knew that even if I didn't. I don't think Roberta knows that. Even if she did we would have a lot more in common if she had one of the dolls and an organdy dress. Besides, they don't have TV sets over there next door because no plugs which means Roberta does-n't even know I'm on TV. So she might think I'm just a little girl like her and she might like me. She always smiles at me.

If we went to the same school maybe we would have something in com-mon and be allowed to be friends and play. But I don't know where Roberta goes to school. I go to a private school, Miss Wetter's at 230 East Lincoln Avenue, and there are only 40 pupils in the whole school and nobody looks like Roberta. I mean not only nobody is a Negro person but also nobody smiles a nice smile at me. At school everybody knows I'm on TV every week so they act like we have nothing in common. Also I'm pretty smart in school and a good reader and have what Mr. Nelson calls "a fast memory," that helps with learning my lines. But getting all A's in school doesn't help me have more in common with the other kids. They think I am a rotten stuck-up pig (Doris Sheidecker said that) just because I'm on TV, and Carol Maloney once tried to burn my face with the sun through a magnifying (spell?) glass when I wasn't paying attention and was reading in recess. Miss Wetter shouted at her and then Carol hated me more afterward. And Harold always pushes me and once he ripped an organdy because there was a photo shoot in the morning before school and no time to change. Mommie says I should ignore it because they're just jealous. I think Roberta would have a lot more to be jealous of me about if she wanted to because she has only one doll that is a Raggedy Ann and no organdy dress but she seems to like me. But since we have nothing in common I guess we can't be real friends. Mommie says I should always smile back of course, and be polite and greet all our neighbors (in the building and even next door) when I see them. But that's not being real friends. I will understand all this when I'm old, Mommie says, and besides the world will change and people won't be poor anymore and she never loses faith. I believe her because she's the best Mommie in the world and she is giving her whole life to me. I hope I die before she does because I wouldn't want to live without Mommie.

I'm too tired to write more so I'll tell you more about myself another time.

Your friend,
with love,
Robin

Dear Diary,
This time I really will tell you about myself. Sometimes I write poems. I am 8 years old, but you know that because you were born on my 8th birthday (which means we have the same birthday, January 29) and I have brown eyes and blond hair. When I was young my hair was *very* blond. You can see it in the pictures when I did the baby food ads and the toddler clothes. But last year it began to get dark and become what Mr. Nelson called "dirty blond" even though we wash it every night and Aunt Sally sets it in curls with bobbypins and hairset while I sit on the toilet seat and study my lines. Anyway, Mr. Nelson and even Miss Irwin (she's our show's Producer) were getting worried, and so they had a talk with Aunt Sally about my hair and now we go every three weeks to Charles of the Ritz on 57th Street in the City to keep my hair blond. I sort of like Charles of the Ritz, because it means I miss half an afternoon of school even if I do have to do makeup homework. Charles of the Ritz is named after a great hairdresser who is either dead or anyway never there. It is very expensive Aunt Sally says so I always sit still and don't waste time. I like the shiny white marble floor and the pink silk coat they put on you and the big soft chair you climb into that turns in every direction and walls and walls and even the ceiling of mirrors. You can see millions of yourselves turning in all directions. The rest I hate. Miss Frances is nice to me and says I am a lit-

tle princess but then she puts this stuff on my head and it stings awfully and the smell makes me sick in my stomach. Aunt Sally and Miss Frances say to hold my nose and breathe through my mouth but the smell even stings in my throat like it does on my head and it goes on and on because they leave it on your head and go away while you do your homework or study your lines or something. You have to be very very careful not to let it drip down your forehead into your eyes if you bend your head down because you could go blind. So I always hold my head straight ahead of me and lift my homework or the script up high which makes my arms tired. After a while, Miss Frances comes back and then it gets better because we have a shampoo to get the stuff out and then conditioner and a set and then I sit under the dryer like the grown women in their silk coats. And then we do comb out and it all is silky golden curls and Miss Frances and Aunt Sally and Miss Irwin and everybody is happy. Your head stays stinging for two or three days and hot water especially on it hurts when your hair is getting washed even at home but then the sting goes away until the next time you have to go to Charles of the Ritz. I wish I hadn't started to be a dirty blond.

Rosemary Rice who everybody but me calls Rosie plays my older sister Katrin and also has stuff put on her hair to be blonder. She has tiny feet and can play the accordion and is beautiful. But I know she doesn't like me. She won't let me call her Rosie, and she hurt my feelings by nick-naming me Toothless Tess when I lost a tooth. Miss Quinlan (Miss Irwin's friend who is Associate Producer on the credits) whispered to me that Rosemary was jealous. I don't know why *she* should be jealous of me because we're *both* on TV. But she sure loves Mr. Nelson. Once at a cast party in Luchow's restaurant she said right out loud in front of everybody "Ralph, I'm tipsy so I've got bottle courage and I'm asking you to marry me." And everybody laughed I guess at the idea you could put courage into a bottle and Rosemary laughed too and so did Mr. Nelson but then it got serious because she started crying and slid down onto her knees and said "Ralph it's been two years and we're going nowhere. I'm begging you Ralph. Marry me. Ralph I'm begging you." Then everybody got quiet and looked away and Mr. Nelson kept clearing his throat and Billy Nalle—he's our musical background director and plays piano and organ and every-thing—he took me by the hand and said Why don't we go into the restaurant lobby and check out the menus. I didn't want to because people are always pulling me away when things get interesting but I had to go so I don't know how it ended except Rosemary and Mr. Nelson still come to rehearsals in the morning together but they didn't get married because I think he already is or something. He used to be married to Celeste Holm a famous movie actress, but that was before.

I'm tired.

Dear Diary,

I apologize because I always mean to tell you about myself but always get tired. Also I'm sorry I was so sleepy I forgot to sign my name last time but you know who writes in you anyway. Today I had rehearsal in the morning and then school and then the lesson with my drama coach in foreign accents. We did French and British today. Tomorrow I have piano after school so I had to do extra practice tonight after homework because I was falling behind. So now I'm too sleepy to write more. I apologize Diary. Oh and I almost forgot. I'm not going to sign what I write in you like I have been, I mean "Your friend, with love, Robin Morgan" anymore. Because way back that is what we decided I should write on the fan pictures I autograph (we are very honest about this and I sign them all myself even if other TV stars use a rubber stamp because Aunt Sally says we have a duty to our fans). But you are not a fan and I don't want to sign this like that. Even if you feel like a real friend and I do love you, those words got used up someplace else. But I don't know what else to sign this with.

Robin

Dear Diary,

Today is February 4 and Mommie says I should always put in the day but I don't see why because I've been writing in you every day since Mommie gave you to me on our birthday so if anybody reads this because you never know they can always count up.

Mommie did read you last night after I was asleep but I guess you know that. This morning she explained to me that it was a waste of time and your creamy paper to fill you up with drivel she said about things like Roberta and Charles of the Ritz. She said a person should be positive and write happy things in a diary or else if anybody looked at it they would get the wrong impression and think life was nothing but miserable. My life is not miserable and I know I am very lucky to be a TV star and have hundreds of loyal fans and go to a private school and have organdy dresses and a doll collection and wonderful privileges like music and dancing lessons and the best mother in the whole world and also Aunt Sally to help take care of me. I apologize, Diary, if I gave you the wrong impression. Mommie explained that even if nobody read what I wrote in you when I was old and read you I might get the wrong impression and who wants to remember bad times an old person wants to remember good times. I have never been old yet so I believe Mommie. I certainly would not want to give me the wrong impression.

Robin

Dear Diary,
This is Friday, February 5 and it was Air Day, which is always special. I don't go to school at all on Fridays (I do full school makeup work at home on Saturdays) not even for a half day like usual because we start rehearsal at ten in the morning in the studio and do a technical run-through and then a lunch break and then a full dress rehearsal and then dinner break and then get our makeup put on and then there's The Show. We don't get out of the studio until *ten o'clock at night!* So I'm going to write in you right now on the train (that's why my writing is bumpy) because when we get home Aunt Sally puts me down right away even if I'm excited because she knows I'm tired and also there's the Saturday makeup schoolwork tomorrow and a new script to learn. And singing lessons, too.

Anyway, today was Air Day, and Miss Wood (she is Peggy Wood who is the Star of our show) and everybody in the cast went around being nervous because it was Air Day and we do our show live and not filmed which means anything could go wrong you never know. But doing our show live is what gives it its magic Miss Irwin says. One time the player piano wouldn't play and Billy Nalle had to fake the music, and *three* times I covered up when grownups forget their lines and everybody said I saved the show. So I wasn't nervous even though I had the biggest part in this episode, which was about Dagmar getting in trouble for being a tomboy until she wins a baseball game for the neighbor kids by hitting a home run. I could have been nervous because I'm not a tomboy and I don't know how to throw a ball or catch one. All week in rehearsal Mr. Nelson had said he "despaired" of me. "Robbie," he said, "I despair of you." I hate it when anybody calls me Robbie. I don't mind Rob so much but I *hate* Robbie. But you can't say that to Mr. Nelson, no matter how polite you say it. I asked Aunt Sally to tell him but she said she didn't dare to either and besides she said everybody else called me something different anyway like Elfin and Sweetie and Princess and Lilliven (that's Dagmar's nickname on the show because it means little one in Norwegian) and between themselves they call me The Baby which Aunt Sally says I should understand because I am the youngest member of the cast and why be fussy? I just REALLY hate The Baby. But anyway Diary I want to be positive and Mr. Nelson is usually nice to me and says I am brilliant and his little Sarah Burnheart (who was the greatest actress who ever lived and died a long time ago). But he despaired of me once before when the script made me ride a bike but I don't know how so I wobbled and rode it right into the scrim that had San Francisco's streets painted across it so it looked like I was crashing into the whole city and they had to change the script even as late as dress rehearsal. Mr. Nelson despaired of me this time too and swore bad words and yelled why can't this godam kid even catch a ball. I kept shutting my eyes tight and sort of ducking down when it came flying at me. I couldn't help it. You never know, it could bust up your face. Aunt Sally talked to me and I really tried to keep my eyes open but then my hands went up in front of my face instead. I don't think it's so silly to duck when somebody throws something at you. It wasn't so silly that time the crazy man threw a rock on the last personal appearance tour. It was good I ducked or Aunt Sally said I could have got a scar or lost an eye or something horrible. They took the crazy man away to an insane place and he was crying and I felt sorry for him but I sure wasn't sorry I ducked.

Roberta next door can throw a ball and catch it perfect every time. I've watched her. After Mr. Nelson despaired of me in rehearsal I thought it would be a good idea if Roberta could teach me how she did it after all it was for my part and she could rehearse me all week on my ball stuff after school just like Aunt Sally or Mommie rehearse me my lines after homework. But Aunt Sally said that was not practical. She and Mr. Nelson and Miss Quinlan all had a conference because nobody wanted to bother Miss Irwin and they solved the whole thing by hiring a double to catch and throw (that's called a stunt) and they would show that scene in a long-shot. It felt funny to see another little girl wearing one of my costumes with her hair done up like mine, being me, except for in the close-ups. They called her the stunt kid and I never even got to know her name. I don't know how she learned to throw and catch like that but when Aunt Sally told Mommie it was going to happen, the stunt kid I mean, Mommie said to me which would you rather know how to do, throw a ball or be a star, catch a ball or get A's in school, and I told Mommie I'd rather be me and we laughed. I love Mommie because she didn't want me to feel bad so she told me to dry my smile and do a good show and remember that anybody could play ball but only I could be loved by thousands of people who never even met me.

The train is getting close to Mount Vernon so I have to stop. But the show went perfect and thousands of people will love me even more because they won't know about my double. They'll think I am the best child star in the world and also that I can throw and catch good as Babe Ruth. Like Aunt Sally says, it was a triumph.

Robin

Dear Diary,

I have been 8 for over a whole week! It was a wonderful week. Before it even started there was my birthday but you know about that. Then I got First in class doing multiplication (spelling? Mommie?) tables by memory. Doris stuck her tongue out at me and Teacher saw her and she got caught and had to write I WILL NOT BE RUDE in her notebook 20 times and was I glad. She is just as good as me in arithmetic but does not have a fast memory ha ha. Also Teacher said my vocabalary (spell?) is remarckable (spell?). But that's not all. Mr. Jones (he's my piano teacher) gave me a postcard with Beethoven looking mad on it because he said I was "coming along so well" and had real talent. Mommie says she isn't surprised because I am a walking talent factory! Today Mrs. Douglas who is my singing teacher said even if I couldn't hardly carry a tune (and Aunt Sally thinks she's crazy wrong about that it's just I'm too little) still I can talk-sing Mrs. Douglas said with "such charm" it didn't matter and Shirley Temple couldn't carry a tune either. (It matters to Mommie and Aunt

Sally, who want the best for me, but it doesn't matter to me because I am a serious actress so I think I don't need to sing anyway.)

Then there was my triumph about the stunt girl and how no one will know I can't throw or catch a ball as if I cared. Mommie rolled her eyes at me and whispered how we should hope none of the writers (Frank Gabrielson is the head writer of our show but sometimes also Gordon Webber writes it) ever writes one where Dagmar will have to roller skate or do something else silly or dangerous! Aunt Sophie once gave me Dorothy's old roller skates, but I'm only allowed to wear them on the rug. Anyway, we crossed our fingers together and giggled, Mommie and me. A person doesn't need friends in school when she has a mother like Mommie. (I don't care if they do write a show like that because now I know they can always hire the little girl who can do these silly things to be me and nobody will ever know.) It's more important and even Mr. Nelson says this that I am such a professional and never complain, which reminds me of the best thing of all but I'll tell you after I tell you this, and that I am so dam (Mr. Nelson uses bad words a lot) smart and can cry real tears any time the script says Dagmar cries. (I can, too. Even better than Margaret O'Brien. They said she always had to think of something sad first. But I can cry whenever they need me to. I don't know how I do it.)

But Pay Attention like Mr. Nelson says when I talk too much. Pay Attention, Diary, to the best part of this whole week. I didn't tell you before because I was too scared I wouldn't be able to finish it perfect. See, every year on my birthday I always give Mommie a present, too. Because, like she says, she was there when I was born. She almost *died*, Diary. Someday I want to have a baby but not almost die. Every night I pray thank you to God she didn't die and leave me an orphan with Aunt Sally. So when I was a tiny baby for my birthdays she would always get herself a little present too, along with the presents for me, because she didn't die, see? But when I was four and already a big girl I started to give her her present on my birthday instead of *her* giving herself one. I only started getting an allowance last year (a quarter a week!) so up until then I drew a picture or wrote her a poem for her present. Last year I saved up my quarters all year and Aunt Sally took me shopping so I could buy Mommie pearl earrings. (They weren't real pearl but almost.) Mommie loved them!

But this year Aunt Sally didn't want to take me shopping for Mommie because Mommie and her had a fight. Aunt Sophie was busy so she couldn't take me either. So how was I going to buy Mommie her present without anybody to take me? (Never mind Mommie if you see this ha ha I'll keep saving it up for *your* birthday, if I can find somebody to take me by then.) Anyway so what was I going to do this year for Mommie's present on my birthday? I didn't want to give her another poem or draw another picture. But then I thought of the perfect thing!

This is what I did. Before my birthday, I mean for maybe a month, I had been a very difficult (spelling?) child. I didn't mean to, but I guess I was. I had talked back and left my white shoes not polished. And also I acted phony because when Mommie let me go to the library for Saturday afternoon story hour all by myself (because the library is right across the street from our apartment building and Mommie can watch me from the window) I went but then snuck out and ran back across to see if maybe Roberta would like to teach me about the ball thing. But Mommie was still at the window and yelled and so I had to come in and I missed even story hour by being a phony. There were more things I did like that but I don't want to remember the bad stuff I want to be positive. I was sorry I made Mommie so miserable during that time. So I thought of the perfect present for her! It was to *promise* for a whole *year* not to make her miserable, the dearest Mommie in the world! I drew a chart and everything. At the top it has the days of the week. On the side it has a list of things I do that give her nerves or hurt her. This is the list I made.

To Obey
Not to Argue
Not to be Lazy
Not to Complain
Not to Talk So Much
Not to be Selfish
Not to be a Phony

Then I gave Mommie the chart and a little box of gold stars I had that you can paste on things. And I told her each week all year we would make up a new chart and I'd try for *perfect* the whole year until I was 9. Mommie hugged me. Then she said what would happen *after* I turned 9? So we giggled and she said my grandpa that I'm named for but never knew would say "Left foot right foot" and most of all *never stop trying* so she said let's just try a week at a time OK?

So we did. And now I can tell you on *every day* of this last week there is a *gold star* beside every thing on the list! Aunt Sally didn't have to report bad stuff not once! I didn't make Mommie miserable or give her nerves *all week long!*

Tomorrow Mommie is getting me a surprise privilege because I'm the best child anybody could ever have. Be in suspense like me, Diary! Good night.

I love you.

Robin

Dear Diary,
We slept till 9 o'clock! And then Mommie made lots of bacon and toast for Sunday breakfast. Aunt Sally went to Canal Street and Orchard Street in the City with Aunt Sophie, so it was just Mommie and me. We made peanut butter cookies. I made the crisscross designs to flatten the cookies with a fork after we rolled the doe (spell?) into balls on the cookie sheet. Then we took a bubble bath together. Then we played tickle and I got her and she got me and we laughed so hard we almost cried. Then we got all bundled up and went for a walk to Hartley Park and fed the ducks in the pond. There was a mother duck with the baby ducks right behind her in a row. I would love to have a pet but they can give you diseases Mommie says. But I'm glad I *don't* have brothers or sisters like those ducks. I wouldn't want to share Mommie. I'm glad it's just us two against the world like Mommie says that even means Aunt Sally. And then we went and ate dinner out at The Beehive restaurant and I had chicken and mashed potatoes with gravy and peach ice cream. Mommie had shrimp salad because she's on a diet. Then we looked in the store windows on Gramatan Avenue and I told Mommie someday I want to buy her a mink coat like Miss Irwin has. And we decided our career was going wonderful and if Miss Mona Monet (she's my agent) could get me that celery raise (I don't know how much money I make but I guess it's not enough yet) then we would just *do* it! I don't know about Aunt Sally but Mommie and me'd move into New York City (that's Manhattan) to a fancy building with an elevator. Mommie would love that, and me too. I don't like the smell in our building hall. It's

like somebody spilled grease and it got old but then you tried to clean it up with cleaning stuff but both smells stuck together.

And we only have one bedroom here anyway, but maybe when we move I can have my very own room and that could maybe mean space for a doll-house! Also like Mommie says, there's almost no closets in this apartment so that's why we have to hang things on the back of all the doors but there's so much hanging there that it sticks out all big and puffy with the sleeves like arms and if you wake up in the middle of the night it makes scary shapes that you don't want to move in bed in case they might come down from hanging there and get you with their flappy arms. And then maybe I can do extra parts in other shows if Miss Monet can get Miss Irwin to not have me in an exclusive contract. After all, I can pretend to be anybody they want me to be. I'd like to play other parts too because sometimes I get sick of Dagmar but still I'm lucky because the cast is like a second family everybody says, with another Mommie who's Miss Wood and a brother and sister and even a father and everything. Oh Diary I forgot to tell you my father died before I was born. He loved Mommie more than anything else in the whole world but he had to go in the war. He was a doctor so he became an army doctor and cured soldiers and never killed anybody but got killed anyhow. Anyway, so we could get out of this apartment and the smell in the hall and Hazel the woman next door who talks to herself on the stairs and Mommie says stay away from and Mr. Tompkins the super who drinks too much and says worse words even than Mr. Nelson and never fixes anything. There's plaster coming off the wall that Mommie says she *hates* but she also says it doesn't matter Mr. Tompkins won't ever paint because we'll probably move soon anyway and besides who wants to take down the pictures from the walls? There's lots of them. They're almost all of me (Aunt Sally says I am the most photographed child in history!) in different show costumes or my ballet tutu (that's a very short dress and is puffy and one of them that looks scary on the back of the door) and modeling and on a horse once (that was for publicity and I got *right off!*) and with famous people and other stuff. So it's OK we don't get painted by Mr. Tompkins. But still, there's this long orange face in the sink from the drips all the time. And there's a green snake in the tub from the drips there. Also sometimes there are bugs in the kitchen and I hate *that*. It's not our fault we're clean and spotless it's Mr. Tompkins's fault and the other people in this building. Aunt Sally says it's maybe the fault of the Negroes to the side of us and she always makes me scrub hard in the tub after we bring them baskets. I don't think it's the library's fault because the library is *really* clean and *very* quiet. I love it there. I'm a good reader (I could read before I started school) so I go every time I can except that once I snuck off to Roberta and gave Mommie nerves.

The library has a big window over the door of different colored bits of glass. It has a huge round ceiling inside and on every wall there are books books books. Also on stands in the middle of the room. Also in glass cases. Also on little carts. You could never read so many books in all your life even if you didn't have rehearsal and school and singing and piano and tap and ballet and Air Day. It's so quiet Mrs. Izzard says Shhhh if anybody makes noise to disturb you or give you nerves. You can learn about *everything anywhere* there. I bet you could learn about balls and bikes and roller skates and surprise everybody by just knowing how to do it! (If you ever get a surprise like that, Mommie, if you're reading this, you'll know what I was doing in the library!)

But really now Pay Attention! So Mommie and I talked about our Future and how even if it's just us against the world we're special enough to triumph. I don't care if it's just us. I'm glad I don't have a daddy, even if that's a terrible thing to say and even if sometimes I miss him but like Mommie says how can I miss him when I never even met him? And besides, I have Judson Laire, who plays my TV father and never got married and has no kids and is so nice I call him Papa even off the set and he likes it. I'd hate to have a wicked stepfather.

So I really have everything and I'm glad Mommie and me had the whole day just to ourselves. She says what do we need with a husband anyway I'm like her tiny husband because my acting brings home the bacon and it will take us far. I want to do that for Mommie, because I can take care of her better than any old husband could. She never punishes me. Even if I give her nerves I just get my privileges taken away, like going to the library that time, or watching Ed Sullivan on TV or playing cards with Dickie Van Patten who plays my brother on the set in the breaks. But privileges are bonuses anyway, like extras, so I shouldn't miss them.

Most of all, there isn't a little girl in America who wouldn't want to be me. Everybody says that. Aunt Sally says if we keep on this way maybe I might be a rich woman all my life even if I decide to stop acting someday and do something else but that it would be a shame to leave our career when I was already a star and going to be an even bigger star. I don't care about being a rich woman all my life but I would like to make Mommie rich so she can have the things she wants like a mink coat.

Well Diary I have to go study my lines now because Mommie and me played all day so Aunt Sally says we better do *some* work before our beauty sleep. Mommie is working on her stocks which are also going to help make us rich. It was a wonderful day and I wish it wasn't going to be tomorrow.

Goodnight, Diary,
Robin

Dear Diary,
Miss Mona Monet who is my agent remember? She committed *suicide* Diary, which means killing yourself with too many sleeping pills! I have never known a real dead person before because I never met my father. It feels scary. Mommie and Aunt Sally said it certainly was an accident but I should never discuss it with anyone. So I'm only telling you, Diary. I'm glad I'm not dead.

Love,
Robin

Dear Diary,
Mommie says I shouldn't have told you about Miss Monet. I'm sorry. Mommie says I should tell you about The Stork Club. Benton & Bowles, the ad agency for our show's sponsors, had a party for the cast there. I wrote this poem about it.

Everyone's sitting and laughing and drinking,
talking and talking
but nobody's thinking.

Anyway, Mommie says I should tell you The Stork Club named a drink after me. That's because Mr. Sherman Billingsley who owns it his little girl Shermane is a fan of mine. They already have a Shirley Temple drink that is ginger ale and cherries and sweet red stuff. So mine is 7-Up but with all the rest the same and also a pineapple chunk. And other restaurants like

Sardi's and The Oyster Bar in Grand Central Station and The Stage Deli and maybe Trader Vic's are going to have the Robin Morgan drink too, for when kids come, Mommie says. I knew I could be anything anybody wanted me to be, Diary, but I sure never thought I would be a drink!

Love,

Robin (gulp gulp)

Dear Diary,

I haven't written in you for a whole week. I'm so sorry. It wasn't my fault. Well, it was, but not because I didn't care about you. I *love* writing in you even if somebody will read it because you never know. I didn't just not pay attention to you for a whole week because I didn't care. I couldn't *find* you.

You see, I did a terrible thing or it turned out terrible and I should have known better. So I had a big privilege taken away and that was you. I couldn't write in you for a whole week. A whole week missed out of my life that you'll never know about because I can't remember all of it but I'll try.

It started with the terrible thing. On Wednesday, because it's sort of an easy day after school with only homework and the script Aunt Sally let me go to the library for a half hour till Mommie got home from work. And I really did go. I am reading Lamb's *Tales of Shakespeare* because in only a few years I will be old enough to play Juliet in *Romeo and Juliet* she was really only 14 did you know that, Diary? I didn't. That's what reading gets you. And I asked Mrs. Izzard to please come and tell me when half an hour was up because when I start reading I forget about everything else. So she did and I left when I was supposed to leave. I was trying for my second Perfect Week with stars but now I've gone and ruined everything for the whole year. Even if every other week is perfect the whole year won't be.

So I looked both ways and was crossing the street all by myself. (I love that part.) Then I saw a little bit ahead up the block by our building this awful thing. It was a fight. It was Benjy and Roger who are these two boys from upstairs in 4-A and Benjy is also 8 and Roger is 10 and their father is not dead but him and their mother Liz are divorced. That means they don't live together anymore and probably hate each other. Miss Wood has been divorced I think lots and I heard she is on her 4th husband but that's a rumor. Still, she says when will she ever learn and that must mean a lot of hating. Anyway, sometimes Mommie and Aunt Sally and Liz from 4-A have coffee together and talk upstairs or down here and when they do the kid or kids in whichever place is sent up or down to the other place. Us kids are supposed to play together whichever place we are. But I hate Benjy and even more Roger who is a bully. If we play up in 4-A they have only airplanes and guns and boring stuff and never want to play house or doctor or *Hamlet*. (I read *Hamlet* in Lamb's *Tales* I told you about and I thought we could act a play on it, with the ghost and everything.) They are very very stupid dumb boys. Roger likes to twist my dolls' arms around and once he broke one. They do not even know how to play poker and you can't teach them anything they are too dumb. Benjy likes to bang on our upright piano and he can't even play Chopsticks. I tried to teach him it was no use. I despair of both of them. So we just watch TV but I think cartoons are boring because I've seen how they do them on these big drawing boards and now it's never the same. But there's nothing else to do with these boys. The only good thing is when it's my turn to go upstairs I can have a Coke because they always have lots of Coke in the icebox. Liz says "Honey (she calls everybody Honey) I'm from Mississippi (spell?) and we just *live* on Coke and cigarettes!" I'm not allowed Coke except on special occassions (spell?) and we never have it in our icebox because Aunt Sally says it will rot my teeth. But I can have a Coke when I go upstairs and that's the only good thing I can think of about Benjy or Roger. And it's no good saying what can you expect from kids who don't have a father around (Hazel says this to herself real low whenever she passes them on the stairs) because after all look at me I'm not dumb and a bully. I know I'm lucky to be me and not everybody especially not boys can be me but still they could be better than they are.

Well, Diary, on that day they were specially horrible. It was Roger I saw up ahead on the street, and he was hitting and kicking at something and then I saw that the something was Roberta! Benjy was helping him and dancing around them and singing yaa yaa niggerbaby and *terrible* words like that that Mommie and me would never ever use (but sometimes if I want to wear new shoes or something right away Aunt Sally says "nigger-rich"). And Roberta was fighting and hitting back and shouting and I was proud of her because she would have licked Roger except it wasn't fair because there was Benjy to help hit her when Roger went down so they took turns but she never got to rest in between. So before I could think about it and I know now I should have thought I ran up and hit Roger hard on the back of his head with the Lamb's *Tales of Shakespeare* Mrs. Izzard let me take out now I have my junior library card and then when he turned around (and was he surprised, Diary!) I kicked him in the shins.

Benjy just stood there. But it gave Roberta time to reach out and sock Roger biff bam wham like in the comic books right on the side of his turned around surprised face. Roger hit me and pushed me and I fell down in the gutter where it's all dirty and my coat I heard it rip and then Roger jumped on me with his knees and he was very heavy because by this time Roberta had jumped on his back and was strangling him around the neck but the two of them together were very heavy on my stomach. And so I reached up to get Roger off me because there was murder in his eyes (I read that somewhere maybe about Othello who really did kill someone or maybe about Macbeth who killed lots of people) so I was worried. Maybe his eyes were just bulging because Roberta was holding on so tight from behind his neck but I didn't want to take any chances and besides the two of them were making me not breathe almost. So I started to bang and bang at Roger's face with my book and his nose started to bleed and the cover got bloody and then once I missed Roger and hit Roberta's arm by mistake and then she got thrown off him which I didn't like because she fell but at least it wasn't so heavy because I was beginning to worry that Benjy would jump on Roberta who was on Roger who was on me at the bottom in the dirty gutter and I'd get squashed flat and die.

Anyway, so then Benjy started to cry like a baby when he saw Roger's nosebleed and Roger got extra mad because not only was he getting beat but Benjy was seeing it. So he picked up this dumb stupid part of one of his airplanes he must have dropped in the fight that was laying on the ground beside me in the gutter and he started to hit me in the face with it like I had hit him with the book. And then there was yelling and grownups and I heard Aunt Sally screaming My God Where Where and her voice was coming closer and then Roger was getting pulled off me and Benjy was crying louder and the snot running down out of his stupid nose and the blood running down out of his brother's stupid nose and Mommie calling from down the street What What on her way home from work and Aunt Sally screaming and bending over me and Liz yelling at Roberta and I turned my head and I saw the front of my coat torn bad and also bloody.

But I didn't know if that was Roger bleeding onto me or me bleeding onto me because what I really paid attention to was Roberta running away. She was running like the wind, faster than Atalanta in my big *Greek Myths* book and she was getting smaller and smaller and she ran even past the Negro houses and kept on running and disappeared around the corner down by the railroad tracks where kids sometimes hid or played you could see them when you waited for the train to go to rehearsal.

And then I started to cry too. Because all of a sudden I wasn't sure if Roberta thought I was joining Benjy and Roger against her or if she knew that the two of us, her and me, were on the same side just us against the world. How could she be sure, because she always smiled at me but I never asked her to play and she never got one of my organdy dresses, and maybe she knew I did play with Roger and Benjy even though I hated to but how could *she* know that? I thought as she got smaller and smaller like the wind and then disappeared that now I'd never get to learn how she was so good at throwing and catching balls. Maybe she just wasn't scared when things got thrown at her so she threw them right back. But she was scared of the grownups that day and none of the grownups were Negro people. They were Mommie and Aunt Sally and Liz and even Mrs. Izzard ran out and she took back the book before I could say I apologize about the blood on it. And there was Hazel out of nowhere talking to herself and Mr. Tompkins saying "These people it's just not right this used to be a good block."

But most of all Mommie was crying and because she was screaming "Your face! Your face My God My God" I knew it wasn't just Roger's nose bleeding on my ripped front then, so I got scared too.

Well, Diary, Mommie carried me upstairs and everybody was crying and the doctor came and it was just a long scratch from under my eye down to my jaw but the doctor said it wouldn't leave a scar. I wonder if anybody called a doctor for Roberta. After Mommie stopped saying Thank God over and over and hugging me she got mad. She and Aunt Sally had a fight that Aunt Sally let this happen but Aunt Sally said it was all my fault. I had done a terrible thing that could have ruined our whole Future and Mommie had a bad bad case of nerves.

So I had my bath and my coat with the rabbit fur collar was "hopeless" Mommie said and she threw it out. Aunt Sally was "disgusted" with me. I was America's favorite child and I had been fighting right in the gutter and it just made her disgusted. And then I had to go to bed early and Mommie took you away and there went my privilege of writing in you for a whole week she said. I tried to explain about two against one and not fair but she said she didn't want to hear it. So that was that.

And the rest of the week just got worse. Mr. Nelson swore at Aunt Sally when he saw my face next day at rehearsal, and Miss Quinlan said she thought she'd have a heart attack. They called up Miss Irwin so you knew it was really bad. She came down to the rehearsal hall wearing her mink coat and the sunglasses she always has on so you can never see her eyes even in the dark studio before the set lights get turned on but you can smell her perfume way before she comes in, so she stood there with her head to one side thinking at me. And it was only after she said like some wise judge or king in a play deciding something while everybody waited around, she said "I think by Friday our magician Pietro can fix it with makeup." And then everyone laughed and said that's what they thought themselves. Mr. Nelson and Miss Quinlan said they were sorry to call her down to rehearsal but they had to be sure.

So then I knew Mr. Nelson and Miss Quinlan were in trouble with Miss Irwin and Aunt Sally was in trouble with Mr. Nelson and Miss Quinlan and I was in trouble with Aunt Sally and Mommie and everybody.

Things didn't get better and by Friday Mr. Nelson said this was the worst week of his directing career dam all of you meaning the whole cast. Miss Wood had three mygraynes (spell?) in one week and Mr. Nelson said I'd probably brought that on because Miss Wood hated violence of any kind (after the husbands and all that hate you can see why). Then it turned out that I had grown a whole inch and one of my costumes didn't fit good and Miss Quinlan said they'd have to start putting bricks on my head and shrinking me like a prune in the bathtub but then she said she was only kidding. Then Dickie (that's Dick Van Patten remember who plays my teenage brother even though he's 23 but looks younger) lost lots of money at the track (which is where they race horses and bet money on them) and wanted his pay in advance but Mr. Nelson said No that's happened too often. I thought poor Dickie. He was once a child actor like me and sometimes he makes me laugh about things but Aunt Sally says what does he know and we have nothing in common but I should always be polite. I still like him because he can't ride a bike even now at 23. But I don't want to grow up and lose all our Future at the track. I heard Miss Quinlan say to Mr. Nelson that it was an addikshun (spell?) like booze (which gets you drunk). Which reminds me that to make everything worse, Papa (that's not my real father you remember he's dead but this is Jud Laire who I call Papa because he acts it) well, Papa came to rehearsal "drunk as a loon" Miss Wood said right out loud. I don't know what a loon is but it must be drunk, because Papa was very happy and kept throwing me up in the air and I loved him even if his breath did smell like our apartment building hall. And then he threw his arms around Billy Nalle and called him "Wee Willy darling" and Miss Quinlan said sharp to Aunt Sally Get that kid off the set.

So you see it was a terrible week, Diary, even if we are a really happy family on our show. You see why I apologize to you for paying you no attention all this time but I couldn't get to you.

Now there's never going to be a Perfect Record of writing in you every single day. That's been ruined for all time. And this terrible week has ruined my Perfect Chart for all year. I had wanted to write in you every single day for the rest of my life, and now I'll never be able to do that. I'm so sad about it. Forgive me, Diary. Try to understand.

Apologetically (spell?)
Robin

Dear Diary,

I know this time I missed two days but at least it's not a week even if I did skip by my own fault and not from losing a privilege. It's just not the same now I can't say I've never missed a day. It's not perfect anymore. But I still love you Diary. If I was allowed to I would show you to Roberta because then she could see from the earlier stuff I wrote in you that I had liked her all along for real and she wouldn't think I had joined in to help Benjy and Roger. But I'm not allowed to do that and I've "medaled enough" Mommie says. Besides, I haven't seen Roberta down by the tracks or playing in front of her little wood house since that day, and I don't know if she's hiding or moved away or maybe even died from being beat up by those dumb stupid idiot bullies upstairs I still hate them and always will. Mommie and Aunt Sally and Liz go on having coffee together but us kids don't play together while they do it. So something good came out of the terrible week anyway. But I hope Roberta's not dead or hurt bad and Mommie says I have a tender heart but I should know better than to medal and she says she's sure Roberta is fine because nobody could run like that and be hurt. But Hamlet gets a mortal wound (which is the kind you die from) and goes on and fights more and even kills a few people and gives a long speech to the audience all between the time he gets hurt and the time he finally dies and while all this is happening he knows he's dying. It makes me worried about Roberta no matter what Mommie says. If her family moved away like Liz told Mommie they should, I'll never even know if Roger and Benjy gave Roberta a mortal wound. But Aunt Sally says there's nothing I can do. And she's right, because I'm not allowed to.

I don't want to write in you anymore right now, Diary, and I hope that doesn't hurt your feelings. Sometimes after Mommie has worked at the stocks that will make us rich she gets that line in her forehead she likes me to smooth out but not those times because she says it's nothing really she's just "deeppressed" (sp?). That means sort of sad like you sometimes get after the show is finished or when you go to an audition but they say they're looking for somebody younger or older or different. You sort of know what it is you're sad about but the sadness is bigger and spreads over lots of things. So I think it must be I'm deeppressed.

Robin

Dear Diary,

I know I skipped again, about a month this time. But Mommie says I have a busy schedule and there are more important things to pay attention to and if I don't write in you every day it's OK. I hope you think so.

There's no big news that's happened anyway. It's not so cold, which is nice because I don't have to wear my leggings. I *hate* them but I'm not old enough to wear tights and we can't afford to have me catch a cold, not after the way I already got us all into trouble about my face.

The scratch is gone, which makes Pietro glad and Aunt Sally and everybody else. But I'm sorry because every time I looked in the mirror I could think how I gave Roger a bloody nose and how Roberta and me fought like the Amazons in the Greek myths even if Roberta might not ever know I was fighting on her side. Roger and Benjy just walk around free when I think Roger at least should go to jail because he could have murdered Roberta you never know. I won't speak to him or Benjy and Mommie says that's OK even if it makes life hard for her with Liz.

So the only big news is that we had the cast party for a whole day out at Miss Wood's country house in Connecticut. (I know that's right because I looked it up. If I use the dictionary for words I'm not sure about maybe Mommie won't have to check in here for spelling mistakes.) She gives a cast party every year but it's always in the summer so we can go swimming in her pool. But last summer we never had it because Miss Wood's husband was sick with something. I think she poisons them maybe like the king was poisoned in *Hamlet* because they always seem to disappear. But Mommie says No they just get divorced but Aunt Sally says she wouldn't put it past Miss Wood to poison a person. Aunt Sally doesn't like Miss Wood, but she's always polite to her because Miss Wood is the Star even if I am more popular with our thousands of viewers and get the most fan mail of anybody, Miss Quinlan says.

So this year we couldn't have the cast party until now and it was too cold to swim in the pool which was OK with me because I don't know how to swim anyway and you never know you could drown like Ophelia. Miss Wood didn't want to wait till later in the year because she's going to do renovations (I looked it up!) and everything will be a mess.

But even if it was just early spring there was already heated water in the pool because Miss Wood likes to swim for her constitution (looked it up again!) which does not mean the Declaration of Independence, Diary, but her health, so she swims even in the cold spring and then runs inside fast. Miss Wood is a magnificent (Looked It Up) actress and she's been on the stage on Broadway and in London too and she sort of acts all the time even out there at her country house where she says she "lets her hair down." (Not really, Diary, she keeps it pinned in a bun on top of her head like always. That's a saying that means she doesn't have to act at the country house, but I think she does at least when anybody else is there I bet even the husbands.) So when Mr. Gabrielson had so much booze he fell into the pool Miss Wood wasn't even worried about Ophelia (he can swim) but just stood there in her hostess gown looking at him through the big glass window that's like a wall by the pool and she put her hand up to her throat and her big blue eyes were open very wide and she sort of sang out (Miss

Wood *can* carry a tune and used to sing with Noel Coward who was very famous and is old now and maybe dead) anyway she sort of sang out "Frank! I am ap*palled!*" But everybody laughed and he climbed out and Jessie (that's Miss Wood's maid who is a Negro lady who smiles a lot but only when she thinks you're looking) she ran and got a towel for him and then he had another drink.

Dickie played pool (not the water kind but a game with sticks and balls on a table) all day inside with Johnny who is our assistant (spell? No, L.I.U.!) director who I love. He always calls me Hey Kid or Trooper or just Rob but never The Baby because he says years don't count and I'm the oldest one in the cast. That's nice because I get tired of always being the youngest. Miss Quinlan sat in the glass room but kept shouting to Dickie in the other room that if he was losing next week's pay he could go to hell before she'd plead for him again with Carol. (Carol is Miss Irwin's first name but *nobody* calls her that except only Miss Quinlan and Miss Wood and Mr. Nelson and the men from The Sponsors which is Maxwell House Coffee and Gaines Dog Food when they visit the Control Room on Air Day. Miss Irwin was somewhere in the house on the telephone a lot.)

Everybody was having a good time and Aunt Sally sat off to one side like she's always careful to do because you don't want anybody to think you're one of those awful stage mothers like other kids in the business have even though she's really a stage aunt. She drank lots of coffee and talked with Betty who's our script-girl lady and Helga who's the wardrobe lady. Helga comes from Hungary and got out before the communists (liu!) came, by the skin of her teeth she says. And Aunt Sally even said I could go for a walk along the forest path all by myself. Miss Wood told her it was "perfectly safe" and not to be "overprotective" (liu!) so what else could Aunt Sally do she had to let me go. I whispered to her that I'd bundle up and only go a little way and come right back, and I'd gone that path once together long ago on a walk with Miss Wood and a publicity photographer so Aunt Sally knew it really was OK and not in anything jungley but just a sort of field with trees back of the house and the pool.

And so Diary I had a whole walk in the country all by myself! It was *magnificent*. I saw a skunk! (But I didn't scare it I stood perfectly still until it went away so it didn't put out its smell.) I saw a brown rabbit for just a minute. The snow was all gone and there were different tiny flowers beginning to peek up out of the dirt and I wanted to pick one but I didn't because you never know there could be poison ivy or something and then I'd get us all into trouble again. So I stuck to the path and looked up at the buds on the trees, and when I squeezed my eyes almost shut, the sun made sparkles (l.i.u.) like the air was a green color. There were lots of birds but you couldn't see them, only hear them. I wish I knew the names for flowers and trees and birds, like a library in my head. I stood like a statue and didn't move a muscle like you have to do when you're being fitted for a costume or if you're posing for a picture where they use a long exposure. But here I stood still just because I didn't want to scare off the birds or the forest or anything. I pretended to myself I was part of the forest, a tree or a wild creature (liu!) just being there. It felt so *real*. And except for the birds singing and the dry leaves left over from winter sort of Shhhing when they blew around in the green color air it was as quiet as the library. Even if Mr. Nelson does despair of me because he says I'm a hopeless city child (he grew up in someplace maybe Montana which is mostly not cities) Aunt Sally always tells him not to worry about me I'm doing fine. I sure was doing fine by myself on my walk in the country.

I kept to the path and remembered my promise and turned around after a while and came back. Well, to tell the truth, Diary, I would have gone on a little more, but I saw something funny through the trees up ahead and I knew I better not make the mistake of medaling. Pietro was there. He is our makeup man who fixed my scratch remember? He really grew up in Brooklyn but is called Pietro instead of Pete because it fits a makeup man better and besides he lived in Rome for three whole years. He is very funny and makes me laugh and calls me his little Garbo. (She is a movie actress who doesn't talk too much, not like me!, in fact she hardly talks at all but is very famous and not dead yet.) Pietro was there up ahead through the trees with Lee, who is Miss Wood's house-boy which means he takes care of her house like Jessie takes care of her self. I like Lee (who isn't a boy at all but old, about 25, and who sneaks me Cokes) and of course I really like Pietro so I was going to run up and say Hi to them. But I didn't. It was funny. Not funny ha ha but funny strange. Pietro was on his knees in front of Lee and Lee's pants were down around his ankles even his underpants. You could see Lee's bare bottom white in the sun against the brown tree stems or whatever they're called. Lee's head was sort of thrown back and he made sounds like he was in pain. So right away I knew Lee had been bitten by a snake or some other poisonous thing and Pietro was trying to save his life by sucking out the venom (liu) like they tell you in first aid books and on TV. I knew Pietro would be very brave about saving somebody's life because he's gentle and tall and handsome. But I hoped he would remember you had to spit out the poison and not swallow any or you could die after you saved the other person.

Anyway, I knew better than to go medal. Besides if there were snakes in that part of the woods I sure didn't want them to bite me and they might because I am shorter than Pietro and nearer to the ground. When Mommie and I play tickle she sometimes acts like a giant and she growls in a loud voice "Ho! Tender baby flesh! Yum!" and I know Mommie is just playing so I laugh but I sure didn't want the snakes to think I was tender baby flesh because the snakes would not be playing. Also I didn't know if a person could suck out the poison from two people one after the other or die themselves so Pietro might not be able to save me and then what? I might die or ruin the cast party and get into trouble again.

So I just turned around very quiet like in the library and pretended I was an Indian walking through the woods in my moccasins (liu) without cracking a twig. I made it all the way back to the house without a sound.

It was a wonderful walk and Aunt Sally said she was proud of me. But when I whispered to her about the snake bite and how we should tell the others and call an ambulance because Pietro might not have got out all the poison you never know she said very fast No and not to mention it to anybody that she would take care of it and I should forget I'd ever seen Pietro and Lee in the woods at all. I tried to explain to her how important it was but then she gave me The Look and I didn't want her to tell Mommie because I'm trying to get back at least to *near* Perfect on the chart so I stopped because one of the things on the chart list is Not to Argue.

Aunt Sally was right because sure enough a little while later Lee and Pietro came back but not together and nobody even asked where they'd been. Lee didn't mention the snake bite and he looked OK. Pietro didn't mention it either, but Pietro would never brag and I guess he also made Lee not tell how brave he'd been. I think Pietro is a good man. He and Papa took me to the ballet once on a Saturday afternoon because they both know a lot of the dancers.

Anyway so that's the big news. Aunt Sally and me went back early by train even though we had drove out in one of the cars along with Helga and Betty. But the grownups were staying later and I felt sorry Aunt Sally couldn't stay with them because after all she is a grownup. But I had to be got back early and somebody had to take me and so of course it was her. We had a nice long train ride which I love because Aunt Sally reads the *Journal American* newspaper and I can just look out the window at things going by and think. You can't think much at home because there's always homework or the script or piano practice or sleep. But there's not much you can do on a train because it bounces too much to write your home-work clear. You can always be running your lines over in your head to save time but sometimes you can just stop and think a little. So I looked out the window and thought and I guess I fell asleep because I woke up with my head on the windowsill which was all dirty and Aunt Sally said I was a filthy-faced baby and what was she going to do with me? I am *not* a baby but I knew then she wasn't mad at me, so I didn't complain when she took out a hankie and spit on it and rubbed my face. I wish she'd at least let me spit my own spit on the hankie if there has to be spit at all when there's no water around. That way I would be smelling my own spit while it dries instead of Aunt Sally's spit at least.

That was the only big news which is not very big unless you think Pietro saving Lee's life and being too much of a hero to tell anybody is big news. I do. But when I told her about it Mommie said we'll keep Pietro's secret, just her and me and Aunt Sally and not tell a soul. So I only told you, Diary, because you're not a soul.

I love you Diary.
Robin the country kid

Dear Diary,
You are a soul, I guess. I have to be more careful what I write in you. Mom-mie was checking for my spelling mistakes even after I told her I *promise* to look up hard words myself to *save* her from having to correct them. Mommie says I haven't got the hang of writing in you yet and if I don't get it soon she'll hide you away until I'm older.

You see, I should not be putting in these things all the time that really don't have anything to do with me. Like Roberta, because Roberta and I had nothing in common. Like Miss Monet and you know what. Like Miss Wood and the maybe husbands and her being an actress even when she lets her hair down. Like Rosemary crying to Mr. Nelson and Dickie and the track and Mr. Gabrielson and the booze and the pool. Especially like Pietro saving Lee's life.

I can sort of understand about everything but Pietro because you could say the other things are not positive and might give me the wrong impression when I am old and read you, Diary. But it seems to me that Pietro's being such a modest hero is *very* positive and something I will want to remember as a happy time of my childhood. And I would never show you to anybody now Roberta is gone. So Mommie would be the only person to read you, and then me when I'm old, and both Mommie and me already *know* about Pietro saving Lee's life so I don't see what was wrong about writing that in you.

But I don't want to be difficult all over again and Mommie almost had nerves over it so I'll just obey which will give me another star on the chart at least. I'm sorry, Diary. But that's the way it is. You never know.

Still your friend anyway,
Robin

Dear Diary,
There are lots of things I'd like to write in you tonight but I don't think they've got the hang of it so I just better say Hello and I love you. Besides, I'm tired. I think maybe I'm sort of depressed, I guess.

Robin

Dear Diary,
I know it's almost Easter and Pesach (spell? I couldn't find it) together and I haven't paid you much attention. I apologize. I've been very busy doing important things but I still love you. I'm going to appear on 5th Avenue on Easter Sunday with Steve Allen (who talks on TV) to do television commentary together about the Easter Parade. Some famous hat person named Lilly Dashay or something is making me a custom Easter Bonnet.

My new agent Miss Olga Lee got me out of the exclusive contract with Miss Irwin and CBS so now I can play Dagmar and other parts too if they don't have what is called a time conflict because playing Dagmar has to come first it's steady. And we had to give up the pay raise in order to get the contract different. So I'll be very busy Diary, you have to understand and not complain. I finished reading *The Snow Queen* by Hans Christian Andersen and it is one of my favorite stories in the world. I *love* the Little Robber Girl. I love Little Gerda too. I even think the Snow Queen isn't so scary. I think she's beautiful, in fact.

Your friend,
Robin

Dear Diary,
Mommie says we're going to give me private swimming lessons at the Dalton swim school so I'll never die like Ophelia. I'm scared of learning but I know it's important not to drown. If I die in the first lesson, remember that I loved you, Diary.

With love, for real,
Robin

Dear Diary,
I know I've missed weeks and weeks, but I'm working hard. I'm doing lots of one-shots on radio and on TV I did a guest shot on *Suspense*. That was with Boris Karloff playing a lighthouse keeper where I got stranded at an old lighthouse in a storm at night but off camera he wasn't spooky at all and sat me on his lap and told me stories about old times when he was young in silent movies where you never had to learn lines. Aunt Sally says I'm making good money. Oh, and I did *Danger* where I got to co-star with Darren McGavin who says all children and dogs are horrible scene stealers. I like Darren McGavin but I have not stole anything and I do not like being put in the same group with dogs.

The best part about doing *Danger* was Sidney Lumet who was the director. He was once a child actor, Diary, so he understands. He always says I should call him Kid Sid Lumet. He's short and very funny and hugs people and never talks down to me. Everybody says he's full of beans which means he jumps around and gets real excited and tells everybody how good they are. I think Kid Sid is like a grownup child and I started liking him last year when he directed *Mama* while Mr. Nelson was on vacation.

That reminds me, Diary, our cast had a *big scare*. Dickie got drafted and had to go in the army for the Korean War! It scared me because of my father dying in the army you know. We had a goodbye party and everything, and there were auditions for another Nels to take Dickie's place. Miss Irwin and Mr. Nelson found somebody and he started coming to rehearsal but it seemed funny. He must have felt left out because he was new. He was real quiet but he had a nice smile. Then, Diary, it was like a *miracle,* Aunt Sally said. Because after only two days of rehearsal, Dickie walked back in! His eardrum was busted up so the army didn't want him after all! Everybody laughed and cried and was happy, except for the new actor who was supposed to play Nels. He just plain cried without laughing. Honest. He put his head down and *cried.* He said "I need this job bad." It was awful. Mr. Nelson and Miss Quinlan told him "You'll find something else for sure, Jimmy." Everybody called him Jimmy, Diary, but his name was James Dean. I felt so sorry for him. He said he was washed up in New York and was going to try his luck on the Coast (that is the West Coast, Diary, which means California). Then he left and we never saw him again but Dickie had to learn his lines real fast.

My swimming teacher, Hank, says I have a terrific (LIU!) backstroke and he could train me to be in the Olympics but Mommie says I should just learn not to drown. She says there I go again, her little talent factory!

Esther Williams
(no, really Robin)

Dear Diary,
Mr. Jones says if I work hard on my piano then in a year or two he might enter me in the New York State piano competition where I could win a medal. Aunt Sally says she always knew I was musical and Mommie says now Snibbin—that's another one of her names for me—winning *that* would be *some*thing, not like being in the Olympics. It gives me nerves so I am practicing hard and won't have much time to write in you.

Arthur Rubinstein
(no ha ha Robin)

Dear Diary,
Like Mommie says, how time flies! Here it is September and school starts soon. I meant to write more in you over the summer but I was very busy

doing a lot of extra shows. Like Aunt Sally says, that was more fun than going to camp like other kids get sent away to. I'm making more money but we're still in 3-A and can't be in an elevator building with my own room yet. Mommie gets depressed with her stocks but we're being positive and we have faith. Maybe next year.

Robin

Dear Diary,

Today is November 18. I know it's been a long time since I wrote in you. But Mommie said I should tell you Thanksgiving is coming, and I'm going to be Queen of the Macy's Thanksgiving Day Parade and wear a crown and the tutu and ride on a float! Phil Silvers who is also a TV star will be the King. I have met *many* famous people, Diary, and Mommie says now *that's* the kind of thing I should tell you and will want to remember when I'm old.

Usually when I meet famous people it's at a personal appearance for publicity or else at a benefit (which means to raise money) for poor people or sick people. I do lots of benefits because Aunt Sally says it's a great way of getting your face out there and also helping people is nice. Once when I was young I met Abbott and Costello who are a very famous comedy team. I did not like Abbott who is tall and serious but I *loved* Costello who is short and fat and can make funny faces. He put my hair ribbon on his head and made me laugh and then he whispered to me about his little boy who drowned in a swimming pool just about my same age back then maybe 4 and I felt so bad for Costello but am I glad I can do a backstroke now. I also met Kate Smith who sings and is very *very* fat, more even than Costello. We sang together on the radio for people to call in and pledge (LIU!) money for research to cure polio. We sang "Home on the Range" and "Buttons and Bows." I met Sister Kenny, too, who has a whole foundation that invented special exercises to cure some kinds of polio and after I made a speech she took off her corsage (LIU!) and gave it to me. Also I met Gloria Swanson the movie star who wore foxes around her neck biting each other on the tail, that was for the March of Dimes benefit. And Rosalind Russell another movie star. And Ernie Kovacks who is on TV and smokes a smelly cigar, that was for PAL which is the Police Athletic League that raises money to help poor children. I did a lot of benefits for

PAL, and so did Sid Caesar who is a comic and Perry Como who croons and Gene Autry who is a cowboy star who made me sit on his lap and then on his horse and I did not like his lap or his horse. PAL made me an Honorary Police Captain with a pin and everything. Once I was on a radio drama show, DuPont's *Cavalcade of America*, with Robert Taylor the movie star and I played Henrietta Edwards the little girl who grew up to marry Eli Whitney (that was Mr. Taylor) who invented the cotton gin that must have something to do with booze. And I met Raymond Duncan who always wears sandals and a sheet even in winter and he said I was an old soul and had a third eye I think he's a little crazy but nice. He is the brother of a famous dancer Isabella or some name like that who died from being choked by a scarf. I danced the part of The Little Girl (that's what I am, after all, Diary, until I grow up!) in *The Nutcracker* ballet at New York City Center, that was with the Ballet Russe de Monte Carlo and so I met the great ballerina Alexandra Danilova and the dancer Frederick Franklin who starred in it. Once when I was five I danced (tap) with Bill Robinson who was also called Bojangles and who had danced with Shirley Temple but was famous for himself. That was at a big benefit for The Negro Actors' Fund at the Apollo Theater in Harlem which is way far uptown and had LOTS of famous people appearing. There was Sophie Tucker who is Aunt Sally's favorite in the world, and Jackie Robinson and Noble Sissle and Fannie Hurst and Sarah Vaughan and Ed Sullivan and Mel Allen who does sports and I met them all. But everybody said Bojangles and me stole the show. Also once when I did a benefit in Lake Worth, Florida (where I was born, Diary, did I tell you that?) I met the Mayor who I heard Mommie say later they put in jail for something and I met Representative Dwight Rogers who is in the Congress from Lake Worth. I got made an Honorary Life Member of the U.S. Congress! (I don't know what that means, Diary.) And I met Milton Berle when we both were MCs at a benefit but he wasn't funny backstage, he yelled. I met Prime Minister Nehru of India who gave me a red rose when I appeared at the United Nations in a benefit for UNICEF which is sort of a company that gives money and medicine and food to poor children all around the world.

Soon Mommie and me will give the food and old clothes to the poor Negroes next door. I wonder if we'll see anybody special. Today was OK. Rehearsal, a tunafish sandwich and milk before catching the train back to school, ballet and modern dance class one after the other, homework, piano practice, the script, supper, and bed for the beauty sleep.

Robin

Dear Diary,

Today was Thanksgiving Day. I have so much to be thankful for. The Parade was nice but it rained. I was *freeeeeeeeezing* cold. Still, I was a trooper and am the luckiest little girl in the whole world. We ate turkey and mashed potatoes and gravy and cranberry sauce in a restaurant. It was very traditional (sp? Help Mommie!). Happy Thanksgiving!

Robin

P.S. We gave food and clothes to the poor Negroes next door and they were thankful. The only little girls over there now are bigger than me so there wouldn't be anybody to give an organdy dress to anyway, even if it would not be an insult which Mommie and me would never ever make. Nobody else was there.

Dear Diary,

Soon it will be Christmas and no school and a *whole week* with no other lessons either. But we still do the show. Every Christmas we do the same script which is now very popular and traditional. I have the biggest part of anybody. I play Dagmar like always but I also play her great grandmother back in Norway (that's a flashback, Diary) who lived on a farm and heard the animals talk on Christmas Eve. It's this old Norwegian myth. Mr. Nelson always swears a lot at this show every year because it means he has to put up with a LIVE cow and a LIVE donkey right in the studio on the set!!! One year the cow needed to be milked even. The first time I ever met a cow or donkey or watched anybody being milked it was in a TV studio! Anyway Mr. Venza decorates us a big tree on the old farm set and another one in the parlor of our regular set. Two trees! Also Norwegian circle cookies called mandelkranser (I asked how to spell it!). And then there are presents, for real, at the cast party. At home we celebrate both Christmas and Hanikuh (couldn't find out how to spell!) and that's more presents.

Merry Christmas and Happy Hanikuh,
Robin

Dear Diary,

Well it's the New Year which is 1951. Happy New Year! It still feels funny to be living in the 1950s, even if we already did that for a whole year. That's because I've spent almost my whole life in the 1940s, Mommie says. What is even more funny is to think way ahead to the 1970s and 1990s and even the 2000s. They don't seem real. They seem like science fiction, and it's funny to think that unless I die or there's a war and they drop the atom bomb and I don't have time to duck and cover under a desk or table in time like we're taught to do in school, then I'll actually be a grown-up and have my own room or maybe even my own apartment or house and not be living with Mommie and Aunt Sally anymore. Of course I would miss Mommie. But probably I'd see her a lot so it would be OK. I think about that, especially around my birthday and New Year's.

I didn't make it through 1950 perfect on the chart and now there's all of 1951 ahead to try and get perfect again and stay that way. I don't know why but that makes me depressed. But I'll try to be positive and have faith, like Mommie!

Happy New Year!

Robin

P.S. I read all the Stuart Little books and loved them. I'm reading W. H. Hudson's *Little Boy Lost* now. I wish there was a *Little Girl Lost*.

Dear Diary,

Life is very busy so you still have to not complain that I write so little or with such long times in between. I lie in bed sometimes and think about what I would write in you. If I wasn't too tired to write it down, I mean. I made up an imaginary (*looked it up*, Mommie!) friend named Bunker who is half girl and half boy and goes with me everywhere. Mommie doesn't mind and says that shows imagination (*L.i.u.M!*) but it shouldn't go too far and carry me away. Bunker is only a kid too and not strong enough to carry me, so I don't worry about it. Anyway, at night I tell Bunker things I would write in you. I hope that doesn't make you jealous, Diary. I hope you understand.

Still your friend,
Robin

Dear Diary,

It's the night before my 9th birthday and I'm excited to see what my presents will be. I can tell you what I got Mommie because she won't read you until tomorrow and by then she'll have it. I saved up my allowance money since July (when I spent the *old* saved-up money to get Mommie *her* birthday present for her *own* birthday). Anyway, I gave the money to Papa in secret at rehearsal and told him what to get and he got her a *magnificent* pink silk scarf from Saks 5th Avenue, all wrapped and perfect.

That reminds me. I didn't want to repeat myself this year by doing the Perfect Chart again. You should never repeat yourself (which is why it's so good I'm doing other parts and not just Dagmar) because it is *death* my new agent Mr. Stephen Draper always says for an actor to get typecast. So I don't think I'll do the chart ever again.

Tomorrow will be my last birthday ever in a single number. The one after that will already be my 10th birthday and I'll be in two numbers then and stay that way for the rest of my whole life, unless I live to be 100 years old. Aunt Sally would be dead by then, and even Mommie. It's hard to imagine the rest of my life. But I guess it will really happen. I made up another poem. It goes:

Some like it hot, some like it cold

But I am afraid of 9 years old.

Happy Birthday to you dear Diary, you're almost one year old. I apologize that I'm so busy I hardly tell you things anymore. Please understand. That's how it is. I loved you anyway. For real.

Your friend,
with love,
Robin Morgan.

All That Glitters

> *It was the best of times and the worst of times.*
> — CHARLES DICKENS

*I*magine that every night in prime time you have your choice of viewing two or more, hour-long or longer, original, written-for-TV plays. Imagine that intermixed with these anthologies of serious dramas and witty comedies are some skillful adaptations of novels, plus an elegant sampling of classics and revivals: Shakespeare, Shaw, Chekhov, Ibsen, Brecht, Pirandello, Anouilh, O'Casey, O'Neill, Isherwood, Williams.

Now imagine the creative energy of certain young, as yet only moderately known writers, busy at their clunky manual typewriters, turning out those original plays: Rod Serling ("Patterns," "Requiem for a Heavyweight," and *The Twilight Zone* series—all teleplays before becoming movies, although Serling would later write such screenplays as *Planet of the Apes* and *Seven Days in May*); Paddy Chayefsky ("Marty," a teleplay before it became a movie, after which he wrote the films *Network* and *The Americanization of Emily*); Reginald Rose (*Twelve Angry Men*, written for TV, later revised for the film and the remake); Gore Vidal ("Visit to a Small Planet," "The Death of Billy the Kid," plus teleplay adaptations from novels by William Faulkner and Henry James); and some guy named Gene

Roddenberry, a television script editor who was always trying to pitch his idea for a science-fiction series. Imagine, too, on a periodic or regular basis, enjoying the written-for-TV work of Orson Welles, Molly Goldberg, Neil Simon, Carl Reiner, Robert Sherwood, and Sam Peckinpah (before he took up directing as being apparently less violent).

Now imagine that the casts of these nightly plays are composed of generally first-rate actors and fine craftspeople—tomorrow's stars, many of them—doing their jobs at a high level of professionalism. Professionalism was crucial, because preparation was bracingly short: rehearsal time for a one-hour drama averaged only five six-hour-long days, and by the second day lines already had to be memorized so the cast could be on its feet to begin floor "blocking"—the director's choreographing of actors' moves, camera shots, and "boom" (elevated microphone) positions. Rehearsals, in various venues around Manhattan, were conducted in large, loft-like halls (sometimes old dance studios with one long mirrored wall), with masking tape stuck on the floor by the production assistant to outline imaginary doors, staircases, windows, and walls of the eventual set, plus a few tables and folding chairs as makeshift furniture. There were also costume fittings and makeup and hair tryout sessions. But there was only one day ever in the studio itself, with the actual set, lights, props, and costumes: Air Day. Imagine, then, all those disciplined, hard-working, up-and-coming actors, desperately eager to land a consistent job in a nighttime series or daytime soap, but grateful for one-shots, under-five-liners (minimum pay), or even walk-ons. Just a sampling is astounding: Paul Newman, Jane Alexander (and her older sister Denise, who several times a year played Dagmar's sometimes best friend), Lee J. Cobb, Joanne Woodward, Sally Field, Marlon Brando, Cicely Tyson, Ben Gazzara, Bill Cosby, Candice Bergen, Warren Beatty, Mia Farrow, Valerie Harper, Jack Lemmon, Robert Shaw, George C. Scott, Andy Griffith, Leslie Nielsen, Julie Harris, Robert Redford, Christopher Plummer, John Cassavetes (before he took up directing), Lee Grant (before *she* took up directing). Imagine, too, frequent appearances by established stars of theater and film: Laurence Olivier, the Lunts, Helen Hayes, Charles Boyer, Lillian Gish. . . .

Now imagine such literary and thespian talent working under the directorial gaze of the young hawks learning their flight patterns in between television test patterns: Robert Altman (who would eventually give us

Nashville and *M*A*S*H*); Sidney Lumet (who would direct such film classics as *Serpico, Dog Day Afternoon,* and *Twelve Angry Men*); John Frankenheimer (*Andersonville, Days of Wine and Roses, The Manchurian Candidate*); George Roy Hill (*Butch Cassidy and the Sundance Kid, The Sting*); Ralph Nelson (*Lillies of the Field, Requiem for a Heavyweight*); Franklin Schaffner (*The Best Man, Planet of the Apes*); and Delbert Mann (*Separate Tables, All Quiet on the Western Front*). These men—and directors were, back then, all men—worked as omnipresent "jobbers," freelancing from show to show, since few were so fortunate as Nelson to be contracted to a steady series with the same cast. They earned their rent and learned their craft by substituting for a vacationing or sick steady director on such a same-cast series as *Mama,* by directing one-shots on such "theme" series as *Danger, Suspense,* or *The Twilight Zone* (all of which had different casts each show), and of course by directing the nightly anthology plays.

Those anthologies offered a feast of work. Nor did anyone yet complain that, in a brazen display of capitalist aesthetics, they were mostly named after the companies sponsoring them, in much the same way as Mobil Oil and Xerox would later come to be identified with quality programming on PBS.[1] In the late 1940s and the 1950s it was *Armstrong Circle Theater, Alcoa Presents, The Hallmark Hall of Fame, Kraft Television Theatre, The Kaiser Aluminum Hour, Ford Star Jubilee, General Electric Theater, Buick Electra Playhouse, U.S. Steel Hour, The DuPont Show of the Month, Philco-Goodyear Television Playhouse, Studio One, Omnibus, Playhouse 90.* . . .

Now. Here's the most amazing part. Imagine that every one of these plays is telecast *live.*

And that's not counting the presence of what forty years later would be termed "classic" comedy: Jack Paar, Lucille Ball, Sid Caesar and Imogene Coca, Jack Benny, Jackie Gleason. . . .

---

[1] At the time, the real power lay with the sponsors and their ad agencies, not the networks. It wasn't until 1961 that Newton Minnow, the new director of the Federal Communications Commission (FCC), openly declared war on the sponsors' greedy reign over the medium; it was thought that the networks would exercise more benign control. Ironically, the first thing the networks did was to pull many of the anthology dramas from the air as being insufficiently competitive and profitable.

And not counting the news—when it was more news than "infotainment." The standard had been set by the visionary news producer Fred Friendly and his on-screen colleague, Edward R. Murrow. It was continued by Murrow's protégé, Eric Sevareid, and *his* protégé, the young Walter Cronkite. These were the folks who created such documentaries as the great "Harvest of Shame."

And *that's* not counting what today is (usually derisively) termed "culture": telecasts of concerts, operas, and ballets not exiled to public television but on mainstream *network* TV; Leonard Bernstein's New York Philharmonic "Concerts for Young People," for example, were on CBS.

Virtually all of it live. No retakes. No second chances.

No wonder they call it the Golden Age of Television. But that's in retrospect, of course.

At the time it all seemed perfectly normal, though exciting in its freshness—as the Elizabethan Age might have felt to Londoners of that period, or the Renaissance to Florentines living through it. The present always masquerades as a beginning; maybe we couldn't endure it if we realized at the time that it was a peak, or even an ending. Writers, actors, and directors became disciplined in and enthusiastic about this demanding new medium, which combined the challenge of live theater with the thrill of a then unimaginably enormous audience. That audience was a fraction of what was yet to come: as late as 1948, only 9 percent of the U.S. public had television sets.

I worked hard, on *Mama* and on every one-shot my agents could book. The scrapbooks bear witness—both the crumbling ones reverently assembled by Aunt Sally and the slick, laminated one later compiled by the public-relations professional my mother hired. Brittle clippings of reviews, features, cover stories, and interviews flutter forth from the *New York Times, Daily News, Post, Sun, Journal American, World Telegram,* and *Herald Tribune* (yes, dear reader, there were that many major dailies in New York alone). Also *Time, Newsweek, Look, Life, McCall's, Variety, Silver Screen,* two *TV Guide* cover stories, and the *Chicago Tribune, St. Louis Post Dispatch, Los Angeles Times, Miami Herald,* and *Minneapolis Tribune,* as well as the London *Times*, the *Bombay* (India) *Standard*, and the wire services. More: the creator of the daily comic strip "The Phantom" wrote me in by name as a character for six weeks. Now I was not only a drink but a cartoon. I definitely got around.

On radio (subsequent to the two years—from age five to seven—of *The Little Robin Morgan Show* and *Juvenile Jury*), I did a three-year run as a featured player on *Hilltop House* (a radio soap opera), and guest-starred on, among others, *DuPont Theatre of the Air*, *The Greatest Story Ever Told*, *Cavalcade of America*, *The Shadow* ("Who knows what evil lurks in the hearts of men . . ."), and *Let's Pretend*—whose sponsor, Cream of Wheat cereal, had a jingle so maddeningly catchy that Gloria Steinem, then an avid listener, can still sing every word, all these years later.

Radio was easy and fun. For one thing, there were no lines to memorize; all you had to remember was not to rustle your script pages too close to the mike. For another, different accents came in handy, and you could play older or younger than you were by pitching your voice accordingly; when I was around age twelve, I could and did play "down" to age seven and "up" to age twenty-five. I liked watching the way radio sound effects got made (hollowed-out coconut halves clomped by the sound man across plywood for a horse's gallop, cellophane crinkled to mimic a crackling fire, liquid pouring from a jug to sound like liquid pouring from a jug). My child's sense of mischief relished the joke that few radio actors looked the way they sounded: a fairy princess on *Let's Pretend* could be voiced by a grey-haired woman wearing wedgies and a housedress; the guy playing the Shadow's heroic, handsome self was in his mid-fifties, short, balding, plump, and given to snapping his suspenders absentmindedly when off mike.

But I, apparently, was deplorably telegenic.

Featured on *Mama* for seven years—by the end of which I had played Dagmar for half my life—I also starred in teleplays on *Alcoa Theatre*, *Kraft Playhouse*, and *U.S. Steel Hour*, as well as on *Danger* and *Suspense*. I worked under Sid Lumet, George Roy Hill, Delbert Mann, Frank Schaffner, and of course Ralph Nelson. I did a fair amount of hack work, too, because there was also plenty of clunky tin being broadcast during the Golden Age, a reality nostalgiacs would prefer to forget. I did a run on the soap opera *Another World*, guest shots on pre-*Sesame Street* days kids' shows like *Howdy Doody* and *Mr. I. Magination* (where, in a bizarre pre-feminist augury, I got to play Annie Oakley, defend girls' rights, and belt out "Anything You Can Do I Can Do Better"), and *Rod Brown, Rocket Ranger* (during which I developed an age-ten, massive crush on Cliff Robertson, whose talent was wasted playing Rod Brown).

At the classier end of the spectrum, I guest-starred on a well-written science-fiction series, *Tales of Tomorrow,* playing a genius child scientist. I remember that I enjoyed the challenge of learning and then rattling off page-long technical speeches on atomic theory, and I liked the integrity of the character, who refused to share her knowledge with the military, because she was bent on saving the world. According to the clippings, that show, titled "A Child Is Crying," won a 1952 Peabody Award nomination, and I won the Science Fiction Galaxy Magazine Award for "outstanding television performance." Rebroadcast live a year later by popular demand, "A Child Is Crying" still sometimes surfaces in a grainy kinescope[2] version on cable channels specializing in vintage video science-fiction. That role remains one of my two favorites, along with playing the lead in "The Tall Dark Man," a teleplay on *Robert Montgomery Presents* in 1955. It was a tour de force for me, pushing psychological buttons of which I was only vaguely aware—a "wolf wolf" story about a young girl so disturbed by her father's disappearance and mother's remarriage that she takes to pathological lying. When she happens to witness a real murder and knows she's been seen by the killer, no one believes her. The murderer waits for her to leave school and, when she hides inside, enters the building after hours to track her down. She must survive by her wits, and in the process learn to overcome both her terror and her overactive imagination. The reviews were uniform raves, and more awards came tumbling in.

Between the ages of twelve and fourteen, I also did a number of "spectaculars," so termed because they were each two or more hours long, and (gasp!) by that time actually in *color*—which in those days meant even more suffocatingly hot lights than usual, plus the added pressure of glitches from this new technology—broadcast live, of course. So I played the title role in the first television production of *Alice in Wonderland,* with a cast that included Edgar Bergen and Charlie McCarthy. In another

---

[2] A format in use before videotape became common; the program was "filmed" off a TV monitor, making it only barely fit for rebroadcast.

"spec," I played the essential "teen," Corliss Archer, in *Kiss and Tell*—receiving, at about age fourteen, my much-hyped first on-air kiss from Warren Berlinger.

Somewhere in all this, time had been found for me to do a screen test for Paramount Pictures, but I see from fragments of saved 1948 correspondence that my mother and aunt regretfully turned down a movie contract—possibly because I had by then entered into exclusivity with *Mama*. But in 1953 there was a Columbia Records deal and, at age twelve, I cut two successful children's albums: "Little Smokey the Runaway Train" and "A Magical Music Box" (still "talk-singing," still—despite the efforts of three different singing teachers—cheerfully unable to carry a tune).

There was also work in "legit" theater. In 1952, Carol Irwin decided to capitalize on the popularity of the *Mama* show, and commissioned Frank Gabrielson to write a new play called *Here's Mama*,[3] based on some of the best-loved episodes of the TV series. The company, again under Ralph's direction, took it out on the summer-stock road. We went off the air for longer than our usual two-week summer break, and were away from New York for two and a half months, rehearsing and then playing to sold-out houses at the Ogunquit Playhouse in Maine and the Cape Playhouse in Massachusetts. Audiences who had never been to the theater flocked to see their favorite TV family in the flesh.

For me, that summer was genuinely enjoyable. Once rehearsals were finished and except for matinee days, there were hours of swimming and beach strolling as if on a real holiday; there were nights of excitement in front of the one-eyed, single-throated "beast in the darkness." There was the challenge of absorbing stagecraft, learning to develop a sense of timing different from that in the studio, to pause for laughs, to project from

---

[3]This was distinct from the earlier John Van Druten play *I Remember Mama*, which had starred Mady Christians on Broadway (with a young Marlon Brando playing Nels), and which had been a direct adaptation of the Kathryn Forbes book *Mama's Bank Account*. The Van Druten play was adapted for film, and Irene Dunne starred in the movie by the same name. Later, there was an attempt to make a musical of the material starring Liv Ullmann, but it failed because Richard Rodgers, who'd written the music, became fatally ill. The only actor who worked in the original Van Druten play, the TV series, and also *Here's Mama* was Ruth Gates, who brought a consistently funny fussiness to the character of gossipy Aunt Jenny.

your diaphragm so the balcony's last row can hear you even when you whisper. There were perks: applause, curtain calls, backstage flowers. Richard Aldrich, owner of the Cape Playhouse, was married to Gertrude Lawrence, who flattered me on opening night by coming backstage and bowing to me with the same deep curtsey she'd just made famous in *The King and I*. There were practical jokes: theater veterans like Peggy Wood and Jud Laire played the requisite tricks on me, their neophyte: I was sent to track down the key to the curtain, and to find striped paint. So I trotted amicably from stage manager to prop man to stagehand, each of whom, after mulling it over, assured me that somebody else was in possession of what I was looking for. (I should've picked up on striped paint right away, but legitimate theater seemed so magical and mysterious, and the technical arrangements were so foreign to my experience with cameras and mikes, that I thought there must *be* a key to the mechanism that rang down the curtain.)

Five years later, around age fifteen, I would do another stock stint—as the young girl in Graham Greene's *The Potting Shed* at the Boston Summer Theatre—memorable to me primarily because it introduced me to Greene's writing, to which I promptly developed a lifelong addiction. A year or so after that, I would spend a summer on the boards in Canal-Fulton, Ohio, playing various parts in repertory, including a fey asylum inmate in *The Curious Savage* (with ZaSu Pitts, of all people, and James Coco, whose campy humor I adored).

I didn't work on Broadway, and to the end of her life my mother never forgave Carol Irwin those years of contract exclusivity that, according to Faith, made me unable to accept the title role in *The Diary of Anne Frank*, despite (so I was told) an offer of the part after my highly successful audition. Given my mother's capacity for verbal as well as needlework embroidery, I can't be sure this offer took place, and it may well be that the late Susan Strasberg was first choice all along. But I do remember Garson Kanin, the director, coming to the footlights in actual tears after my audition and embracing me, amazed that I'd completely memorized all three scenes I'd been given to familiarize myself with one day earlier. (Overachiever was apparently my middle name.)

Looking back, I can thank a benevolent fate that I was *not* signed to Paramount Pictures and did *not* play Anne Frank. The former would have meant a move and resettlement to Hollywood hell. The latter, given the long run of that play, would have made my eventual attempts to get out of the business even more difficult than they were destined to become.

But not playing Broadway theater didn't mean I was safe from the proscenium stage. There were the accursed benefits, including radio marathons before live audiences and, later, telethons for cerebral palsy and polio research. There were fundraisers for the Red Cross, the Fresh Air Fund, the Lighthouse for the Blind, the National Cancer Fund, and many more. There were—judging from the scrapbook-collected thank-you notes—intolerable numbers of religious charities (Jewish, Protestant, Episcopal, and Roman Catholic). There were appearances at philanthropy breakfasts, charity teas, and fundraising luncheons, where my speeches were applauded by ladies wearing flowery hats with tiny veils. There were also visits to last-dying-wish children.[4] And there were publicity visits to schools, hospitals, orphanages, and summer camps for euphemistically "underprivileged" and "disadvantaged" children—all of which were detested, I'm sure, even more by the children I visited than by their visitor.

These appearances left me feeling bloated with guilt about my own advantaged existence. They also left a residue of patronizing, toxic pity for the recipients. Over time this heated, fermenting toward a rage that probably has had a considerable influence on my politics. I loathe the notion of "charity," with all it implies: contempt, hypocrisy, condescension; token largesse bestowed by the elite upon those who've been deliberately *kept* from their own fair share *by* that same elite. Furthermore, when "charity" becomes an industry, the corrupt siphoning off of monies from those in genuine need is a scandal waiting to happen: the money goes to keeping the bureaucracy afloat and to paying generous corporate salaries for those running it—what my friend, the writer and activist Theresa Funiciello,

---

[4]Not one but two different New York *Daily News* full-front-page photos display me on such grim missions: once accompanied by the movie starlet Gloria de Haven and by Bess Myerson (post-Miss America crown, pre-financial scandal), and once with the baseball player Monte Irvin. It was always claimed, of course, that the last wish of these terminally ill children was to meet me (or whoever was in the arranged foray). But I clearly recall that the visit to the leukemic little girl had been arranged by my PR agent and that, in the other case, the little boy with bone cancer (who really *did* want to meet Monte Irvin) had never heard of me.

terms "the poverty industry." Were there sane government priorities (more money for medical research than weapons research, for instance), and authentic social-justice programs empowering people as is due them by *right*, with dignity, there would be no need for the fraudulence of charity. But of course charity *is* useful—in inviting contributors to garner tax deductions while feeling good about them*selves* plus neatly preserving the status quo. I didn't understand any of this back when I was four, and seven, and ten, and fifteen—distributing donated toys, auctioning off my gold barrettes, shaking bandaged hands, cutting ribbons on newly donated wheelchairs, signing autographs, and smiling for the cameras. I went where I was taken, did as I was told, and couldn't comprehend why I would sometimes need to excuse myself, retiring to the nearest bathroom to vomit as quietly as possible.

My enforced Good Samaritanism apparently was contagious to my fans. According to a CBS Network press release, by the time I was thirteen, there were 3,500 members in Robin Morgan Fan Clubs across the United States—not only watching, following, and fantasizing about their idol but imitating her "charity work"as well: collecting used clothes and old toys for the Salvation Army and holding bake sales to raise money for the Community Chest. But by that age, I already had a growing distrust of the values for which I was being used as a conduit. I had simply seen too much of what goes on "backstage." I knew it was really about people using my celebrity to publicize their cause, and about my PR agent using a cause to publicize her client. To this day, when I hear of some athlete or actor being lauded for "humanitarianism," I gag.

I too was actually rewarded for these publicity and promotional gambits, which only made things worse. The hardest part about receiving honors was that my mother insisted I was deserving of them, while I knew there was a big difference between helping and hyping. The presentation events didn't feel flattering, merely irrelevant. I knew these honors had nothing to do with who *I* really was (whoever, I would think to myself, *that* might be). But little Robin Morgan was somebody else.

Among her other honorific identities, Robin was UNICEF mascot at age four, honorary Kentucky Colonel, Police Athletic League Mascot, Mascot of the Children's Aid Society and of the Sister Kenny Polio Foundation, honorary Boy Scout (don't ask; I don't know why), honorary Girl

Scout (never mind getting to be a real one: no time), Queen of the Boy
Scout Explorers' Ball, and recipient of the President's (Eisenhower's)
Prayer Award from the U.S. Secretary of the Treasury (for promoting sav-
ings-bond sales).

Religion, patriotism, law and order, humanitarianism, family values,
obedience, the sanctity of money. Drums and whistles. The works. The
only surprise is that I didn't grow up to be a serial killer. Perhaps if I'd been
a boy . . .

While my mother didn't expect me to believe I was really a Boy Scout,
she did require the pretense of conviction—balanced by an appropriate
show of humility—that I was worthy of what she called "our finest hour so
far," my being named at age twelve "the Ideal American Girl," as designated by the eleven million members of the General Federation of
Women's Clubs of America.

The ornately inscribed parchment scroll read:

THE RADIO AND TELEVISION DIVISION

OF THE GENERAL FEDERATION OF WOMEN'S CLUBS

PRESENTS THIS CITATION TO

YOU,

ROBIN MORGAN,

AS THE CHILD WHO HAS CONTRIBUTED MOST TO THE ADVANCEMENT

OF RADIO AND TELEVISION IN 1954.

FOR YOUR GRACIOUS EXEMPLIFICATION OF THE IDEAL

AMERICAN GIRL, AND FOR YOUR ARTISTRY DISPLAYED IN THE

CBS TELEVISION AWARD-WINNING SERIES "MAMA."

ALSO FOR YOUR ENCHANTING INTERPRETATION OF ALICE

IN "ALICE IN WONDERLAND," BELOVED BY

GENERATIONS OF THE ENGLISH-SPEAKING WORLD.

I recall little about the ceremony, except that it was staged in the Convention Center in Denver, Colorado, before popping flashbulbs, and the
stiff parchment scroll kept threatening to snap back up into its roll. A
glossy photograph informs me that my Peter Pan collar was starched, my
long blond hair pushed back by a silk ribbon headband, my smile fittingly
grateful. I do remember thinking the designation weird, partly because I

knew I was *nobody's* ideal (I had just upped my secret daily masturbation rituals to three), and because I must have intuited with the common sense of a child that no such ideal could or should exist except perhaps as a joke.

It would be years before the full irony of the award would reveal itself. Today, when I think of all those women's club members—all those gloved, hatted, corseted, volunteers-for-every-good-cause women who managed to organize efficiently around everyone's needs but their own—today I grin, as if they might somehow have divined that this dutiful young girl not only exhibited periodic symptoms of committing poetry but also harbored the gene for—could it be?—*feminism!*

Had they only known.

I wish I could have said, curtseying politely and snapping the parchment scroll,

"Thank you *so* much. I promise you that I will try to surprise your wildest expectations. America's Ideal Girl will, in my case, grow into an iconoclastic writer, a political radical in the civil-rights and anti-war movements, and a founder of contemporary feminism; she will elope with a gay poet and stay married to him for twenty years, spend time in jail and underground, survive experimenting with the sexual and drug 'revolutions,' give birth to someone who will grow up to be a rock musician and her close friend, leave the marriage, enjoy men and women lovers—and retain a threadbare, somewhat surreal sense of humor through it all. Put that in your apple pie and smoke it."

It was an oddly prophetic twist of fate that *women's* clubs were the source of the honor. For decades, women asking questions or offering comments after a feminist speech or poetry reading of mine have shyly added the query "This is crazy of me, I'm sure, but weren't you also—?" To save time and awkwardness for both of us, I've learned to interrupt gently: "A child actor, yes." At which point the questioner's eyes widen with delight. Even feminist leadership isn't immune. My friends and colleagues all have their own amusing stories to tell of how my childhood unknowingly affected theirs. Among them, Susan Brownmiller whoops that she was a fan who watched *Mama* religiously every Friday night; Andrea Dworkin insists she wanted to *be* Dagmar and live in that idealized TV family; the late Audre Lorde laughed at recalling that she'd been mesmerized by my *Alice in Wonderland*. And Gloria Steinem and I have tried to work out whether it's possible that I—at age four or five a guest judge for Ted Mack's *Amateur Hour* radio show—could actually have sat in decision over Gloria's own Mack audition when she was twelve, in her desperate attempt to tap-dance her way out of the "wrong" side of Toledo, Ohio. If so, I wish I'd had the foresight to vote for her.

But how could any of us have realized we would blossom into flower children of the radical Sixties? Perhaps the only hint was the sense of suffocation we endured as if it were regular oxygen. This, after all, was the Fetid Fifties.

This was the period that political conservatives and religious fundamentalists regard as "the good old days." It was the ghastly era of "I Like Ike," of Nixon and Checkers and the Red Menace, Wonder Bread, racial segregation-as-the-norm, and Fallout Shelters. Bishop Fulton J. Sheen glared and flapped his cassock about, propagating the faith on TV, and the series *I Led Three Lives for the FBI* glamorized counterspying on that omnipresent Red Menace. Senator Joe McCarthy pretty much ruled the Senate and, for a while, the nation. Fashion was calf-length full skirts, waist cinchers, Capezio shoes, and mink stoles. African Americans were "Negroes" or "Colored people," Native Americans and indigenous communities were "Red people" or "Indians," and Asian Americans were still considered suspect in the wake of the U.S. government's having hauled Japanese Americans off to internment camps during World War II. Other groups were subsumed under a generic, assimilative "white," though ethnic stereotypes about the alcoholic Irish or dumb Poles or miserly Scots went largely unchallenged. Anti-Semitism thrived, so much so that *Gentleman's Agreement* was considered a controversial film: it wasn't uncommon for clubs to be "restricted"—a euphemism for No Jews Allowed. America's stunning dual capacity for homophobia and denial showed itself in the immense popularity of a closeted yet outrageously flouncing Liberace. Abortion was illegal and, for all but wealthy women, tantamount to backstreet butchery with no anesthesia and a high morbidity rate. Contraception consisted mostly of condoms and diaphragms (the Pill was still in the laboratory stage; a headline from a 1952 *New York World Telegram and Sun* clip proclaims "Birth Control Pill Works on 24 out of 30 Rats"). Acquaintance rape, date rape, and marital rape were nonexistent concepts; spousal battery a whispered shame; child sexual abuse a not-even-whispered-yet shame; sexual harassment a fact of life; and equal pay a fantasy. Married women couldn't legally retain their "maiden" (i.e., fathers') names or obtain credit independently from their husbands. Newspaper and magazine ads (in the corners or on the reverse of those scrapbook clippings) reflect the same hideous norm promulgated by TV commercials of the day: smiling (all European-American) women caressing refrigerator doors, sporting frilly aprons while serving "him" hearty casserole dinners, vacuuming (such miracle labor-saving devices!), going to church, and sleeping in a twin bed (*not ever* a double, which might imply sex)—but never seen behind a desk or the wheel of a car, much less in any nontraditional job such as wielding a gavel, dangling from a pole in a telephone-repair harness, or holding a press conference as secretary of state. Most such job openings would, in time, require lawsuits.

It's heartening, in the moments when one despairs of real progress ever being possible, to remember the Fifties—and celebrate not living in them any longer.

Those contented all-American families hid brutal secrets behind their toothy smirks. Those charity industries and "brotherhood" charades never engaged commonplace racism and poverty. That "Pledge of Allegiance to the Flag" babble we had to recite in school was part of the chauvinistic, anti-Communist propaganda poisoning the country. And with the rise of McCarthyism, the television industry would develop its own corrosive rust—the too-little-remembered tarnish defacing the Golden Age.

Television blacklisting entrenched itself in 1947.[5] That was the year three former FBI agents began publishing *Counterattack,* a newsletter with the stated aim of exposing "Communist influence" in the entertainment industry. Actually, it was a shrewd protection racket: any actor, director, or writer listed in *Counterattack* as "unacceptable" or "unclear" could be ruled "politically acceptable" for one-time work *for a fee,* seven dollars per

[5]See *The Box: An Oral History of Television, 1920–1961,* by Jeff Kisseloff (Penguin, 1997).

person per clearance. (One producer who opposed the process waggishly listed Santa Claus, who was subsequently cleared—for a cut-rate five bucks.) But by 1950 the accusers had grown in numbers and in clout, and the industry was paying serious attention to the whispered-about "graylist." Vincent Hartnett, a fanatic who'd been involved in *Counterattack*, also published *Aware, Inc.* as well as *Red Channels*—all of them booklets listing people accused of being Communists or "Communist sympathizers," though you might find yourself on the list simply for criticizing the notion of a blacklist, or supporting racial integration, or saying you thought the UN was probably a good organization.

The blacklisted actor John Randolph recalls that Procter & Gamble[6] and Borden's had a list of 151 names of "radical" or "obstreperous" actors, except that in some cases the names were of nonexistent people, or were misspelled or mixed up with other actors' names. But it didn't matter. Why let a picky detail like accuracy impede the rush to accusation and judgment? Like all smears, once the accusation had been made, it stuck. The victim had little choice. You could confess (even if there was nothing *to* confess), recant, and name others. Or you could protest in defiance and face the certainty that your career would be destroyed. Randolph, who had been a courageously hostile witness before the House Committee on Un-American Activities (HUAC), could get no work in television, radio, commercials, or movies from 1951 to 1965, although he was able to land a few parts on the stage.

Soon it wasn't only rabid witch-hunters like Hartnett, or powerful sponsor-advertisers and ad agencies, who were circulating lists. The FCC

---

[6]Ah, the joys of consistency. In 1990, when I returned to *Ms.*, this time as editor in chief, our first ad-free issue featured a silence-breaking exposé by Gloria called "Sex, Lies, and Advertising," in which she revealed the extent to which advertisers have for years used (and still use) their economic power to control and manipulate editorial layout and even content in magazines—women's magazines in particular. She wrote, "Procter & Gamble, one of this country's most powerful and diversified advertisers, stands out . . . its products were not to be placed in *any* issue that included *any* material on gun control, abortion, the occult, cults, or any disparagement of religion. Caution was also demanded in any issue covering sex or drugs, even for educational purposes." Plus ça change . . .

began to make threatening noises. The networks themselves became actively involved.

As Jeff Kisseloff wrote in the *New York Times* (May 30, 1999), "Each of the networks caved in to some extent. NBC abruptly canceled *The Aldrich Family* in 1950 . . . until an actress could be found to replace Jean Muir, its star [who] did not work again in television for eight years. The actress Kim Hunter recalls being blacklisted by CBS, ABC, and NBC, in that order. Delbert Mann [director of "Marty" for *Goodyear TV Playhouse*] has said he was so fed up with NBC's blacklist that he had to be talked out of leaving the network." The blacklisted radio star John Henry Faulk became unemployable, but at least he lived to sue his accusers, win a landmark decision in court, and write a book about the blacklist, titled *Fear on Trial* (later, in 1975, made into a TV movie). Not so fortunate the actor Edward Bromberg (dead of a heart attack in the wake of being forced to testify before HUAC, after he'd been named by the director Elia Kazan), or the actor Philip Loeb, co-star of TV's *The Goldbergs*. CBS canceled that award-winning show in 1951 when Gertrude Berg, its producer, star, and primary writer, refused to jettison Loeb though he'd been blacklisted. But when the series reemerged the following year on NBC, it was without Loeb—who never again worked in television, and who committed suicide in 1955. Berg's attempted defense of someone accused was unsuccessful and tragically rare—although dear Sid Lumet became famous (or notorious, depending on one's perspective) for finding creative ways to justify hiring blacklisted talent for shows he was directing.

No one was immune. The distinguished newscaster Howard K. Smith was named. The world knows about the Hollywood Ten, but the hard-hit writers in broadcasting were less well known, among them Allan Sloane, a prominent radio writer, and Walter Bernstein, whose scripts had been sought after for television; Bernstein later wrote the movie *The Front* as well as a memoir of the period, *Inside Out,* in which he described the financial terror and despair he and his colleagues and their families faced.

In 1999, around the time of the furor over Kazan's being given a Lifetime Achievement Award by the Academy of Motion Pictures Arts and Sciences, the New York chapter of the National Academy of Television Arts and Sciences bestowed a comparable award on Frank Stanton for "lifelong work defending First Amendment rights." Stanton, at this writing ninety-one years old, was president of CBS—and overseer of its blacklisting policies—throughout the 1950s and 1960s.[7]

Kisseloff again: "In 1950, Mr. Stanton approved a company-wide loyalty oath to reassure advertisers and self-proclaimed patriots. . . . [In 1951] with [CBS Chairman of the Board William S.] Paley's approval, Mr. Stanton took the network beyond Red Channels with the creation of a security office staffed by former FBI agents to investigate the political leanings of its employees." In fairness, it should be said that later in his tenure, Stanton risked jail by defying President Richard Nixon's attempts to censor CBS newscasts and documentaries, and he led the triumphant fight to have TV cameras permanently on the floor of the U.S. Congress. It should also be said that Stanton—unlike Kazan, who to this day claims he sees nothing wrong in having named names—has at least stated that he wishes he'd had the wisdom back then that he has now. Nevertheless, Kisseloff is not exaggerating when he notes that in the late 1940s through the 1950s, CBS went further and more willingly than any other network in collaborating with and enforcing the blacklist.

That was precisely the period *Mama* was on the air.

On CBS.

In the early years I knew nothing about all this. Who would bother to tell me? On the contrary, my experience was that grown-ups clammed up whenever I entered the room. Naturally, any bright child quickly comes to know this means the adults were talking about sex, politics, or money. It wasn't until the early 1950s that I would strain my ears while pretending to do my homework in a corner of the rehearsal hall, trying to pick up

---

[7]As Kisseloff has pointed out, blacklisting persisted, especially at CBS, into the Sixties, marking Lee Grant, Jack Gilford, and Pete Seeger, among others, as unhirable. As late as 1963, when the writer Reginald Rose, creator of the CBS series *The Defenders*, approached network executives to propose doing a show about racism, they refused—but he at least won the right to do a show about blacklisting. Yet when Ernie Kinoy finished writing the script, CBS's program-practices department insisted the plot be shifted from television blacklisting to the movies, denying there had been much of a blacklist in TV. Then, in a perverse twist, the same program-practices people demanded that a cast list be submitted to them—for *clearance*. John Randolph was one of the actors being considered, and he hung twisting in the wind for days. It was only because Rose and Kinoy insisted it was madness to do a show denouncing the blacklist while still engaging in the practice that Randolph was finally hired.

clues from the discussions and arguments adult cast members had during breaks.

Decades later, in Los Angeles during a book tour, I decided to recon-
nect with some of my erstwhile TV family. Conversations with Doris
Quinlan, Dick Van Patten, and especially the late Ralph Nelson were
interesting, alarming, and validating of what I thought I'd overheard all
those years earlier.

There was a three-way political split in *Mama*.

On the left were ranged Frank Gabrielson, Gordon Webber, and most
of the other writers (those writers—ya can't trust 'em), plus (quietly) Jud
Laire, Jac Venza, and Doris Quinlan, and (more openly) Ralph Nelson—
who even dared wear a provocative "Adlai Stevenson for President" button
to work.

In the noncommittally safe Gee-I'm-just-in-show-biz-don't-know-
nothin'-'bout-politics category were Dickie, Rosie, and most everybody
else, including my mother and aunt.

Then there was Peggy Wood.

Peggy—the working-class, compassionate figure of Mama herself—
was actively involved with the *Aware, Inc.* group.

Peggy, who within moments of meeting people would inflict on them
the information that her American heritage dated back to the Revolutionary War, used to trill elegantly, "Whoever thought that *I*, with *my* background, could play a poor Norwegian immigrant?" Her memoir was
actually titled *How Young You Look*. She had worked in the theater since
1911, peaking in productions of *Naughty Marietta* and Coward's *Blithe
Spirit*, and she regarded herself still very much in the grande dame tradition: her maid would brush Peggy's hair fifty strokes at a time and kneel to
lace up her shoes.

I suspect that Peggy (I called her Miss Wood or Mama until I was
twelve) never quite forgave television for putting her in the position where
she would choose to sacrifice her patrician, "legit" image for the sake of
earning considerable money and stooping to become a household word.
She seemed to harbor a mild, chronic resentment of the situation,
although she was probably nicer to me than to anyone else in the company. I was unthreatening; I couldn't sing (she had starred in operettas); I
gratefully overachieved when she decided to teach me how to knit; I was

a *child*, after all. In fact, Peggy was one of the few people who actually encouraged my scribbling of poetry—that encouragement a legacy, no doubt, from her first marriage and great love, the not particularly inspired American poet John V. A. Weaver, by whom she had a grown son. Compensating for her bargain with the populist demon TV, Peggy consolidated her power in real life. Shuttling between the Connecticut estate and the Park Avenue apartment she shared with her second husband, William Walling, a wealthy printer (not an oxymoron in those days), she was a vice president of the American National Theater and Academy and of the Episcopal Actors' Guild, a council member of Actors' Equity—*and* a board member of the American Federation of Television and Radio Artists (AFTRA).

AFTRA was our union. I was a charter member, in fact, since I'd already been a member of AFRA—American Federation of Radio Artists—at age four, before the *T* for television was added. During the worst years of the blacklist, AFTRA apparently was in a state of internal agony, caught between trying to protect its members on the one hand and on the other trying to protect itself from the McCarthyite suspicion that all unions were hotbeds of "Commie symps." There was consequently an *Aware* contingent *within* AFTRA: arch conservatives who argued strongly for purging the union of "undesirable elements" who might "threaten its survival." This faction—of which Peggy was a leader—urged cooperation with the blacklist, including suggesting names for addition to it, even if the guilt of those hapless candidates was based only on rumor or the random Stevenson button.

So Peggy was very much part of the problem. She also must have spread powerfully protective wings—and political censorship—over the cast and company of *Mama* in her Torquemadan capacity, because to my knowledge none of us were ever listed.

Between the pages of an old script, I've come across a one-scene spoof written by Gabrielson and Nelson, to be read at a cast party during this period. It parodies the individual character clichés that had become company running jokes (Dagmar's mantra line was "Mama, can I have a cookie?"; Nels's was "I'm hungry, when do we eat?"; Papa's was always something about his boss, Mr. Jenkins; Aunt Jenny's was reporting gossip, and so forth). But the Gabrielson-Nelson one-scene spoof also tweaks blacklisting, and Peggy's role in it. Here's an excerpt from what they titled "Russian Roulette":

> Papa: Marta, I just discovered.
> Mama: What, Lars?
> Papa: That Jenkins is a capitalist. Come the revolution—
> Nels: Papa. The revolution has already come.
> Papa: Oh. Yah.
> Jenny: Marta, guess what I heard from Mrs. Johnsrud!
> Mama: Don't mention that woman's name in this house.
> Jenny: Why not?
> Mama: She has been listed in Red, White, and Blue Channels.
> Papa: For what?
> Mama: Accepting Lenin-lease.
> Katrin: Golly, Mama, what will happen to her?
> Nels: What do you think, stupid? She'll starve.
> Dagmar: Why should she be different from the rest of us?
> Nels: Yeah, I'm hungry.
> Katrin: So am I.
> Dagmar: Me too. Mama, can I have a cookie?

Long after I'd left *Mama*,[8] I ran for office as a delegate to the AFTRA annual convention. By that time I was grown, out of the business, writing, and married. But I'd kept my membership out of a sentimental union loyalty and, when urged by some members to bring my by then activist politics home to my own union, decided I'd run for delegate. I remember that

---

[8] I was contractually bound to renew so long as the show was telecast live. But in 1956 Carol Irwin decided to join the trend toward taping, which meant that all contracts had to be renegotiated. By then, I wanted out of the business entirely, but taking such a stand got me nowhere. So I adopted a step-at-a-time strategy I knew would work with Faith: urging that we not renegotiate so I could do movies or plays instead. It worked. Ralph Nelson left at the same time, Frank Gabrielson wasn't writing for the show anymore and, after eight years at the top of the TV series heap, *Mama*'s days were numbered. There were only thirteen taped episodes with Toni Campbell, a young girl who had the unenviable task of being the replacement Dagmar, before the series folded.

Peggy had invited me and my husband, Kenneth Pitchford, to a cast-and-company reunion at her apartment. I also remember that we left early, reeling out onto Park Avenue after Peggy's eruptive attack on my having *dared* to run for AFTRA delegate when I was so clearly "pinko" as to be active in the civil-rights movement and against the war in Vietnam. She would see to it, Peggy warned, that I would lose. She fulfilled her threat. Elected AFTRA delegates that year included Peggy herself, and even the sweet, mild-mannered, apolitical Dick Van Patten. But not me.

That was as late as 1965.

The Museum of Radio and Television, formerly the Museum of Broadcasting, has—god help us—Robin Morgan archives.

In the early 1990s, when I was editor of *Ms.*, one of the odd time warps that sometimes hiccup through my life occurred. The Museum, then based only in New York, now with a California branch as well, wanted to do a *Mama* retrospective. Museum officials were assembling those members of the company still alive and presumably coherent for a public panel, and hoped I would join them.

In the Sixties and Seventies, I'd spent considerable energy ignoring although not denying, my working childhood. I'd refused to discuss it when I was being interviewed as a writer or feminist spokeswoman, because I'd learned that it tended to overshadow and trivialize any real content in the interview. By the Eighties, though, I'd opened the skeleton-closet door to play with the notion of writing a quasi-autobiographical novel, eventually published by Doubleday in 1987 as *Dry Your Smile*. So by the early Nineties, the thought of appearing at the Museum with the *Mama* cast and reminiscing in public, while hardly an idea I'd have dreamt up myself, didn't provoke acute indigestion. Peggy was dead by then, as were Jud, Ruth Gates, Carol Irwin, and Frank Gabrielson. But I was curious about what was left of my TV family. And I had an agenda of my own.

Reviewing the tape of that panel, still in the Museum archives, reminds me that I rather like the woman little Robin Morgan had become, at least that day. I didn't trash anybody, didn't dwell overlong on how we, as an "ideal" family, were just as dysfunctional as other American families.[9] I even joined in (with restraint) to some of the ecstatic reminiscing: all that "Yes, I was a flower girl at Dickie's real-life wedding" stuff.[10] I noted that if one's childhood had to be laid on a performance altar, I was glad much of mine had at least been spent on a program with a female lead, strong women characters, and an immigrant, working-class setting—as opposed to, say, *Ozzie and Harriet, Life with Father,* or (bite your tongue!) *Father Knows Best.* With writerly loyalty, I praised Gabrielson, Webber, and the series' other writers for trying to inject real issues into the show—World War I fears, discrimination against non-native English speakers, kids' shame at their father's being a manual laborer. I urged Jac Venza to take a bow from the audience, as *Mama*'s former set designer who's gone on to produce most of PBS's major cultural events, including *Live from Lincoln Center* and *Live from the Met.* I'm particularly glad I got to pay tribute to the present but ailing Ralph Nelson, who would die not long after, publicly honoring not only his directorial skill but his political courage. And, while everyone else there was waxing misty-eyed over the dearly departed Peggy Wood (for whom most of the panel would have privately wished a stake in the heart), I paid due respect to Peggy's acting craft—then "outed" her as a blacklister.

They say that radio and television signals are long-lived. They say that the waves broadcast all those years ago are still beaming out into the universe, standing an excellent chance of becoming the first communications ever received from our planet by intelligent life elsewhere—especially since

[9]Even Kathryn Forbes, who'd written the book on which all the *I Remember Mama* spin-offs were based, invented her perfect family. She was actually a neglected only child of divorced parents, raised by a mother and three critical aunts. Presenting her book, *Mama's Bank Account,* as fact instead of fiction, however, intensified the heart-warming factor.

[10]Dick, also present that day, spoke proudly of his grown, firstborn son, named Nels after his character on *Mama.* Back when Nels was named, I remember thinking, "If I ever have a child and it's a girl, I'll *never* name her Dagmar."

deliberate SETI communiqués from high-powered radio transmitters and satellites antedate them by decades. I find it a horrifying notion that some-day when I'm ashes and only my books can speak for me, some intelligent life-form might be trying to understand our species by viewing me flip back my braids and whine for a cookie. I hope to god they at least also screen the *Tales of Tomorrow* episode about the child scientist trying to save Earth; hope they receive more Serling and Rose teleplays than episodes of *Leave It to Beaver*. But I know that sheer volume favors the worst assumption. It's a sobering thought that we'd approach program-ming differently even today if we regarded what beams over the airwaves not just as hypnotism for the largest share of a lowest-common-denomi-nator market but as ambassadorial signals to intelligent creatures, describ-ing who we as human beings really are—and who we might yet become.

Since the retrospective, I've been back to the Museum only a few times. Both Dr. Robert Batscha, president, and Ron Simon, curator, have been warmly welcoming in helping me whenever I've needed to . . . well, I guess, access myself. Nevertheless, whenever I visit the Museum I feel like an ambulatory potsherd.

It's passing strange to sit in a carrel, re-tapes of kinescopes at hand, ear-phones on, watching little Dagmar, and Annie Oakley, and Alice, and other incarnations of this small professional self doing her job: a child playing at being a child. Her eyes are sharp and older than her years, but her face is round with chubby cheeks. Those "baby fat" cheeks were a plague in childhood (I used to think I'd get cancer from so many people apparently feeling free to pinch them) and remained so into adulthood (when I smile broadly, I still look like a squirrel storing nuts for the win-ter). Watching the wee actor with a critical eye, I tend to think she over-acts—too breathy, too eager. But I also recall being directed that way, and find I think other people's performances on the tapes are similarly over the top, so maybe that was the style of the period. I know this child intimately, and at the same time she's utterly foreign to me. Her energy is high, her intelligence obvious. She doesn't ever fluff, forget a line, use a teleprompter, or steal a glance at the camera. The absolute *control*, in one so young, brings tears to my eyes—more of sorrow than pride. Once in a while, I'll stop a tape, rewind, and replay in slow motion, as some detail flashes by that shocks a recognition up from memory's depths: how Edgar

Bergen made Charlie McCarthy try (but fail) to break me up into laughter during *Alice;* or how, though you'd never know it from my serene expression during the barn scene of our annual Christmas show "The Night the Animals Talked," I was desperately trying to ignore the stink of a cowpat freshly deposited on my foot.

Then again, it wasn't only on-screen that you'd never have known from my expression what was really happening. With each passing year I grew, my internal subterranean landscape expanded. This is true for everyone, but was unusually intense for a child trained to inhabit differing realities. By age thirteen, I regarded the internal me as an alternate universe forced to coexist with the antimatter of my external, daily life. I couldn't see how the two would ever somehow come together and merge, or even come into balance, without an explosion. I didn't yet know the word "implosion."

$\mathscr{A}$ $\mathscr{L}$ittle $\mathscr{L}$earning . . .

Only in darkness is thy shadow clear.
— HART CRANE, "THE BRIDGE"

$\mathscr{L}$eaving aside atoms, bacteria, sugar and spice and puppy-dogs' tails, electricity, and 90 percent water, just how much is each of us more than the sum of our parts? I write this early in the year 2000, as conventional wisdom, affected by recent leaps forward in genetic research, tends toward crediting heredity with more influence than environment in shaping who we are. The pendulum swings; the reverse was thought true as I was growing up. Anyway, since I know more about my formative environment than my formative genetics, practicality tilts me in that direction.

Environment is complicated enough.

A sense of place shapes us, for one thing. Alice Walker's rural American South, Willa Cather's Midwest prairies, Henry James's (old and New) England(s). Location, location, location—what Toni Morrison calls "the site of memory." For me, that place of influence is New York City, by which I mean—no doubt unfairly, but too bad about that—the island borough of Manhattan. I happily lack the capacity for patriotism, preferring by temperament as well as politics to dance in step with Virginia Woolf's anti-pledge of non-allegiance: "As a woman I have no country. As a woman I need no country. As a woman, my country is the world." Furthermore, once I took advantage of the Freedom of Information Act to obtain my files from the U.S. government in the 1970s, any patriotic remnants I might have retained were buried under the avalanche of paper—from the FBI, CIA, National Security Council, Secret Service, and even the U.S. Air Force. So much for claiming my identity as an American. But being a New Yorker, that's different. Were Manhattan to secede from the USA, I'd grab my fife and drum in a New York minute.

Until I turned twelve, my remembered childhood home was Mount Vernon, but most of the color, excitement, and rewards—from Air Days to special treats—took place in what was called the City, which seemed, like its Emerald cousin, bright with enchantment. This part of my childhood *was* highly privileged—and it was unadulterated pleasure.

I grew up going to the Central Park Zoo, including the old Children's Zoo, which, while not as biodiversity conscious and educational as the lovely new one, was still charming, replete with nursery-rhyme statuary. I loved being taken for a browse through the massive FAO Schwartz toy store, enjoyed sliding a nickel into the slot for Aunt Sally's coffee at various now nonexistent Horn & Hardart automats, and relished visiting the elegant but also now extinct Rumplemeyer's Cafe on Central Park South, where they served the coziest hot chocolate and cinnamon toast imaginable on a wintery day, surrounded by a decor consisting of life-size stuffed zebras, giraffes, lions, and gorillas. Enthralled, I watched skaters twirl across the Rockefeller Center ice rink (where I skidded around on skates atrociously a few times but was photographed frequently, posed in front of the golden, floating god Mercury, my ankles bowed in and my stance wobbly, but my smile intact). At Coney Island I devoured my first Nathan's hot dogs and survived the only two roller-coaster rides of my life—one as a young teenager, the other as an adult, both terrifying. I became a familiar at the Waldorf Astoria, the Pierre, and the Plaza, because fashion shows and benefit appearances at which I appeared were often held at those chic hotels; at the Plaza's Palm Court, the maître d' knew me so well he nicknamed me "the real-life Eloise." Various cast members, producers, and friends of my mother's took me to ballets at the old City Center and to operas at the original (pre–Lincoln Center) Metropolitan Opera House.

At the latter, I heard so many performances of *Die Fledermaus, The Magic Flute,* and *Carmen* that I knew certain arias by heart before age fourteen (these were the three operas somehow thought appropriate for a child, although how *Carmen* quite fit into this category eludes me); in my teens I got to hear a wider repertoire: a memorable Callas (and also Tebaldi) singing *Tosca* (with such a sexy, velvet-throated George London as Scarpia that I've utterly forgotten the tepid tenor who sang Cavaradossi), Callas's *Norma,* Sutherland's *Lucia di Lammermoor,* Tebaldi's *Madama Butterfly,* and her Violetta in *La Traviata* (I didn't encounter Wagner, Strauss, Berg, Poulenc, or contemporaries like Menotti or Barber until my late teens and early twenties). I saw Martha Graham dance, and Nora Kaye, and Tanaquil Le Clercq; I was thrilled by Maria Tallchief's electric *Firebird,* by the newly defected Nureyev partnering Margot Fonteyn in their lyrical *Romeo and Juliet,* and, some years after, by another new defector, Baryshnikov, first soaring across the stage in *La Bayadère.* By age nine, I'd learned the constellations not from the night sky but from the planetarium at the Museum of Natural History, and during my adolescence I spent hours alone, roaming the Metropolitan Museum, the Frick, the Museum of Modern Art, the Guggenheim, and the Morgan Library (secretly pretending it belonged to distant relatives but knowing better).

It was pure glee to pass along such a New York City childhood to my son, Blake—that rarity, a Manhattan-born *real* New Yorker—when he was little. This city's offerings, many of them free, make for a magical, healthy context in which to grow, one not only of splendor but of depth, width, and texture: I'll take Shakespeare-in-the-Park, the Bronx Botanical Garden, the trash-talking Knicks and dysfunctional Mets, all-night restaurants and movie theaters and delis, street fairs, street foods, and street smarts any day over the prospect of growing up in the plasticine picket-fence blandness of suburbia. By now, since I've lived all over Manhattan, certain sections of it have come to represent different periods of my life to me, entire neighborhoods functioning as sense memories: East 57th Street and its Sutton Place environs (to which Faith and I moved from Mount Vernon) makes me think of my adolescent rebellion; the Upper West Side stands for my days haunting Columbia University; the Lower East Side (fatuously euphemized by some as "the East Village") is redolent of my elopement, my twenty years of married life with Kenneth Pitchford, "summers of love"and subsequent hippie hells, and Blake's birth and childhood; the Upper East Side represents my "diaspora"—many months of staying with friends after the marriage broke apart in the early 1980s; the Brooklyn Bridge will always resonate for me with the recollection of walking across it with Kenneth as he shouted Hart Crane's great poem "The Bridge" into the wind; the narrow, winding, tree-lined streets of Greenwich Village—where I longed to live for most of my life—are what I now finally call home. . . .

I didn't always grasp this sense of place in myself, partly because I confused it with that loathsome patriotism but mostly because I refuse to be sentimental about New York in a mawkish, Liza Minnelli way. This city is noisy and crowded; it can be maddening, smelly, costly, and scary; and it's a perfect place to live if you don't trust air you can't see. Moreover, I can imagine living in the country, and contentedly spent many months on a fairly isolate farm in New Zealand, itself a fairly isolate country. But for cities, there is simply no equal to New York, certainly not in the United States, much as San Francisco, Chicago, Boston, and New Orleans—nice enough places—preen themselves trying. (We won't even *discuss* Los Angeles, conceived by Dante on a slow day and executed by Bosch when his eyesight was failing.) There really *is* a reason—reasons, in fact—why New York is called the capital of the world, and it's not only because of the United Nations.

I noticed this the more I traveled abroad, especially in Europe, as I felt an odd sense of displacement on ordinary streets. Part of it was pace: my characteristic impatience, which around more leisurely people can make me feel like a ball-bearing spinning to escape being drowned in a bowl of Jell-O. But there was something else I couldn't quite grasp. The feeling intensified in Copenhagen once, following a visit to Oslo—although I adored the former's Tivoli Gardens and the latter's Munch Museum. Finally I recognized what the unease was: everyone on the street was so terminally *white* I felt in danger of going snow-blind. They were all tall and blond, with lemon-yellow eyelashes. Where was the palette of patinas— blueblack, walnut, bronze, amber, olive, teak, cocoa, ginger, saffron, ocher—that brandishes its glorious spectrum along New York streets, in parks, in subways? Where were the towering Kikuyu descendants, or the diminutive Asians who made me (at five feet one inch) feel statuesque? In

Copenhagen and Oslo, conversations of passersby sounded like mellifluous tracks from an Ingmar Bergman movie (with no subtitles), but where was the counterpoint of Spanish and Chinese, Arabic and Italian and Korean and Greek, where was an English transformed by Yiddishisms, mixed with a Jamaican lilt, a Philippine twang, a Haitian patois, an Indo-Pakistani singsong percussion?

As a woman I need no country. As a New Yorker, my city is the world.

Where we set our roots forms us, yes. And certainly we're formed by what we're taught, although what we're *not* taught affects us as much or perhaps more. Lessons come in many guises and images. When I was a child, air travel was just becoming commonplace, so we journeyed to other cities largely on trains with sleeping cars (which I fancied greatly), attended by elderly gentleman porters, all of them black; I didn't know then about the organizing history of the Brotherhood of Sleeping Car Porters, but travel delivered clear if unstated lessons about race, sex, age, and class. I came to adulthood, like everyone, staggering under a million such subliminal messages. Being a European-American child, I was cooed over especially for my golden curls and peachy-cream skin, and there were further lessons: Aunt Jemima's pancake mix, Uncle Ben's rice, radio's Amos 'n' Andy and Jack Benny's valet Rochester, pink "flesh-colored" Band-Aids, Eddie Cantor singing "Mammy" in blackface—all popular, all unquestioned. My mother labeled whomever she considered vulgar as "white trash," and Aunt Sally described independence in a then conventional phrase, as being "free, white, and twenty-one."

If our education came only from those persons formally called "teachers," that would exclude the people responsible for our earliest, deepest, most enduring imprints. As, for example, when I was ten years old, and my mother decided to enlighten me about menstruation. After explaining the physical process, she spoke emphatically about how there was *nothing* shameful in menstruating, how I should *never* let anyone make me feel embarrassed about my body or its functions, how reproduction was a miracle and sex a joy, how neither was unclean or sinful, and how I should strongly repudiate any philosophy or attitude that attempted to make me think so. Such rational, healthy support! It would take years of bafflement and six months of feminist consciousness-raising in my late twenties to figure out how I had nevertheless fallen prey, albeit secretly, to believing the stereotype of the unclean female, when my mother had tried so valiantly to free me from it. It was a revelation when at last I remembered that Faith, Diva of the Double Message, had delivered her entire peroration—even after making sure we were alone—in a whisper.

Probably it's the unofficial teachers who make the real impact: relatives, friends, lovers, bosses, rivals, therapists, mentors, and definitely one's own children. Animals, too, and gardens, can be teachers.

But then there are the ones who are *supposed* to teach, from whom we're *expected* to learn, if not wisdom then at least knowledge, if not truths at least facts, if not talents at least skills.

Shirley Wetter was decidedly one of those. I have no recollection of how Faith or Sally found her, or how they fashioned the arrangement about my working schedule. All I know is that, when I was not quite six, after a one-month bout at the Professional Children's School in Manhattan, I was out of there and enrolled at the Wetter Private School in Mount Vernon. My mother said it was because the academic standing at PCS wasn't high enough, even if it did grant priority status to my career. She was right, but she must have suffered a conflict between her longing for this child to become sufficiently rich and famous to pull the family up from its immigrant origins ("to better ourselves" was the phrase), and her equally strong desire, culturally implanted by those same origins, for the child to become well educated ("improving your mind is *so* important"). In retrospect, I'm touched that she tried to invent a middle way.

Shirley Wetter (Miss Wetter to me) was of indeterminate age, with a youngish face but graying hair; she ran a one-woman small private school out of her home in a "nice" residential section of Mount Vernon. Her mother and sister had originally run the school with her, but both were now dead. I realize that she was perhaps only in her late thirties or early forties, yet there were whispers about her being a spinster—yes, the word was in active use—because of a tragic love, something to do with his having died as they were about to be married. How much of the legend was apocryphal I'll never know, nor did Miss Wetter make you feel you could probe into personal matters.

She wasn't a cold woman, though. Partly it was the house itself that intimidated: a large, dark, wood, beautiful house about seventy-five years old. Only once, when I took sick in class and was sent to the upstairs bathroom and then given permission to lie down in a guest room until my aunt picked me up, did I ever get to see the upstairs—dusty lace curtains and mahogany furniture stood out against the wallpaper's faded mauve roses. Mostly we were confined to the downstairs, to the hall and two rooms.

I can still remember my first visit to that long, dark hall, the little bench on which I sat while my galoshes and leggings were tugged off, the different-height pegs for coats belonging, respectively, to the Big Kids and the Little Kids. The main schoolroom—originally, I imagine, a dining room— was a pleasant octagonal shape, with three large windows in three of the walls. A round table at which four students could sit stood in the center of the room, and three smaller tables, each capable of seating two students, were off to one side. Miss Wetter herself sat at an even smaller table in front of a marble fireplace mantle. The adjoining room was originally, I assumed, the front parlor or sitting room: another fireplace, a long library table, bookshelves with the big reference books, and a sofa-and-chairs set lived there. And the piano, a splendid piece of furniture that hadn't been tuned in so long it was hardly any longer an instrument: a *rectangular* piano, in full Victorian carved mahogany majesty. I used to fantasize that Shirley Wetter, who seemed to have no relatives, would leave that piano to me when she died.

Miss Wetter taught an intensive two-session day—grades seven through twelve (the Big Kids) in the mornings, from 9:00 to 12:30, and grades one through six (the Little Kids) from 1:30 to 4:30 in the afternoon. Once I'd begun working on *Mama,* my rehearsal and on-air schedule dictated my other activities. We had no rehearsal on Mondays, but we rehearsed from 10:00 to 1:00 on Tuesday, Wednesday, and Thursday mornings, and on Fridays we were in the studio all day. An efficient if peculiar arrangement was worked out, so that I could attend my missed Friday afternoon school session on Monday mornings, sitting in with the Big Kids (until I finally became one), breaking for lunch, then returning for the afternoon session with my own group. Tuesdays through Thursdays I attended the afternoon session immediately after the train from rehearsal in the City had deposited Aunt Sally and me back in Mount Vernon.

Mondays were my favorite. First, I got to be with the Big Kids, which meant I got to sit in the piano room and soak in by osmosis what would become my future curriculum. Also I got to have a real lunch break instead of a quick sandwich wolfed down while lurching along in the train. Some days this lunch break meant that I walked five blocks to Aunt Sophie's apartment to be indulged in her cooking, but that was allowed only after I grew older, about nine or ten. When I was littler, I brought a sandwich and thermos with me and ate alone, sitting in Miss Wetter's hall, reading, which was a mild form of bliss. But other days, when it was warm enough in spring and early fall, Faith or Sally would bring me lunch, and we'd picnic on the broad steps of the Methodist church at the corner. They each ran true to form. Sally would bring a bologna, salami, or liverwurst sandwich on pumpernickel (which I came to fully respect only as an adult, yearning instead for bland white Wonder Bread like other kids ate), and she'd sit and read her newspaper while I munched. But my mother, characteristically, would make lunch into an occasion. Coming on her own lunch break from work at Lerner's, she might surprise me with Chinese egg rolls, or hot dogs in still-warm buns, or sliced chicken-breast sandwiches and thin sweet pickles on white bread with the crusts removed . . . and suddenly it would be a real picnic, a conversation, an intimacy. Sometimes I would put my head in her lap and doze while she stroked my hair. Those quiet moments of sitting, eating, talking, and simply being together on the sun-warmed granite steps live as treasured memories; even now they can render me temporarily able to forget whatever else she did that at times I've feared I might be unable to forgive.

At school we did the basics: the three Rs, plus geography, world and U.S. history, penmanship (sic), English (grammar, essays, book reviews), and what was then called social studies or civics. Study was taken seriously. Twice a week, we stood "on line" in a circle, waiting to be called on for rapid-fire math answers calculated mentally with no paper or pencil: multiplication tables, long division, fractions, and, later on geometry and algebra. On line (what a different meaning it has today!) also served for Doing Questions once a week: state and national capitals, match-the-author-to-the-book, naming grammatical parts of different sentences. I'd been reading well before first grade, so that was never a problem, and, given my memory, I was good at these firing-line spontaneous tests, enjoying them. In fact, I loved school. I was smart and knew it and knew that Wetter knew it, too.

The problem, of course, was that this tendency to know stuff and

worse, to *flaunt* it, hardly endeared me to the other kids. I didn't *mean* to
ace out anybody; I just got genuinely excited about the work itself, and
even more enthusiastic when I knew the answers. Furthermore, by age
eight, I had already tried to ingratiate myself every way I could imagine,
already failed miserably, and already given up hope of being liked for
myself: I'd lost that contest to my image. It was painfully clear what my
peers felt about this classmate who manifested herself on television live
every week: awe and resentment. At the time, I didn't know Lao Tzu's
warning that "the creation of envy in others is a great crime." On the contrary, with their dismissive refrains of "So-and-so is just jealous," Faith and
Sally made me feel that the creation of envy in others was part of my job
and that I should try to do it well. Still, I desperately wanted a real
friend—not just Bunker the imaginary companion, not just the occasional
kid actor hired for a one-shot on the show, and not just my dancing
teacher's daughter who, while affable enough, was the handpicked girlfriend my mother chose for me.

I knew exactly who I wanted. I wanted Doris Scheidecker.

She was my age but taller than me, with sandy, tousled hair and blue
eyes. She wasn't at all pretty, and she wore corduroy pants and flannel
shirts. Some of the kids whispered that her family was poor and that she
had a three-quarter scholarship, which didn't surprise me, because Doris
Scheidecker was very, very smart. I skipped a grade twice, and so did she.
She was, in fact, my only real competitor in the gold-star-high-marks-who-
is-smarter department, and I loved her madly for that. I was ecstatic when
I beat her at answering a question, but I even enjoyed losing to her, and
the frequent times when she and I would be the only two left on line
(when you erred you had to sit down) were so exhilarating that my mouth
would dry out and my palms would sweat as if I were about to hear the
floor manager's Stand-By backward five-count to going live on air. But
Doris Scheidecker did not requite my lust for friendship. Doris Scheidecker did not like this little sissie who wore dresses and never coveralls,
who disappeared every Friday but got to study with the Big Kids Monday
mornings, who must have seemed rich and who really was famous and, as
if all that weren't enough, was obnoxiously smart to boot.

I tried to show Doris who I really was. In my pursuit of her friendship I
jettisoned all pride. I brought her little presents: a paper origami bird I

learned to make from a Japanese actor who did a guest appearance on the show; a watered-silk violet ribbon I'd stolen from Faith's sewing kit, for Doris to use as a bookmark; one of my lace hankies Faith had mono-grammed *R,* from which I'd secretly picked the monogram, patiently working with a pin and nail-scissors at the initial's limbs until I'd got it to look like a tiny mangled *D* instead. But Doris always shrugged, muttering, "I don't want that," and turned away. I was slow and I was stubborn, but after three long years of this even I got the message. I told no one about the rejection, because I didn't want to hear the Job's comforters Faith and Sally always became in such cases. I kept my hurt to myself, over time acidifying it into a fuel that intensified my competitiveness. And when I won first in academic standing the fourth year in a row and Doris, as four-time runner-up, was forced again to congratulate me, I shrugged, "I don't want that," and turned away.

Perhaps we might have developed a different camaraderie, a team spirit, had there been any teams. But there were no sports and no physi-cal education, which doubtless relieved my mother and aunt. In clement weather the Little Kids were taken into the backyard for a fifteen-minute recess each afternoon. Supervised games were the order of the day, but these sometimes ran the Olympian risk of falling down on the grass, so I usually didn't get to participate. To her credit, Shirley Wetter disapproved (she always insisted I at least come outside for some air), but my playing nothing except musical chairs or circle dancing must have been part of the special arrangement for my "safety."

Real dancing took place elsewhere, but that was part of my career preparation. Once we moved into Manhattan and I'd graduated to toe shoes and work *en pointe* in difficult combinations, I took class five times a week under the tyranny of the revered, tiny, unintelligible Madame Nevelska at Carnegie Hall studios. But I'd already attended dance classes in Mount Vernon for six years—ballet, tap, and modern (most kids took only one, but I took all three), each taught by Grace Liccione, a striking woman with ramrod posture, huge dark eyes, and gleaming black hair worn in a long ponytail or wound in a chignon. She had a daughter (Faith's choice for my girlfriend) named Georgiana, who'd had been born with a slightly clubbed foot but who had been lovingly, mercilessly trained by her mother to, as Grace put it, "transcend" the disability and become an accomplished dancer; Grace and Faith shared a friendship as well as an identification in maternal ambition. Each year the Liccione School of the Dance held a big recital at Wood Auditorium to which all the families came—as many as four or five hundred people. I remember dancing through various recitals as a Valkyrie, a Petunia, a Cowgirl, a Day Hour in "Dance of the Hours," the Virgin Mary, and a Powder Puff. But my biggest moment came when I was cast as Cinderella in a special PTA night at the Robert Fulton School auditorium, for which Liccione presented a grand finale ballet. My narcissistic recollection of how hard I worked to earn the part and dance it well was humbled recently when, going over old scrapbooks for the writing of this memoir, I came across the program for "Cinderella": blazoned across the front is the announcement "Featured Artist: Robin Morgan, TV Star." Admission, you see, was being charged, and I was considered a draw.

But at the time, I didn't resent dance classes or feel particularly displayed or exploited. Grace Liccione had an authentic passion for all forms of dance and communicated that passion to her students. She made *everyone* want to excel, so I felt less alone in my drive to overachieve. But I *did* like the rest breaks we'd get. That was when Rosina Tinari (who was younger than me but bright) and Dorothy Drewes (who was older and wanted to become a professional ice skater) and Carol Sherman (who was kind of snotty about her dimples but played my prince in "Cinderella"), and all the other girls would get to collapse onto the wood floor, surrounded by mirrored walls. We would sit cross-legged in our sweaty leotards, facing each other's backs in a circle, and give each other back rubs or slowly brush each other's hair. Oh, the sensuality of that exercise! Young girls, ranging in age from eight to fourteen, in a giggly, innocently orgiastic ritual wherein you gave pleasure to the girl in front of you while being pleasured by the girl behind you! Mrs. Liccione would retire for her own ten-minute break, but Mrs. Cordes, who played piano for our classes, kept watch—and let us know she disapproved of the way her charges transformed themselves into voluptuaries, moaning Ooooohs and Aaaaahs of delight along with directions specifying "Ouch! Don't brush so hard!" and "A little more to the *right*, Dumbbell."

Fortunately, Mrs. Cordes did not teach me piano. My piano teacher was Mr. Edwin Jones, who was young, gay, closeted, handsome, talented, and wretchedly unhappy to be teaching piano to Mount Vernon children instead of touring the world in the concert career he had envisioned for himself. Sometimes he appeared with a black eye that, with hindsight, I suspect was caused by his church-organist battering-lover "roommate," though he would explain it away as having been caused by various falls, open cabinets, and unseen doorjambs. But he was a fine teacher, and I made my way fairly rapidly up to "Für Elise" and then "Solfegietto." He was also sharp enough to see that (a) I loved playing the piano, (b) I was a fast enough learner to fudge practicing technique and sight-reading, (c) I had been raised to be a killer competitor, and (d) my aunt and mother were enamored of prizes and awards. Consequently, after studying for only three years, I was informed that, with my aunt's permission, I'd been entered in the New York State Music Association Festival, competing at the five-year level, playing Mozart's "Fantasia I in D Minor." I was about ten.

I distinctly recall those weeks of fervent practice (while, of course, the show, and school, and other lessons continued as usual). I remember that period building up to the competition as the first time during which I consciously resented being put on display, particularly since I felt I'd been forced to exchange what had been a private pleasure in making music for yet another kind of performing, this time under intense pressure. When the day arrived, I twice threw up from nerves, but managed to get through the piece clinker-free, despite what one judge noticed as "somewhat uneven pedaling." In fact, I felt a shooting pain in my right foot every time I pressed the pedal, but was too scared to dare stop and investigate what was wrong. Only afterward did I see that a thumbtack had got stuck into the thin sole of my Capezio slipper, and was puncturing the ball of my foot with every pedal press. Ever the pro, I'd dutifully won my medal, and then endured a tetanus shot for my pains. But afterward, I deliberately let my music drop. I knew that was the only way to keep it from getting processed into more performances. Content with their medal, and not seeing piano as necessary for my career as singing, accents, and dancing might be, Sally and Faith agreed that I could stop playing. I've wondered if Mr. Jones didn't actually understand, because that last day, as we were saying our goodbyes, he whispered in my ear, "It's a pity," and then he bent and gallantly kissed my hand as if I were a grown woman. I learned years later that he'd been found dead of a gunshot wound. A pity, indeed. As for all his work with me and my music, it would take well over a decade, until early in my marriage, for me to allow myself the luxury of sitting alone at a piano to rediscover the satisfaction of playing simply for one's self.

Meanwhile, once I'd turned twelve and Faith had ditched Sally, moving herself and me to East 57th Street, the tutors began to come and go, talking of Michelangelo—because I was now already doing the equivalency of high-school work. They were a varied and peculiar mix.

The absolute worst was Mr. Margolies. Tall, lanky, dour, droning Mr. Margolies—I never learned his first name; perhaps he never had one—carried a two-dimensional effect about him: Flatman. He was even slightly concave in the chest. Though he was only in his early thirties, his flesh was a library greenish-taupe color. His voice sounded as if it had been disguise-enhanced or was being played at the wrong speed—too low, too drawn-out. He moved slowly. He wrote slowly. He thought and talked slowly. He even blinked slowly, his lids drifting closed and then rising again with supreme effort in the long, almost expressionless face. The effect was soporific. Mr. Margolies was the Sominex of teachers. Even now, writing about him, I find myself yawning. He had taught me math during my brief stint at the Tutoring School, immediately after Faith and I settled in Manhattan, and he must have spotted a golden opportunity, because he somehow ingratiated himself with my mother. The next thing I knew, he was my sole tutor, arriving four times a week at our apartment.

I despised him. I cannot be fair to him even now. I cannot remember a single thing I learned from this man, and since his specialty was supposedly math, his teaching methods bear testimony to my now sharing the math anxiety of most of my female contemporaries. Did he actually "track" me away from math, which I'd enjoyed and at which I'd been good back at Miss Wetter's? I don't know. But I do know that after a year of Faith's insisting, "Give it a *try*, Robin," I managed to communicate the intensity of my loathing for Mr. Margolies to her with sufficient pathos. Besides, the loathing was showing up in my grades. So he was let go. There were one or two others, staying a few months at a time, leaving no impressions but those of mediocrity, opportunism, and insultingly low, stereotypical expectations about the intellectual capacity of a child star.

But then there was that one teacher who changes your life.

There was Jean Distler Tafti.

In the early 1990s, I gave a poetry reading up near Columbia University, when a new-and-selected volume of my poems had just been published. After the reading, a man in his mid-thirties came up and introduced himself to me as the son of Jean Tafti, who had always "spoken highly of you." I was so glad to have the chance to communicate to him the enormity of what his mother's gift had meant to me, what a quietly brilliant, generous teacher she had been.

That first session after Faith had hired her as my tutor, Jean studied me across the coffee table in the living room. She'd asked whether we should work in my room, and raised her eyebrows slightly when told I shared the one bedroom in our posh 57th Street apartment with my mother (so much for any hoped-for change *there*). She leaned toward me and suggested we use the first session to get to know each other. Then she asked me who I really was, and I knew she did not mean my name, rank, and Employed Minor registration number.

I remember I said I was a labyrinth, a maze. I was thirteen, and eager to show off how much Greek and Norse mythology I'd read. I said the labyrinth had a starting place and a center, but between these two lay an enigma. I heard myself telling her I wanted to be a writer. I'd never said that aloud before. Then I started to talk about my acting career—but she went directly back to the writing.

"What kind of writer?" she asked.

We were off from there. I exploded about how words were mystical, living things. Then I think I babbled that I wanted to make people laugh and cry and think and change, to move people the way I'd sometimes been able to as an actor, but with my own words and thoughts instead of someone else's; that as an actor one could interpret multiple lives but as a writer one could *invent* and *inhabit* multiple lives. Jean sat, silent, nodding. She was one of those perceptive educators who actually listen, who then can sum up a pupil's inarticulate gurglings in a few succinct words so the student feels totally understood.

"I think," she smiled at me, "you want to be of use."

"Oh yes and even worse," I heard myself blurt out. "I want to change the world. I know that sounds hopelessly thirteen."

"*Or*, hope*fully*, a sign of positive evolutionary mutancy," she shot back. "I believe you, Robin."

I thought I'd perish with gratitude.

For the next four years, from 1955 to 1959, Jean Tafti was for me a life raft. Severely challenging in content but mild in style, she had a wry sense of humor and an unpatronizing respect for the people she taught—mostly foreign students at Columbia Teachers College, which was her real job. A white woman from a southern border state (Kentucky, I think), she'd married a Parsi from India. She was a small woman with a heart-shaped face and a gentle, grainy-gravel voice, and she fed my voracious hunger to learn things as if I were a starving beggar and she the teacher right out of *The Corn Is Green*. She never treated me like an adolescent performer dabbling in intellectual pursuits. And the woman knew how to teach.

We discussed writers and language and human rights and politics and comparative religions and psychology. She introduced me to the work of Karen Horney, Margaret Mead, Ruth Benedict, and Edith Hamilton, explained the differences between socialism and communism, helped me understand how the Korean War was complicated, taught me about apartheid and South Africa. It was impossible to do science without a lab (though she managed to devise some experiments we could perform in the kitchen), so she announced that if I couldn't quite have a well rounded education I could at least have a well-focused one, possibly of greater value, she added, since I already knew what I wanted to do: write. So we studied Latin and French and German, moved swiftly past high-school English into the college-level and soon graduate-level English curriculum. Because of Jean's grace and skill, I felt free of self-consciousness and competitiveness, unembarrassed by my failures and my ignorance. I remember one occasion in particular. She'd given me a *Collected Poems of William Butler Yeats* as a Christmas gift; I still have it, dated 1956, inscribed "with deep affection." She must have assumed (accurately) that I'd fall under the triple spell of Yeatsian myth, politics, and verbal music. At our next meeting, I raved on about Yeats—but since I'd never before heard his name pronounced aloud, I uttered it as if it rhymed with Keats—the sort of error that, once realized, normally would have mortified me. As Jean offhandedly corrected my pronunciation, she also praised my assumption which, although wrong, made perfect sense, she said, since the two names were spelled similarly.

With and for Jean, I read Plato, Aristotle, Homer, and (in Latin) Virgil;

Goethe and Schiller and Thomas Mann (in German); Danton, Baudelaire and Verlaine, Sartre, Gide, Camus, and de Beauvoir (in French). My life-long love of Kafka (especially in the Muir translation) began with her, in no small part because she encouraged me in my opinion that his writing wasn't merely "surreal" or "spooky" but darkly hilarious. Through Jean I also met Tolstoy and Dostoyevsky, Chekhov and Turgenev. She was the annunciating angel who first brought Donne, Marvell, and the other seventeenth-century Metaphysical poets into my life, as well as more of the Romantics—Blake and Wordsworth, Shelley and Byron, Barrett and Browning—on up through Eliot, Pound, Auden, and what was termed the Moderns. We read Austen and both Georges—Eliot and Sand—the latter in the original French, along with Balzac, Colette, and Malraux. I'd got myself addicted to the entire Brontë family on my own, but Hardy, Forster, Woolf, Conrad, D. H. Lawrence, and James Joyce now broke over my awareness, as did Cervantes, Lady Murasaki, Neruda, and Lagerkvist. By the time I was fifteen, under Jean's urging and aegis, I was starting to take nonmatriculated classes at Columbia, sitting in on (and sometimes even daring to pipe up in) Gilbert Highet's graduate courses on Virgil and Dante, auditing Moses Hadas's survey of classical Greek drama, Mark Van Doren's lectures on Shakespeare and the Jacobeans, Maurice Valency's course on Provençal poetry, and workshops on contemporary poetry with Van Doren, Babette Deutsch, and Louise Bogan.

I was drunk with joy.

My mother, glad to see me happy (and having little idea what I was really reading—particularly the Baudelaire-Gide-Joyce-Lawrence-Colette axis), was proud of what Jean termed my "exceptionally high degree of proficiency" in the subjects she was teaching me. My career was proceeding: I'd left the *Mama* show and was doing guest-star stints on various dramas. All was well. The problem set in when Jean took a stand supporting my desire to attend college formally.

Faith, as might have been expected, balked. I was too young; I was too well-known to act like or be treated like a regular student; I might attend sporadic classes but going full-time would harm my career. Especially and repeatedly, I was just too *young*. Jean Tafti somehow managed to apply on my behalf to the University of Chicago, where a program pioneered under the progressive educator and former chancellor Robert Maynard

Hutchins was admitting students as young as fourteen so long as they could do the work required. I was sixteen. I was accepted.

It blew up in my face. The notion of my going to another city—alone!—to college was unthinkable to my mother. Not all Jean's persuasive calm nor all my tearful pleas would make a difference. On the contrary, Faith—who actually snarled at me, "A little learning *is* a dangerous thing, I see!"—now regarded Jean as a traitorous viper in our midst, and the Tafti tutorial came to an end. But the emancipating damage had been done.

For some years after, into my twenties, I considered going to college. Then, as I came to realize how superficially educated most college graduates, as well as many with graduate degrees, are, I began to distrust the pedantry of formal academia. As it turned out, Jean was right: a well-focused education, plus the knowledge of how to expand it by research on my own, would best equip me for my chosen work. To this day I've never dissected a frog or lit a bunsen burner, and I miss neither (though I enjoy reading physics and biology). It's true that some of the emotional and social experiences of being in college might have been helpful and fun. Then again, I've not been overly impressed by the social ambience on the hundreds of college campuses where I've guest-lectured or read poetry, or on the four at which I've been a "distinguished" visiting scholar or guest professor (New College in Sarasota, Florida; Rutgers University; the University of Canterbury in Christchurch, New Zealand; and the University of Denver in Colorado). To this day, I have no B.A., although, ironically, some of my books have been adopted as basic texts in a variety of disciplines, from international affairs to literature and women's studies, and although I've been the recipient of an occasional honorary doctoral degree—the bestowal of which is a kindly ritual only sometimes bound up with a university's connivance to wring a free commencement speech from you while you trip over your gown and the funny hat with the tassel keeps sliding off your head.

Whenever I lecture or talk with students, I make certain they know that I never graduated from college. Whenever I guest-teach, I announce at the beginning that there will be no grading other than pass/fail, that I consider marks to be irrelevant and tests abhorrent so there will be neither, that the required reading list is three times longer than what they are usually assigned, and that we will be attempting to bypass the vapid bureaucracy of the contemporary credit-grade-tuition education-industry mill so as to get to the *point*: the challenge and elation of *learning* something about the subject before us. Such pronouncements might make some professors and school administrators uncomfortable, but what I see in the students' widening eyes and incredulous grins, and what transformations they blossom through as the course proceeds, remind me of a young girl who wanted to be of use and, worse, change the world.

I like to think Jean might be pleased.

Sex, Lies, and Fatherly Love

> *Cruelty has a human heart,*
> *And Jealousy a human face;*
> *Terror, the human form divine,*
> *And Secrecy, the human dress.*
>
> — WILLIAM BLAKE

In the late 1960s, at the beginning of this wave of feminism in the United States, a standard question asked of movement spokeswomen was "What childhood trauma did you suffer that made you become a feminist?" Patiently, we would explain that no specific trauma had been necessary, reciting until we were hoarse statistics on rape, battery, butchered illegal abortions, and gross inequalities in education and employment as well as in virtually every other area. Such moronic psychological reductionism drove me nuts, so sometimes, when in a mischievous mood, I'd "confess" in a low voice that something *had* in fact happened to me around age three. With my interrogator salivating in anticipation, I'd spring the scandalous revelation: my trauma lay in having discovered I'd been born female in an androcentric society, the same trauma every girlchild endures.

It's taken thirty years for contemporary feminist politics to enter the so-called mainstream, and now this sort of trivializing dismissal by psycho-babble is attempted less often. We're all more aware of the intimate intri-cacies of oppression, those small but steady erosions of spirit that can exact as great a toll as do blatant outrages to human dignity. Society has begun to glimpse (though not yet grasp) that there exists an emotional equivalence of foot-binding; that self-regard is connected with having access to capacity, agency, power. Furthermore, thanks to three decades of feminist research and organizing, we've also become more aware of the tragically high proportion of *literal* trauma—verbal, emotional, physical, and sexual abuse—that children, in particular girl children, suffer.

This changed consciousness now makes it possible to tell truths less "aslant." One such, in my case, consists of a rather bizarre relationship with the Roman Catholic priest who functioned as my father surrogate from the time I was about four until early in my teens.

Father Joseph Melory Collier—Father Joe—came into our all-female household's life when, having attended one of those religious-charity ben-efits at which I too frequently had to perform, he came backstage to meet the "dear little girl with Franciscan brown eyes."

Then, somehow, he was there. For years.

I was not privy to any discussions my mother and aunt may have had about him. But each of them had said more than once that neither would ever remarry because, since no man would put up with their focus on me, marriage for either of them "might interfere with Robin's career." At the time, I didn't question such a rationale, though it got added to the pile of their sacrifices about which I felt guilty. Given this mindset of theirs, plus concern about my fatherless state (women-headed families in the 1940s were still considered "fishy" even by the women themselves), I can well imagine that a celibate priest might have seemed the perfect daddy-surro-gate candidate. He never proselytized conversion, so the Catholicism was no problem, especially since my mother prided herself on her ecumeni-cism, which was probably more indicative of a flight from her own Ashke-nazic origins than she was able to acknowledge. Faith was hilariously, almost promiscuously, ecumenical. She celebrated all secular, Jewish, and Christian holidays, plus Chinese, Russian, and Persian New Year's; when she discovered Ramadan, she celebrated *that*.

Whatever the justification for Father Joe's presence, I was glad of it. He had a debonair Irish manner and liked to "take off the collar and go incognito." He told terrific stories—mostly about the saints and the Irish, who apparently were synonymous. He called me "Kitten" or "Princess," and about once a month took me to the Bronx Zoo or for rides on the Central Park carousel, always with ice cream afterwards. Of medium build with a ruddy face and balding scalp, he smelled good—of lime cologne, incense, and mellow pipe tobacco. He was gentle and sheltering, never patronized me, and displayed a nonpompous, self-deprecatory sense of humor that extended to singing "Jingle Bells" in Latin ("Tintanabulum, tintanabulum, tinta via cora . . ."). He always remembered my birthday, phoned in praise the day after a show, and sent me flowers on Father's Day.

His presence made Christmastime magical. It became a tradition that my family joined his parents to see him celebrate Christmas Eve midnight mass (usually in Paterson, New Jersey, where for a time he had a parish), and I must say that watching him up there trailing the full regalia was pretty sexy. The Church has always been canny enough to mount superb theater: colors and candlelight, costumes and music, smells and bells galore—all the while torturing witches, burning heretics, forcing conversion on indigenous peoples, denying women reproductive freedom, sacralizing homophobia, and inflicting other such fun dogmatic infallibilities. After the midnight spectacle, I was permitted to stay up into the wee hours of Christmas morning, since we would all adjourn to his parents' apartment in Washington Heights for late supper. There, the entire living room had been given over to a mounted extravaganza of miniature towns, forests, mirror lakes, and hills, transected by a system of eight Lionel train sets, all of it aglow with tiny lights and achurn with moving parts—the whole surrounded by six towering, fully decorated, twinkling Christmas trees. One year, well into this tradition, by which time I was perhaps ten, Father Joe's elderly mother was too ill to leave the apartment, so he got special dispensation to say mass there, at home—and I was his attendant. This was before the Church changed its ruling that only males could approach the sacrament, so I suppose I was the first de facto altar girl in Church history; certainly the first non-Catholic one.

Mom and Pop Collier, Father Joe's parents, fussed over me greatly. Nell Melory Collier was a tiny, wrenlike matriarch in her seventies, a poor woman's Rose Kennedy—puckered face beneath hair dyed coal-black, fiercely Irish, fanatically devout, and obsessively reverent of her Only Begotten Son the Priest, whose responding solicitude she welcomed as her due, reminding anyone who would listen that she'd been dying for all forty-five years since his birth. It seemed she would go on dying forever. In the meanwhile, she made world-class oatmeal cookies nubbled with chocolate chips, and her laugh invited—demanded—the company of others' laughter.

Pop Collier was another matter.

He was never without a beer in his hand, despite his wife's glares and his son's cajolings. Retired, after having worked all his life as a locker-room attendant handing towels to the New York Giants baseball team, he hung out nostalgically at the (now long-gone) Polo Grounds. It was there I attended my first baseball game, trying to learn the rules while chomping my way at Father Joe's expense through a delirium of foods normally forbidden me: hot dogs, popcorn, peanuts, crackerjacks, sodas, pretzels, and cotton candy. Father Joe was what Catholics call "a worldly priest," with a tad of entrepreneurial ambition. He'd found a way to, as he put it, "wield the collar" to develop his father's lowly connection with the Giants into his own relationship with the ball club and capitalize on that. Consequently, he was often able to pair a well-known baseball player, including even a few stars from other teams, with me, for appearances at—what else?— Catholic charity benefits (the *Our Lady of Fatima* film premiere, St. Joseph's Orphanage in Totowa, New Jersey, the Kennedy School for Retarded Children, among others). Had I known enough to get Willie Mays's or Hank Aaron's autographs on a baseball during one of these duets, I would've made my son one ecstatic child some decades later. But I didn't. Nor did I like listening to Pop Collier's long-winded baseball lore, related in the context of how "All the guys know and love me, their ol' locker-room buddy." But there was another reason I didn't like being plonked down on Pop Collier's lap while he went through his repertoire. The instant other people left the room, his hand insinuated itself under my skirt and underpants to wedge itself between my legs. When I fought to get away, he grasped me tighter, claiming it was a lesson: "See, honey, this is to teach you *never* to let boys touch you *there*. And don't you never tell nobody it was me that taught you. *Understand?*"

I understood. He frightened and revolted me. By age eight, after two or three years of this, I began trying to avoid visits to Mom and Pop Collier, because I also understood, with that amorphous knowledge children have, that it would hurt Father Joe and might kill Mom Collier (always at death's door anyway) if I were to tell them; it never occurred to me that they might already half know, because then what would that say about *them*? So I kept my silence and tried to keep my distance—understanding, too, that if I told Mommie or Aunt Sally, they might even stop me from seeing Father Joe himself.

He never did anything like that. He praised my homework, my acting, my attempts to write poems. He taught me to play chess and gave me books. He told me over and over how "special" I was, and I felt more special with him than surrounded by a horde of autograph seekers. When I was eleven or twelve, he introduced me to the poetry of Gerard Manley Hopkins. Respectful of what he called "God's gift of Robin's precocity," he talked to me about philosophy and theology, Aquinas and Augustine and even Duns Scotus. He told me about Hildegard von Bingen, Saint Catherine of Siena, and Saint Theresa of Avila, presenting them as intellectuals and leaders, not just devout nuns or martyrs. He introduced me to the ideas of Carl Jung. He told derisive jokes about Dominicans and Jesuits. Together with smells, bells, *and* carousels, this made for a heady combination. Besides, I was a pushover for anyone who appealed to the erogenous zone called my brain, so I loved him dearly.

Father Joe had a master's degree in psychology, and for a while, when I was around age twelve, he was sent by his provincial office to work as a chaplain at St. Elizabeth's Hospital (for "the Insane" as it was then termed) in Washington, D.C. My mother and I visited him while we were in Washington on a publicity appearance, and he took us on a personal tour of St. Elizabeth's, showing off his young friend the TV star to the minimum-security patients and vice versa. (I was by this time an unflappable hospital visitor, smilingly unfazed by people in bandages, casts, traction, iron lungs, manic states, or catatonia.) As we were leaving St. E's, Father Joe spied one patient sitting alone, apart from the others strolling or sprawling on the expansive but enclosed lawn. Saying he thought I should meet this man because he wrote poetry, he walked us over to the patient. I remember a pale, wrinkled face with rheumy eyes peering out from under bushy brows. Father Joe introduced me this time not just as a TV star but also as someone who wrote poems. I grasped the man's hand and shook it.

"*I* write *poems*," the man snapped, yanking his hand back.

"I know," I answered politely. "I'm sorry, I haven't read your poetry yet."

"You wouldn't understand it. Most people don't," he barked.

I knew enough to feel embarrassed, knew that if he was a real poet he must be disgusted by this TV kid being pushed at him. I said I might understand his poetry if I worked hard, and that I liked working hard if it was to understand poems. He snorted. Glancing at Father Joe, he asked me if I was Catholic. When I answered no, he asked what religion I was. I replied as I'd been taught to for interviews:

"I'm a believer in all religions."

"A kike," he laughed, "as well as a cunt. Forget about poetry."

Faith tugged sharply at my arm and Father Joe moved us away, soothing my mother's feelings with comments about the man's instability and his bitterness at having been forcibly committed to St. E's. Apparently some important writers had brokered this arrangement: that he be committed in lieu of serving a prison term on the charge of treason, for having broadcast a series of virulently pro-Fascist radio programs from Mussolini's Italy during the war. That day, I was busy asking what "kike" and "cunt" meant, though neither Faith nor Father Joe would enlighten me, both of them hissing I must never say either word again. It didn't fully register with me until years afterward that I'd met Ezra Pound.

Birthdays, holidays, and special events like recitals and graduations inevitably included Father Joe, and I took comfort in his reliable presence. Yet he always made me feel time's winged chariot was not just drawing near but bearing down hard.

"Ah, Kitten, soon you'll outgrow me," he'd sigh, "You'll get bored with your old Franciscan pal"—and I'd ferociously insist, "Never!" Still, I half believed his warning and began to develop anxieties about puberty. As I entered my teens, however, *he* started to withdraw. I remember wondering if his priestly vows forbade any friendships, however pure, with teenage girls or grown women. I made quite a pest of myself, but the thought of losing him was so painful that I clung all the harder. If I was that special, I was positive I ought to be able to figure out why he was distancing himself. Detection and decoding are among children's survival skills: what they can't learn directly, they overhear; what they can't overhear, they intuit.

Only gradually did I learn how unspecial I was. I found out about the others. Lots of others, all of them pre-pubertal kittens and princesses. Father Joe was paternal surrogate or uncle stand-in or father confessor to a whole stable of girls, including a pair of twins he'd actually nicknamed Candy and Cake. The pattern was constant: he lost interest in a girl when she showed signs of adult womanhood—budding breasts, first blood. Father Joe, it seems, had the emotional version of his father's physical perversion: nympholeptic lust.

I mourned the loss of him and suffered an intense but private jealousy; I didn't share what I'd discovered with my mother, wanting to protect him from what I suspected would be her rage. I let her think we had just drifted apart. When I turned sixteen, he resurfaced, sending me a sterling-silver charm in the shape of a tiny carousel for my birthday. I took it as the final farewell gesture to a "sweet sixteen" grown girl, but I called to thank him, anyway; the conversation was polite and cool.

About fifteen years later, married and newly a mother, I picked up the phone one afternoon to hear his voice whispering hoarsely, "Hey there, Kitten. How's my special girl?" He said he was in a monastery hospital in New England, gravely ill with cancer, that he weighed less than ninety pounds, had only days left to live, and could receive no visitors. He said he'd called to ask my forgiveness. I gave it, quickly—though neither of us mentioned for what—and I refrained from asking if he was making contrition calls to every one of us. The goodbyes were restrained. Then I hung up the phone and wept.

During my adolescence, I again tried to keep a journal, despite my fears that if Faith discovered it, I might as well step in front of an onrushing camera and end it all. But I needed a place to confide what had become a crushing weight of self-consciousness, an eerie feeling that unless observed by others, I barely existed. Some of this was classic adolescent hormonal angst, but some was unique to the surreality of the child actor's experience. In one poignant entry, at age thirteen, I wrote,

It's as if anything that *would* be the real me is transparent, one of those clear plastic sheets you write on but when you pull it up from the treated slate beneath, the words vanish. As if, when I passed in front of a mirror, I would show myself no reflection. People once thought that meant you had no soul.

Preoccupied with trying to find out if I could feel anything real, I spent quite a bit of time in churches. Catholic churches (yes, Father Joe's influence), but also Episcopal, Greek Orthodox, Methodist, whatever—and synagogues when open. Since I had no room of my own, a church provided a space to myself—the same reason, it turns out, women all over the world tend to compose the majority of the devout. I even made sporadic attempts to pray. But my studies on comparative religion got in the way of faith, as did my atheism (this had made for some lively arguments with Father Joe). I remember being quite little when I first realized there was no god, which I didn't find particularly disturbing. I was, however, willing to explore the concept of a pantheon—Greek, Roman, Norse, Hindu, Wiccan deities. But since there already were constellations, planets, the ocean, and life greening up right out of the ground, there seemed quite enough miracle in the universe to suffice.

Still, probably the main reason I couldn't concentrate on praying, meditating, or much of anything else done in solitude was that same exhausting self-consciousness a character in *Present Laughter* by Noel Coward (himself a survived child actor) described with lethal accuracy: "I'm always acting, watching myself go by." Later, Alice Miller would write about this as the narcissism imposed on a gifted child. I wrote about it to try and get free of it.

JOURNAL ENTRY *(age fourteen)*:
Jean does her Socrates act with me, trying to help, and asks, "Do you agree that all the world's a stage? Then what *is* real?" She's right. Are Faith and I a "family"—a widow and her half-orphan? Is age real? Not only can I act older or younger, I can *feel* older or younger, depending on the situation. Is ethnicity real? Apostate Jews that we are, is it hypocritical that Faith plans a seder every Pesach (*boredom-producing annual event attended by her broker, my agent, a few of*

her "girlfriends," and helpless me)? And are Jews a race or religion? If nonobservant, am I a Jew? At fourteen, am I a girl or a woman? An actress or writer? A daughter like Goneril or Cordelia? Or stark raving mad?

Sure, I know everyone's always acting: lawyers, politicians, businessmen, spies. And clergymen and soldiers in their different costumes, like Virginia Woolf wrote. But they seem able to do it at *will,* while I feel *trapped,* noticing the noticing, like mirrors that reflect each other's image into infinity, until I'd do anything to stop the wheels inside my brain. I've asked Mommie if I could see a therapist. But since that might involve insight, it makes her uneasy. Her reply? "Trust me. I do not have a crazy for a daughter. It would be a waste of money."

Faith and I began to have fights, major screaming bouts that left both of us debilitated for a whole day afterward, red-eyed and puffy-faced with crying. I didn't want to do any more benefits. I didn't want to go on any more auditions. I was convinced that Portia's "quality of mercy" speech, or Shaw's Saint Joan bleating about the little lambs in the green grass would stick in my memory until I died. But refusals got me nowhere ("You have a responsibility to your talent, Robin. You can't just abandon that."). So I began getting clever, making just enough subtle small errors to screw up an audition.

I had no idea how deeply angry I was. Nor would I find out for a long time to come.

JOURNAL ENTRY *(age fifteen)*:
She keeps saying I'm "in a difficult transition" from child stardom to adult stardom. Yesterday, I told her again that this is not just a temporary "slump." I want *out* of the business. *Permanently.* Big Fight # 7,643.

I've already decided that I want to be a writer. I've tried to tell her that. But whenever I say I want to write, she says, "Write what?" Which makes no sense and isn't the point and I can't answer.

Certainly she knows I've scribbled stories and poems since I learned to hold a pencil, but she merely takes that as another sign of

The Baby's multi-talented sickening little self. Like her arranging for one of the poems I wrote when I was nine to be sealed in a time capsule with city documents and newspapers during the Mount Vernon Centennial Festivities. I know she meant well, but it was *awful*. Cutesy gumdrop poem plus publicity shot of The Baby. To be opened 100 years from now. *Mortifying.* I do *not* want to be remembered like that.

I don't know what to do. As an actress, all you can be certain of is that you're something other than you are. (I always suspect I'm really someplace else.) You're sure you can be everything, but not sure you can be *one* thing thoroughly. All you know is you have to overachieve at whatever you're doing even if you don't know what you're doing to begin with.

A few nights ago I dreamt I had absolute power, like an empress or goddess. I had them all lined up—the agents and managers and PR reps, the old *Mama* company, the casting directors and photographers, the wardrobe fitters sticking you with pins, the school kids who hated my guts and gave me Indian burns and liked each *other,* the old singing and swimming and accents coaches—and there, at the end of the line, standing apart by herself: Faith. They were all taller than me, as if I were still a child. But small as I was in the dream, I went down that line carrying an armful of sharp stakes. I drove a stake deep into each of their hearts, and as I did it I curtseyed and smiled to each one, "Thank you very much." But when I came to Faith, she was crying. Then I saw why. She already was riddled with stakes—a pincushion, a female Saint Sebastian. There wasn't one inch of room for me to hurt her more. So I gave up and tried to embrace her instead. But as I pressed myself against her, my embrace drove the stakes deeper into her. Then the stakes turned double-edged, so I was also impaling myself. She and I both screamed at the same time, and I woke up with my heart banging.

Conflicts about my career spawned arguments about my going to college, which spawned quarrels about my future, which spawned battles about marriage, which spawned fights about boys. In my mother's plans, I would soon become a prize fit to be the bride of the young Aga Khan or of Britain's Prince Charles ("Royalty *like* actresses, you know! These days, even to marry!"). Or a billionaire industrialist. Or at *least* a *doctor*.

In the interim, while awaiting my coronations, I had crushes and tried to date boys.

My crushes weren't restricted to real-life people; I fantasized about such fictional characters as Brontë's Heathcliffe, Scott's Ivanhoe, Andersen's Little Robber Girl, and even Kipling's sensual jungle panther, Bagheera. There was also the human-but-tragically-dead-artist category: *I could've saved Chopin where Sand failed.* As for living heartthrobs—with the exception of yens for Cliff Robertson and James Lipton (both grownup actors with whom I'd worked) and one young boy with red hair whose name is now forever lost, who'd also studied piano with Mr. Jones—my crushes, like those of most teenage girls, centered on movie stars.

My taste was certainly eclectic, ranging from Paul Henreid to Dorothy Dandridge, from Richard Greene (specifically in *Robin Hood*), to Ingrid Bergman (especially as Joan of Arc), from Dirk Bogarde to Harpo Marx, and from Sidney Poitier to Laurence Olivier. I was the only girl I knew who fantasized about both Yves Montand *and* Simone Signoret, and who tottered away from multiple viewings of *Gone with the Wind* longing not for Clark Gable but for Leslie Howard. The most formative movies of my life come from this period. One was *The Seventh Veil*, with silken-voiced James Mason alternating between cruelty and tenderness as the Svengali-esque guardian of Ann Todd, playing his ward, a neurotic young concert pianist (no mystery as to whom I identified with *there*). Another was *The Red Shoes*, with flame-haired Moira Shearer torn between loving her composer husband and her career as a ballerina, where she was in turn manipulated by Anton Walbrook, playing a charismatic Diaghilev figure who alternated between cruelty and tenderness as the Svenagli-esque . . . you get the point. Romantic masochism—one theme, many variations. It was the central erotic message to girls and women until fairly recently. But at least the suffering heroines with whom I identified had artistic careers. And there *were* other films I relished, in which the women dared to fight back: *His Girl Friday*, with Rosalind Russell and Cary Grant parrying thrusts of fast-paced dialogue in Howard Hawk's remounting of the

Hecht-MacArthur play *The Front Page*; virtually everything Katharine Hepburn did on screen (and off); even *A Star Is Born*, which seemed radical, because it reversed *The Red Shoes:* he died, she survived.

The crushes were easy and many, compared to the real boys. Being privately tutored, I had no classmates. But clippings from this period remind me that by the time I was fifteen, in order to smooth my "transition" to adult stardom, my press agent had already begun placing discreet items about dates that had been deliberately constructed for the purpose of the item. So there just happened to be photographers present when I "dated" Sal Mineo—who was pleasant enough, though I was well aware he was considerably older, totally uninterested in me, and gay (which, in that tightly closeted time, was probably the reason *his* press agent agreed to the item).

I did become friends with Warren Lyons, one of the four sons of the *New York Post* columnist Leonard Lyons and his wife, Sylvia. The "romance" had been arranged at first, but turned into a real friendship, and I liked visiting the cheerful chaos of the Lyons household at The Beresford apartments on the Upper West Side, where the toddler, Jeffrey—today a film critic—would run around laughing, half-naked, while his older brothers played indoor basketball. My name appeared frequently in Lyons's column during these years, which might be why my mother so approved of the Saturday afternoon "dates" I had with Warren—tea dances, movies, rowing in Central Park, matinees, Scrabble matches. Then there was Ronnie Welsh, who had briefly played Dagmar's first date on *Mama* and had become my sole kid-actor pal. Our mothers loathed one another, but Ronnie and I spent many happy hours acting sophisticated, fancying ourselves as blasé characters from a Noel Coward play—preferably *Private Lives*—and we managed to stay in touch even as adults, until his untimely death in the early 1990s.

There were other so-called dates, organized by my mother throughout my teens. God knows where she found these guys—some were sons of men at the brokerage firm where she went to play the market. One of them was a Harvard medical student she liked. He had the unfortunate name of Floyd, but he did introduce me to the pleasures of paella. He was unhappy about my being an actress but relieved when I told him I planned to stop. However, when I added (rather haughtily, I'm sure) that I intended to be a writer, he mulled that over, then offered his unsolicited reassurances with a wink: "I guess that would be okay. Every young wife should have a hobby. Some women do ceramics." That was it for Floyd. Back home, Faith and I had a screamer over how I should cultivate him for his "potential." I remember yelling, "*Why* should I cultivate him, Mommie? He's a med student, not a garden!"

There was also Tony, a quiet young man from a wealthy Boston family Faith found acceptable, whom I liked for other reasons: he waltzed divinely and was (secretly from his parents) a Quaker. But when he and I started to *be* friends, my mother changed. Whenever I saw him, she'd ask, "girlfriend to girlfriend," how it was going, what had we done and talked about. Since I no longer would tell her every detail, that was the kiss of death to my seeing Tony.

Faith had an eagle eye. Her theme song could have been the folk ditty "Silver Dagger." I became a jittery wreck for fear of discovery during the short period I was seeing Johnny, an alto-sax jazz musician I'd met all on my own up at Columbia. He was smart, funny, made sultry musical love to his saxophone, and never came on to me crudely—which I appreciated since I was still a nervous virgin. One morning, however, when at two o'clock I tiptoed into the bedroom I still shared with Faith, all hell broke loose. I offered the generic adolescent excuse that I'd been "just walking and thinking." No fool she, my mother swore that at daylight she'd enlist a private detective and throw whoever I was seeing in jail. Considering where I'd just come from   dancing, in Harlem yet, with Johnny, who was African American—her threat terrified me. The next day, I told him I couldn't see him again.

The guys came and went, while the abiding connections, each with their own unacknowledged erotic undertones, remained. Jean Tafti. Father Joe. And the greatest passion of my teens—the one boiling and erupting with love, possession, hatred, rage, and obsession, the one that trivialized whatever I felt for anyone else—was with *her*.

JOURNAL ENTRY (*age fifteen*):
I want to write about her. She's gone to dinner with that ghastly lawyer who pronounces the word "business" as "bidness." Hallelujah. If only she'd marry him, it might take some of the pressure off me.

To her it's so simple. She's given me her entire life, she expects only love in return. Who could be so warped as to deny her that? She only did what she thought was best for me. That's also a truth. A truth caught in the subway rush-hour of truths. Because yet another truth is: she made me. Frau Frankenstein and her Creature. She's always been a fighter, and she made *me* one. Whatever confidence I have is rooted in her belief in me. But how can it endure against the opposition of the one who created it?

It's as if Faith has no notion of her power over me. She can whine and she can thunder. She can crack me like an eggshell so that I splatter out with pity for her. I used to watch how she tried to avoid being a stage mother, a role that never overly daunted Aunt Sally, and it would break my heart. But I hated her for it, too, because it meant my own mother didn't defend me or contradict anybody who had power. In private, *there* waited the expectations, criticisms, advice to "Forget what the director said. Stand a fraction upstage but if you're caught don't say I told you to because they'll bar me from the set."

This is so *mean,* so *petty.* I ought to put down some of the good moments. Like yesterday, when I learned that years before I was born, she'd loved a poem of William Blake's I'd just discovered in *Songs of Innocence.* Who would have imagined that? Her rare shocking miraculous *comprehension.* The way her smile can make me feel. She always manages to send me white lilacs on my birthday, and they're sure not in season in January. But she knows I love them, and I guess she orders them way in advance; I bet they're flown in from somewhere at a huge price. Oh *damn.* Why does running away from her tyranny also mean running away from her love?

If she were to read this! She'd be so hurt it would kill her. She'd never speak to me again. She'd throw me out. She'd cry till her eyes bulged and then, still sobbing but icy as the Arctic, she'd turn on me and say, "You are a vile, inhuman, uncompassionate, spoiled brat. You've accepted everything and preened yourself and had the world's adoration while I lived in your shadow. You've played into every bit of what you claim to detest, and enjoyed it. And for this I've given you my entire existence—which you've destroyed."

And she'd be right about that, too.

From the time I was fourteen on, the war intensified. I would lose on the college front, and I would eventually lose the Tafti tutorial. I would also lose the battle to stop working: it was during this period that I did many of the one-shot television dramas, as well as cut the two Columbia records and play summer stock. The bane of doing benefits continued, but later in my teens I won a skirmish on that front—the right to decide some of the "worthy causes" myself. By age sixteen, I'd become an avid newspaper reader, and Jean Tafti's influence encouraged a sense of outrage at social injustice. Capital punishment and civil rights were beginning to surface as issues of the time. So I appeared at the various vigils that appealed for more stays of execution for Caryl Chessman (who was finally killed by California in 1960). One clipping reminds me that I played Desdemona to Robert Earl Jones's Othello in a benefit performance to raise money for Bayard Rustin's early attempts at organizing for integration in the South. I also took pride in having manipulated my hapless fan clubs into becoming support chapters for the work of the United Nations; doubtless bewildered as to why they were being urged to hold bake sales and get newspaper routes to raise money for UNICEF, the loyal fans did what their idol asked of them.

It's lucky I didn't turn completely schizoid, considering the abyss between the political message of such actions and the molasses content in my press coverage during this period. My salvation was to heighten a sense of irony and develop an affection for bitter humor.

There I'd be in the magazine interviews: the perfect 1950s junior miss, described as "unspoiled," "courteous," "fresh-faced," "bubbly," and "completely natural." As one writer admiringly put it, "No rock 'n' roll fan with violent outbursts of antagonism against established society, Robin is the ideal girl-next-door." (Little did the poor reporter know that he was describing a future Beatles addict, Deadhead, Police fan, Nirvana lover, and mother-to-be of a rock musician. As for violent antagonism against established society, we'll deal with the Weather Underground period in later chapters.) Photo spreads showed me baking pies, doing an arabesque *en pointe* in a leotard, brushing my waist-length hair, shopping for "a prom dress" (*what* prom?), and peering thoughtfully at a typewriter to compose a "teen advice" column for *TV StarParade* magazine. The copy, complete with "good grooming tips" for skin care, manicures, and light makeup, certainly would have made the future editor in chief of *Ms.* gag. On boys: "Bone up on his interests. Always be sweet and feminine. And no dungarees. Boys like girls to look like girls!"

No wonder I had a reality problem. In print, "Most of all, teens should trust the wisdom of their parents. I don't know what I'd do without my wonderful mother." In real life, "Mommie, I can't *breathe*. Can't you understand? I'm growing *up*. I need to find out who I *am!*" In public, "I rely on the three P's: Patience, Perseverance, and Prayer." In private, only perseverance felt relevant. I sometimes tried to speak in code, albeit with a sappy-happy spin to the sub-rosa message; one interview quotes me as saying, "I'm glad I began my career at an early age. I don't have to start out as a starry-eyed girl in show business. I got the glossy, tinsely ideas of show business out of my mind as a child." But whenever I'd let the mask slip, Faith would be there to do her part in fostering the image. In public, "Robin has a whole crowd of girlfriends her age, and they do crazy things like old-fashioned taffy pulls and getting it in their hair. She fills up the apartment so with kids I don't know where to go." In private, no girlfriends, never pulled taffy in my life, didn't know enough kids to fill a walk-in closet.

I began to feel that with every interview, every appearance, I was collaborating in the hypocrisy, and I blamed and despised myself for it. But things came to a head when my agents, then MCA, began negotiating a TV network deal for a teenage series along the lines of *Kiss and Tell*, starring young miss vivacious herself. Faith and I had a monumental fight over my having added seven pounds to my ninety-six-pound weight (my height—such as it is—had stabilized at five feet one inch by age fifteen). I knew I'd been snacking a lot, and I certainly knew I was miserable. So, having read my Jung, Freud, and—bless her!—Karen Horney, I decided I must be eating from depression. But it was my mother who unwittingly handed me the tool of rebellion when she screeched,

"You *know* the camera adds ten pounds! You better drop that weight *fast*, kiddo, or we could lose the MCA deal!"

There it was. The route to freedom.

I could *eat* my way out of the business.

And so I did, turning depression into revolt, sneaking food into my mouth whenever she wasn't looking, cutting dance classes, discovering

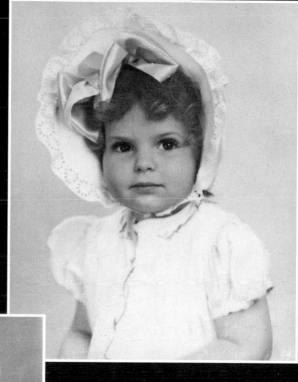

RIGHT The prize-winning
baby, around age
one and a half.

ABOVE Sally (Teitlebaum) Berkley:
"Aunt Sally."

RIGHT Faith (Teitlebaum) Berkley as
a young woman, visiting Mexico.

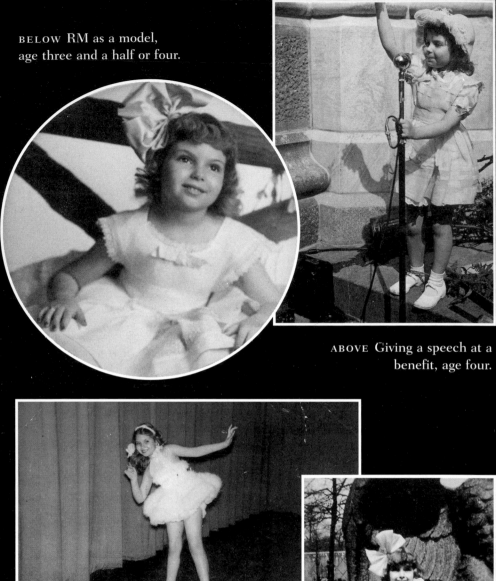

BELOW RM as a model, age three and a half or four.

ABOVE Giving a speech at a benefit, age four.

ABOVE In the Powder Puff tutu, age seven.

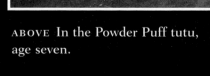

RIGHT Under the Central Park Zoo's stone eagle's wing, age three.

ABOVE On air: "The Little Robin Morgan Show," age five.

ABOVE With Jack Barry and other Juvenile Jurors, age five.

ABOVE RM at age six, with Frederick Franklin and Alexandra Danilova, in "The Nutcracker."

ABOVE With Bill "Bojangles" Robinson, after the two tap-danced together at a Negro Actors' Guild benefit, reenacting Robinson's famous routine with Shirley Temple.

ABOVE With Rosalind
Russell at another benefit.

LEFT With Milton Berle,
at yet another benefit.

LEFT Age six, with the Robin Morgan doll.

IS THIS THE END FOR GODFREY?
...See Page 3

TV GUIDE

LOCAL PROGRAM LISTINGS
WEEK OF MAY 7—13

15¢

Robin Morgan
Peggy Wood

ABOVE Age thirteen: one of the *TV Guide* covers sporting RM, this time with Peggy Wood.

LEFT The first *Mama* show: RM at age six and a half.

ABOVE The Hanson family, seven years later.

LEFT A press "item": RM, age fifteen, on the fake date with Sal Mineo.

RIGHT Presentation of the Ideal American Girl scroll.

LEFT RM at sixteen, with Faith—smiling while private battles of adolescence raged.

the delights of candy bars and pizza, deliberately developing my own version of an eating disorder before I'd ever heard the phrase. But it worked.
In six months, despite all the enforced diets and raging arguments, I
gained thirty-five pounds. The MCA deal fell through. Audition after
audition turned me down, and after a while my agents called less frequently. I'd managed to make myself virtually uncastable. (Unfortunately,
there were still radio jobs to pay the bills.) But there was a personal price
to pay, in body-loathing. Nor was there yet any feminist movement to put
that self-contempt into context.

JOURNAL ENTRY (age sixteen):
It's very hard being a teenager, because you think and feel everything
strongly and at the same time everyone is telling you that you only
believe you're in love, only *think* you're depressed, only *imagine*
you're confused. (This feels like Charles Boyer secretly turning the
gas lights up and down in order to drive Ingrid Bergman daffy.) Also,
you'd give anything in your life not to be a sophomoric "teenager."
Which in fact you are. Disgusting state.

I'd love to peel me off myself like Faith peels herself out from a
corset. I wish my body was removable like those custom-made
braces I could take out before a show so they wouldn't flash in the
lights when I smiled. It's creepy that I came out of her body. I don't
feel as if I'm in *mine*, but I know I was in *hers*.

Where I really live is inside my head. Well, there's one thing I *do*
do in my body: masturbate. Of course, never having had a damned
room of my own, even here in the promised holy land of a Sutton
Place apartment, I learned long ago how to develop speed while hidden in the bathroom. I must be the swiftest hand in the East. Door
locked, sink-faucet running, zip bang whoosh three minutes flat: Ta
Da! Then flush as if you'd used the toilet, and emerge not even
breathing heavily before she growls Why is the door locked Why are
you taking so long Don't you know reading on the toilet will give you
piles.

Somehow it's all connected to the way I feel about my body.
Short, short-waisted, small-boned, tending toward the plump—like
hers, dammit—and currently *way* overplump. Yet I lack her good fea-

tures, her pale skin, large eyes. My breasts? Ample (have been since I was thirteen; they had to use binders to flatten them for certain roles so I could look younger). Nose too large. Eyes too small. Hair thin and given to oiliness—and I'm still fighting the Battle of the Blond to get her to let me return to my own color, which, judging by the roots, is probably a revolting mousey brown. But I'm stuck with the principle of the thing.

I make me sick.

Given the immediacy of adolescence, no precocity could have comforted me that I would ever feel better about my body. Yet after a year or so—once the casting directors seemed to have given up on the pudgy teen who hadn't made "the transition" after all—to my amazement and my mother's exasperation, the weight melted away.

Not only did I not need protective poundage anymore, but romance had entered my life. Not with boys this time. There was a man—in fact, two of them. They even overlapped.

Petter Juel-Larsen was a handsome, talented, concert pianist in his early twenties. The hair was wavy dark blond, the body was tall and muscular, the Chopin "Ballades" were to swoon over. Petter (aptly named, but pronounced "Peter") was the son of a well-to-do Massachusetts family presided over by a concert-mother version of a stage mother, so he knew the drill and was smart enough to go out of his way to charm *my* mother. She had him over for frequent dinners, and on occasion, when he stayed late talking or playing a private concert for us, she actually encouraged him to sleep over on the sofa or, in warm weather, on the double lounge on our apartment's small back terrace. She knew I'd tiptoe out to him the moment I thought her asleep, so I can only surmise that she must have decided what she couldn't stop she would control: any heavy petting would happen under her supervision. For almost a year, these foreplay-for-its-own-sake sleep-overs took place in between dinners, études, and conversations about art, literature, and music. I fancied myself in love with Petter and played it for Melodrama Center Stage. When his family finally sent him off to England for advanced conservatory study, I was crushed. But at least I was now only technically a virgin, and the Ideal American Girl had practiced enough five-finger exercises to develop jack-off artistry.

Then there was Ron Fieve. He was a bit older, in his mid-twenties, a
Harvard medical school graduate, a psychiatric resident at Columbia
Presbyterian Hospital, a shrink-in-training. He was not as tall as Petter
and not as picture-book pretty, but he had his own rakishly handsome
attractiveness, a voice like a cello, and a Thunderbird convertible—so as
Petter faded, Ron brightened into focus. With him, there were fascinating
conversations about dreams and the unconscious, realms of exploration
particularly appealing to a prematurely sophisticated and narcissistic adolescent girl. With Ron I continued my erotic education about (almost)
everything sexual except actual intercourse. (I seem to have presaged the
Clintonian prohibition on *that*, as well as the self-deluding defense that
nothing else was "real sex.") I had fun with Ron. We went for long drives
with the convertible top down, went dancing, picnicking, to movies and
plays. He brought me to hospital social events as "his girl," which felt
delectably grown-up. Since he regularly did volunteer medical work at
clinics in Bedford Stuyvesant and Harlem, he seemed to have no problems with my nascent politics. About my writing he seemed agnostic, neither particularly supportive nor opposed, and I think he genuinely loved
me. So I talked myself into falling in love with him.

But his shrink felt it was time to think of the future and Get Serious,
and Ron began talking engagement. My mother—who had maintained a
vigilant hospitality similar to that she'd exercised with Petter—moved in at
the speed of light. She needn't have bothered. I didn't want to marry Ron.
I didn't want to marry, period. I wanted freedom, time, a room—an apartment of my own. I wanted to find out if I could dare really write.

Ron Fieve later met and married someone else, built a family, and went
on to become a well-regarded figure in his chosen field, as one of the pio-
neers of lithium treatment for bipolar disorder, back then called manic-
depression. (Twenty or more years later, he would be helpful when I called
him out of the blue, at Kate Millett's request, for help in getting Kate into
a special treatment program more civilized than the "loonybin" treatments
about which she has so courageously written.) So the Petter affair ended
with a bang, and the Ron relationship with a whimper, subsiding with
some tearfulness into a friendship, then into silence.

I missed the non-sex sex. I wanted desperately to rid myself of my virginity. But I also wanted the liberation to happen with "the right man," as

they used to say in the Fifties, and I wanted him to be someone I would love. In the meantime, I could wait. The waiting didn't matter all that much, because two core elements of what constituted my internal reality were beginning to tremble under the surface of daily life, like tectonic plates beneath the earth's crust prior to a quake.

For one thing, I'd begun to write in earnest, and I was loving it. I lived for the workshops and classes at Columbia, and hung out in coffeehouses where I thought real poets might congregate, dreaming of being part of a literary circle. I sent out poems to little magazines, whence they came shooting back as if by return mail. The fights with Faith continued, but were now being waged on another field. She was refocusing from my acting career (which, she decided, was "adrift for a while") to my writing.

She must have shifted emphasis as an act of will and, undoubtedly, an act of love. Once she finally realized I was sincere about wanting to write, it would have seemed perfectly natural to her that she would elbow her way in to help. "Literature" would have sounded high-minded and elite to her, the immigrants' daughter so fixated on self-improvement, and since she'd never been supported by her mother in any of her own youthful desires, she mightily overdid things in the other direction. Faith never understood that possibly the most important thing a parent can do is learn how to respond to a growing child by saying "goodbye," with grace and celebration, in a thousand different ways.

I was alarmed at her interest. I wanted her blessing, but our history showed that whatever I invented she took over. I hadn't forgotten how my backstroke narrowly escaped Olympic training, how my piano playing had become another "talent" ripe for competition, how my romantic entanglements had dwindled to whispered diddle scenes with my mother on the other side of a thin wall. I knew she never meant to harm. Indeed, she never destroyed outright. Instead, she somehow cheapened what I did—then left me with it. When I made the fatal error of confiding I was trying to write poetry instead of stories, the next thing I knew, she'd made the acquaintance of some people at a vanity press and began plotting to bring out a first book of heavens-look-how-she's-grown-into-a-poet Robin Morgan.

But one day she overstepped herself. "For the good of your writing career" (*what* writing career? I fumed to myself), she insisted we go to a soiree being thrown by a professor friend of her vanity press cronies. I'd already met the man, Livingston Welch, a pompous ass who fancied himself a sculptor and writer and was neither. But my mother was insistent.

"*Think*, darling, of the artists and writers you'll meet there! A whole new *universe!*"

She ground me down. We went. What neither of us knew was that at the soiree I would ignore everyone else once I started to talk with a young man who was leaning against a bookcase regarding the scene with obvious disdain. He knew blessedly nothing about me, hadn't seen me on TV, had only just learned from someone at the party that I was some kind of actress. He was twenty-eight (older than Petter or Ron), and he smoked a pipe (echo of Father Joe); he was lean and sandy-haired with pale, piercing blue eyes (echo of Doris Scheidecker); he was gay (echo of Judson Laire, my affectionate TV father); he unashamedly introduced me to his lover, a pianist and composer. By the end of our conversation, I'd learned that his ancestors had been in the United States since Colonial times, that he'd been born in Minnesota of a working-class family, and that the faint vitiligo mispigmentation on his hands was probably the result of mixed ancestry between pale-skinned forebears from Norway and the British Isles intermixing with black Americans who were slaves in the pre–Civil War South (echo of Johnny). So many elements came together in him that he was a living prescription for rebellion. But I wasn't thinking about rebellion that day.

That day I saw a man of extraordinary intelligence, dressed in simple khakis and a white cotton T-shirt, puffing his pipe and peering at me through narrowed eyes across a cloud of fragrant smoke. He was safe to have for a friend: he was gay, after all. I'd grown up around gay men in show business (the women had to be much more closeted), and I trusted them. But neither was he campy; he was serious, even brooding. I liked him.

But the revelation was yet to come. When the party settled down, a few people began reading their poetry. Despite my mother's prodding, I refused. I knew I was writing rot, and I was not about to embarrass myself. When it came his turn, he also declined. Only after a chorus of urgings and a whisper from his lover did he agree, sweeping the room with a scornful glance that recognized he was clearly not among literary equals. Then he read some of his poems.

"A whole new universe" indeed. They were dark, lyrical, audacious, executed with technical brilliance and frightening intensity. His language sang, his images seared; the story embedded in each poem was memorable as an entire novel. This poetry reminded me of Yeats's work, even of Donne's. Then, with the casual insolence of someone recently named one of the finest poets in the U.S. under the age of forty, he suggested playing his favorite parlor game: the one-minute, spontaneous sonnet.

Thunderstruck, I watched as people called out a subject, image, or first word—"Shakespearean, Spenserian, or Petrarchan preference?" he would coolly ask—watched him scribble on the back of an envelope in one minute flat an accomplished sonnet. Five times.

At the end of the evening, my mother had to drag me away. But he and I exchanged phone numbers, while I gratefully wondered why in hell he would possibly want to know me.

Faith was delighted. She planned to ask "those two nice gay boys, the poet and the musician," to dinner soon. "See? *See,* darling, didn't I *tell* you that you'd meet important writers and artists?"

She had no idea that we were living on top of a major fault line, beneath which that night one tectonic plate had begun to slide toward a fated overlap with another. She had no idea, nor did I, who it was I'd met.

His name was Kenneth Pitchford.

He was the man I would marry, the man who would father my son.

Meanwhile, the other tectonic plate was rising and grinding forward. It had been on the move for a long time.

I described it in the last entry of my adolescent journal.

JOURNAL ENTRY (*age seventeen*):
I can't avoid it any longer. I'm going to write it down. Even though all my searching has so far led nowhere, still I have to tell it *some*where or explode. Even though neither of us have spoken about it since I was thirteen. She acts as if it never happened, but it haunts me. Maybe if I write about it here—though if she ever found this journal she'd view that as yet another betrayal—I can get free of it. I can't

remember exactly when it started. I know I'd already been accumulating clues here and there, and a previous visit of Aunt Sophie's had yielded up some juicy ones to an expert eavesdropper like me. (Train an actress, and you *get* an actress. I can walk in my sox across a parquet floor to eavesdrop without a single creak of the floorboards. I can detect the difference between the shifting of her weight in a kitchen chair and the other kind of shifting, prior to rising, so I can scurry soundlessly back to bed with no discovery.)

But this time I almost forgot my technique, given the shock of overhearing, through their mix of English and Yiddish, the *present* tense. When the rising weightshift creaked from the chair, I barely made it back to the bedroom in time. My heart was pounding so loudly I was afraid it would heave through my "sleeping" body when she peeked in.

How long after that did it take me to build up the courage, to wait for the perfect moment? A few months, I think. But eventually I must have felt the time was right. Which was a mistake. It was during one of those mirage oases of her comprehension—the ones that turn out to be quicksand. We were lying in our twin beds in the dark, having the close conversation we seldom have anymore—the kind that goes rancid in my mouth when I hear her tell a reporter "We're real *girl*friends who can tell each other *any*thing with total honesty!" What a joke. But the mood *seemed* right.

So I maneuvered the conversation around to get her discussing the time before I was born, her girlhood and adolescence and the war—all of which I'd heard before anyway. But sometimes a new nugget drops, you never know. Then, softly, I asked,

"Mommie?" (she hates me to call her Faith), "Mommie, tell me more about him."

"Him?" she said into the room between us.

"You know. My father."

"I've already told you, Robin. You know what a clever man he was, what a fine doctor. The languages he spoke, how well-educated he was. We loved each other so much. We could have been so happy. It was tragic when the war killed him."

"The war killed him, Mommie?"

"But you know that, honey. I thought I'd die of grief. I would have, if it hadn't been for you. You kept me going."

I could hear her smile through that last sentence. I remember calculatingly putting into my own voice all the tenderness it could communicate, with every vocal skill I'd acquired in my thirteen years, whispering gently,

"Mommie? . . . Mommie . . . he's alive, isn't he? He's still alive."

There was such a silence in the room that for a second it felt as if I were there alone.

"Mommie, it's all *right*. I love *you*. Nothing can ever change that. But, Mommie? I know. I know he's—alive?"

The bedtable lamp clicked on, the room sprang into light, and her face seemed to fill all of it.

"Spy!" she hissed. "Traitor! How did you find out? Who in hell do you think you are to dare—"

"Mommie, darlingest little Mommie—" even now I can taste my panic as I ran from my bed and tried to get into hers, under the covers, the way I used to fall asleep when I was little.

She wouldn't let me in. She was sitting up in bed staring at me as if I was an intruder, burglar, murderer. I burst into tears and tried to sit on the edge of her bed, but she stuck out a foot and kicked at me. So I stood there in my pajamas, crying.

"Honest, it's *okay*! I still love you more than anything or anyone! I always will, *always*! I just want to *know*, don't you see? Mommie, please—"

"What. What do you want to know," she asked, but it came out as a statement. Her tone was flat, like that of somebody who'd been dreading this moment, for years, living under a delayed sentence of death.

"Anything, Mommie. Everything. Whatever you want to tell me. Please?"

"Anything," she repeated dully. "Everything." Then she looked at me, sharp and deep.

I could hardly breathe.

"Then I *will* tell you, Robin. Sit down."

So I sat at the foot of her bed. I waited. I didn't dare hurry her.

"Everything you already know is true. But what I never told you . . . well, I always intended to, when you were older, better equipped to handle it. You're a highstrung child, you know. Sensitive, fragile. That goes with your talent, but still . . . what I would have told you when you were older, if you hadn't turned *spy* on your own *mother*"—the hiss in her voice rose again, then receded as if reined in—"is that he changed. I'll never know why. Maybe he wasn't ready for the responsibility of being a father after what he'd been through. He'd escaped from the Nazis, he'd lost every single human being he'd ever loved. That must have been it. Because, Robin— since you want the truth—he deserted his wife and child. He abandoned us."

"He—abandoned us?"

"Totally. He disappeared. At first I tried to have him traced. I thought something had happened to him, maybe an accident. But as time went by, I started remembering how cold he'd grown while I was pregnant with you, how remote. Then one day I got a letter from him—no return address—somewhere in New Jersey. He said it was finished. Over. I was devastated. But I knew how futile it would be to try and find a man who had managed to cover his tracks all across Europe—false papers, false names—with the Gestapo on his trail. This man knew how to hide."

"Was he— Couldn't you look up Matthew Morgan, Mommie? Or Mates Morgan? I mean, in the telephone book? Or ask information? Couldn't you just look up Morgan?"

"Morgan?" she laughed strangely. "His name wasn't Morgan. It was Morgenstern. Mates Morgenstern."

"Not Morgan? But Mommie—"

"Why should me and my child bear the name of the sonofabitch who abandoned us? I had to recover. I had to survive. I got a divorce on the grounds of abandonment. Then I went to court and had our name changed. Legally. To Morgan."

"But—who's Morgan then?"

"*Nobody's* Morgan, you fool!" she snapped, "*We* are. You and me. I made it up. I liked it. That sorceress in King Arthur stories, she's

Morgan Le Fay, and I thought since my name's Faith I can be Faith Morgan. So I took it. It's a good name. For you too. It's a beautiful name. What's wrong with it?" She glared at me.

"Nothing, Mommie. It's fine. It just feels—strange to think that—"

"There's nothing goddamned strange about it. People change their names all the time. It's normal. Your Aunt Sally and I had already changed our maiden names from Teitlebaum to Berkley. You knew that."

"Yes . . . but that was *you* two. This is *my* name. All this time I never even knew . . . I mean I thought—"

"You thought. You never knew. What do you know about life, about anything, Robin?"

"I guess I don't, Mommie. But all I mean is, it feels—it's . . . peculiar. Not being my real name."

"The hell it isn't!" she shouted. "It's legal, it's real, it's mine, it's yours. The whole goddamned country knows you by that name. That name is *famous* because of you and me. What could be more real? Are you crazy?"

I remember thinking to myself: Back off. Don't aggravate her further. Get more facts if possible.

"Mommie?" I reached out and touched her hand. She pulled it away. "He never . . . I mean, in thirteen years he never once—"

"*Never.*" The word hit like a fist in my face. "And don't cook up romantic fantasies in your overheated brain about finding him, either. *Never.* He didn't want you. He still doesn't. Get it?"

"But how do we know for sure? Maybe—"

"Do you hear him pounding down the door to get in to see his cherished daughter?"

"No."

"He didn't want you. *I* wanted you."

"Yes."

"I bore you, raised you, sacrificed for you, loved you. He didn't give a tinker's damn for his precious daughter. He only wanted a son."

"He did? He said that?"

"He didn't have to say it. Or maybe he did say it, I can't remember. It doesn't matter, I knew it. Your father, Robin, is a Prussian iceman, arrogant and fancy. The kind from a long 'bloodline' who wants to extend it. A son he would have stayed with his wife for. A *son*."

I just sat there, crying. She looked at me and seemed to relent.

"Baby. What would I do with a son? *I* wanted a *daughter*. Look. Put it out of your mind. It's always been us against the world, you and me, remember? Back in Mount Vernon, when we'd go window shopping and plan our future and bake cookies and laugh? We've still got each other. That's really all we've ever had. But that's all we need, you and me."

She reached out to me. I took her hand.

"Robin, baby, you're thirteen now, a big girl with a wonderful career and life ahead. There's no stopping us. Remember what I've always told you: *you can be anything you want, there's nothing you can't be*. So what's the point of mooning after some scum who never wanted you? Even if you *could* find him—and you can't and he's moved on by now and he might be dead for all I know—believe me, Robin, he'd throw you out on the street. I won't have you hurt like that. I *love* you. More than life itself."

I looked up at her and when I saw she was crying too, it burst inside me and I hurled myself into her arms. This time she took me under the covers, inside next to her, warm and safe.

I remember the softness of her breasts under her nightgown, the sheet wet with our tears, and her murmuring, "Some kind of monster, the war must have made of him. That he could be so loving. Marry me. Father you. Then—goodbye, farewell, *auf wiedersehen*. Some kind of inhuman *creature* . . ."

The last thing I remember, before we cried ourselves to sleep in each other's arms, was my whispering,

"Like Zeus in the myths, huh Mommie? He appeared as a swan, or a rain of gold coins, or a bull, but then he always vanished afterwards . . ."

And her crying, answering softly,

"Yes, my baby, yes. Just like in the myths."

After that night we never spoke of it again.

But the knowledge that he might be out there wasn't silenced. At first, I was just so grateful to her—for having wanted me, for having kept me. And for finally telling me the truth. Then the anger started.

Why had she lied to me all those years? Why had she been so *nasty* when it turned out I knew? Why did she imply I was "fragile," as if unstable? Then the guilt started: *Hello again, guilt*. Because she *was* the one who raised me. Then the feeling, growing like a tumor, that I owe her so much I'll never be able to get away from her. And through it all, loving her. For having survived. For having loved *me*.

So here I am, almost eighteen, still locked in battle with her. And still obsessed—with the phantom of myself, the unreality of him, the too vivid reality of her.

Last night I read that in parts of rural China, to this day the most dutiful of Chinese daughters cuts out a piece of her flesh to make a soup for her ailing or weak mother.

Today I felt Chinese.

EIGHT

Storming the Gates of Mycenae

Father, if I had the voice of Orpheus
if I could sing rocks into rising,
if I had words to move all hearts, or only yours,
I would have used them.

—EURIPIDES, *IPHIGENIA IN AŪLIS*

Finally, I was on my way to meet him.

It had taken five years of sleuthing, patching fragments of evidence together from eavesdropped-on conversations between my mother and her sisters, five years of library trips on literary excuses to research my way through the telephone books of New Jersey cities. Five years of imagining what it would be like, what *he* would be like.

There was the scenario in which he refused to acknowledge me, in which I was denied outright, annihilated on the spot. The scenario in which he physically threw me out the door. The scenario in which he broke into tears and flung his arms wide, crying, "My daughter, I knew you'd find me someday." Five years of lying in bed at night, fantasizing how he would look, which of my features I might recognize in his face, what his voice would sound like.

Since the confrontation about him with my mother when I was thirteen, a deceptively calm silence had descended on the subject. Only once, on my eighteenth birthday, had I dared gingerly raise the subject again. But there were no fireworks. Faith's version had simply picked itself up from its position five years earlier and ambled sideways, settling down not far from where it had been. So he was alive, what of it. He had deserted us. Why be curious about a so-called father who'd never taken a particle of interest in his own child—especially when such curiosity wounded the other parent, whose entire existence had been given over to that child? Faith neither understood nor would grant a millimeter of sympathy to the notion that one could be obsessed about a mystery parent. There was nothing to learn from or about Mates Morgenstern; he *was,* in effect, a dead man. And so should he be to me. Hadn't eighteen years of his invisibility made that clear?

My obsession went into hiding, taking inventory of all the ways he might have tried to contact his daughter but been impeded by Faith. Had she destroyed letters? Deflected phone calls? I knew that nothing was beyond her when struggling for what she believed was her survival and her daughter's love. So the mystique of him had ripened, tended in secret by my imagination.

Now, riding in the window seat of a dingy bus en route to the university town of New Brunswick, I began for the thousandth time to number the minimal facts I knew about him, telling the beads of memory through one last novena.

He was a doctor, an obstetrician/gynecologist. Born in Vienna, of a middle-class Jewish family. About ten years older than Faith. Well educated. A linguist: spoke German, English, French; reportedly had read the classics in the original, for pleasure; particularly relished Greek drama. Knew and loved music—but Faith would go into no details there. Was brilliant, handsome, arrogant; could be cold, cruel, "emotionally aloof unto sadism" (Faith's phrase). Indeed, my mother's virtuosity in the skills of exaggeration had to be weighed against every detail. To drop one's guard about that for even a second was to be assaulted by such doubts that I would again surrender any idea of contacting him. That had already happened three times, as I tried to reconcile myself to eternal ignorance on the subject, even after I had finally learned where he was: the city, the address, the telephone number.

That moment, sitting in the wooden library chair with the phone book for New Brunswick in front of me, is etched in my brain. How the room froze, how utterly still everything became when the name leapt at me—in the same fine print as those above and below it but with the impact of emblazoned letters flaming ten feet high: Morgenstern, Mates, M.D.

Mates: the Hebrew for Mattheus, heroic Maccabee leader. Morgenstern: the German for morning star.

In the little games I played with my obsession, this had been the next-to-last trip to the library phone books I was going to permit myself. It was ludicrous, thinking someone might still be in the same state where he'd been eighteen years earlier—if he'd been there to begin with. Like an alcoholic trying to clamber on the wagon, I now had a history of refusing to permit further self-indulgence. I first stopped searching for him after confiding the matter to my journal. But when Faith escalated her interest in my writing, I stopped keeping the journal and hid it away more securely, so there would be no evidence. But then there also was no longer any exorcism of him on the page. As long as he'd been confined there, I had relative peace of mind. Now he was loose, so the library trips started again. Then, with only one more self-allowed trip to go, it was suddenly too late. I'd found the name. Now none of us could escape from any of us anymore.

It was overheated in the bus, and the window was sealed. I felt my palms begin to sweat and stripped off my gloves, remembering how my hands had shaken the day I'd made the first call—in a British accent, pretending to be a researcher doing follow-up on Jewish war refugees—to confirm that this was indeed the same Dr. Morgenstern who had emigrated from Austria in 1940. The very thought of that phone call, placed just before my eighteenth birthday, still could make my hands tremble now, a full year later.

The wife had answered. I hadn't known that at the time; possibly the nurse-receptionist, I'd thought. But those well-contrived, British-accented questions of the researcher from the mythical American-European Jewry League had amazingly enough elicited a fair amount of information—certainly sufficient to mull over for another year—until the next call, the second call, to make the appointment toward which this bus steadily sped me.

"To whom am I speaking, please?" the British researcher's voice had inquired.

"This is Mrs. Morgenstern, the Doctor's wife. I also work in the office of his medical practice."

"I see. And may I ask how long you and the doctor have been married?"

"Since 1941."

"1941?" Impossible.

"1941, ya." How amazingly obedient she was to this inquisitive stranger. Yet she responded only to what was asked, volunteering nothing.

"I see. And may I have your first name, please?"

"Viga."

"Spelled—?"

"V-i-g-a."

"Any children, might I ask?"

There was a pause so slight it might have been imagined by the British researcher.

"Ya."

Acknowledged, after all. And how had she coped with *that* for so many years?

"Will that be all?" The accent, though faint, was there. Stall for more information.

"You were born in Vienna, as well?"

"Ya."

"And you met Doctor Morgenstern in—"

"The Doctor and I were childhood friends."

"So you emigrated to the United States in—?"

"In 1941, the same year we were married."

Each answer blasted open further underground deposits of questions. But these were questions no American-European Jewry League volunteer could get away with asking. Besides, although I retained my Oxbridge tone of inquiry, I had to get off the phone, because more than the hand holding the receiver had begun to tremble.

Who would have thought it might be so easy? Just say thank you for your cooperation and hang up the receiver. Then sift for months, solipsistically, through the new information—which certainly did not relate to the details I'd already lived with for years.

She was clearly confused about her dates. But he'd obviously remarried. Yet he still acknowledged the child of the first marriage. Then why had he never—or had he?—tried to be a presence in that child's life? Furthermore, the second wife, Viga, clearly knew about the child. Or did she think the child was dead? And how could they have been married a year *before* the child was born? Or was the man a bigamist? I cursed myself that the league volunteer hadn't pressed for more information about the child. Viga's respect for authority seemed so entrenched that she might have gone on answering whatever questions were put to her.

At times, my speculations reeled down side paths leading to dead ends, swamps, precipice edges. What if Faith were not my biological mother? Nonsense: the genes showed themselves physically. What if Faith had told him their child had died, just as she'd told me *he* was dead? Rat in a maze, my mind retraced every route, no matter how irrational.

Forget it, I ordered myself. What will matter in your life is what *you* make of it, not your ancestors' influences. *There is nothing you cannot be.* Then I would remember who had taught me that. And I would reenter the obsession—the state of mystery, terror, longing, nausea, the place I now felt truly at home.

I glanced at my watch. The delicate gold face—Faith's gift for my eighteenth birthday—announced we were only twenty minutes away from New Brunswick. This was happening. I was approaching the Gates of Mycenae. I brushed a piece of lint from the jade-green wool suit in which I'd carefully costumed myself, and readjusted the collar of the white blouse. Stocking seams straight; I could feel them. Black high-heel pumps, new, still unscuffed, still uncomfortable. Black gloves in lap, along with matching black purse and neatly folded camel-hair coat. The well-dressed young woman, prepared for anything.

I had lied to Faith, of course; the genes showed themselves more than physically. I'd told her I was attending an all-day seminar up at Columbia, suggested by Ken Pitchford, on how to get published. He would have winced at the idea, but I knew she'd find that subject more appealing than a seminar on villanelles and sestinas. Besides, Kenneth was, after a year of casual friendship, now ensconced in her mind as my literary guru (as he was in my mind, but for different reasons). In order to make the appointment, I had lied to the wife-receptionist—although, I told myself, *that* lie fell more into the category of hint than outright falsehood. But its being a hint depended on how accurate Faith's stories were about my father. Lies teetering on a foundation of truth, or the reverse? At this moment, everyone concerned had been lied to. Only Robin Morgan, riding on a bus in New Jersey, knew whom she was going to meet.

Think tactically, I had directed myself. Plan it. Stage it. Costume it. That's the only way you can get through it. He was a classics scholar, Faith had said, and he loved Greek drama in particular. He'd refuse to see you, Faith had said; he wants no part of you. Calculate. How can you make an appointment but be assured you get to see him? Certainly *not* warn him it will be Surprise Daddy. Faith just might have been telling the truth. But *can* you surprise him totally? The man was a concentration-camp survivor, a refugee. How merciless can you get? What if he has an on-the-spot stroke from your little bombshell? What if you murder your own father out of curiosity?

No. Better to stage it. *Do what you know how to do.* But give him at least a hint, a half-lie yet a clue—the same way you've lived with half-lies and clues all your life. Something with wit, with style. If he's as smart as you hope he is, as educated as you've been told he is, as obsessed with his daughter as you've dreamt he is—then he'll figure it out. He'll know and be prepared for the young woman who walks through his office door.

So I had made the second call. And again got Viga. This time I wore a French accent—but a light one, to safely confuse things. I wished to make an ob/gyn appointment. I hadn't expected to be asked who referred me to Dr. Morgenstern. It threw me. But years of live TV performances, where you improvised if something went wrong, came to my rescue.

I tossed out a made-up-on-the-spot name: an old friend who lived in New Jersey had praised Dr. Morgenstern's skills. Since I had only recently moved to New York from California and had no ob/gyn of my own, why no it wasn't too far to travel an hour or so to find a really good doctor.

But, ventured Viga, the name of the referrer was not familiar as one of the Doctor's patients.

"Ah, yes." I backed-and-filled rapidly. "My friend married a while ago and I never *can* remember his name. I know her by her maiden name. Doubtless she's registered with you by her husband's name, you see."

Viga saw. Viga, faithful to her role as a walk-on character unwittingly furthering the plot, helpfully made an appointment for me.

In the name of Atreus.

"First name or initial, please?"

"E."

If he knew his classics, then. If he remembered. If the House of Atreus put him on alert. If the name *E. Atreus* snapped into place as the final piece of the puzzle; if the magic words opened a passage through the great gates; if Sophocles and Euripides were still read by him for pleasure; if he were brilliant or merely cared, if he were vigilant or merely wary, *if.*

Then he would *not* be surprised. Then he would be well warned that no one in the world but his daughter would be appearing in time to keep the appointment of Electra Atreus.

And if not? If he were stupid or unsubtle, uneducated or forgetful, complacent, dense? If he hadn't ever cared at all?

In that case—some Sophoclean chorus intoned inside my proscenium brain, an ancient menace of revenge hissing its sibilant cunning—*in that case, let him be surprised.*

I was suddenly sleepy. It was absurd to be sleepy now, when we were entering the outskirts of this quiet suburban town—neat snow-patched lawns, skeletal trees that would be lush in summer, tidy white houses, window boxes sporting miniature evergreens, and here and there a few Christmas lights and porch decorations not yet dismantled in early January. But I was sleepy. It was as if the years of lying awake were now taking their toll. Years rebuilding his face from one faded photograph, tracking him down—his daughter the post-war Gestapo. Years of Electra living under Clytemnestra's ruthlessly loving hand, hunching at the palace gate on guard for the encounter that would set in motion a final avenging of her father's honor—the meeting that might tell me who I was.

I live life far too dramatically, I thought absently, *but it's because that's all I know. Which makes me weird. But that's not the whole of it,* I had to admit to myself. *It's also true that the great dramatists depicted the deepest reality of how life really is lived, even if that intensity is unspoken or denied. Which is why their work can still move us 2,500 years later.* Still, I felt a newfound sympathy for all the people who chose *not* to risk realizing that. All I wanted was to pass the stop, let it slide past the window, and stay on the bus so its motion could rock me to insensibility. Stay on the bus and get off someplace else, become someone else.

"This isn't me," I whispered to the gold watch face. "I don't want to live this. It's all the fault of a bad script." But the bus stopped. There was no way out but to rise, listing slightly on the new heels, and straighten my spine as if I were about to make an entrance.

And so you are, I added silently. *You will get down this aisle—and off this bus—good. Now you will look around for a taxi. There's one, that's it. Now you will give the address. There.*

This was really happening. The taxi reached its destination with distressing speed. Two blocks to the right, three to the left, and the houses became larger, the front lawns broader, the juniper bushes luxuriant even in winter. There was no mistaking *the* house. I sensed it ahead just as the taxi began slowing down. The corner house. There, in polished brass swinging from two posts on the lawn, his shingle. The Doctor's House.

Not the Gates of Mycenae, but formidable. The Doctor's House differentiated itself from the uniform white of neighboring homes on the block. This one was painted a soft gray; the sunporch at the back was half visible from the side, glass-enclosed for year-round use. A back-lit stained-glass panel—imported, from the looks of its quality, possibly an antique—had been mounted in the front door: jewel tones of garnet inlaid on sapphire. The block, the neighborhood, the town itself might be suburbia, but the Doctor's House was still trying for Old World.

I tried to focus and fix the moment as I paid the cab driver. Twitches of emotion—excitement, terror, elation, urgency—were now so rapid in their quicksilver shifts that I could barely separate them one from another. But there was no time for self-examination. I didn't dare linger on the sidewalk; I was still afraid of telegraphing my identity before I got to him, and it wouldn't do to appear suspicious. The twitches jerked their puppet up the front walk.

The doorbell didn't buzz like most American doorbells; it chimed, echoing from somewhere inside the bowels of the house. A respectable wait. No answer. I pressed the bell again, watching my own gloved hand begin to tremble slightly. Get control, I scolded myself, what is this—stage fright, like a baby? Had I—or Viga—got the date or time wrong? Had all those damned fake accents confused the facts? Had Mates read the Atreus clue *too* clearly, and left the house rather than face his Electra? Or was he at that moment hiding inside, refusing to grant her admittance?

The door swung open. A plump, dark-haired woman in her early fifties stood there, offering a tentative smile.

"Ya?"

"I have an appointment with Dr. Morgenstern?" It came out as an appeal. Correct the tone. Needs more authority. And don't forget the French flavor.

"Ah. You are Mrs. Ahtraiyeoos?"

"Miss Atreus, yes." *Stupid,* Robin. Let her think you're married. And why repronounce the name more accurately? Maybe nobody got the clue just because of Viga's mispronunciation. Because this, decidedly, was Viga. The Other Woman. No mistaking the voice or, for that matter, the type.

Mates Morgenstern was in one thing, then, consistent. He had a weakness for a distinct type: The Doctor's Woman. Short, zaftig, with dark hair and large eyes. Viga and Faith could have been sisters. But I couldn't avoid noticing the milder quality of this woman, an almost deliberately projected pliancy—or was that perhaps required to conceal the strength of the woman who had won? The vibrant, sometimes offensive, sometimes electrifying energy my mother radiated was lacking here. Where Faith would confront and defy, Viga would manipulate and appease. Where Faith might be compelled to appease, Viga would concede. And where Faith would—hard to imagine—concede (which she would do only with privately articulated vows of vengeance), Viga would surrender tractably. She was a more unsavory, because more pretentiously genteel, version of my mother. Even her physical features, I thought with some satisfaction, were coarser: the eyes not so lustrous, the hair not so fine. The complexion was ruddy, unlike Faith's alabaster skin. The voice was a shade too high-pitched, too cheerful in its hausfrau poise. Following the jelloid hip motion of Viga down the Persian-carpeted foyer, I was startled to find in myself such unforeseen loyalty to Faith. Nevertheless, I couldn't help thinking that Mates Morgenstern had settled for a Roman copy of the Greek original.

Viga ushered me into the waiting room. It was Modern American Doc-

tor, an abrupt departure from what little I had been permitted to glimpse
of the rest of the house. This room might have been moved intact to any
professional building of doctors' and dentists' offices: pastel yellow walls,
the wifenursereceptionist's desk toward which Viga homed like a contented pigeon, a leather sofa. The coffee table displayed copies of *Time,*
Ladies' Home Journal, and *McCall's,* plus two stacks of pamphlets: "How
to Raise a Healthy Baby: What Every Mother Should Know" (in a pink
cover), and "Fathers Can Help, Too" (in a blue one). A spray arrangement
of pink silk carnations stood stiffly on Viga's grey metal desk, where that
pudgy dovelet now sat, offering me a clipboard and pencil with her ladylike menial air.

"You will please to fill out the information form, Mrs., uh—"

"Yes. Thank you."

I glanced at the form and swallowed a bubble of panic. Mother's name.
Father's name. Date of birth. Medical history. But the Greek chorus
remained steadfast inside my brain, swaying in rhythm to its chant.

It's a standard form. Make up any answers you like. He'll have his answers
soon enough. What matters is how close you are now, all but inside the door,
that door, there, which must lead to his office. You're inside the gates. Now get
inside that door.

I scribbled my answers rapidly and handed the board back. Viga disappeared with a courtier-like scuttle through the door to the inner sanctum.
Every second of waiting for her return seemed interminable. Finally the
door opened and she emerged. I stood up.

"He will see you soon, Miss Iytreeoos. The Doctor."

Viga pronounced his title with such veneration one could hear the
undertones: Herr Doktor. Poor Viga. Had she, like her predecessor Faith,
once dreamed of a different life? Had the handsome doctor swept her off
her feet, too, promising romance and a vicarious career as the soulmate of
an altruistic physician and chatelaine of his manor—only to set her down
here, in however fancy a house on a suburban New Jersey street, doubling
as his receptionist? Surely this demure creature had never envisioned herself a second wife, co-conspirator for years in the Gothic-novel plot of her
husband's skeleton-child rattling in the closet of his past.

But Viga seemed the essence of gemütlichkeit, puttering contentedly at
her desk among his papers. I tried to picture them in bed together, my

father and this placid woman, an exercise complicated by my ignorance of what he looked like. It wasn't possible to imagine anybody making love to Viga without sinking into her ductility like a dazed child into a featherbed. Whereas Faith—whom I had never seen in an erotic situation with anyone beyond the flirtations conducted with brokers, agents, and headwaiters— Faith was as clearly, and with as little evidence, capable of grand passion: ever-hyperbolic Faith.

"Please to be patient," Viga simpered. With an effort, I slowed my pacing. Viga pantomimed formally toward the couch—she tended to make gestures out of a badly directed Schnitzler play—but I declined and continued to stroll around the room. The windows looked out onto a carefully landscaped lawn punctuated by yew shrubs. The pictures on the walls were stock prints of landscapes, not worth a second glance.

Viga's intercom made a burping sound—like that of a cyanide pellet dropped into acid under the seat of a condemned prisoner, I thought, shocked at my mental associations. She was already hanging up the phone and rising, again smiling that ingratiating *moue* of sycophancy.

I slid straight into panic.

He knows. He read the form and found the answers peculiar and put them together with E. Atreus and he's told her to oh-so-politely throw me out. Oh god, what if he knows? But what if he doesn't?

"The Doctor will see you now." She bowed her head at me.

Then she opened the door and took a step backward. I walked through and heard her muffle the door shut behind me.

This office was only slightly smaller than the reception room, but just as impersonal. This desk, however, was burnished mahogany, facing into the room in front of glass French doors that looked out—as he now did, his back toward me—over what in spring and summer must have become a modest flower garden. Another door led, presumably, to the examining room. The details around me would blur forever in my remembrance, except for three specific imprints: the dapper-suited back of the man of medium height who stood behind the desk, and the two large silver-framed photographs on a side table. One was obviously the young Viga, that obedient smile already in place decades ago. The other was an instantly recognizable baby photograph of myself.

I stood just a step inside the closed door, waiting. Everything seemed to have stopped: my heart, my breath, time itself. He turned, his gaze fixed on the clipboard in his hand, and glanced up at me. What I saw then, more than registering any of his features, was a man's face suddenly paling to chalk before my eyes.

"Hello, Mates. I'm Robin. Your daughter."

His eyes jerked down to the clipboard, then up again to me, then down again, then up. So he hadn't deciphered the clues. I could hear his mind skidding, braking, careening around the silence of the room.

He regained control, and looked at me evenly. By the time he spoke, the voice was already contained, almost suave.

"Yes. I know."

"Oh? You seemed surprised."

"You look—very like your mother did when—when I knew her."

So that, too, had worked. Set the stage, design the makeup, let no detail escape you. I was wearing my hair as Faith had worn hers in old pictures— parted in the middle, with the sides loosely brushed back, shoulder length, even though I usually wore it knotted in a bun, to look and feel older than my eighteen years. So it had worked.

He came toward me. Each movement now was weighted with years of fantasy scenarios, and as the gesture rose and entered reality so rose the possibilities. In that instant, as it hovered, his motive hung in a balance. Then, as it chose one action only, all other possibilities fell away forever, just as the striking of a first chord ends silence but limits music.

He did not embrace me.

He continued past me, opened his office door, put out his head, and curtly told Viga he was not to be disturbed. Then he shut the door and locked it. Then he went to the examining-room door, and locked that. So part of the hoping died forever, while part of the fright was resurrected in its place, wildly, irrationally. We were locked in together. What did that mean? Why had he done that?

He retreated to the safety behind his desk.

"You will please to sit down?" He all but clicked his heels. The Viennese accent was unmistakable, as if intentionally retained.

I moved to the chair in front of his desk and sat down.

Before me was a man in his late fifties, well preserved and well dressed—spotless white shirt, discreetly expensive tie, cufflinks. The silver hair was worn in a fashionable haircut, but slightly longer than common, more in the European style. His features offered me nothing of myself.

His eyes were dark grey, his complexion a smooth-shaven olive. The high forehead rose from a long, straight, delicately flared nose. There was a slackening line around the jaw from age, which didn't belie the sensuous mouth or the thrust of a square chin below it. Faith was right: there was a real dimple in the chin. I could see that when he had been younger, and blond, and the face and body lines sharp and slender, he must have been very good-looking.

"Well," he said, leaning back in his chair, now in possession of himself, "I can say I *am* a bit surprised."

"I . . . wasn't sure you'd know who I was."

"I knew who you were the moment I saw you. You really do look very much as she did."

"Any other features you recognize?" I smiled.

"I see nothing of myself, if that is what you mean."

"Well, the genes must be there. I wasn't an immaculate conception." I'd meant to sound witty, but it came out edged with sarcasm. I flinched. He peered at me, the physician making a diagnosis. Then he said coldly,

"What do you want?"

So this was to hate him, then.

That the same man who had against all explanation kept my baby picture in his office for almost nineteen years could, on finally meeting me, think of nothing to say but *What do you want.*

"I want nothing from you. I'm here because I . . . isn't it obvious?"

"Perhaps. But not to me."

"For all my life I've wanted to meet my father. Is that so strange?"

He shrugged elegantly. "A great many people have never met their parents. It doesn't seem so uncommon."

"It's uncommon enough to have become something of an obsession in my case."

"That's unfortunate. I understand young girls often are romantics. But surely the world does not revolve around anything so trivial as—"

"Excuse me. You can't possibly realize my position. This isn't trivial to me." Perhaps if I shifted from the emotional realm, demonstrated my intellectual . . . "Look. If I'd been a son in search of my father, I'd have been reenacting a major archetype. Oedipus. Theseus. Horus. Does my being a daughter in search of the same thing make it a trivial quest?"

He shrugged again. "And so you want . . . ?"

"Only to have met you, seen you face to face, talked a while with you. Heard your side of the story."

"My side?" he smiled. "There is, I am afraid, very little story."

"Nevertheless, I want more than you can imagine to hear it from your lips. And that's *all* I want." I added, trying for a note of dignity that would betray neither humiliation nor bitterness, "I haven't come to blackmail you, you know. Or harm you or your new wife in any way."

"My new wife? You mean Viga? What is so new about Viga?"

"Well, I mean . . . your second wife."

He swiveled slightly in his chair.

"I see," was all he responded. Then he leaned forward and began playing with the silver letter opener on his desk.

"And may I ask," he murmured, "why the elaborate pretense? This strange name in which you made the appointment? And after so long, why now, suddenly? Is your mother no longer alive?"

Something was going wrong. I should be asking the questions. But so eager was I to show myself to him—to be known by him, to have him comprehend how indomitable I'd been in my pursuit—that I knew I'd reply to any question he put. *And,* chanted the chorus, *it must mean he is curious. He cares. He cares.* Hoping to impress him with my erudition, I put on my most disarming smile, and asked,

"You mean the false name I gave means nothing to you?"

He studied the clipboard.

"No. And please to not play games with me."

Another chord, the death of more music. So this is what it was to fear him. I crawled back toward what remained of my raggedy courage.

"It's not a game. My mother is still alive. She doesn't know I'm here. I made the appointment in a false name because I had no idea whether you would receive me as myself or not. I traveled a long way to this meeting, and not only in mileage. I didn't intend to be turned away. But I gave that particular pseudonym as a possible clue. Please understand that I have been told very little about you. But I *was* told you were once very fond of classic Greek drama. Aeschylus. Sophocles. Euripides."

"That was many years ago. I fail to see—"

"Miss Atreus. From the House of Atreus. That family had only one daughter with the initial *E*. Her name was Electra, as it seems you've forgotten."

He looked mildly amused.

"And I was to decipher this—this clue? How ornate, my dear."

So this is what it was to recognize each other. My tragedy interpreted by him as farce.

"Perhaps not ornate to one who remembered his Sophocles or his Mycenaean history," I ventured, as politely if insultingly as he had. *You are his daughter,* the chorus murmured, *you can hold your own with him.*

"Perhaps not. But a great deal of modern history has intervened and— preoccupied me somewhat." He forced a brief laugh.

So this is what it was to feel a lifetime of defenses shatter in pity. *This is your father, Robin, and he only has escaped alone to tell thee.*

"I would like to ask you a few questions . . . You don't have to answer anything if you don't want to, of course," I added hastily.

"I may not know the answers, and I have no idea—or perhaps I do— what you've been told, but . . ."

Like a biblical blessing: the permission. But of all the firmament of questions, where to begin?

"Why did you never . . . *Did* you ever try to see me?"

"I saw you once. You were an infant, a few days old only."

"That was all?"

"It was . . . unpleasant."

"Seeing me?"

"The circumstances. Your mother, her sisters . . ."

"And you never tried after that one time."

"No."

"How could you just—I mean, did you never want—"

"It was not that possible—or that necessary—to follow up. Those women, your mother and her sisters, made it difficult. Distasteful. They were, I regret to say, quite, ah . . ."

"Vulgar."

He raised his eyebrows.

"Exactly."

How will it ever be possible for me to erase from my memory the shadow of approval cast by his surprise? And if it had been real approval—at what cost? Denial of the women who had cared for me sufficiently to live the lie that permitted my existence? Somewhere in all my famishment for acceptance, I had to find at least an appetite for honor.

"How did you *imagine* they'd regard you? As a prince with *droit du seigneur*? I realize, of course," I threw in casually, speaking of my life in the third person and the passive construction, "that the child was unwanted. But you were the doctor, after all. You were the one who might have thought about a contraceptive."

"I had other things to think about. Food. Shelter. Survival—as much as possible on my terms. Or what the world had left to me of my terms."

"Some might think that a convenient excuse."

He shrugged. "You are your mother's daughter."

One honor gained, another lost.

"I'm also your daughter."

An indifferent smile. "On one meeting?"

"No. On fact. Or do you deny it?"

"I don't deny it, my dear. But I think it has little relevance to either of our lives."

There was no way to batter down a door barred with such politesse. I felt tears rising and forced them down. *That he will not have. He will not see you cry.* But the voice that asked the next question embarrassed me by its childish treble.

"Did you ever love her? At all?"

"What a traditional question for a modern young woman." Was he teasing me? Was this his way of being kind? "But," he went on, "I fear I must tell you, the answer is no."

"Never? Even—"

"Even when you were conceived? No. Oh"—that tight smile—"you are shocked I know what you were really asking? You forget that I am a gynecologist—which means I know women better than they know themselves.

I know their sentimentality about conception. Nature is not sentimental about it in the slightest."

"Faith loved you. You knew that."

"I knew that, yes. And certainly I was fond of her. Your mother was an attractive woman. And she was good to me, I will say that. But she was totally unrealistic in terms of what she expected from me. A possessive woman, Faith. She wanted my life, my soul."

"She wanted you to love her, perhaps. That might be the simplest reason for what later became her possessiveness." How odd to defend the rights of one's enemy, as if to keep that adversary worthy of one's own best in a lifelong contest of wills. "She shared her life with you. Was it so bizarre for her to want you to share building your new life with her? It wasn't as if you had an established existence anymore. You'd lost your entire family, crawled through the nightmare of the camps, were a fugitive from the hell Europe had become—"

He shifted abruptly in his chair. His posture stiffened, as if an old fencing master had entered the room.

"My dear young woman. I cannot tolerate all these maudlin assumptions. I am not responsible for your misinformation about my life. But you ask. So I tell you a few hard truths. I was never in a concentration camp. Nor were any of my family. I already was a full surgery and medical graduate, having just commenced my practice in Vienna. My father had died some years earlier, peacefully, in his sleep, of a heart attack. My mother wished to emigrate to Israel, so my sister and her family also settled there to be near her. They are still there, quite healthy and happy—except of course for the stress caused by these demented Arabs. But it was felt there were more career opportunities for me in the United States. And so it was arranged, through friends who had influence and with considerable bribery, that I be put on the priority list of émigrés with the Jewish refugee committees—although the company I had to keep in that category was often quite unpalatable."

I didn't believe him. I thought he must be repressing his experience of the Holocaust, out of survivor guilt. But his manner seemed too relaxed for that.

"You never escaped from a camp?"

"It would have been difficult for me to escape since I never was there to start with. As for escaping from concentration camps—that was hardly a common occurrence, my dear girl."

"Faith said you'd crawled through the sewers of Europe to survive. That was her phrase. She *believed* it. She believed that was the reason for your callousness. She wasn't lying about that. . . . Oh my god. *You* lied to *her*."

Again the aristocratic shrug. "I did not tell her those things. She had her own preconceived notions. She assumed many things. I simply refrained from telling her otherwise. It seemed kinder. And she was, for a crucial period of time, my lifeline."

"My *god*," I repeated. "It's stunning. You really are a cruel man. You 'simply refrained from telling her otherwise.' *God*."

"And why should I have told her otherwise?" His voice never rose, but the accent became more clipped. "Your mother believed what she wanted to believe, what they all wanted to believe. She believed it even before she met me. It was like one of your pre-cut mass-produced American coats she slipped over my shoulders when I walked off the ship. She never bothered to ask whether I liked it or not. But *my* clothes had always been custom-tailored. All the American Jews pitied us—and some of us were indeed pitiable. But *every* one of us *needed* that pity to begin new lives. Many, even most, who came here were not only pitiable but, it must be said, contemptible. Less than human. Even before the Nazis, they had been like this. The stock your mother comes from: peasants, shtetl dwellers, peddlers, ghetto denizens. Little or no education. Little or no culture."

"The 'stock' . . . my mother's father was a rabbi. He—"

"You asked. So be answered. To American Jews in their cushioned nests, all European Jewish war victims were the same: worse off than their own immigrant ancestors had been before coming to the New World. In their view, we were all scrawny, hungry, filthy, desperate, groveling, half-crushed insects. Objects that were pathetic and a little disgusting. It let them feel how far they had come from being what we still were. Ghetto mentalities, Yiddish speakers, whiners, *Mussulmen*—the newsreel skeletons, the walking dead of the camps—that's what we all were supposed to be. The world's most reliable victims: the first and last resort for persecution. Greasy, itinerant, superstitious. Am I to help it if your mother projected *her* family background onto *mine?*"

"Her family—"

"And I should have told her otherwise?" he snorted. "The background differences were evident, anyway. Also, I could not always stop myself from speaking aloud the enormity of my loss. Not people, not family, no. But a distinctive . . . way of life. You could never understand. Certain rituals. The opening night of the Philharmonic, the sound one's footsteps made on the marble of the Kunsthistorische, summers in Bad Ischl, winters on ski holidays in the Austrian Alps, the annual excursion into Grinzing to sample the new wines. The young Schwarzkopf in concert the first time she dared attempt 'Im Abendrot.' The Ringstrasse, the Stadtpark. These things mean nothing to you. To us they *were* our life, leisurely, reliable, lending a graceful rhythm to the seasons. My great-grandfather was a surgeon-captain in the Austrian army—and he was not the first or last Jew to hold such a rank. My family was *Austrian,* do you understand? More than that: *Viennese.* All of us—surgeons, solicitors, professors. And the women—accomplished, able to draw nicely, play at least one instrument, dance charmingly, preside over a well-kept home. These things I could not stop myself from saying aloud to Faith, as if I were mourning Kaddish like some devout synagogue fanatic—which no one in my family ever was."

I stared at him. He barked a short laugh, at ease in his bitterness.

"What little I did tell your mother merely made me more pitiable in her American Jewish eyes. Lo how the mighty have fallen. I could hear it in her voice, suffused with a love only the powerful can afford. But destroy *all* her pre-cut illusions? If she had known I never, how you said it, crawled through the sewers of Europe, never was in or heroically escaped from a camp, would I then have been a sufficient victim? I think not, my dear. And there was something else. I had my pride. Which no one—not the peasant Jews of Europe, not Hitler's lack of discrimination, not your mother—could take from me. With *that* pride I survived. Not a crude pride of endurance, like the Hassidic peasant scurrying around under the Cossacks' hooves. A pride of blood, a long line—"

"So you not only didn't love her. You despised her."

"Oh, really. Such excess of language, such psychologizing. I was fond of her. Grateful, even. I might perhaps have remained a friendly distant acquaintance, except that—"

"A friendly distant acquaintance with your deserted ex-wife, the mother of your child? A friendly distant *acquaintance*—"

He rose to his feet, and for a terrifying moment I thought he would order me from the room. But he turned, paced around his desk chair, and stared out the window. When he spun again to face me, I was confused by his expression—what seemed a clumsy encounter between sympathy and his features.

"Robin," he began softly, "you came here seeking some revelation, a happy ending to your girlish fantasies. When you have lived longer, you may understand there are no happy endings. But there are revelations. Some of which by their nature preclude the happy ending."

I folded the gloves in my lap and forced my hands to lie perfectly still.

"I do understand," I said quietly. "I'm not afraid of the truth."

"That is good. It is best to not be afraid of facts. I take you at your word that you wish to know what there is to know. So then."

He returned to his chair and sat down. I waited. Years of waiting densified into that pause.

"So then," he repeated. "Your mother is not my ex-wife. Viga is not my new wife. Viga is my only wife. Your mother and I were never married."

Certain statements fall, as if through stratospheres of shock, with the gravity of the inevitable. Only then can we comprehend they had always been intuited and were merely delayed en route to the doom of confirmation.

"Viga and I have known one another since we were children in Vienna. Our families were old friends. We grew up together. We knew someday we would marry. We had been betrothed before the war came. She went to England, I came here. As soon as I could, I sent for her."

"I see. Did Faith know this?"

"No. It was not possible to tell her. At first it seemed not necessary. Later, when I came to understand she had been making all these plans in her mind—well, I still needed her. Then she claimed she was pregnant. So it became unavoidable *not* to tell her. She was of course upset. Her sisters were hysterical. That I should marry her."

"And you? You weren't 'upset'? You felt no pity for her?"

"My dear child. We came from different universes. We had nothing in common. She craved what little I still possessed—my education, my culture, my suffering. It would never have worked. I suggested she get an abortion. She would not hear of it. It was her decision. She had miscalculated that someone whose world had been destroyed by the coarsest of people for the coarsest of reasons through the coarsest of means, could still feel pity."

"So you just abandoned her."

"That is harsh. I urged her not to have the child. I knew doctors who would have helped. She refused. What could I do? At her request—her pleading—I did see the infant. I know she believed I would be so moved I would be overcome with love for her and her offspring and thus the happy ending. Au contraire. It was an unpleasant occasion."

"And that was it? You never tried to connect with the child, to see the child, again?"

"It was too difficult. I had my own life to think about, to begin again. There was no way I could keep track of a child who—"

I burst free of the third person.

"Actually, Mates, I would have been a hard child to lose track of. You can't possibly be unaware that at a certain point I was probably the most famous small person in this country?"

"I read something about that. But I rarely watch television, you see. And after all, it was none of my business. Even Faith by then would not have welcomed my interest. She had changed her name again, and you had never borne my name. Also, you see, I had my pride—"

"Your pride." Stung, I began to talk rapidly. "I'm beginning to understand. Tell me your scientific opinion as a doctor: don't your bastards carry the same bloodcells, the same genes of such pride?"

Had his expression not been so controlled, I might almost have imagined he winced.

"I really can't say, my dear. One doesn't—"

"Follow them up. So how *would* one know. Or is it that you follow up the sons but not the daughters? Surely not those from peasant stock."

"Ach, my dear Robin," he laughed, "so you are the young radical, too! A television star, a celebrity, and also political. How very American. Like

your new President Kennedy. But perhaps that is more excusable in someone like you, only twenty years old. I too was once going to change the
world. I was a pseudo-Communist, can you believe it? It was the chic attitude for Viennese intellectuals between the wars. Such self-righteous fervor!" He chuckled, inviting me in as an accomplice to his bonhomie.

"But once in this country, you settled into the comfortable life of the
bourgeoisie? You recovered from all that youthful idealism, eh?" I heard
the edge in my voice, but my interior listening was alive to something else
he'd said, something not even aimed at me, but something that had penetrated fatally and was coursing through my blood like an embolism.

"Once in this country, I determined to build a life here. I knew that
even after the war would be over, Vienna—my Vienna, as I and my family
had experienced it—would never be the same. I've been back to visit, naturally. Many times. But to be 'repatriated' and 'recompensed' like the mer-
chant class, that was not for me. Anyway, it is not possible to be on this
planet and escape America. I can imagine a day when one will be standing
in the Belvedere Gardens and look up to see the hideous golden arches of
McDonald's not far off. So, since I could not escape this country, I determined to survive *here*. This is why I changed my field from surgery to
gynecology and obstetrics. They seemed—obstetrics, especially—more
positive. When I came to this country, you see, I learned that my medical
education—the finest, in the world's most honored medical city—was not
good enough for raw young America, so self-confident of its own destiny.
It would have taken more years of being dependent on and possessed by
your mother, to take the required additional courses and board examinations for surgery, my old specialty, than it did for ob/gyn."

"And the latter was also easier, perhaps?"

"Easier? Oh my dear child—"

"Please don't call me that." The embolism was still traveling through
the veins, approaching the brain. What was it he'd said, *what?*

"My apologies. A manner of speech. But 'easy'? Can you imagine what
it is to try and minister medically to women? Their emotionality, their lack
of judgment? Their excessive alarm over minor illness and their self-
deluding home remedies for major diseases? They *resist* you, these
women. They ask for your advice and claim to obey it—but they fight you
as if to the death. It doesn't matter what age they are, they act as if—"

There it was.

"You said something, Mates. A moment ago. Something about my being a young woman twenty years old. You must've lost track of that, too. I'll be twenty *next* year, Mates. I'm about to turn nineteen, later this month."

I couldn't tell whether the astonishment in his expression was from my having dared interrupt the direction of his thought, or whether it was the content of what I'd said. Then his eyes narrowed, and he leaned forward across the desk.

"No. You are about to turn twenty later this month."

This was a direct engagement, one I had to win. For my mother's sake? For the few things I had believed solid among so many shifting unrealities? Or was it one I actually hoped to lose—for the savage, awesome freedom that would imply?

"I was born January 29, 1942. This is 1961. I'm about to be nineteen."

"You were born January 29, 1941, Robin. You are about to be twenty years old."

We stared at each other. Then he rose, strode to a filing cabinet across the room, took out a set of keys on a silver pocket key chain. He selected one and unlocked a file drawer. It took him only a moment's search to find the paper. I watched, mesmerized.

"This is your birth certificate. Perhaps you have never seen it."

I started to speak, then stopped myself. How suddenly irrelevant to explain to him that there *was* no certificate, that there had been a fire in the registry of the little Florida town and all the records had been lost, that it had been necessary for Faith to swear a deposition to a judge years ago so a new certificate could be issued. I started to speak, then stopped myself in one last hopeless gesture of protection for the young mother whose terror and despair, I finally realized, must have been overwhelming.

But there it was in my hand. The original one, the one with the seal. *Robin, female, born to Faith Berkley, nee Malkah Teitlebaum. Father: Mates Morgenstern. January 29, 1941. Lake Worth, Florida.*

"It's an odd feeling. To lose a year of my life. Just like that."

"Your mother lied to you about this also? But why?"

How dare he.

Why indeed?

"No," I answered. "No. She didn't lie. I think we both understood it would be helpful in my career, to . . . shave off a year. As time went on I just . . . must have lost track myself."

Not enough to have had my own radio program at age five; more precocious at age four. A whole year lived somewhere, somehow—doing what? Lost, gone forever. While a young woman tried to cover what she thought was her shame by doing the only thing she knew how to do—pretend the real into being, by pure will. And he dared speak of pride! *Nothing* about me is real, I thought, I am a figment of Malkah Teitlebaum's imagination, her *golem*.

"Would you like to have this?" he asked, holding out the birth certificate.

"Yes," I said, "I would."

"Keep it. I have no use for it. I kept it all these years in case . . . actually, I don't know why I saved it."

He began to straighten out small items on his desk. It was time to exit before the room spun completely out of control.

"Well. Thank you, Mates. For seeing me. For telling me what you've told me. And, for this—" gesturing with the paper. "I—wish you well."

"Thank you," he replied formally. "I must ask, what you intend—"

"I won't bother you. I agree, our relationship is irrelevant." I lifted my chin and smiled, both prides—my mother's and my father's—alive in that smile, but recognized by neither one nor, at the time, by their daughter. "I don't intend to tell Faith about this meeting. Not for a while, at least. It would only give her more pain. So. I'll be going." I rose and went to the door, unlocking it, then turning to let my eyes sweep the room and record it a last time. "Oh. There is one thing more."

"Yes?" he asked, and with a stubborn rush of longing I thought I heard an eagerness in his question.

"Mates. Why does the man who saw his child only once and never 'followed up' still keep, ninetee—twenty years later, her baby photograph framed in silver by his desk?"

If it could have been said: *I exist. Look at me, tell me, let me know, speak it once and for all O my father, let free whatever syllable of love for me you might have strangled all these years*—if it could have been spoken, what shone in my eyes, what braced my body upright while my spine hummed like a tuning fork for his answer, *if*. If it was ever to be known, let it be learned now.

He looked at the picture. When he turned to me again, his expression was tinged with what once might have been grief, and something else I could perceive but not yet understand: the addictive self-contempt knowable only to a survivor.

"That photograph is not of you. That is my elder son, Danny, when he was a baby. He is twelve now. You see," he turned around another frame, on his desk, one that had been facing him, "there they are. That is his brother, Gil. Both of my boys, taken last year."

I said, "Thank you, Mates. Goodbye."

You smile, I directed myself. You exit with dignity. You thank Viga in passing, you do not break your stride, you grab your coat from the brass rack you get through this corridor and this stained-glass door and out to the street and you walk in the general direction the cab had come from toward the bus depot somehow you do it a bastard a year lost wiped clean out of your past *ya* she'd said on the phone how could you have assumed a child was you wishful hearing 1941 half-crushed insect a year the son he always wanted two in fact do two half-brothers make a whole one Faith was right no she lied he never loved her he lied he never wanted you she lied she never wanted you a son two he lied she lied the only real choice in life is a choice between lies. I am the child of lies. I am a living lie.

By the time the bus deposited me back in New York City, I had remembered there was one human being on the planet in whom I could confide these raw, bleeding truths. One person so scarred from his own bleak and violent family love that he would hear me, understand, be able to see something real in me. One person who knew if you could turn suffering into something of use—into art, into politics—yes naively try to save the whole lying blood-sick world with it, then you might do more than just survive it, calloused and sardonic. You might understand it, forgive it. *Not repeat it.*

I ran to the first booth I saw after getting off the bus. I was in luck, the phone wasn't broken. I dialed, whispering *Please let him be in, please.*

The familiar voice answered.

"Kenneth? Thank god you're there."

"Oh, hi, Robin. What's the matter? You okay?"

"Kenneth. I need to talk to you. And Kenneth, can we walk across Brooklyn Bridge? You said we might someday. I've still never been."

"Uh, yeah, sure. Wait a minute, you mean right *now*? But it'll be freezing! It's *Janua*—"

"Right now, yes. Right now. If that's humanly possible. Please. There's stuff I've got to tell somebody. Meet me in fifteen minutes at the Manhattan side of the bridge? *Please?*"

And he said he would. And he wasn't lying. He did.

NINE

A Doom of One's Own

Actress: also **actrice**. Middle English. **1.** A female doer or actor (one who acts, takes part in an action), 1569. **2.** A female player on the stage, 1700.
— OXFORD ENGLISH DICTIONARY

 othing, short of falling in love or learning you have a terminal disease, so invests life with concentrated intensity as discovering you've just lost an entire year of it.

Acutely aware of each moment yet in a daze, I reeled through that first week after meeting my father feeling literally, *spatially* off balance, cut adrift from my past, unable to imagine my future. I didn't know then that for the rest of my life I'd be a fraction of a second late in replying (while mentally double-checking) whenever I was asked my age, and that by noting the year as well as the age, so as to be certain (e.g., when you're forty-nine, you're in your fiftieth year), I would somehow infect those close to me with the same confusion, so now it's become a running joke that friends and lovers are comparably unsure of how old *they* are, too.

Back then, the one thing I knew was that I couldn't yet tell my mother I'd met him and learned I was a year older than she'd always said I was. Confronting Faith with *that* would be a watershed moment, and I had to prepare against it. Meanwhile, beneath the mourning over that year's loss, relief and anger were bubbling, as every day another new realization popped up into place, a domino effect in reverse. So I'd been precocious but *not* freakish, after all; so my first period *wasn't* all that abnormally early; so I *hadn't* been too impossibly young to have gone to college. But what I still couldn't work out was why she and Sally had shaved off that year; I was certain those two had conspired but unsure whether Sophie had been part of it. Still, the emotional vertigo caused by such instant aging felt oddly like a symptom of health. Even though only two people— Kenneth and myself—knew it, I was twenty now, not nineteen. *Twenty.* It sounded powerful, adult. I clung to that twenty as if it were a life jacket. Twenty meant that in only a year I would reach my legal majority. Twenty-one meant Faith could do nothing to stop me from being or doing whatever I chose.

But what would that be? I needed to be ready. I needed to reinvent my life according to my own terms—whatever those were. I kept reminding myself that if I didn't know what in hell I was doing, it was all right because everybody else was secretly making it up as they went along, too. I remember feeling as if the days were passing in such slow motion that I might have been sleepwalking under water, yet in retrospect I'm impressed at the speed with which that young woman flew into action. Within three months I was in an onerous weekly poetry workshop with Kenneth and his friends; I was taking my writing seriously, had found myself a job, was working as a secretary at a literary agency, and had begun hunting for my own apartment.

Such changes had not come about smoothly, openly, or truthfully. "When in Rome, lie as the Romans do," I muttered to myself. Apartment hunting was my dark secret; I'd no idea how long it might take me to find one, or even to save enough money for the first two months' advance rent. As it turned out, I wouldn't be able to move away from my mother until June of the following year, and the intervening thirteen months found us not always on the coziest of roommate terms. In the meantime, I'd convinced Faith that my search for an office job was sort of a lark and only temporary, until I could (a) win the transitional role that would establish me as an adult actress and/or (b) write her a best-seller. Naturally, she saw no contradiction between the two.

Actually *landing* a job was another matter. Like millions of wanna-be writers, I hoped to work "in publishing somewhere." But I had no office skills other than an acquaintance with the alphabet that would qualify me for the post of file clerk. I knew no shorthand and although I could type accurately and rapidly I had never learned touch-typing, so my technique required glances at the keyboard and a weirdly Wanda Landowskan style of pianistic hand crossovers. I didn't lie to the employment agencies about this lack of skills, figuring I'd be found out anyway. But more than that was discovered at the first placement agency with which I registered. A seedy man named Louie interviewed me and recognized my face and my name.

"Hey, you were a kid star. TV. Big stuff," he chewed the words past his mustache and into his cigar. "So Miss Big Stuff, what's a millionaire like you who got rich from doing nothing but be cute want with an office job, huh? Huh, Baby?" I bit back my humiliation and explained to him that all that was long ago and I wasn't a millionaire and wanted a job.

"How come? Spent all your dough on caviar lollipops? Don't think you can play *me* for a patsy, Baby. What are you, researching some role you're gonna play? There's gals really *need* these jobs, ya know, Cutie."

I told Louie the truth, that my mother controlled all my money and had stated I wouldn't get a penny if I moved out, and that I was desperate to gain my independence. I begged. Louie refused to send me out on interviews.

"Because I have no skills?" I asked. "But I swear I can learn very fast and I'm willing to do any—"

"Nah. Skills shmills. Just on accounta' you're *you*, Baby."

I slunk away to other agencies. But after days of pavement pounding and being told to go to secretarial school (which Faith had refused to pay for: "Secretarial skills for a genius like you?!"), or else being told, "Get some on-the-job experience first" (*how?*), I'd gained the painful insight that my attempts to "live the real," as I put it, were false starts. So I returned to Louie's 42nd Street office, filled out a new card, and sat again in front of his desk.

But this time my own skills were being practiced. Louie glanced at a card listing my accomplishments as typing sixty words per minute, rapid-write shorthand, fluent French and German, previous experience three years in executive-assistant positions with convincing-sounding small businesses abroad. The signature at the bottom of the card was Roberta Moran. Louie was impressed. Louie looked up to see a young woman wearing glasses, earrings, bright red lipstick, and an aqua chiffon scarf wound in a turban covering her hair. She smiled winningly at him. He never stood a chance—especially when she began to respond to his questions in her boarding-school voice with the faintly British high pitch, acquired from all that time working abroad. He began to riffle his files for something "worthy" of her, since she was "one classy broad." Together they chose Curtis Brown, Ltd., an established literary agency—the post of executive assistant to the head of the periodicals department. Louie told her whom to call in the personnel department and how to approach them. It was only after she'd thanked him and turned to go—job address and contact's name secure in her purse beyond reclamation—that poor Louie wished her well, making the temptation to respond too strong.

"So, Baby, lotsa luck. If you land it, you'll buy me a drink, huh? And lissen, if it don't work out, you sashay right back here and I'll find you something else. Something sterling, Cutie."

Which permitted his classy broad the supreme moment of turning, whipping off the glasses and scarf, and smiling, "Call me Robin Morgan. *You* remember. Don't call me Cutie. And *never* call me Baby."

I swept grandly out of his office—not yet having learned that while such a triumph may warm the victor with a temporary satisfaction, it leaves ashes of doubt that one has not only failed to educate the person one was trying to impress but has in fact confirmed his prejudice. Nevertheless, I got the job.

I'd gambled correctly—that Louie would be too embarrassed to call and denounce as an imposter someone he himself had sent over. Nor, to be on the safe side, did I cite him as a reference. I claimed I'd heard about the job opening from a (nameless) friend at another agency, thus saving both Curtis Brown and myself from paying commissions. It had been surprisingly simple. I'd called for an appointment and gone to the Curtis Brown offices, on Madison Avenue just off 57th Street, looking like myself and using my own name, but inventing my office skills and references, which, it turned out, weren't even checked. Nor did anyone do a double take at my name or my face; either people in the publishing world hadn't watched much television or they had short memories. I was hugely relieved—and blissful when asked to start the following Monday. Even Faith shared some of my excitement ("while it lasts" it would help my "writing career"), though she expressed reservations about my ability to adjust to a nine-to-five, five-day-workweek schedule. I proved her wrong.

Mrs. Sewell Haggard—Edith Haggard—was my boss. I smile now just thinking about her. A widow for thirty years but "a career woman" all her life, she was in her sixties, under five feet tall and still a beauty, with an upswept mane of luminous silverwhite curls, sharp grey eyes, high cheekbones, and an elegant taste for quietly expensive clothes. Edith was a *grande dame* legend among literary agents because she was as literate as she was irascible. But I didn't find her difficult, merely crisp and businesslike. Of course I called her "Mrs. Haggard," but she also chose to address me as "Miss Morgan," thus paving a two-way street of professional respect no other boss at Curtis Brown deigned to tread with any other secretary, and she won my heart for that. In the two-and-a-half years I worked for this woman, I came to have real affection for her, which, to my pleasure, was reciprocated. When she retired, so did I—at least from wage slavery into freelance freedom (and attendant financial insecurity); I was flattered to be offered other jobs at Curtis Brown, but couldn't imagine working for anyone else there. By then, she called me Robin, and had invited me to call her Edith. We remained friends until her death in 1995 (when she was in her nineties). She rarely missed a publication party for one of my books, and always invited me to her celebrated New Year's Eve literati parties.

At first, however, our relationship was built on quicksand. I handled phones, filing, and typing well enough, though the other secretaries were mystified by my keyboard sleight of hand. I overachieved reliably at punctuality, being discreet, booking her travel, theater, and luncheon reservations, watering her plants, fetching her coffee, and greeting visiting authors. My shorthand, however, was pure prestidigitation.

Basically, I *memorized* the letters during dictation, and as mnemonic flags I invented my own written code: a check mark meant "the"; the symbol @ (pre-email) meant, depending on context, "at," "about," or "approximately." Vowels were dropped or truncated, abbreviations were chronic, and numerals replaced words where they could: cn u pls rtrn ✓ ms. 2 me b-4 nxt 2sdy, or s sn s psbl; my shorthand read like a cross between what would later be 1980s rap-album titles and 1990s cyberspeak. Once in a while I had to claim to Mrs. Haggard apologetically that I couldn't be *quite* certain of my own shorthand in just *one* spot and what exactly *was* it that she'd wanted to add in that postscript to Daphne Du Maurier . . . ? Appreciative of my compulsive attention to detail in all other aspects of the job, she was forgiving and would repeat what I'd missed. Mostly I was astonished that my system worked so well. Years later, of course, I learned that Edith had surmised early on I couldn't take formal shorthand, but had cannily chosen to ignore that.

"You see, dear," she told me at her apartment one of the last times I saw her, over very dry martinis (which I happen not to drink but which she enjoyed and so served without asking my preference), "you see, anyone who can memorize twenty or so letters a day needn't *bother* to learn shorthand, that's what *I* say. You wrote excellent reader's reports on manuscripts, were good over the phone, enchantingly fanatic about meeting deadlines, and soothing with authors. Why should I have cared about *squiggles*? Really!" She sank back on her satin chaise longue and cackled.

Proximity to authors certainly was the best part of the job. But it was gratifying to be an apprentice learning tools of the professional writer's trade, too: proofreading and copyediting marks; terminology of newspaper, magazine, and book production; the syndication process; copyright procedures; the contractual mysteries of commissions, kill fees, royalties, subsidiary rights—knowledge that has stood me in good stead to this day.

It was enjoyable, too, making a few friends near my own age. In time, I was admitted into the "secretaries' circle"—which was composed of three gay young men, one black and two white (all of whom were witty, chic, and well-dressed far beyond their means), and three straight young women, one Polish-American and two Italian-American (none of whom were witty or chic, all of whom lived with their parents in Queens, and all of whom longed to get married so they "could stop working"). Leave it to *this* circle to recognize the Ideal American Girl. But their warmth took precedence over their suspicion while their sympathy outlasted their questions—which I duly answered until the novelty of me as a former child star finally wore off—so they included me in the Wednesday cheap-Chinese-restaurant lunches and the Friday drinks-after-work ritual. Lubricated by sickeningly fruity, toy-umbrella'd mai tai's, we royally dished

the mannerisms of CB higher-ups, certain inept agents, various rude editors, and the most temperamental of our authors, enjoying that rib-aching
mirth shared by peons at the expense of our so-called betters. I had my
favorite targets, but I was careful to protect Haggard and her authors, not
just out of loyalty but out of respect.

Ah, the authors. Sure, some were hacks, and others simply jobber pro's
making a living out of writing for the then many periodicals publishing fiction as well as journalism. But most of Edith Haggard's clients were literary writers. Furthermore—although strictly speaking she and I handled
the periodicals market and other agents at CB dealt with book authors or
represented playwrights and screenwriters—quite a few of Haggard's
longtime clients worked in more than one genre and preferred that she
handle their work in every medium. (This didn't always sit well with the
other departments. Cindy Degener, who ran the theater department with
noisy élan, was a good sport about it, but some of the other Curtis Brown-
ies, as I secretly called them, resented such rabid authorial fealty to Haggard.) Haggard's client list was impressive, so I got to read raw
manuscripts by Elizabeth Bowen, Lawrence Durrell, Mary Renault,
William Golding, Clare Boothe Luce, C. P. Snow, Ogden Nash, Nadine
Gordimer, Patrick White, Thomas Merton, John Cheever, Christopher
Isherwood, and Kenneth Tynan, and to deal with the literary estates of
Sinclair Lewis, Joyce Cary, and A. A. Milne. I got to read mail from these
luminaries, speak with them by phone, and sometimes meet them in the
flesh. From experience, I learned that Sir Charles and Lady Snow preferred fresh pink roses and freesia in their hotel suite when they visited
New York, that Mr. Durrell never even approximated making his deadlines, that Miss Bowen had a devilish sense of humor, that Mr. Nash had
almost none. From tidbits confided by Mrs. Haggard as she gradually
came to trust me, I also learned that Mr. Cheever "drank more than was
required *even* of a writer," that Miss Renault "had a live-in lady companion, you understand," that Mrs. Luce "was rich enough to afford being
quite mad," and that Joyce Cary and Haggard had once had "a bit of a
fling." Mostly, I learned that all writers great and small were fixated on
when the check had been mailed.

But when W. H. Auden appeared in person one day, I lost it. I was sitting at the outer office desk, substituting for Irene Petrovitch, my pal the

receptionist who also worked the switchboard (yeah, lines and plugs, a classic I prided myself on learning). Reenie was on her lunch hour and I was reading a manuscript in between making pert announcements into my headset—"Good afternoon, Curtis Brown literary agency, may I help you?"—when Auden slouched in through the glass doors, his unmistakable, heavily lined face peering at me with diffidence. He had dropped by "to see Edith" without an appointment, "was that all right?" I stared up at probably the greatest then living poet writing in English, and my tongue solidified into a plinth. But the rest of my body, still capable of movement, flung off the headset, vaulted over the desk, charged the poor man, and then stood there, clasping and unclasping my hands, terrifying him until I managed to blurt out the words "Haggard out. Lunch. Back soon. Wait! Please? Coffee?" He was kind (probably thinking I had a speech impairment and wondering why they'd posted me at reception), though he was less kind when I nervously brought him the second cup of coffee, having poured the first one on his shoe. Meanwhile, the board, by now lit up like Times Square, was beeping with unanswered calls. Alan Collins, the president of Curtis Brown, came stalking out demanding why in Christ's name he couldn't get an outside line. Seeing Auden, he stopped in mid-glare at me and swept the poet away to his office to wait for Haggard there. I'd lost my chance. Back at the switchboard, answering, apologizing, wrestling the octopus of lines back into a semblance of efficiency, I thought of all the things I might have mentioned without appearing too much the worshipful fan, things mercifully left unsaid—such as that I too wrote poetry, or that I'd met Pound when he was in the booby hatch. By the time Irene rescued me and Edith Haggard returned and sent me to escort Auden from Collins's office to hers, I was calmer, and was further sobered by Auden's wince when he saw I was to be his guide. So I showed him the way in silence and then, holding her door open for him, merely whispered that I found his sestinas particularly brilliant. It was worth it for the look of shock that rippled through the wrinkles before he turned toward Edith's melodious "*Wystan. What a nice surprise!*" A few years later, I would meet him again, with his longtime lover and partner, Chester Kallman, on St. Mark's Place, where they'd lived for many years. It was only a few blocks from where I was by then living with Kenneth, with whom I was out walking. In the manner of people who've been a couple for many decades (and sometimes even pets and humans who live together for years), Auden and Kallman had come to share a startling resemblance: they could have been brothers. Kenneth knew them both, and Auden, thanks to a compassionate lapse, did not remember me. We four stood chatting on the sidewalk for maybe half an hour. But I was the odd woman out, since the conversation revolved raunchily around news that the fleet was in, and there was amicable disagreement about which country's sailors were hotter. Poetry was not mentioned, though I stood there silently quoting to myself "Lay your sleeping head, my love, / Human on my faithless arm; . . ."

But there *were* the weekly poetry workshops at which I felt lucky to be included. These were worlds apart from the workshops I'd attended up at Columbia, with Mark Van Doren, Babette Deutsch, and Leonie Adams; those had been more like classes, with as many as seventy would-be poets attending; you were fortunate if the teacher/poet scanned even one of your poems during the entire semester.[1] At the weekly poetry workshops I now attended, there was no place to hide. There were only a few of us— Kenneth, Jim Rosenberg, Barbara Romney, and David Galler—all of them accomplished, published poets ten or more years my senior. They chain-smoked cigarettes, drank jug wine or cheap brandy, and seemed to have lots of sex (Barbara and David with each other; Jim with men and alcohol, the combination of which would eventually kill him; Kenneth with his lover as well as with other men, sometimes with both together). They all lived downtown, on the Lower East Side. We usually convened at Barbara and David's small loft, which I found to be gloriously "real"—reality taking the shape of burlap curtains, chipped pottery, and home-baked bread (actually, Barbara-baked bread, since the sex roles were as traditional as

---

[1]Van Doren did take a liking to me, reading and commenting on about thirty poems of mine. But I suspect his interest was influenced less by my work than by my having silently brought him a single red rose the day after his son Charles had been all over the news for having cheated on Barry and Enright's TV show *The $64,000 Question*. Van Doren would have had no way of knowing that my sympathy for his paternal embarrassment included an element of special pity for all victims corrupted by Barry and Enright. That day (the day of the rose), Van Doren surprised the class by summarily announcing he would not be giving his planned address, on *Macbeth* and ambition. Instead, he delivered an unforgettable, extemporaneous lecture on *Lear*, analyzing the play as a failure of fatherhood without once mentioning the headlines.

the context was "bohemian"). Around this time, I started smoking, later to cease temporarily for six years during pregnancy and Blake's babyhood, halt unsuccessfully three times thereafter, and finally stop permanently in 1993. I'd buy a pack of Kool filters on my way to the workshop session, puff away until nausea threatened, throw the pack out after leaving, and chomp cinnamon Dentyne all the way home under the delusion my mother wouldn't smell tobacco on me. I also marched myself off to Charles of the Ritz and got my hair colored back to match my eyebrows, an ash brown (my mother, like Queen Victoria when told a tasteless joke, was "not amused"). I sought refuge from Faith's predilection for all shades of pink and my lifetime of pastel clothing by wearing anything brown or black I could buy cheaply. I was trying to save as much as possible of my take-home pay—$61.34 a week—toward getting the longed-for apart-ment, little knowing that, as the months went by, Faith would figure that out and start requiring me to pay her half my salary in rent, thus slowing the process considerably.

I lived for those workshops, but I lived in fear of them, too. We each would bring a new poem and read it aloud as well as pass copies around; the work would then be critiqued or, more accurately, verbally *shredded*. Kenneth was a survivor of infamous Seattle workshops run by Theodore Roethke, and earlier he'd pulled off his master's thesis in the form of a long poem under the supervision of Allen Tate at the University of Min-nesota, so he set the tone: pitiless criticism of others. Especially me. Then again, my work warranted more criticism then anyone else's. It tended to preciosity and melodrama, and was crudely crafted. I was miserably aware of my deficiencies, and terrified of being regarded as a dilettante, so I accepted all criticism with the facade of a stoic, but dreaded criticizing the others' work since I didn't know what to say and thought their poems impressive to begin with. Nevertheless, I was stubborn in my refusal to be put off. From the moment Kenneth casually asked me if I wanted to "sit in on" one of these evenings of exquisite torture, I resolved I was going to keep coming back week after week so long as they'd let me in the door.

Galler mostly ignored me; he was solipsistically focused on Oedipal struggles with his wealthy father, and he exhausted easily under the pres-sure to appear civil. Jim Rosenberg was friendly, tried to put me at ease, and on occasion even defended some of my work. But in a odd foreshadowing of the future, it was Barbara Romney who mostly protected me and sometimes actually praised an image or two in one of my poems. If this was female solidarity, it definitely masked itself from both of us. On the contrary, Barbara, a skilled poet, tended to put down other women, as many female intellectuals of that period felt compelled to do, in order to "pass" with token status among the boys. She'd escaped from Utah and lethal Mormonism to New York, liberty, and this Jewish passive-aggressive lover, but when her eventual marriage to Galler foundered, she returned home with their child to vanish again among the latter-day saints. In vain I've scanned poetry magazines for her name, and when giving the rare speech in Utah I've asked feminist activists if they've heard of her, but Moriah's seraphic wings seem to have closed round her and hidden her from sight. Back in the early 1960s, however, Barbara seemed to me a model of independence, female power, and bohemian glamour.

More than these poets' style of living, I coveted their style of writing. Their subject matter was personal, analytic unto the Freudian, packed with images as violent as the emotion was intense. Juxtaposed with a strict elegance of form, this could produce a powerful effect. In the jargon of "schools," I suppose they were "academic" poets— not because they were based in academia (though Kenneth was teaching undergraduate English at NYU's uptown campus), but because they mostly chose to write sonnets, sestinas, ballades, and other traditional forms (Kenneth was in fact inventing new forms, including one he named his "mystic stanza").

Now, four decades later, in this era of rap and poetry slams, some readers might find it pitiable that I was so surrounded by a "white male Western tradition" of poets and poetic techniques. God knows I profoundly wish there had been more than the few token women poets, poets of color, and cross-cultural poets who were then visible as inspiration and enrichment. But it can be valuable to learn a discipline for the discipline itself; afterward, one can keep or jettison different skills as one chooses, or vary them as I have and still do. I sometimes write "formal poetry," but when I write blank or free verse, I do so more concisely and precisely because I do so from choice, not inability to do otherwise; when the technique is there so the challenge of form *can* be met, it *needn't* always be met. It's taken these forty years for me to understand how much each poem demands its own unique shape—perhaps a traditional Western form, perhaps one borrowed from a non-Western culture, such as a Turkish ghazal or a Japanese haiku or tonka, perhaps free verse, perhaps a form invented afresh for that individual poem—and it's taken forty years for me to learn *how* to uncover *which* form will fit a specific poem's function.

Nor does poetry exist in some rarefied atmosphere beyond politics. It never has, which is why Dante got sent into exile. Thanks to the cultural explosion called feminism, an entire new poetic vocabulary would open up in the late 1960s. Until then, it was acceptable—even laudable—for a poem to contain images from an androcentric universe (*rods, members, wands,* and *staffs* from the traditionalists; *cocks, pricks* and *dicks* galore from the Beats), but it was unthinkable for a poem to contain such words as *clitoris* or *vagina*—or even *dishtowel, tampon, mop, diaper.* Except for clues glinting in Millay's irony, Parker's sarcasm, and Rukeyser's lonely feminist intimations, the experienced reality of half the human species was invisible; female imagery—unless as the object of male perception—was considered not the stuff of poetry. (Since we also were told to "write what you know," this sent a double message that silenced or deranged more than one poet who happened to be female, and helped drive some, like Plath and Sexton, to early graves.) Consequently, any serious woman poet in the 1950s and 1960s bent over backwards—often literally, spread-eagled—to prove she could keep up with the boys in choice of subject matter, fearing to be classified alongside "nineteenth-century lady poet-esses with three names who languished neurasthenically on their sofas, twitching their smelling salts," as Kenneth put it.

Nevertheless, when I was only twenty (still nineteen, officially), any strict discipline of craft, albeit patriarchal in origin as well as in style of delivery, was useful training. As a young poet, I might otherwise lazily have been tempted to believe that poetry was about "having something to say" or "experiencing deep feelings," or might have let myself believe that prose could be called a poem if it had "high-sounding language" and was typed with jagged right-hand margins. Robert Frost famously said that free verse struck him as senseless, "like playing tennis with the net down," and Kenneth sternly lectured me, "After you manage to write your first thousand sonnets, then *maybe* you *might* begin to write poetry." I took both comments seriously, though later I realized that Frost was exercising, well, Frostbite, and Kenneth hyperbole. Still, we wouldn't let just anybody wander into an OR to perform brain surgery, and the craft of poetry is at least that difficult. So although I often sat in the bus riding uptown after a workshop evening sniffling tears of humiliation as I chewed my Dentyne cud, I don't regret those workshops or the lessons drilled into me:

Concrete images, not abstract ones: never write "tree" when you can write "aspen," "birch," "willow," "ash." Read Cleanth Brooks's *The Well Wrought Urn: Studies in the Structure of Poetry*. Study the sixteenth- and seventeenth-century English poets, especially Donne, Marvell, Herbert, and Crashaw, for wordplay, meter, wit. (It was quite a day when I came across Mary Sidney Herbert and Katherine Fowler Philips, same place, same periods.) Read Whitman for excess, Dickinson for economy, Yeats for music. Read Wallace Stevens for imagery, T. S. Eliot for philosophy, Robinson Jeffers for audacity. Read Randall Jarrell for astringency, Robert Lowell for psychology. Read William Carlos Williams for his eye, Roethke for his ear, the strength of his individual line. (I discovered Phillis Wheatley, Amy Lowell, H.D., and Zora Neale Hurston by myself, but it was Kenneth who recommended Christina Rossetti, Charlotte Mew, Kathleen Raine, and Ruth Pitter.) *Read, read, read.* Don't think you can find refuge from low-level clichés in high-level clichés. Read Strunk and White's *The Elements of Style*. Dissect Marlowe's mighty line; analyze what Shakespeare does with vowels and consonants. Get yourself a good rhyming dictionary. English is rhyme-poor (unlike Italian, for instance, with all those supple vowel endings), so work through slant rhyme and subtle internal echo rhymes and save strict rhyme for rare dramatic resolution, if at all. Tread lightly on alliteration. Read Fowler's *Modern English Usage*. A refrain should up the ante on itself each time it returns, or else it's mere repetition. Never settle for simile if you can manage metaphor. Never settle for approximate metaphor: only exact will do. Tighten, then tighten again. Poetry is about essence. Poetry is distillation. Read Empson's *Seven Types of Ambiguity*. Watch those jog-trot rhythms, or your work will sound like "The Song of Hiawatha." (Naturally, there are exceptions to every rule: did you ever notice that most Emily Dickinson poems can be sung to the tune of "The Wabash Cannonball"? The format of hymns must've got stuck in her head.) Respect etymology. Don't over-rely on onomatopoeia. Get yourself a good thesaurus. Trust no translations of poetry until you learn how approximate they are. Use adjectives sparingly; if you have the right noun, you may not need an adjective at all (tell it to Faulkner). The verb is all-holy; it moves the line forward. Read *poetry,* read *about* poetry, *read*.

I drank it all in, in long draughts that intoxicated me. I watched a poem I decided I'd *finally* finished get ripped apart line by line, dactyl by iamb by trochee—then reassembled with suggestions from the group into something rich and strange. In time, Kenneth would tell me it was my stamina that had won their respect, that he'd been impressed by my endurance: no matter how much "homework" he gave me—books he urged me to read, exercises he suggested I do, classic poems he told me to analyze so as to learn how they'd been structured—I did it all, and came back for more. "You may have been a pink ex-child star from a Sutton Place pink apartment with all but pink turds floating in the pink toilet," he once said, with characteristic off-putting charm, "but you loved poetry and dearly wanted to write it well. And you just refused to be stopped."

Refusing to be stopped seems to be a character flaw (and/or strength) of mine, one that aging already moderates and death will assuredly cure. While a blessing in certain circumstances, this tendency has been a curse in others. For example, during the fourteen laborious years, from 1970 to 1984, of compiling the anthology *Sisterhood Is Global,* the motto I hung above my desk was "Only she who attempts the absurd can achieve the impossible." Such doggedness qualifies as a form of obsession, and in a sense, one definition of talent could be the gift of a capacity for obsession. Still, this stubbornness, this fanatic belief that sheer *will* can see you through, can also be a form of hubris. It's beguiled me into staying too long in certain relationships better exited earlier. It's blinded me regarding people who lack (or are free of) the same capacity, so that I assume intolerantly they just aren't trying hard enough. On one occasion, it inspired me to keep driving nail after nail into a concrete wall (positive that if I could only do it *right* the shafts wouldn't buckle). "There is nothing you cannot be," Faith had said, "if you want it enough." The imprint had taken.

In the workshop period, something certainly was driving me on, despite secretarial workdays at Curtis Brown, nights and weekends spent rewriting drafts of poems and fighting with my mother, and periodic forays to an audition here or there because it was easier to just go and louse it up than wage another fight about not going. Meanwhile, I completed a verse play,

Their Own Country, a youthful but somewhat subversive work about what the three Magi really might have seen in the stable. To my ecstasy it actually ran for a week of performances at the Episcopal Church of the Ascension on lower Fifth Avenue, in a Christmas-season production directed by Warren Bayless, who was one of my Curtis Brown secretary buddies and a member of the church congregation.

During those months, I drew closer to Kenneth as a friend and confidante. In return for all I felt he was giving me, I was happy to be of use to him, too. He was writing plays during this period (probably why I monkey-saw, monkey-did too), and I organized several readings with actor acquaintances and myself participating, sent scripts to the few theater people I still knew, persuaded Cindy Degener at the office to take him on as a client. Faith didn't (as yet) mind my being in his company. He and his lover, Robert Phillips, the pianist and composer, would have me over for long, hospitable dinners, let me play with their cats Castor and Pollux, and sympathetically share their own horror stories at having fought and fled parental strictures. They solicited and enjoyed anecdotes of my working childhood, but seemed genuinely more interested in who I was becoming than in who I'd been. I was actually more at ease with Bob than with Kenneth; I sought Kenneth's approval too thirstily to be able to relax fully around him.

Bob was tall and dark, campy, temperamental but talented, and unashamedly omnivorous where men were concerned. This was back in the age of freewheeling pickups—the docks, parks, "meat-racks," and bathhouses—well before HIV/AIDS rudely woke the gay male community out of its denial into a brutal realization that casual sex could get you dead. Committed relationships had always existed among gay men, of course, but weren't all that respected or enduring (especially in metropolitan centers) until the epidemic's tragedies inspired a maturity affirming relationships more than passing fancies.

From the first, Kenneth gave off a sexuality different from Bob's. He talked openly about women of whom he'd been enamored, of having had several heterosexual affairs, and of wanting someday to father a child. I knew from his poetry that he was not a man to use words lightly, so I listened closely to what he said, listened at many levels of hearing. Given all the gay and bisexual men I'd known in show business, none of this seemed

particularly strange to me. I'd already developed a Galatea/Trilby attraction for and ambivalence toward him, casting him as my Pygmalion/Sven-
gali. I already loved his poetry, his intellect, his intensity. I loved everything
he stood for: rebellion against convention, refusal of simplistic definitions,
insistence on the centrality of art to human consciousness, and the
courage to be ironic yet lyrical. To me, Kenneth *was* poetry. It was a simple step from there to loving the man himself.

I've always confused my lovers with Art, God, or Revolution. Such
unfairly inflicted expectation has ensured their foreordained shortcoming
and my inevitable disappointment. But it's taken a while for me to comprehend this pattern. Back then, what I felt drawing me to Kenneth—
unlike what had drawn me to previous attractions—was at least rooted in
a healthy self-interest: he possessed knowledge I lusted to get near. (Perhaps had Faith let me go to college . . . but even so, it was the contents of
his brain I yearned for, which no courses in poetry could possibly have
equaled.) That my lust was perhaps more for his knowledge than for its
imperfect, simply human host seemed as irrelevant as the motivation for
his desire, which he candidly admitted was perhaps more concerned with
affirming his D. H. Lawrence-model bisexuality than for me as a specific
love object. Ours was a dance of denial as much as of courtship. We
flirted, awkwardly in person but skillfully in poems. We even discussed
having sex, but he was taken aback by my virginity and refused to be my
First. This was frustrating, since to my mind he was an ideal First, being
both a friend and a poet. I knew myself well enough to grasp that I wanted
to feel *some* surge of authentic love for the first person with whom I had
actual intercourse. During a brief trip to Puerto Rico the previous year,
when I'd managed to extricate myself from Faith's company, I'd maneuvered myself into bed with a sexy young man I'd just met—only to gaze
into his stranger's face, freak out, leap to the door, and, when he refused
to leave, yell that I had *both* syphilis and gonorrhea and he *must* go *now*.
Whether thinking me honest and infectious or lying and insane, the poor
guy fled, and I learned that my First needed to be at least a friend.

Kenneth was a good friend. That autumn, with his support, I finally
created the moment to tell my mother that I'd met Mates Morgenstern,
that I'd found him sadly not so very different from the man she'd
described to me back when I was thirteen, and that I still loved her

deeply—for having survived him and raised me. To my surprise, she handled it well. Perhaps she'd intuited it was inevitable. Or perhaps I'd found the right way of telling her—as proof of choosing her over him; as reassurance, not accusation. We talked late into the night, a good talk, about how his power felt lessened now that he was no longer a phantom. When I hazarded the subject of the lost year, there was a nervous moment. But Faith must have been weary of carrying her secret for so long. She told me the story quietly, as if it were not at all unusual, as if she were innocent of the hair-raising implications in what she was saying.

"When I got pregnant and then he broke the news about his fiancée waiting for him in England, I just didn't believe it. It was like a nightmare I couldn't wake up from. He said I had to have an abortion. But I'd known two girls—one from the lingerie shop and one before that, back in Atlanta—who'd died from abortions, and I was afraid. I knew how he talked about having sons, so I thought, well, what if it's a son? I thought, he'll dump his fiancée and marry me, that's what. We argued and fought, and then one day he moved out. Then Sally and Sophie and me, *we* argued and fought—to have the baby, not to have the baby. Sally and I insisted. So then we three decided Sally and I should go away, to Florida, to have it, so nobody in New York would know the details until after—because we all were sure he'd marry me in the end. That's why you were born in Lake Worth. I felt so sure you were going to be a boy that all your baby blankets were in blue, initialed RK—for Robin Kenneth. You were going to be named after my Papa Reuben, and I always liked the name Kenneth. Somebody told me once it meant 'knowledge' or 'wisdom' or something like that. Anyway, you were a girl—a gorgeous little girl. But I thought, she's so perfect her father will change his mind and want us after all. We came back north and arranged a meeting with him. It didn't go well. Sal and Soph took matters into their own hands. They said if he didn't marry me they'd make an anonymous report to the U.S. government that he was a spy. This was still wartime, remember, and though eventually he'd have been found not guilty, they'd have clapped him in prison for the duration and he'd have been damned uncomfortable, as well as probably denied a medical license forever. Sally said—I'll never forget it—she said, 'You're Austrian and educated and somehow *you* got away while all the other Jews got gassed? You think the U.S.A. is going to buy *that*?' Well, in the end, we made a deal. He'd marry me, give you a name, then I'd get a divorce right away. Which is what happened. But then I decided I didn't want his damned name for me *or* you, so I went to court and changed it, like I told you. As for the year . . . well, this wonderful doctor, Dr. Grady Brantley in Lake Worth—he delivered you—he understood that things were backwards, that the wedding had happened after the birth. It wasn't all that unusual in wartime, Robin. He understood that changing one little number, 1941 to 1942, would make all the difference. It would make the birth *follow* the marriage and divorce. It would make you legitimate, save you from a lifelong stigma. So he issued another birth certificate, and that's the one we've lived by. It wasn't until you had a career that the extra year came in handy for reasons we'd never planned, making you seem even smarter than you were. By then I was sure it was God, laughing together with us—you and me, Sal and Soph—at Mates."

Each revelation blasted open more deposits of mystery and melodrama. Altering legal documents. Medical collusion in a felonious action. Blackmail. Accusations of espionage. A shotgun marriage, an instant divorce. But *he* had said, "Your mother and I were never married"—so which of them was lying this time? Or didn't he consider a coerced brief marriage being married? But if *she* was lying, what other reasons could she have had for the falsified year? On the contrary, her story made sense—surreal sense, but sense. Then again, what if—

I gave up. It was a deliberate act of will. I drew a curtain over the mystery, feeling that the path of its pursuit wound through madness, and finally comprehending that no details in this saga would ever fall into a rational pattern with all versions in agreement. I didn't know then that most families have similar secrets, contradictory explanations, onion-skin layerings of truth, half-truth, untruth. I knew only that I was glad to have told my truth to my father, glad to have told the truth about meeting him to my mother, glad she had taken those truths in stride. I knew that beyond all our power struggles I loved this hurt and hurtful woman as strongly as a daughter could love a mother, and knew just as strongly that I was embarrassed and exhausted by the histrionic facts of my life. I wanted to be free from obsessing about them, to be born anew and entire, not Athena sprung whole from the forehead of Zeus, but myself sprung whole from my own brain and heart. I wanted to turn my back on their past and face my future—and I wanted that future to be literature, in part because I knew that good literature means the employment of language in the service of truth.

Since literature seemed incarnate in a particular man, whose name was to have been my own middle name, it seemed almost fated. When I told Kenneth Faith's story, he shared my sense of awe, as if this were an eerie sign that the universe had a sense of humor and a sense of wordplay. Those two halves of one name helped us to understand that we really did love one another.

So it came to pass that on a soft May evening in 1962, after a party at the loft of one of Kenneth's friends, a ballet dancer named Thatcher, Kenneth swept out the last of the partygoers—the boozy bikers and stoned, hallucinating Joffrey dancers and Rockettes—waved goodbye to Bob, who was departing entwined with an actor he'd picked up, sent Thatcher away from his own home, lit every votive candle in the place, put Dvořák's "New World" Symphony on the phonograph, and became my First.

Afterward, we emerged into the grey spring dawn, walking for hours through the still city, winding up on a bench in Stuyvesant Park, near Kenneth and Bob's place. There we sat, talking, as morning billowed into full light. All the street trees—including the puffy white callery pears—were in bloom. I remember that a beggar came shuffling by, and Kenneth, normally frugal with every cent, emptied his pockets and poured all his loose change, largesse, into the beggar's cupped hands.

"Here. And here, and here," he laughed. "I'm so rich today, I don't need money." He smiled at me. "You have such an air of *possibility* about you, Robin. It makes me believe *any*thing can happen."

"And you're a great writer. So we *can* make anything happen," I smiled back.

It was decidedly the road less taken. At the time, we didn't know that those two statements would define our behavior for the following two decades. Neither of us thought it would be more than an affair leading, hopefully, to a lifelong friendship. But the pace of events was about to quicken again.

Claiming that "I was just out for a long walk and to think" wouldn't cut it with my mother anymore than it had a year or so earlier regarding that late night out with Johnny; worse, this was *all* night and well into the day.

So I didn't even try. I told her the truth. Then I ducked in time for her solid brass bed-table clock to dent the wall instead of my skull. It was the first time she had ever acted to harm me physically.

"Go have your little shudder in bed then!" she screamed, her face swollen with crying at my betrayal. "Repeat the pattern. Ruin your life. *Ruin* it. I've done my best to save us, done everything I could. I failed. The rest is up to you."

She was correct in that at least. It was up to me.

Being liberated from my virginity seemed to have a galvanizing effect. Less than three weeks later, I found an apartment—a sixth-floor walk-up at 516 East 78th Street—plonked down the first month's rent and security, borrowed fifty dollars from Kenneth and Bob to tide me over until payday, and, sobbing as loudly as Faith, moved. All she would let me take as I staggered past our goggle-eyed elevator man and doorman was one shopping bag of clothes and toiletries, my portable typewriter, and a small bag of books. I borrowed a pot, a pan, some cutlery and dishes, one set of sheets, two towels, and a washcloth from my secretaries' circle buddies at work. Carl Stepney, one of that circle, had a sewing machine and stitched me up curtains. Jim Shue, another secretary, offered to give me an extra (three-quarter size) mattress he had. But he lived way over on the West Side so, balancing it on a little red wagon borrowed from one of *his* friends, Jim and I trundled it across town and through Central Park, convulsing passersby with the periodic collapses of mattress, wagon, and movers. We then lugged, panted, paused, and again lugged it up all six flights. It took us an entire Saturday. Ronnie Welsh, my one ex-kid-actor friend, helped me beg or steal wooden milk crates from neighborhood grocery stores; these became my bookshelves, stools, tables, and, with the addition of a plank found on the street, "desk." Kenneth, Bob, and the workshop poets instructed me in New York scavenge techniques: how to pick up good stuff that's been discarded on the street. First you had to find out which morning in your area the sanitation department accepted bulk items and furniture; then you knew that the previous night was when people would leave their old paraphernalia out on the sidewalk—everything from sofas to dish racks to air conditioners. There were basic rules. *Don't* take in anything upholstered (it can be alarmingly alive inside). *Do* pick up lamps (you can learn to rewire them), chairs (who cares about a missing rung?), and anything decent made of wood even if painted (you can strip it down to the grain). *Do* go foraging late, preferably with a friend to help carry. *Don't* be tempted by records; they're probably scratched beyond use. *Do* realize that file cabinets with drawers that still work are the best find of all. And so forth. With such advice and help, I made myself a home.

It was hardly homey. That apartment—a studio—had a tiny kitchen, a tinier bathroom, and one window overlooking a back court. It did have a ledge that passed for a balcony, on which I put out crumbs to seduce pigeons for company, until they began attacking my windows at night as if they were extras on leave from a Hitchcock set. The floor was unpolished concrete painted black, which meant that no matter how many times I mopped it, it showed every footprint. The neighborhood, just off the East River, was a bit unsavory but not unsafe. I didn't know that I wouldn't be spending a long time in this apartment, that I'd be there for only three months, in fact. But during that time I learned some crucial lessons.

I learned what I could do without. Because I'd left precipitately and still hadn't saved enough money to equip a home with fundamentals, I survived on a miserly budget. To save bus fare, I walked almost thirty blocks to work each day, then walked home again. I brought lunch to work, went without a visit to the morning coffee wagon, and regretfully declined lunches or drinks with the gang. I made as many phone calls as possible from the office, not from home. I pilfered toilet paper, paper towels, and bar soap from the ladies' room; stole pencils, pads, paper, and typewriter ribbons from the supply room. I confess I reveled in discovering I could do all this.

I also learned the value of planning ahead, learned in fact to become an inveterate maker of lists. The motivation was clear: once you got downstairs from that apartment to the street, you did *not* dash up again. Each flight was a cruel sixteen steps, with a brief landing in between. So you made damned sure you had the requisite sweater or umbrella *before* walking out your door. If you were proceeding on somewhere after work, you made certain you had with you whatever would be needed later—change of clothes, ticket, address—because there'd be no popping home blithely to change. On the return trip every day, you bought not groceries, but *a* grocery or two. *Only* one or two, because doing a full shopping was out of the question—for money reasons but also because with even two moderately heavy shopping bags the ascent required Sherpas.

Last, I learned I was capable of doing something I was sure I never would. I'd been sophomorically impressed by Albert Schweitzer's phrase "reverence for life"—and no doubt subliminally influenced by my mother's stories—so I had always been sure *I'd* never have an abortion. But I also harbored the fear that I'd repeat my mother's life and become pregnant with an unplanned child. So I'd taken care that the de-virginizing intercourse had occurred while I was having my period, under the misapprehension that this meant I'd be safe from conception. (It's amazing how little anybody knew—or would say—about women's bodies, only a scant three decades ago.) A few days after the loft night, I'd hied myself to a gynecologist recommended by one of the women at work, to get fitted for a diaphragm. Then, suddenly, once I moved to 78th Street, my usually clockwork period was late. Three days late. Five. A week late. I told no one. I spent one Sunday afternoon running up and down the stairs to my apartment twelve times, until I thought I'd pass out on my concrete floor, trying to bring on the period. Later, I took a long walk by myself along the river and stood leaning on the railing, watching the lights wink on across the water in Queens. Faced with Schweitzer plus reverence on the one hand and Faith's life plus reality on the other, I heard myself softly announce to the dusk, "If it turns out I'm pregnant, I'll have an abortion. I'll find out where and who. *Somehow.*"

It was another of those defining moments that take on such importance in retrospect, more so because there was no support in those days for reaching such a decision. I did confide in one of my pals at work, Anne Tedesco, who had found me the gynecologist, hoping she might also know of someone who could do such a procedure. (I'd already called the gynecologist, who had promptly hung up on me for having even asked her.) Anne was horrified, partly because of her Catholic background but also because she, like virtually every woman of that time, knew of somebody who had died on the table of a back-alley illegal abortionist, or died of complications thereafter. But I was not to be deterred. Finally, I managed (through show business, of course: a contact twice-removed via Ronnie Welsh) to obtain a phone number in Pennsylvania. The piece of paper sat for two days on my milk-crate nighttable, until I finally resolved to call the following morning. That night, like a reprieve, my period began.

The next time I saw Ken, I told him, assuming he'd be sympathetic, after the fact, about this close call. He was furious. How could I have *considered* an abortion? How could I have even *thought* of doing such a thing? How could I have not told him? I was baffled, but touched by his concern for me—until he added other outraged questions. Didn't I realize it was his child? How dare I destroy his child? We had a huge fight, during which I distinctly remember that I felt on shaky ethical grounds for daring to express such an unheard-of idea that what took place in my body was my concern and how to deal with it my choice. Ken and I didn't speak for about a week. Then, I vaguely recall due to Barbara's intervention, we patched it up. Many, many menstrual cycles later, in the early 1970s, the young feminist movement assembled signatures under a now famous statement: "I have had an illegal abortion." It was signed by hundreds of courageous women, well-known and lesser-known. I never signed it, because I was one of the luckier ones who had been "let off with a scare."

While I was nervously watching the calendar, the situation with my mother was in stasis. She was the last person in whom I would have confided, but the problem was solved anyway by noncommunication. Faith had refused to speak to me since I'd moved, hanging up the phone whenever I called for over a month. I stubbornly persisted. One day she relented, and we began to speak tentatively. Finally, to her credit, she accepted my invitation to dinner at my apartment. How insane it must have seemed to the woman, as she laboriously climbed those ninety-six steep steps, hauling with her, naturally, inappropriately de luxe housewarming gifts. A Wedgwood bowl. Irish linen dishtowels. Steak knives. I couldn't afford steak, but I remember that once she had recovered, greyfaced and gasping, from the trek upward, I cooked her chicken breasts with rosemary, garlic, and olive oil. She sat on my one rickety chair (I perched on another ever useful milk crate) and she tried to enthuse over "what interesting things could be done with the place." When she left, I walked her down to the street and saw her to a taxi. She hugged me, and we both teared up. Then I left base camp to mount the north face again.

That summer passed quickly. I loved to stroll around my new neighborhood, basking in almost anonymity, rarely being recognized except as a familiar customer at the laundromat, the A&P, the all-night deli, the Korean produce stand that sold cheap cut flowers. This is as good a place as any to confess to a lifelong, self-indulgent weakness for fresh flowers. I've gone without food on certain occasions in order to buy flowers or plants. One of the joys of now having a garden of my own is wandering through it early in the morning, steaming coffee mug in hand, while the dawn chorus is still celebrating its alleluias. That's the best time to notice what's begun to bud, what's blossomed overnight, what can be plucked from the cutting garden. As I write this, one of the last roses of summer, a homegrown Michele Meilland, drowses its garnet head languidly over the rim of a bud vase on my desk. Back during that summer of 1962, when I received the unexpected windfall of a ten-dollar check from a magazine accepting two of my poems, did I use it sensibly toward purchasing any one of the fifty items I so needed for my apartment? Of course not. The Korean stand had anemones on sale. I bought them all: two armfuls, fragrant splashes of black-centered red, purple, and blue petals nodding on slender loopy stems. I filled—damned right—the Wedgwood bowl with them, and spent all evening sitting looking at this spectacle of color, moving my one chair around for differing viewpoints, while I dined on five Saltine crackers.

It was a good summer. On July 4, Kenneth, Bob, a musician pal of Bob's named Franco Renzulli, Thatcher, and I all went to Coney Island, part of a sea of lemming-humanity trying to swim, bask, and watch fireworks. I noticed rather quickly (not that it was difficult to see) that Ken had a crush on Thatcher, who was possessed of a classic well-exercised dancer's body unfortunately accompanied by a classic under-exercised dancer's brain. But Thatcher claimed he was straight and Bob accepted Ken's affair with me, so hey, who was I to complain? I was more interested in being in touch with my freedom than with my feelings. Anyway, we were all being cronies together. Bob had to go out of town on some musical gig for a week and suggested I spend time "playing house" in his and Ken's apartment. Welcome to Bloomsbury, I thought!

During that week, I experienced firsthand what Bob referred to as Kenneth's "bull in the china-shops of the world tendencies": a refusal or inability to learn the most basic hypocrisies of polite social congress, and an absent-minded-professor air that caused Kenneth with running-joke regularity to drop vases, spill drinks, misplace tools, and lose eyeglasses, keys, and wallet—all the while insightfully holding forth on anything literary from "Beowulf" to Berryman. But none of that mattered. On the contrary, such awkwardness struck me as attractive: a working-class, boyish vulnerability that balanced out his ferocity on other fronts, a sort of Heathcliffean "unmannerly stableboy."

We had fun that summer. We knew enough artists and performers to cadge free tickets to concerts, poetry readings, Ailey and Joffrey ballets. We went to museums and to Shakespeare in Central Park, argued about literature, painting, sculpture, music. We drove across the Brooklyn Bridge in someone's borrowed convertible: top down, jug wine, hair in the wind, the works. Once, after Ken stayed over at my apartment, he walked me all the way to my office building, and we stood at the corner of Madison and 57th not wanting to separate even for a few hours; I was wearing a sleeveless blue linen shift, and he said I was beautiful. That summer I wrote lots of poems, made diligent love with Kenneth, and reconciled with Faith, who released more of my clothing and books to me. I went to work every weekday, but I didn't attend a single audition. I even learned to drive and got my license—with the real birthdate on it. I felt self-possessed, poised to start my life.

Then, one day in September, Kenneth phoned me at work. He was breathing rapidly. I remember I was standing by my desk, looking at my green-and-white-striped spider plant and absently pulling off a brown edge or two as we talked.

"Are you all right?" I said. "You sound breathless. What's the matter?"

"If I come uptown can you get off for a quick cup of coffee?"

"Well—yeah, sure, I guess so. I didn't take any lunchtime today, so— But what's up? Give me a clue, at least. Is something wrong?"

"It's—it's that . . . Bob just told me he's involved with somebody else. A conductor, who's also a pianist. You've met him. Franco Renzulli."

"Yes, but—you and Bob. I mean, you two are hardly exclusive or monogamous or . . . I mean, what's the—"

"This is different. It's not a fling. He says he loves Frank. He wants to live with him. He wants to spend their lives making music together as a duo-pianist team. He wants to compose work for Frank to conduct."

"Well, but—"

"He's in *love* with him. They have it all worked out. Bob wants to leave me. Don't you see?"

"Oh. Oh Kenneth. Oh, I'm so sorry. I—"

"So, I thought— what I mean is— what I wanted to ask you is— Robin, will you marry me?"

The woman I am now finds it an absolute astonishment that this conversation went the way it did.

But the woman I was then replied instantly, with no uncertainty, no hesitation, no backward glance.

"Yes. Unequivocally," I said.

Part
Two

TEN

. . . .

Alice in Bloomsbury

And whilst our souls negotiate there,
we like sepulchral statues lay; . . .
Love's mysteries in souls do grow,
but yet the body is his book.

—JOHN DONNE, "THE ECSTACY"

Nine days after he proposed, Kenneth and I were married.

Those were a busy nine days. Everyone we knew disapproved of this match, except of course for Bob, whose heart had its own reasons. All of Kenneth's gay friends, all his artist friends, all the radical intellectuals and bohemian types, flipped at the notion that he would (a) marry at all, (b) marry a woman, and (c) marry an only recently virginal former child actress ten years his junior. (Well, we *were* an odd couple.) In my circles, the assembly of forces arrayed against this marriage ranged from the workshop poets through my actor buddy Ronnie Welsh to my friends at work. Then there was my mother.

When I first tried to tell her, stammering as I led up to the announcement of my plans, she interrupted me.

"Honey, *what?* Are you sick? Are you pregnant? Were you robbed or mugged? Were you raped?"

"No, Mother, no. I'm fine. But—"

"If it's none of those things, then don't worry. Whatever it is, Snibbin, we'll see it through together."

Oh, how I knew this was something we would not see through together. Sure enough, once I managed to get the news out, the ensuing scene was so debilitating that it was all I could do to hold the discussion at Stage One ("Kenneth and I plan to get married") while cravenly avoiding Stage Two ("Imminently").

I hadn't yet made up my mind how or when to tell her *that,* though I did want her to be at the wedding. The truth is that I was still grappling with the concept of getting married, and so soon, since an engagement wasn't even discussed as an option. I apparently lacked the common sense to question why the schedule was being driven by the double urgencies of Bob's and Frank's desire to live together and Kenneth's desire not to live alone. Somehow, with every passing day, more decisions got made. We discussed eloping to Maryland, but opted instead to find someplace in New York with a pleasant setting but a civil or nondenominational ceremony (not as easy in 1962 as it is now). We went for blood tests, went to get the license, actually set a date. Then, just as I was about to break it to Faith, the matter was taken out of my hands by Anne Tedesco from my office. She'd met my mother once and liked her, so she called her to tattle on me, in hopes of stopping the onrushing ceremony. I was outraged at this betrayal of confidence by someone I'd regarded as my friend, livid that my mother's reach could stretch into the realm of my work relationships, and infuriated at yet another person's doing what she considered was best for me without consulting me. But I barely had time for indignation because the firework theatricals that burst forth from my mother concentrated the mind, as they say, wonderfully.

In tears, moans, and shouts, she and I Had At It—sometimes in whispered, hissed phone conversations from my office, as Faith was no respecter of workspace when her daughter's future was at stake. She roused both of my aunts, my agent, my managers, distant acquaintances, even former cast members from *Mama* to call me and denounce this marriage, all of them asking, "*What* are you *doing* to your *mother,* Robin?"

I ignored them. I attempted to convince her this was not about *her* but about *me*. Fatuously, I tried logic, reminding her of the days following my announcement about having gone to bed with Kenneth that past spring. I reminded her that she had threatened to throw him into jail for corrupting the morals of a minor—until I'd pointed out I could now prove I was no longer a minor; reminded her that she'd actually brought forth a dainty pearl-handled revolver and, to my horror, had begun brandishing it, threatening that he would damned well *marry* me or die. I reminded her that I hadn't *wanted* to get married *then*, although now was different. (I was on slippery footing here, a mere three months later, but she never paused long enough to notice.) I begged her to attend the wedding and be happy for me. But when she found she would not be able to stop me, denying me her presence was the one thing she could control. And probably, in her rage and grief, she felt that if she didn't witness it, the ceremony wouldn't really have taken place.

Meanwhile, Bob made plans to move in with Frank, and his shared household with Kenneth entered the property-division stage. Since they'd come to New York from Seattle together and had lived as a couple for seven years, this was not simple: grand piano to leave with Bob, upright piano to stay with Ken; scores leaving with Bob, books staying with Ken; dishes, linens, cookware, and cats in contention—while everyone strove to appear magnanimous and sensible. In the meantime, their friends came and went, and people were bursting into tears, embracing in corners, wiping their eyes, shaking their heads, and muttering, "I don't know. I just don't know . . ."

This was hardly the atmosphere I'd thought would surround my impending wedding. On the one hand, unlike most young women, I'd harbored no particular fantasies about the Day, the Dress, or the Ceremony, and had contentedly decided I didn't want to marry for a while or maybe never. On the other hand, I wasn't the only one who'd heard *"unequivocally"* issue from my lips with the knell-like absolutism of a prophecy by the Delphic oracle. I did feel that none of us quite knew what any of us were doing or why, but I also thought—after a lifetime of being told what to do and having to do it—that such uncertainty couldn't be worse and might be an improvement.

Being disowned and poor didn't help. It meant that "the bride's side" could pay for nothing. That was humiliating, since I knew I was hardly marrying into money, and especially since my childhood earnings were still paying rent for Faith at the posh East 57th Street apartment. But Ken's largesse-to-the-beggar-in-the-park impulse revived, and he not only footed the bill for the blood tests, license, ceremony, and flowers but volunteered to spring for a bash of a party afterward, back at his apartment, complete with champagne punch. He even offered to buy me a new dress for the wedding. But the one I wanted I couldn't tell him about, as it would have cost him a quarter of a year's salary teaching. I had spied it in the window of Bergdorf Goodman's: a burnt-sienna crushed-velvet evening gown with medieval slashed sleeves of deep bronze satin and a short, flared train. I envisioned myself in it, a walking resplendence of earth colors: my brown eyes glowing, autumnal flowers—burgundy mums, tawny asters, wheat stalks—twined in my sable greengold hair and bundled as a sheaf in my arms . . . Persephone on her triumphal procession toward winter. I settled instead for a dress I already owned—a knee-length, sleeveless, teal-blue velvet. But the flowers came true; we bought heaps for the party, and I assembled my bouquet from the same batch. I've kept a stalk of the wheat all these years.

Dickinson's "bustle in the house" takes place not only on the morning after death. Somehow, I missed only one day at work during all this frenzy, needing to call in sick after a flattening three-hour phone battle with Faith the previous night. Otherwise, I functioned. I weathered Ronnie Welsh's Noel Cowardice suicide attempt (he swallowed three bottles of aspirin, then immediately phoned me), rejected Anne Tedesco's apologies, asked Irene Petrovich to be my maid of honor instead of Anne, and reassured Edith Haggard (who had by now heard the rumors) that no, I didn't intend to take a honeymoon but yes, having the day off after the wedding *would* be pleasant, thank you very much. I still had so few furnishings at 78th Street that packing would be a minimal task. But I did insist on real wedding announcements, engraved on thick cream paper stock. I can't remember why. Was it because words on paper seemed solid, trustworthy, alone capable of making things real? Or was it a practical reason? Given my poverty and the depleted household into which I was moving, I know I was brazenly hoping for wedding gifts. Whatever the motivation, I managed to order the announcements, pay for them myself, address them, and send them out to everybody Ken and I knew—thanks to Curtis Brown's postal meter, not quite *de rigueur* for elegance but most helpful in the circumstances. Since there were no proud parents of the bride announcing anything, the text read,

MISS ROBIN MORGAN AND MR. KENNETH PITCHFORD

ARE HAPPY TO ANNOUNCE

THAT THEY ARE AT HOME

AS

MR. AND MRS. KENNETH PITCHFORD

109 THIRD AVENUE

NEW YORK 3, NEW YORK

Somewhere in the midst of all the rushing about, one night, alone in my short-lived apartment, I made time to write a letter to myself. I no longer kept a journal, but needed at such a moment to turn to the sanctuary of the page, for me the one reliable place of honesty, insight, peace. This letter fascinates me, for all it reveals about what I knew, and didn't know— and didn't know I knew. Do any of us ever really *hear* ourselves? My words were both prophetic and naive.

12 September 1962

So I am, after all, going to marry K. And for my own benefit, I want to put into words below what that—and the very living of my life entirely, which only really begins now—will entail:

I will learn to love him even as he loves me, from knowledge and not abstraction. I will use him to find more of myself, and be at his hand for the same purpose. I will not lie to him, nor deceive him, no matter what the cost. I will insist on mutual honesty between us, whatever it discloses. I will not be subject to his life or work, be beset upon by him or any other; neither will I ask that of him. I will assert my selfness, my work, my desires and hours, not at the cost of his but to bring about between us a separate wholeness, threatening neither, reinforcing both. I will not play the girl-child to his father, nor will I patronize him, emphasizing his impracticalities or awkwardness in the technicalities of this world. I will work toward becoming a woman rather than a wife, knowing that the latter need not include the former, but rather the former can with ease and a whole graciousness bring about the latter. I will remain me. I will fight all images that sprout between us of unconscious making. I will find the strength to be with him, or without him, as the case may be. I will try never to hurt him, within the bonds of loving or awareness. I will try to make him love me more each day, surprising his own limitations. I will not be overly dependent upon him, his potential as an artist, or his opinions—nor allow him to be tricked into leaning overly much on me. I will respect his actions all, his motives all, his ideas all, reserving that individual right of persons to differ.

I will survive my mother's hurt and horror, until such time as she can know me—and him—again. I will never stop a barrage of love toward her that must someday break her hatred and despair, and bring her to me. I will watch her always and be there when she needs me. I will find the strength and humor to cope with friends and acquaintances and their shock or disapproval. I will not let them touch me deeply, where I dwell, but will retain compassion, with action, toward those I care for. I will not be ashamed of what I am doing, but will compel acceptance on my own terms. I will not justify, excuse, explain, or plead. I am what I am, in pride and excitement.

I will follow him into any paths he chooses, however alien or dark, or blinding, and at the same time seek my own paths. I will respect myself and my work, alone and to his face. I will strive to enjoy his bed truthfully, his work critically, and our life, with all the endurance, passion, and honesty I, as a separate me, can bring to them.

And I will love him enough, and more. And that will make everything possible.

R.M.

The alarms raised by that vigilant twenty-one-year-old were startlingly on the mark. Her assumed earth-mother capacity for making everything possible through love was another matter altogether.

In any event, on the rainy, chilly Wednesday afternoon of September 19, 1962, I married Kenneth Pitchford in a nondenominational chapel way uptown at Riverside Church. Irene was my maid of honor, Bob was Kenneth's best man, and Ronnie insisted on coming along (to Kenneth's irritation), in hopes I might suddenly change my mind and require an escort to go someplace else. At the last minute, it seemed proper that I wear something on my head (a chapel, after all), but the only dressy head covering I owned was a lacey net square kerchief. Its inappropriate color made Bob jittery, but made me smile. Persephone was wed wearing a black veil.

We returned to Ken's (and for the time being still Bob's) apartment, where about forty friends—almost all *theirs*—were gathered for the party, hell-bent on making the best of a bad thing with style. I would be vacuuming up grains of rice for months to come, but there *were* wedding gifts, and toasts, and dancing to live piano music. Frank, deliriously happy at inheriting Bob, played for hours on end, and fortunately he had a repertoire that, unlike Bob's, wasn't snobbishly limited to "serious" music. Then Kenneth and I lugged flowers and leftover champagne back up to my apartment, where we'd set up camp for the next week or so, while Bob moved the last of his things out. Finally, during the first week of October, we moved back downtown and I entered my new home.

The apartment was one of those New York "finds" over which people gasp. I counted myself wildly fortunate that Frank hadn't wanted to live there with Bob, who had dibs on the place because he'd been the one who'd actually found it; luckily, Frank couldn't bear feeling he'd be the new partner moving into Manderley. But I—already an experienced enough Manhattan-apartment hunter to recognize a fabulous thing when I saw it—had no qualms about running into Rebecca's ghost or Mrs. Danforth's revenge. The rent was staggeringly low—$150 a month, gradually rising to the august sum of $300 over the next two decades—and the space was enormous. It was on lower Third Avenue between 13th and 14th streets—not quite the Bowery but almost—and the neighborhood, pre-gentrification, was fairly squalid. Across the street from Ken's building, the old vaudeville Variety Theater still flashed its original neon marquee, but had fallen on bad times and offered porn flicks; next door to it, the Faith and Hope Mission promised salvation and soup. The building itself was an early nineteenth-century two-window-wide row house now bereft of its row-mates, squeezed between taller, latter-day tenements. On the street floor was (still is, at this writing) an idiosyncratic herbal shop, later to become popular for its worldwide mail-order business: Kiehl's

Pharmacy, owned by the ancient, tottery Mr. Morse, who also owned the building. The second floor, pungent with dried herbs, was used by the pharmacy for storing inventory, although eventually we would colonize and rent it, too. The third and fourth floors constituted the apartment, a *duplex* of two full floor-throughs, each approximately sixty feet long by twenty feet wide. There were working fireplaces, exposed-brick walls, original wide-planked wood floors, and dormer windows peeking out from the eaves on the top floor. Part of the anguish of my mother and aunts was based on my moving to "a tenement slum" on lower Third Avenue—but if moving from Sutton Place to the Lower East Side was regarded as a step down by them, moving to this space from my six-flight walk-up concrete-floored cell was, to me, quite a coup.

If the good news about 109 Third Avenue—or as we called it for short, "109"—was the cheap rent, the bad news was that Mr. Morse did nothing whatsoever as a landlord except collect it. He'd originally rented the space to Bob and Ken because he hadn't wanted to bother fixing it up and he'd heard that "gay boys did that sort of thing well." He wasn't wrong. Over the years, they'd gradually supplied what basics had been lacking—replaced broken windows, installed radiators, repaired antiquated plumbing and wiring. But they'd divided up the space with each man having his own floor plus a shared space, so now—entering this status called Married Life—I was informed there was apparently more work to be done. Cheerfully game about it since I had absolutely no idea what renovations might entail, I stood ready to help with my clean blue jeans, T-shirt, new work gloves, and headscarf. Then, one Saturday soon after I'd moved in, Kenneth went up to the attic above the top floor, stomped his foot repeatedly through the plaster, and brought down the ceiling.

It was the beginning of what would be years of tearing out walls and ceilings one by one (then, in time, *building* other walls and ceilings), chipping plaster off the huge wood beams and then shellacking them to a glow, building more bookshelves, exposing more brick, opening yet another fireplace, building closets, and learning how to make one floor cozy whenever the other contained enough plaster rubble to qualify as bombed-out Berlin after World War II. I was never very good at any of this, except for being able to locate where Ken had last put down his hammer or screwdriver. But I was useful with the daily clean-up part, though my pulse would race when we had to make midnight forays to street trashcans at least three blocks distant, to dispose illegally of bags of rubble, since we couldn't afford cartage. Yet we managed somehow, returning home from our jobs every day and transforming ourselves into construction workers—by each evening's end a prematurely aged couple, muscles aching and hair and eyebrows white from plaster dust.

Kenneth had decided the previous winter to quit teaching at NYU, since otherwise he'd have had to pursue the loathsome doctorate more assiduously than he was willing to do, and he'd taken a job at Funk & Wagnalls, the publishing firm that produced dictionaries, synonymies, and other reference books. I was to continue for another year or so at Curtis Brown until Edith retired, at which point I would take up freelance work, as a manuscript reader for literary agents and publishing houses and, later, as a proofreader and copyeditor. Meanwhile, we settled into marriage.

As might have been anticipated, our version of matrimony was not your garden-variety wedded life. We had a vision of ourselves as modern-day Webbs—Sidney and Beatrice, the literary couple—"two typewriters clacking as one." Indeed, the first thing Kenneth built was a desk for me—a sanded and shellacked door laid across filing cabinets rescued from the street. I cherished my first real desk, but I wrote little during that first year or two, because right there in the middle of the literary world where I'd wanted so to be, I was busy turning myself into the Ideal American Wife.

I could try now to excuse my rush to domesticity in various ways. Not counting the three-month temporary residence, this was my first real home away from my mother, so I was flexing independence muscles. Furthermore, I "nest" by temperament. It was also apparent early on that the division of labor between Bob and Ken had not been so untraditional after all: Bob did most of the cooking and was always complaining about the infrequency or superficiality of Ken's housework, so that was an area I could slide right into with proprietary confidence—which Kenneth certainly didn't require but definitely didn't resist. Beyond those reasons, though, I suspect two others. I was a product of the 1950s, after all, barraged while growing up with images that defined any adult woman as a person wearing an apron—and I really, *really* longed to feel adult. It's also true that Wife was a new part, a challenging role to play well and at which to overachieve. For all these reasons, I threw myself into housewifery with

energetic insistence. Although the two men had employed a weekly cleaning woman, I took that work over myself. I scrubbed and soaked, polished,
mopped, and waxed so hard you'd have thought I must be scouring away
all vestiges of previous occupants. With my new kitchen utensils, now liberated from my one-pan-only recipes of 78th Street, I dove into cooking as
if the Aunt Sophie gene had suddenly become activated. (But not
sewing—never sewing: that was Faith's terrain.) I'm talking heavy-duty
cooking here. Coq au vin. Crown racks of lamb. Seafood crepes. Roast
Cornish hens stuffed with wild rice. Mandarin-orange and chocolate souf-
flés. Home-churned granita de café. And that was just for *us*. When we
entertained friends at dinner, I did something *really* fancy.

Poor Kenneth. His cholesterol levels, about which we were ignorant
back then, must have skyrocketed. He tried hard to be appreciative. But
at heart he'd wanted to be a vegetarian ever since he'd worked in an
Armour slaughterhouse and meatpacking plant to put himself through
school back in Minnesota. The man worshiped macaroni and cheese; he
loved soft edibles because his teeth gave him problems, and he adored his
working-class childhood's comfort-food casseroles with plain ingredients.
His favorite—"Ken's baked dish," the one thing he liked to cook himself—
consisted of pasta (usually rigatoni), onions, tomatoes, melted cheese,
and, in a grudging bow to the carnivores who surrounded him, crumbled
hamburger. It wasn't bad; the problem was that he only knew how to make
it in vast quantities in a massive army-mess pot that could have served as
a bathtub for a three-year-old child. Consequently, whenever he made the
baked dish it was for a party, or else we'd be eating it for weeks.

There *were* parties, though, and celebrations to show off the latest carpentry accomplishment, or how the upstairs looked as one impressive
peaked cathedral loft with all the walls down and the beams exposed
above ranked bays of bookshelves and our two imposing desks. We liked
being by ourselves but we also loved showing off, and friends were curious
voyeurs as to how this experiment was going. I admit we royally enjoyed
giving them something to talk about; it was fun being considered beyond
the pale by people who were rather outlandish themselves. But as the
years went on, that sense of fun would harden into a modus operandi that
adopted outrageousness as its standard. This was intensified by an Us vs.
Them attitude, a draw-the-wagons-in-a-circle-around-this-marriage

stance that was nowhere near as necessary or healthy as we pretended, even on those occasions when it may have seemed called for. Kenneth adopted a Promethean style: fist shaken in defiance at the gods. I tended more to identify with Sisyphus: rolling the stone up the mountain again and again in characteristic denial of gravity—a pretentious version of The Little Train That Could. In 1962, though, it really did feel like us against the world. When I look now at the photographs of us during that period, I see two people slightly stunned at their own accomplishment, at having flown so in the face of conventions both bourgeois and nouveau, at having stepped off the precipice into a void—two people who, as if caught by the camera in the act of falling, steal a glance at each other to see if maybe the other one knows what in hell we're actually doing here.

We were, at least briefly, "hot" in downtown artistic social circles. That meant loft parties where Andy Warhol would reel through with his blank stare, trailed by his vapid catamites; where the poet Anthony Hecht, whose work I so admired, would laugh, on my being presented to him, "But, my dear, women should *be* poems, not *write* them!" I backed off quietly, found the bathroom, and threw up in disgust. This reaction would become fairly common, an at-the-time-unrecognized sensible response to unswallowable crap. But it was the early 1960s. Acknowledgment of racism was only beginning to surface in general American society (including among so-called radical artists), consciousness about sexism was a long way off. On social occasions, Kenneth was lionized and I was introduced (if at all) as "Oh! And this is, um—Ken's, uh, wife." Now and then a charitable host might add, "She, uh, also writes." Then again, Kenneth had had a book of poems published, was working on a second, had published a novella, and was writing a novel. I'd had a few poems appear in literary journals and was wobbling uncertainly from apprentice to journeyman (sic). The word "sexism" didn't exist in my vocabulary. "Ego" did— but so did "humility."

The best social events were the salons of the composer Ned Rorem. Ned, who remains a friend to this day, and who was the longest-term "life witness" present at my fiftieth birthday party, lived in Greenwich Village then; this was long before his Pulitzer Prize, although he was already regarded as a major figure in American music and the preeminent composer of contemporary art songs. Kenneth and Ned were friends, and Ned had set some of Ken's poetry to music (the first time he chose one of *my* poems to set, I was certain I had Arrived). Because Ned set contemporary poets' work, knew and liked writers, and wrote essays and diaries himself, he bestrode both literary and musical society as well as gay and straight. There were usually two sets of guests at Ned's soirees, because of limited apartment space: those invited to dinner, and those invited to "join us for dessert and coffee after dinner." On different occasions, Kenneth and I revolved into one or the other of these groups. My mouth hung open no matter what was being forked into it, because you never knew whom you'd meet at Ned's. All you knew was that everyone except yourself would be madly clever, probably famous, *au courant*, and arch.

A youngish, erudite Susan Sontag, sitting in a corner defending the ideas behind her essay on "camp." Paul Goodman, whose success had come too late, bitterly denouncing anyone who had the misfortune to stray across his path. Allen Ginsberg, stoned out of his beard but the essence of sweetness to every man present (the younger the better) and coolly dismissive to the women. Caresse Crosby—with other luminaries from the Black Sun Press, a center for expatriates in Paris, where Ned had spent so many years—literally flipping her feather boa into the osso buco one night. The *Paris Review* crowd warily circling the *Chelsea Review* crowd. Frank O'Hara, usually surrounded by his own mini-circle of painters, poets, and hangers-on (including a barely-out-of-adolescence Stephen Holden, now music and theater critic for the *New York Times*). One night, O'Hara, John Ashbery, and Janet Flanner had a huge argument; I do wish I could recall what about. Elizabeth Hardwick (yet again re-separated from Robert Lowell) was a regular, as was Hortense Calisher, and both went out of their way to lessen what must have been my painfully obvious reticence in such glittering company. The poets Richard Howard and Howard Moss (then poetry editor of the *New Yorker*) were regulars, too. I first met Gore Vidal at one of Ned's evenings; he was especially cordial to me on god-knows-what grounds, a gesture I've not forgotten, and one we remind each other about in various greenrooms of TV studios around the United States, whenever we happen groggily to bump into one another during overlapping book tours. At Ned's I met Edward Albee (who was especially *not* cordial, to *any*body, but then who would be, living as he was with Bill Flanagan?), and David Windham, Paul and Jane Bowles, Jules

Feiffer, and James Dickey—all of whom, it must be said, were as normally boring in person as any other dinner guest you might find to your right or left. Writers, artists, and composers rarely talk about "Art," I learned. Everyone is too busy gossiping about lovers and ex-lovers, and carping about money problems, agents, publishers, gallery owners, conductors, and, most of all, reviewers.

The music world was represented even more impressively than the literary world. One night Alice Tully—yes, as in Lincoln Center's Alice Tully Hall—got piggily possessive over Ned's homemade orange cake. Eleanor Steber came by briefly another evening, croaking with a cold like any ordinary voice, and demanding hot tea "with lods of lebon, blease." Eugene Istomin must have said *some*thing, primarily to the musicians perhaps, but I only remember him chewing blissfully. Ned's circle of composer mentors/rivals/friends extended from Aaron Copland through David Amram and Gian Carlo Menotti to Samuel Barber and David Diamond. Diamond surprised us by being actively supportive of Kenneth, me, and our marriage; David had been for years in a relationship with a married man, was godfather to his lover's children and would in time put them all through school—so this "transcending of petty sexual categories by carrying a passport stamped mere Human," as he put it, was nothing new to him. Meanwhile, Virgil Thomson would be pontificating from the most comfortable armchair about every subject, whether he knew anything about it or not a sort of chubbier Peter Lorre bestowing judgmental aphorisms in a high, petulant wheeze. But everything froze when the Entrance was made: the electric presence of a composer-conductor at the height of his fame (though not of his powers), arriving freshly damp from some podium, French-kissing *every*one—male *and* female, friend *and* stranger—and requiring a towel *instantly* because "Oh God I'm still *so* sweated up!": Leonard Bernstein or, simply, "Lenny."

And in the center, there was Ned himself—blessed with both beauty and talent, basking in the certainty that every man in the room wanted (or had already had) him, and every woman in the room believed *she* could turn him straight (that is, if *she* were). Ned, radiating rampant egotism but always managing to get his work done nonetheless, dripping with sophisticated ennui yet touchingly inclusive of his parents, lifelong Quakers who remained political activists into their eighties. I was nervous and excited about going to these soirees, and some evenings I'd spend most of the time in the kitchen chatting with whoever was Ned's always unfamous live-in lover of the moment. But I shyly liked Ned. He was hard *not* to like. His sometimes studied superficiality has always masked genuine depth (a refreshing switch on the usual), and he was/is a kind man who, unlike some others in those circles, has never hated women. Certainly he found my acting background fascinating (as, to my unease, did many of the literati, once word leaked out—certainly not from me). But he knew I was en route to another identity and respected that. He never treated me as Kenneth's appendage, regarding me as a serious poet well before my first book of poems came out. Years later, he would urge me to apply for a residency at Yaddo, the arts colony, and offer to stand as my recommender. But Ned, who like Colette has never made the mistake of trivializing vanity, once also startled me by announcing to a gathering at his home that he believed "Robin is one of the great beauties of our time." Naturally I knew then we'd be friends for life, despite my awareness of the obvious fact that I was not a great beauty and never would be. Mostly, I was so thankful that Ned neither patronized nor marginalized me (not for *him* the "She's, uh, also . . ." introduction). He set a generous standard I've tried to follow myself with younger artists over the years.

Kenneth never patronized or marginalized his new wife the also-poet either. On the contrary, he defended me with flaring-nostril gallantry and was shocked at the bigotry of most of his male peers. (We'd both simplistically assumed that gay male artists would somehow be more welcoming to a woman than would their straight brothers. I now find this notion side-splitting.) Ken, especially during the first years of our marriage, was extremely influential on my writing, and it flowered with his support, patience, and humor. Draft after draft of my poems would improve with the aid of his keen eye and ear, and his voluminous knowledge of poetry. I was euphoric when he would admit to being impressed by a line or stanza of mine. Bliss was it to be critiqued, but to be *praised* was very heaven.

Several years later, we would go on a trip to Moorhead, Minnesota, and to Minneapolis, to visit his birthplace, childhood friends, and the teachers who had influenced him as a young adult, and then on to Seattle, where his family had moved, so I could meet his parents and older sister, Norma. At each stop, poetry readings had been arranged for the returning prodigal son—who insisted they be turned into joint readings for both of us. I appreciated this hugely, since my work was just beginning to come into its own and his was already established. (Not that being established made sufficient difference for the writer who was a woman in those days.[1] I recall attending a joint reading at the 92nd Street YMHA in New York, where the prize-winning poet Isabella Gardner came onstage quickly reassuring the audience that she was "merely the brief curtain-raiser for the one you *really* came to hear, my husband, Allen Tate.") Of course, every couple manages to believe, "*We* will be *different*," and I was grateful to Kenneth because I was living in a state of aesthetic excitement. Daily life had become a perpetual poetry workshop.

Nightly life was different. Here, dear reader, we draw a veil across certain specific memories. Not to consign them to the total privacy some would say they warrant, because the truth is they've already been bled across many pages (Kenneth's *and* mine) as subject matter, explicitly in poems and implicitly in prose—neither the first nor the last time writers have mined their lives to fuel their work. But anyone famished for graphic details must read elsewhere to find them. Here a few facts must suffice, and those only because they are unavoidably central to the story. These facts are simple enough, though the attempt to put down even the barest outline of them, and to do so without blame, remains complex.

Kenneth's crush on Thatcher was not a crush. He was in love with him, for a while perhaps obsessed with him, and further seduced by Thatcher's casting him in the role of intellectual guru (as, in truth, *I* had also done). Thatcher's sexual games enjoyed flirting with Ken's adoration, but for physical intimacy he required the additional presence of a woman so as to comfort himself that he wasn't godforbid "queer." I, meanwhile, had let myself be convinced that I knew nothing about my own desires and nothing about sex, despite those heated adolescent encounters that had stopped short of the "real" thing. I was less than six months out of literal

---

[1] In his book *Partisans: Marriage, Politics, and Betrayal Among the New York Intellectuals* (Simon & Schuster, 1999), David Laskin charts the standard use and abuse of Mary McCarthy, Jean Stafford, Caroline Gordon, Diana Trilling, and other women writers of the period at the hands of (respectively and sometimes revolvingly) Philip Rahv, Edmund Wilson, Robert Lowell, Allen Tate, Lionel Trilling, and their brotherhood.

virginhood, too, and curious, and pathetically more eager to be pleasing than to be pleased.

So the Ideal American Girl bought into every sexual myth the guys could fling at me—about Bloomsbury, sexual liberation, not being a puritan; about keep-on-doing-what-you-don't-like-because-the-more-you-do-it-the-more-you'll-like-it; about D. H. Lawrence's ideal quartet (two women, two men, all possible sexual permutations). I never questioned *whose* needs and self-interest these models served.

The first threesome was only two months and a day after Persephone embarked on her stately black-veiled journey to wed her chosen netherworld lord. It was followed by encores, and by foursomes, and by various numerical combinations with other people (always with Kenneth present)—ordeals my memory still can neither purge itself of nor fully grasp. I know I partly dissociated my consciousness in order to survive them, an attempt to compartmentalize and contain the experience of violation. It hadn't struck me that there would be such an exorbitant cost to this brand of "free love," one that would beggar my emotions for years to come. I did understand I was jealous of Thatcher in a way I'd not been of Bob, and in time that intensified to a loathing for his grinning ignorance, the way he treated his chorus-girl dates, the sexual power he knew he held over Ken. To me, my husband's Greek ephebe was a male dumb blond.

But hadn't I married an openly gay man with complete knowledge and acceptance? Hadn't we often discussed "pansexuality" as a goal for being "truly human"? (Had bisexuality seemed too limited or what?) Hadn't I insisted that I lose my virginity to Kenneth, even when he was reluctant to be my deflowerer? Hadn't I, for that matter, then done what any good 1950s girl was raised to do: marry the first man I went to bed with? Hadn't I known, after all, what I was getting into? (Well, yes and no. That's a book in itself, one I intend never to write.) More to the point, I was now *in* this situation—so what to do?

The reply came resonating up from a place so deep in me I'd forgotten who'd put it there: *Wasn't I a competitor?* If I was facing the avant-garde version of keeping up with the Joneses, by god *I'd* show 'em. Sexually, I was desolate. My sin, if such, in this was never lust. But pride? Arrogance? Oh yes. *I* could handle it, *I* could be the ideal American *swinger* if necessary. *I* could be *"anything anybody wanted me to be"*—except that I still wasn't even *one* of the people doing the defining of who this latest-model Galatea would become.

It would take me almost four years of self-loathing, bouts of nausea, mysterious hives, eyelid twitches, nightmares, writing poems that were trying to tell me what I refused to acknowledge I knew, and other unconscious acts of resistance, until one evening, as Kenneth and I stood in the kitchen washing and drying dishes together, I said quietly,

"I never want to have group sex again, Kenny. I hate it. I feel that's my failure, but it's the truth. I believe in Lawrence's ideal and all that. Really. It's just that I'm not up to it. I don't want other men—or other women. I don't want to go to bed with people you choose for me. I don't even want to choose other people for myself. Maybe I'm hopelessly heterosexual. But I just want you. I want our marriage. I don't want my limitations to crimp your style, though. Monogamy was never part of our bargain, I know. So you're free to sleep with whomever you like, and I'll still love you and still be your wife. I hope you can accept that. I'm sorry, I can't do the other. I *won't* do it, not anymore."

I spoke calmly, but I was trembling so much I was afraid I'd drop the soapy pottery bowl in my hands. I was terrified of losing the marriage but even more terrified of losing my mind if we continued as we had been. I wonder, now, where the courage came from. Utter desperation, probably, because there was in our social world no external validation for my "prudery"—though some years later, as feminism trickled into and then flooded all our lives, one of the first hypocrisies to be exposed was the "sexual revolution" that had happened for men but had exploited women. Today a friend, woman *or* man, might cry out to that young wife washing dishes, "What *were* you, an emotional masochist, apologizing for *your* limitations? Why in hell didn't you say NO and just tell him to *stuff* it?!"

Today is not 1962. I knew no such friend then, and that kind of counsel would have come only from people who hated sex, not people who hated sexism. One barometer of how profoundly this consciousness has changed all our lives—including the lives of those who dismiss it, disown it, or take it for granted—is how difficult it is today even to conceive of the isolation, the self-condemnation, the feelings of madness, despair, and dread inherent in such an individual act of ungainly valor as I attempted that precarious evening. In time, Kenneth would try to understand and try

to take responsibility for his part in this small domestic tragedy, asking forgiveness for and from himself. I gave it gladly, even if neither of us yet
understood that something had been permanently shattered in me, and
even if I was as yet unable to forgive myself for what felt like collaboration
in my own debasement.

Today my heart can finally go out to that young woman who had already
spent her few paltry No's on her mother in order to come as far as she had,
and who had so longed to shower her husband-liberator with a cornucopia
of Yesses. Today I can forgive and even respect her, not for being a victim
but for refusing to remain one, for standing alone as so many women of my
generation had to, literally shaking with the intensity of trying to bite out
those words.

Kenneth seemed shocked and confused: "But if you didn't *like* it, why'd
you do it, Rob?" And I was too much the ingenue to challenge his reaction
as disingenuous.

But he said he'd accept my decision regarding my own behavior. He
even chuckled and candidly admitted to being flattered by it. Indeed, in
flight from one (modernist) double standard of sexual practice, I had
taken refuge in another (traditionalist) double standard. My proscription,
being focused solely on *my* actions, wouldn't limit his behavior—except
possibly with Thatcher, who was beginning to show tin patches under the
golden-boy plating anyway. Still, Thatcher stuck around for years, sometimes managing to be sexually available even without the cover of a
woman. But Thatcher, it would turn out, was merely Charon rowing the
boat in a general direction.

I had no way of knowing then that my own capacity for sexual passion
would be hibernating through a very long winter. One of life's questionable little mercies is that you don't miss what you haven't had, and I settled like so many others into a routine of joyless but usually amicable
lovemaking (helped along by my active fantasy life), thinking, "Well, that's
just marriage," while grieving guiltily. I knew that such pedestrian physi-
cality was a great disappointment to Kenneth, too, though he at least
enjoyed alternatives. But like me he'd co-cherished a romantic vision of us
more in the impassioned mode of Barrett and Browning than in the discreet arrangement of Virginia and Leonard, so each of us mourned the

same loss with a separate grief. Over the years, we would both come to assume that—as he lamented and I agreed—"Robin is just not a very sensual person." Neither of us noticed that this verdict conflicted oddly with my lust for backrubs, garlic homefries, Schumann, bubble baths, sueded silk, winter beaches, and a thousand other sensualities modest or major.

We simply tried to do our best. For us, this meant turning it all into poetry. It's a fair question to ask if we had lived this drama in the first place in order to provide ourselves with subject matter, and I wouldn't put it past artists to do so. (This may have been a sub-agenda of the original Bloomsbury, come to think of it.) But in truth I don't think we would have been quite so brutish or stupid.

When my first book of poems, *Monster,* came out in 1972, it would be both celebrated and denounced for its "rabid" feminist poems, some of which, like the title poem and "The Invisible Woman," were fated to become poetry-anthology staples as well as instant classics with women; lines from these poems showed up on T-shirts, stationery, bumper stickers, and picket signs. Other poems, like "Arraignment"—which accused Ted Hughes of intentionally causing the death of Sylvia Plath—became causes célèbres and/or scandals in their own right, about which more later. But what got noticed less or not at all, yet what I now find most moving, are the poems at the beginning of that collection: tightly crafted poems (perhaps too much so) on which I'd been working well before the kitchen announcement and which I continued to write over the following five or six years. It amazes me now that I could so effectively deny the depth of my pain by convincing myself I was transcending it.

In such poems as "The Improvisers," "Twins," and especially "War Games: A Mescaline Quartet," my flat-out rage and anguish at our sexual predicament are unmistakably clear. "Static," "The Invisible Woman," and "Revolucinations" read like smuggled-out notes calling for help from a sensibility believing itself at the edge of breakdown. "Annunciation" reeks of displaced fury, false militance, and the familiar earth-mother stance— in this case protecting and defending Kenneth's sexuality. "Rendez-Vous" and "Quotations from Charwoman Me" resonate with longing for what might have been "if only." And "Satellite" is a shocker. The identification with other women, including Plath, erupts here for the first time. The sexual damage is openly articulated:

> Effortlessly faithful
> I wax toward curves he charts himself
> for straying. I couldn't care more. No woman, either, smiles back
> sleeping in my arms. Not even
> I—not now—lie there. He has no rivals.

Yet "Satellite" manages to connect the sexual distress with everyday life (where playing superhousewife had clearly lost its allure), and in a bitterly ironic tone tries to imagine a politics that didn't yet exist:

> "We are equal," he says and says. I will write
> my poems in indelible ink on the laundry then
> while lost buttons roll where green-marbled meat
> molds books unfinished, unvacuumed ovaries, self-pity.
> Women ought to be born one-breasted or male
> or mindless. "We are equal," he says. We find me wanting.

It makes me wonder if I ever bothered to read—to myself, that is, not just aloud to others—what I'd written. This same poem begins with the line "I wonder if I hate him yet" and ends,

> Who set me orbiting this bed?
> My two escapes: to kneel before the oven
> or hang his wrung-out love to dry,
> each leaving these windows unwashed of that moon—unless
> I turn to rouse his sleepless fear
> with mine. I wonder if he hates me yet.

The answer was probably yes.

Ken meanwhile had of course begun writing his side of the story—a story of his own fears, longing, guilt, anger, conflicting selves. But there was a double catch to all this revelation. First, our refusal to settle for a mere confessional mode, trying instead to transform our subjective truths, through craft's crucible, into poetry, felt like a joint triumph of our circumstance—one so strong it might be capable of transforming *us*. Second, given our aesthetic ethics and mutual loyalty to each other's work, we each insisted that the other's poems be published, no matter how discomfiting. That's easy to call crazy but hard not to admire. Such a principled stand was one reason we stayed together. This was our way of turning the sorrow inward into art, and simultaneously turning outward to face the world in a united, brazen defense of our choices.

Kenneth, I came to realize, had actually had very little sexual experience with women; in me he faced what was for him uncharted territory. (Well might we ask, "Then what excuse do *heterosexual* men have?" Not until I was six months into my first consciousness-raising group did I realize the women there were enduring almost identical frustrations with their husbands and boyfriends, none of whom were gay.) But while Kenneth's brain and soul were those of a brave cartographer, his heart was homebound to the loves and lusts of the terrain he'd known lifelong.

And I? I also had a familiar terrain on which I ran true to form: I refused to be stopped. (Ned nailed it in his *Nantucket Diary*: "Robin finds what she seeks, whether it's there or not.") Leaving the marriage was out of the question. It would be tantamount to giving up. It might also mean Faith had been correct. And I was haunted by a skill that had nothing to do with writing poetry. "You can do this," I told myself. "You're an actor. You can do this *well*."

Such neurotic reasons for staying were obvious. But there's something else, and it mustn't be denied or discounted. The ferocity of Kenneth's spirit, authenticity of his talent, and breadth of his intellect were real, and absolutely lovely—and I was not a fool for choosing, as I did a few years later, to mingle my chromosomes with his; that was, in fact, a *wise* decision. Besides, I still *loved* him: Kenneth the poet, Ken the friend, Kenny the Minnesota kid who laughingly dismissed the New York cold that first winter of our discontent, who showed me how to make snow angels in Stuyvesant Park, who brought me hot chocolate while I thawed out afterward in front of the crackling hearthfire of the home we'd created with our own hands.

So fifteen more years would have to pass before I'd be willing to discover that what I was sure was my whole life was after all merely a phase of it. I wouldn't realize for all those years, and wouldn't admit for even longer, that there was another reason I refused to be stopped: I still believed in perfection, in *willing* things to be perfect, in insisting I could love enough, bear enough, do enough, to *be* perfect myself—because then surely I would be loved. It never dawned on me that fallibility is what's lovable.

ELEVEN

Revolucinations

The revolution must be ongoing and permanent.
— MAO TSE-TUNG

*D*on't panic. I'm not given to quoting Mao, and haven't for more than thirty years. Even then, I usually restricted myself to the tasted-of-the-pear bit, which, though somewhat Garden of Eden for my taste, at least suggested a concrete image: socialism with a human face might leave little cadre tooth marks in a Bosc. Did you know that Mao—along with Castro, Guevara, and Quaddafi—considered himself a poet, and that they all have written perfectly awful poetry? As bad as Jimmy Carter's, which *is* impressive. It's tempting to wonder if they settled for political power because they couldn't get published; what's a state publishing house, after all, but a vanity press writ large?

Still, the visionary old tyrant or his "Quotations of" staff writers had a point in that statement I've used as an epigraph above. It's like a rule of entropy: whatever seems fresh and new will get crusted over with amazing rapidity, until the original content ossifies into something almost wholly surface. Human curiosity yearns to discover the unfamiliar, but human attention span is embarrassingly short. We bore easily. Having discovered something, we frequently dismiss it: politics become co-opted, enlightenment dwindles to ritual, art gets banalized, creativity commercialized. But that necessitates reinvention: a new thesis, antithesis, synthesis; a fresh turn of the wheel. Or the screw.

I've just relearned the obvious again because I've been trying to write this damned chapter for weeks. The problem? We were now up to the mid-1960s, so politics had officially clambered into the memoir, excreting rhetoric in its wake like a slug trails slime—many words ending in *-ism* and *-tion*. Furthermore, as draft after draft emerged—each more awesomely dull than the next—despite all my efforts to focus on the personal, each draft sounded ominously *familiar*, like a codified set-piece, the subject matter already tackled before, many times. In fact, it *has* been—in my poems, fiction, essays, and book-length works of "feminist theory" (meaning attempts to demonstrate with the facts of our lives answers to that dumb Freudian question "What is it women really want?").

There truly is a limit to how many times and ways you can say something, no matter how inventive you tell yourself you are. Even a summary is preferable to another repetition. This way the disinterested reader will be spared, and the interested reader can find the information elsewhere easily enough. Consequently, we now pause for a (*brief!*) aside:

"And Then I Wrote..."

My introductions to both anthologies, *Sisterhood Is Powerful* and *Sisterhood Is Global,* are studded with personal anecdotes about the impact feminist consciousness (domestic and international) made in my life.

Going Too Far focused on my earlier activism in the so-called New Left and the beginnings of the "women's liberation movement." There I wrote at length about the influence of that politics on my marriage, comparing "B.C." (Before Consciousness) ways in which we had communicated with later ones—which at the time seemed fresh and hugely helpful, even if we did couch many of them in the political jargon we called "being in struggle." I looked at how the rhetoric of the period corrupted many of us who worked with words, how in order to write for the so-called underground media that we deemed so necessary, we were pressured to sacrifice what verbal or literary skills we possessed to the Marxian gibberish of the Left and the hippie gobbledygook of the counterculture, which in turn—as

Orwell knew well—affected our thinking itself. I sniped, for instance, at what I termed Failure Vanguardism: the then trendy but unadmitted notion that if your political project fizzled, your constituency ignored you, and your personal attitude was sneeringly more-radical-than-thou, you were obviously a Revolutionary—but if you actually *succeeded* in any of those areas, you had sold out and were a Running Dog Capitalist Swine. (Not only was this patently unfair to puppies and piglets, but the purism was *literally* terminal: imprisoned was preferable to free; life sentence had more cachet than felony; corpsehood had status in the most enviable vanguard of all.) In *GTF* I also wrote about my fleeting fantasy of building feminist "basic training" guerrilla camps (an idea that luckily died before Ramba could be born and buckle on her weaponry). Last, attempting to have form follow function, I stirred all this personal-life-plus-political-analysis eclecticism together in a comic verse play at the book's end, a somewhat wild exegesis on "metaphysical feminism."

In *The Anatomy of Freedom* I explored reasons underlying what I named the New Left's "ejaculatory tactics," unacknowledged masculinist agendas that corroded its vision and diminished its constituency to reflect finally only its own entrenched leadership: middle-class, young, straight, pale males who could afford to preach downward mobility since they had the option of re-elevating themselves with a single collect-call home. In writing about the personal lessons as well as the organizing techniques gleaned from that experience, I suggested that advanced theoretical physics could constitute a witty metaphor for sophisticated feminist politics, parsing the physics as well as the politics. But I grounded the abstractions by writing about my own body (and flesh loathing), sex (and fantasies), dreams, the politics of aging, and the possibility of "a good death." I wrote about the marriage there, too, about the nonverbal code between a wife and husband that neither admits to but each continually transmits; "The Marriage Map" section tracks what happens when the tsunami of feminism hits and they both think No Problem! Why, We'll Be A Liberated Couple!

Dry Your Smile was a quasi-autobiographical novel, so what do you *think* I wrote about?

In *The Demon Lover*, I revealed the period of my pre-feminist involvement with small, militant individuals and groups (predating but overlapping with the Weather Underground period): the intoxicating drama of living on the edge as well the nausea of fear that permeated daily life, the bitter fights over making warning calls after incendiary devices had been placed in buildings (the women wanted to place calls, the men considered such concerns bleeding-heart sentimentality). That book, subtitled "On the Sexuality of Terrorism," began as an attempt to fathom the process of what had been my personal descent into political violence and the struggle to break free of those tactics—which I was lucky enough to do, thus managing not to wind up, like many of my colleagues, underground, in prison, or dead. This personal exploration of violence—its odd seductiveness, rewards, demands, and despondencies—grew into a study of women and global terror, yet returned repeatedly to the autobiographical. That forms the premise of the entire book, so to summarize it is no more feasible than repainting a mural as a miniature.

For the essays collected as *The Word of a Woman*, I assembled the unabashedly nonobjective "participatory journalism" I'd done for mainstream as well as alternative media from the mid-1960s through the mid-1990s, with contextual commentary—from my days of Leftist-defined priorities and the "women's liberation" early years through my becoming a feminist, the mother of a son, an international activist, and the partner of another woman.

As for the six books of poems—well, the *real* story is in the poems . . .

All of which is to say, in other (so as to avoid the same) words:

Been there. Wrote that.

"But I Digress . . ."

You see the problem. This period in the memoir has already been written and published, years ago. All that's left of the pear is the core.

Well, let's look at that, then, because it *is* fair to wonder *why* I mined my life for the ore of subject matter and drafted its details into political service.

Partly, I believed that such explorations into the impact of politics on my life (and the reverse) were required by the essence of the politics themselves, feminism in particular. It was an experiential essence, so it invited, even demanded, a reaching out to others, mostly but not exclusively to women, not only through words on the page but through a willingness to risk exposing one's private realities (plus an equal or greater commitment to learning others' realities). I'm not sorry I took that risk. I admit to being a romantic, but frankly, I also think it's *sensible* to trust politics rooted in experience, reality, and passion more than those based on some central-committee-devised abstract theoretical blather, or those emanating from certain post-commonsense academics too busy deconstructing tropes to go on a march for reproductive rights.

But that might not be the whole story. Perhaps I was hoisted by my own petard: that phrase "the personal is political" returning to stalk what unfamiliar privacy I'd managed to achieve as an adult. Or possibly it was recurring egotism, albeit in a benign form, a gambit to remain onstage but through a volunteerism of self this time pressed into service to illumine a political point. Likely it was a bit of all of the above. Mostly, it was just what *writers* do.[1]

In any event, one thing is bracingly clear on having plowed through this chapter's earlier drafts of stale epiphanies: if I were to be bored writing it (again), then reading it would have put you in a coma.

So. We'll try an entirely different approach. I'd *really* like to pull this off as a sonnet sequence or a farcical playlet, but they'd never let me get away with it. However, I promise you that whatever follows will *not* be:

(1) A chronicle—personal or otherwise—of the New Left, civil rights movement, anti-war movement, counterculture, or Summer of Love.

---

[1] Of the fortuitous explosion of feminist books at the start of this contemporary wave in the United States, almost all were authored by women who had never considered themselves serious writers: psychologists, academics, visual artists, theologians, attorneys, and so on, with one or two sometimes-journalist types thrown in for good measure. I can no longer count how many times these otherwise brave women have expressed shock (sometimes admiringly, sometimes derisively) at the "personal" and "intense" quality of my writing—as in "You expose your own life so! How *can* you make yourself so vulnerable?" Only now do I realize that such reactions might have been based on a simple lack of understanding about the basic vocation that for me predated and transcended even the imperative of the politics themselves. To me, the question would be "How can I *not* draw from my own life?" This is what writers *do*.

(2) A history—political or otherwise—of "women's liberation," contemporary feminism, the Women's Movement, or "gender theory."[2]

(3) A sensationalistic confession, personal or political, listing details of the illegal political actions ("armed propaganda," we called it) I did—or revealing when, where, and with whom.

These last are delineated at some length, only mildly disguised, in *The Demon Lover*. I could write—carefully—about them there, because by the time I was working on that book (published in 1989), the period fixed by the statute of limitations for incrimination regarding certain acts had lapsed; regarding some other acts, it's still not up. Moreover, unlike some militants of the Sixties and Seventies who in their zealous recantations veered so far Rightward they chose to volunteer colleagues' identities in an orgy of confessional writing, I won't name names. There were actions I took that not even Kenneth knew about, but I don't intend to endanger those who did know, either—even persons I no longer respect or trust, people with whom I wouldn't now stoop to wire a woofer or tweeter, let alone anything incendiary.

In general, from here on in we encounter another challenge, which a traditional memoirist would probably not admit: How can I tell the truth without ruining my credibility? Unlike the majority of souls who populated the first part of this memoir, most of the persons in this part are *alive*. What's more, they have lawyers. Many are friends—the people, not the

---

[2]See? *Damnably* hard to resist. Along with Coca-Cola, Kentucky Fried Chicken, and McDonald's, the U.S. infatuation with and export of "gender" is at this writing wildly popular in those geopolitical areas of the global Women's Movement where people clamor with equal ferocity to imitate the United States while denouncing its imperialism. That is to say, "gender" is popular in policy and academic circles—as opposed to the populace of those countries, where average people, in their varying languages, still relate to the concept of "women." I could inveigh at length against the political manipulation inherent in the practice of replacing "women," "women's studies," "sexism," "male supremacy," etc. with the bland, obfuscating, and inaccurate idea and word "gender." As someone who cares about the precision of language, I could also fulminate against the widespread misapplication of the word "gender," even by well-meaning persons who innocently adopt this grafted-on word without fully grasping its implications. But I'll restrain myself, except to note that what Coke does to teeth and KFC/Big Macs do to cholesterol levels, "gender" does to that part of the cerebrum in which political clarity might otherwise reside.

lawyers (well, even a few of the lawyers). Unlike the late poet Robert Lowell or the arguably living pugilist Norman Mailer, I've always tried to respect what I feel is a fine-line border between my right to explore my own life as subject matter and other people's right not to be subject matter. If, however, the other person has already given her/his "side of the story" publicly—why then, all's fair. Nor do I intend to hide the *fact* of someone's being part of my life. But I might employ that handy proscenium device, the scrim, letting it descend over certain scenes so their details can be viewed with softened edges, as if on a London street corner through fog or across the blue spaces of a smoky bar. So we enter a new terrain, where, in order to *be* honest, truth-telling must sometimes put aside its homespun cottons and array itself in more artfully draped silks that whisper subtlety. While this might be a loss in terms of gossip-quotient buzz and prepublication excerpts appearing in periodicals (another blow to my patient publisher and long-suffering literary agent), it could be a gain for literary style. Rather an agreeable trade-off, that.

Anyway, I never promised you a Tell All. Only a Tell Some.

If you're the sort of reader I suspect you are—you've traveled this far, after all—then such an announcement will actually come as a relief. If it strikes you as a disappointment, though, go read something else. I'll be hurt but I'll act understanding. Meanwhile, I'll just tell some stories, preferably some I've never revealed before.

Politics becomes a part of your life once you realize it has been all along. Kenneth and I had been "political" before we knew each other, albeit in the mild-mannered fashion of, respectively, literary people and show-business folk. The son of a working-class man proud of having once ridden the rails with the Wobblies, Ken grew up in a more consciously Leftist household than mine. While teaching at NYU, he'd tangled with his department head over the attempted imposition of faculty loyalty oaths, and had refused to trot out his students for air-raid drills, noting that nuclear holocaust would hardly be survived by ambling to the basement. Later, when Funk & Wagnalls—where he worked as an in-house writer and editor— was purchased by the conservative Reader's Digest Association, he would get into principled hot water for daring to put up anti-Vietnam War posters in the privacy of his office cubicle; he was finally fired because he refused to take down a famous poster showing the bloody My Lai massacre, its caption quoting testimony by the GIs who'd torched the village, killing all its inhabitants: "Q: *And children?* A: *And children.*" He would in time become a founder of the Gay Liberation Front, as well as one of the first men to respond to this feminist wave in ethical, supportive ways, both on the page and in daily life. But that's getting ahead of the story.

As for my political development, a voice from the past speaks out to remind me: my own, interviewed by Peter Babcox for his February 9, 1969, article in the *New York Times* (Sunday) *Magazine*, "Meet the Women of the Revolution." In the piece I pompously refer to Kenneth and myself as a "two-member commune," doubtless in a silly attempt to co-opt emerging criticism of such "bourgeois" institutions as marriage or couple-dom. On the whole I sound like the deadly earnest twenty-eight-year-old I was, prematurely reminiscing: "My first approach to politics had been that of the artistic community. Most of the actors and artists I knew were Fifties artists who had just barely survived the McCarthy years. They were either apolitical ivory-tower types or superficially political in the best liberal tradition. During the Death Valley days of the Eisenhower years when nothing was possible, nothing imagined, about the most political act you could commit was participating in a benefit for the UJA."

Subtext: those childhood benefits still rankled like hell.

The article mentions a brief experience with the Democratic Reform movement, but rushes past it. Yet it was an important episode in teaching me what I *didn't* want to do. Early in our marriage, Ken and I had flirted with Reform Democratic Party insurgency, opposing the party bosses and their political-machine ward politics. Their bully boys roughed us up physically when we did volunteer poll-watching at a local election, which had a radicalizing effect—the first of what would be many—inspiring me to run for county committeewoman on the Reform Democratic ticket. (I was forced to run as "Robin M. Pitchford," because although I continued to use my own name after our marriage, legally it was then still required that a ballot, as well as a bank account, driver's license, and other legal documents, reflect a woman's "legal," i.e., "married," name.) Fortunately, I lost even that humble race. It was the only time I've been remotely tempted to run for political office, having learned I lack the sanctitude to suffer fools gladly. I admit to being amused at having received party overtures on two occasions since, and to being flattered over the years when women have urged me to seek various candidacies. Certainly I'm relieved that there are quite a few smart, good-hearted women (and men) who *are* willing to tread that necessary route, and I support them every way I can. But for me, seeking or holding office has the appeal of having to be a child star all over again though now old enough to know there are better ways to live.

The *Times* interview goes on about my involvement in the civil-rights movement by 1964. It was indeed as I depicted it—a frightening, exhilarating period, from the mass marches to the quiet, grinding, dangerous work in the hells of Mississippi, Alabama, Georgia. That era flaunted some of the most sadistic faculties of the human brain and illumined some of the most invincible capacities of the human spirit. But I did *not* share with the *Times* any "backstage" stories—say, about how many black radical men had hit on white radical women with the inventive line "If you're serious about fighting racism, gimme a little of my civil-rights tonight, Baby," *and* how many of the white women had guiltily caved in, *and* how many of the black women—rejected, ignored, or exploited by both these so-called brothers and sisters—dried their eyes and went back to work on the next voter-registration drive.[3] And I did *not* tell the *Times* another story from that period, one I did subsequently relate in *The Demon Lover* but choose to repeat here because it's so devastatingly symptomatic of the entire New Left's attitude toward women.

I was one of seven women—three of us white—at a joint meeting in the CORE (Congress on Racial Equality) office with members of SNCC (Student Nonviolent Coordinating Committee—which later was to renounce nonviolence but retain its anagram). More than twenty men, black and white, were present, running the meeting. Three young CORE

---

[3]One superb documentation of the civil-rights movement is *But Some of Us Were Brave*, ed. Gloria Hull, Patricia Bell Scott, and Barbara Smith (The Feminist Press, 1982). Its title is based on black women's sarcastic phrase from that era: "All the men were black, all the women were white, but some of us were brave."

workers—one black man and two white men—had disappeared in Mississippi, and the groups had met over this crisis. The lynched bodies of the three men—James E. Chaney, Andrew Goodman, and Michael Schwerner—were later found, hideously tortured to death. Meanwhile, the FBI, local police, and National Guard had been dredging lakes and rivers in search of the bodies. During the search, the mutilated parts of an estimated seventeen different bodies of African Americans were found. All of us in the CORE office were in a state of shock. As word filtered in about the difficulty of identifying mutilated bodies long decomposed, we also learned that all but one of the unidentified bodies were female. Incensed, a male CORE leader muttered, "There's been a whole goddamned lynching we never even *knew* about. There's been some brother disappeared who never even got *reported*."

My brain went into spasm. Had I heard him correctly? Had he meant what I *thought* he'd meant? If so, then was my racism showing itself in that I was horrified? Finally, I managed, nervously, to hazard a tentative question. Why *one* lynching? What about the sixteen unidentified female bodies? There was total silence. Every man in the room, white and black, stared at me. Every woman in the room, black and white, stared at the floor, more embarrassed by my question than by the situation in which I felt forced to ask it. Finally the answer came, in a tone of marked impatience, as if the speaker were addressing a political moron: "Those were obviously *sex* murders. They weren't *political*."

I sometimes think that women are the last true keepers of the flame that called itself the New Left. At least we're still at it. As a few examples out of thousands: Eleanor Holmes Norton who, fresh out of law school, was special counsel to our women's caucus in SNCC, is wonderfully, consistently active, as a feminist leader, an African-American leader, and the congressional representative for Washington, D.C. So is Elizabeth Martinez, civil-rights organizer who founded *El Grito del Norte* newspaper and is still going strong, working with Chicana and other Latina women. So is Nancy Kurshan, one of the few European-American counterculture leaders I can think of who's still doing serious political work, in her case with women in prison.

The men? They virtually collapsed—maybe from deflation of ego, because once women began to shift energy into our own groups there was no one around to do what we inelegantly but accurately termed "shit-work." When the men resurface at all, they're mostly an embarrassment. They either wax misty-eyed like veterans about World War II, nod off into a druggy or religious daze, or affirm their recently acquired right-wing conversions. A disturbing number of New Left male leaders veered precipitously off the edge into looniness or to the Right, which may be a redundancy. Jerry Rubin traded his head bandanna for a bowler and tried to morph into a Wall Street entrepreneur. Abbie Hoffman—so notorious for his sexist behavior that his later claim to have founded feminism stands as one of the more surreal statements of the era—became a drug dealer, went underground after being busted, and wound up committing suicide. Stokely Carmichael (he of the infamous announcement "The only position for women in SNCC is prone") moved to Africa and lived off the singer Miriam Makeba until she ditched him. Tom Hayden at least turned into a vaguely progressive California state senator, but Rennie "the Fox" Davis ohhhmmed toward ashrams and gurus. And Eldridge Cleaver—having already shifted from being a convicted rapist to a Black Panther leader—moved through wife-battering into promoting velvet codpieces as a fashion fad (*honest*, could I make this stuff up?), then to being born again in Jesus and realizing that the Pentagon was one helluva grand place after all.

Who *were* these men? Not that it matters. Every time I've granted permission to reprint my notoriously furious 1970 essay "Goodbye to All That,"[4] I've had to expand the footnotes identifying sexist male Leftist leaders I polemically attacked by name. At the time I wrote the piece, they seemed to bestride the world like proverbial colossi, but they made themselves so irrelevant that with each intervening year fewer people had any clue as to who they were. It will be poetic justice if they squeak into history as footnotes because they were once lucky enough to have been denounced by an angry woman writer.

Meanwhile, back at the revolution, Ken and I had done the usual letter-writing and petition-signing, gone on the occasional march or picket line, then become interested in organizations with which literary friends

---

[4]Collected in *The Word of a Woman: Feminist Dispatches 1968–1992*, Second (Updated) edition 1994 (W. W. Norton).

like Marge Piercy and Ira Wood were becoming involved. One such group was Movement for a Democratic Society (MDS), "the SDS for adults." Writers (or "word workers," as some of the Marxians obnoxiously termed us) were welcome volunteers, since press releases, manifestos, and leaflets didn't pen themselves, and we were a writing pair: a two-fer. But petitions and polite demonstrations were having a zero effect on policy— which gets forgotten by those who think that we all leapt at radicalism overnight because it was fun or chic. We didn't and it wasn't. Being ignored by our own government drove us there, in heartsick disbelief.

A leisurely pace regarding political principles was a luxury fast disappearing. The nation was beginning to boil. Medgar Evers and John F. Kennedy had been assassinated in 1963, the same year of the Birmingham, Alabama, church-bombing slayings of Addie Mae Collins, Denise McNair, Carole Robertson, and Cynthia Wesley, four little black girls at Sunday school. Malcolm X was assassinated in 1965. Three years later, 1968 would witness the murders of Martin Luther King Jr. and Robert F. Kennedy. The TV screen flickered news nightmares each evening. Protesting the war, Buddhist monks sat calmly in the lotus position and immolated themselves, their silhouettes outlined amid triangular pillars of flame. Shots of wailing, bleeding women and napalm-seared children became as commonplace as those of body bags filled with the corpses of U.S. soldiers.

Kenneth and I were changing, along with everyone else. The *Times* article reminds me that in 1966 we "participated in Angry Arts Week, reading National Liberation Front poetry on flat-bed trucks around the city."[5] But soon our protest chants were shifting from "Peace Now!" to "Bring the war home!" and from "Freedom and Equality!" to "Black Power!" Slogans like "Make love, not war" were giving way to pronouncements like "Level everything; *then* we'll talk politics." The *Times* proceeds to chart my shift

[5]Misleading: we each read our own versions of transliterated poems by both classical and contemporary Vietnamese poets. Some of my versions were later published in my first collection of poetry, *Monster* (Random House and Vintage Books, 1972). We'd worked with translators to forge moving English versions of the poems—only some of which were openly against the war, but all of which revealed the complex aesthetics of Vietnamese culture. And we read our own poems against the war—as did other poets we knew—on the flatbed trucks and anywhere anyone would listen to them.

from opposition to insurgency in terms of a fashion statement: "On the [April 1967] peace march to the United Nations, I wore a conservative skirt to show that I was a member of the law-abiding but morally outraged middle class. . . . Since the Pentagon [demonstration], I never go into the streets without jeans and boots. . . . [In MDS, we had] thought there must be something we could do as artists and writers. But there wasn't, and we were beginning to get a little disillusioned by what seemed to be a joyless-ness in the movement, an over-ritualized ideological seriousness. Then I walked into the Yippee [Youth International Party, YIP] office one day. There was this hysterical loft with the groovy posters and people sitting around rapping, and coffee spilled on the floor, and whoever picked up the phone would yell 'Yippee!' It seemed life-affirming, myth-making, just beautiful! It was . . . a real feeling of *communitas*."

Well, that's a bit over the top. I didn't tell the *Times* that counterculture style began annoying me within days:"Shake a chick's tit instead of her hand" was one Yippee lifestyle rubric, and their postrevolutionary vision of an ideal society consisted of "free grass, free food, free shelter, free chicks." Besides, the dirty-feet-in-sandals, bearded-and-beaded look never quite cut it with me, who had only recently been contending for Superwife and who still took visceral if secret pleasure from a well-waxed floor. But Ken truly enjoyed YIP's style, which chimed with his own capac-ity for genuine bohemianism; he grew a beard and Fu Manchu mustache, and the two of us tie-dyed almost everything we owned. Kenneth was never totally accepted by the Yippies, because he was almost ten years older than most of them but even more because he was open and proud about being gay well before that was chic or a political position—but he was at least *male*, and that counted for a lot in the New Left and the coun-terculture. In YIP as in MDS, the anti-war groups, and the civil-rights organizations, men made policy while women made coffee. We were expected to make havoc, too—but only on directions from the men. We were to be traditional nurturers, serene commune types, sexy foxes, and fearless militants. It was tiring.

I opted for the one other role, which was open to only a few female per-sons: the "heavy." This referred neither to weight nor villainy, but to being "a tough chick," i.e., the token woman who could barter her way into inner circles by means of some bargaining chip—usually by being the appendage of a powerful man or, if unattached, donating substantial cash to the group. In my case, the chip was verbal and writing skills. A heavy would not roll joints for the men, bring them more beer, schlep water from the well in a commune, rise at 4:00 A.M. to cook for the Panther Breakfast Program, or be relied on as an object for sexual sharing. (I was saved from having to sleep around because I was already spoken for, and, based on the previous debacle in the marriage, both Kenneth and I gave off the clear message that we "weren't into group stuff anymore.")

But being a heavy was frightening, because you had to out-tough the guys. The *Times* again: "Once, I was a pacifist. I had such a strong, self-righteous feeling then. Now, as each day goes by I get more scared. It's the kind of terror that comes with the realization that with each passing day I am a little more willing to fight and to die."

The thing is, I actually was. We both were. A line from one of Kenneth's poems of the period comes to mind: "It's no longer making beautiful things that I like, / but making things beautiful . . ."[6] Actually, each of us still wanted to do both, but everywhere we looked, there was an acute need for making things bearable, to say nothing of beautiful. Poor people were rising in the ghettos; students were rising on the campuses. We spent more than a few days and nights in support demonstrations for protests at New York area colleges, and we joined the fray outright at Columbia University, as part of the human blockades formed around the clock to keep riot police from storming the campus.

I've sometimes reflected that my (lack of) height had a major influence on my tactics, notably my growing preference for militant small-group actions as opposed to large-scale demonstrations—though I certainly recognize the need for the latter and went to more of them than I can count. The problem was that I could never *see* what was going on beyond the shoulder of the person in front of me, so I came to dread the moment when a voice off in the crowd would shout, *"Here come the TPF!*[7] *They're charging into the crowd! Watch out, here comes the tear gas!"* It was bad

---

[6]From the poem "(Working Title)," in *Color Photos of the Atrocities: Poems*, by Kenneth Pitchford (Atlantic Monthly Press/Little, Brown, 1973).

[7]Tactical Police Force—the mounted, heavily armed, notoriously testosteronic riot police.

enough being attacked by rioting cops for having committed the sin of exercising one's First Amendment rights, but it was worse being trampled by one's co-demonstrators as they surged this way and that while I screamed futilely into the din, *"Where?"*—sometimes running directly into the fire hoses or rearing horses. Is it so surprising that I became more interested in small so-called affinity group actions—a well-aimed brick through the window of a U.S. Army recruiting station, for example? I could run, after all, even if I couldn't loom. At my height, such actions seemed *safer* than a peaceable march.

Feminism had begun trickling into my awareness by the mid-1960s. The New Left was rife with women's caucuses (ladies' auxiliaries, really) wherein women might critique men's offensive behavior but never question the issues, focus, political analysis, or tactical strategy of the group itself; on these, male leadership was assumed. To challenge that, as eventually some of us did, was to invite being pelted with raw eggs, ripe tomatoes, and actual stones, as happened at more than one SDS meeting. If rebellion persisted, ultimately one walked out or faced expulsion, but only *after* having been denounced by the men (and most hurtfully by their loyalist women) as being "shrill, selfish, divisive, counterrevolutionary,"and that standby, the unkindest cut of all, *"bourgeois."*

Yet I continued to be torn for almost a decade between my emerging feminist priorities and my allegiance to the Left (which I would in time call the Boys' Movement), even in its violent period. As if I were compiling an adult Perfection Chart, a ghost of that long-ago childhood one, I made a frantic attempt to cover all bases *and* retain male approval—no easy task. I became involved in a union-organizing attempt at Grove Press, where I'd become a part-time editor, but I also wrote for underground papers (Leftist points on my chart); joined a women's consciousness-raising group (feminist points); organized demonstrations supporting the Panthers and the radical Puerto Rican group The Young Lords (Leftist points); co-founded the first New York Women's Center (feminist points); carried the *Manual of an Urban Guerrilla* or *The Second Sex* to meetings (double points) and actually read both; did underground abortion referrals (feminist points); salivated when a Weatherperson was busted and rushed to be rent-a-body for courtroom support (Leftist points plus a red star).

By the early Seventies, I felt like a veteran. My police mug shots show a young woman whose eyes gleam with exhaustion and whose jaw is set firmly in defiance. My days were filled with juggling editorial work, house-work, and street demonstrations that ended in acrid clouds of tear gas; my nights were filled with meetings, candlelight vigils, stolen moments of writing, fearing the knock at the door—and "engaging in struggle" with Kenneth about sexism. My body was honed by karate training, my lan-guage salted with expletives. I had sat-in and smoked-in, made phone calls and made bail, raised funds and raised hell, been beaten up, busted, and afraid—for years already. I was in my late twenties, and I wasn't the only one convinced that I'd most likely be killed before I turned thirty-five.

It was hard to choose which front to fight on and difficult to focus on which tactic. The Nixon administration had begun calling for preventive detention camps for radicals; friends were going underground or to Canada or being sent to prison on twenty-year sentences as punishment for political actions. People we'd known or demonstrated with were sud-denly dead of gunshot wounds in the middle of their college quads or on a city sidewalk two blocks away. To dare invest energy on "mere" women's needs was seen as constituting a betrayal of humanity—the operative syl-lable in humanity being the second one: the draft (affecting men) was considered a universal issue, but childcare (affecting parents and children of both sexes) was considered a marginal, self-indulgent, "special-interest group" issue.

Here I must indulge in a caveat and then be done with it. The New Left was terminally diseased with sexism and toxic with characteristic U.S. arrogance—but the right to criticize is earned fairly through love. To this day, when I hear anyone inveigh against the Left from a Rightist view-point—a reactionary dismissal of unions, or "socialism produces a society of ants" rhetoric—my blood starts to simmer. To this day, when I encounter women or men of my generation who somehow managed to sit out those years indifferent and unaffected—or who, like Bill Clinton, were already worrying about how whatever they did might look on their future political or corporate résumés—I wonder at their lack of moral vitality. And when I encounter those who *were* in the streets and on the barricades against war, racism, and poverty—but who are now comfort-ably settled into establishment niches of academia or the business world while considering themselves lucky to have "outgrown" politics, I also wonder. For me, the problem was never one of retrenchment from a radical position or from fighting to stop an epidemic of misery. It was that the Left never went far *enough*, in analysis, vision, or practice; that Leftist men, for obvious and shameful reasons, were unwilling to include the larger half of humanity in their plans for changing the world. (What remains of the Left still seems unable to grasp this—although the fatigued jargon has been recycled to encompass women as "a target constituency." They still just don't get it.)

Yet if I'm to acknowledge fairly the factors in my formation, then it's important to say that I, who take back not one of my denunciations of that phallocentric movement, nonetheless preserve a loyalty to what we all— women and men alike—*hoped* to stand for. We did change something in this country, for the better. If I feel saddened at how that movement failed *because* of its narrowness (regarding issues of sex and race and age and class and disability, and-and-and . . .), I'm still proud at having shared in the idealism, and in an energy that at times expressed itself in humorous, creative organizing tactics; proud of having shared in all the hotheaded-ness, and all the outrageous beauty.

But while living through it, I was every day more unable to escape the awareness of my personal frustration. I was unable to deny that, even given Leftist priorities, the men's leadership style reeked of egotistical power games; unable to deny that another woman could better teach me how to handle a rifle in a single afternoon than five of my condescending Leftist brothers could in weeks. I was angry at the commonplace use of grass and acid to get women high before gang-raping them—a counter-culture tradition peaking in practice at Woodstock. I was livid at watching myself and other women grow depleted from fighting for "mankind's" free-dom while staggering under inequalities of housework, childcare, sex, and similar "woman questions" the men dismissed as our personal hang-ups, not *serious* politics. I was enraged at a "sexual revolution" taking place for men only, leaving in its wake women who were pregnant, infected with STDs, drugged out, and desperate. In the *Times* piece I was cautious to understate it: "It was clear to me that the movement didn't really make room for women . . . here was a new politics, a new lifestyle, a new freedom, and still, the notion of a liberated woman was someone who is indiscriminate about whom she sleeps with, not a realization that women don't want to be objects."

Subtext: those group-sex years in the marriage still rankled like hell.

Ironically, Ken and I drew closer during this time. There were so many Thems it made uniting as an Us easy. We might have formally rejected splitting up as a time-wasting bourgeois self-indulgence—at least that would have been a convenient argument for staying together "for the sake of the revolution." But we shared an intellectual shorthand and now had mutual emotional scars binding us—and for me, he was solid, safe, trustworthy.[8] The boorishness of movement men threw Kenneth's intelligence and sensitivity into sharper relief. Besides, unlike them, he was authentically radical, not just due to his working-class origins, but because he was always drawn to the most original, even extreme, issue, position, solution, or tactic. His character was gripped by what Yeats called "the fascination of what's difficult," and he had the courage to endure his convictions. This meant he was supportive of my being a heavy, even when that didn't include him. When I became more of a women's liberationist, he supported that, too—even after some of our Leftist brothers and their molls cruelly nicknamed us "the Ball-less Wonder and the Castrating Bitch."

They weren't the only ones calling us names, though. In the 1970s, I was one of a number of radical activists who applied for access to files the government had kept on our activities (this was made possible by Bella Abzug, then a congresswoman from New York, who as chair of the House Subcommittee on Government Information and Individual Rights,

---

[8]The one exception to such trust was when I would get stoned on grass, or trip on mescaline or acid. Certainly there were great moments—eating a single grape for an hour, laughing until rib-ache set in, flashing on him as a Viking sailing into the dawn— but more often than not I'd hit a wall of paranoia that would include him as part of the problem, not part of the solution. This may have been based on the way hallucinogens had been employed to facilitate the earlier group-sex scenes. In any event, although grass was a frequent ritual and tripping a special occasion, I came to do less and less of both, since for me they had become highly unpleasant. As usual, I was sure this was *my* failing. Imagine my surprise when I discovered that many women of my generation had the identical reaction around their husbands or lovers. Imagine my greater surprise when I discovered that sampling such substances when alone or with other women (and even, years later, with certain men) yielded a delightfully different reaction.

pushed through changes in the Freedom of Information Act, sometimes known as "the Sunshine Law"). Some of my files are permanently held back as classified; they've never said why. But those that were released were hilarious.

The FBI and CIA were so wide of the mark that their operatives should have been fired not only for infringing civil liberties but for incompetence and misuse of taxpayers' money. Most of the files consist of newspaper clippings, including interviews quoting me as being against racism, the Vietnam War, and what Eisenhower himself had termed "the military-industrial complex." The Feds, working with New York City's hated Red Squad, apparently got an absurd amount of their information from the media—articles I'd written for *WIN* (the periodical put out by the War Resisters' League), *Liberation,* and other underground journals, as well as interviews in mainstream media. Files list me as "aka [also known as] Mrs. Robin Pitchford"—as if that were a code name, and as if I ever used it. Interestingly, the FBI and CIA didn't share the Left's dismissal of burgeoning women's activism as irrelevant. *They* were *really* paranoid. They were certain that telephone conversations (referring to editing jobs, or books I was reading or writing, or errands being done) were secret signals for militant actions—as if I would have been dense enough to discuss such things, even obliquely, over a telephone line so tapped the static sometimes interfered with conversation; Ken and I would jovially ask, "May I have an outside line please?," through the hum of their tape recorders.

Yet it was educative that voluminous files had been compiled on me not only by the CIA and FBI but also by other agencies and even branches of the military. Despite the fact that I'd never been involved in any violence against *persons*—only property—and never been convicted of any charges, I was on the Secret Service list of "dangerous radicals" to be tailed whenever the president journeyed to New York, and on a list of people eligible to be picked up without charge and held in (illegal) preventive detention. The U.S. Air Force file remains a mystery; did the agents think I was organizing Amazons to zoom in over the Pentagon, darkening the skies in perfect formation on a thousand witchy brooms? The intelligence community just didn't have very much. One jewel of an FBI report from 1972 notes, "The WLM (Women's Liberation Movement) in New York City is no longer functioning as a group, but only as a movement."

Bless 'em, they were tailing me a lot during certain periods, so various reports read sternly,

> *To All Appropriate Agencies and Field offices: Robin Morgan aka Robin Pitchford aka Mrs. Kenneth Pitchford.* Subject—born 1.29.42 in NYC [wrong date, wrong place, guys]—is an anarchist housewife [don't you *love* it?], reported to be a writer of poetry ["reported to be": you'd actually have to *read* it to check *that* out] concerned with revolution. Subject attended a filming of "Pig for President" in NYC and attended a June meeting of the National Committee to Combat Fascism.

Or this one:

> Subject joined the April 1967 peace march to the UN; in October 1967 she went on the March On The Pentagon; in November the demonstration against Secretary of State Dean Rusk, then the demonstration against the Whitehall (NYC) induction center. In April 1968 she joined in demonstrations supporting the student "uprising" at Columbia University. . . . Subject is listed as one of the individuals on the CORE Southern Education Committee.

Interestingly, the more involved I became in women's liberation activism, the more my files proliferate. One report notes that my propensity for violence must be increasing because I'd written an "extremist" statement calling for "secretarial sabotage against white male power gone mad." (And they say *feminists* have no sense of humor.) The surveillance continued through the late 1970s (probably even later but, bored with their prose style, I stopped demanding my files), and the Feds tracked me when I appeared in other states:

> *From SAC, Tampa, Florida, to The Director, FBI:* A confidential source advised that Robin Morgan, white female, age approximately 30 years, has been active on campus of New College, Sarasota, Florida. . . . Morgan organized minor protests concerning Women's Lib [sic] activities. All have been peaceful and nonviolent. However,

source is concerned that violence may occur should she continue pushing her ideas. Bureau is requested to check indices on Morgan.

The protests were to pressure for the hiring of a female gynecologist in campus medical services, and the installation of better lighting near dorms where there had been a rash of sexual attacks. True, we did end up occupying the college president's office—which was not something I, as visiting guest professor for one semester, was supposed to do—but that was only *after* polite petitioning, picketing, and press conferencing had got us nowhere.

In sum, most of the time, the FBI and the local gumshoes got it *wrong*—missing what serious mischief I *did* do and fulminating over my innocuous acts. Meanwhile, I'd become more interested in bringing both sets of tactics I'd learned in the New Left (serious and innocuous, guerrilla actions and guerrilla theater) to working with women. Kenneth seemed to understand this well enough, but it shocked other radical men, who couldn't fathom why I might prefer attacking silly old sexism when I could continue to be a token woman in their impending apocalypse.

I remember a particular meeting in the spring of 1968. It was a gathering of the secret central committee of YIP (Yippee postured itself as leaderless and anarchic), at Jerry Rubin's "pad" on St. Mark's Place. Jerry was his usual manic self. Nancy Kurshan, then his lover, the only other woman present, was saying little. Tom Hayden was wearing his fetching Mao cap with the wee red star, Abbie was stoned as always, Rennie Davis was stoic as ever, and Kenneth sat off in a corner drafting some manifesto praising Jerry as "a young Lenin." We were planning massive demonstrations—"Days of Rage"—to take place "spontaneously" at the upcoming Democratic convention in Chicago.

Then I announced that I had decided not to go to Chicago after all, because I intended to organize a different protest.

There was shock, then astonishment, when I told them that I'd be going to Atlantic City—to take on the Miss America Pageant.

"That's *crazy!*" Jerry gasped, his eyes bulging as he sanely twirled his bandanna and passed a joint.

"No shit, man," Abbie grinned foggily at me, reaching for it. "You're puttin' us on. *Nobody's* that wild. Oh wow. No shit. Bummer. Yeah. "

"Incorrect," Davis pronounced flatly.

Expectedly, it was Hayden who was serious, albeit patronizing. His first, about-to-be-former wife, Casey, had been an early fomenter of "women's issues" and New Left women's caucuses. So *Tom* knew *all* about *women*.

"Robin. I realize women need to be taught political consciousness, educated to a proper analysis, and organized to fight against the war and racism. I understand Miss America would be a perfect symbol to attack, and it's a ripe media opportunity to spread the word. But you don't want to miss *Chicago*! There'll be riots in the streets! People will probably be killed! We'll make sure the whole world is watching! Don't you *get* it? The second American *revolution* will take place in Chicago!"

From the manifesto-writer in the corner came the mumble,

"It's *you* guys I think don't get it. Somebody pass the joint? My money's on the second American revolution taking place in Atlantic City."

TWELVE

Fits and Starts

For rebellion is as the sin of witchcraft.

—I SAMUEL 15:23

There's a riveting moment near the end of Arthur Penn's 1967 movie *Bonnie and Clyde*, when the bank-robber fugitive pair realizes that it's an ambush, that they are cornered and are about to be killed. They exchange a long look of complete understanding—then break into a grotesque dance propelled by the rain of machine-gun bullets sieving their bodies. That's a somewhat gruesome image with which to identify, but it's revealing that in the manner of some couples having "our song," Kenneth and I considered that gaze "our moment," like a signature chord of our marriage, as the 1960s drew toward a close. Our Us-against-the-World defensive posture gained greater validity every day, given the objective realities of the time.

Nevertheless, there were intermissions in the relentless drama of the period, and the good moments were very good indeed. The more frenetic the tantrums we threw in the outside world, the cozier an island Kenneth and I tried to create at home. We were house-proud, and wore the aches and scars to prove we'd earned that pride with our own hands. We took satisfaction in the gleam of our wide-plank floors, burnished to reflect the dance of firelight in the hearth, the few paintings by artist friends shown to advantage on the whitewashed walls, stripped and refinished furniture we'd rescued from the gutter, the big slab of butcher-block wood we'd splurged on buying for the kitchen counter—and somehow, always, a few fresh flowers arching from a vase on our round oak dinner table.

When the New Left's white sons and daughters of CEOs and military leaders[1] turned downwardly mobile, Ken and I were already *there,* at least in terms of income. Yet we lived well, if humbly. When the Left descended into anti-intellectualism, however, we balked. I recall one Weatherman snarling at us that the only good use for a typewriter was to heave it out a window onto the head of a "pig cop." Other such troglodytes denounced us for having so many books, and demanded that we sell them to raise money for the movement. But we clung fiercely to our typewriters and never considered liquidating the library. If that meant we were reactionaries, at least we'd be literate ones.

Our household had become recatted early in the marriage. Since Bob had taken Castor, Pollux, and Helen with him in setting up a household with Frank, we began anew with Hektor and Cassandra. One of the things for which I'll always be grateful to Kenneth is that he introduced me to cats, the beginning of my passionate attachment to feline beings. At one critical point in the 1970s we were actually up to owning—or, more accurately, being owned by—as many as five cats at once. We eventually branched out in the name department, expanding from strict adherence to characters from the *Iliad* to the Cabalist classic *The Zohar* (from which we borrowed the seraphic name Sandalphon), Wiccean tradition (for Grimalken), the Welsh epic poem *The Mabinogian* (for Bran, singer-poet son

---

[1]Not exaggeration. Mark Rudd, who postured himself as leader of the Columbia University uprising, was the child of an army general, as was the autocratic sometime-feminist Ti-Grace Atkinson, and a disproportionate number of Weatherpeople came from elite corporate backgrounds. This might prompt us to wonder just whom they were really rebelling against, and when the crunch came they could and did rely on Daddy Warbucks. For example, some Weatherpeople (from poorer or more politically active backgrounds) are still underground or still serving out life sentences, but Bill Ayres, a Weather Underground leader, served no serious time and is a university professor in Illinois, where he lives comfortably with Bernardine Dohrn, another Weather leader. Ayres's father owned Commonwealth Edison of Chicago.

of the Great Goddess), and even science (for Phosphor, a lilac Siamese who did almost glow in the dark). Although we had sufficient space for such wildlife, we did have to engage in a twice-a-day spectacle not unlike feeding time at the zoo. It was especially challenging to persist in our perpetual renovation of some corner of the apartment with twenty tiny paws poking into every pile of rubble, scampering underfoot, rolling nails and screws across the floor, hiding behind stacked plasterboard, and playing spring-and-pounce with our ankles. But we managed. And I became a lifelong cat person, at this writing catless for the first time in decades, because I'm still mourning Bran. It was Bran who moved in with me after Ken and I split up, who outlasted all his contemporaries, and who died two years ago at the venerable age of twenty-one. Bran—who possessed not only intelligence but wisdom and humor—was a classic all-black cat, an ideal Familiar and, it must be admitted, the Cat of My Life.[2] He saw me through it all, purring in celebration at the highs and, at the lows, rasping away my tasty salt tears with his coral tongue and comforting me with his knowing, emerald-eyed gaze.

During the mid-1960s, I'd written a series of letters to Kenneth—not while traveling but while at home. There were things I simply couldn't say to him, which is not to imply that we didn't talk. We talked about everything. Especially the marriage. All the time. We were perceptive, eloquent people. We were also getting to be bored, morose people—or so I thought, which may have been a projection of what *I* was feeling. Neither of us was willing to admit being less than happy. But whenever we did admit it, then—since Ken could claim to have known "happiness" pre-marriage (a claim I wasn't sure I could honestly make)—we both blamed me. What Kenneth confusingly praised but also rebuked as "Robin's overly developed self-critical faculty" was based on my personal adaptation of Solon's statement "To a really good [wo]man, everything is [her] own fault." I didn't yet know this was a socially fostered belief shared by many of my sex. In my case, it was also a residue of the childhood lesson that I was respon-

[2]Bran forms a central figure in my long poem "The Fall of a Sparrow," originally published in *Depth Perception: New Poems and a Masque* (Doubleday, 1982), and reprinted in *Upstairs in the Garden: Poems Selected and New, 1968–1988* (W. W. Norton, 1990).

sible for, well, everything, and another facet of my insistent perfectionism, which was hard on those around me and harder on its judge herself.[3]

But under the self-blame was anger, and more than a little of that was directed at Kenneth. I've never expressed anger well, although as a political activist (and, inescapably, former actor) I learned how to do *public* anger apparently well enough to be called a "harpy" and a "man-hater," as well as your basic termagant, bitch, gorgon, and shrew. But both my mother and my husband conveyed anger so effectively there seemed to be no space left for mine; I felt theirs sucked up all the air, like the old wives' tale about flowers in a hospital room, making it impossible to compete or even get heard enough to be a contender. Consequently, I would stake out the placid, "rational" approach in arguments—but I'd manage to *leak* anger well enough. This self-censoring tic was another trait that I would come to realize many if not most women shared across geography and culture. Exacerbated by my personal background, it resulted in my rarely being able to speak anger clearly and cleanly, especially to Faith or to Kenneth. Hence the letters—some loving and tender, but the bulk written out of choked feelings I feared I could never articulate.

I regarded the letters as diary leaves written for my own sake. But I must have harbored the hope that one day I'd be able to show them to Kenneth, which eventually I did. It's to his credit and his loyalty to the printed page that later, when I was writing *Going Too Far,* it was he who urged me to include them, as artifacts of a couple's difficulties "pre-struggle," and they did appear in that book. Most of them could serve as classic examples of a woman trying to find a personal solution for problems she is sure are singularly hers, and usually her own fault. A "Various Failures of Me" list is included in one of the letters, an inverse catalog ominously reminiscent of that Perfection Chart from my childhood. I was in real distress about my failures, and just beginning to acknowledge that I was in real distress about the marriage itself. In neither case did I yet rec-

---

[3]"Loyalty Oath," another poem from the same period, begins, "Ungrateful Daughter, Intolerant Friend, / Officious Associate, Malcontent Wife: / these signs, hand-lettered in uneven print. / The oppressed carry them around inside my skull / in shifts. They want to organize, despite my efforts to negotiate / an individual settlement with each." See *Lady of the Beasts: Poems* (Random House, 1976).

ognize the pain as something shared and commonplace, thus political—
though it's also undeniable that "love is more complex than theory," as a
later poem, "Easter Island," would note.[4]

The letters were written from a pre-feminist perspective that saw our
marriage and its problems as unique. Of course, every marriage is unique.
Ours may have appeared more so, but therein lies an irony. It was precisely what made us *different* that constituted our strengths and bonded
us: two intense poets, a decade apart in age, from widely divergent backgrounds, each obsessed with words, art, audacity. Obversely, it was what
we had *in common* with most other couples on the planet that would frac-
ture and eventually fragment the marriage, particularly after exposure to
the erosion of time and the harsh clarity of feminist light: housework,
money crises, sexual conflicts, ego clashes, work habits, career problems.
In other words, Bloomsbury wasn't so very different from Bloomington.
Doesn't this fragment from one letter sound familiar?

> We've got a conflict of life-styles here, Kenneth. I know that I work
> best when my life is cleared away, things in order, no bills or errands
> or laundry on my mind. So I do them. It's not easy when I'm also try-
> ing to drift along with your schedule instead of ignoring or fighting
> it. . . . You, of course, also work best when things are in order, except
> it will never be you who orders them, by god. I'm tired of all this.
> Tired of doing the things I actually love to do: cook, clean, etc. Tired
> of your constant criticism, tired of failing and feeling it myself *and*
> tired of your alternating condemnation and condescension. Tired of
> your god-like manner, all the while you're complaining that people
> cast you as an oracle. Tired of your equality-in-our-marriage talk,
> which I've always heartily seconded, silently planning the dinner or
> how to get to the bank on time meanwhile. Tired of your moods,
> which you indulge in freely (mine, of course, are unfortunate—you
> can't help being sensitive to them, and they upset you and you can't
> get your work done). Tired of the way you come to a mutual project
> late, reluctantly, and then take it over completely. I *like* our home,
> our life together. It's the two of *us* I can't stand.

[4]See *Lady of the Beasts* and *Upstairs in the Garden: Poems Selected and New.*

But love *is* more complex than theory. Another letter:

> Where [do we go] from here? Tonight, coming home on the bus
> together, we saw a beautiful mother and baby . . . healthy, rare, com-
> monplace. I want to have your child. Unsure again, afraid again, now
> it seems a fantastic dream. Still, I want that, us together, raising it
> and writing and talking for twelve-hour stretches. . . . This moment,
> when I'm numb and tired and want only to sleep and know you are
> lying in bed a few feet from my desk, one thin wall between us, waiting
> for me to lie down beside you, hating, fearing, and loving me at this
> moment when I've no heart for it, for anything but to finish this . . .
> and sleep, this moment when to feel even hopelessness is impossi-
> ble, let alone hope—this is like being at the center of some simple
> emptiness . . .

Finally, there was a breakout, an explosion, an acting out of the anger I
couldn't fully admit, even to myself, that I felt.

I tried to play sauce-for-the-goose, thinking maybe that would equalize
things. I had an abortive affair with a young painter. The childhood patterns reasserted themselves handily: it was a situation ripe for lies and
half-lies, self-consciousness, theatricals. But when it came to actual lovemaking, I couldn't go through with it, feeling that would be as much a
betrayal of myself as of Kenneth and our marriage.

When I told Ken about it—which may have been the reason I did it in
the first place—he erupted in fury. My confessions consisted of a series of
coffeehouse meetings where the painter and I had talked and gazed
mooney-eyed over candlelight, which seemed pretty tame in the circumstances. I'd anticipated Kenneth's being hurt, but I was stunned by his
rage. I'd assumed a single standard, thinking Bloomsbury worked both
ways. Arguments, tears, thick silences—the misery was constant between
us for weeks, ceasing only long enough to lend us a faint renewal of energy
sufficient to prolong the woe further. Then I broke the cycle, cracking the
pattern of my usual refusal to stop. One freezing December night in 1966,
I left him.

Our separation lasted only twenty-four hours. I stayed overnight with a
woman friend, another painter, but when I came home the following day

to collect some clothes (having stormed out with only my purse and, naturally, a blank notebook), I was glad of the excuse to see him again. He, meanwhile, had cleaned the house and stocked it with wine, candles, and flowers. None of which, even so, might have tempted me. But the planes of his familiar, loved face, the sound of his loud tears and quiet voice, the words he said, met my longing at least halfway. So I stayed.

Within a year, I was positive I had *now* discovered the tools with which I could *really* speak to him. I was in a small women's group that met on the Lower East Side each Tuesday night, talking about our lives.

I was en route to the words *"the personal is political."*

That phrase has been so misinterpreted that it's time once and for all to clarify its origins and meaning. Therefore, we'll pause briefly for

Another Aside:

Unless you were in hibernation on Mars during the late 1990s, you know only too well that an ostensibly antisexist president of the United States brought his satyriasis hang-ups and hang-outs right into the Oval Office. Since it's always open season on feminists, we too got blamed. If we defended Clinton, we were Democratic party hacks; if we denounced him, it must be that we shared the puritanical mores of his most rabid conservative detractors.

True, some of my feminist-spokeswoman sisters spun Clinton's sexual actions as private (in the *Oval Office?*) and as consensual. Mutual consent *would* have made a defense—except that after three consciousness-raising decades, most people finally understood that a power imbalance in the workplace *or* out makes "consent" a moot or at least highly questionable factor. Other feminists attacked Clinton with the wrath of a woman betrayed by the man she'd trusted. Most of us, of course, never trusted him to begin with—merely voted for him as the preferable alternative to a candidate and party in thrall to a religious-fundamentalist Right that plans to time-travel women back to the twelfth century—earlier, actually: twelfth is perilously near that pesky Eleanor of Aquitaine. As we've frequently had to remind politicians, women were *not* born Democrats, Republicans, or yesterday.

Yet the same folks who'd condemned our lack of pragmatism for decades now complained that most of us were practicing realpolitik: deploring Clinton's behavior while supporting many of his policies, which were *still* preferable to the alternative. Adversaries sneered "Inconsistent!" at what was to them this apparently mind-boggling complexity, and they played Gotcha!—by wielding the phrase "the personal is political" against us. I could quote Emerson that "a foolish consistency is the hobgoblin of little minds," but the truth is that we *have* been consistent (*and* large-minded) all along.

If the norm was men occupying the public realm (the political), and women being largely sequestered in the private realm of home and relationships (the personal), then how *does* that offstage half of humanity enter political discourse? Who defines "political," anyway? "The personal is political" was born of the small-group, consciousness-raising process, as we compared notes, for instance, about how our men all seemed to think the issue of who did the housework wasn't political. But the phrase became an open sesame toward general visibility, because it had wider applicability.

During the Sixties and persisting through the next decade (when people refer to the Sixties, they're really talking about the mid-Sixties to mid-Seventies), it wasn't only the New Left that vehemently opposed most of the emerging feminist agenda. The human-rights and civil-liberties groups—run by gentlemen accustomed to defining "human," "rights," "civil," and "liberty" as reflections of themselves and their needs—were even more recalcitrant adversaries. (The American Civil Liberties Union, then under the leadership of Aryeh Neier, was proud to be the *most* resistant to us crazy women. In fact, concerned women in ACLU eventually split off to form a separate reproductive-rights group, since the harassment of their reproductive-rights unit within the organization was so beleaguered by Neier and ACLU men.)

Every feminist issue had its own backlash from these purported brothers. Rape? An accusing woman often lies; besides, she probably asked for it. Battery? Criminalization would be an invasion of privacy of the home; besides, she most likely incited him—*and* she must enjoy it or she'd leave him (the option of shelters barely existed yet). Marital rape? Outlawing it would violate the marriage contract; besides, she must have provoked—or exaggerated—it. Violent pornography? First Amendment absolutism must reign—except of course in silencing critics of pornocrats. Sexual harassment? Hallowed free speech; besides, she probably welcomed—or imagined—it. And so on . . .[5]

Today, most women and many men see through these Blame-the-Victim smokescreens. Yet in the late 1960s, such reactions from our alleged brothers were devastating. They periodically drove each woman back to anguishing, "Maybe it *is* just me, *my* fault, *my* problem." So although much ridicule was visited on C-R groups as hen sessions, therapy circles, gossipy gabfests, or ladies' coffee klatches, *this* is why the modest format of sharing real-life experiences was such a reality check. Whenever we broke through individual isolation to compare notes, what I termed The "You *too*?!" Moment was electric. Practically speaking, it helped build a movement: it connected us to realizations about sexism's dynamics, institutionalized male entitlement that comprised patriarchy, power patterns embedded in the social/economic/legislative *systems* surrounding us—in short, the *politics* of it all. But the thrill of mutual discoveries that ricocheted through us gets muted in the rhetoric of that preceding sentence. The real point is that this process connected us to each *other*, and most of all to our*selves*.

In time, the phrase would gain still wider usage. We would become disgusted by senators who voted against a woman's right to reproductive choice yet arranged safe, secret abortions for their mistresses; congress

---

[5]Many of the U.S.-based human-rights groups have carried this attitude into the global context. For years, arguing "cultural relativism," they derided women campaigning to end the practice of female genital mutilation (*in their own cultures*); only when the UN was forced to acknowledge this issue did the human-rights groups opportunistically jump on board. At this writing, these groups are ranged in opposition to international feminist organizing against the sexual traffick in women and children. Still trying to convince themselves and others that women really *want* to be impoverished, prostituted, and exploited, they cynically revive old anti-union "right to work" arguments and misappropriate "pro-choice" phrases for the ostensible "right" of a human being to be trafficked into sexual slavery by pimps they've conveniently renamed "migration facilitators." But they're savvy enough now to preach (abstractly) that "women's rights are human rights."

men who moralized about family values yet gutted legislation to protect battered spouses or incest survivors or child-abuse victims; politicians (in this instance, like Clinton) who preached the sanctity of motherhood and preciousness of children while denying poor women the support of a *decent* welfare system to raise their kids. These were the *policy* hypocrisies we also confronted with "the personal is political."

For the record, then:

We did *not* say the personal is *public*; that's been the tabloids' and the paparazzi's position.

We did *not* say the personal is *prosecutable*; that was Independent Prosecutor Ken Starr's claim.

We did *not* say the personal is *prurient*; that was the pornographer Larry Flynt (in addition to Ken Starr).

We did *not* say the personal is *puerile*; that was several neo-antifeminists trying to revive Blame-the-Victim theories with confessional yarns about their lust for belching cowhands and bikers.

We did *not* say the personal is *predominant*; that was certain lesbian and gay activists who—though motivated by understandable grief about young lesbians and gays committing suicide partly for lack of public role models—pioneered "outing" with a cold indifference to the rights of those being outed.

We simply said "the personal is *political*." Because politics is about power.

That insight has genuinely altered our national consciousness. The old-boy network had always looked the other way regarding politicians' sexual misdeeds, as the press did with FDR, JFK, LBJ, and many others. But starting with Ted Kennedy and Chappaquidick, through Gary Hart, Clarence Thomas, and Bob Packwood, right on up to Clinton's stupidity and womanizing (magnifiable to "high-crimes" status only by a rabidly partisan prosecution), understanding that the personal is political has helped change the way we see things, and helped change the rules.

By the way, the political is also personal. That's just another way of phrasing former Speaker of the House Tip O'Neill's maxim "All politics is local." But enough ideological etymology. To return to our narrative:

Forward to the Past

Once a month our little Tuesday-night group came together with other such groups from around Manhattan, in what we boastfully referred to as a "coalition" called New York Radical Women. This coalition, which topped out at the critical mass of perhaps thirty-five women, was composed of three basic groups. There was Redstockings, which had pioneered consciousness-raising (calling it, in Maoist jargon, "speak bitterness meetings"), led mainly by Shulamith Firestone.[6] There was the October 17th Group (later revamped as The Feminists), which had been formed by Ti-Grace Atkinson when she stalked out of the New York chapter of the National Organization for Women (NOW), declaring it insufficiently radical. And there was us.

We were nameless, just "the Lower East Side group" or "the Tuesday-night group" until I, carrying both my Yippie sense of mischief and addiction to wordplay with me, came up with WITCH, soon destined to become our identity as well as our adaptable anagram.[7] The other two groups and outriders in New York Radical Women were understandably suspicious about our mixed loyalties: most of us in WITCH were still active in male-led organizations, had a Marxian or at least generally Leftist analysis, and exuded a "hip" counterculture style—that is, we were "politicos" as opposed to their being "feminists." I deprecated the word

---

[6] Firestone would eventually write *The Dialectic of Sex* (William Morrow, 1970), an astute work of feminist theory unfortunately flawed by its naive assumption that technology would be an unmixed blessing that would automatically free women. Firestone would suffer a breakdown and drop out of political activism.

[7] It originally stood for Women's International Terrorist Conspiracy from Hell. But as it caught press attention and people's imagination with its humor, activist style, and guerrilla-theater tactics, women around the country picked up on the image and adopted the name. Variously, the anagram came to stand for Women Incensed at Telephone Company Harassment (operators on a wildcat strike), Women Indentured to Travelers' Corporate Hell (a group trying to organize a union at the insurance company), Women Intent on Toppling Consumer Holidays, Women Inspired to Commit Herstory, etc. For more information about WITCH, see *Sisterhood Is Powerful* (Random House and Vintage Books, 1970) and *Going Too Far: the Personal Chronicle of a Feminist* (Random House and Vintage Books, 1977).

SATURDAY'S CHILD

"feminist" as being "boring, a nineteenth-century left-over of a word." I bragged that the women in our group weren't "anti-male" like those dreadful feminists. While *they* went about calmly talking and writing papers that would become classics,[8] *we* in WITCH were into *action*.

These decades later, given my genuine regrets about the way we squandered WITCH, I have to admit that the group was lovably irrepressible. What's more, we were onto a real mother lode—identifying with the witches—although it was years before any of us would begin to give the tradition of Wicca the serious study it warranted, either as an ancient pagan religion, a contemporary belief system, or part of the buried history of women's rebellion—"herstory," as I would rename it. I *meant* to read the anthropological, theological, and mythographic data on witchcraft—but I was busy doing actions. I *meant* to do research on the nine million who'd been persecuted as witches during The Burning Time—but I was too busy doing actions.

How I did love actions. Ideologically I identified with the confrontative tactics of the Left, stylistically with the proto-anarchist conniptions of the Yippies, temperamentally with anything romantic, and by training with anything theatrical—so naturally it seemed to me intolerable that we should "just sit around talking." *Subtext: the talking was getting uncomfortably close to the bone.* When I discovered in one meeting of our small group that I wasn't the only woman duplicitous enough to have faked an orgasm, I was retroactively enraged at inept men in general and Ken in particular—but also so relieved that I thought I'd have one on the spot.

Whatever its excesses and errors, over the next two or three years, WITCH made its own mischief, fun, and headlines. Early one Halloween morning, having alerted the press, thirteen of us in full costume descended on Wall Street and hexed the New York Stock Exchange (for its capitalism and male supremacy) with an elaborate spell to seal its doors. When the bronze doors could not in fact be opened at 9:00 A.M., we were an instant media sensation. Nor did we blemish our reputation by informing the press (or the cops) that we'd helped the spell along with generous

---

[8] "The Politics of Housework," by Patricia Mainardi, for example, and "Resistances to Consciousness," by Irene Peslikis—both of which I included when compiling *Sisterhood Is Powerful*.

applications of Krazy Glue oozled through the door locks a few hours earlier, just before dawn. One February, we demonstrated against the Bridal
Fair being held at Madison Square Garden, offering the target-consumer
brides-to-be free hot cocoa as they waited in line to get in, and distributing free ShopLifting Bags for sample products. The cocoa and bags were
a success, other gambits a disaster. As we picketed, we sang "Here come
the slaves, off to their graves" (*not* the friendliest approach), then released
150 live mice inside the Garden (I know, I *know*, playing on a stereotype
of women's fears *plus* exploiting mice). Leftist and counterculture men
"dug" us as being "Harpo Marxists," but we began to understand that we
were alienating women—the very people we wanted to reach. Finally, the
original "mother coven" of WITCH, still composed largely of that Tuesday-night group, decided to retrench, in order to engage our own lives and
that "man hating" thing called feminism.

But before any of this, there had been a demonstration redolent of
WITCH style even before WITCH existed, a demonstration that *was*, as
it turned out, a kind of American revolution—in 1968, in Atlantic City,
New Jersey.

On the Boardwalk

I've written so often about what did and did *not* happen at that first protest
that for those details I refer curious readers to *The Word of a Woman*. Suffice it to say here that No, we never burned bras (a myth perpetrated by
an article in the *New York Post* likening us to the young radical men who
were then burning draft cards), and Yes, we did crown a live sheep Miss
America on the boardwalk (*not* one of my finest hours: it insulted the con-
testants and irked the ewe; my animal-rights consciousness had a long
way to go). Also: No, I did not regret missing the Chicago "Days of Rage"
for a moment, and Yes, to my amazement women arrived on the boardwalk
from as far away as California and Florida, responding to pre-protest publicity, to join with us.[9] Ken's money was on the right bet: it *was* historic.

---

[9] An impressive number of attendees would "graduate" to become feminist authors and
local or national activists, including Donna Allen, Charlotte Bunch, Jacqui Ceballos,
Leah Fritz, Kate Millett, Pamela Kearon, and Alix Kates Shulman.

But at the time it seemed merely exhilarating. It was heady to be using the organizing skills I'd learned in the Left—getting the demo permit, booking the buses, writing the press releases, marking up the picket signs—but this time for *ourselves,* not for the guys. I even had buttons made, with a new feminist logo in red on a white background: a circle with a cross beneath (the universal sign for the female) and a clenched fist raised inside the circle. Almost a decade later, in *Going Too Far,* I finally came out of the closet and admitted having designed this symbol—which, astonishingly, has become the global sign for feminism. Since I draw badly, I'd described to Kenneth what I envisioned; he'd sketched it accordingly and skillfully; I'd had the first buttons pressed for the 1968 Miss America protest. Since then, I've seen the fist-in-the-circle-above-the-cross as graffiti in the Gaza Strip, Soweto, and Sicily; on rice-paper stationery in Nepal and posters in Rio, Manila, and Beijing; as jewelry in San Francisco, Sydney, and Tokyo; and on T-shirts sporting feminist slogans in most of the world's languages. Women physicians' organizations use it entwined with a caduceus. Women lawyers' organizations show the fist grasping the scales of justice. Lesbian activists draw the circle doubled and linked. It keeps being reinvented, and always gives me a private smile. It will be ironic if this turns out to be my most enduring contribution to feminism.

But I could predict none of that back then, as I proudly pinned on the new-minted button and watched women snatch up and pin on theirs. Intoxicated with our own leadership and freedom, we picketed, leafletted, chanted, and sang all day outside the convention hall where the pageant was taking place. Ever-impertinent Florynce Kennedy held reporters captive with her sound bites about how racist the pageant was (at the time there had never been a black finalist), while others of us pointed out connections between the pageant and commercialism (Miss America hawks products), militarism (Miss America is always sent to cheer up the troops, wherever they are), and most basically, the sexual objectification of women. The hot September sun and the site gave the event the feel of a day at the beach. Not all the passersby shared the goodwill, however. While most women seemed amused and were willing to accept leaflets, the men almost without exception appeared to feel threatened by this group of about three hundred women chanting, "No more Miss America!"

As the day wore on, the group of men on the other side of the police barricade grew larger and uglier, spitting out chants of their own.

"Dykes! Commies! Lezzies! You don't deserve to be Americans!"

We demonstrators exchanged glances of revolutionary sanctitude and bravado. We viewed ourselves, with a certain unsteady hauteur, as seasoned radical patriots used to accusations of being communists, scum, and the like—but for some of the women there, this was the first time they'd been called lesbians, and at *that* accusation many strong Leftist women dissolved into tears. (It would be almost a decade before we would come up with the button reading smartly, *How dare you assume I'm straight?*) Meanwhile, as the accusations of pervert and un-American drifted past, I chuckled to myself at a personal joke none of the other demonstrators knew about. The choleric men had no idea that their epithets, especially when screamed at me as the demonstration's organizer, were aimed at the Ideal American Girl.

There's an untold story of that protest that I can now tell here. It regards Charlotte Curtis, then editor of the *New York Times's* Style Section (for which read: renamed Women's Pages). Curtis was a rarity of the period, a well-known woman journalist. She'd been a foreign correspondent, but that didn't save her from being assigned, on her return, to fashion, flower shows, society, and—even when she was promoted to being an editor—to Style. Her revenge was to dip her pen in perfumed poison, and she became known (and feared by some) for her wit and trenchant writing about the social scene. It was Charlotte who coined the phrase "radical chic" in her wry coverage of Leonard Bernstein's notorious cocktail-party benefit for the Black Panthers. In later years, after she finally became editor of the *Times's* Op-Ed page (but never rose higher, though less-experienced men did), Curtis sometimes found herself in the position of being middle management, awkward for her as younger women began to organize against sex discrimination at the paper. Yet the truth is that for a woman of her generation and prominence, Curtis was unusually supportive of women *and* feminist ideas and actions, even if she had to express that support behind the scenes. Her mentoring of younger women journalists is well-known. But she went further, and therein lies my tale.

Charlotte, in an interview with me days before the first Miss America protest, had gone off the record to inquire personally about our guerrilla theater tactics. Did I believe they'd be effective? Might we alienate instead of persuading? Should we be more genteel, or was she being overly so? These weren't baiting questions. She was warm, curious, open, and our discussion was candid. I was touched when she left saying she now understood and would try to convey through her coverage what she termed the "eminently reasonable politics" behind our protest. She did. In fact, she made us seem downright wholesome—so much so that a few of my sister protesters cringed.

But Curtis did more. She came *along* to Atlantic City, elegantly dressed in black (gloves, pearls, and heels) amid our colorful informality, gamely warbling "We Shall Overcome" with us as we bounced along in the rattle-trap buses. She stayed all day on the hot boardwalk with us, brought us cool drinks, laughed and applauded when we would recognize and respond to women journalists only. At the pageant that evening, we had snuck some of our demonstrators inside, where they managed to disrupt the then live telecast; they were arrested and hauled away. I stayed on after the buses left, raising bail by phone, and being sent from precinct to precinct in search of where our friends were being held. Finally, at 3:00 A.M., I learned they'd been released hours earlier, on cash bail put up personally by "some older woman" named Charlotte Curtis.

When I phoned the next day to thank her, she asked me to keep it quiet, as "these dreary grey guys running the *Times*" would not be amused. It's time to tell the secret now. She died some years ago, only in her fifties, of cancer. But Charlotte Curtis had a style all her own. She was what they used to call "a real lady." But she was a real feminist, too. In her, this was no contradiction.

It wasn't surprising that some of the demonstrators had been offended by Charlotte's coverage making us look reasonable; they were scared their men might think they'd gone "bourgie." Various members of New York Radical Women had helped me organize the protest and most had joined it, yet several disapproved sternly. Carol Hanisch, a former reporter and civil-rights worker, circulated her polemical critique. Kathie Amatniek, a Radcliffe graduate who, with her leprechaun haircut and grim bent was our pixie Robespierre, expressed grave concern about any press coverage at all. Aghast, I asked if she thought a protest taking place in secret would be effective. Kathie, ever uncorrupted by a sense of humor, snapped that we weren't ready to spread the word; other women "out there" might get involved, and we had to "complete our analysis" about women's oppression before, at some point, serving it to the world. This sort of Lenin-in-a-closed-train proprietary thinking didn't sit well with me. Besides, we were just beginning to glimpse the enormity of this "analysis," so I figured we wouldn't be winding it all up very soon. Meanwhile, I couldn't imagine sitting on what we *had* learned, from each other and our own lives, through a process that was part of the lesson itself. Last, I was damned if I'd let that "analysis" be left to a handful of young, white, middle-class, ex- or still-Lefty women, either.

Imagine my wicked delight then, when, to Kathie's indignation, at the next meeting of New York Radical Women after the protest, almost two hundred women appeared, crowded into one room. Too late to control storming the Bastille. We were on our way.

Yet Another Aside: Historical Context (But Only a Touch)

It was terribly unfair (and highly satisfying) that the media termed that 1968 Miss America protest "the birth of the feminist movement."

The 1960s had already seen two streams of the Women's Movement emerge: a reform-oriented "equality feminism," represented by such dues-paying, formalized membership groups as NOW, and a radical feminism represented by us, younger women activists seasoned in the student, civil-rights, and anti-war movements.

At its inception—under the influence of NOW's New York chapter, which mostly meant Betty Friedan and her colleagues—the moderate, reform-oriented wing was almost totally white, heterosexual, middle class, and politically middle ground, though later NOW would grow beyond its founders and become happily more risk-taking. The looser "revolutionary" wing of the movement, on the other hand, was from the start a mix of races, ethnicities, classes, sexual preferences, and ages, no matter how much the media claimed that only white women were interested in feminism. Despite the campus-centered activism of the period, the radical wing embraced neighborhood groups and welfare-rights organizations. Despite the homophobia of the time, lesbian feminists were at the forefront of those first groups (though, deplorably, not always with the freedom to be out). Clerical workers and secretaries, pink-collar workers and household workers, disabled women, older women, rural women, and institutionalized women were all part of this eclectic, quarrelsome, enormously energetic wing of the movement.

To the more mainstream groups fell the unglamorous but crucial job of tackling legislative reforms, helping women integrate male preserves and nontraditional jobs, bettering the lot of employed women in general and professional women (assumed to have already made it) in particular, attempting to absorb and organize the literally hundreds of women who every day clamored to locate and join the Women's Movement, and trying to encompass each new issue as it arose. That could mean fighting discrimination against females as sportscasters or ministers one day and as firefighters or orchestra musicians the next. This wing had the foresight to urge more women to run for public office and to create support systems for those candidates, such groups as the bipartisan National Women's Political Caucus. Generally, at least from the 1960s through the late 1970s, many of these moderate groups shied away from what they then considered controversial or alienating "sexual politics": lesbian custody rights, for instance, or the outright repeal of abortion laws (as opposed to reforming them), or confronting the industries of pornography and prostitution, or in some cases even challenging laws on battery (considered a "domestic" problem). But what they may have lacked in impudence or vision they compensated for in organizational skills: most of the institutions these women forged *lasted*. Moreover, their impact has grown and, fortunately, so has their political inclusiveness.

The same could *not* be said of us, the more sensational revolutionaries who bravely risked and regularly endured tear gas, beatings, and jail—but were apparently unwilling to risk any kind of coherence. We were nothing if not fluid. Many of our groups formed, split, reformed, disbanded, and resurrected themselves within weeks, making it difficult for movement newcomers even to *find* us. However, we were the women who ambitiously unearthed and confronted issues broadside, despite being divided ourselves into those two camps of "politico" or "socialist feminist" (who had a residual overriding loyalty to male-defined Leftist priorities) and "radical feminist" (who made *women's* needs, condition, and organizing the priority). After September 1968, we were on the map, whether Hanisch and Amatniek were ready for us to be there or not. So separately or together, both politico and feminist twigs of the "revolutionary branch" created a high-energy frictional heat of activism: C-R groups, demonstrations, *and* "zap" actions. Groups proliferated nationwide, from, of, and for particular constituencies of race or sexuality or focus: the Combahee River Collective, the Lavender Menace, Older Women's Liberation (OWL), Cell 16, the National Black Feminist Organization (NBFO), La Mujer Chicana Group, Radicalesbians, Asian Women United, First Mothers Native Americans—it seemed there was a group being born every day.

I felt right at home, because we never stopped. We marched against the Vietnam War as the "Jeanette Rankin Brigade," so named in honor of the first elected congresswoman, who had also voted against U.S. participation in both world wars. We demonstrated against forced sterilization of poor women and women of color—while also providing underground abortion referrals when both the procedure and counseling it were illegal. We participated in seizures and occupations protesting advertising's objectified images of women.[10] We helped organize women's groups at all major newspapers and television and radio stations. We staged speakouts and speakups and began conceiving such terms as "battered woman," "sexual harassment," and "date rape." We hardly ever sat still, too much awhirl setting up storefront women's centers, childcare groups, women's health and self-help clinics; producing the first women's studies programs and self-defense courses; creating what would be called a "women's culture" in music, visual and performing arts, literature, even spirituality. We founded festivals, galleries, theater groups, record companies . . . we meant to leave no battle unjoined.

Our branch did, however, mostly shy away from legislative reforms and from the push for more women in public office or in positions of corporate, media, or "establishment" power. Furthermore, self-righteous politi-

---

[10] The sit-in at the *Ladies' Home Journal* was a particularly newsworthy one. See Susan Brownmiller's *In Our Time: Memoir of a Revolution* (Dial Press, 1999) for specifics, and for further information on this period.

cal purity frequently infected us with contempt for those groups "working inside the system"—as if anyone could manage to work totally outside it. (This more-radical-than-thou scorn would turn in on itself, with periods of infighting: between those radical feminists who considered themselves "separatist"—which had at least ten different definitions—and those who didn't, between mothers and childless/child-free women, and expectably along the already vulnerable fault lines of race, class, and sexual-preference differences.) The larger estrangement went both ways: the exasperation felt by radicals toward moderates was tartly reciprocated—with the moderate women (their wing suffering its own schisms meanwhile) characterizing us as hairy-legged, wild-eyed, and unpragmatic.

It's taken thirty years of contemporary feminist activism for the movement to outgrow these rancorous categorizations. The bad news is that it took that long and that some people never outgrew anything but their birkenstock sandals or, in the other camp, their mink coats. But the good news is that there were more of us able and willing to work with each other across all barriers, ego games, and deflections.

In part, the splits paralleled comparable fractures in the nineteenth-century women's suffrage movement; herstory repeats itself, too. There were also generational schisms—daughters fighting against, with, and sometimes for their mothers and mother surrogates, and the reverse. That was a battle I knew in my bones.

The Personal Is _Personal_, Too

Like many people in their late twenties, I was during this time still trying to resolve my ambivalence about my parents, all the while claiming that such struggles no longer had any hold over me. Ever since our wedding, my mother had refused my phone calls and returned my letters unopened. We didn't speak for almost four years, and then fitfully. It seemed that anything could set off another bout of phone hang-ups, and often did.

Perhaps in recompense, and with Kenneth's support, I began thinking about my father again. I'd given up on him once before, but that had been when I was in a state of shock after the meeting, and besides, I told myself, things were different now. I was a wife. I was an activist. I was a grown-up. So I phoned and told him I was married, and invited him and his wife to dinner. I thus initiated a series of manufactured social occasions where people who have absolutely nothing in common except some strands of DNA congregate and pretend to be civil. Most families endure such periods annually, calling them "holidays."

First, Viga Morgenstern came into Manhattan from New Jersey to test me out with a woman-to-woman lunch, in order to protect her menfolk. I must have passed muster, because then she and Mates accepted our invitation to dinner. I can't remember what I cooked, but I recall it took days, so it must have been elaborate. They were both sniffy about our neighborhood, commenting on the empty glassine envelopes strewn by the junkie sleeping on our doorstep. But once inside they were startled at the size and beauty of the apartment, by now a standard reaction. The evening went passably, in a strained sort of way, until they requited the gesture by actually inviting us to dinner at *their* home.

I was euphoric—until Mates and Viga made it clear that when I met their sons, I was to be presented as "the daughter of an old friend," not as their half-sister. Viga obviously knew of the liaison with my mother, but the boys—then in their teens—had not been told. What's more, they *wouldn't* be. Kenneth rose to my defense, since with a glance he'd gathered I was unable to. He asked when, if ever, Mates intended to tell them who I really was.

"Ahh, later. Much, much later. Perhaps when they turn twenty-one, perhaps even . . . it's important that they not lose respect for their father," was his reply, with Viga chiming her little *moue* of agreement. Given my own experiences of retroactive family information, I did manage to pipe up, "You don't think that suddenly getting this news at age twenty-one is worse?" But the question might as well have been rhetorical.

I was hurt, but didn't want to seem intolerant. Besides, I thought in time things would change, sooner rather than later. And oh, how I was curious. So one icy February day in 1965, Kenneth and I trooped to the Port Authority Terminal to catch the same bus for New Brunswick, New Jersey, that I'd taken four years earlier. We stopped at the newsstand to pick up a paper, jolted by the headlines: Malcolm X had been assassinated the night before. We spent the bus ride talking and crying, and were still declaring our sorrow and anxiety when we arrived at the Morgensterns'—where we were met with the diametrically opposed view that "the world was a better place without this terrorist Negro."

Not a good beginning. The ensuing argument was played out in full hearing of the Morgensterns' African-American maid, who scurried in and out with drinks, readjusting her uniform and glancing sidewise at Kenneth and me—while the words "Oh, her, she's just like one of the family" actually issued from Viga's mouth.

It was like discovering Hell as the crossroads between Mississippi and the Ringstrasse. The atmosphere was formal. The two stiffly polite boys wore shorts and knee socks in the European style, and you suspected they'd never heard of Elvis. The older one, Danny, struck me as being overly young for a sixteen-year-old. His future was announced by his parents while he stared vacantly into the middle distance: he was being tracked to follow his father's footsteps into medicine. The younger, Gil, at eleven and a half, was sharper, apparently a bit of a prodigy violinist; parental pride was voiced at the certainty of his eventual concert career. Dinner was, to say the least, uncomfortable, made more so by arch comments about that old friend whose daughter I was. At one point, Gil leaned across the table and said to me, with a pointed wink that stopped my heart, "Children know more than grown-ups think they know," making me wonder if he and I shared a familial talent for eavesdropping.

But it was hopeless. The charade made me feel slimed, as if I'd been asked to deny my mother, asked to collaborate in my own erasure all over again. I got through the evening but knew I couldn't repeat the pretense. The long road to my phantom father had led to a cul-de-sac presided over by a man terrified the truth about my existence would upset the carefully constructed lie of his. I could sympathize with his fear, but not with his cowardice. I *was* drawn to building a relationship with this family, however slowly, now more to be in touch with the mysterious promise of my half-brothers than with the boring, suburban, Prussian Mates had turned out to be. But there seemed no way to accomplish that relationship without further compromising my already tattered sense of integrity. I explained this, as courteously as possible, in a follow-up phone call, and Kenneth and I proffered no further invitations. On their side, Mates and Viga were clearly relieved to let things drift into silence.

But did I *really* stop, this time? Well, hardly. I resurfaced from invisibility on three more occasions.

Almost four years later, after Blake was born, I phoned to tell Mates the news; after all, it was his first grandchild and (I was thinking strategically) it was a grand*son*. Viga answered, congratulated me, and said she'd give my father the message. But he neither called back nor sent a gift, not even a tin spoon, much less a silver one. For a while I told myself Viga might not have given him the message. But I knew better.

Still, obstinate as one of those weighted balloon dolls that pop back upright each time they're knocked flat, I called again in 1983, when Faith lay dying—and I actually got Mates on the phone. I said the doctors had told me my mother had only a few days left and if he wanted to see her or say anything to her, I felt I should offer him the chance. What obtuse, tenacious yearnings were still rooted in me! What foolish longings—for him to want to see her, ask forgiveness, lay the ghosts to rest, once and forever heal it, end it! No, he said, he had nothing to say to her.

The final attempt came a few weeks later. I phoned my then sole living parent to give him the particulars about when and where Faith's memorial service would take place, in case perhaps he . . . No, he answered stiffly, he saw no need for such information. He offered formal condolences. And that, finally, was the end of it.

For years, on and off, I wondered about the boys. There have been times when I considered looking them up, the younger one especially, since he seemed capable of a rebellious spark. But an emotional lassitude set in regarding them. It spoke to my soul in a wearied voice, reminding me that there's just so much rejection any sane person cares to risk. Eventually, I was just too busy doing other things. I feel fairly certain my father and his wife never told my brothers about my existence at all—but that's because I find it hard to imagine being one of them, having that information, and not seeking *me* out. Which is probably one of the most naive projections I've come up with, in a lifetime filled with them. I do wish I had more information about that side of my genetic inheritance, even if just to fill in the blank half of my medical history. But time, in the end, is the best tutor of indifference.

I turned back to the family I knew. I recommitted myself to mending my relationship with Faith. I recommitted myself to Kenneth and to the marriage that, whatever its conscious or unconscious lacks for each of us, was never bereft of intimacy, tenderness, humor. And poetry.

We'd begun writing more openly political poems, though fortunately we were both vigilant about not descending into socialist realist art. These new poems may have intensified the political heat, but they took some of the psychological heat off writing about our own lives. After all, no matter how many times we had quoted Donne's "The Canonization" ("For God's sake hold your tongue and let me love . . .") to others in defending our marriage, there's a limit to the number of times we could effectively quote it to ourselves. We had by then fairly exhausted the inward analytical landscape of our relationship—or at least we'd done so within certain parameters, ones that seemed brave at the time but now strike me as sophomorically Freudian.[11] Poems affected by the epiphany of *feminist* politics were yet to come.

Nor was that the sole epiphany on the horizon. We decided to have a child.

We were now twenty-eight and thirty-eight, respectively, and we'd spoken about it for years. Kenneth had always wanted a child, children in fact. The younger of two, he'd really been raised more by his seven-years-older sister, Norma, than by his mother. I—an only child to my fingertips, a status left unaltered by those two ghostly half-brothers—couldn't imagine being or having multiples, although I'd always assumed that someday I'd have a child. I wanted to know what it was like to give birth and be a mother—but for selfish reasons, for *my* experience. I realized this, and it made me nervous. Certain as I was Ken would be a good father, I was petrified I'd fail utterly as a mother. What if I reenacted Faith's suffocatingly possessive love? Or overcompensated in the other direction and turned out to be as unfeeling as my father? Then, too, there was the real world where, as friends reminded us, we might be arrested, killed, or, as we not infrequently considered, forced to go into exile.

---

[11] One of my poems from this period, "The Covenant," dedicated to Kenneth, has the following as its closing stanza: "Bodies, to brave what dreams dare show, / must recognize each faceless ghost. / Give me my father. I give you / your sister, and procure her rest / from wanting him. So we fulfill / their final promise with our first— / and you and I, who share this hell, / again lose what was always lost" (from *Lady of the Beasts*).

Counsel came from all directions. What a bourgeois step! What a dangerous course! What a ridiculous time and situation in which to plan having a child! This decision was life-affirmative but impractical, daring but illogical; it was also radical and romantic. A perfect fit for us.

As for our watchful friends in the government, they got it wrong again:

> By means of a suitable pretext on August 25, 1969, by an SA (special agent) of the FBI, it was further ascertained that the subject is expecting a baby very shortly and as a result of her pregnancy is employed only [*sic*] as a housewife.

These guys just couldn't get with the program. Actually, I'd continued working as an editor at Grove Press until two weeks before I gave birth—on July 10, 1969—making it impossible for me to be expecting a baby very shortly one month later.

Of course I wrote about it.

Wrote about it beforehand and afterward, and if I could have, would have written my way *through* it—but that, as any woman who's been there can attest, is not an option. Writers are genuinely weird beings. In the early stage of labor, before we left for the hospital, I carried out a plan I'd contemplated for some months: I sat down at my typewriter and wrote two letters, one to Kenneth and one to the child I was carrying. Since my pregnancy and childbirth were "natural," the actual writing was punctuated by breathing during a contraction every second paragraph or so, while Kenneth was timing the length of the contractions, Lamaze style, with a stop watch. At my request, he didn't read either letter until he returned home alone from the hospital, after the birth, some twenty hours later.

Like any woman with her first childbirth, I was prey to almost archetypal feelings that I must be ready for the possibility of losing the child, or of dying myself, in some mishap. No matter how modern we become, it will take still more generations, consciousness, and changes in medical procedure before the imprint of a million ghosts dead in childbirth will be erased from the secret thoughts of a pregnant woman anywhere in the world; depending on her geography, class, age, and race, her death in childbirth may still be a commonplace occurrence. The letter to Kenneth was written, as was the one to Blake, out of an acute awareness that these might be the last words I would ever write. Here is a fragment:

Wednesday, 9 July 1969
Dearest K.:
It's almost six o'clock in the afternoon now and we know we definitely are in labor because of the bloody mucous plug having loosened, and we've had our baths and are all ready, just playing hide-and-seek with the irregular contractions. And you're running about crazy loon with our color Polaroid camera taking pictures of me typing this very letter to you—images of images, visual of verbal—as we each try to reach and make permanent contact with and of and for each other.

And all I really wanted to say in this letter was and is and will be that I love you very much and am very happy at this second of our absurd existence. These last days have been so beautiful, as we finally seemed to find a way of growing closer out of all the difficulties we've been having these past months. . . .

[I]f anything should happen to the baby or me, I know that we still have—in truly remarkable ways—each other, and that the years I've lived with you have taken me in directions I've so wanted to go, since I can remember wanting anything. What I'm trying to say, rather badly, is that it's *already* been worth it, after all, you see, even if there isn't any more. . . . I'm less afraid now than I've ever been, although with more reasons to fear for us all . . .

We had chosen a "genderless" name for our child, whether it was to be a girl or a boy. I still have the final short list, and it's horrifyingly funny. Thank god we didn't take the militant path with Che, or the touchy-feely route with Leaf. We chose Blake, because the name means "bringer of light" or "illumined one," and also for William Blake, the eighteenth-century poet and mystic. (There was a political slant to it, as well: Blake knew and had been influenced by the politics of Mary Wollstonecraft, as well as by those of Catherine Boucher, the painter he married.)

Rereading this second letter now, I'm struck by the false consciousness of it, the simpleminded views on oppression, revolution, sexuality, parenthood. The language is striving *so* hard to be "hip" that it makes me groan. My predictive calendar of the future is staggeringly off-kilter. All my self-doubts are in play again, together with my confident auguries about Kenneth's parenting skills; after all, I thought, *he* at least knows how to *play*. Mostly, though, I'm touched at how deeply this letter still moves me, how much I recognize its urgency, and how intensely I still validate what was happening there—in that woman's body, and on that woman's page.

I actually got some things really right—about loving, about letting go. I had no idea that I was about to learn what love might really look like—a love beyond self-consciousness, beyond pretense, beyond fear.

But I got some things right, after all.

Wednesday, 9 July 1969 6:38 p.m.
Dear Blake:
I've written you no poems or letters while carrying you these past nine months, and somehow feel I can write you now only because we know, K. and I, that our labor with you has definitely begun, and so you seem finally very real, beginning your own struggle into the conscious universe.

First, I ask you to forgive us for having coalesced you via our genes from that whirling matter and energy that you were before. A planetary famine is likely within ten years; nuclear, biological, gas, and chemical warfare are all possibilities; our species is poisoning what little is left of the air, water, and soil that is our natural Edenic heritage, and it is moving out later this very month to land on (explore? contaminate?) our satellite, the moon. You are part of a population explosion which may well be alone responsible for the destruction of life on earth. Overbreed and overkill begin to be common everyday phrases.

Yet we have conceived you, from our sex and love, from the blending together of our brief tissues, K. and I. I could cite excuses, some of which I believe and some of which I don't: our own egos, our curiosity about what our genes would produce, our callousness, our desire to make an ongoing revolution in our own lives, on and on. Perhaps none is the truth, or all are. Perhaps none is really relevant.

The fact is that you are now being born, a woman or a man, but mostly yourself, Blake for now (later you might want to change that name to one nobody has a right to give you but yourself), into a dimension we are all struggling to space out, to make freer, until we are ultimately free from it, into some new life or death—some meaningful way of living, or dying at least, in ecstasy.

Some people are arming themselves—for love.

Some people are refusing to bear arms—for love.

K. and I will be trying to find new ways to save ourselves and our sisters and brothers from suffering and extinction under the greedy powers of a few madmen, and you will be involved unavoidably in that struggle. But on your own terms, as soon as you know them and make them known.

We have no claims on you. We are your genetic mother and father, and beyond that, and more important, merely two people who will take the responsibility of you while you are still small and helpless, love you to the best of our ability, provide you with whatever tools of knowledge, skill, humor, and emotional freedom seem to interest you, respect your own individuality, hope you dig us as people but hardly dare insist on that (only try to earn it)—and let go.

Of course, I already envy you. Despite the horrors that oppress people around the world, those people are rising up to fight for their freedom. You are born into the age of worldwide revolution. You will be thirty-one years old in the year 2000. You may well travel to other planets. More prosaically, you have one hell of a groovy father, which I never had, and in some ways I trust him more with you than I do myself. I know you two will have crazy beautiful fun together. I have to get my ass in gear so I can join in.

If you are a woman, you will grow up in an atmosphere—indeed, a whole Movement—for women's liberation, so that your life will be less reflective of sexual oppression than mine, more human.

If you are a man, you will also be freer; you will not need to live a form of stereotyped masculinity which is based on the oppression of the other sex.

If you are a woman, you will be free to think—unlike so many women today. If you are a man, you will be free to feel—unlike so many men today.

K. and I are trying to be humanly unisexual, or pansexual. Join us?

If any of us survive these next decades on this planet, you will live to make a society where people share and love and laugh and understand each other. If none of us survive, it won't matter, because then we'll be free. Meanwhile, we can play with each other, and create poems and colors and songs and orgasms together, and learn to fight not so much for what we believe in as for what we love.

Dear Blake, I love myself right now.

Dear Blake, I love K. so very much.

Dear Blake, I love you, even though we've not been introduced.

Dear Blake, leave my body behind you quickly. K. and I together, throughout labor and delivery, will work hard to aid you in your struggle toward light and air and independence.

Dear Blake, welcome to the universe.

Dear, dear Blake, goodbye.

R.

THIRTEEN

Montage

I want a women's revolution like a lover.
I lust for it, I want so much this freedom,
this end to struggle and fear and lies
we all exhale, that I could die
just with the passionate uttering of that desire. . . .
— ROBIN MORGAN, "MONSTER"

ursing Blake, I lie sprawled beside him, staring down at him
where he sucks, all twenty-two inches of his little body of a piece with
my flesh, erotic, symbiotic. For him, I am food; for me, he is relief from
the pressure of milk-full breasts. He stares back into me, mouth busily
working, fierce blue eyes the color of Kenneth's not yet darkening to
what will become the deep brown of mine. We study one another, awed.
He elicits from me an expression I've never felt move across my features.
Perhaps this is his way of getting me to show him how to smile in wonder, to teach the shapes tenderness can take, how joy laughs. There is
nothing abstract about him; he *is* his senses. His eyes roll slightly: satia-
tion, pleasure, sleepiness. He gives himself up to a voluptuous yawn.
His tissue-thin, lilac-veined eyelids flutter, then droop slowly closed,

glowing alabaster curves lit from within. He breathes, softly, steadily. He is absolute and exquisite.

So this is what is meant by being in a state of grace.

A whole new poetry begins here, miraculous, celebratory; a whole new politics begins here, too.[1] I clasp him and drowse, musing about the hypothesis that in ancient societies the model for all relationships was originally the bond of love between mother and child, not as we know it today—in its corrupted form where women can at times misuse power over children because child-rearing has been the one area where they're allowed to exercise power, but in a pristine state of mutual love and sensuality, interdependence, sensitivity to unspoken need, true nurturance. I suddenly realize that to live in such a culture might mean that I could feel about everything—male and female, child and adult, human and animal and plant—the way I feel about this small being asleep against my heart. All at once I'm in tears with a longing I sense is more authentic than every word of political rhetoric in any language, because it vibrates with loss, because it surfaces with the intensity of the desire boiling beneath that loss.

It's impossible to negotiate this period—roughly the Seventies, with cusps on either side—in a linear fashion, as if one event neatly followed another in discrete or even overlapping continuity. Living unwraps more like a piece of music, in layers, in folds: melodies, counterpoint, motifs, syncopation, dissonances, harmonies. Certain periods of everyone's life are even more extreme, surpassing music, which, after all, moves sequentially through time. Such periods erupt in simultaneous, vivid images displacing one another so rapidly they virtually coexist, more like a painting: revealing in detail, but with perspective, viewable entire—immediate, whole, out of time, everything happening at once.

[1] Among the poems, "The Network of the Imaginary Mother," first published in *Lady of the Beasts* and included in *Upstairs in the Garden: Poems Selected and New*. For the politics, see, for instance, the section on children's suffrage in *The Anatomy of Freedom* and the essay "Every Mother's Son," in *The Word of a Woman*.

But our medium here is language, and words require sequence and progression in being spoken, written, or read; they exist in time. A compromise form, though, might be borrowed from film: the montage . . .

Although women all over the Third World carry their babies in side, back,
or front slings, in 1969 Snuggli pouches are not yet common in the United
States. Being ahead of one's time can flatter one's ego but apparently challenges other people's manners and finally exhausts one's own patience.
Older women on the street feel free to stop and berate me for "warping the
baby's spine by carrying it that way." Since he isn't garbed in blue or pink
(then the only options other than white), but rather in a home-tie-dyed
layette of bright jewel-like vegetable-dye colors, every passerby, of either
gender and any age, feels compelled to inquire as to his sex and seems
actually hostile to the child until such curiosity has been satisfied. All this
stopping and chatting makes Blake crabby. It makes me even crabbier.
After enough of these interrogations have turned every outing into an
ordeal, I develop a repertoire of brisk responses deliverable while not
breaking stride. These efficiently discourage sidewalk chitchat, though
they earn me a nutty-lady reputation in my neighborhood:
    "Girl? Boy? Dunno. Never looked."
    "Both."
    "Oh, dear no, it's not human. An alien, you know."
    "Don't care, so long as it's a healthy, happy homosexual."
    But the women who nightly patrol our street corner of Third Avenue
and 13th Street are different. They think I'm amusing; they coo adoringly
over Blake in his pouch, they watch out for us protectively when I return
from evening meetings with the baby asleep like an infant marsupial. We
get to know each other. I invite them in for coffee breaks when the
weather turns cold. They each have searing stories of why they're in the
life, why they detest it. They all have dreams of getting out, but they're
also clear about their lack of options. One is a single mother of a little boy
with a cleft palate, hustling to raise money for an operation for him; she's
a college graduate but believes she can only earn the kind of cash she
needs quickly by hustling. From these meetings comes the first attempt to

form a prostitutes' union—which collapses when two of the women are murdered by their pimps. "This isn't work anyone should unionize," one woman says to me. "This is work that shouldn't exist."

~ ~ ~

At first, I avoid speaking to the press about the burgeoning Women's Movement, encouraging others to pick up the mike and run with it. My own skills in this area feel tainted by having been learned in a context I never chose, so in fleeing my childhood history I also disdain the tricks of my old trade. But it soon becomes clear that no one else in our activist group wants to handle the press—or, more accurately, everyone *wants* to, but is scared witless.

No *problem*, I think: I can be useful here! It's skill-sharing time! I start informal, free, media workshops, first for a few women in my own small group, later expanding to any women interested. We desperately need articulate spokeswomen, yet almost everyone is scared of facing a microphone, TV camera, or audience. I explain terminology—boom, take-outs, slug, segment, sound bite. I construct exercises to build confidence: "Imagine you're looking into the lens. Inside it, imagine a tiny woman wearing a housedress, her hair in rollers, standing by her ironing board, watching TV. She wants and *needs* to hear from us, so look through the lens at *her*, talk to *her*," or "If you're nervous facing an audience, close your eyes for a second and un-dignify them. Visualize them sitting not in auditorium seats but on rows and rows of toilets, pants down around their ankles, butt-naked. Now really, what's to be afraid of?"

Finally, they're ready. At the next demonstration, I stand back like a proud stage mother—and watch them clam up, stutter, go blank, fall silent. What's been programmed into my bones to regard as *anathema* happens: dead air on live radio, glassy stares from a picketing spokeswoman during a live remote TV feed; collective foot-in-mouth disease while talking to print reporters. I know the only cure for their fright is experience, but in order to do it they have to *do* it—a catch-22. I try not to be intolerant, and I work hard to hide my judgmentalism, but my background and characteristic impatience make me unable to grasp the depth of their terror. They want to give up, but of course I won't hear of stopping.

So we do the training all over again, longer, more carefully. With the same result. Twice. At last, they persuade me to speak to the press; they *promise* they'll watch, learn, and "join in." So, starting with the Atlantic City protest, I do it. Since I've been brought up to do it well, I do it well. Idiotically, I think my sisters will like me for doing what they asked me to do.

~ ~ ~

Naming really *is* a form of logos, breath, reality. Kenneth and I call each other by our own names to Blake—never "Come to Daddy" or "Sit here with Mommy"—and consequently we keep our identity, not as roles but as real, fallible human beings. This might turn out to be the most important thing we do in all our radical child-raising. It helps to empower Blake—and will make for a much easier transition as he comes to maturity. Around age three he wants to experiment with calling us Mommy and Daddy, as he hears other kids calling their parents that. We say it's up to him, we'll answer no matter what he calls us. After about a week, he shrugs and reverts to Robin or Rob, and to Kenny.

Naming. I call Kenneth "K" in the letters I write to him, partly for brevity, partly in homage to Kafka, whose work we both love, and partly as a solution to the various names of Kenneth Pitchford. Casual acquaintances call him Ken, closer friends Kenneth, which is what I usually call him. But as the years go by, I more and more come to call him "Kenny," as his older sister, Norma, always did. It seems the name with which he's most at home, the one that really fits him. Blake grows up hearing it and calls him that, too. Kenny likes it, and it's an endearing term of affection (though as unwelcome as "Rob" when superficial aquaintances think they can adopt it). Yet at times I wonder if, as a diminutive, it isn't also one that infantilizes him. . . .

Naming. Young radical white women begin mimicking a trend in the black community to adopt "freedom names," as opposed to the slave names left over from Reconstruction days or, in the case of women, the patriarchal names of one's father or husband. I appreciate the importance of renaming, but most of the names chosen seem to me coy, derivative, unintentionally comical, or plain hypocritical (especially when used only in movement circles, not out in the "real world"). Some women, like Laura

X, choose what strikes me as a path too imitative of black male militance for comfort, especially questionable for white women to be treading. Others try for a matrilineal approach and adopt a form of their mother's first names; Kathie Amatniek becomes Kathie Sarachild, which comes across as ersatz Amish. Some drop the patronymic and resort to a first and middle name, as does Judith Weston Duffett in our group, becoming Judith Ann; this last seems to me the most tasteful solution. But it's a brightly ironic day when I realize I already *have* a matronymic, because Faith had invented Morgan and legalized it for her and for me. Morgan: half-bowdlerized (and Anglicized) from my father's name but half-based on Fata Morgana, the powerful female character with whom Faith identified. What in my adolescence had weighed on me as a mortifying negative turns out to be a feminist convenience.

Feminism—and motherhood—reinspire me to try to *truly* connect with Faith. I don't yet understand that the last person in the world you can organize is your mother. *You* may suddenly see her in a new light: she's an oppressed woman! she's a *sister*!

She still sees herself as your mother.

Faith cannot understand why, now that *I'm* a mother, I'm still: (a) writing poetry, (b) working as an editor, (c) going to meetings, demonstrations, and marches (forgod*sake* Robin!), (d) living on the Lower East Side ("that slum!"), and (e) returning to karate class—where I am about to make brown belt but have slipped behind, having had to fudge it and avoid front falls when I became pregnant and then stop class in my fifth month. My *sensai* is not amused that I dropped out to have a child. My mother is not amused that I returned and have a *sensai*. At least my child enjoys imitating my *kiah* yells when I practice my *kata* at home.

I'm trying to learn I can't please everyone. I fail at that, too.

I've been shifting from freelance editing to in-house work in publishing. Having been a "slush-pile" reader of unsolicited manuscripts at various literary agencies and publishing houses, as well as an itinerant proofreader and copyeditor, I begin a steady editorial job at Grove Press in 1968. It seems ideal. The office is within walking distance from our home, and at first I'm assigned books by radical authors—Régis Debray's book on Che Guevara, Alex Haley's *The Autobiography of Malcolm X*. Since as a free-lancer one of my jobs had been constructing Sammy Davis Jr.'s so-called autobiography, *Yes, I Can!* from taped transcripts, these new assignments are a relief.

Once Blake is born, I shift to part-time: half-days. Kenneth manages to change his status at Funk & Wagnalls to part-time, too, and we both res-urrect our freelance editing contacts to compensate for the financial cut-back. Between us, we construct a job routine around Blake: a five-morning workweek for me, a five-afternoon workweek for Ken, a prompt changing of the guard at lunchtime. Both our employers consider the arrangement odd, but since we're underpaid for our skills anyway (and are both perfectionists about the quality of our work), it's not a bad deal for them, either. For us, this solution involves financial sacrifice as well as being bone-tired most of the time, what with the baby, publishing jobs, freelance work, movement activities, housework, and trying to find any spare second in which to write. Yet we know we're privileged to be able to forge such a solution, and we feel incredibly lucky. Blake gets both of us. And we both get to be there for the delight that is him, golden, growing.

When the small women's groups meet in monthly coalition, it's clear that leadership battles, power struggles, and ego fights are upon us. Shulamith Firestone announces to Redstockings that she is a Great Thinker and therefore cannot be forced to take turns sweeping the floor at their tem-porary storefront headquarters; this is not received as a sign of sisterhood. Ti-Grace Atkinson purges certain members of The Feminists, who in turn pronounce her a Stalinist. Barbara Kaminsky (now calling herself Barbara Susan) confronts Kathie Amatniek (Sarachild) over Kathie's flirting with her husband, Hank Kaminsky (whose name remains Kaminsky); this come-on is embarrassing Hank and upsetting Barbara. To the alarm of all present, Kathie concedes her flirtation and further proclaims that although she is pro-monogamy, there are simply too few men with any feminist consciousness around, so their wives ought to be willing to share them in the name of sisterhood. Being an excessively fair person, Barbara actually considers this but then declines, remembering that the reason Hank has any consciousness at all is that she's labored to develop it. Meanwhile, a well-known British Marxist-feminist and Freud defender (which should have warned us) goes chirpily to bed with the husband of one of our New York Radical Women colleagues—while a houseguest in the New Yorker's apartment *and* while her hostess is in the hospital giving birth to her host's child. This is pretty odious stuff. "Sexual revolution" casualties litter the ground like the last-act cast of *Hamlet*.

We activists work hard to keep these troubles out of the courts and the press, because we know the freedom to fail is one of the freedoms denied us. Where differences among male politicos are covered with respect, the slightest disagreement among political women is regarded as a "cat fight"—and if word were to get out about any *sexual* scandals, the reporters would have a field day. So we whisper and hiss among ourselves, but having to conceal our altercations while engaging in them seems to make them more intense.

All things are relative, and we in WITCH consider ourselves by comparison fairly sane. We don't always succeed, but we *try* to avoid what we call "horizontal hostility," try to take out our ire in actions undermining patriarchy, not each other. We're a tightly knit cabal, ferociously loyal and snottily proud of our risk-taking, high visibility, and humor. We snitter among ourselves that because we are "more together" than Redstockings we ought to call our group Pantyhose. Our attitude is reminiscent of the Us-versus-Them tendency I know well from my marriage; it's a not always unprovoked proclivity of radicals in general, and it fits the paranoia of the day. We in WITCH consider ourselves the incarnate quiddity of revolution—blending female rebellion with Leftist revolt. We will suffer our own casualties in years to come, but for now we love each other, trust each other, laugh helplessly in curative recognition at our C-R meetings, offer each other dinners, solace, and Kleenex, baby-sit for each other. We are mostly white, mostly young—in our twenties and early thirties. We are ready not only to change the world but to do what we don't yet know is harder: change ourselves.

There is a core group in WITCH, plus outriders who come and go. Judith Ann is our calm rock of integrity, her quiet, unsought authority, our center; what Kenneth calls her "sword-steel eyes" can gleam a warning nobody wants to mess with.[2] Peggy Dobbins, a southerner trained as a sociologist, is our resident political analyst; she is nursing her son Jeb at the same time I'm nursing Blake; we sometimes switch babies during meetings, hoping to make them "milk brothers."[3] Florika—she of the cappuccino skin, wild gypsy mane, keen mind, and love of puns—has survived being a child-prodigy violinist in Europe; she never touches the violin now; she and I understand one another in private ways.[4] Bev Grant is our singer-songwriter-guitarist; Page, a would-be filmmaker, heaves her cumbersome 1960s video equipment along to our actions; Marcia is our graphic artist, in between doing her own woodcuts.[5] Barbara Susan comes to us, a welcome refugee from Redstockings. Sue Silverman/Silverwoman is our youngest member, in her late teens; Lynn Laredo is our den mother (maybe all of forty, which is *ancient*); Cynthia Funk is our resident wit, with beauty (she looks like Liv Ullmann and gets irked when men ask why *she* "needs feminism"). Mary, Perry, Ingrid, Jackie, and Naomi round us out, and Alix Kates Shulman[6] sometimes sits in on meetings. It is to Judith that I can finally admit how damaging the group-sex years in my marriage were for me, crying for hours in her arms.

[2] She and I stay in touch to this day. Judith, now divorced, remarried, and working in theater-therapy, has relocated to California.

[3] When last heard from, Peggy was a professor of sociology at the University of Alabama. She published a book of feminist theory, *From Kin to Class* (Signmaker Press, 1981), but complained humorously that her two sons were growing into southern "good ole boys."

[4] Florika Remetier will die of a drug overdose at age thirty-three in 1979. The poem "Elegy" commemorates her (in *Depth Perception*, and collected in *Upstairs in the Garden: Poems Selected and New*), and *Death Benefits: Poems* (Copper Canyon Press, 1981) is dedicated to her memory.

[5] Marcia Patrick will die tragically of breast cancer in the 1980s—cancer she chose to treat solely with alternative, herbal remedies until it was too late.

[6] Alix and I also remain in touch. She will go on to write the highly successful *Memoirs of an Ex-Prom Queen*, as well as the historic first "Marriage Contract"; still a feminist, she is still writing.

All of these women seem so damned *wise*. Each is an expert—on her own life, certainly, but that in turn relates to *all* our lives. Each has a special slant to contribute. The revelations I experience in an atmosphere of safety, support, and laughter among these women make me want to shout to the world how amazing this politics is.

I want to help them *back*, to help other women help *other* women. I want *millions* of women to connect with this consciousness, not just those we try to reach by handing out our smudgy mimeographed papers on street corners. I've already been the poetry editor of a small collection, *The New Woman*, published by *Motive* magazine—but if only there was a more effective, practical use for writing and editing skills! If only . . . it hits like Newton's apple falling on my head.

"*I know!*" I think to myself. "*An anthology!*"

In what will later be termed "networking," I start to reach outside the WITCH group. I hear about a woman who's a sculptor and also an academic; she's writing her dissertation on what she calls "sexual politics" in literature. I get in touch with her, read a draft, ask if she'd be willing to have an excerpt of it appear in a women's anthology. She thinks that's a great idea, confessing she yearns to publish the dissertation as a book, "even if nobody wants to read an academic thesis." I say she should try, that maybe the excerpt will help her land a book contract. Her name is Kate Millett.

I watch a woman being interviewed on William F. Buckley's TV show. She's presented as a feminist Roman Catholic theologian by Buckley, himself an arch-conservative Catholic. His description of her sounds oxymoronic. But she mops the floor with him, wrings him out, and proceeds to dust up the Vatican. I must have *her* in this anthology. I track her down. Her name is Mary Daly.

My old friend from SNCC days, Eleanor Holmes Norton, agrees to write one of a number of essays I plan to include on black women. Another pal from the civil-rights days, Elizabeth Sutherland Martinez, is happy to organize a section on Latinas. Interestingly, I can't find anybody willing to admit she's old enough to write an essay on ageism or on being an older women (which means, in the context, only over *fifty*), so Marge Piercy generously volunteers to write it under a nom de plume, even though she's too young but has, she reminds me, a novelist's imagination—and she'll also contribute an essay on sexism in the Left, under her own name. Martha Shelley, an early activist in Gay Liberation, will write on radical lesbians; the Daughters of Bilitis, the first lesbian civil-rights organization in the United States, formed in 1955, will also be represented, by Gene Damon, a foremother; Rita Mae Brown offers a poem on loving women. . . .

My brain goes into overdrive. In the middle of the night, I sit in the rocking chair, baby at my breast, notepad and pencil in my lap. *Young* women's voices, high-school students, have to be represented! And women in medicine, the military, the media! What about how psychology creates the norm of what's then considered "natural"? There *must* be an article on mothering! And statistics—*have* to have statistics! And those basic early documents we've been handing out: the NOW Bill of Rights, the Redstockings Manifesto. . . . We'll need a big appendix, listing sexist sayings and fight-back sayings—I'll call it Verbal Karate—and oh! there *has* to be a listing of groups to join, with addresses and contact people, so readers can *act*, and as complete a bibliography as can be assembled, so people can study more, think more. There should be poems, too, and songs for demonstrations. The book should be a primer, a key. The book should be *alive*. The book should be an *action*.

I begin to play with titles. I'll call it *Women in Revolt*. No, I can see the reviews—"a book on revolting women." I'll make up something funny, like *The Hand That Cradles the Rock*.[7] No, best to go with something simple, like a slogan we use on marches but also whisper to each other when our spirits sag. Something plain and true. Something like "sisterhood is powerful."

---

[7] This was the title up through advance notice in catalog copy, until it turned out to my surprise that S. J. Perelman had written a short story with that title decades earlier but now threatened to sue if we "harridans" used it. Some humorists have *no* sense of humor.

The men in relationships with the women in our group are not happy. They are just now discovering that this consciousness pertains to sex. And housework. And money. We women are not happy to discover that our men really and truly are just now discovering this. Big scenes. The men storm about. Some leave, some return, all of them complain of being depressed. They have no friends anymore, their old male buddies sneer they're "pussy-whipped," and most of the women they know are interested in being friends with each other, not with men. They are lonely for us, envious of the fun and energy we generate for each other. We women joke that our men need a play group more than our babies do. We try to reassure them that this is all in their own self-interest. They're having a hard time seeing the act of ceding power as being in their self-interest. Among ourselves, we defend them, feel guilty when we defend them, feel guilty when we don't.

Our men decide to form a men's group. They will be each *other's* friends! They will meet weekly, cook together and eat together, share their problems! They're elated. We're uneasy but can't locate why. Don't we *want* them to challenge and support each other in changing? Don't we *believe* in solidarity? Of course we do! Why are we so jittery?

It takes only a few months to explode in our faces. John wants to know why *he* has to do the laundry when it turns out that's not one of George's tasks. George wants to know why John gets off with laundry, a once-a-week task, when he's stuck with dishwashing and drying, a three times-a-day task. Kenneth and Hank quarrel over whether it's a one-upping, masculinist, elitist gesture to bring Häagen-Dazs ice cream to a group potluck dinner. There is competition about who is the most antisexist revolutionary man. There is competition about who knows his Engels better and who can quote most from "Resistances to Consciousness." There is competition about which man is more sensitive, about who cries more. There is serious discussion about whether they should all "turn gay" as a political statement of support for not pestering women.

We women are in a stupor of disbelief. We're being set against one another. First only two of the Witches spend hours on the phone mending fences after their men have traded private sexual stories; soon all of us are spending hours on the phone doing damage control. We decide that, at this moment in history, men in groups bond to reinforce their power, not to divest themselves of it. We march together to disband their next meeting.

Things are pretty sullen in everybody's home life for a while.

Random House will publish the anthology. John Simon, a politically engaged person and a senior editor, will be its shepherd. But he is a man, and white to boot—a combination virtually required to hold power in the publishing world at the time.[8] In a leap of principle, I proclaim that John can be the titular editor but that all hands directly involved with the book must be women's, even if women at Random House are mostly assistant or junior editors. To my surprise, he graciously concedes—but I learn later from these women that he thinks me terrifying. I don't feel terrifying. I don't think it extreme to want the first anthology on women's liberation to be in women's control.

Meanwhile, back at WITCH, several women are uncomfortable with the idea of the book. They worry that it will make me rich and famous and that they're not in it. I explain that the advance doesn't even cover the permission fees, that I've already *been* famous and found it overrated, that I'd be delighted for us to do the book as a collective, and/or that I'll gladly put them in it—so what would they like to write about? Silence. But the majority supports the book. I'm grateful, because I suspect I'm so far gone into it by now there's no turning back. This is the first time I've dared "defy" anyone in our own tight group, so I'm a wreck with the stress of losing even one woman's approval.

Meanwhile, Random House editorial and production folks are pressuring me to deliver the manuscript ahead of schedule. They worry that "this women's liberation fad" is peaking and will soon decline, so if we don't get the book out fast, we'll miss the boat.

[8] The situation, of course, is markedly different thirty years later. Now, tokenism abounds.

The year 1970 hits like a meteor.

In January, I get a phone call from Jane Alpert, one of the women at the "underground" newspaper *Rat*. She says that women have decided to seize the paper for an issue and need ideas and support from women's liberationists. I'd written some pieces for *Rat* in 1968 and 1969, but hadn't been able to tolerate the paper's lifestyle emphasis aimed at young white straight males—sex-wanted ads, pornographic articles and graphics, and Rolling Stones coverage had begun to bury political reporting of any substance. So I find it wonderful that the few women on *Rat* have finally had enough, too.

We come from all parts of the nascent Women's Movement, most of us knowing zip about putting out a newspaper. But we do it. A few feminist newspapers have already begun—*Everywoman*, *It Ain't Me, Babe*, and *Off Our Backs* among them, but this is the first time women have seized a male-run periodical, and it creates ripples all across the Left, with women in other cities taking over local media on a temporary or permanent basis. We do not, in fact, *ever* give *Rat* back to the boys, although we never manage to change it into a real feminist paper, either.

"Goodbye to All That" is my contribution to the first issue. It simmers with fury at Leftist men's betrayal of women. To my astonishment, it becomes an instant classic, having apparently articulated the experience of most women in the Left.[9] The piece is quoted, read aloud in struggle meetings, cried over, fought about, excerpted on posters and banners, and widely reprinted. I receive my first death threats. They're from my Leftist revolutionary brothers.

~ ~ ~

The year 1970 accelerates.

In March, Kenneth is fired from his job at Funk & Wagnalls for refusing to take down his My Lai poster.

In April, I am fired from my job at Grove Press for union organizing. We're bringing the war home indeed.

---

[9] For a thorough depiction of the *Rat* seizure, the reaction to "Goodbye to All That," and the essay itself, see *The Word of a Woman*.

I've been working at Grove as an editor for two and a half years when I'm summarily fired, along with five other employees. The official reasons are "reorganization needs," but the real motive—as later confirmed by the National Arbitration Association of the National Labor Relations Board—is union busting.[10] Grove Press has built a reputation as a Left-liberal, avant-garde publisher, but much of its output consists of sub-imprints (the Venus, Zebra, and Black Cat lines) of soft- and hard-core porn paperbacks. I've refused to work on these, though I did edit a critical edition of the Marquis de Sade for them, which gave me nightmares. But I can't refuse to engage the unequal treatment of women employees, from janitor to editor, all around (and including) me.

In 1970, publishing—a white-collar business, and one of New York City's largest industries—is experiencing feminist and union stirrings in general. The two issues merge, since more than 80 percent of all publishing employees at the time are women, and we are virtually all at the bottom of the pyramid.[11] There is talk of forming an industry-wide vertical union. With the help of two notably anti-war, anti-racist, progressive unions—the Fur, Leather, and Machine Workers (FLM) and District 65 (hospital workers)—organizing efforts have begun in a number of publishing houses, including Harper & Row, which previously had managed to co-opt such efforts into a "company union." At Grove, we few who've volunteered to be union organizers are warned by our superiors that we could be fired, but we know that's illegal. Each of us has also withstood pressure to name employees who signed union cards toward holding an election. Then the purge hits. The Grove Press firings serve as a warning to employees throughout the industry. In this at least Grove is avant-garde.

[10] On August 4, 1970, Arbitrator Thomas Knowlton ruled that Grove had illegally discharged employees "solely for union activities," and ordered our reinstatement with back pay. I could never go back, but the money was useful—it paid the pediatrician, and it paid the printer for two issues of *Rat*. For the full story of the Grove Press union-organizing effort and subsequent firings, seizure and occupation, jailings, etc., see *Going Too Far*.

[11] As with pediatrics in medicine, the exceptions to male control in publishing are the juvenile-book departments. This too is not so drastically different in the year 2000.

It is also avant-garde in playing unwilling host to a seizure, barricade, and occupation of the executive offices by myself and thirty other women—protesting the firings, the union busting, discrimination against women employees, and misogynist publications. This is the first such militant action of the current feminist wave. It's also the first time women declare pornography a form of hate propaganda against women. My rallying cry will be "Pornography is the theory, rape is the practice."

We are ensconced in the executive offices. I have marched us all in at 8:00 A.M., claiming to the security guard that these are friends come to help me carry out personal stuff from my office, now that I've been fired. He thinks it odd I need so *much* help, but we move into the elevator and up to the sixth floor before he has time to stop us. Once upstairs, I sever some of the elevator cables, strew vaseline-coated thumbtacks on the stairs, lock the doors, and pour glue in the locks. Then I hang our Women's Liberation banner out the window of the executive office—a white cloth emblazoned in red with the feminist symbol. Some of us lug furniture to barricade the doors; some hit the phones to inform the press, other publishers, and union officials of the seizure; some patrol windows. Martha Shelley, unfortunately, busts open the executive liquor cabinet to have a "symbolic" drink. I start inspecting the financial files of Barney Rosset, Grove's founder and owner. I suspect we'll find that Betty Shabazz, Malcolm X's widow, has been bilked on royalties from his autobiography, and find correspondence in which Rosset admits he'll fight union organizing to the death. It turns out I'm not wrong: "Grove Press won't tolerate a revolution; Grove Press *is* the revolution." We laugh with glee and chomp potato chips.

As word gets out, a crowd gathers down on the sidewalk, at the corner of Mercer and Bleecker streets in Greenwich Village. Secretaries, junior editors, women from other publishing houses appear in solidarity. Union pickets start circling. After five, when work lets out, the crowd swells, spills into the street, stopping traffic. Police arrive. Journalists and camera crews are everywhere. Our lawyer and spokeswoman, Emily Jane Goodman, talks with the press on the street.[12] She displays a pornographic paperweight found on Rosset's desk, and conveys the news that in addition to demanding our right to unionize, we insist that the proceeds from the pornography imprints be used to set up a fund for prostituted women's bail, rehab, and tuition, and that Malcolm X's royalties be properly paid to his widow. Emily is soft-spoken, blond, lovely, smart, *and* recently corporation counsel to Grove itself. Some male journalists can't grasp why *she* "would want to be a feminist." She informs them that Rosset "never knew how to treat a woman lawyer like a lawyer."

The hours wear on. Rosset, in Denmark screening porn films for U.S. distribution, is apoplectic on the phone. This exposure is disaster for his would-be radical image. Fred Jordan, vice president and editor of Grove's *Evergreen Review*, calls to scream obscenities at me. Dick Seaver, another VP, who heads Grove Books and is my former boss, calls and offers me my job back if I'll leave. I remind him we have political demands. Later, he calls again to warn me arrests are imminent, at Rosset's and Jordan's insistence, though he too has "been forced to" sign the complaint. He begs me to go, asks why am I doing this "to him," and whines, "Robin, *I've* done *nothing!*" Borrowing a retort from the British suffragists, the Pankhursts, I reply that this is happening *because* he's done nothing. Tension grows. Police vans arrive. Some of our group can't afford another bust on their record; others are scared. We sneak them down the back stairs and on out with help from sympathetic secretaries at another firm. The "Grove Press Nine" who remain with me are Martha Altman, Ti-Grace Atkinson, Barbara Chambers, Suzanne DeVincenzo, Beth Katz, Barbara Kevles, Geraldine Maleba, and Wendy Roberts.

The arrest finally comes. The elevators are still out of action, and it takes a while for the police to wend their way up the back stairs. When they do, they find us barricaded and have to de-hinge doors and heave furniture to get at us. My colleagues go peaceably once arrested. But I'm sailing with it now.

---

[12] Emily and I had become friends when, as former counsel for Grove Press, she'd worked with me as I edited *The Bust Book* (a what-to-do-till-the-lawyer-comes arrest primer for radical readers) for Grove. She will be standing by me as my attorney for many a trauma during this period. Still a friend, she now sits as a judge on the New York State Supreme Court bench.

I declare that I refuse to recognize male authority and will surrender only to policewomen. For a few minutes everyone huddles, considering whether to call for women officers; then the cops jolt back to reality and remember their own power. When the policemen approach me, I go limp, trained in the civil-rights passive-resistance tradition. I'm charged with resisting arrest on top of criminal trespass and criminal mischief, a felony, and hauled out and down six flights—like Pooh bear being dragged by Christopher Robin, my head bouncing unceremoniously on each step.

The crowd roars in support as I emerge feet first, but I can't see anyone, surrounded as I am—one short woman bobbing in a sea of blue-clad men. I do register the presence of Red Squad reps. And I can spot, from afar, Emily, smiling reassuringly, fist raised. And farther back, John Simon, my non-editing editor at Random House, looking shell-shocked but with *his* fist gamely raised.

We are detained for arraignment. This is a first bust for some of the women, and they require hand-holding. It's all very well having to mother them, but personally I'm worried about my real baby: Blake's been having a mild reaction to his smallpox inoculation and is running a low fever. Only after using my one call to phone home am I reassured: "Fever's down. We love you. Give 'em hell!" Kenny says. I can hear Blake piping, "Yaaaay!"

I breathe easier, but soon realize I have committed a major tactical error by including Ti-Grace Atkinson in the group. Divas and detention are a lousy combo. Her imperious, patrician attitude has been irritating enough throughout the long hours of the occupation; she has also brought along a friend—a woman who behaves so suspiciously that some of our group think she's an agent.[13] Atkinson's haughty behavior would actually be comic—if it weren't under the circumstances dangerously provocative

---

[13] She will turn out to be a would-be journalist smuggled in secretly by Ti-Grace—violating pledges we've all made that no press will be permitted inside the group—to cover Atkinson during the demonstration. The poor woman, Barbara Kevles, who never intended to be arrested, gets pressured by Atkinson into going the whole way. Kevles pouts through the action, trembles through the arrest, and barely talks with anyone but Ti-Grace. Later, she will write the story of her rebellion and incarceration—an interesting if embarrassingly written piece of fiction—but be unable to find a periodical to publish it.

of the police, in whose custody we decidedly are. This is 1970, and sensitivity training for cops is as yet unheard of. She rants at them, calls them
vermin, says she will sue to have her mink jacket cleaned from police van
"filth," reminds them their parents were probably immigrants whereas
hers have been here for generations, screams she's being tortured when
the desk sergeant tries to fingerprint her, and refuses to be searched,
threatening the matrons who come near her. I catch myself being concerned for the matrons' safety, then decide my sense of sisterhood must be
getting bleary. When one of our other women, a diabetic, faints, I wheedle
a decent young cop into getting food for her *fast*—which he manages to
do, so Ti-Grace loudly castigates me for "collaborating with fascists." Fortunately, Emily appears, with the attorney Flo Kennedy in tow. Emily
bears the news that John Simon will put up bail for me—quite a gesture
considering the trouble it may get him into at Random House. I gratefully
refuse, I can't leave the others behind. Message comes back: okay, *okay*,
bail for all *nine* protestors. To the mixed reactions of my sisters, I again
decline—unless bail can be extended to include Kitten, Candy, Peaches,
and the other six women with whom we're penned, women busted for
prostitution, women I consider political prisoners. John's purse isn't big
enough. We're taken to holding cells for the night.

There's a peculiar freedom about being in jail. You have nothing to do but
wait. In southern jails, somebody's usually humming a spiritual off in some
neighboring cell. You feel pure, light, weightless, momentarily unbur-
dened of duties, no bills to pay or phones to answer, cut loose from your
responsibilities and personas, from the physical moorings of familiar
places and *things*. I rediscover that I am, after all, not the Tiffany shade on
the living-room lamp, much as I love its greengold swirls. I am not my
clothes or my furniture, I am not my husband, not my child, not the books
I have read or written. I am simply who and what I portably am, in my
mind, emotions, and body. I have been stripped of everything—even my
tampon, which the matrons insist I replace with a sanitary napkin they give
me. I ponder why, and decide it's because they're afraid I'll hang myself

with the two-inch string. Laughing, I fall asleep on the hard wood slab, my pea jacket for a blanket, one sleeve for a pillow.

On the other hand, awakened repeatedly during the night, I have second thoughts about the meditative qualities of this jail. I don't know how in hell Marx wrote *Das Kapital*—or even his name—in prison. Maybe European detention is quieter than Manhattan detention. Or maybe long-term sentences yield some silence. Or maybe men's prisons do. But New York women's jails are a cacophony of screams, sobs, talk, giggles, singing, cursing, snores, and shouts. Furthermore, Ti-Grace is shrieking that she's having a nervous breakdown from having been tortured and that she must have lightly poached eggs for breakfast, real cream—*not* milk—with her coffee, and fresh—really *fresh*—croissants. After such a night, Helen of Troy would appear at her arraignment looking bloated.

The next morning, soft-voiced, sharp-brained Emily gets us released on our own recognizance. Hundreds of women are in court, where they've been all night, waiting for us; one has been arrested for banging her tambourine. There are cheers, crowds, and a rush of interviews to do—but everything will just have to wait. Nothing in the universe is more important than the fragrance of Blake's baby hair, the instant I can clasp him in my arms while he waves his little fist, hugs my neck, and laughs.

In strategic terms, the action is a success. Not only women's liberationists but much of the Left supports us. Carl Oglesby, Kathy Boudin, Julius Lester, and James Forman side with the protest, and Boudin and Oglesby even withdraw their books from the house list; the Leftist guru Paul Goodman and publisher André Schiffrin publicly denounce their old friend Rosset.[14] Boycotts of Grove Press books are mounted (and eventually will be so successful that Grove as a publishing house will fail, existing merely as an imprint out of other houses).

A few weeks later, the judge throws out the charges, actually lauding us for protesting against pornography, but lecturing me for resisting arrest. The other women manage to restrain Ti-Grace, who wants to complain to

---

[14] Certain other Grove or *Evergreen Review* authors are deafeningly silent on the whole matter, including the attempt at unionizing—among them Abbie Hoffman, Dennis Hopper, Jack Newfield, Dotson Rader, Allen Ginsberg, and Nat Hentoff.

the court that she should have pulled down an extra charge, too, because she *meant* to resist arrest and besides she was tortured. Meanwhile, I get the feeling that this judge is railing against porn because he's against *sex,* not sex*ism*—but it's not the moment to quibble.

There's still the whole arbitration battle to fight with Grove. Rosset and Jordan, in print, declare me "a brown-shirt, fascist, would-be book burner" for my comments about their porn lines. Carl Oglesby, in print, resigns as a contributing editor to *Evergreen Review* and declares me "the *real* wolf of the revolution" that Rosset, by publishing radical books, has invoked but cannot deal with in the flesh. I do not feel like a fascist or a wolf. I am linguistically disgruntled by the way "fascist" is thrown around, and by all this anthropomorphism regarding animals. What I do feel like is a human, quite worried about the matter of survival, which will mean more reliance on freelance editing again. And where's that supposed to come from? I now have a union organizer's reputation in the book industry.

It's yet another radicalizing experience. Which is becoming a daily occurrence.

Sisterhood Is Powerful is published in the fall of 1970. It will be become a best-seller but not be listed as such on the *New York Times* list, because in that day the list excludes anthologies. It will become the "click," the first feminist epiphany for hundreds of thousands of women, and the staple of mushrooming women's studies courses around the world. Toward the end of the 1990s, the National Association of Librarians will choose it as one of the World's 100 Most Influential Books of the Twentieth Century—up there with Marx's *Das Kapital*, Einstein's *Theory of Relativity*, and Freud's *Interpretation of Dreams*. Random House's anxiety about missing the boat will be a touch off the mark: the book will remain steadily in print for thirty years, up to the turn of the millennium.

The dedication reads: *For Faith, my mother. With love. Finally.*

My mother says, "That's nice, dear."

I swear I will never compile another anthology.

Meanwhile, the thought occurs to me that there really is a need for an international version. . . .

~ ~ ~

Book promotion. Movement promotion. The talk-show circuit.

The instant I hit the TV world, *they* know who I am—or rather, was. I insist my former career not be mentioned, not because I'm hiding anything, but because I know that this subject, once allowed in, will take over and bury whatever feminist ideas I'm there to discuss. Selfishly, I do dread gurgles of "*Look* who's grown up to be a *feminist!*" But I also worry that once I'm identified as a former child star, the tiny woman inside the lens, the woman in curlers and a housedress, ironing and watching TV, might dismiss me as being a celebrity too distant from her reality to carry a political message of any relevance to *her* life.

While still pregnant, I've had to do Merv Griffin's show, when another activist cancels from stage fright. This entails smiling grit-teethed while explaining the Basics ("*No*, women *don't* want to be drafted. Actually, we'd like to end the draft for men, too. *No*, rape survivors *don't* 'ask for it' . . ."), only to have Griffin fixate on my belly, asking, "How can you be a genuine feminist if you've got a bun in the oven?"

A few weeks after Blake's birth, I do *The Tonight Show*, at that time still aired live. The staff promises not to raise "my past," but to treat seriously issues of my present. While on air, citing statistics on employment and education discrimination, I glance at a monitor and see that I'm really doing a voice-over, while clips from the network film morgue are being run: little Dagmar eating that eternal cookie, Alice arguing with the Cheshire cat. Mortified, I interrupt myself and call it. Carson puts on his quizzical, raised-eyebrows, whywhatssamatter look. Big laugh from the audience. I explain courteously but firmly that I agreed to do the show in order to publicize issues that affect women's lives, and that his staff had sworn not to trivialize that by focusing on my having once been a kid actor. He manages to turn my indignation into a joke. This is a no-win. I rise, politely wish him good evening, and walk off—off camera, off stage. There is panic behind me as I leave the stage door. *Nobody* walks off *The Tonight Show*, live, on air.

I'm certain they'll never have me on again, but I'm wrong. By this time they're pre-taped, though. Bob Hope is a substitute host for a vacationing

Carson, and another guest, Glenn Ford—a pro-gun, anti-choice conservative, it turns out—has at me. But several years have elapsed, and consciousness has begun to shift. This time I ignore Hope and Ford and
appeal directly to the woman inside the lens, asking her to complain if she
thinks it's unfair for men to gang up on and make fun of a woman trying to
talk about women's rights. Hope makes a joke about rape and rapier wit.
The LAUGH sign flashes, the audience titters. I save my laugh until later,
when a feminist mole on the show's staff informs me that protest letters
are inundating them, mailbag after mailbag.

The Phil Donahue Show is live, originating in Dayton, Ohio. They want
me to debate an editor from Playboy magazine, a man unforgettably
named Anselm Mount. I tell them I don't debate such basic issues as
human freedom. They promise they'll have us on in separate segments.
When I check into the hotel in Dayton, Mount has left a chummy little
note, asking me to have a drink with him in the bar so we can discuss
tomorrow's debate. It's been a trap. I decline his drink and once in my
room, get on the phone and start calling around Ohio to women's groups I
know. All night they drive and arrive in stages—sixty women, from Cincin-
nati, Cleveland, Toledo, Akron. A women's media group from Antioch College comes, complete with video equipment. We strategize in my room.
The next morning, they all show up, smiling, docile, in line for the studio
audience. Once on air, seated beside Mount (it *is* a trap, no separate segment is planned), I seize the mike from a startled Donahue and refuse to
give it back, announcing that we will not be debating after all, that women
are taking over the program. Indeed, they rise from all over the audience,
the Antioch video women calmly elbowing aside the cameramen to take
possession of the cameras, women moving up onto the set, women moving to guard the doors. Mount is reduced to jumping up and down, throwing a hissy fit, screaming that we're all just jealous that we're not cute
enough to be a Playboy centerfold; he finally slumps into a sulk. Phil, to
his lasting credit, goes with the flow, unprotesting that his show has just
been yanked out from under him. He knows his audience—mostly
women whose hair has been in rollers—and his audience applauds us.
The switchboard is jammed with questions and call-ins of support. I stay
in the studio for two hours after the show, answering women's phone calls.
The producer claims this was the most watched Donahue show to date.

On subsequent appearances over the years, Phil will take naughty pleasure in starting each interview with me by running video clips from that first takeover.

~   ~   ~

As I knew he would, Kenneth makes a superb father, especially for a young child. His irrepressible creativity is given full vent, as if he and Blake were both children. They don't just *finger*-paint; they *body* paint, smearing their daubed bare torsos on big sheets of paper, making a joyful mess of which de Kooning would be proud. Kenny can make toys from nothing; he whittles a plastic milk carton into a knight's helmet with visor, bends and cuts a large cardboard box into a castle. (Kenneth is still a writer, though, so naturally he *writes* about his fathering, in articles for alternative media and in poems.)[15] Our shared love for this child has knitted us together, more closely than in a long time. I, meanwhile, am in a state of vigilant pleasure to discover that I'm not a half-bad mother, after all—neither a Faith nor a Mates reincarnate. It's so *easy* to love Blake, which makes it easy to be a good mother.

Of course, I feel guilty all the time: not being there every single second for Blake, not there every second for Kenny, not there every second for the movement, for *Rat* and WITCH and *Sisterhood Is Powerful*. Not earning enough money. Certainly not writing enough poems. I'd feel sanctimonious about my sacrifices, but I'm too busy feeling rotten about my deficiencies. The triumphs seem ectoplasmic; only the failures seem real. But guilt is a homey, familiar emotion for me by now. I'm also learning it's not just me; it comes with the territory of being female—guilt, plus fatigue so pervasive as to be invisible and normal. The word "multi-tasking" has not yet been coined, and won't be until men discover decades later that they too can do more than one thing at a time. The word "proletariat" *has* been coined, however. Etymologically, it means "bearers of children." I understand why.

---

[15] See especially *Color Photos of the Atrocities.*

Relentless 1970 draws to a close with the book tour for *Sisterhood Is Powerful*. The anthology has generated requests from women around the country—to lecture, organize, advise, agitate. Well, the movement needs money and so do I, colleges can pay, and local groups need benefits, too. I can cleanse my old skills by putting them to work for a cause *I* choose.

At this point, the montage accelerates into a blur that I will later try to describe in *Going Too Far*. The spontaneous circle dance of hundreds of women in a Michigan gymnasium after a speech. The physical eviction of an especially obnoxious heckler from a seminar in New Mexico—all six-and-a-half-foot football hero of him being hefted out the door by five petite women. Forty-degree-below-zero dawn in Saskatchewan, Canada—sitting up and talking all night (as usual) with women before catching my 7:00 A.M. plane on to another town, another college, another feminist community. The closing circle around me of about twenty jocks on a Pennsylvania campus, drunk and in an ugly mood, each man carrying a lit torch and screaming, "Burn the witch." The growing presence of women of color in audiences, the growing presence of housewives, community women, working-class women. The Jesus freak who lunges at me from four feet away as if in slow motion, cursing me to eternal damnation, his knife raised high, glittering in the Los Angeles sun, at an outdoor speech. The sixty-year-old woman who stands up at the rap session after a lecture and, crying softly, says she's just realized she's been raped almost every night of her thirty-five-year marriage. The bomb threats in auditoriums before or during speeches, the pickets carrying signs declaring me a baby killer, the menacing letters and phone calls. But also the radical feminist nuns in Washington State doing secret abortion referrals who present me with an embroidered banner reading "Saint Paul was Just a Big Prick." The women's faces, women's voices, tears, laughter, electricity, energy . . .

In 1971, I attend the Radical Feminist Conference in Detroit, organized by Kathleen Barry, Joanne Parrent, Barbara Burris, and Joanne DeLor, women who had written *The Fourth World Manifesto*. This groundbreaking manifesto is in part a response to Charlotte Bunch (a former Christian youth leader then husbanded and hyphenated as Bunch-Weeks) and a group of women who'd formed the self-termed Anti-Imperialist Women's Movement, rather insultingly implying that anyone who wasn't in their group was pro-imperialist. I still consider myself a women's liberationist, but now find these omnipresent schisms tiresome. At the Detroit conference, I will re-meet Joanne Parrent[16] and Kathleen Barry,[17] a striking woman with prematurely white hair, a crisp wit, and a radical feminist mind. I don't yet know that Kathy and I will become lifelong friends, only that apparently her patience as well as mine has broken at the agonizing rhetoric of several Trotskyite women who have infiltrated to break up our "bourgeois, reactionary, divisive-of-world-revolution meeting." One such woman has planted herself in the entrance way, cross-legged amid bundled piles of her lethally boring newspaper, the *Militant*. She shouts slogans and hurls half-punches at all who pass, refusing to budge, no matter how nicely or frequently asked.

I suspect rightly that Kathy will be not just a sister but a friend when, on the second day, with only a glance exchanged between us, we gently lift the Trot and place her, still in lotus position though in midair, stunned, together with her newspaper stacks, in the elevator. Then we smile and wave goodbye, press the Down button, and, as the doors close, shake hands and reintroduce ourselves.

Kenneth, who was part of the Stonewall demonstration—the formal birth of the Gay Movement—has co-founded the Gay Liberation Front (GLF). The same ego games, leadership fights, correct-line squabbles are taking

---

[16] Joanne will go on to form the first Federal Feminist Credit Union and eventually move to California, where she currently writes and produces films.

[17] Author of *Susan B. Anthony: A Biography of a Singular Feminist* (NYU Press, 1988), *Female Sexual Slavery* (Prentice Hall and NYU Press, 1979), and *The Prostitution of Sexuality* (NYU Press, 1995), editor of *Vietnam's Women in Transition* (St. Martin's Press, 1996), and founder of the International Coalition against Trafficking in Women.

place there as among women—but worse (gay or straight, these guys are *guys*). Meanwhile, lesbian women in GLF are ricocheting between the misogyny of their gay brothers and the homophobia of their straight sisters in women's liberation.

Kenneth is looking frayed around the edges, too. Apparently he's "too pro-feminist" for some of his gay comrades; besides, if he's married that *must* mean he can't be gay (though most of these men damned well know better). Since he and I have been quietly killing ourselves for years trying to work out this arrangement—with his practicing a guilty freedom and my practicing a guilty monogamy—the irony of this oversimplification is not lost on us. And since I wear the scars of being "insufficiently radical feminist" for certain women, because I'm married and a mother (of a *male*, yet), our wagons are drawn in a circle again.

Ken, Steven Dansky, and John Knoeble form a pro-feminist gay men's group and publish several issues of a journal, the *Effeminist*. It contains the earliest thoughtful antisexist writing by men in the current feminist wave, and lasts for a year or so. Ken is persona non grata in GLF now, for being too "pro-woman." But at least Steve and John, together with some of the women from WITCH, help make a chosen, extended family for Blake.

Back in New York, the women at *Rat* announce they've decided I write "too well" and must drop my byline. Humbled, I submit. A few months later, they say I *still* write too well, that my pieces are identifiable even with a pseudonym. I try to oblige. I stick in lots of mutha-fuckin'-pig-dog conspiracy stuff, but fail miserably in sustaining sufficient solecisms. I am caught using the word "antithesis." Finally, they tell me I may not write for the paper at all—but not *leave* either, which would be letting me off too easy: I must stay and just do office work instead.

God forbid I should act like Firestone and think I'm above sweeping. So I do it, all the shitwork, for some months, feeling morally superior in secret. I'm getting tired, though, of having to argue that a Miss Havana Beauty Contest is no better just because Fidel says it's different in a socialist country; tired of having to explain why feminism is not necessarily defined by a woman with a baby on her hip, a rifle in her hand, and a tractor under her ass. I realize I'm tired of having to be in the feminist cau-cus—tired we have to *have* a feminist caucus at an all-women's newspaper in the first place. The lives of those "unrevolutionary masses" of women I've met in Montana and Iowa and Kentucky and Maine echo back at me. *That's* feminism, I think. It dawns on me, more than two years after hav-ing written "Goodbye to All That," that it isn't just the *men* in the Left but the *politics* of the Left that are failing women.

I resign from the *Rat* collective. I stop calling myself a women's libera-tionist. I start calling myself a feminist. A radical feminist, of course.

Blake and I are caught in a summer rainstorm. Impetuously, we decide to walk home singing, not avoiding the puddles but splashing directly through them, skipping and holding hands. I am in my early thirties and have never done this before.

With the zeal of a convert, I seize the torch and loft it high for those sis-ters still standing where I stood five minutes earlier.

Having already required universities to have signers, wheelchair access, and free childcare at my lectures (greatly resisted at first but later standard procedure at feminist speeches), I now stop taking questions from men. I carefully explain that this is not meant as anti-male but as pro-female, to correct the imbalance in a discourse men tend to dominate. I explain that women's questions should be the priority because we must be the agents of change over our own lives, and that clever men will see this as a chance to listen in on what women ask and answer each other. A few men under-stand, come up quietly afterward or pass notes of support, but most are offended at this challenge to what they feel is their entitlement. So it's just as well that I offer the above reasons instead of admitting that I cannot bear *one more time* a man's question so moronic it could have been posed by an inebriated gnat.

My mother actually *marries*! All through my adolescence I'd longed for this, thinking it might take the heat off me; I'd laughed aloud in recognition when I first heard the song "If Momma Were Married" from *Gypsy*. Now finally resigned to the fact *I'm* married, and expectably ecstatic about her grandchild, *she* finds herself a husband. Hallelujah.

But. I don't want to carp, yet I find myself loathing her choice. Archie Thurman, a wealthy businessman "in textiles" is a widower with grown children of his own, who in turn loathe my mother.[18] This is the kind of man who is incapable of commenting on anything without revealing or inquiring about its price.

Me (trying to be nice): Nifty tie, Archie.

Him: Nifty? *Nifty*? You wanna know nifty? This tie cost eighty-five bucks!

Or:

Me: I'm excited. My book of poems has been accepted for publication.

Him: Pomes. How much d'ya get paid for a book like that?

But my mother is a surprisingly attentive, even obedient wife to him. She joins his temple and goes regularly to services. It occurs to me that I disapprove of her marriage as much as she disapproves of mine. I wonder if that makes us even.

For the first time, Gloria Steinem registers on my consciousness as someone worth knowing. Until now, in different ways, she and Betty Friedan have been driving us radicals batty. Friedan too vociferously denounces us, exaggerating our message toward androcide; Steinem too helpfully explains us, blanding our message toward insipidity. On the few occasions I find myself stuck with them, doing a radio or TV show, Friedan is downright rude (not just to me but to everyone, especially Steinem, which is oddly comforting). Steinem is always warm, yet she strikes me as being

---

[18] An unanticipated benefit, which I will discover later, is in being remotely related by this marriage to his niece Judith Thurman—referred to by *her* family as Judith-who-lives-in-the-Village-with-a-loft-bed. She will eventually write acclaimed biographies of Isak Dinesen and Colette.

largely irrelevant to serious feminism at this point. She's written sympathetically about us for *New York* magazine, and she's fine on liberal
causes—against the war and for the Farmworkers—but she's one of the
Beautiful People, she's chic, dates powerful men, and actually campaigns
for Norman Mailer in his short-lived attempt to become mayor of New
York. I don't *dis*like her but, being a bit of a literary and political snob,
regard her as a well-meaning but glitzy jet-set journalist, not an activist.

Then we're scheduled to appear together at PS 41 in Manhattan, discussing violence, women, and women's liberation. The panel will also
include Ti-Grace, Kate Millett, and Anselma Dell'Olio, a filmmaker active
in NOW. We assemble on stage in the auditorium. While the audience is
still filing in, Gloria slides a manila envelope in my direction.

"I, um, thought you might like to have these. Anyway, I thought you'd
prefer them not floating around," she murmurs, rather shyly.

I peek into the envelope. Glossy photos of me as a child star—publicity photos, photos from *Juvenile Jury,* from the *Mama* show, from *Kiss and
Tell* . . . I stare at her.

"I have friends who work in the photo morgues at some of the newspapers, so I just thought . . ," she smiles.

"*Thank* you," I say, and mean it from the heart. I do an emotional
double take, thinking *That's an interesting woman*—someone who understands certain subtleties about the uses and abuses of celebrity and public perception, as well as about power and access . . . and how rare that a
stranger should want to protect *me*, the one used to doing the protecting.

This night will be memorable for other reasons, too. Ti-Grace, barefoot
and wearing flowing Vietnamese pajamas, strides to the stage microphone
to announce that her friend the recently gunned-down Mafia boss "Sister
Joseph Colombo" was a *real* feminist since he was an outlaw, as opposed
to the rest of us, "who refuse to challenge the system." Since the Colombo
family controls drugs and prostitution in New York, the audience responds
with an appalled silence before breaking into boos. (I must be slow, but
this is actually the first time it occurs to me that movements for social
change attract all *sorts* of people, for all sorts of personal and not necessarily healthy reasons, who carry with them all sorts of pain and serious
imbalances, and that just *maybe* not *every*body is *automatically* my sister.)
Gloria, in a trembling voice, admits as a pacifist to having dreams about

doing violence to violent men. Then, since the subject is violence, I decide to use my panel time to offer the first public reading of a poem I've just finished. It begins, "Listen, I'm slowly dying inside myself tonight . . ." The poem is called "Monster."[19]

~ ~ ~

Blake grows, rapidly, beautifully, precociously. He has walked early, talked early, and adores music. This will be his eventual vocation—both escape from and loving revenge against his logorrheic wordsmith parents.

Every detail about his raising *matters* to us, passionately. We don't lie to him, ever. (This is hard sometimes, and will be harder when the marriage eventually ends, but it's the complicated *lies* that have scarred most people's childhoods; for us, truth is a form of respect for him and each other.) We only promise what we know we can actually deliver, and the result is trust. We tell him bedtime stories about strong women and gentle men, making the stories up ourselves[20] or basing them on historical characters, since virtually no antisexist children's books are yet available. We talk politics with him, explaining whatever we can, admitting where we've been wrong, saying what we've learned. (Like any kid, he wants to do what the grown-ups are doing—so by age six he has paper cuts on his tongue, from having begged to help lick envelopes during Bella Abzug's campaign mailings.) He knows about and is proud of Kenneth's being gay. We proscribe nothing—no television shows, books, or movies are forbidden—but we do Talk About It afterward, at length (*endlessly*, he will tease us as an adult). We construct alternatives to patriarchal holidays, like Wiccan sabbats— and wind up celebrating both traditional *and* alternative (like mother, like daughter). He plays with dolls *and* trucks. Later, war toys are unwelcome in the house, but to combat peer pressure we devise a substitute: medieval legend, the Round Table. At least then battle will be distanced from reality: maces and lances aren't standard issue in Vietnam. The hope is that

---

[19] First published in *Monster: Poems* (Random House, 1972), collected in *Upstairs in the Garden*.

[20] In 1991 The Feminist Press at CUNY published *The Mer Child: A Legend for Children and Other Adults*, which I wrote for Blake when he was about seven.

he'll turn out less accepting of the idea that contemporary weapons are toys and vice versa (which works, by the way)—and there's a bonus in his affection for *Morte d'Arthur* and poetry relating to Arthur, Guinevere, and their crew. *Every* detail matters to us, passionately.[21]

~ ~ ~

Sisterhood Is Powerful is selling out, reprinting after reprinting. I decide that all the money from the anthology must go to set up a fund to support women's projects. This upsets Kenneth, since I'm already tithing or halving my speaking fees with the movement as well as doing a lot of benefits for women's groups (ah, the revenge of my mother and aunt). He's right. There are months when we barely make the bills and are late with the rent. I'm still taking in freelance editing, but can do less because of speaking dates and travel, and Blake-care at home. Ken's still taking in freelance, too, but can do less because of caring for Blake half-time when I'm home and full-time when I'm on the road. We both realize I'm becoming the breadwinner, which is all the more reason for *not* setting up a fund.

Kate Millett lectures me that I should provide for myself, and put the money "into land" as she's doing; the success of *Sexual Politics* is buying her a farm she'll enjoy and eventually share as a women's arts colony. But I say women need the cash for projects *now*. Emily helps me incorporate the Sisterhood Is Powerful Fund. It is the first feminist grant-giving foundation in the United States.

Emily and I, the sole officers, keep the bureaucracy to a minimum. No office, no staff; she and I do all the paperwork. No proposals are required, only a letter about the project. The sole stipulations are that it's first-come-first-serve, that the recipient group has to be all women and autonomous (that is, not a caucus of or auxiliary in a male-led organization), and that grants will go to groups, not individuals. Twice a year the royalty checks come in, and twice a year the Sisterhood Fund checks go out. Simple, clean, direct. The process gladdens my heart because so little money—a few hundred dollars here, a few thousand dollars there—goes so far. The fund gives seed-money grants to what will become a

[21] See "Every Mother's Son: On a Feminist Raising a Son," in *The Word of a Woman*.

massive alternative feminist media: newspapers, magazines, publishers. We help establish the first-ever rape crisis center (in Washington, D.C.), the first shelters for battered wives and incest survivors, many of the first constituency-focused organizations: African-American, Latina, Asian-American, Native-American, lesbian, disabled, welfare women's groups.

On one occasion, I sit at our oak table signing fund checks to the movement by candlelight because Con Edison has turned off our electricity due to failure of payment. It doesn't occur to me that I've now positioned myself to support movement women in sacrificial ways not so dissimilar from those in which I supported my mother and aunt. Kenneth says I'm nuts. Kate says *Don't do this*—and pretty much everyone, including Adrienne Rich, Eleanor Holmes Norton, Mary Daly, Phyllis Chesler, Susan Brownmiller, and Rita Mae Brown, concurs. But Emily, my legal buddy, understands. In our nonexistent spare time, she and I have founded the New York Women's Law Center, and she's taking on so many pro bono cases she can barely make *her* rent.

Meantime, while I write checks, Blake sings songs he's invented and makes shadow pictures with his fingers in the candlelight, to keep me company.

The crises keep coming. They provoke me. I provoke them. Am I confusing stress with excitement, or even fun? Am I becoming addicted to adrenaline? Stopping is unthinkable. I might not be able to start up again.

Random House is about to publish my first book of poems, *Monster*, including the title poem I read at the violence panel—which has now taken off, prepublication, in taped and mimeo'd form, and become an underground rallying cry for women. But there's another poem in the book, called "Arraignment," in which I flatly accuse Ted Hughes of the murder of his wife, the poet Sylvia Plath.[22] The poem is deliberately hyperbolic and symbolic, but I also do intend to imply that Hughes's well-known womanizing and his physical, mental, and economic cruelty, before

[22] "Arraignment" also appears in *Upstairs in the Garden*.

and after their separation, drove Plath to suicide. I rest my arguments on the testimony of her own words—her accusations of betrayal, rape, battery, and poverty—in her last poems, letters, and journals. My book is in galleys when it's stopped cold.

Random House lawyers have read the galleys and on their recommendation, the house threatens to kill the book unless I cut the poem. I'm a young poet about to have her longed-for first book, and the news lands like a punch in the stomach. A six-month nightmare ensues: endless meetings with Random House lawyers—grey-faced, grey-haired, grey-suited men versus me and trusty Emily, who bases her defense of my poem bravely if unsuccessfully on free speech, poetic license, and Plath's own testimony. We try to subpoena Plath's last journal—but Hughes announces that he has deliberately destroyed it, claiming he has done so for the sake of their children. We suggest that Random House publish my book with a blank, black-bordered page where the poem *would* have run, stamped simply CENSORED, but the house refuses. I feel censored for acknowledging that I'm being censored. The RH lawyers and executives tell us candidly that a lawsuit doesn't scare them, that sometimes they even welcome one, because it can help sales—but only for a book that might *sell*—which would mean *prose*, fiction or nonfiction, certainly never *poems*. I am having difficulty comprehending why Hugh Hefner, Al Goldstein, and other pornographers can have a field day traducing feminist spokeswomen by name as sluts, whores, and bestialists in the pages of their newspapers and magazines, and calling the smears "fact,"[23] and *that*, somehow, is free speech, but my poem—a *poem*—is unprotected by the First Amendment. All Emily's arguments get us nowhere. I foresee my life as a published poet ending before it begins.

"By any means necessary" means just that—as Galileo knew when he genuflected to the pope while muttering, "Nevertheless, it moves." So I attempt another approach: a revision to 'scape hanging yet get the point across. Thank *god* for the rhetorical question:

---

[23] Larry Flynt had not yet surfaced as a porn king, but he would eventually take such attacks to new depths.

How can
I accuse
Ted Hughes
of what the entire British and American
literary and critical establishment
has been at great lengths to deny,
without ever saying it in so many words, of course:
the murder of Sylvia Plath?

And god *bless* irony: I recast the entire poem in a tone hovering between that and sarcasm—which, with the addition of a stanza about Hughes's second wife's suicide, possibly makes it even more powerful:

What a coincidence.
But only paranoiacs would assume
that such a curious redundancy constitutes
a one-man gynocidal movement.

I also add in various *J'accuses* against A. Alvarez, George Steiner, and Robert Lowell, who, along with other "critical necrophiles," have gone to some lengths to protect Hughes after her death, writing about his talent but her instability. In a sense, this poem of mine will have an effect similar to that of "Goodbye to All That" regarding the Left—but this time in terms of the literary establishment.

I seem not to worry about crossing a bridge until I get to it and am ready to burn it behind me.

Random House goes with the revised version of the poem, so the book finally is published in 1972. The *Feminist Art Journal* promptly prints both the original *and* the revised versions of "Arraignment," plus an essay of mine exposing the entire censorship process. To everyone's shock, *Monster* takes off: it *sells*, fast and well. Thirty thousand hardcover copies in the first six months alone is unheard of for any book of poems, much less for a first book by a young poet. What no one, including me, has anticipated is the size and hunger of the new female readership.

The 1970s are a renaissance period for poetry, especially that by women poets and poets of color. These previously stifled voices are singing, and people are coming to listen and be moved, to laugh and cry as if in ancient bardic days around campfires. Poets are accustomed to audiences of twenty loyal souls, but now readings draw hundreds of people; on three occasions I give readings for packed auditoriums that seat a thousand or more. The white, gentlemanly poetry establishment is disturbed by this new popularity of the art; Robert Lowell is actually quoted as saying, "Too many people are reading poetry these days."

But the establishment isn't finished attacking *Monster*.

In 1973, Kenneth, Blake, and I spend three months in Sarasota, Florida, where I am to be guest professor at New College—holder of the Visiting Chair in Feminist Studies, to be precise—by invitation of the student body in a popular vote. I go down a week early to orient myself, lease a car (and relearn how to drive it), rent a bungalow, and stock up on groceries before they arrive. It will be like a vacation! It will be a quiet, bucolic, beach-walking, family-cuddle, writing-poetry time! Yeah, sure.

Blake at least turns tow-haired and bronze-skinned in the sunshine, splashing through the waves and watching for dolphins. Kenneth's fair skin and vitiligo alternately burn and tan him in patches until he must stay hatted, sleeved, and shaded. I drive them around when necessary, since Ken doesn't drive. I also wind up spending more and more time at the school, not just teaching but organizing: students, faculty women, faculty wives. Things heat up when I set different requirements for male students (practical politics: set up a childcare center) than for female students (keep a personal journal, then write one element of feminist theory based on it). The administration has a ho-hum attitude about campus rape, so petitions must be initiated. Meanwhile, Jane Alpert, an old *Rat* colleague now a fugitive from the FBI on bombing charges, visits us for a brief, secret holiday. I end my short tenure in academia supporting my students by sitting in with them in an occupation of the president's office.

Blake starts preschool. He's bored because he already knows his alphabet and has begun to read, and he can't comprehend why one little boy in particular keeps hitting him for carrying a doll. Kenneth and I embark on what will be years of visits to principals, defending him and getting school policies changed. We tell each other that we really *must* be more selective about which issues we'll take on, but life doesn't permit us this indulgence, and temperamentally we rise to the bait every time.

Showing a fascination for music early on, Blake fiddles around at the piano every chance he gets. Ken's childhood ghosts rise and wrestle with mine. He'd always longed for piano lessons but his family couldn't afford them, so he wants Blake to have every advantage he lacked, to start lessons at once. I, of course, don't want Blake to have to go to *any* lessons *whatsoever*, much less ever have to perform in recitals or be prey to *any* enforced knowledge unless and until he himself demands it. Back and forth we go. Blake solves it one day by asking for lessons.

~ ~ ~

Canadian friends phone, asking me if I know why *Monster* has disappeared from their bookstores; they've been informed the book has been withdrawn by the publisher, Random House of Canada. On investigation, I learn the Random House consortium has, without a word to me, made its separate peace with Ted Hughes, who threatened to sue even on the basis of the revised, irony-suffused poem. The publisher agreed to withdraw all copies from any markets in the entire Commonwealth, and Hughes then agreed not to lodge suit. After a flurry of activity by stalwart Emily, it's clear there's nothing I can do.

But I'm underestimating women. When I tell them what I've learned, the Canadian women are outraged. They decide to publish a "pirated" edition—but "pirated" with my permission. Within a month, Australian women and New Zealand women contact me wanting to publish their own pirated editions, which they do—with my permission. This happens all over the Commonwealth, spontaneously, furiously, wondrously. Each edition is different, some with graphics by women, some with photos of Plath, some with *both* versions of "Arraignment," picked up from the *Feminist Art Journal*. Then, bearding Hughes in his own den, an English women's group publishes and distributes *its* edition, an act of special courage, since UK slander laws are draconian, carrying heavy sentences for printers and distributors as well as publishers and authors.

These remarkable women all over the Commonwealth carry it further. They make it impossible for Hughes to give public poetry readings in his own country: English feminists picket the venue with signs quoting lines from "Arraignment." His reading tours in Canada, Australia, New Zealand, and the United States are canceled because of threatened mass protests by what come to be called "Arraignment Women." I am dumbstruck with admiration and gratitude.

The literary establishment puts in its two cents, pressuring me to "call off" these women, who are planning their own actions quite without consulting me anyway. I get phone calls from gentlemen literary critics whose voices are shaking with disgust at having to descend to lobbying the likes of me. I get notes from James Silberman and Jason Epstein, the Olympian gods at Random House. I keep *trying* to explain that this campaign is neither at my direction nor under my control, although I do admit I support what the women are doing. I keep *trying* to explain that we are not a conspiracy but a synchronicity.

The one pressure letter that reduces me to tears is from Doris Lessing. I have loved her work, and *The Golden Notebook* has been germinal for me both as a writer and as a political being. She urges me to withdraw *all* versions of the poem from publication *anywhere*, and to call off all protests because, although she makes a point of not denying these problems regarding Hughes, she insists that we literary people must not wash our dirty linen in public.[24]

The reactions to the poems "Monster" and "Arraignment," make me think of Auden's line "Poetry makes nothing happen," and beam.

---

[24] This seeming anomaly became chronic a few years later, when Lessing—herself so insightfully feminist on the page—took it upon herself to denounce the Women's Movement and individual feminists publicly and repeatedly. It is one of the saddest persona splits—where the brilliance and bravery of the writer desert her when she rises from her desk—that I've ever witnessed.

Apparently not having enough to do, and feeling I'm falling behind on the home front, I initiate a series of political-literary dinners.

Subtext: Kenneth and I can't talk literature with our political colleagues, but often get into political fights with our literary friends. We feel schizoid. Never mind. *I*—Earth Mother Redux—will ride to the rescue. *I* shall meld these worlds together.

It is not what Martha Stewart would call "a good thing." At one dinner party guests are faint with hunger since we don't eat until almost 11:00 P.M., because I am so busy holding people back from each other's throats that I fall behind on the overly ambitious kitchen front. Another evening founders when Kenneth argues hotly with the poet Howard Moss, then the *New Yorker*'s poetry editor; Kenny is claiming that a person has every right—indeed, a moral responsibility—to lie during jury selection, pretending to be neutral about capital punishment in order to get *on* the jury so that later, if there's a conviction, the person can argue against the barbarity of the death penalty from *inside* the jury. I kick him under the table, privately fearing that he'll never have another poem published in the *New Yorker*, and that I'll never have one published there at all. At another dinner, Ned Rorem and Kate Millett get along well enough so long as they stay on the subject of adoring Paris, but when Ned announces he's about to set a series of Sylvia Plath's poems to music, *I* take umbrage. He's my friend; I care for him, his wit, and his music; but I feel rabid that at this moment in history it's arrogant for any male artist to think he can interpret women's experience, especially one so redolent of female anger as Plath's; besides he has pressed my Plath button. Ned takes umbrage at *my* umbrage. He will set any poet he bloody well chooses, and besides, he tells me, he's as feminine as any woman, probably more so than most feminists. I get a crazed look in my eyes at such a statement. Kenneth kicks *me* under the table. Ned publishes it all in his next *Diary*, adding slyly that Kenneth is perhaps too quick to defend the cause of women rather than letting *them* speak.

Embattled again. Or is it consistently?

Valerie Solanis decides she despises feminists, especially me, since I have committed a double sin against her. First, in *Sisterhood Is Global* I've published—with her permission and full payment of the agreed permission fee—an excerpt from her "SCUM Manifesto." I've regarded it as a grimly funny example of extremism (SCUM was an anagram for Society for Cutting Up Men), which by comparison reveals radical feminist statements to be quite rational. My second sin apparently is having come to her support after she shot Andy Warhol, was then deemed psychotic, and sentenced to a state asylum; I'd organized a petition and raised funds for her release to a private institution where she would receive better care. Now, suddenly, she *is* released—and livid. She decides that (1) she is not now and never has been a feminist but is a "killer dyke biker," (2) I have defamed her by printing her work in the context of feminism, and (3) I am somehow responsible for her having been sent to a mental institution in the first place. She phones repeatedly, informing me that she plans to throw acid in my face and blind me for life. I try to reason with her, finally stop answering the phone, shudder a lot. The local precinct is already shadowing a man to whom Kenneth unthinkingly gave our home address, who, it turns out, is stalking me for having "destroyed his life" by "inventing" feminism. Just getting Blake to school in the morning is becoming a challenge. But Solanis is something else. By now I'm used to getting threats from men, but being menaced by another woman corrodes the spirit.

Meanwhile, I'm attacked in a startling manner by one of the contributors to *Sisterhood Is Powerful*, who has asked me for a personal grant from the Sisterhood Is Powerful Fund. I remind her of what she and all the contributors already know and in fact supported: that the fund gives grants to groups, not individuals. We have only so much money, and much as we'd like to be able to support individual women, the collectively decided-on priority is to build alternative institutions of and for women. This particular contributor now demands to be the exception to the rule; I apologize but say I cannot oblige her. She says if *she* can't have the money, nobody else will, either—and hangs up. I dismiss it as hyperbole, but it's dismaying nonetheless. Not as much as what's to come, though.

She proceeds to sue me. For plagiarism. She claims that in *Sisterhood Is Powerful*'s bibliography I have plagiarized a mimeographed handout bibliography she once compiled. She wants almost half a million dollars in

damages, plus all copies of the anthology recalled, the printing plates
destroyed, and any foreign editions of the book stopped.

I think it must be a sick joke. First I go into a spin on the basic question. How in hell can a bibliography be plagiarized, since it's a list of
books? I know firsthand the months of collective labor that I, with the
help of Connie Brown and Jane Seitz of Random House spent creating the
anthology's bibliography, surveying the various woman-centered book lists
that existed but deciding to build our own from scratch despite the additional research entailed. I know that this woman, a contributor herself,
received a complimentary copy of the book well before publication—and
that she has not once mentioned a word to me about any problems regarding the bibliography in the intervening *four years* since the anthology was
published. I know she knows that the fund is the sole recipient of the
book's royalties, and that such a suit will drain it. I cannot believe this is
happening.

Better believe it. This woman and her male lawyer, who's working for a
share of the profits, will not listen to Emily, my valiant if exhausted attorney. Nor will this woman listen to other women who call her and beg her
to stop. She will not sit down and try feminist arbitration. She *wants* to
involve Random House—which means their Park Avenue lawyers, which
means the clock ticking on skyscraper legal fees, which means the publisher has the right to indemnify itself by garnisheeing the royalties, not
only from the anthology but from *Monster* and any future books of mine at
Random House as well. Everyone—Kenneth, Emily, all my women
friends and colleagues—urges me to settle, reminding me that it's done all
the time and doesn't mean surrender. But it's so *unfair*, I moan, I'm *not* a
plagiarist, and it *will* wipe out the fund. So do I stop?

I make Emily countersue, for slander. Months pass, during which I
throw up a lot. The law's delay, depositions, affidavits, movement rumors,
frozen royalties, frozen fund. Finally, physically and emotionally depleted,
and fearing there won't be enough money in my entire future writing life
to indemnify Random House sufficiently for their five-hundred-dollar-an-
hour lawyers' zillions of hours, I agree to settle out of court. The plaintiff
and her lawyer get a few grand, plus the excision of *our* bibliography from
all future editions of our book. (By that time, feminist books are prolifer-
ating, as are feminist bibliographies, so this loss doesn't worry me that

much.) The plaintiff, sad woman, gets something else, too: virtually ostracized in the Women's Movement.

I feel compelled to write a "Report to the Movement," with appended legal documents, explaining the entire debacle, why it has erased our fund, and why there can be no more grants. Yet this brings it all back again, and makes me literally ill to write. Friends say not to bother. But I can't stop, feeling it's owed to the community.[25] The Report appears in most feminist media. Support letters in response are many and gratifying.

Yet I feel bitter for the first time, having fallen prey to that particular acridity of soul suffered by an idealist who now feels something of a failure and a fool. My responsibility tic reminds me that I brought all of this on myself and that I have no right to act martyred or sanctimonious. Yet I keep wondering if I'm the only one crazy enough to have really believed in trying to *live* this politics.

Of course it's hardly just me. Resentments, personal envies, and ideological schisms are imploding viciously all over the movement as if, in our rush to sisterhood, we forgot about sibling rivalry, or as if we'd fallen for the myth that suffering ennobles, when it actually degrades. Certain disturbed women with personal, vituperative agendas are becoming career "trashers," spending their lives sniping at other women in the name of their own apparently patented brand of feminism. God knows I am a judgmental, snippy person, but I've devised some rules for myself regarding this and try to abide by them. Fulminating up to 20 percent of any given period, time, or space (as in an article), though probably tasteless, is grudgingly allowed as polemic or "venting"—but raving on for more than 20 percent becomes *trashing* and should not be trusted, in oneself or anyone else.

Meawhile, having done *Sisterhood Is Powerful,* I'm now beginning *Sisterhood Is Global*—but privately I joke that I should compile an anthology titled *Sisterhood Is Suicide.*

---

[25] Years later, I will counsel Gloria Steinem similarly: not to spend precious time writing an open letter defending herself against Kathie Amatniek/Sarachild's spiteful and bizarre charges that Gloria is a CIA agent—but Gloria will do precisely what I did: throw up a lot and spend weeks writing what "sisters have a right to know." Double moral: (1) it's easy enough to advise others, and (2) you're more often punished for the rights you've done than for the wrongs.

Still, in its brief life, the fund has made history, set a precedent, and given a considerable amount of money ($35,000 in its last year alone) to hundreds of women's groups across the United States. That seed money will flower into century plants.

~ ~ ~

Kenneth and I expand our miraculously cheap, spacious apartment to *three* floors, since the landlord no longer needs the other floor for pharmacy storage. More tearing down of walls, building of walls. Separate studies, with working fireplaces, for each of us. This is great, because the strain has taken a heavy toll on the marriage. This is also great because it's the first room of my very own—excepting the three-month sojourn in the 78th Street walk-up—in my entire life. I'm in my mid-thirties.

We also colonize a mostly shady rooftop off the back of the new floor, which we turn into a small garden, "making the tar bloom." I grow herbs and a few annuals and cacti in pots; Kenny nurtures a sapling jacaranda tree. I discover a favorite time of day—dawn, sprinkling plants with my watering can and listening to birds.

I love birds. I love plants. I love cats. I remember I once yearned to love everyone in some way approximating what I feel for Blake. That thought provokes a crooked little smile. I am in danger of becoming one of those revolutionaries who love humanity but can't stand people.

FOURTEEN

Mount St. Helens

To write is to sit in judgment over oneself.

— HENRIK IBSEN

If suffering doesn't teach us anything, then it's ever so distasteful.

I know good women who are achingly nostalgic for the early "women's liberation" years. Partly their nostalgia is plain human longing for one's romanticized youth, this being the female version of war-story reminiscences by old New Left men; there's even one group calling itself VFW— Veterans of Feminist Wars—which I've respectfully declined to join, finding myself still on active duty. In some melancholic cases, the nostalgia appears to be the longing of persons who feel their lives have slid downhill in terms of relevance and excitement ever since "the good old days." Others apparently believe political engagement fitting for younger folks, as if it were a phase—idealistic and much missed—to be outgrown by any sensible realist. Then there's my grizzled old warrior-colleague Susan Brownmiller, by temperament a feisty scrapper who relishes a good political brawl, who thus managed to enjoy even the spite of the period, and who believes, grieving needlessly, that radical feminism perished along with "women's liberation." (Anyone has the right to stop being an activist, but I think it *is* a bit silly to rationalize that with the sullen claim that nothing is any longer worthy of one's activism.)

Not me. I cherished the insights gained during those early years, tried to weather the blows, and delighted in the organizing—so much so that I decided to persist in it, employing, I would hope, an expanding tactical repertoire. I've loved watching the intersecting dynamics of consciousness shift and movement growth, loved having the opportunity to feed that shift, foster that growth, help that energy spread, catch, and recognize itself *already* indigenous in countries all over the planet.[1] In other words, what's become the vast transformative force that is the national and especially the international Women's Movement—*that's* what quickens my political heartbeat, *that's* what I call the Politics of the New Millennium, and I mean none of it as hyperbole. Which leaves me no time or inclination to mourn a season when a few young, urban, educated, largely straight, mostly white, U.S. women, however plucky or clever, actually believed they had created and could control this explosive consciousness.

Some of them paid dearly for their hubris. To paraphrase a line from Ginsberg's "Howl," I've watched some of the best *feminist* minds of my generation go mad with impatience, despair, horizontal hostility, or—I'm afraid it has to be said—laziness. We've certainly had our casualties. Many "original" radical feminists have been lost, having themselves lost the vision, having let themselves be driven into irrelevance: bright minds squandered to alcohol, drugs, "personal solutions," corrosive negativity, religious conversions, easy-chair feminism, single-issue obsessiveness, shallow celebrity-politics, or frozen central-committee thinking.

If this sounds overly severe, so be it. My impatience with ego games, whining, and the lack of political will stands in an honorable tradition: for *real* judgmentalism read Elizabeth Cady Stanton's writing during the last twenty years of her life. Some of these women never worked on a tangible project like storefront legal counseling or a crêche or a self-help health clinic; most never had or long ago lost touch with women outside their own local, exclusive feminist-café-society circles. Such alienation from

[1] "Oh *well*," Susan shrugs glumly, "you're into that international thing." "Oh *well*," I snort huffily, "*yes*. Merely the *world*."

the world of most women's acute needs and desires makes for a solipsistic attitude inimical to becoming a political long-distance runner (which, I can testify, carries its own moral perils), one into which I might have fallen had I not been fortunate enough to be lured out of the serpents' nest by the traveling that *Sisterhood Is Powerful*'s publication initiated. It was in small towns, on welfare lines, on factory floors during break time, in shelters, farmhouse kitchens, and student cafeterias—listening to women—that I learned a durable politics with multiple, interconnecting priorities, what I've come to call a multiplicity of feminisms. Little wonder (and little credit to me) that, when I simply turned that politics around and sent it back out in my speeches, the most commonly used adjectives in audience reactions were "life-changing" and "inspiring."

Admittedly, at first it wasn't only sharing the emotional and intellectual "high" generated by these women all across the country that was so exciting. It was also the adventure of travel—which I'd done to death in my working childhood but which the intervening years had glossed over with misremembered glamour. All those airplanes! All that toy food served with toy plastic cutlery by flight attendants who were treated by most male passengers as toy women! All those podiums and phallic lavaliere microphones! All those junk-food-for-the-ego academic receptions at which one was lionized, then criticized; deified, then crucified. Except that, after years of such questionable exoticisms, getting there was no longer half the fun; the high from the women endured; the high from the travel went flat. Life had become a round of airports echoing flight announcements, of waiting for connections in deserted terminals at 3:00 A.M., of rarely being able to sit at my desk for more than four days at a time without having to pack again. Life became long-distance phone calls squeezed in after the guest seminar (which I would promptly rename "ovular") and before the evening lecture, while I hunched over a sandwich and nursed a container of rapidly cooling tea for my ever-present cold. Life was trying to pack one carry-on bag for a February trip that would span Vermont and Louisiana; life was revising poems and drafting essays on seat-back tray tables in every airborne vehicle from 747's to four-seater commuter tin cans seemingly powered by squirrels on treadmills. Life was a chronic stiff neck from dozing off in trains, buses, waiting rooms, and backstage green rooms.

Life was also learning that the at first temptingly homey stay at the local feminist commune was to be tactfully avoided since, with a few memorable exceptions, it meant one or all of the following: (1) being kept awake through the night for the intimate, "exclusive" workshop—the unstated but equivalent price of room and board—after which the local sisters went to bed while their bleary guest tottered to the airport for another flight, city, and round of the same; (2) being fed gummy brown rice puddled with soy sauce topped by a bean sprout; (3) feeling compelled to insist on washing up after dinner because one did *not* wish to be a snooty New York–type star-leader honcho who let other people wait on her and consequently doing dishes for ten people after the lecture and before the "private" rap; (4) discovering that rest, at least for the ten minutes permitted, was to take place in a sleeping bag on the floor—sometimes, unsettlingly, with a would-be-groupie-young-lesbian-feminist fan hovering hopefully over it. To complain and be a rotten sport was not an option. These were women trying to treat their guest as best they knew how. (Besides, wasn't I trying for Perfect on *their* chart?) So I grinned, talked, rasped cheerfully hoarse, sucked lozenges till my tongue glistened chartreuse, diplomatically declined intimate overtures, learned to enjoy it all—and tried to nap on the plane.

Later, to be sure, I rediscovered the bliss of privacy at hotels and motels, although given sufficient time and recurrence they began to appear hallucinatingly identical, town after town. I shall probably never forget those iridescently orange cabbage roses with which it seemed most rooms in one motel chain were papered, the design coyly carried through in the bedspread fabric. Since the boreal air conditioner usually couldn't be turned off and an extra blanket was nowhere to be found, I'd appropriate the bedspread for additional warmth—only to find, once tucked in, that its matching pattern gave me the sensation of being absorbed into the wall, my head peeping out from a rip in the design. There was, too, the radicalizing experience of being a woman traveling alone, which would require a book in itself—another one I don't intend to write. Yet there was also an unexpectedly swift trust and friendliness between traveling women strangers, particularly where children were involved. Entire vocabularies can be wordlessly exchanged in the simple gesture of offering to hold her baby while a mother wipes off vomit from the front of his toddler sister.

With hindsight, I confess to wishing I'd spent more of those years quietly at my desk; I would have written more books, been more solvent financially, and relished lots more sleep. Still, for me that would've required living in another era, perhaps a hundred years or more in the future. Given the historical moment in which I found myself, ethically there was no other choice. I had to fight, and not just for other women. I was fighting for myself.

There are, however, genuine dangers that come with the territory of being an itinerant political organizer. Physical attack and threats of assassination are among them, yes. But except for some near misses and bad scares, a broken rib, a graze from a knife, and a well-aimed rock that probably cost me some precious brain cells I could ill afford to lose, I've been lucky. The subtler perils are less commonly acknowledged; they're psychological, intellectual, even aesthetic. There's a real danger in seeing too many faces, shaking too many hands, facing too many audiences, answering too many of the same questions, repeating too often what was once fresh and sincere until it's inevitably reduced to a platitudinous set piece. There's a danger in watching complex issues "of necessity" simplified, then *over*simplified toward precisely the sort of nonthought you fancied you were opposing. To anyone other than a sentimentalist given to convenient self-delusion, an infection of cynicism contracted in this exercise is unavoidable, as is an elation-exhaustion seesaw, an emotional megalomania, and an accompanying self-dislike. The process slackens your spirit and tempts you toward contempt for the very people on whose behalf you're purportedly acting; they begin to appear like a faceless, manipulating, manipulable mass. And you begin to feel like a faceless, manipulating, manipulated demagogue.

Think, then, of what happens to a campaigning *politician.*

I should have recognized these hypocrisies from my childhood as an actor. But there's a warped honor, at least, in that profession, where your *job* is to appear as something other than yourself, and everyone knows your skills are bent toward that end. That's not comparable to the politician (or political organizer) who *claims* to be her/his self but learns not to expose authentic aspects of that self, for fear of losing the attention or affection of the constituency. In our society the political message depends to a lamentable degree on who delivers it, and how.[2] The pretense of the actor is a translucent art, therefore oddly honest. The pretense of the political figure is an opaque charade, a deliberate deception that can deceive even its deceiver into thinking no deception's taking place.

There have been times when my life seemed to curve back on itself like a Möbius strip and mockingly return me to the same progression of stages, cameras, and mikes I fought so hard to escape as an adolescent. Yet the responsibility for one's life ultimately is one's own—at least after society's various bigotries and the other cage bars of existence have set the boundaries within which that choice can be made—though sometimes it can be made courageously enough to bend those bars a bit. During this siege of disillusion, I learned that the forging of a public face, necessary to a performing artist and seemingly useful to a political creature, can be pernicious to a creative artist. How could it be otherwise, when your replies become shortened into sound bites, self-protective and superficial?[3] A Q-and-A session is neither the time nor place to be confidential or candid—though I would find myself trying, sometimes sustaining internal emotional injuries in the attempt. Yet the authentic answers—and, more important, the questions themselves—*self*-asked, are the very stuff with

---

[2] Ronald Reagan's popularity, for instance, was no coincidence. He was the logical apparition conjured up by a public conditioned to trust the worth of celebrity and distrust the work of cerebration. Things seem to be getting worse before they may get better; the borderline between governance and entertainment is becoming a permeable membrane labeled "Fame" or, even worse, "Notoriety."

[3] I did get some good ones off now and then, but usually only when exhaustion rendered me unable to self-censor. Once, when a man interrupted a woman questioner in midsentence, prefacing his question to me by sneering, "So, Miss, ah, Missus, or *Miz*, uh, what *do* you want to be called?" I snapped, "Your Majesty will do. Now sit down." At another Q-and-A, a militant teenager with a crewcut, her new fatigues still creased and shiny boots squeaking from the army-navy store, demanded to know how I *dared* call myself a radical feminist if I wasn't living in a lesbian commune. Usually my answer to such a question would be lengthy and thoughtful—but on this occasion I was too tired to be edifying, and I heard myself reply gently but firmly, "Let's make a deal. If you'll forgive me for not answering that question, I'll forgive you for asking it."

which the artist should work, in a markedly different process where length, depth, and self-exposure must all be assumed.

The more I age, the more I appreciate perspective—which itself changes with, well . . . perspective.

In the enthusiasm of the 1970s, breaking free from the incestuous infighting of elite metro-feminism gifted me with a perspective that the movement was far more than the sum of its sororicidal leadership parts. By the end of the decade, a different perspective helped me figure out that my growing irritability with being on the road was not about the estimable women I was encountering but about my loss of writing time and family time, plus the fatigue of trying to pacify rising childhood ghosts as I found myself again the family's sole breadwinner: the old conflicting prides, guilts, resentments, and martyrdoms.

Now, two decades later, perspective offers another, different surprise: the realization of what I've left *out* from this period, not even from choice but simply from having overlooked it as just not being important, although at the time it happened it seemed absolutely crucial. There are so many examples of this in the writing of a memoir that any sample of the genre might as easily be termed a forgettoir. Perspective comes into play because certain occasions or relationships that seemed integral to one's existence reveal themselves with time to be totally irrelevant to who one really is, always was, or has become. So they fall out of the story, not from a wish on the writer's part to hide them, just from their retroactive irrelevance to the narrative and from the indifference of the narrator.

There was, for instance, some cadre-type organization in San Francisco run by Lynn somebody, who was petrifying most Bay Area women's groups by garroting them with correct lines; I remember being asked to come and confront Lynn whats-her-name in public, and agreeing (part of the responsibility of the "outside" agitator who can, after all, visit but then gets to *leave*), and I recall being anxious about my decision for two months before the trip to California. Finally, a mobile bundle of nerves, I went. We had a confrontation where she and her group were faced down publicly and successfully, and I learned later that they never wielded their mini-tyranny effectively again. The whole movement buzzed about it for the better part of a year, but the substance of the debate, along with her name, has vanished, leaving only the spoor of stale adrenaline. I'd love to go back and warn myself not to spend such angst on something so trivial, but all I can do is try to fritter less in the present.

Perspective's lack of pity in denying do-overs *is* compensated for, however, by the merciful humor it can bestow on what once felt earth-shakingly serious. An example of this would be my relationship during the 1970s with a once vivid presence in my life: Jane Alpert,[4] a Leftist militant who'd been involved, together with her lover Sam Melville,[5] in anti-government bombings; she became a fugitive from the law, surfaced after some years underground, turned herself in, served a prison term, and was finally released into middle-class obscurity. In that single sentence (thanks to semicolons) resonates what was once an impassioned alliance: years of friendship, actions taken together and separately, journeys in various disguises to meet in various cities; years of support, risk, and financial aid, of long letters sent to and from false names, of poems written for and dedicated to her;[6] a conceited tutorial pride in watching her outgrow her old politics and gain a sense of self as she discovered what feminism really was (and an accompanying despair every time her feminism *and* sense of self went out the window because some cute stud came in through it, this vulnerability self-indulged even at the risk of exposing her identity or infuriating the guys' girlfriends, who were sheltering her as a favor to me). Then there were more years of finding attorneys to help her surface, doing damage control over her flirtation with an FBI agent, visiting her in prison, orchestrating her move to a minimum-security facility (then doing damage control over her affair with a male inmate *there*), mobilizing support to defend her against accusations of having informed on her colleagues. . . . Well, an expense of spirit in a waste of shame all *that* turned out to be. Which is a somber way of saluting the amusing power that perspective has in clarifying how what we once were sure was central was quite marginal.

[4] Alpert is the shadowy figure referred to as "the particular woman" in chapter 7 ("Longing for Catastrophe") of *The Demon Lover*.

[5] Melville was later killed during the 1971 prisoner uprising at Attica state prison in New York.

[6] "Letter to a Sister Underground" in *Sisterhood Is Powerful,* and various poems in *Lady of the Beasts.*

You see, in writing about the Sixties and Seventies, I *forgot* to put any of this *in*. But shorthand does it justice.

Now we approach the Eighties, though, when what I'd assumed was marginal turned out to be central. And *un*forgettable.

Breaking Down

The marriage was in trouble, trouble by now so chronic it felt normal. We worked hard at being soulmates, yet every time we heaved ourselves up toward the stature of archetypes, life smacked us into the pratfalls of stereotypes. As a gay/bisexual man and an artist, Kenneth had already opted out of most aspects of John Wayne masculinism, but as he became more publicly pro-feminist, the cost increased. Although he continued to produce poetry, political essays, stories, and a novel at an admirably pro-lific pace, he faced more and more difficulty getting into print.[7] Publish-ers had finally realized there was a huge new women's market, that women wanted to read women. But they didn't want to read men at this particu-lar juncture, not even an antisexist man, and men *certainly* didn't want to read "a traitor to his sex."

So we'd extricated ourselves from the plot of *The Red Shoes* only to find ourselves cast in *A Star Is Born*, as one career flowered and the other wilted. Not fools, we acknowledged it, swore we could get through it, insisted we wouldn't let "them" play Either/Or games with us. But any inequity eats away at its hosts over time. Writing, which had always been the primary bond between us, was becoming a delicate subject. Kenneth could hardly be active in women's groups, so we couldn't work together politically as we had before. Eventually only Blake would remain as the strong connection between us. Meanwhile, we veered steadily apart while clinging tearfully to one another.

Partly in an attempt to travel less but not feed my family less, I became a contributing editor at *Ms.* magazine in 1977. My acquaintance with Glo-

---

[7] His *Color Photos of the Atrocities: Poems* was published by Atlantic/Little, Brown in 1973, but his next, *The Contraband Poems,* was privately printed (Templar Press, 1975), with my support.

ria Steinem had over the years slowly developed into a friendship, especially as I came to know the real, vulnerable woman behind the glamorous
image—the woman who was at heart, as she puts it, "still a working-class,
fat brunette from the wrong side of the tracks in Toledo, Ohio, with a
mentally incapacitated mother, yet." Gloria, already a celebrity as a journalist, had been anointed by the media boys as a feminist leader the
moment she showed interest in the Women's Movement, but she was
growing into that role by working seriously at becoming a skilled feminist
organizer. I'm not always fond of her public persona, although I recognize
the at times strategic value of such an image. No, to me her most important contribution lies in the thousands of beneficial actions, large and
small, that she's made discreetly, behind the scenes, for absolutely no personal gain. Refreshingly, our friendship from the first was one in which no
punches were pulled regarding what political and stylistic differences we
had. For example, my rather droll defense of Gloria in 1972, when Friedan
mounted yet another diatribe on the "female chauvinists" and "man
haters" of the movement—that is, anyone who criticized men and/or disagreed with Betty. In this case, she attacked by name both Gloria and
Bella Abzug (for daring to run for Congress against a man who had only a
minimally tolerable legislative record on women). The *New York Times*
quoted my statement on the contretemps: "As I've just told Gloria, I've
never seen her as a raging feminist, man-hating broom rider, but rather as
a wimpy moderate." I meant it. A movement needs all kinds of activists,
but if Gloria and Bella were foaming-at-the-mouth radicals, then I must
be off the map. As for my relationship with *Ms.*, it too began in my characteristically dissident fashion.

In 1972, a group of us from New York Radical Women had come to the
Ms. offices after the pilot issue to complain about advertising we considered sexist and racist.[8] On the one hand, I was impressed by the editorial
staff's openness to criticism and apparent willingness to include radical

---

[8] I was particularly disturbed by a Clairol ad with the slogan "If I have only one life to
live, let me live it as a blond," and I pointed out that a black woman also has only one
life to live, and it's not likely to be as a blond. Once *Ms.* came into its own, it would
develop precedent-setting policies in the magazine industry regarding advertising content, but this wasn't yet evident in its preview issue—which was as an insert in *New
York* magazine, whose staff had solicited the ads.

RIGHT Kenneth Pitchford at Oxford on a 1956 Fulbright, shortly before he and RM met.

LEFT With Robert Phillips, Kenneth's best man, toasting "the transition" at the wedding reception.

ABOVE Kenneth and Blake (age three and a half).

LEFT With Blake at age two, after a bath; the bathroom walls were irreverently bedecked with RM's childhood awards.

RIGHT RM and Blake in Quebec, 1981.

ABOVE Blake with his (by-then-separated) parents, at his graduation from the United Nations International School, 1987.

RIGHT Blake Morgan in the photo from his 1997 album *Anger's Candy*

ABOVE RM tossing a bra into the Freedom Trash Can on the Atlantic City Boardwalk at the first Miss America Pageant protest, 1968.

ABOVE The Grove Press bust, 1970.

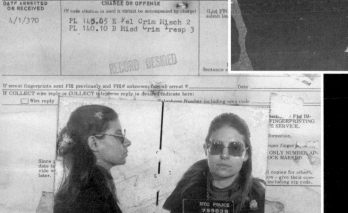

LEFT Mug shot and rap sheet, 1970.

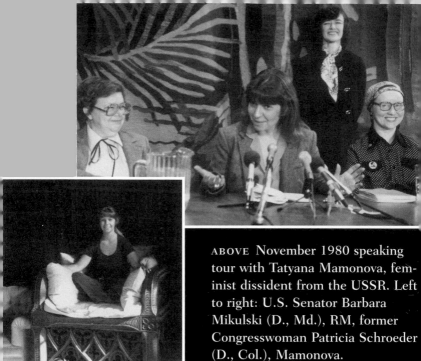

ABOVE November 1980 speaking tour with Tatyana Mamonova, feminist dissident from the USSR. Left to right: U.S. Senator Barbara Mikulski (D., Md.), RM, former Congresswoman Patricia Schroeder (D., Col.), Mamonova.

LEFT RM at Yaddo, May 1980.

ABOVE The 1979 Women Against Pornography March on Times Square. Front row, l. to r.: RM (under "porn hurts women" sign), Gloria Steinem, Bella Abzug, Andrea Dworkin, Frances Patai, Barbara Mehrhof, Dolores Alexander, Amina Abdur-Rahman, Lynn Campbell

ABOVE The *Sisterhood Is Global* staff (partial), 1983. Back row, l. to r.: Karen Berry, Marcia Landsman, Jane Ordway, Fran Rosen, RM. Front: Wendy Wolff, Toni Fitzpatrick, Annette Fuentes, Donna Santos Yamashiro.

ABOVE *Sisterhood Is Global* contributors at the 1984 book-launch party: back row, l. to r. : Carmen Lugo (Mexico), Omolara Ogundipe-Leslie (Nigeria), Gwendoline Konie (Zambia), Margaritta Chant Papandreou (Greece), Marilyn J. Waring (New Zealand), Fawzia Hassouna (Palestine), Anna Titkow (Poland), Vanessa Griffin (Fiji), Devaki Jain (India), Hilkka Pietilä (Finland), Isel Rivero (Cuba), Lidia Falcón (Spain), Claire de Hedervary (Belgium), Peggy Antrobus (the Anglophone Caribbean). Middle row: Farida Allaghi (Libya), Carola Borja (Ecuador), Paola Zaccaria (Italy), RM (holding the book), Slavenka Draculié (former Yugoslavia), Luz Helena Sanchez (Colombia), Hema Goonatilake (Sri Lanka), Manjula Giri (Nepal). Front row: Berit As (Norway), Danda Prado (Brazil), Marjorie Agosin (Chile), Mallica Vairathon (Thailand).

LEFT RM and
Marilyn
Waring, New
Zealand,
1989.

ABOVE At the farm,
early 1990s.

LEFT 1984, photographed
by "Iliana."

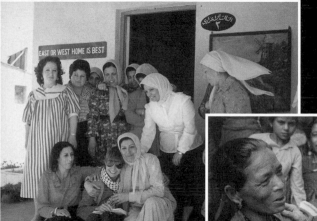

LEFT With Palestinian refugee women in Rafah Camp, the Gaza Strip, during the Intifada, 1989.

ABOVE With village women in Baluwa, Sindhupalchowk District, Nepal, 1994; two hundred women walked miles from six different villages for an electrifying all-day meeting.

ABOVE The first defiant, illegal NGO demonstration in Hairou, China, during the 1995 UN World Women's Conference at Beijing. RM holds aloft the "Don't Forget Tiananmen Square" sign, which no one else would carry and which nearly caused her arrest.

ABOVE With Sarah and Evelyne, fifth-generation farm workers in the Afrikaner-owned vineyards of Stellenbosch, South Africa, 1998.

LEFT With former U.S. Congresswoman Bella Abzug, mid-1980s.

RIGHT RM's 1989 publication party for Waring's economics book; l. to r.: RM, Waring, Steinem, Kate Millett, Andrea Dworkin.

LEFT The 1990 *Mother Jones* cover story on relaunching the new, ad-free *Ms.*

RIGHT After addressing the rally of half a million people, at NOW's 1989 Washington, D.C., March for Women's Lives.

perspectives alongside the more "mainstream" feminist issues—reproductive rights, job and education parity, legislative reforms—which formed the bulk of their content. But on the other hand, I was suspicious that our critique was being smoothly co-opted and would produce no real change. In fact, it would be two more years before I agreed to publish in *Ms.*, and then warily, contributing poems and, a year after that, an essay. In 1976 Gloria, editor Suzanne Braun Levine, and publisher Patricia Carbine took me to lunch to propose, as Mary Thom wrote in her history of the magazine, *Inside Ms.*,[9] "a more formal connection." Still, although I certainly could have used the salary starting then and there, it wasn't until December of the following year that I came on board as a contributing editor, having come to respect the importance of the magazine's existence (and its potential) as outweighing any of its weaknesses. For the next decade[10] I would write regularly for the magazine, attend editorial meetings, help expand the presence of radical and literary writers in its pages, assign and edit pieces, and periodically write snarling memos to the advertising department when it tried to foist what were in my opinion unacceptable ads on the rest of us in the editorial fortress of political integrity.

Not surprisingly, far from being the hotbed of man-hating that Friedan claimed *Ms.* was, the magazine bent over backward to be persuasive to men, and bent further, into pretzel shape, with gratitude to pro-feminist men. *Ms.* was one of the few places that would publish Kenneth's antisexist writings, and Gloria personally brought the manuscript of his novel to Jacqueline Kennedy Onassis, by then a book editor at Doubleday (Jackie loved it and pushed for it, but even she couldn't get it past higher-up male editorial resistance—which certainly taught us a lesson about the limits of female power). *Ms.* tried hard to bring feminist values into a marketplace

[9] *Inside Ms.: Twenty Years of the Magazine and the Feminist Movement* (Henry Holt, 1997).

[10] In 1988, after the magazine's sale to Fairfax, Ltd., of Australia, the new regime repositioned *Ms.* politically and restructured most of the editorial staff. In solidarity with Suzanne Levine, who was being forced out (Anne Summers of Fairfax coveted the job of editor in chief), and in disapproval of the slick, corporate, editorial slant, I formally severed my relationship with *Ms.* and requested that my name no longer appear even honorifically on the masthead. When that name reappeared in 1990, it was as editor in chief of a considerably different magazine. About which, more later . . .

context.[11] The magazine also prided itself on being a family-friendly work-place, and Blake soon became one of "the Ms. Kids," visiting the office on school holidays or during a weekend when we were closing an issue. He made friends with Letty Cottin Pogrebin's son David, Yvonne Peace's daughter Tammy, and Alice Walker's little girl Rebecca (Alice was another contributing editor during this period, and we shared an office for a few years). Blake especially liked "doing childcare," minding the younger tod-dlers and babies; it seemed to him a grown-up manly job, since he'd wit-nessed his father doing it. Cursed with his mother's craving to bring order out of chaos (as well as the illusion that one *can*), Blake decided one sum-mer to reorganize the Tot Lot, a room put aside for *Ms.* Kids and child guests. He spent days painting shelves and fixing and tidying toys. His pride—and subsequent anguish at the mess when other children began playing there again—touched me; it's what women have felt millions of times, and I remember thinking the experience would stand him in good stead as a part of a new breed of men. But meanwhile I was busy trying to comfort the outrage of an eight-year-old.

Since he was five, Blake had been a student at the United Nations International School (UNIS). Like Lisa Simpson in the TV cartoon series, he had a personal frame of reference different, to say the least, from that of other kids his age. This at times made his life difficult. Kenneth and I supported him strongly, but he had to weather his schoolmates' reactions alone, and I recall watching him learn to do so with the heartache of any

[11] Sometimes this effort failed, sometimes it succeeded, and sometimes it was simply hilarious. I remember one editorial meeting during the fight for the Equal Rights Amendment. I staggered in, having flown the red-eye from California after two weeks on the road with a book tour answering imbecilic questions like "Does the Equal Rights Amendment mean feminists want to share men's toilets?" The consciousness gap between Out There and the *Ms.* meeting widened to a chasm when one editor pas-sionately pushed for a story on some new counterculture toys intended as playthings for ill children, and then demonstrated them: multiracial, anatomically correct, male and female cloth hand puppets suffering from various terminal diseases. Partly from lack of sleep but mostly from culture shock, I started giggling uncontrollably. Suzanne tried to deflect my hysteria but caught it instead. I remember laughing so hard I slid from my chair down to the floor. The whole staff got infected with helpless laughter, and the indignant hand-puppet editor took weeks to forgive me.

parent trying to let go and at the same time longing to protect. Academic learning is the challenge for most children starting school. For Blake, that was a relative breeze compared with the challenge of trying to bridge his home context with that of the general society, trying to integrate himself into a world where other kids looked at him blankly when he innocently made offhand references to Shakespeare, Susan B. Anthony, the Lady of the Lake, or Zeus. We'd hoped the transition would be eased by the atmosphere at UNIS, where, we assumed, every child might feel unique because of the multicultural composition of the school. But we'd under-estimated the seduction of what we then called "cultural imperialism." I remember sending him off, around age six or so, to a birthday party for a little Japanese girl in his class. I reminded him to take off his shoes before entering the apartment, not to be nervous about the chopsticks because he already knew how to use them deftly, and not to act squeamish if sushi was served. It turned out that shoes were to be left on, hamburgers were served, and his present—a Queen Elizabeth I coloring book—bombed beside the gifts of Barbie accessories. All three of us tried to adapt, and we weren't always successful. But Blake found—or forged—his own way. He was a small child, who wouldn't shoot up until his early teens, but he dis-covered that baseball was both enjoyable and a way of sharing popular cul-ture—a practice and insight accomplished totally on his own, eliciting admiration but no functional advice from his parents, both of whom were sports ignoramuses (I've improved somewhat since). Because of Blake, the baseball team was opened to girls, gymnastics was opened to boys, Thanksgiving Day and Halloween decorations were challenged (since Native Americans got a raw deal and witches were *not* green warty hags), and women's studies was introduced as a subject, first in Tutorial House (high school), then downward through Middle House into Junior House, where he had begun. Clearly, the poor child never stood a chance of not being "political," given his background—yet he always put his own stamp on his politics, and he survived the passing cruelties of other children by his sense of humor, which eventually got him accepted. He was a true New York kid, sophisticated, street-smart, articulate, funny. But he was also the child of two artists, and he grew up understanding what the cre-ative process involves: how the most important thing money can buy is time in which to do your work, how certain sacrifices and disciplines are part of the bargain, how the triumphs might turn out to be solitary and the defeats public, but how the completion of work you know is really good is the best goddamned fun to be had in the universe.

The best that can be said of Kenneth and me during this period is that we took pains never to use Blake as a battleground, and we almost succeeded. Virtually everything else was becoming one, though. Kenneth surely felt as trapped in his way as I did in mine; and though he never stopped writing, he withdrew more and more into anger and depression, increasingly magnified by brandy. He must have been able to glimpse no escape without seeming to turn into the type of man he deplored. I should have let us end then and there, as we discussed—but naturally I refused to admit, even to myself, that it was time to quit. On the contrary, I initiated another round of literary dinners in the hopes of helping his publication chances. I corralled him into interviews and public forums[12] because he seemed to want to do them and acted hurt if not included, and because I hoped a raised profile would help his career.

Most of this backfired, as I might've surmised if I'd paused for a moment in my perpetual-motion frenzy. Publicly, he was turning into a "feminist prince," disliked by some women for his pontifications. Men made "Mr. Robin Morgan" jokes about him. We were sarcastically referred to as "Feminism's Holy Family," which was all the more outlandish considering what was going on under the tarnished halos, where we felt like hypocritical wax figures or, as Kenneth put it, the candy bride and groom on the movement cake. Privately, his economic dependence on me was resented by both of us. Yet he seemed unable to take steps toward landing an editing job or returning to teaching, though his "house-husbanding" was no longer as preoccupying as it had been when we went half-and-half during Blake's preschool years or when I'd been on the road more, during which period he shouldered a lot of the childcare. We still lived moderately, but UNIS was expensive and, as every parent learns, raising a child costs more money than you ever planned. Between my lecture fees, book

---

[12] See, for instance, *Not a Love Story*, Bonnie Klein's award-winning film about pornography's effects, distributed by Studio D of the Canadian Film Board.

advances, royalties, freelance journalism, and job at *Ms.* (which paid humbly but steadily), I was dancing as fast as I could, yet it was still never enough. Every freebie poetry reading I did to benefit some women's group coffers became a subject of contention between us, as did the "if only" specter of the indemnified *Sisterhood Is Powerful* royalties and the now dead fund. And while Ken may have felt bad for envying my being published, I felt bad for envying the time he had to write.

I remember crying a lot in the bathtub or in my study, wherever I could manage a few minutes alone. I believed the despondency was impenetrable and permanent, believed Ken had made major sacrifices for me, my politics, and my career, and that I owed him accordingly. (I noticed no leitmotif in such beliefs, though I couldn't avoid noticing a recurring dream of mine in which he turned into my mother.) Most of all I believed in commitment, believed I had to stick it out, although I wondered if I could live the rest of my days in a state of such personal joylessness.

Attempting to find some way of feeling honorably resigned to the situation, I saturated myself with the work of such Anglo-Roman Catholic authors as Graham Greene, C. S. Lewis, Dorothy Sayers, and Charles Williams. Their unsimplistic serenity, combined with their British urbanity and irony—especially Greene's darkly lustrous vision—was comforting, and seemed to offer clues for forbearance and survival. That helped for a year or two, but in the end the spirituality felt imported, artificial. It revived memories of Father Joe, and an inchoate uneasiness—as if he'd secretly baptized me while I was napping, inflicting a proprietary blessedness without my knowledge or consent that was now exerting its eerie magnetism as on a Greene character. So I wound up back at existential Go, quoting Camus to myself that the only real task was trying to be a saint without god.

The more Kenneth inhaled brandy, the more I exhaled sanctity, and vice versa—a bleak symbiosis and yet another stereotype. In 1978 I took a drastic step and told no one. I deliberately stopped writing, thinking it would equalize things between us for a while, since at that time virtually anything I wrote seemed to get published, nothing Ken wrote was seeing print, and the imbalance was intolerable. This was one of those self-destructive gestures one makes ostensibly for another person's sake but actually in order to jettison guilt and feel holier than him.

The impasse couldn't last. Editing, speaking, and organizing kept me drained, but not writing felt like suffocation. Then, in 1979, I was awarded a National Endowment for the Arts grant in poetry. Every penny of the ten thousand dollars went to get us out of debt, but left us back at square one: I needed to hustle more journalism assignments and speaking dates so we wouldn't slide back down. The grant, which was supposed to be used for writing time, had bought me not a single hour.

Something began to crack, spidery lines webbing across my resolve like craze along a piece of pottery. Once too often I found myself mulling Yeats's line "too long a sacrifice can make a stone of the heart." I started wondering aloud whether to apply for a stay at an arts colony, away from everything—marriage, money-earning, magazine, activism—for once in my life, have to do nothing but write, even if only for a few weeks. Ken thought it wasn't a bad idea; we both assumed it would serve as a kind of brief separation to freshen the relationship. He suggested Yaddo, in upstate New York, where he'd had a residency himself. I applied. Ned Rorem, a frequent guest there, was my recommender. I was accepted for the summer but felt I could spare the time only for a three-week stay in the spring.

I remember that my *Ms.* colleagues gave me a little going-away party in the office conference room, because I hadn't taken any vacations since starting at the magazine three years earlier, and because some of them knew about the home-front battles. Suzanne—with whom I'd invented the TGIM (Thank God It's Monday) Club, since at the time she too was enduring marital tribulations each weekend—gave me two reams of crisp typing paper. Gloria gave me five boxes of number 2 Venus Velvet pencils, our mutual favorite, sharpened just so. There were waggled eyebrows about "those art colony frolics, ya' know." I laughed uproariously, reminding us all that I was a fuddy-duddy old married lady one year short of turning forty, and stating for the record that I was traveling with a portable typewriter, baggy jeans, and a most unfetching flannel nightgown for chilly spring nights in the country. Then I went home, obsessively finished my child's costume for the upcoming UNIS play, and made to-do lists for Kenneth about household needs in my absence. Last, as I'd promised him I'd do for some time, I organized all of Ken's papers into a coherent filing system, a goodbye present before I left.

Meanwhile, out in Washington State, some officials were ignoring seismic readings coming from Mount St. Helens, which was thought to be inactive. "Oh, she's just like one of those women's libbers, letting off steam," said one wag, famously. "A menopausal lady threatening to throw a temper-tantrum," chortled another. It was May of 1980.

Breaking Out

Yaddo was paradisaical. I'd published five books by then, all of them written on the run, in the corners of my existence. Now, for the first time in my adult life, meals were cooked for me, laundry done for me, phone messages taken for me, the world kept at bay so I could work uninterrupted. For a woman writer especially, this is mind-boggling (most male writers have live-in arts colonies called wives). There were days and days of silence, spring woods through which to amble, a cabin in which to work at any hour without disturbing anyone. I broke this blissful rhythm only once, dashing to Manhattan to watch Blake play the lead in his school presentation of *The Pirates of Penzance,* but then I returned to Yaddo and resubmerged in its luxurious peace.

If anyone got stir-crazy, there were other writers and artists for socializing in the evenings, but I mostly relished the solitude. Moreover, it was problematic being regarded as the Feminist Leader whom almost every male artist or writer felt compelled to interrogate, as in "What is it you people really want?" But I found friends in the novelists Mary Elsie Robertson and Jewell Parker Rhodes, and the painter Katherine Kadish. We devised a ritual of late-afternoon Bloody Mary imbibing on the Great Lawn or in the Rose Garden, where we'd sit and cackle at the pomposity of our artistic brethren, cheered by the thought that our clique was making them even more paranoid about us than they already were. There were two exceptions among the men. One was the poet Al Poulin Jr., who wasn't politically obnoxious and who became a bit of a pal. The other was a sculptor calling himself (fatuously) Vladimir Urban.

Yessss. He was tall, dark, and Gothic-novel handsome. He was stunning in other ways, too: whenever those sensual lips parted, inanities came dribbling out with awesome reliability. But he had the common sense to keep his mouth shut most of the time—certainly at first—so that his silences and brooding gaze seemed symptomatic of depth rather than ignorance about every subject except plaster of paris and the weather. Still, this man knew how to flirt.

I had never really flirted. But it was peachy to be flirted *at,* and once I applied myself, was I ever a fast learner. Feeling miraculously freed from every stricture, I was writing poetry daily in a rush of creativity, and I convinced myself this flirtation was a symptom of that energy. Besides, it *must* be meaningless because he was a dim bulb and I naturally could be attracted only to a genius.

Then, one moon-drenched spring night—after I'd spent the day revising poems as I lounged beside a lilac bush in full fragrance—I drank a critical amount of red wine while watching shooting stars, and went to bed with him. It was May 18, 1980. Three thousand miles to the west, fuddy-duddy Mount St. Helens erupted.

It was good. It was *very* good. It was so good I did it again the next night (and the next, and the next). I rationalized that I could afford to repeat such a significant experiment because (a) he was not my intellectual peer and therefore it was inconsequential; (b) if this meant I was objectifying him, why then it was turnabout for the eons men had objectified women; (c) contrarily, when I caught myself feeling infatuated then it must mean I *wasn't* merely objectifying him; (d) I knew that Michael, Kenneth's friend and sometime lover, for whom I'd cooked almost as many breakfasts and dinners as I once had for Thatcher, was staying at our home in my absence; and (e) *surely* by now Ken and I had the Bloomsbury-equality stuff thoroughly worked out between us.

Lovemaking in our marriage had of late been rare, mechanical when it happened, and a relief when it didn't (for both of us, I suspect). In earlier years, it had been at least warm and affectionate, and I could always rely on my own internal fantasy life to contribute considerable climactic excitement (as, I'm sure, Ken's was doing for him). But *this*, in a sense, was my first experience of pure, delectable, raucous lust. I could manage to get over the embarrassment of being a late bloomer engaging in remedial living, but it was more difficult for me to stomach the fact that such a revelation could happen with a nitwit for a partner. Nevertheless, it was undeniable that so long as Vlad didn't get chatty, settled for looking like a Pre-Raphaelite angel, and did what he knew how to do, the results were spectacular. For my remaining two weeks at Yaddo, I felt I was a poet again—and, for the first time, a beautiful woman, a free woman, a *sexy* woman.

Truth's supposed to be a good thing, although in retrospect I sometimes can't remember why. Denser in my way than Urban was in his, I *still* believed I had a single-standard marriage. So when I came home, of course I told Kenneth the truth about the affair, and of course I was shocked when of course he suffered what some might call a nervous breakdown. I saw no way not to tell Blake as well, who, at age eleven, had a considerably more mature reaction than his parents. He was naturally taken aback and upset at first, then, as we talked more, he said philosophically, "Well, I'm glad for you, Rob, because it's made you really happy. I can see it in your face. But," he sighed, "Kenny's going to take it badly. So this is going to be damned inconvenient for me." He was right.

We entered into a drama that was part tragedy, part farce, part surrealism. Qualities I'd so loved in Kenneth in the first place—his capacity for going to extremes, his fervor—careened into boomerang play. There was weeping, shouting, moaning, stomping about. There were public and private scenes, suicide threats, and Ken's attempted tit-for-tat affair with another woman.[13]

I didn't know it yet, but this was the start of the beginning of the end. The drinking got worse, then better, then worse. *My* addiction was to stubbornness abuse (and I didn't yet know beans about codependency or enabling): I *insisted* we could save the marriage. Pat Carbine lent me the money to get Blake out of the house for the summer, sending him to the same progressive arts camp his pal David Pogrebin attended; David's mother, Letty, pulled strings to arrange his last-minute acceptance; Suzanne sat up with me most of one night while Kenneth was out, labeling every item of Blake's clothing as the camp required, and somehow making me laugh, weepy-eyed, while we did it. With Blake safely off, I started therapy. Then I maneuvered us into couples therapy. Finally Ken

---

[13] Gorier, and sometimes funnier, details can be found in the chapter on romance, "A Stake in the Heart," in *The Anatomy of Freedom,* and in many of the poems in *Depth Perception: New Poems and a Masque* (Doubleday, 1982).

agreed to begin his own therapy. We were getting in touch with our feelings all over the place.

Repeatedly, we'd separate, reconcile, separate. Women friends were marvels during this period. It was as if the safety net I'd spent decades helping to weave for others was suddenly, all unasked-for, stretched for me. Kenneth sometimes seemed worse in my presence, so when things got really bad I'd stay elsewhere, all around Manhattan—what Suzanne termed "sleeping around without sleeping around"—with different friends so as not to put too much weight on any one woman's hospitality: at Gloria's, at Suz's, at Bella Abzug's, with my old chum the designer Lois Sasson, with the poet Adrienne Rich, with the short-story writer Ann Beattie, with the philosopher Dorothy Dinnerstein, with the biographer Marion Meade . . . at one point I held keys to the homes of more distinguished women than had attended the first Seneca Falls Convention.

Suzanne, Gloria, and Pat conspired supportively so that *Ms.* sent me to Europe on assignments twice that summer. In the fall, they packed me off on a U.S. lecture tour with Tatyana Mamonova, to publicize the cover story I'd written on her and three other exiled Soviet dissident feminists. If Robin was going to be in a diaspora from her own home, the trick was to keep her moving productively. They knew I was a workaholic and in need of cash to boot, so they mobilized, providing opportunities and deadlines that I drove myself to meet. It was the sole pleasure I had left, at least until I was booked for an autumn lecture in Alaska and brought Blake along for a much needed short vacation where we could watch salmon, spot great bald eagles, learn that the inside of a glacier, where it "calves" or splits off a section, really *is* ice blue—and where we could recall, fleetingly, how to laugh.

By the year's end, things had quieted down. I was convinced the marriage would survive, tattered but intact. My brief foray into luscious sexuality had ended—forever, I thought, mourning it silently. It just wasn't worth the ensuing punishment, the crush of grief. Kenneth, calmer now, kept saying that it wasn't the fact of my having had an affair that pained him so; it was that the affair had been with another man.

"Your whole *life* is spent with women," he explained plaintively. "Women are your colleagues, sisters, friends—your world. I acknowledge that. So I would've easily *understood* if only the relationship had been with a *woman*."

We both smiled at how far-fetched *that* would be.

Breaking Away

In July of 1980, with Blake at camp, I flew to Copenhagen, Denmark, to cover the United Nations World Conference on Women and, preceding it, to a week-long smaller gathering in Oslo, Norway, sponsored by the UN International Institute for Training and Research (UNITAR). I was tireder than I'd ever been in my life, but relieved to be getting away, and I knew that both meetings would also afford networking chances for choosing contributors to *Sisterhood Is Global,* which had been steadily percolating as a project ever since *Sisterhood Is Powerful* had been published ten years earlier.

The networking was indeed fantastic, and being around vibrant women from all over the world put my personal troubles in perspective and replenished my energy. At the week-long UNITAR conference called "Creative Women in Changing Societies,"[14] I reencountered old friends: the Brazilian theater director Gilda Grillo, the Egyptian writer and physician Nawal El Saadawi, the Thai feminist Mallica Vajrathon, and my U.S. feminist colleagues E. M. (Esther) Broner and Phyllis Chesler.

I also met for the first time a number of extraordinary women who were to become friends, allies, anthology contributors, and long-term colleagues. There was Gwendoline Konie of Zambia, who movingly described the realities women faced in postcolonial Africa, and former Portuguese Prime Minister Maria de Lourdes Pintasilgo, wise, jolly, unpretentious. There was Keiko Higuchi from Japan, whose militance was masked by her genteel demeanor, and the Ghanaian novelist-playwright Ama Ata Aidoo, with whom I talked through the glimmering, midnight-sun summer night not only about our struggles as women writers but

---

[14] See *Creative Women in Changing Societies: A Quest for Alternatives*, edited by Torill Stokland, Mallica Vajrathon, and Davidson Nicol for UNITAR, with a Foreword by Robin Morgan (Dobbs Ferry, N.Y.: TransNational Publishers, 1982).

about our same-age, precocious, chess-loving children. And there was a New Zealander with short blond curls and an air of calm authority, who gasped as we were being introduced, "Robin Morgan! You're one of my heroines!" A jeans-and-boots-clad streak of energy, she turned out to be a sitting member of Parliament, but acted like no MP any of us had ever met. This was charismatic, twenty-eight-year-old Marilyn J. Waring. Her tactical brilliance and impatience with intellectual sloth would become as evident in the daytime working-group sessions as would her emotional fragility and musical flair in the evenings when, accompanying herself on her guitar, she sang folk songs for us all in a classically trained lyric soprano.

These women would become part of the Sisterhood Is Global projects over the next twenty years—first the anthology, then the strategy meeting the book would inspire, then the institute the meeting would in turn spawn, then the various translations and editions of the book again—and they remain allies still.

But with Waring there was from the first something different. Not just a bond: a danger, an electricity. I was certainly not about to act on *that,* although the invitation was subtle yet clear, both in Oslo and a week later in Copenhagen, where she'd exchanged her blue jeans for the silk designer print frocks appropriate to her rank in her country's delegation. I, however, still a zombie from the consequences of my last run-in with erotic energy, was hardly about to take another such leap, especially with a woman; I reassured myself that the *frisson* must be residual libido from Yaddo, and that furthermore—considering my dismal experiences back in the group-sex days—I was hopelessly heterosexual. Anyway, I had my hands full: a kid at camp, a marriage to salvage, a conference to cover, potential contributors to network, *work* to do. Thank *god* for work to do.

There were caucuses and fracases. There was more than the usual backstage friction in the U.S. delegation, which greedily availed itself of the expertise of Koryne Horbal and the extensive groundwork she'd done for the conference's preceding two years (Horbal was an architect of the UN Convention to Eradicate All Forms of Discrimination against Women, or CEDAW, and at the time U.S. representative to the UN Commission on the Status of Women), but then denied her minimal courtesies in Copenhagen because she'd been openly critical of certain Carter administration policies on women. There were sign-ins and walkouts and sit-downs.

But most cherished among my Copenhagen memories[15] is the way that Abzug and I worked in tandem. Bella lobbied the Israeli delegates, who had confidence in her; I worked the Arabs, where I'd managed to earn trust. The two of us knocked heads and twisted arms to arrange early breakfast meetings for dialogue outside formal channels, knowing that if you got people together at 6:45 A.M., they would be so catatonic they would actually *want* to listen more than to talk. Iran was still holding fifty-two U.S. hostages at the time, but Bella and I managed to extract a pledge from the Iranian delegation's women that if U.S. mothers would demonstrate in Washington, D.C., for the shah's ill-gotten millions to be returned to Iran's women and children, then Iranian women would march simultaneously in Tehran for the hostages to be returned home "to their mothers." All of us were already in the TV studio, about to go on air and announce this, when the man who headed the Iranian delegation stormed in, mullah-flanked, and shooed his countrywomen away like a flock of black-winged ravens. But it was one fine try, and seeing Bella work—the way she alternated cajoling, bullying, wheedling, reasoning, and humor— was to be spellbound, watching a political virtuoso. She too refused to stop. But unlike me, she was selective in her choice of issues on which to persist.

I returned to the States to write about the conference for *Ms.* and for the *Los Angeles Times,* to bring bagels and Chinese dumplings up to Blake at camp (where he was suffering Manhattan-withdrawal symptoms), and then to spin around and fly back to Europe for a four-day in-depth interview and cover shoot in Vienna with the feminists exiled from the USSR. On every flight, I filled pages of legal-sized pads with notes for the emerging anthology. We would have to transcend standard geopolitics. We would have to include both Israel and Palestine, both Germanies, both Irelands. This time there couldn't only be personal voices, though those would be the soul of the book. There would have to be statistics about

---

[15] For further details about the conference and the non-governmental-organization forum, see the "Blood Types" chapter of *The Anatomy of Freedom.*

women's status in each country, facts that would be tools in the hands of activists and useful for women's studies, international studies, policymakers, funders. Much of this would mean original research. The rest would mean finding, assembling (and checking for reliability) existing data from sources all across the globe. *My god,* I would catch myself thinking, *this will be a veritable international encyclopedia on women. And there are no precedents.*

Then I would get petrified.

The best way to deal with fear is usually to keep forging on. Besides, the time felt right; anyway, the project drove me as if I were its plowhorse. Still, organizing *this* epic would be a task to make the years on *Sisterhood Is Powerful* by comparison seem lethargic. There was no way to do this one by myself. I needed a team.

FIFTEEN

. . . .

Exiles

When a woman loves a woman, it is the blood of the mothers speaking.

— CARIBBEAN PROVERB

For the next four years, until Doubleday's November 1984 publication of its almost nine hundred printed pages, *Sisterhood Is Global: The International Women's Movement Anthology* would devour most of my literary and political energy. Considering what else was going on during those four years, the book would also serve as an anchor in the tempestuous seas of my life. In the Introduction, I wrote, "Somewhere in these pages there vibrates for me much personal mourning, fear, grief, celebration, and plain living. But the book continued. At times feeling like a curse of inexorable deadlines and self-chosen responsibility, it has been far more often a blessing of focused work and sanity, a demanding preoccupation which has borne me up even in moments when nothing else anymore seemed real. . . . [It] has functioned in my life like the rare gift of a creative obsession."

The team came together, slowly at first, then swiftly as the project gathered momentum. It started with Jane Ordway, a smart young woman who'd been interning with me at *Ms.*; she worked for two years on the project as a volunteer before there was a penny of funding available for salaries. Soon there was Karen Berry, who had worked in *Ms.*'s advertising department as a secretary, had become a friend, and had aided me with research when I was writing *The Anatomy of Freedom*. We began working in the corners of *Ms.* and in my study at home, but after a particular scene on the home front we moved the anthology files and its growing library to my office at the magazine. *Ms.*—chronically enduring its own financial crises as a result of advertisers' tantrums and attacks from the extreme Right—generously contributed support in postage, long-distance phone calls, and toleration of my divided attention. I was now writing the "World" column as well as doing in-house editing and being a gadfly on foreign coverage, which, considering much of the international subject matter, meant that I earned the office nickname of Atrocities Editor.

But it didn't take long to realize that *SIG* needed space to itself, and a production staff, a research staff, translators, a library . . . which meant rent, payrolls, phone, cable expenses (ah, had faxes and email been common in the early 1980s, our lives would have been much easier!). All of this meant fundraising. So now I was Alice in Foundationland, getting tips and contacts from Bella and Gloria, Pat Carbine, Koryne Horbal, Susan Berresford,[1] Donna Shalala.[2] One person led me to another. Alida Brill, the author and social critic who would become a dear friend, was then working in the foundation world and took me under her wing; without her guidance my fundraising would have stayed at the level of rattling a tin cup. I was learning how to construct budgets and draft proposals in Fundingspeak: stay away from words like "feminism" and "patriarchy," write "discrimination" instead of "oppression," and when in doubt, bland it out. I was also studying a new role: how to recostume myself from my comfortable slacks, shirts, and boots to what the *SIG* staff would call "her fundraising look," in order to perform the requisite fast shuffle at various foundations—in dresses and high heels.

---

[1] Susan would later become the first woman president of the Ford Foundation.

[2] Donna, whose life has been spent trying to heave the ideas of social-justice movements into the circles of political power, was at the time president of Hunter College. She is, at this writing, U.S. Secretary of Health and Human Services.

The front matter and the acknowledgments of *Sisterhood Is Global* read like credits for a film with a cast of thousands—with reason, given all the people who made various kinds of contributions and had assorted involvements over the years. The steadiest financial backing came from two sources. One was the Ford Foundation, which, under the then presidency of Franklin Thomas, was the first major philanthropic institution to support not just women (who still receive only about 5 percent of all funding) *and* not just international issues but the juncture *between* them—precisely where *SIG* broke ground. The other source was a lone woman: Genevieve Vaughan, a feminist Texan so shy she insisted on being anonymous at first. Gen matched Ford dollar for dollar and, astonishingly, did so with no baroque proposal process. She said she knew my work and merely needed a letter outlining the project.[3]

We found space, sub-renting from the Women's Action Alliance, which had offices on Lexington Avenue where *Ms.* had once been quartered. We could have much-needed twenty-four-hour access; eventually we'd work in shifts and, toward the end, around the clock. The Alliance women had *no* idea what they were getting into—but then neither did I—yet they were excited by the project and absurdly hospitable. We began renting one room, then gradually expanded until we swallowed virtually the entire floor and the Alliance staff was cooped up in two small offices, patiently waiting for the book's completion. By the end of our sojourn there, we had a functioning tiny kitchen, foam pallets and blankets for dozing breaks, a medicine cabinet (full of aspirins, No-Doz, vitamin C, Midol, and tampons), a periodically resident cat (with litterbox), and a frequently visiting poodle.

Hiring staff was another new role for me, an uncomfortable one I probably would have handled abominably, too guilty to turn anyone away, had it not been for Karen, who would become the de facto assistant editor of the book and day-to-day coordinator of the project. Word spread, and the staff—not counting contributors—grew at its height to eighteen salaried

[3] Gen Vaughan—now out of the closet as a feminist philanthropist—still is a good friend; having given away most of her wealth to women's groups around the globe, she's devised yet another way to contribute, by writing serious political theory: *For-Giving: A Feminist Criticism of Exchange* (Plain View Press, 1997).

women (subsistence salaries, admittedly), *plus* interns, volunteers, and translators. When Toni Fitzpatrick joined us, the quality of research bumped up impressively—as she reminds me to this day.

Karen is now an attorney, and will always be dear to me. Toni—also now an attorney (and a therapist: one of those overachiever types)—lives in California but visits at least once a year with Shira, her wee feminist daughter. Karen, Toni, and I—the hard-core of *SIG*—sometimes get out the old scrapbooks and convulse with hilarity at anecdotes evoked by certain snapshots. About those days at *SIG* I *am* nostalgic, although I'd do something drastic in order not to relive them. Blake—who was our token male and all-around helper, frequently hanging out at the *SIG* offices—now says he thinks that those years were the equivalent for me of what most people experience as part of a normal youth: summer camp or college-dorm heydays. It's a fair insight, in that our offices became home to me more and more as the book moved into its final crunch years, and I sometimes slept there. We became a family, a workaholic commune. People left but, recidivist, returned. Love relationships bloomed or withered, people fell ill, recovered, survived migraines, breakdowns, root canals, funerals, arrests, abortions, and personal crises. We were there for each other through it all.

We spent weekends and holidays poring over demographic charts, we rose at 3:00 A.M. to place phone calls to some country where it was midday, we typed and translated and fact-checked and proofread until dawn, or straight on through the next day. I tried to forge a work system that would reflect feminist vision, a balance between anarchic self-responsibility and practical professionalism. This did *not* always succeed, and there were endless meetings, arguments, sometimes tears. But there was as much or more laughter, understanding, and teamwork. We ranged in age from adolescence to the mid-sixties, and were of an ethnic and racial composition as varied as the U.S. Women's Movement itself. Job functions sometimes blurred, as did day and night, exhaustion and elation, pride in our efforts and humility at the valor of women around the world whose lives we were discovering and describing. Every one of us who worked on the anthology emerged forever changed.

Ultimately, the buck stopped with me, named by the staff "Attila the Hon" (*sic*). The fundraising—ongoing and perpetual—was my responsibility, as was dealing with Doubleday via my forbearing editor there, Loretta Barrett. Mine were the final decisions on assigning contributor essays and country research, on content, staff administration, format and style, translations, and scheduling. As hands-on compiler and editor, I compulsively line-edited every article and every statistical preface. This had to be done repeatedly since updates kept coming in, necessitating, as we joked wearily, going "Baaaaack to Afghanistan" *just* when we'd managed to make it all the way through to Zimbabwe. Mine, too, of course, was the responsibility of dealing with the contributors I'd chosen from almost eighty countries. Some of them had to use pseudonyms for safety, some were in forced exile, and some were temperamental divas, but most of them were cooperative and enthusiastic, taking seriously the responsibility of being a voice for their countrywomen.[4]

Choosing, editing, and dealing in general with the contributors lent me even more perspectives regarding the multiplicity of feminisms I'd learned to affirm earlier. Choosing contributors also led me to the woman who would give me a markedly different perspective on my being "hopelessly heterosexual."

Breaking Through

In June of 1981 I was still filling in some crucial gaps where contributors were concerned. By and large, once word got around that Simone de Beauvoir had agreed to be the contributor from France, soliciting essays had got considerably easier. Yet there was a problem we regularly faced regarding countries with varying degrees of totalitarian government. "Official women" from their National Federation of Women or their Women's Bureau were eager to contribute, but while off the record they would vent their rage openly, their written submissions parroted their political masters. This was understandable but maddening. If the dictatorship was a right-wing one, the line was that feminism was a Communist plot, that in

---

[4] For details about the methodology of research, the staff, contributors, funders, and in general "the making of *Sisterhood Is Global*," see the book itself, preferably with the updated preface I wrote for the edition reissued by The Feminist Press at CUNY, 1996.

their culture Women Were Women and Men Were Men so they had no need for women's rights. If, on the other hand, it was a left-wing regime, the line was that the revolution had solved all such problems, so any rumors of sexism were CIA lies and capitalist slanders. Finding brave, independent voices willing to go public from such countries wasn't easy—yet with enough obstinacy usually turned out to be possible.

But one such country, with a left-wing dictatorship, had me stymied. It was in the Caribbean, and I was intent on including it, concerned that if I didn't, it might seem I automatically agreed with the United States's strong opposition to its government. Sure enough, the Federation women offered a "No Problem *Here!*" essay droned onto paper in sleep-inducing jargon. But the women I located in the exile community who *were* willing to critique their government all took a virulently right-wing line (written, I might add, in an equally insipid style). I was on the verge of admitting defeat when saved by Claire de Hedervary, a Belgian feminist working as a political adviser to the UN Security Council.[5] Claire mentioned she thought she knew the perfect woman: a UN colleague in exile from the country in question. This woman had fled because she felt the revolution—of which she'd been a part—hadn't gone far *enough,* that it had abandoned its ideals and had exploited and then betrayed women. She spoke and wrote fluent English (as well as Spanish, German, French, and Italian), was a published poet, *and,* although she worked at the UN Centre in Vienna, was currently in New York for a week at Secretariat headquarters. I embraced Claire and told her that *she* was as helpful as she was chic (which was very), and that I owed her a bottle of champagne if this worked out. Then I rang up Iliana de Costa and invited her to lunch.

Pause.

Iliana de Costa is not her real name. It's the name I invented for a fictional character based on this woman, in my novel *Dry Your Smile.* But it's the name I perforce return to here, at her request, since she still works with the UN—an organization not yet as free of homophobia as we would wish it to be. So she is pseudonymous in this memoir, but all other details

[5] Claire would write the anthology's critique of the UN itself, a witty article titled "Good Grief, There Are *Women* Here!"

of our relationship are accurate, albeit subjectively related. Only the names—of the individual and of her country, since it would identify her—have been disguised. To protect the guilty.

We had a lovely lunch, our conversation ranging from the lives of Sor Juana de la Cruz and Virginia Woolf to feminist insights, poetry, and international politics. Iliana was a multicultural intellectual, possessed of a rich sense of humor, a mellifluous voice, large expressive eyes, and Latin American buoyancy. Only a little taller than me and five months younger, she nonetheless seemed the elder, very much a woman of the world, and she exuded a stubbornness that I recognized and found invigorating. She couldn't have survived going into exile, alone, at age nineteen, without being stubborn. I felt I'd made a friend, and invited her to be a contributor on the spot. She accepted, but said she'd have to write under a pseudonym. Given her critique of her country, I could understand why; she wasn't the only contributor whose identity we were protecting, via a tight security system to which only Karen and I were privy. There was definitely a buzz between Iliana and me, but I didn't think much about it. I was accustomed to the exhilaratingly high-energy exchange often generated between feminist activists in cross-cultural encounters.

Kenneth's therapy, and mine, and ours, had all been moving right along, and hope sprang eternal in my obstinate breast. In July, once Blake was at summer camp (now an annual ritual, not an emergency flight), I swept Kenneth and myself off to the Yucatán, in Mexico. It was supposed to be the honeymoon we'd never had, a week together in hopes of kindling the spark we'd either never felt or had felt so briefly and so long ago it wasn't an ember anymore. The trip had its poignant moments, but it generated more billing than cooing, thus only increasing the financial pressures. Afterward, I returned to New York and work, and Ken went on for a week's vacation in Key West by himself.

Iliana wrote and telephoned, but not perceptibly more often than other contributors, and she was incredibly helpful in obtaining statistics and reports for the research staff that would otherwise have taken us months to locate and extract from UN bureaucracies. In one phone call, she said she'd been immersed in reading everything I'd published, and asked if I'd be interested in coming to Vienna to speak on a panel with Nawal El Saadawi and Germaine Greer at the next UN observance of March 8,

International Woman's Day. I replied that I'd love to, if my schedule allowed it.

That September, Blake and I went to Quebec for a long weekend. We needed it desperately, since the marriage had taken another downward turn. (Such occasions are precisely the reason credit-card debt was invented.) Blake practiced his UN-school French and gorged on escargot, discovering that snails are the gourmet's excuse to eat quantities of garlic-butter-soaked bread. We stayed at the Château Frontenac, took carriage rides, got merrily lost wandering the narrow streets of the old city, walked along the St. Lawrence, laughed, cried, and hugged a lot. But coming home was no fun.

When, at the turn of the year, I finally accepted Iliana's invitation to speak in Vienna, I told Kenneth I'd like to bring Blake with me for his first trip to Europe—especially since Vienna was a music city. The Vienna UN Centre would pay for a business-class ticket, which I could convert into two coach seats with only a small additional payment, and my per diem expenses could stretch to cover both Blake and me. It would be spring break at UNIS, so we could eke out ten days. Ken thought it was a fine idea—but only if he could come, too. There was a flurry of calls to Iliana, who, ever resourceful, found an excuse for another ticket.

Would I be willing to give a poetry reading? Because then, more money might be—

Uh, well, could Kenneth and I give a *joint* poetry reading?

Yes! She would arrange it. Ever vivacious, she insisted she'd love showing off Vienna to my whole family, that we'd have a proper holiday. So the feminist holy family took flight in March of 1982.

Breaking Open

It was to be *eine kleine* hell. The only unalloyed delight of the trip was when, during the panel Q-and-A, Blake politely asked Germaine Greer why she had granted an interview to *Playboy* when the magazine was built on contempt for women. Insulted (and hung-over), Greer fumbled her response rather badly, and the audience wound up discreetly hissing her but applauding her twelve-year-old questioner. The other public events went well enough, and I threw a dinner in honor of those *SIG* contributors who were present.[6] The "vacation" part was touching, even overwhelming. Iliana had arranged for opera and philharmonic tickets, museum trips, visits to Mozart's house, drives to the Venus of Willendorf site and to Dürnstein, the medieval castle on the Danube. She was extraordinarily generous with her time as well as with her wallet. She and Kenneth got on royally, having in common their passion for Goethe, Schiller, and Wagner, not my favorite trio. Blake liked her. We were all grateful.

I was also a nervous wreck. It was becoming evident that Iliana had, as I first regarded it, a "crush" on me. The intensity of her gaze was flattering, and the champagne and sheaf of orchids arriving addressed to me at our hotel after the poetry reading raised my temperature and Kenneth's eyebrows. I said I needed to talk with her alone. It became apparent, after that conversation, that she felt she'd fallen in love with me.

Who knows, after all the libraries filled with analyses on the subject, why anyone falls in love with anyone? Some say you really fall in love with the person you yourself become in the beloved's presence. All I knew was that no one in my life had *ever* looked at me the way Iliana did, with such a luminosity of desire. Oh, how I liked the woman I saw mirrored in her eyes, the woman I became in her presence! Added to that was the startling sense of freedom in feeling erotically drawn to someone who, being a woman, spoke the same emotional language, someone who was already a friend, a *sister*. Nevertheless, I told her the story of Yaddo, and I said flatly that nothing could ever happen between us.

She was perplexed. She'd read my poems. She'd now read Kenneth's. He'd talked to her proudly about our Bloomsbury "open marriage," which didn't shock her; she was a sophisticate accustomed to moving in European art circles. She knew he had lovers. "My gay brother," she'd called

---

[6] Nawal and her husband, Sherif Hetata, the two Austrian co-contributors Edit Schlaffer and Cheryl Benard, Iliana, and Claire de Hedervary, who was visiting at the time. Some of them brought more people at the last minute, until, with Kenneth and Blake, we were up to twenty—in a pricey restaurant, with champagne. In the circumstances, I saw no way to disinvite the extra guests or ask people to chip in. I distinctly recall seeing the bill with hundreds of thousands of zeros in Austrian schillings, blithely handing over my credit card, and then waiting with a fixed, dazzling smile while internally dreading that the waiter would return to whisper that I'd maxed out. That time I was lucky.

him, and "my lesbian sister," he'd responded, as arm in arm after dinners they had careened tipsily ahead of Blake and me down the cobblestone streets of Vienna's First District, loudly singing "Ich grolle nicht" from Schumann's *Dichterliebe* together. She made it apparent—to me and subsequently to Kenneth—that she was in no way out to destroy our family. Rather, she wanted to earn a place in my life alongside it. I actually thought, for the space of that afternoon's conversation, that this time things might be possible. I arranged for the three of us to talk. After all, Kenny had said repeatedly that he could have understood if only I'd been involved with a woman . . .

Boom. Crash. Bang. We hadn't even gone to bed together, but there were scenes, storms, weeping. . . . Look, we can do this shorthand, right? I mean, to hell with the details. You get the drift.

The holy family left Vienna with the adults barely on speaking terms and poor Blake in gloom. I recall feeling devastated, waving goodbye not just to Iliana but to the woman in myself I'd glimpsed, might have become, and knew now I never would be.

Yet this time there was a different factor. I had underestimated how seriously Iliana took her Taurus-horoscope characteristics. She was a stubborn little bull. She was also a romantic. Huge boxes of ivory lilies arrived for me at *Ms.* (raising eyebrows *there*). She phoned. She wrote. She was sure she could convince her brother Kenneth of the injustice of his position. I felt *wooed*. I realized I had never been desired to the point of being wooed before, and decided there was certainly something to it. Sixteen days later, like the battleship *Intrepid,* Iliana arrived in New York.

She'd come to give a poetry reading herself, at Womanbooks, then New York's feminist bookstore, but she remained for eleven days, having taken personal leave from the UN. She stayed with my friend Lois Sasson, who was becoming the godmother of my peripatetic adventures in passion. I'd met Lois in the early Seventies; we'd become buddies when I participated in a Broadway reading she produced to bring attention to the plight of "the Three Marias," imprisoned Portuguese feminist writers.[7] I had seen her through some trying times of her own, but during this period, well—god *love* Lois, she put up with a lot. I was to stay with her during my various

---

[7] See *Going Too Far.*

exiles from home so often that we renamed her spare room the Robin Morgan Memorial Den.

But now Iliana was ensconced in it.

Sometimes life conspires with chance and compels you into living when you're doing your best to stay safely dead. Or, as the psychologist Mary Jane Sherfey wrote about sexuality, "the strength of the drive determines the force required to suppress it."[8] During those eleven days, I had two overnight trips for speeches in Virginia and at Brandeis (during which time Lois took advantage of my absence to interrogate poor Iliana, concluding that the latter really loved me, and that she, Lois, approved—but that she worried Iliana, a Taurus like herself, might be possessive). Kenneth meanwhile made a good-faith effort to live up to his own rules: he, Blake, Iliana, and I had an indigestion-provoking Chinese dinner. Then he announced he could not sustain the proximity, for which I actually didn't blame him—wondering only why, for so many years, *I* had sustained it regarding *his* relationships. He took off for Key West again. As fate would have it, Blake went on a five-day school field trip. And Iliana de Costa and I became lovers, right in the Robin Morgan Memorial Den.

Breaking Up

What gets lost in such *Sturm und Drang* is the rhythm of daily life, which manages to persist no matter what. I leaf back through old datebooks in amazement at its consistency. Somewhere in all this, *Depth Perception's* galleys arrived for me to proofread, and *The Anatomy of Freedom* manuscript went back to the copyeditor with my comments and changes. Somewhere, somehow, taxes got done, clarinet and piano concerts and teacher-parent conferences got attended, political meetings were held, writing deadlines met, *SIG* contributors soothed, funds raised, speeches delivered, planes boarded, money borrowed and repaid, laundry done, groceries bought, meals cooked. Women are indefatigable. So it's just as well I was one.

But things would get worse before they got better.

---

[8] "A Theory on Female Sexuality," in *Sisterhood Is Powerful.*

The relationship with Iliana was not to be dismissed. This time Kenneth's resistance only fed the passion. She and I *both* wrote. We *both* phoned. Throwing caution (and *her* credit cards) to the wind, she came to New York for ten days again in late May, and brought me to Vienna for five days early in July. She came again for a few days in August, then again in September. Kenneth dug in and wanted me to live elsewhere than our home, even when she wasn't around. I refused to leave Blake. This time I foolishly tried to fight for both the relationship and the marriage. There were ghastly battles wherein I questioned why Ken's new friend, a sweet young man named Rafi, was allowed to stay in the home I was financially supporting, but I wasn't. (It's remarkable how much courage it takes you to screw yourself up to ask such an obvious question—only to find that your big-deal heroic asking of it gets you nowhere anyway.)

There was a lot of to-ing and fro-ing. Blake went to camp again—this time no doubt *eager* to get there. In the early fall, he spent as much time as possible with me in my latest diaspora—mostly at the apartment of Suzanne and her husband, Bob Levine, when they were away and we could have it to ourselves—to do them a favor, as they gracefully put it, and "cat-sit." In November, Doubleday sent me on a twenty-city book tour to promote *The Anatomy of Freedom*. In December, Iliana arrived to stay, having got herself transferred to the UN's New York headquarters, and having found herself an apartment.[9] Throughout it all, *Sisterhood Is Global* ground on, as did the lectures and my work at *Ms.* From the serenity of today, I look back on the ten months following April 1982 as one of those relentless periods of turmoil you cannot imagine having survived, although you know you did.

Then again, I do know how I survived. I had to, because something more important was happening, something that added heavily to the burden of other crises but emotionally dwarfed everything else. In July, I'd had a phone call that my mother had been taken to the hospital.

At this point Faith hadn't spoken to me for almost three years. When

---

[9] In one of those spooky coincidences that trick you into thinking momentarily there's meaning in the universe, Iliana's apartment was in the now residential building that had formerly housed Grove Press's offices. Visiting her there was like returning in triumph to the place from which I'd been hauled out feet first.

Archie Thurman had died in the mid-1970s, we'd grown closer for a while. I'd been so glad to be there for her, to defend her—the interloper second wife—against Archie's family, and to help her through the mourning process, which, to my amusement, hadn't taken her all that long. Then one day, I'd noticed tremors in her hands, but in reply to my questions she'd replied sharply that it was her nerves. It took weeks of prodding to get her to the doctor. The verdict was Parkinson's disease, a particularly hideous blow for someone who only ever had one thing: her pride. She'd defended it fiercely, fighting for it, lying for it. Now she would be forced to surrender even that.

As time went on, the medication produced results as bad as or worse than the disease: periodic blindness, bouts of depersonalization, paranoid delusions. She was in and out of hospitals all through the late Seventies. I grew adept at smuggling in Chinese food and her favorite rotisserie chicken, since she loathed hospital trays. If I could coax her into a good mood, we would *shhhh* and giggle while she ate and I stood watch, in an echo of our long-ago two-person church-step picnics. But there were distressing days. Once she attacked me physically, screaming that I was an imposter imprisoning her and bringing her poisoned flowers in order to steal her money. She flew at me to bite my wrist, but her teeth closed on my watch. She bit so hard she broke the crystal.

Sometimes she did have clarity, returning like Persephone from her hell as I, in our role reversal, paced the world like Demeter searching for ways to reclaim her. In those moments of comprehension, we would discuss what to do. It was obvious that on her return home, she'd need a professional aide to look in on her on the alternate days when I couldn't get there or if I was out of town, someone who would help with groceries, maybe cook a little when I couldn't do my usual cook-for-a-week-and-leave-portions-in-Mommie's-freezer. She didn't want that. She wanted me. In person. All the time. She offered to buy us a town house (with the invested earnings from my childhood) *if* we would all live in it together. Kenneth and I did consider it, but decided it was hardly a helpful development for an already endangered marriage. When we declined, she raged that I was abandoning her.

Grave illness, like any crucible, can transform people into their best or basest selves. Faith's disease was cruelly degenerative, and exacerbated

her worst traits. She did hire a long-suffering aide, but she switched doctors every month; they were all incompetent if they didn't agree with her
opinions of what she needed. To me, she grew more intractable and dom-
ineering than ever before: I had destroyed her life and I was selfish,
ungrateful, "like Lear's bad daughters." Denouncing me seemed her primary pleasure. Every time I went up to see her in her Fifth Avenue co-op,
I felt I was going through a loin-girding ceremony for combat. Finally, after
one blowout, she refused to speak to me—the standard ritual—but this
time she stuck to it no matter how often I kept phoning. So I stayed in
touch with the aide, her doctor, and her few last friends, who began to
complain that she wouldn't see *them* anymore, that she was becoming a
recluse. She fired the aide and hired another when she learned I'd "been
spying" on her. At last, all my sources were cut off by her executive order,
and she still wouldn't speak to me. Her latest doctor suggested I have her
declared legally incompetent, but the idea revolted me. So I just kept calling, positive that one day she'd relent and not slam down the phone at
hearing my voice.

In July of 1982, however, the voice on the phone was that of an older
woman with a Jamaican accent. She was one of my mother's two current
companion-aides, she said, and she was calling despite Faith's having forbidden her to do so, because she didn't know what else to do. I was on my
way to the hospital as I hung up.

Mercifully, the future veils itself from us. I didn't know I was entering
into a real-life drama of such magnitude that it would diminish my toler-
ance for all fabrications thereof ever after.

I was shocked at how she'd changed: tiny, wizened, virtually paralyzed,
her body cramped into the distorted tensions of last-stage Parkinson's. The
disease seemed to have advanced with terrifying speed—until I discovered, tucked away in her apartment, a shoebox crammed with unfilled
prescriptions for medication she'd refused to take, since doing so would
have been to acknowledge the diagnosis, and since she must have feared
the delusions even more than the rigidity. She was in the hospital this time
because she'd fallen out of bed and fractured a hip, lying on the floor for
half a day until the aide arrived at the usual time. The doctors had also put
her back on medication for the disease, but they announced that she

couldn't possibly return home. Once they stabilized her, they said, she had to be put in a full-care nursing facility.

"Why? Why me? What'd I do to deserve? Mama, I'm not a whore, not a whore, notawhore," she kept muttering, in a slurry singsong to rupture the heart. Her other refrain was "Home. Wanna' go home. Where's home? Is there home?" Nothing I could say was understandable to her, and she didn't react to my stroking her, kissing her, holding her. She was in exile from her own mind.

From then on, the discoveries broke and broke again over my life like waves intent on convincing an abandoned lighthouse it was time to fall dark at last. Once before, buffered by the distance fiction bestows on a writer entering its environs, I revisited these months, in *Dry Your Smile*. There's no way to parse them in comparable detail here. Reality, like poetry, requires distillation.

The discovery of what it was to search for a nursing home not functioning on a circle of hell. The discovery that there was no way legally to arrange for Faith's transfer or access her finances to pay for it unless I went to court to become her guardian-conservator, which meant having her declared incompetent. The discovery that there were moments when she had perfect clarity, making the incompetency approach all the more repulsive, even though imperative. The discovery, then, that there was almost no money in her bank account, that her stocks had been sold and her savings withdrawn, that her jewelry and furs—including the mink coat I'd triumphantly bought for her years earlier—had vanished. The discovery that hundreds and hundreds of checks, ranging from sums of $50 to one at $60,000, had been forged—and cashed. The discovery that letters purportedly written and signed by her, instructing her brokers to liquidate her stocks, had also been forged. The discovery that neither her brokers nor her bank had ever questioned these unusual instructions, drastic withdrawals, or squiggly signatures, and claimed they weren't liable. The discovery that Medicare would not pay for her to be in a nursing facility so long as she owned a co-op, which meant it had to be sold as soon as possible, even if at a loss, to pay the nursing-home fees of $4,000 a month. The discovery of evidence that it was her aides, two women in their sixties, one from South Carolina and the other from Jamaica, who had managed to make off with more than $400,000—all of Faith's investments and savings from the entirety of my childhood earnings plus whatever Archie's family had settled on his widow. The discovery that my mother had been willing to trust two strangers rather than her daughter. The discovery of how odious it is to spend one's life in meetings with doctors, lawyers, and accountants. The discovery that the district attorney's office now wants to locate and prosecute these two elderly black women, who have for the moment vanished, for grand theft—*but* that the DA cannot locate or reclaim any of the money. The discovery that the trail grows cold after one of the women had donated hundreds of thousands of dollars to her pentecostal church down South and the other—well, the other had a heroin-addicted son whose child she was raising, so we can surmise where *her* share had gone. The discovery that the DA won't prosecute those truly responsible—the brokers and bank officers who never blinked when stock-liquidating documents and checks for huge sums came their way because, as the young ADA shrugs, "Those guys have power. It's a lost cause. *You* can sue them. *If* you can find a lawyer to take your case. But it'll take a decade. And you'll lose." The discovery that he's correct. The discovery that since no funds are recoverable anyway, I realize I will discourage what I regard as the purely vengeful prosecution of these two aides—women who have spent their entire lives cleaning up after people who could afford to make messes. The discovery that all the lawyers—the DA's office *and* mine—don't understand why tracking down and sending these two women up for thirty years, and placing the grandson (who is Blake's age) in foster care, is an unacceptable conclusion. The discovery that they can't prosecute without my cooperation and that I dare announce I'll be a hostile witness. The discovery that social workers and doctors can keep Faith in the hospital only so long, once she's stabilized, meaning money must be found *fast* to pay for the one humane nursing home I've finally located. The discovery that it's possible, with the help of women friends, to plow through the mad attic her apartment has become, sort things out, clean and scour, have certain items appraised for sale, and sell them; have the place painted, fumigated, and waxed; put it up for sale, convince the co-op board of the reliability of almost the first buyer, sell it, and pay for her to enter the best nursing facility in Manhattan—all within eight weeks. And the discovery that nowhere amid all her pack-rat-saved papers and documents is there anything resembling a marriage license or divorce decree, neither of which ever existed.

Kenneth tried to be comforting. But his own pain and his own demons preoccupied him during this time; he would alternate between expressing sympathy for Faith and inveighing against her as the bitch who deserved to suffer because she'd caused all my, and thus his, problems to begin with. Blake was exquisitely tender, but there was little he could do juggling, as he already had to, school and problems at home. As it was, I died a little every time I saw how rapidly the whole situation was maturing him. It was Lois who mostly housed me. It was Suzanne who first went through Faith's apartment with me. It was Gloria who lent me the money to carry on. It was Karen who kept *Sisterhood Is Global* moving on schedule. And it was Iliana who seemed to be always there, like a rock emanating security and a cornucopia lavishing love.

What an irony *that* discovery, to be exploring another woman's body in love while the body of the woman who gave me life was moving daily, inexorably into decay. Or was that in fact the reason? However many the dimensions, Iliana was friend as well as lover, mother as well as sister. She was the person who toured nursing homes with me, who argued with doctors when I couldn't bear to one more time, who scrubbed apartment items before appraisal, who kept me (relatively) sane after meetings with lawyers, who reminded me to eat something or sleep a few hours; the person who held me when I couldn't stop crying and shaking.

All through that summer, I saw my mother almost every day, usually twice a day. When I had to be briefly out of town, I was consumed with getting back. I was possessed by her; haunted by her past while going through her papers, albums, and books; submerged in her present as I sat hour after hour at her bedside editing *SIG* articles while she dozed or murmured half sentences or railed against her mother, or her doctors, or me. Some days she called me Friend and whispered that the doctors were pimps and the nurses madams and the place was a brothel at night. No reassurances to the contrary worked, so I entered into her delusion and together we clung and huddled and plotted her imaginary escape, which made her laugh with delight. Some days she knew who I was, but thought I was four years old again. Some days, she implored me to tell Robin she was sorry, sorry, so *sorry,* and *please* to come visit her.

The medical personnel scuttled about, cheerily exuding what de Beauvoir termed "ritual facetiousness" in the account of her own mother's dying, *A Very Easy Death,* which became my bible. Summer surrendered to autumn and autumn to winter while Faith lay in her bed staring or mumbling and I came and went from the magazine or the meetings or the *SIG* office, to sit at her side watching the light dim and shrink across the floor. She seemed improved enough for me to go on the November book tour—but I broke it on three occasions to fly back for overnights in order to visit her. She was stabilized enough that I went with Blake and Iliana for three days over Christmas to the Levines' country home in upstate New York, while Rafi spent the holidays with Kenneth at our home. The moment we returned to the city, I went directly to see her.

She was sleeping, her jaw slack, her mouth open with labored breathing, the lines in her forehead a tortured knot of tension. I dropped my coat and sank into the familiar chair, waiting. Maybe she'd wake up and take a little spoon-fed food. Maybe she'd want Friend to sing to her. Maybe she'd tell Friend that the Baby had given a good performance, like a real little trouper. But she slept on, and the night nurse looked in to warn me that visiting hours were almost over. Then, as I gathered up my things, my mother opened her eyes.

They were brilliant and clear, black stars in the bone-colored pottery skull that was left of her face. They focused on me. They *focused.* I watched through tears how those dark novas glowed toward recollection, how the forehead knot slowly released its lines, how they radiated like a rose window until the entire sunken, twisted constellation of her features caught and blazed into recognition and love, the dry lips leaking spittle but cracking into a luminous smile.

"*Robin!*" she cried. "It's *you!* You're all grown up but you still came home to me!"

I dropped whatever was in my arms to gather her up instead, crying, "Yes, Mommie, it's me. All grown up and still here. Never really been anyplace else. Oh yes, little Mommie, it's me."

We stayed that way a long time, as I rocked and whispered to her while she drifted back to sleep. Then the nurse came, insisting I leave. I could now, because I knew that for the rest of my days, this would be the face of my mother I would choose to remember. This was a woman whose passion knew no middle way, saw no distinction between love and hunger, lies and truth—but this was a woman who had managed to surface from the depths where she now semi-lived swimming through the wreckage of her life, to grant her daughter one moment of grace.

The next day, she was suddenly worse, and had to be rushed from the nursing home back to the hospital. Her heart was strong, but she had pneumonia—"the friend of the dying," her doctor called it. I asked for no extreme measures, canceled as much of my own life as I could, and began the vigil. When I couldn't be there, Lois or Iliana managed to be.

They say that of all the senses in a dying person, hearing is the last to go. I murmured and sang and told her stories through those last weeks, read to her from the books she'd once loved—Blake, Kafka, Lao Tzu. I talked about the Orozco murals in Mexico City that she'd seen when she was seventeen, laughing into the wind and daring her future to be as beautiful as herself. She never regained comprehension. When she lapsed into unconsciousness, I kept on whispering into wherever she might be lingering to listen.

No matter how expected, death is always the ultimate surprise.

She died in the month and hour she'd borne me, a chill January dawn.

In certain parts of the Amazon rainforest, bromeliads—partly parasitical plants that attach themselves to trees and live on air and water—can grow as large as three feet across. Since they are deep-centered, they contain small pools of rainwater, up to several gallons, in which entire miniature ecosystems flourish. Among the life-forms found there, high in the treetop lagoons, is a tiny frog, which is born, grows, lives, mates, spawns, and dies in the same pond, believing those few cupfuls of water are the world.

By Jewish law, the deceased should be buried before sundown the next day or, at maximum, within forty-eight hours. I knew that my mother had wanted a plot in the Conservative Jewish cemetery where the Thurman family graves were, and that she would have wanted a Jewish ceremony, though I would have opted for cremation and a secular memorial service. Well, politics teaches even its radicals the art of compromise, so—with the help of those indefatigable women friends—I was able to devise a middle way, one that bestowed its own comic tenderness even in the midst of grief. If it was going to be a religious ceremony, then at least it would have a womanly style.

Joanne Edgar, a friend and *Ms.* colleague, helped make the necessary phone calls. Letty Cottin Pogrebin found me a woman rabbi (in 1983 they were rarer than today) and even a woman cantor, who at the time was one of two in all of New York State. The rabbi told me we'd need a minyan for the burial—the minimum ten people required by Jewish law for ritual prayers—but that a minyan was traditionally male, at least among Conservative Jews; she herself was Reform. Never mind, our minyan would be different. Lois, meanwhile, flew into action, remembering and locating an old acquaintance, Angie, then one of three female funeral directors in the whole country.

Angie had inherited the business from her father and was bent on showing that a woman could act, dress, and undertake as solemnly as any man. She was an old hand at this, and she would deal with everything, although, she warned me, she was used to organizing funerals in the tradition of her own background—which was Italian and Roman Catholic. Never mind, she could adjust. She did, managing to find the homespun white shroud and plain pine coffin with a Star of David on top required by Conservative Jews, instead of the elaborate caskets, clothing, and cosmetics to which she was accustomed. But that was nothing compared with her alarm when she realized that a special washing of the body had to take place, not by her own employees, but by Jewish women recommended by the cemetery, whose job it is to perform this washing as a religious act. The additional catch was that no Conservative Jewish cemetery would receive a body that had been "desecrated" in any way. With the ritual washers waiting suspiciously in her outer office, Angie phoned me in a panic, hissing into the phone, "The eyes! Holy Mary Mother of God, what am I supposed to do about the *eyes*?"

In the hours before my mother's dying, I'd asked to sign the requisite papers at the hospital, to donate her corneas for transplant after death. Now, Angie was afraid the washers would regard this as desecration. I didn't know what to tell her. I recall stammering how sorry I was but that I carried a universal organ donor card myself and so I'd thought Faith's beautiful brown eyes at least should be used to help someone see and—

Angie, ever practical, cut off my meanderings with a curt, "I got it. Marbles. I'll deal with it. G'bye."

Whatever she did, it worked. The ritual washing took place. No desecration was found. My friend Lesley Gore—herself a child-singing-star survivor—rose to her assignment and managed to find, in midwinter, a massive armload of white lilacs. The next day three cars bore Faith and the nine-tenths-female minyan to the cemetery—where we were promptly barred at the gate for not being all men, and for having a female rabbi, wearing slacks, yet. But a rabbi she was, using her powers of moral persuasion, and they finally permitted us to proceed to the gravesite. Blake, the minyan's sole male, never let go of my hand. Iliana hovered protectively. And there was Lois. And Lesley. And Joanne, Suzanne, Gloria, Letty, and my friend and literary agent Edite Kroll. With me, ten.

The rabbi and cantor had never experienced what they called a "full feminist funeral" before (neither had any of the rest of us). They said later they'd found it profoundly moving. Still, both of them—and most of the minyan—almost lost all composure when, to oversee the moving of the coffin to the site, Angie emerged from the hearse: a tall woman with cropped black hair and a crisp but compassionate manner, impeccably attired in a full cutaway tuxedo.

We gathered round in the cold grey morning, and the rabbi and cantor led us in reading the Kaddish. In women's voices the prayer for the dead seemed to take on a keening quality sharper with grief than in men's, the traditional words of mourning flayed raw again by the unexpected treble. We each threw a handful of earth on the coffin as it was being lowered. Last, I lifted the sheaf of lilacs, stepped to the edge of the open grave, and flung my arms wide so the flowers descended, wingspread like a great pearl bird, into the earth.

Two days later, my twenty-two-year-old marriage ended forever. Two days after that, Faith's memorial service was held. Although I'd made calls and posted notices in the newspapers, those few people who attended were my friends, because my mother had so alienated her own. In her honor, I read the closing lines from Elizabeth Cady Stanton's final speech,

"The Solitude of Self." At the end, after almost everyone had gone and I was waiting to thank the rabbi, two women came slowly up the aisle from where they'd been sitting by themselves at the very back. They offered their condolences and said they'd keep me in their prayers. We embraced. Nothing more was said, and they retraced their steps out of the temple. One had a southern accent. The other spoke with a Jamaican lilt.

It was over.

The following day, Karen and the *Sisterhood Is Global* team insisted I pause work for an hour to celebrate my forty-second birthday with a lovably lopsided carrot cake Toni had baked. And Blake appeared, to give me something I'd never been allowed as a child, and had always longed for: a dollhouse.

"To tide you over, Rob," he smiled.

It was now the only dwelling I had.

Rights of Passage

> *Every day*
> *the past gets revised . . .*
> *You say*
> *turn the page*
> *see the bloody light prints*
> *of your fingers . . .*
> *take responsibility for your heart*
>
> — ISEL RIVERO, "MEASURED WORDS"

If you've played chess, you've probably experienced a stalemate, that moment when nothing of significant value seems movable without too great a sacrifice to contemplate. So each player slides a pawn forward here and there, until some development—an opening on the board or a flash of insight (or guts) on the part of one of the players—inspires a meaningful move. At which point everything shifts: new risks, losses, and gains surface; pieces relocate and tumble rapidly across the board until the game is all but unrecognizable.

So with the period following my mother's death. Was it mere coincidence that she died never knowing my marriage, initiated and sustained in defiance of her, wasn't a perfect match after all? Was it coincidence that now there was no necessity (or possibility) of proving anything to her, that I no longer had to prove (or tolerate) certain things for myself? Did her dying give me permission to burst out of the emotional bomb shelter where I'd been hunkering, and start trying to save my life?

I left the home I'd helped build for more than twenty years, and for which I'd been the financial support for more than thirteen, under (by now run-of-the-mill) melodramatic circumstances. I'd been reassured of Blake's security by both therapists—Ken's and mine—by Blake himself, and by my certainty of Kenneth's love for him. My own security seemed to be another question, in everyone's mind. In a sense, I could almost sympathize with Kenneth, who was trying his damnedest to get me to give *up*, to *stop,* in the only manner of which he apparently felt capable. I already had files, some books, and a few changes of clothes at the *SIG* offices. With little else, I encamped at Iliana's apartment.

She was more than glad to have me there, but my women friends were uniformly affronted. Why did *you* leave? Why aren't *you* getting that great triplex? Why don't you *fight* him—for the apartment, your home, your property? (Bella quipped, "Dahlink, you are the most spineless militant I've ever met.") I would have counseled the same thing, and had, many times, because too many women take the high road to avoid further confrontation in such situations. Well, now I was one of them. But there are moments when the loftiest feminist rhetoric must be grounded in reality. That period gave me insight into what motivates women in abusive marriages, how and why they stay, and why and how they go. Kenneth was *not* physically abusive, but fear tastes acrid no matter what engenders it; in the months following Faith's death, I would tremble during phone conversations with him. He was deeply angry at what his life had become, and it must have seemed convenient to blame me for even more of his problems than those for which I was responsible. Karen, with whom I shared an office at *SIG,* would watch me lower the receiver, shaking, after he'd banged down the phone on his end, then wordlessly bring me a cup of tea or offer a backrub or Kleenex, let me talk if I needed to, let me not if I couldn't. But I'll say this for fear: it focuses you on what is and isn't crucial.

Finally realizing that you must get out is crucial. Finally feeling that you must save yourself and your child is crucial—as is finally understanding that you need to do the first *so that* you can do the second, like the order in which adults with children should strap on oxygen masks in a depressurized airplane. Material goods? Less crucial. Besides, there are times simply to cut your losses and get on with living. For all these reasons, I walked away from another home I'd supported, taking with me little but the clothes on my back. It was the second time in my life I'd had to do this, reminiscent of the flight from my mother's co-op to my walk-up. This time, like a carrot-gnawing Scarlett O'Hara, I swore to myself, "as God is my witness," it would never happen again.

I continued as sole financial support for my former household for almost nine more months, which also infuriated my well-meaning friends. But I had my reasons. First, for the time being, Blake was living there. Second, even if he weren't, I couldn't very well see Ken being put out in the street. Third—you guessed it—I couldn't see a way to stop. At last I built up the courage to tell Kenneth that I had to start putting money aside toward renting someplace of my own and, although I'd continue paying all of Blake's bills and tuitions, I couldn't manage everything else as well; Ken would have to find some sort of job. That went over rather badly. I gave eight weeks' more notification of when the partial financial shift would have to take place, then extended that another two weeks. Of course, once that safety net *was* finally withdrawn, Ken managed to find a job within three weeks—earning more than I did at the time. You have to laugh at these moments, or you'd slit your wrists over the nearest basin.

We weren't formally divorced for another seven years. Today, that strikes me as ridiculous, but at the time there seemed no urgent need to legalize the situation, since neither of us was about to remarry, and I had other financial priorities—survival, relocation, pulling out of debt—so attorney's fees fell low on the list. I finally divorced Kenneth in October of 1990. At this writing, I will soon have lived apart from him as long as I lived with him. In the subsequent decades, freed from me and from being "the candy groom" on the movement cake, Kenneth has been able to pull his life together and live it honorably, always continuing to write and to be there for Blake in the special ways only he can.

On my side, I've been "happily divorced" although, ironically, I might now even argue that for much of the relationship I was "happily married." Considering the hurt we caused each other, that could sound bizarre. Yet just because the marriage ended doesn't mean it failed. In fact, given what

I've seen of certain other marriages, I might actually count it a (qualified) success. For more than two decades, we helped each other write some fine poetry, contribute to social progress, and birth and raise a wise, good-hearted, talented human being; we parented fairly well, to judge from the result—which is more than can be said of many marriages. A mismatched pair from the start, we were nothing if not creative in trying to make the best of it. I was already a senior citizen as a child, and I attained my womanhood before I had a chance to grow into my adolescence, a living example of Bob Dylan's line "I was so much older then, I'm so much younger now." As for Kenneth, he tried on various masculinities like cloaks, none ever quite fitting, but at least he was *open* to different ways, which is more than can be said of most men of his—or, sadly, any so far—generation. It's for him to say what I gave him of value in our relationship. For me, he was integral in the three mainstays of my life: a vital early influence on my poetry; a support of (as well as a cause for) my feminism; and most of all the father of Blake, chief joy for us both. I'm grateful to him for this triple benefaction. For the rest, I can best describe Kenneth by paraphrasing his own beloved Walt Whitman: "He was the man, he suffered, he was there."

So Much for Labels

Now, regarding all this about my being "hopelessly heterosexual."

I flatter myself that I'm an intelligent human being, but some of the gaps in self-insight are whoppers. It literally had not occurred to me that my previous attempts at encounters with another woman had failed because they had either been at Ken's behest (obviously *not* a turn-on) or, once, because of caving in to movement pressure (also a decided turn-*off*). It never struck me that if I wasn't *attracted* to the women in question, much less in love, the result was doomed to be dreary. When, with Iliana, I found myself drawn to a woman who clearly desired and loved me, and was someone I already cherished as a friend, the eroticism was an epiphany.

I've often hypothesized that in a sane culture we might see a bell-shaped curve of human sexuality. At one extreme would be people who are totally heterosexual, at the other people who are totally same-sex attracted (both extremes being "born that way" folks). The great bulge in the middle would contain *most* people, who—unless socially conditioned otherwise, as is the case today—would probably be variations in the mix, and who might change the expression of their sexuality a number of times at different stages during their lives. At the very least, I credit human sexuality with far more fluidity than we're taught to believe. Colette, that great crone of sexual wisdom, offered the entertaining opinion that men (plural) might be best for a woman when she was young and reproduction was at issue, but that only another woman (or women) could equal her as she matured. I'm not at all sure I agree, but I do think that affectionate, varying, erotic relationships will be more the common state of affairs when our culture eventually outgrows its narrowness.

As things now stand, such relations become acts of rebellion.[1] I didn't become involved with a woman for the sake of rebelling. Yet it's true that I'd rebelled enough about other issues so that when love actually beckoned in a shape unanticipated (in fact already relinquished), I at least knew how to exercise the emotional muscles of rebellion. I still believe that the more people acquire a taste for rebellion, the more that behavioral curve will emerge—about all sorts of differing behavior, not just sexuality—once and for all exposing the concept of a single standard for "natural" as the preposterous idea it is.

By the time I met Iliana, I'd had a long, complex political history with lesbian issues. I'd been straight-baited by some separatist women ("You *can't* be a radical feminist unless you're a lesbian") and gay-baited by right-wingers ("You're a radical feminist, so you *must* be a lesbian"). As early as 1968, when the *New York Times* inquired about our "open marriage"—which really should have been called an ajar marriage—and asked if I defined myself accordingly as heterosexual or bisexual, I hesitated. I *had* after all been to bed with women (albeit unhappily at that point), and I didn't want to disown that. So I replied that in the circumstances I'd choose to identify myself with the people suffering the heaviest discrimi-

---

[1] Some people tried to fake the rebellion without the acts. There were a few women in the 1970s who declared themselves "political lesbians" without having once loved or felt attraction for another woman, and in certain cases without even *liking* other women much. Atkinson was one, wielding the label (in a way that naturally incensed lesbians) to demonstrate that she was more purely feminist than anyone else—including lesbian women.

nation, and that since a woman could lose her job or custody of her child for being a lesbian, *that* was the label I'd wear, if labels there had to be. In 1973, I'd been asked to keynote the West Coast Lesbian Conference in Los Angeles, and had accepted—to the later consternation of several lesbian-feminist women who felt that my living with a man, albeit their gay brother, disqualified me. In retrospect, I agree with them—not so much because of my living situation but because of my sexual reality at that time. (The speech was one of my better ones, though, and fairly prescient.)[2] From the early Seventies, I remember a lively conversation that went on for some months with Adrienne Rich about the desirability of "androgyny." Adrienne, at the time new to the Women's Movement, considered it a feminist ideal. I didn't. I was worried that in such trendy attempts to "blend" femaleness and maleness, somehow the Frankenresult would again be a male generic with femaleness as appendage, the female subsumed into the male the way women were "meant to be" included in the concept of "mankind" but somehow never actually got there. Although at that point neither Adrienne nor I had ever been in love with another woman, our androgyny discussion ranged over same-sex attraction, both of us wondering how much social conditioning had really formed our sexuality and whether either of us would ever really know. (This is another one of those moments when you'd like to travel back in time and smile, "Awww, girls, don't worry. Have some more tea. Give yourselves time. Will *you* be surprised!")

All told, specifics of sexual preference and lesbian oppression—from discriminatory health-care issues to homophobic violence to workplace and housing discrimination—had been fixtures in every speech I'd given or article I'd written for almost twenty-five years before Iliana rhumbaed into my life. But it's another thing altogether, and rather bracing, to find that you yourself have become one of the people you've been defending. This "learning it in your bones" had happened more than once before. After years of pushing for decent, community-controlled, childcare centers, it was only when I had a young child that I fully realized, "Omigod. This *is* a major issue!" Now, as I bustle toward decrepitude, with each increasing year my consciousness is forcibly boosted on issues of ageism.

[2] See "Lesbianism and Feminism: Synonyms or Contradictions?" in *Going Too Far*.

The lesson is, you *are* "the Other"—or at least you may well become it. Disability activists wryly refer to nondisabled persons as "temporarily abled." Given my years of international work, I've joked that one of these days I may wake up to find myself grinding sorghum in Ouagadougou.

Nevertheless, I would never compare the minor inconveniences of discrimination I've experienced regarding same-sex love with that suffered by women who've been lesbians lifelong. On the contrary, I brought with me a sense of experienced heterosexual entitlement that startled my lesbian friends; after all, since I'd been allowed to kiss a *man* in public how *dare* anyone suddenly tell me that now I couldn't, just because the lover was a woman! Lesbian friends and colleagues received me with genial responses ranging from "I always *knew* you had potential!" to "I would have *sworn* I'd never see the day!" (So much for those invisible vibes of recognition.) Some were concerned this was one of those notorious flings in which the straight woman uses the lesbian for "experimentation" and then returns, re-energized, to her marriage—not bloody likely in my case. Others were apprehensive that I was a babe in the Sapphic woods and might be taken advantage of—until they met Iliana. My heterosexual women friends and colleagues made a point of being effusively supportive ("Do you feel *loved*? Really *loved*? That's the main thing. Then I'm so *glad* for you"). Meanwhile, they unconsciously shifted the posture of their embraces from the former relaxed variety to the contorted shape of a number seven—that peculiar upper-body clasp/lower-body arch away that heterosexual women use to hug their lesbian sisters. There were a few feminist colleagues who actually seemed dismayed at my new situation, which confused me since I knew they weren't homophobic. Then I realized that a monosexual pattern—that is, a lifelong heterosexual *or* lesbian pattern—didn't alarm them, but blurring fixed borders made them feel unsafe. If I, long married as they were, could discover another component in myself, what might that imply about them?

Happily, the impact of such slights is inconsequential, especially when one is in a state of emergence from a traumatic period, or in a state of flushed new loving, or in a state of awe that intimacy with a lover can be *combined* with the intimacy felt for a woman friend. Or, as I was, in all three states at once.

Love Conquers All (most)

Life is a series of recoveries as much as a series of blows, and the former can be even more challenging than the latter. The calm descending in 1983 was relative and temporary but welcome. I lived partly with Iliana in her apartment at the old Grove Press building, and partly at the *Sisterhood Is Global* offices, where the anthology was moving into last-stage madness. I cut back on work at the magazine during that year, having my hands full with *SIG*, fundraising, and continued travel for organizing, benefits, and any university lectures that would pay. Continuing to shoulder Ken's financial needs paralyzed plans for a place of my own. I didn't even have enough money for the two month's advance rent and security needed to get an apartment.

Iliana was more than content with the situation. A homebody who'd been traveling the world since her exile, she'd yearned to nest somewhere, and now she yearned to nest with me. She wanted us to get a larger apartment and live together, and she returned to the subject repeatedly. From the start, I demurred. I'd lived for almost twenty years with my mother and for more than twenty years with my husband, having three months to myself in between. I was fanatic about needing a place of my own, at least for a while—"turf" for my child and myself. I didn't mean this as a rejection of Iliana, although at times she took it as such. Having unilaterally decided to uproot her life in Vienna and move to New York to be near the object of her love, she couldn't grasp why I didn't share needs she felt so keenly. Eventually this would become an issue between us. My insistence on wanting my own space activated her old anxieties about homelessness and fears of abandonment. Her determination that we live together pushed my buttons and made me feel crowded, possessed, infantilized. The first time I dreamed that *she* turned into my mother, I woke up drenched in sweat. You can bet that my therapist and I spent more than a few hours on the question: were all adults I loved condemned to become Faith—either because they showed those characteristics to start with or because I somehow managed to turn each of them *into* her?

But for a while, at least, love conquered all. We'd had only one period of wild sweetness, during the first months of the relationship the previous spring and summer, before the fateful call came about my mother being in the hospital—and even that period had been clouded by Kenneth's dis-

tress and wrath. Nevertheless, those first trips of Iliana's to New York and
the brief second trip I'd taken to Vienna were a full-tilt *swoon* I'd never
experienced: the way in which the entire atmosphere is so charged that
the most ordinary things you do together—laundry, cooking dinner, brushing your teeth—are eroticized. Eating oysters or peeling a mango or listening to Rachmaninoff's "Trio Elégiaque"—all become acts of foreplay
positively *suffused* with pheremonic humidity. This is the zero-gravity
phase, where you make love horizontally, vertically, and aslant, on the
floor, on the sofa, against the wall, on the kitchen table, in the car, and—
after leaving a trail of clothing strewn all the way from the front door to the
bedroom—on the bed. In this universe, morning fades into afternoon and
evening brightens into dawn as the phone rings on ignored, the mail piles
up, and the dog whimpers piteously to be walked—while you consider the
possibilities of wringing him out over the sink so as not to have to leave for
even five minutes. In this dimension, you are capable of a famishment
that has you devouring paté, cornichons, and champagne at seven in the
morning, and cocoa and scrambled eggs at nine in the evening, because
there's nothing else left in the fridge but that's *okay* they're the *best* scrambled eggs you have *ever* eaten in your *life*.

Iliana's hobby was photography, and she took a lot of pictures—
cityscapes, landscapes, people. There's one photograph she shot during
this time: of a tousle-haired, ravishingly sexy woman, head thrown back,
graceful throat exposed, utterly self-possessed, laughing with absolute
abandon. When Iliana showed me the print, I was filled with admiration
and envy, and although I didn't want to make her jealous, I couldn't help
asking her who it was. Her expression sent me back to the photo, and only
then I felt tears rising in shocked recognition. It was me.

But the following year and a half of acute stress would take its toll.
These were the months when Iliana was forced into functioning more as
friend and caregiver than lover—months of nursing-home visits, doctors'
and lawyers' meetings, scenes about and with Kenneth. These were the
months she spent waiting—for me to get in from the airport, for me to
come back from dinner or a weekend with Blake, for me to deal with a
crisis at *SIG* while she lingered in the next office helping with translations, for me to stop in at the magazine, for me to return from the hospital, for me to get home from the anthology office well after midnight, only

to leave again at six in the morning. A proud hedonist who celebrated life's sensual delights, Iliana was highly efficient at her UN work but not a workaholic, political but not a dedicated organizer, a poet but not a driven one—so my pattern of passionately juggling chosen commitments was alien to her sensibility. She adored Blake and never questioned my time with him, and she respected completely the hours spent with and on my mother. But she did come to regard my political responsibilities, and especially the anthology, as being in another category. She was supportive of the project, but came to resent the time devoured by it—and I came to resent her resentment. She began to be jealous of the *SIG* staff, as if she was competing against individual women plus an unbeatable rival whose name was global feminism. I felt as if I was having to defend what was keeping me alive. We quarreled over her possessiveness and my obsessiveness.

It's undeniable that work was, all through those months, my salvation. It fed me, literally and figuratively. There was no serenity in which to do my own writing, but work on the anthology made me feel as if, even though my life was in flux, I was making some meaningful contribution. That addressed the earth-mother syndrome, which, let's face it, is as much (or more) about feeling capable and in control as it is about generosity. During the previous year, I'd been forced to learn how to ask for and accept help. That sometimes felt embarrassing despite my gratitude for it. Now I was eager to redeem my own dignity and hungry for independence. The path to both, for me, led through work.

Furthermore, all psychological niceties aside, the anthology *was* a jealous god. In the stress of the project's final stage, staff members were regularly at war with lovers, partners, and husbands; I wasn't the only one. Even two staff members who were lovers with each *other* broke up, partly because of deadline pressure. We *Sisterhood Is Global* women had reached the point when the only people who understood our shorthand—written, verbal, *and* emotional—were, for the time being, each other.

In December of 1983, we delivered the final manuscript to Doubleday in four supersize shopping bags. Iliana thought it was over—but she was wrong. Working with Loretta Barrett, we continued to exert quality control over every production detail, including the typeface, book design, and jacket design. In January we moved out of the Women's Action Alliance, putting the *SIG* library and my own books, some already in the office and more now liberated from 109 Third Avenue, into storage. Iliana thought it was over—but she was wrong. I picked up my duties at *Ms.* I also began writing fundraising proposals for the Sisterhood Is Global First International Feminist Strategy Meeting, an idea that had emerged from conversations and correspondence with anthology contributors. There was a frequently expressed need for more coherence in global feminist tactics, a longing for the cross-cultural brainstorming that men in the Club of Rome or Club of Dakar get to do—up to that time an unattainable opportunity for women. Moreover, if I could raise funds for travel and housing of twenty-five representative contributors for a week's brainstorming in New York that November, Doubleday would time a major book launch to honor their presence.

Meanwhile, galleys came and went—and as we proofed them we kept updating statistics to the last minute.[3] On May 15, 1984, we delivered corrected page proofs, the now reduced *SIG* staff having worked on them with me every night at the *Ms.* offices. The proposals for the Strategy Meeting went out to funders. And Iliana decided that enough was enough. We had to have a real holiday, she demanded. No, *not* just like the few evenings at the opera or concerts where I'd doze off from lack of sleep, and *not* just like the three days she'd hauled me off to Florida or the weekend we'd spent in Maine: a *real* vacation, with *no* paperwork smuggled along, *no* phone calls back to Karen. Two, almost three whole weeks. Greece, where I'd never been. Crete, where I'd always wanted to go. Away from everything, including the Women's Movement. The honeymoon we'd never had. That should have been enough to warn me.

The trip *was* lovely, with moments of pure enchantment—at Knossos, at Ephesus, at Delphi (where we both drank from the oracular spring, as poets should), and especially on a side trip to Thera/Santorini, the archaeological site of what became mythified as Atlantis. But en route to Greece,

---

[3] When cornered, my writer-editor persona can turn on my political one. I remember my frustration on learning that a progressive new law in the family code had been enacted in Greece, and that the Argentinian military junta had fallen—both coming too late for inclusion, thus making those country entries out of date even before publication. "How *could* they!" I kept muttering, feeling undercut by such inconveniently wonderful news.

I'd needed to stop in London, you see—for the International Feminist Book Fair. And although we managed to make that a holiday, with obeisance-paying visits to the tomb of Elizabeth Tudor and the statue of Emmeline Pankhurst, I had meetings with *SIG* contributors at the fair, so the politics sort of, well . . . took over. On the plane to Athens, Iliana exhaled. *Now* we'd be free of the Women's Movement for a while.

But on landing, we were paged over the plane's intercom. It seems we were being met by Margaritta Papandreou, the Greek contributor to the anthology and at that time the First Lady of Greece. There was the greeting on the tarmac, the VIP lounge, limousines with flags flying, a parliamentary party to receive us, the works. I'd dropped a note to Margaritta weeks earlier, to say that since I was coming to Greece for a holiday, I'd love to see her if she had a spare moment, but understood that she was very busy and might not have time. Since I hadn't heard back, I was flabbergasted at this response. Of course, the stay in Athens and environs was transformed. There was still sightseeing, but there were also meetings with women parliamentarians and with activists in nongovernmental organizations. There was a memorable organizing visit to a mountain village with Margaritta—herself an indefatigable woman who used her position to leverage more women's rights and who had founded and was president of the Women's Union of Greece.[4] There was a special invitation to the island of Aegina, the Greek "weekend White House," where Margaritta and her circle of feminist colleagues frequently caucused. I had a terrific time. Greek hospitality welcomed Iliana into all these activities, and she participated in and enjoyed them. But it was *not* what she had planned for us. When we were on the plane to Crete, she shot me a sulky glance, sat back, and again exhaled. Now, *finally* we *would* be free of the Women's Movement.

[4] Margaritta—born Margaret Chant in Oak Park, Illinois—had spent most of her adult life in the service of her adopted country, including having been jailed and exiled by the junta before it fell and before her husband, Andreas, became prime minister. She lives there still, regarded by the Greeks with an affection they no longer bestow on her late husband, who divorced her to marry a younger woman and then fell from power. The blunt American side of her still surfaces now and then, as when, during an interview some years ago, a reporter simpered, "As a little girl growing up in Illinois, did you ever dream that one day you'd actually be *married* to a *prime minister*?" "No," Margaritta replied tartly, "I dreamed I'd *be* a prime minister."

In Crete the late afternoon air was fragrant with hibiscus, the Aegean was stippled in turquoise and aqua, the cream-colored sand had the texture of silk. Riding in the taxi from airport to hotel, we heard the sound of shepherd's flutes from the hills. Iliana chuckled in triumph, linking her arm with mine.

At the front desk, a basket of flowers awaited me, with a card: "Welcome to Krete! We come at six to take you to dinner! Much is planned! Your Sisters, the Kretan Women's Movement."

Poor Iliana went ballistic. It was no good explaining about the feminist grapevine and how Margaritta must have mentioned to her Cretan colleagues we were coming because I *hadn't* since I really truly didn't even *know* them but *surely* we couldn't just rudely *reject* . . .

Beware of having the honeymoon you've never had. If you didn't have it when you should have had it, forget it. By the time we returned to New York, more stuffing had leaked out of our two-and-a-half-year-old relationship, though both of us would have denied it if asked. Iliana was dour about returning to work. I'd loved Greece, but I was eager to get back to my desk at *Ms.* and catch up on funding for the Strategy Meeting. Karen had news of some funding guarantees, but nowhere near enough.

The pressure was on again. It was already July. A venue for the meeting had to be found and booked, airline tickets purchased, a stupendous number of details yet to be resolved. Dare we go ahead and formally *invite* twenty-five women—the majority from the Global South—with no guarantee? They had tight schedules and couldn't keep holding the November weeks open indefinitely. I stepped off the edge and decided to wing it. Audacity can feel *so* satisfying.[5]

---

[5] This was my period of daily audacities. Karen says she will never forget one incident when we needed to get our stored *SIG* boxes out of the Alliance office on a Saturday but were forbidden access by the building guard. I insisted he call his superior, but the superior backed him up and wouldn't speak with me. Little did the hapless guard know he was dealing with someone who'd been told "you can be anything anyone wants you to be." I took the phone to call again, but covertly held down the receiver button as I dialed. Then I faked an entire conversation in which I listened attentively to and answered a dial tone, otherwise known as "the superior"—who heard my appeal, changed his mind, granted permission to move the boxes, instructed me to tell the guard (standing there wide-eyed) that it *was* okay after all, and added that the guard

On my first day back at *Ms.*, Joanne Edgar leaned over from her neighboring desk to cheer me with news I'd missed while abroad, news of another bold act. Marilyn Waring, still an MP (and New Zealand contributor to *Sisterhood Is Global*) had brought down the government and her own political party in an historic parliamentary vote to keep New Zealand nuclear free. I immediately called to congratulate her.

"Just doing my job," Marilyn replied, with Kiwi understatement. I could almost see her characteristic shrug over the long-distance line. It was now four years since we'd met in Oslo, and we considered ourselves friends. We'd kept in touch by mail, and Marilyn had been through New York on business three or four times in the interim. She always called to say hello or stopped by the magazine or the *SIG* office to visit. Sometimes we'd have lunch or dinner. At every encounter there was personal warmth and political collegiality, but never *ease*. On the contrary, there was always that sense of danger, an intellectual sparring, an almost tactile purr of electricity. At one point, Marilyn was in the United States for three months as a visiting fellow (*sic*) at the Institute of Politics, Kennedy School of Government, at Harvard. She arranged for the school to invite me up for three days to speak, give a political workshop, and read poetry at a women's event she was organizing there. We'd combine the visit with an interview *Ms.* wanted me to do with her. It's indicative of the edginess I felt when around Marilyn that I brought a de facto chaperon to Boston in the person of Jane Ordway, who was interning with me at the time. The interview went well, albeit tensely. At the women's event, I read poetry and talked politics as requested, but declined to dance, although I watched Marilyn dancing—and noticed that she moved like smoke. This was in April of 1981, two months before Claire de Hedervary would suggest I meet someone named Iliana de Costa.

In conversations during the interim years, Marilyn had mentioned the end of one relationship with a lover and the beginning of a new one; I'd told her about the death of my mother and demise of my marriage, and the

---

needn't bother to ring him back because he was about to go on a break. It worked. We moved at the speed of light to get the boxes out before we'd be discovered. Then Karen and I, dumbfounded, celebrated with Howard Johnson's fried clams while recovering from the fact that we'd gotten away with it.

unexpected element—a woman lover—in my own life. Ever since Oslo, there'd been a refrain: she wanted to bring me to New Zealand for a lecture tour. She felt it would be a tonic for the isolated feminist movement there, and admitted she'd like to show off her country, of which she was so proud. I'd been invited there once before, during the 1970s. Back then I'd regretfully but firmly declined because I wanted to show solidarity with Gloria, who had just been disinvited because the NZ women had foolishly fallen for the smear that Gloria was a CIA agent. But I'd heard about the famed natural beauty of this small country, and had always wanted to visit. Annually, Marilyn inquired about my schedule. By early 1984, with the anthology winding down—and feeling myself safely shielded from any interpersonal electricity by the protective mantle of my relationship with Iliana—I agreed to go.

I wrote Marilyn that the following September would be the best time, after final page proofs and before last preparations for the book launch and Strategy Meeting in November. She wrote back on her parliamentary stationery that the timing would be perfect—enough advance notice to organize the lecture tour, and besides, September would be springtime Down Under. What neither of us knew was that in June, while Iliana and I were in Greece, Marilyn would not only bring down the NZ government and her party but put herself out of a job. That didn't change anything, she said the day I rang with congratulations; in fact, now she'd have time to tour the country with me, to show me its wonders.

Iliana was not pleased at my going, yet resigned to it. She even teased me, with a decided edge to the humor, that she was jealous of this Marilyn person who'd first become an MP at age twenty-two, had cut a rock 'n' roll record in New Zealand, was taking flying lessons, and exuded such notorious charisma. But by then I was used to Iliana's feeling jealous of most women with whom I worked—the accusations all baseless—so her statement just seemed familiar and mildly annoying.

Throughout July and August of 1984, Karen, Toni, and I, together with interns and volunteers, scouted locations for the Strategy Meeting. We finally found a beautiful old inn with an excellent restaurant on Long Island. I booked the entire place, main house and cabins, for six days in November, with my heart in my mouth about funding. It was a fair risk. By the end of August we had the funding commitments. Gen Vaughan had again flown to the rescue like a good witch on her broom, to match another Ford Foundation grant. Karen and I flew into action with preparations: airline bookings, reserving hotel rooms for the five additional days in Manhattan after the Long Island meeting, and lots of liaising—with Doubleday about the book party and the media, with Ford about the reception/seminar they would host, and with Donna Shalala about public panel presentations and a formal dinner she, as president of Hunter College, wished to sponsor. As September rolled around I was reluctant to leave. But I'd given my word, the New Zealand lecture dates were set, and Karen would be in New York to handle things in my absence. So I flew off, myself, for the place called by the Maori "Aotearoa"—"land of the low-lying white cloud"—where the seasons were reversed and the water swirled down the drain counterclockwise and the very stars in the heavens were alien, and where my life, too, would turn upside down.

Little Match Girls

The journey from New York to New Zealand takes more than twenty hours of flying. Over the next decade, I would do it so many times I would get it down to a science. But that first time, seasoned flier though I was, I found it an unsettling experience, compounded by walking out of my Northern Hemisphere autumn into a verdant spring, plus losing an entire day as we crossed the dateline (you do reclaim it—flying into yesterday—as you return, but this merely heightens the feeling of irreality).

On that first visit, New Zealand struck me as being quaintly poised in a 1950s time warp; in terms of the Women's Movement, *may*be the 1960s. In the not always friendly rivalry between Kiwis and their cousins across the Tasman Sea, the Australians growl that the New Zealanders are "pommier than the poms," meaning more British than the Brits—which isn't an exaggeration (on the other hand, the Aussies sometimes try too hard to imitate the worst of what they think of as American). Aotearoa's Maori communities are their own world: complicated, artistic, insurgent, passionate, and oppressed. But *pakehas*—the Maori word for New Zealanders of European ancestry—tend to be veddy English, exemplifying that syndrome in which colonials, feeling inferior, try to imitate or outdo the original, fail pathetically, then feel inferior all over again.

The people were affable, though, even puckish, and you couldn't not like them. In public appearances and private encounters, I tried to hold up a metaphorical mirror to the women, who were laboring under a double (national and female) inferiority complex, so that they might see their own strengths. I kept reminding them that theirs was the first country where women won suffrage, the first to establish a form of social security, the place that shelters more endangered species than any other nation in the world. I kept saying that the country's small size and population (three million people, less than the New York City borough of Brooklyn) made possible a laboratory effect regarding progressive social change, so that as activists they could afford to take greater risks, be leaders, set more examples for the rest of us. They were as thirsty for affirmation as for news of global feminism. So many women attended the lecture in Christchurch that we wound up doing an entire second presentation later that evening for those who'd been turned away at the earlier one. In Wellington, in addition to other appearances, I spoke at the farewell party thrown for Marilyn by other women parliamentarians, announcing, to a roar of applause, that I brought regards from Geraldine Ferraro, who was then running for vice president of the United States. In Auckland, Hamilton, Palmerston North, at universities and public venues, I guest-taught classes and ovulars, delivered lectures, read poetry, held workshops and Q-and-A sessions. In between there were meetings with women's groups, Maori and *pakeha* both, focusing on health, media, violence against women, connections between sexism and racism, reproductive rights, funding—the usual. That was the foreground.

The background was the joltingly strong erotic energy that vibrated between myself and Marilyn Waring. It hit me in the face, not quite at the moment of arrival, because the flight left me walking into walls, but within the first twenty-four hours. I realized then that far from providing a protective mantle, my relationship with Iliana had intensified the possibilities, in that I now knew I could be drawn to a woman. But this was one relationship I started *out* trying to stop.

It had everything going against it. I had a lover. Marilyn had a lover. The idea that I'd be betraying not one but two women made me literally sick, and I kept disappearing into bathrooms before speeches, losing my previous meal. I dropped nine pounds in the first five days. For her part, Marilyn seemed to enjoy the power of the allure between us; her sexual history was markedly different from mine, and her friendships seemed casually peopled with former women lovers from previous affairs. Except for the one with Vladimir, I'd never really had an affair, and I considered my relationship with Iliana, however rocky at the time, a *relationship*, one I'd assumed would continue.

Yet it was undeniable that seeing Marilyn in her own element heightened her attraction, as perhaps she'd known it would. For one thing, only recently out of Parliament, she was at the apex of her popularity; people would stop her on the street to thank her for having kept New Zealand nuclear free. But it was nothing so simple as the aphrodisiac of power, because hers had substance. It had been earned and exercised for principled reasons, at considerable cost, and with little personal ambition. There was, too, the sheer delight of the way her brain worked: a lightning-swift intelligence that had a fatal allure for me, particularly since it was combined with her own gift for audacity. She had a flair for the dramatic (which the old professional in me recognized and appreciated—but coolly appraised as that of an amateur). Unlike Iliana, she wasn't possessive and didn't question my actions or intentions. That was pleasant. It felt as if I'd regained a sense of my own agency. More: she *understood* my passion for work, even shared it—and that in itself was magnetic. The cultural differences were apparent: where Iliana had a hot, effusive manner, Marilyn projected understatement; after the previous months this felt like a soothing hand on my fevered brow. I remember thinking Iliana was like a great adoring Labrador puppy, and Marilyn like an aloof, patient cat. (Since I considered myself a cat person, I didn't take my own simile lightly.) Most important, Marilyn was the only adult I'd ever met, male or female, whose peculiar energy equaled mine. She could work incredibly hard and play just as hard. Whatever she chose to do *mattered* to her, and she focused like a five-foot-four-inch human laser beam of intensity on whatever that was.

After six days of flirting that wasn't flirting (but *was*), of double entendre that twittered awkwardly at itself, of self-disclosures and exchanged confidences interspersed with ponderous silences that were then followed by raves about how perfect our respective lovers were, I couldn't bear the hypocrisy. I needed to name it, expose it, kill it. At dinner that night I said as much.

"Look, Marilyn, I don't know what's going on. But I can't play these games. I mean . . . Marilyn, what are we *doing*?"

She paused for a moment before answering, with a mournful grin.

"Our very best."

Neither of us could breathe for the next ten minutes, from laughter released in recognition and admission. At least the tension was broken. We then entered into three more days of Seriously Discussing It. All this was interwoven, you understand, with television appearances, radio interviews, more guest teaching of classes—in American studies, women authors, feminist theory—and side trips to meet flightless birds at the Auckland Zoo and wander through the splendid public gardens in each city visited. Seriously Discussing It meant we could now spend every spare moment assuring each other This Cannot Happen.

Certainly any relationship was out of the question, considering my lover, her lover, and our locations. All Asia yawned between us. Even if it were only a brief affair, the fallout would be severe (she didn't see that, but then she also was aghast at my propensity for telling the truth to people I loved). We found scores of reasons why Absolutely Nothing Could Possibly Take Place—all the while talking about It and thinking about It, thus magnifying the desire.

That desire was unlike any I'd felt in my scant history of erotic experience. With Kenneth, my mind had been drawn to his literary brilliance and my heart to his bull-in-the-china-shop dependence; there hadn't been that overwhelming a physical attraction—which I didn't much notice at the time, being so young and knowing myself so little. At Yaddo, it was moon and art colony and breakout and the safety of what's temporary, mindless, and pretty. With Iliana, it was she who'd initiated the attraction and pursued it, doing so with such headstrong elegance that I responded; I'd been as much in love with the idea that *she* was in love with *me,* and with the idea of *being* in love, as I'd been in love with her. But here, everything locked into place: brain, heart, body. Despite her greater experience, Marilyn was equally thrown by the intense pull between us. She confessed she'd been haunted by it for four years, since Oslo, but had been afraid to make that clearer for fear of losing our friendship. Now, she said, it was as if we'd each finally met our match.

Discussions of political strategies felt like a dance of twin intellects indulging in a singular pleasure. We shared the addiction of longtime politicos who arrogantly believe themselves capable of saving the world, plus the private, bitter fatigue of idealists for whom only the failures feel real. We shared a passion for art, although not the way I had with Kenneth or Iliana, both poets. Not an artist herself, Marilyn was nonetheless extremely well-read, and her former training as a musician, which she'd abandoned for Parliament, gave her insights into the aesthetic process that she expressed knowledgeably, longingly. A bit of a rake, she carried herself with the rapscallion grace of someone who'd been an athlete when younger, and this chronic roguishness lent to her moments of tenderness an acute poignancy. The body was slender, angular, wiry; the voice was rich and mellow—and she knew how to use it. Her large dark eyes, high forehead, prominent cheekbones, and sharp chin gave her face the features of a wild falcon.[6] For the first time in my life, I not only desired to *be* desired in my old narcissistic fashion; *I* desired. If we had indeed each met our match, we certainly were tinder. Ultimately, the energy was stronger than the resolve. We struck flame.

The remaining week of my stay in New Zealand was a haze of nonstop lovemaking, passionate conversation, public appearances, and hilarious attempts at discretion. Through it all, by ourselves or around others, politics functioned as an ongoing, ever-intensifying erotic foreplay between us. And all this was taking place amid the natural beauty for which the country is justly known—a beauty that served to intensify the sensuality. Black-sand volcanic beaches. Fields of scarlet heather. Rolling green hills dotted by puffs of frisking newborn lambs. Snow-capped mountains, crystalline pools, ancient *kauri* forests, glowworm caves, hot-spring baths, bubbling mud pools, white-plumed geysers, boiling lakes. The whole damned landscape was steaming, over-the-top, orgasmic.

By the time I left New Zealand, I was a woman in love, in the grip of a passion that would sustain a level of white-hot ferocity for ten years.

---

[6] On first seeing a photograph of Marilyn, my friend Lois, who is capable of one-liners approaching aphoristic pith, snorted, "Definitely not a vegetarian."

Back then, however, we both said it was an affair from which we were returning to our respective lovers. Marilyn was not going to tell her lover, which disturbed me, and she thought I was wrong to tell Iliana, but it had never occurred to me not to. We both were red-eyed with weeping on the day of my departure, and Marilyn, who'd driven the roads of her small country so often she could've done so blindfolded, managed to get lost on the way to the airport, almost making me miss the plane. I remember striving for a sophistication that might redeem us, saying at the flight gate, "Come on now, no more tears. Surely we know how to do this."

We didn't. When I landed in Hawaii for my planned overnight stopover, I was wretched, already missing her so much the ache felt physical. I also seriously questioned my mental and moral health. I walked the beach outside my hotel for hours, flagellating myself, wondering if after decades of marriage, I was now turning into some kind of omnivore, a selfish maniac, a sex fiend—and a recidivist crisis addict to boot. I dreaded telling Iliana. But I knew I couldn't not tell her, partly because she'd sense it, mostly because I couldn't lie to her.

I've thought about this fetish with honesty a great deal. God knows I understand that truth is subjective and plural—and that it can be used as a bludgeon. But the private ways in which lies are excused and the political ways in which truth is manipulated have always repelled me. In close relationships, especially, it seems to me that by not hazarding honesty—which is really simply the longing to know and to be known, the longing I believe is synonymous with loving—we doom intimacy. Even when you make up your mind to tell the truth, it still is an onion, and you peel skin after skin. But if you aren't even trying to do *that*, what's the point of the masquerade? I'm sure that my fixation on honesty has its roots in my childhood, in the swamp of lies about my identity. My name was not what I was told it was. My parentage was not what I was told it was. My age was not what I was told it was. This, combined with the too early imprint of being a working actor, would give anyone a skewed sense of what's real. As a young adult, I tried to discover what reality was—or, if it didn't exist, to invent it. Even now, no matter how odious the truth may be, I'd always rather know it. Writing, for me, is a process of discovering and recording truths—about myself, other people, consciousness itself. Politics, for me, is about communicating and protecting those truths.

But in my mulishness I've at least learned that honesty takes two—the teller *and* the hearer—and ultimately I've come to trust only two partners in that exchange: my son, and you, my reader. Still, Iliana was the kind of hearer who wanted the truth, went through its sorrow, and survived— which is why, though we were lovers for less than three years, we'll likely be "family" for the rest of our lives. I rang her from Hawaii. As I thought she would, she heard something in my voice. She asked me the direct question. I gave her the direct answer.

She was hurt and furious, her heartache centering around having been cast, as she put it, "as the annunciating angel." I certainly couldn't blame her, since I was busy blaming myself: I'd used her, relied on her support in my time of need, and now betrayed her. This was only part of the story, of course, but everything gets oversimplified in an atmosphere of reproach, and I was more comfortable with self-accusation than with counter-accusation. My return to New York was followed by days of misery, tears, and attempts to repair the relationship.

Meanwhile, those artifactual datebooks display the shorthand of how life swept mercilessly on. Catching up with Blake. Seeing Margaritta Papandreou, in New York for a visit. Drawing up the invitation list for the big Donna Shalala dinner. Writing a magazine piece on New Zealand so gushingly prurient about its natural glories that I might as well have invented a new genre: landscape pornography. Phoning Riyadh repeatedly to ensure that the Saudi contributor, Aisha Almana, would be attending the Strategy Meeting. Dealing with the Israeli embassy, consulate, and mission to the United Nations, all three of which were blustering about the presence of Palestine as well as Israel in *Sisterhood Is Global* (the Israeli contributor, Shulamit Aloni, a member of the Knesset, feminist, and peace leader, knew this all along and understood perfectly). Delivering promised campaign speeches at fundraisers for Gerry Ferraro. And working with Karen on all the yet-to-be-resolved crises looming around the imminent Strategy Meeting, to which, by the way, both Iliana and Marilyn had already been invited—the thought of which gave me cramps.

October was filled with pain and recriminations, guilt and rebellion, false reconciliations. No longer sure I could heal the relationship with Iliana, I also saw no future with Marilyn. The latter wrote ardent love letters and phoned daily, yet was schizophrenically proceeding with plans to buy a farm, raise Angora goats, and live happily ever after with a lied-to lover who was moving to New Zealand from Australia to share this bucolic future. All lovers aside, I more than ever wanted space of my own, and *soon*. I'd begun to suspect that Iliana and I would not be walking hand in hand into the sunset.

Off the Page and into Action

On November 10, Karen, Toni, the Strategy Meeting staff (what remained of the book staff), and I drove out in rented cars to Long Island. The plan was to have one quiet day to ourselves when we could settle in, make sure all was in order, and get the meeting rooms ready. The plan was also to give the staff a well-deserved day and night of being peacefully pampered before They arrived. This was naturally shot to hell by the appearance of the Nigerian contributor a day ahead of schedule, with no notice and many imperious needs. But we carried it off nonetheless.

We *really* carried it off. For decades, feminist activists had been meeting in storefronts and basements, while men had been assembling in luxury hotels to talk policy. For once, I wanted women to be treated *well*, and I'd raised the money to do it. So we'd arranged with the airports and with feminist moles in the State Department for VIP treatment, streamlined passport procedures, priority baggage handling.[7] Each contributor was met by a Sisterhood Is Global volunteer (we had identifying sweatshirts made up for the occasion), presented with flowers, ushered to the VIP lounge and thence to a limousine for the drive to the Three Village Inn. Special care was taken over dietary details. There were flowers and fresh fruit in every room, a complimentary bottle of Ouzo in Margaritta's, a borrowed guitar in Marilyn's. We even had arranged and paid for a twice weekly dialysis treatment for Slavenka Draculić, the Yugoslav contributor, who at the last minute had informed us she had kidney disease.

---

[7] This was easy enough to organize for Margaritta, as First Lady of Greece, and for Maria de Lourdes Pintasilgo, as former Prime Minister of Portugal. What was fun was managing to pull off the same courtesies for the others: for example, Carmen Lugo (who worked with indigenous women in Mexico) or Manjula Giri (a grassroots activist from Nepal) or Fawzia Hassouna, a stateless Palestinian with no papers other than a Jordanian passbook.

On November 11, they arrived: a regionally representative cross section
of the anthology contributors—from Barbardos, Brazil, Chile, Colombia,
Cuba, Finland, Fiji, Greece, Italy, India, Kuwait, Libya, Mexico, Nepal,
New Zealand, Nigeria, Norway, Palestine/Israel, Poland, Saudi Arabia,
Spain, Sri Lanka, Thailand, and Zambia.

It was a memorable six days, and it was moving to see how touched the
women were at being treated with such respect. The inn proved an ideal
setting, surrounded by autumnal golden woods through which people
could take walks during meeting breaks. Berit Ås (Norway) and Hilkka
Pietilä (Finland) actually took morning swims in the nearby lake—their
Nordic heartiness impressing everyone but inspiring no imitators. Simone
de Beauvoir, ill with flu in Paris, had to cancel but sent support by phone
and telex. Devaki Jain landed a day late from India, barely having got out
at all in the wake of turmoil following Indira Gandhi's assassination. Marilyn arrived just out of the hospital with pneumonia, whispering, to my dis-
traction, that her relationship with her lover might be over. Iliana came for
two days, found it too painful, and pled off with job obligations. Nourah
Al-Falah could get permission to leave Kuwait for only three days—so
spent two of them flying in order to have one precious day with us. Luz
Helena Sánchez (Colombia), who was a medical doctor, brought me
around when I passed out from control-freak exhaustion on the fourth day.

But everything went off without a hitch. No press were allowed, so the
talks could be honest, and I knew we were home free when the first
woman felt safe enough to cry. We talked for hours—in full meetings, in
regional caucuses, in the dining room, in the individual cabins—about our
personal lives, political priorities, differences, similarities, hopes. Issues
now taken for granted as basics in the international Women's Movement
first surfaced into codification at that meeting, including globalization,
women's unpaid labor, the threat of religious fundamentalisms, the
increase in sex trafficking, and the impact of national debt on women. At
one point, I remember Karen, Toni, and I hugging each other, sobbing
with accomplishment. The meeting had magic.

In the meantime—despite our both having solemnly declared This
Cannot Happen Again—Marilyn had been creeping from her cabin into
mine each night like a character in an operetta. Since Karen was

ensconced in the cabin next door, she knew, but no one else did. Iliana had spent only one night at the inn before returning to New York.

As the six days came to a close, everyone was a bit tense about the transfer into Manhattan for the public events. On the penultimate day, the regional caucuses came back to the full meeting with a proposal that made my heart sing and sink at the same moment. The women didn't want it to end. They wanted something permanent, an ongoing institution that would function as the first international feminist think tank but also have an activist component. They wanted to "lift the book off the page and into action." They wanted the Sisterhood Is Global Institute. They wanted Robin to make it happen.

I was flattered, honored, and appalled. I'd been waiting for the day when the anthology would be published and the Strategy Meeting done, so that I could turn my attention to getting an apartment and writing again. I already had the next book planned: *fiction*, by god, no research necessary. There was also the little matter of finding myself madly in love with someone who lived on the other side of the planet, *and* being in the middle of a breakup with Iliana.

Consequently, I tried to foist the Institute back on those who wanted it. No fools they. One by one, they declined, citing clever reasons for why and how I should be the hapless soul to found it. The only dissenters were Marilyn and Iliana—who'd returned for the last half-day—who supported my plea for release in two distinct appeals. (I wondered darkly to Karen if it was necessary to sleep with everybody around the table to get unanimous permission to be left alone and write.) It was finally Margaritta, the senior stateswoman as it were, who lovingly entrapped me, building a case that I was a victim of the anthology's success, and that if the Institute were not at least begun with my participation, contacts, and funder networking, it wouldn't happen at all. One good entrapment deserves another. So I persuaded valiant Karen Berry to be the first executive director, promising my help behind the scenes. I trusted her politics, ethics, cross-cultural sensitivity—and workaholism. The assembly agreed, and we spent the last day at Three Village Inn drafting a press release about the Institute's founding, with de Beauvoir signing on to it by phone.

The next four days were high pressure. We drove into the city and rebased at the Tudor Hotel, near the UN. I didn't return to Iliana's in Greenwich Village, but stayed at the hotel, near where the events were. That night, Doubleday threw a lavish book-publication party for contributors, press, and guests—so large it was held in the ballroom of the New York Public Library for the Performing Arts, at Lincoln Center. Champagne flowed, as did major press coverage. In addition to the twenty-five women who'd been on Long Island, other contributors were in attendance, including some based at the United Nations and some living in exile in North America, so it made for a hearty representation. Many came in national dress. A representative pantheon of the U.S. Women's Movement attended or sent messages as well, and my old *Ms.* officemate Alice Walker issued a statement calling the book "one of the most important human-rights documents in history." Of course both Iliana and Marilyn were in attendance—the former breathing deeply, the latter drinking champagne deeply. I'd slept an average of four hours a night for weeks, so by now my eyes were glittering and my teeth grinding from stress, manic excitement, and double espressos.

Afterward, Lois threw a smaller party for the *SIG* staff, Iliana, and myself at her apartment. We somehow got through it, though the staff was wiped out too, Karen was zomboid, and Iliana was in a state of controlled anguish. As a surprise, she'd reserved a suite at another hotel, more lavish than the one where we all were staying, and she shanghaied me to it, where more champagne was chilling, along with her fragile hopes. I fell asleep, half dressed, after one glass.

The next morning the two days of Hunter College panels began, sandwiching between them the dinner that Donna hosted at the Eleanor Roosevelt House for approximately three hundred guests. It poured an icy rain. Marilyn ran a fever and remained at the hotel that night, so Iliana felt more relaxed. Donna, Gloria, Margaritta, and I spoke, and each of the contributors present—now also co-founders of the Institute—were introduced to applause. De Beauvoir graciously sent yet another greeting; she was functioning like a daily pen pal, bless her, but she understood the impact of her support. Blake impressed everyone by adeptly pronouncing the names of Motlalepula Chabaku (South Africa) and Hema Goonatilake (Sri Lanka), the result of all those months of his hanging out at *SIG*. My former attorney Emily Goodman and I stole a private moment so she could show me photographs of her daughter; Kate Millett had a bit too much wine and jovially tried to play kneesies with a radical nun; Karen and Toni went around with copies of the book for all contributors present to sign, for history's sake; and I smiled until my jaws hurt.

The following Monday saw the last of the ensemble events: a formal press conference preceding the Ford Foundation reception and seminar. The press conference went smoothly, but several contributors had to become invisible regarding it, since their governments would not have approved and it might have put their lives in danger. At Ford, my level of indigestion rose when, as we gathered around the polished conference table and Frank Thomas welcomed us, one of those eruptions euphemized by diplomats as "candid exchanges" burst out. Some of the women had decided to vent vociferously about the lack of attention funders give women internationally. Marilyn (who should have known better but who was still smarting from a reporter's having assumed she wasn't a radical, since she'd been an MP) joined them. Fortunately, the soothing presences of Margaritta and Devaki helped ameliorate the situation, in which the sole foundation that *was* paying any attention to women was being tongue-lashed for the sins of all the others.

The next day the departures began. But I was still booked into a week of radio and TV promotion for the anthology. Marilyn decided to stay another week, so I corralled her into doing some of the appearances with me. Iliana had managed to carry off the public events with dignity and a certain hauteur, admirable given the predicament. But it was now clear to all three of us that what had happened in New Zealand was not a passing fancy but a continuing fascination. When it was time to vacate the Tudor Hotel, I couldn't return to Iliana's.

Naturally I called Lois. Having just seen me exude smiling *bonfemie* at the Lincoln Center book party and her own soiree afterward, she was taken aback to learn, in one phone call, the whole sub rosa crisis: New Zealand, Marilyn, grand passion, Iliana, serial monogamy turned to granola, place to stay needed . . . but she was solid as Gibraltar. That night I was back in the Robin Morgan Memorial Den.

Marilyn had moved to stay with a friend who worked at the UN, but in a few days she joined me in the RMMD. By the time she left for home, we both knew we were in far deeper than anticipated. She was in love with me, said so, and kept bursting into tears at the thought of leaving. Yet demonstrating a remarkable capacity for compartmentalization, she also felt compelled to pursue her long-planned scenario for the impending year: the (still in the dark) lover, the farm. That seemed odd. But I couldn't see myself as either a home wrecker (even if my own had been wrecked), or a "backstreet woman." So I accepted her departure, assumed we were finished, and began the process of mourning. At least *Sisterhood Is Global* (the book) was a publication *accompli*. (It would remain in print with Doubleday/Anchor for twelve years. In 1996, The Feminist Press reissued it with a new preface, an updated overview I wrote for the occasion). The love affair had died, but the book had been born.

Dropping Anchor

I may have been grieving over Marilyn, but there was as always the solace of work: more anthology promotion, a *Ms.* roundtable on what feminist foreign policy might be, a gathering at the International Women's Tribune Center. And—surprisingly, as my datebook reminds me—by December 9 I'd finished the outline and sample chapters of *Dry Your Smile*, the novel, which went off to Loretta at Doubleday.

That Christmas I was still in the den. Marilyn was spending the holidays with her lover in Australia, having fights and sneaking away to phone me while I urged her not to, or else to tell the truth and clear the air. Iliana and I met frequently for long, painful, brave, and loving talks about how we might rebuild our relationship as close friends. Since Lois had gone abroad, I had her apartment to myself, so Blake came to stay over. He and I made dinners, took walks, saw movies, and talked for hours. But for the moment he was still living with Kenneth. He'd handled the excruciatingly overlong breakup with extraordinary grace, even humor. Well, at least nobody had lied to him. When people are tearing their hair out but pretending, "It's nothing, really," for the so-called sake of the children, that's when the children are driven batty, since they *know* something's happening anyway. If the truth is admitted, at least that's one less source of pain. My real concern during these months was that Blake was becoming a classic prematurely caregiving child, taking the place I'd just vacated in codependent hell—but I was happy to be proven wrong. He sought his comforts with friends, at school, and mostly in his music, for and in which he already lived with the certainty of a life's vocation—and in that I knew he'd always find his own safety and sanity.

On New Year's Eve I wrote a long letter to Marilyn telling her that it was truly *over*, that the phone calls had to *cease*, and that I wished her joy in her plans. Then I sat cross-legged on the fold-out sofa bed in the den, surveyed the latest ruins of my life, and rearranged priorities.

For the next three months, I focused on apartment-hunting, pounding pavements all over Manhattan but always returning to Greenwich Village, where I'd yearned to live for years. At last I found a two-bedroom apartment (reassuringly well to the west of the Iliana-Grove Press building) at the corner of Perry and Bleecker streets. It was small, and two flights up— but it had a working fireplace, an eat-in kitchen, lots of light, and access to a roof that I knew I could transform into a container garden. With the just-arrived advance for the novel from Doubleday, I paid off my debts, rented the apartment, and in March of 1985 moved in, heaving my books out of storage, where they'd been languishing. I had no furniture, but was so desperate to *be* there that I slept on the floor until the bed I'd ordered arrived. In Blake's room I had a loft bed built for him above his desk, as he'd wanted. Kenneth and I felt the living arrangements should be Blake's decision, and he chose to alternate staying in the Village and at 109 Third Avenue for each school semester. But the following year, 109 was sold and Ken had to leave, so Blake moved to Perry Street full-time.

Eager as I was to settle in and start writing, the Institute loomed. Karen, when she returned from a long-overdue vacation, would begin the work of incorporating it as a nonprofit, tax-exempt organization, and I'd be back at the fundraising stand to garner its start-up money. Marie Wilson at the Ms. Foundation for Women had kindly given us a cut-rate rent on tiny space in its offices, so the Institute had a mini-home.

It was over with Iliana, though we knew now we'd always be friends. It was over with Marilyn (I thought), though we also would be friends. I had no lover, but I had a *home*—for myself and my kid. To hell with sex, anyway, I thought. Like a shipwreck survivor, I paced the apartment in a state of delirium at just being there—touching walls, opening and closing windows, building my first fire and sitting in front of it, weeping with relief.

My mother's estate was now out of probate. Almost all the proceeds from the sale of her apartment had been swallowed by her medical and nursing-home bills. With the remainder—the only money left of my childhood earnings—I bought Blake a Steinway. Once the piano movers had angled it gingerly up the Perry Street stairs, his expression told me all I needed to know. He understood it as an instrument of confidence in his choices, as well as an instrument of music. It was a gift of triumph, across time, from one child to another.

SEVENTEEN

Gaining the World

> *"You have to help us," she said. "You have to help us.*
> *They are shooting us down in the street." By "us" she*
> *meant women who wrote against the grain. "What*
> *can I do?" I asked her. She said "I don't know. But*
> *you have to try. There isn't anybody else."*
>
> —TONI MORRISON, THE DANCING MIND

*C*risis can be an addiction as powerful as any other, one to which romantics like myself are especially prone, and one in which the universe will play a willing enabler at the slightest invitation. It takes time to wean yourself from dependence on this particular high, because going cold turkey merely serves to induce another crisis. I count March of 1985 at Perry Street as the beginning of what would be a lengthy, uneven process of self-induced detox. At least it was the beginning of discernment between provoked imbroglios and unavoidable urgencies, external demands and internal imperatives.

I spent that year writing the novel *Dry Your Smile* and functioning more as a contributing editor to *Ms.*, as I had at first, than as an in-house editor. I'd pulled out of debt for the moment and was living off my book advance, augmented by a reduced lecture schedule and a little freelance journalism. Politics went on as usual: meetings, actions, organizing, and that activity I loathe only a little less than collective writing but more than being teargassed: fundraising, in this case, for the Institute. Blake was in his junior year of Tutorial House (high school) at UNIS, aiming for the International Baccalaureate, and he reveled in living in the Village as much as I did. Bran, the beloved black cat, moved to Perry Street, surveyed the surroundings, approved, and took ownership immediately. The roof garden came alive that spring in containers bright with jonquil and tulip bulbs, and the summer was resplendent with boxes of herbs, lettuce, peppers, and tomatoes (grown from seed), vats of roses, tubs of wisteria and lilac, and an expanding collection of potted succulents. There was no shade, so fuchsia languished until I got the point and gave up on it, but rich blue clematis climbed rapidly, splashing the whitewashed chimney with velvet flowers, and the lacy dwarf Japanese maple in its half-barrel container flourished into a gorgeous maroon flecked with burnt orange.

Life was more peaceful than it had been in my adult memory, which doesn't mean it wasn't punctuated by convulsive periods. In the preceding paragraph I've skipped over the element of Marilyn Joy Waring.

A particular challenge in memoir writing is to convey a past state of mind now so altered by hindsight that it's difficult to access the original topography for oneself, let alone describe it to others. This is especially true about the state of being deeply, wholly, lethally in love. The present self keeps muttering How in god's name could I *ever* have done that/put up with that/felt that? (This is a variant on Whatever did I see in *him/her?*) Nevertheless, the past self *did*. And it's no good simply announcing that the whole thing ended badly but took ten years to do so. One must reenter that past terrain so as to convey at least part of the reason why in hell one was there to begin with. This is imperative for at least three reasons.

First, cardboard villains may be permissible in real life, where in fact we meet them all the time, but they're not acceptable on the page: too simplistic and, frankly, boring. Second, if Our Heroine (in this case, laughably, me) loved and stuck with a demonstrably not-so-good-for-her person for such a long time, what does that say about Our Heroine? Third, it takes two to tangle, so it's just as well to accept responsibility for one's actions. Granted, it's easier to exercise restraint when a relationship rusts twenty years in the past. Furthermore, if a union has produced offspring, one is more motivated to strive for generosity, if only for the offspring's sake. But when the situation is both more recent and less generative . . . you see the problem. So bear with me. And do realize that if at times I descend into exasperation, that's *after* six layers of revision.

The poetry I wrote to Marilyn helps me remember the absolute beauty I perceived in this woman, beauty of which she was sadly unaware— "greensilver sapling, her body," I named it in one poem; "silk breasts and brain erotic," in another; "voice indigo as a violin's," "antic grin that struck and blazed me glad / to be alive," her "particular face, lit with love to see [me] enter the room." As always, the poems, like amber, preserve distilled memory: how she was capable of a sudden, disarming sweetness, how adroit her perceptions could be, how my ribs would hurt from laughing, how girlishly happy I felt . . .

Marilyn had not, after all, gone quietly into the antipodean night. On the contrary, she began what would be a veritable commute to the United States.

This was largely my own fault. Some feminist leaders hide their contacts close to their chest, but others take real pleasure in matchmaking, seeing it as one aspect of activism. I fall into this latter category. For years I'd made it a practice to suggest others—my countrywomen as well as internationals—for jobs, funding opportunities, speaking engagements, and so forth, delighting when a match worked. Long before we'd become lovers, Marilyn's name was one of a number I'd raised on occasion, since I thought her a dynamic speaker with important things to say about women, labor, and economics.

I admit that once we fell in love, I intensified this effort—especially since I knew she was in financial difficulty, having sacrificed her seat in Parliament as well as the pension that would have accompanied it had she completed her third term and not brought down the government. I also empathized with her being in her own diaspora—the staying-with-friends, books-in-storage nightmare—since she'd sold her house before their shared farm plans were postponed by the Australian lover, who was having second thoughts, obviously sensing something, despite Marilyn's still not having told her about us. It did occur to me that my promotion of Marilyn was not necessarily in my self-interest, once I realized that what she needed the money *for* was to buy her share of the farm with her *other* lover.

But carrying off noble self-sacrifice was something I now had down to a fine art. I got off on it the way an anchorite thrills to nestling in a hairshirt. Besides, it did seem tacky to withdraw needed support from a sister whose work I still respected. Or so I told myself.

Consequently, when Genevieve Vaughan was planning a spring strategy retreat in Texas and asked me whether she should invite Waring as the economics person, I said yes. Meanwhile, international feminism was catching on in the United States, in part thanks to the warm reception *Sisterhood Is Global* had received from press and readers. This created a climate where I was asked all the more for referrals, and Marilyn's name was one I suggested.

It took a while for me to realize fully that she wasn't about to break it off with me *or* her other lover, that each of us was a standby in case the other didn't work out, and that I was in an all-woman version of a cliché situation: being involved with the married man who's always on the verge of a divorce. Then it took more time to make myself grasp that her presence in the United States was just too tempting for me to ignore, and was therefore personally destructive. Once I understood both unhappy truths, I stopped promoting her so energetically. By then it was too late. She'd begun to be known a little, and was being invited independent of my prompting.

In late March of 1985, less than a month after I'd moved to Perry Street, she came to New York for a few days before Gen's Texas meeting, to which we both were going. She was to sleep on the sofa because we were in the This Can No Longer Continue We're Just Friends mode. Which lasted twenty-four hours. I wonder now why we bothered to go through such ornate motions of denial at all, as if we were exotic birds hoooing at one another in a bizarre mating dance on the Discovery Channel. By the time we left for Texas we could barely keep our hands off one another, even in public, and by the time she departed for New Zealand we were distraught with goodbyes all over again. Worse, I now *loved* her, as well as being besottedly *in* love. That summer, passionate letters and phone calls burned back and forth, with me repeatedly saying goodbye forever, confident she would ignore that. I should have bought stock in AT&T, but I hadn't the foresight, stomach, or extra cash.

In October she was back. She had speeches in California and Indiana. I had organizing lectures in Iowa and Utah, so we met in Arizona—yes, I know, never mind the geography; it was all west of the Hudson River— and we spent her thirty-third birthday together at the North Rim of the Grand Canyon, where she'd never been, with side trips through the Painted Desert, Zion, and the sculptural glory called Bryce Canyon. (It was satisfying to show off *our* natural grandeur, so I indulged in a burst of eco-patriotism.) She returned to New York with me and remained in the United States until early December, based at Perry Street but flying in and out on overnights for speeches in New England. We spent a weekend at Kate Millett's farm in Poughkeepsie, where Kate enjoyed playing the maternal figure to us. We weathered a rare, tiny earthquake in Manhattan, where earthquakes aren't supposed to happen. I cooked an excessive Thanksgiving dinner at which Lois, Lesley, Marilyn, Blake, and I gorged ourselves to stupefaction. Life almost seemed normal.

It was a bittersweet two months, though. Marilyn was torn, still trying to have it both ways, which would periodically make me feel like the girl in this particular port. Ultimatums, to her or to myself, did me no good; after a lifetime of feeling I had to be in control and had to feed the emotions of everyone near me, I was now in a state of emotion that could not be controlled—and conscious of my own hunger. So my longing undercut my resolve, and Marilyn knew that, relying on it. I assumed her fierce intelligence would surely come to grips with what she was doing. What I should have grasped at the time, even given my limited experience with husbands and lovers, was obvious. Yet I wouldn't understand until it got branded onto my soul years later: intellectual brilliance is not necessarily a reflection of emotional maturity.

Many of the poems in *Upstairs in the Garden,* love poems shadowed with ambivalence, were written during this period. Marilyn's somewhat schizoid rationale was "I can't help it if I'm in love with two people at the same time." Mine was "I know that this is bad for me, and that I'll pay for it later. But I'm so happy—and don't I deserve to be reckless for once?" Self-delusion is a potent justifier, particularly when mutually reinforced. In fairness, her resolve was undercut, too, by *her* longing. We were always poised on the brink of final farewells, which intensified the poignancy and urgency of every moment. At the same time, as if living in parallel dimensions, we were making our own chipper plans for future encounters. Every time I thought it *was* over and felt reconciled to that, she'd unsettle me. She ultimately flew off with tearful adieux to lectures in Montana and Washington State, then to proceed westward home to New Zealand—but suddenly decided to fly back across the entire United States to see me again, even though only for two more days. At such moments she was as helpless in the clutches of this obsession as I was. Finally, exhausted by trying to figure out who in hell was driving, I decided to sit back and ride. At least having my own place gave me stability; Blake's presence helped keep me going; and I continued, no matter what, to write. Marilyn left for home on December 3. I delivered the manuscript of *Dry Your Smile* two weeks later.

A Doubleday contretemps ensued. Loretta, loyal to her authors, backed me solidly, but the firm had just been bought by the German multinational conglomerate Bertelsmann A.G., and the new management was interested in cash-cow biographies of celebrities or the sort of nonbooks that have titles like *1000 Exciting New Ways to Cook Yams* or *The 7-Step Zen Diet to Success, Orgasm, and a Perfect Golf Swing.* They were unimpressed by the few Doubleday authors producing "litrachur." I was told, furthermore, that my quasi-autobiographical roman à clef was too unrealistic; *no*body lived that way. Their special concern was that no couple could exist in which the husband was gay/bisexual and the wife later had a woman lover. Citing Vita Sackville-West and Harold Nicolson, Jane and Paul Bowles, or the facts of my own life elicited blinks of nonrecognition. Their bottom line was that I had to straighten *some*body out—preferably *both* but at least *one*, the husband or the wife—or no publication. This is how they get you: not so much with fire hoses or jail, but by pestering you to death.

After months of such hassle, rather than cut the protagonist's relationship with "Iliana de Costa," I went into extensive rewrites and de-gayed her husband. (It's comforting to know the First Amendment is of use to someone in this country, though unfortunately it's to an abuser like Larry Flynt.) We got the book past the censors in this manner, and it came out in 1987, the year Blake graduated from UNIS. *Dry Your Smile* did well abroad, but was barely visible in the United States, because Doubleday/Bertelsmann's revenge (for my not having straightened *every*one) was to publish it nearly in secret. They placed not a single ad.

That was the last work I would publish with Doubleday, departing at the same time as did Kurt Vonnegut and their few other remaining literary or political authors. The best way to recover from postpartum book-delivery depression is to start another one as soon as possible, which I did. For some years, I'd wanted to explore what had *really* drawn me (and others) to the tactics of violence during the late Sixties and early Seventies—and I mean the emotional, sexual sub-agendas, not the rhetoric about smashing imperialism. That's how *The Demon Lover* began. But something had changed in me during the *Sisterhood Is Global* years. My brain couldn't think in a solely national context anymore. Too many dots were connecting themselves: the high rate of spousal battery found in the homes of policemen in both Chicago and New Delhi, for example. So my initial research about other women militants in the U.S. New Left grew to encompass more countries, then stretched backward in history, until the book emerged as a cross-cultural study of how violence has been eroticized in patriarchal society, and how and why women and men have colluded with that or resisted it. It required considerable research, the kind of reading that makes for troubled dreams. But I was so glad to be writing almost full-time that I had no complaints.

At the end of December 1985, I fell ill with a bad flu and bronchial infection that lingered through January, compounded by the anxiety provoked by Doubleday's first reactions to the novel. Marilyn, on holiday in Australia with you-know-who, was aware of my being sick and beleaguered, but didn't phone or write for weeks, and she knew that I would never phone her when she was with her Australian lover. Later I learned that she'd finally been forced to admit my existence and then had agreed, after a huge fight, to reconcile permanently and faithfully with the lover. Meanwhile, I could do nothing but feel wounded and insulted by her silence. Nor could I do anything on the book front except wait passively for Loretta to try to change Doubleday's decision. So I spent most of that January wheezing, popping antibiotics, sitting before the fire wrapped in flannels, and filling hundreds of handwritten pages with what I called "The Fever Zone Journal," meditations on what writing was, what love was, what silence and betrayal—including mine of Iliana and of Marilyn's other lover—was. By the end, I'd reached the decision that the person I loved more than anyone in the world other than Blake wasn't acting even as a friend, much less as a lover, and that this affair *had* to *stop*.[1]

A banana peel lay waiting for my instep. Ever since I'd met her, Marilyn had talked about her dream of spending time at the United Nations doing in-depth research on the UN System of National Accounts, which basically defines what's of value in world economics (women's labor does *not* count, a GDP invisibility). I'd told her I thought there was a book wanting to be written on the subject, one that could demystify economics and would be especially crucial for women, and I encouraged her to pursue the idea, promising help with writing it, with a literary agent, and with publishing contacts. During 1985—in one of the On periods in the On and Off relationship seesaw—I'd generated an invitation from Rutgers University for Marilyn to be a visiting scholar with support for this research, and also had recommended her to funding sources regarding the project. The irony was that now, in early 1986—just when I really *did* want to begin getting over her—all these chickens were coming home to roost. And lay egg on my face. Next door in New Jersey at Rutgers. And in Manhattan, at the UN. Close proximity. For three months.

I was due in San Francisco that February, to be the token woman on a panel about the future, an invitation I'd accepted for three reasons: Fritz Capra was on the panel, and I liked his work; I'd stay with Toni Fitzpatrick, and we'd get to visit; and Marilyn and I had planned earlier that when she landed in California that week for the Rutgers sojourn, I'd drive her down the coast and show her Robinson Jeffers's Big Sur country before we both flew back to New York and she settled down in New Jersey. When she did finally phone in late January after the weeks of silence, I told her I did not intend to meet her in California, and that from here on in, it was over for good. I said I'd see her civilly in New York and that I wished her good luck at Rutgers. Period. I then went to San Francisco and came directly back with no Big Sur asides, although I wept my way through a lot of Toni's Kleenex, herbal tea, and cabernet.

It's not so easy to undo carefully laid plans, especially when the spirit is

[1] The poem "Famine" with its refrain "This must stop" comes from this period. See *Upstairs in the Garden*.

only three-quarters willing and the flesh is tofu. Marilyn would be arriving in New York a few days later, *and* a few days *before* her lodgings in New Jersey became available, and now had no place to stay. Of *course* I should have told her to look up her old UN friend or explore that interesting phenomenon called a hotel. Of course I didn't. Of course I thought I had it under control. Of course I was kidding myself.

If all this had been going on with a man, I like to think that I would have recognized my emotional masochism and not been such a moron. But women were supposed to be *different*, you see. Anyway.

Lover arrives in blizzard. Long conversation by blazing hearth. Both parties crying. Expressions of love, loss, rage, pain, betrayal, ethics, confusion. Decision: This Time We Both Mean It, Merely Dear Friends.

Oh yeah. Forty-eight hours of *that*, and we were off and flying. Soon we were making plans for a Vermont weekend where she would teach me how to ski and for a trip to Bethlehem, Pennsylvania, later in the spring, for the annual Bach Festival. When I drove her to New Jersey some days later, I took her past my father's house—as life would have it, in New Brunswick, the same town where she'd be quartered. We parked across the street from the house, and sat and talked quietly for a long time in the car, watching no one come or go along the snow-shrouded sidewalks.

I think now that that was a turning point, one of those moments when you decide that if, no matter how you try, you cannot stop yourself from feeling something—in this case, a passionate loving—then you might as well go all the way. I think now that the deliberate vulnerability I showed her that day I meant as a sign, a kind of surrender—not to *her*, but to *It*, this power that so gripped me with loving her. One must be careful not to mistake the poignancies in one's life for tragedies, but it's possible that one loves this way only once—and is willing to risk being left by such loving utterly devastated only once. I would in time come to regard it as an existential loving, a devotion in the face of nothingness. But that day, without understanding the connections I didn't know I was making, I spoke about my father—his legendary intellectual ability versus his demonstrated capacity for withholding emotion. She spoke about her own childhood, having been a too-bright, too-spirited, too-tomboyish working-class little girl in a prim culture that embraced conformity like a straitjacket and regarded the battery of children as ordinary discipline. We talked about how cruelty coarsens the spirit, how lying corrodes the soul. For that hour, we were just two grown children trying to comfort each other, huddled in a chilly car while snow crystals spent their symmetries on the windshield to melt against an invisible wall.

Once Marilyn was established at Rutgers, she lived as much at Perry Street as in New Jersey, or perhaps more, with the excuse that the UN library was in New York. Again, life adopted fairly sane rhythms. Friends came to dinner and met her. She and Blake talked music. In March we took the big ski trip—which, as far as I was concerned, was heaven for the Jacuzzi and hot-toddy part but not so great for the careening-downhill-on-slippery-stuff-while-wearing-long-waxed-pieces-of-metal aspect. (Marilyn, who'd skied since age four, insisted on being my teacher—not her brightest idea.)

In April, as I was wrestling with the novel's revisions, Simone de Beauvoir died. News of her death came on the same day the United States bombed Libya, killing and maiming civilians "by accident" in a so-called smart-bomb surgical strike ostensibly to stop terrorism from killing and maiming civilians. In tears, I pushed the revisions to one side and sat down to write a tribute to her that would run in *Ms.*[2] She had been to me an intellectual mother, reliable, generous with her support, astringent in her advice. When I first tackled the novel, I'd written to her about my nervousness in attempting it and my guilt at stealing time from political work in order to indulge myself in fiction. She'd answered swiftly and firmly, writing, "For now, forget politics and write the novel, Robin. For you, in any event, they will be the same thing. It will demand an act of courage. Bon voyage." Now she was gone. Yet she comforts me still, oddly, all these years later. Recent biographical revelations and publications of her sweet, at times insipid love letters to Nelson Algren[3] help me laugh at my own sillinesses; her lifelong disastrous decisions about money and love help me forgive some of mine. She was always one freelance assignment away from *almost* getting out of debt, always torn between her political

[2] Expanded, this became the essay "The World without De Beauvoir," in *The Word of a Woman*.

[3] *A Transatlantic Love Affair: Letters to Nelson Algren by Simone de Beauvoir* (New Press, 1998).

responsibilities and her longing to be left alone to write. She was as vulnerable in her heart as she was formidable in her brain. And she had, as they say, "issues" with her mother. I miss her.

The months with Marilyn living so near or at Perry Street seemed at once a beginning and an ending. Shopping for groceries together, ambling through Greenwich Village arm in arm, going to concerts or movies, gardening on the roof, getting happily stoned on grass and talking for hours on end or laughing until our face muscles were sore, making love even longer and better as time went on—it seemed so promising that I gave myself to it totally. But I also believed that we were doomed, that when she returned to the other side of the world at the end of May it would be the last time we would see one another. I was trying with all my heart to live "in the moment," but was afraid that when she left I'd crash into depression, so knew I'd need the demands of work to prop me up. With the revisions at last finished and the novel entering production, I'd begun research on *The Demon Lover*. But I needed more than cerebral work; I needed some preoccupying activism that would insist I function and be of use. There's nothing like practically addressing other people's suffering to give one perspective about one's own puny dilemmas.

In 1985, I'd been approached by the UN Relief and Works Agency for Palestine Refugees in the Near East (UNRWA), with an invitation to visit the refugee camps and write about the condition of women. It had taken a year of negotiations, because I wanted to go alone, not as part of a journalists' group busing from camp to camp as if touring zoos; I wanted to wander through the camps, to see a minimum of buildings and installations, and to focus on women and children; I wanted to be free to avail myself of extra-official contacts acquired through my own networking with Arab feminists, and, most important, I wanted female interpreters—because the kind of intimate communication I hoped to inspire would be impossible through men. By the spring of 1986, these apparently unorthodox requests had been met. So on May 29, the day Marilyn left for New Zealand via California, I flew to a briefing at UNRWA headquarters in Vienna, then on to a sweep of Egypt, Israel/Palestine, the Gaza Strip, West Bank, Lebanon, and Jordan, for a six-week stay in the refugee camps.

That trip is described at length in *The Demon Lover*—probably the most excerpted and quoted part of the book. My return to the region two years later, during the *Intifada* ("Uprising") is covered in a long essay in *The Word of a Woman*. Both trips were brain-searing and heart-rending, and it would be a violation of the many Palestinian women I came to know and love (and the Israeli feminists and peace activists I also grew to know and respect), even to attempt to abridge those encounters here. How to summarize the memorable women in the camps of Jordan, Egypt, Lebanon, West Bank, Gaza—former peasants, teachers, artists, ex-guerrillas, housewives, doctors, students, factory workers? The personal stories, the confidences entrusted, the mutual tears shed, the defiant laughter, the whispers when men were around, the radicalization of the women interpreters? How to summarize Rashideyeh Camp in Lebanon, where the hunger became so great that, after the rats had been caught and eaten, the men petitioned the mullahs for dispensation to eat human flesh—but no one had to ask who would cook it, because everyone knew that was the job of women, who were already "unclean"? Nor is it possible to express the flush of proud humility when word has spread about one's coming—all the way from the southern tip of the Gaza Strip to the north part of West Bank—so that women rush up in welcome, exclaiming through the translation, "Ayee, we know about you. You are the woman whose eyes weep with us. My cousins in Rafah Camp call you 'the American woman with an Arab heart.' *Marhaba*. Welcome."

Much of my nonfiction prose since the early 1980s consists of first-hand reports about the lives of women in different countries across the globe, and none of that can be summarized, either. Yet this memoir would be absurdly incomplete without at least a sampling of the vivid presences of those women. For me, they *are* the international Women's Movement, despite, at this writing, fashionable trends in what might be termed a pseudo-feminist "establishment": slick professionalization of a leadership willing to work hand-in-fist with corporate globalization, overly academic emphases that can wind up having a neocolonial effect, attempts by some in the human-rights movement to co-opt global feminism into being a ladies' auxiliary of narrowly defined "human rights," and donor-driven funding that ignores what women need, want, and specifically ask for. Well, these, like past fads, will run their course. Meanwhile, it's the real, flesh-and-blood women, who live and die far from any kind of establishment in New York or Washington, D.C., who will eventually transform society. Certainly such women have permanently transformed the way I view the world. Many of them have honored me with their trust and their insights; their realities have become part of my reality, and so belong in this memoir. I can at least offer samples of their voices, the way their unforgettable stories have sequined my life, like koans.

Tahrir is only fifteen, a refugee who has fled Burj el-Barajneh Camp in Lebanon, one of the Beirut-area camps under steady siege by Israel in 1985. She's proud of her English and honor-student grades at an UNRWA school. She's beautiful, a bud of young womanhood flowering into her own energy.

"I want to teach," she says. "I want to end the killing and start the living. I hate death so much. I hate people being cruel." When I ask her, as I've asked so many others, what message she wants to send to women in the rest of the world, she thinks for a long time. Then, her smile a dazzle of optimism, she's ready.

"Tell them," she says carefully, "what my grandmother and mother always told me—that it is women's job to save the world. In our *own* way, which isn't the men's way. Tell them," she adds, "that whenever a woman anywhere fights for herself, she fights for me. My name, Tahrir, means 'Freedom.'"

We embrace. "*Bahibbik ya ukhti*," I murmur, "I love you, my sister."

Later I learn that the day after entrusting me with her message, Tahrir is killed by a shell.

When I began working in an international feminist framework, it was largely at conferences. That's all very well, but big meetings are, like any self-selecting group, unrepresentative of most "real people." I discovered that there are international globe-trotting jet-sets of feminist elites just as there are national ones. To get at the authentic situation, you have to go *to* it—to the women in the region, in the villages, to the people who never get to go on delegations. There you find depths of human suffering you could not have imagined and, sometimes, heights of human courage you might never have believed.

But first you have to do your homework, because these women have more pressing things to do than educate your ignorance in a private tutorial. That homework must also include ongoing self-scrutiny. It's delicate to be an activist in a global context when your country is currently the only superpower. I've sarcastically referred to myself as a sensitive Roman at the height of the Empire, well aware that my sisters abroad—especially in developing countries—may perceive me as that Roman, no matter how much cross-cultural awareness I labor to develop in myself. This, by the way, has nothing to do with guilt politics, which I regard as conveniently paralyzing, ripe for backlash defensiveness, counterproductive, and boring. It has to do with responsibility and a political will to change—and change doesn't happen without some clumsiness. But it *is* possible, for example, to transform privilege into access. That means you learn to say, "Okay, so I have certain skills and connections. Rather than hoard these, ignore them, or pretend to divest myself of them, how can I make of myself a bridge so that other women can acquire those skills and take advantage of that access?" Or to say, "Okay, so I got invited. I'm a European American, which means I better make damned sure that the U.S. presence is plural, and not lily-white."

Actually, I'm rather vain about how the U.S. Women's Movement usually functions in international situations. The French and Germans, for instance, will be there with their brazenly homogenous delegations, claiming that their own immigrant populations "aren't interested in feminism." Then in we'll tromp, Yankee Doodle Dandies. Let's say there are five of us. Immediately you know there has to be a Native American, an African American, a Latina, an Asian American, and a European American. But wait: there also must be representation beyond race or ethnicity, which means doubling or tripling up. So the Native American might be in a wheelchair (and married), the African American a Jew (and single), the Latina a small-business entrepreneur (and a mother), the Asian American eighty-four (and a lesbian), and the European American a fourteen-year-old rural quilt maker sporting baggy pants, a be-ringed pierced belly button, and an Appalachian drawl. This makes for a comical motley crew, and when we caucus all hell breaks loose—but in public we're not separate fingers, we're one fist. At such moments I indulge myself in a sentimental fit of matriotic pride, although the Europeans sometimes ridicule our multicultural pains. Hélène Cixous once huffed Frenchly at me, "You Americans! You are obsessed with this race fairness issue!"—a glass-house comment if I ever heard one, from the folks who brought us colonial Algeria, Senegal, and Rwanda, for starters.

The trick is to pull off this balancing act—conscientiousness but not guilt, respect but not servility—steadily, never forgetting it has everything to do with fairness and nothing to do with charity. After decades of teetering on this tightrope, I admit to some vanity at being one of the few trusted U.S. women in the international Women's Movement; I've worked hard to earn that trust. Then again, you never *can* earn it. It's a gift.

At first, my idealistic naïveté got bruised. After decades of rhetorically idolizing "the Third World," what a shock to discover how profoundly racist the Chinese can be, how xenophobic Japanese culture is, how deeply tribal enmities are rooted in parts of Africa, how dismissive of indigenous populations most South Americans are, how many national women's movements resist noticing the inherent connections between sexism and bigotries based on caste, class, homophobia, disability, or age. Sometimes I wonder where my head was during the early years of hardly daring to criticize another culture's cruelties with the same frankness I aim at my own. Actually, such criticism is a form of respect, since it implies a belief in the capacity to change. Not daring that critique shows the limits of a radicalism blind for its own sake, when what's needed is harder to achieve and even more difficult to sustain: an idealism that persists while fully noninnocent about the underside of human nature.

Staying silent in the face of any inequity (for fear of coming across like the Roman) does no good. Speaking up risks provoking the cultural relativism reaction—"What do *you* know about it, you outsider? *We* have no such problems. These have always been *our* ways." This specious argument never ceases to amaze me. First, if an idea is good it doesn't matter where it comes from—which cultural relativists understand well enough when it comes to the light bulb; pasta originated in China, but the whole world thinks pasta is Italian, so what. Second, what's old and traditional is not necessarily affirmable: think slavery, bound feet, monarchy, stale Christmas fruitcake. Third, if you look and listen carefully enough (which is where those villages come in), you discover people right *there* who've been speaking out against "our ways" all along.

~ ~ ~

After a week in the Himalayan foothill villages outside of Kathmandu, I begin meetings with the many women's groups in the city. They are energetic, competitive, overworked. The landlocked little country has Least Developed Nation status, and a 5 percent literacy rate for women (33 percent for men); women have almost no property or inheritance rights and very limited reproductive, divorce, and custody rights; hereditary temple prostitution still thrives in this Hindu fundamentalist society. When I am there, in 1994, the country is newly emerging into fragile democracy after centuries of god kings followed by decades of "hereditary prime ministers." So the feminist NGOs have their work cut out for them. Yet I notice they are all composed of Brahmin or Chetri (priestly or warrior caste) women. Where, I ask, are the lower-caste women? I am told, "Oh, *they're* not interested in feminism"—an answer inevitably more revealing about its speaker than its subject.

When I seek them out, not surprisingly I find they're very *much* interested. Formerly called "untouchables," renamed by Mahatma Gandhi *harijan*, or "children of God," they've now chosen for themselves the name *dalit*, or "the oppressed." Durga Sob, a small Dalit woman with a lovely heart-shaped face, about thirty years old, is a natural leader. She exudes warmth but has a sweet steeliness about her; she's an anomaly in having managed to get herself educated and even learn some English, although we work with backup interpretation. Quick to grasp the opportunity, Durga makes it clear that she and other Dalit women had approached the women's NGOs repeatedly but had been told that feminists could never come from a low caste. She has heard that there are Dalit women's groups in India, but since none of these call themselves "feminist" Durga wonders if the upper-caste Nepali women aren't right after all. She herself recalls being beaten at school when, at age seven, she mistakenly drank from a well reserved for upper-caste students. But she finds the feminist rejection especially frustrating because "Dalit women are doubly persecuted—by the caste system and by our own men. Where can *we* find support?"

It takes only a few hours and a few stories. About the separate water fountains in Mississippi in the old days. About the sit-ins and marches. About the founding of the National Black Feminist Organization. About a *good* kind of refusing to stop. Before we leave the room, Durga and her colleagues have formed the first feminist untouchables' group in the world: FEDO, Feminist Dalit Organization. She asks me to be godmother patron of the group and makes me an honorary Dalit. I'm so honored I blush, and my red face provokes giggles and hugs all around.

For the remainder of my three weeks in Nepal, we are joined at the heart. Whatever meetings I attend—with high-caste women in Parliament, in NGOs, in the aid community—Durga and/or some of her Dalit sisters accompany me, at my invitation. The Brahmin and Chetri women are eager to meet with this international feminist visitor from New York, to discuss organizing, to ask about international funders, to raise their profiles in interviews so that I will write about them, to hear different strategic approaches that have worked elsewhere in winning legislative and judicial reforms. But if they meet with me, they find they're meeting with Durga and FEDO as well. At first it seems simple enough: the upper-caste women are stiff but courteous. Then I spy them in a corner sprinkling their heads and hands with water to purify themselves after having sat at a lunch table polluted by the presence of Dalits. Still, after an intensive three-day workshop I conduct on tactics—opened by an exercise where each of the forty women present has to speak as if she came from a caste other than her own—I spy a new mix of women in those corners, this time arguing animatedly, crying quietly, sometimes embracing for a moment, awkwardly, across caste. It's just a beginning. None of us are so naive as to believe it won't take a *long* time. But Durga slips a gift of bangles onto my wrist, then gives me the high fives I've taught her.

As I write these words, the one image from the global Women's Movement I keep on my desk is a photo showing the garlanded, festooned front entrance of the FEDO office on the day it opened. The legible plaque reads, in Sanskrit and English, "First Feminist Dalit Organization."

~ ~ ~

By the end of 1987, the novel was out, I was finishing *The Demon Lover*, and Blake was at his chosen school, Berklee College of Music in Boston, coming home at least once a month, with the snobbery of the Manhattan born, for his fix of garlic bagels and "*proper* Chinese food, not served with *bread*, forgodsake." Meanwhile, the Sisterhood Is Global Institute, with Karen Berry as its executive director, had pioneered the first Emergency Action Alerts ever to be focused on the plight of women persecuted specifically for work on female human rights.

The romantic tumult had calmed down. Marilyn's Australian lover, understandably enough, had *had* it, and definitively broke off the relationship. Marilyn continued her lecture trips to North America, which were quite lucrative since the exchange rate was almost two to one. She then proceeded to buy a farm herself, about an hour's drive outside of Auckland, and begin fixing it up. I'd started to trust that we weren't always about to say farewell. In fact, we were easing into our own coupledom, mocking our situation by claiming we were like any other middle-class pair with a city pad and a country home—except that in our case one happened to be in New York and the other in New Zealand.

Once I had completed *The Demon Lover,* I hit the road again. These days, when I was invited to another country for a conference, or to speak, organize, or write about women there, I asked if they also needed a feminist economics person since I just happened to know an excellent one. This was the start of our meeting all over the world—oh, the anticipation, the excitement of those encounters!—doing our political work, then stealing four or five days of vacation alone together before flying off, wet-eyed, in opposite directions.

One such meeting took place in Brazil in 1987, when Bella and I were the U.S. presence at a gathering of CEDAW (the Committee on the UN Convention to Eradicate All Forms of Discrimination against Women), and I arranged for Marilyn to be invited as an expert witness on women's unpaid labor—which in fact she was. By the third day I'd managed to miff Bella by apparently insulting the president of Brazil when, during our audience with him, I politely inquired about a timetable for direct elections. When abroad, Bella had to act like the former congresswoman she was, but I didn't. I was under instructions from poor women in the favelas and from indigenous women who wanted me to raise this question, so what the hell, glad to be of service. When the meetings were over and Bella had grudgingly forgiven me, she, Marilyn, and I went off for a brief holiday first at the home of then Deputy (Congresswoman) Ruth Escobar, and later at the ranch of my old acquaintance the theater director Gilda Grillo. Gilda put us all on horseback—to Marilyn's alarm, my dismay, and Bella's glee as the one horsewoman among us. Bella also trounced everybody at poker until we plied her with cachaça, which slowed her down and made her head wobble enchantingly.

Much as I adored the vacation part of these trips, I also relished working politically with Marilyn. Though we had markedly different styles—she was even more impatient than I am, but was unafraid of acting abrupt or snappish—we learned much from each other. The poem "Two Women"[4] captures that connection, describing a large part of what drew and held us together. But I'd deftly forgotten how I'd once tended to embody all poetry in Kenneth. Now I was confusing Marilyn with feminism. I'd once written the line (in "Monster") "I want a woman's revolution like a lover." Had I all along really wanted the reverse?

The year 2000 is Brazil's 500th anniversary (the indigenous peoples surely have something to say about that). When news coverage shows crowds celebrating Brazil's "racial democracy," I think of Maria Alice Santos. I met her in 1987, but later lost her. Since 1994, mail has been returned from her address, and none of my Brazilian contacts know how to find her. I'm afraid she's dead.

She was, in 1987, a tiny, birdlike woman of indeterminate age, bright black skin, a sardonic smile, and a gaze that punctured your ego. She had agreed to meet me because I "came recommended" by some of the favela women, one of whom, who spoke English, kindly came along to translate.

---

[4] *Upstairs in the Garden.*

It turned out that Maria Alice had seen me before, at a full-moon Candomblé ceremony to which I'd been invited a few nights earlier.

That led to talk about female spirituality, and then we turned to talking about her work. She wanted to explain her name first, laughing: "Whenever you meet someone called Santos, you know it's almost always because they're born out of wedlock. In Brazil, you see, having no father automatically makes you a saint." Maria Alice Santos was a secular saint. She'd been working with prostituted Afro-Brazilian women in Rio's backstreets for more than twenty-five years. She'd been talking about HIV/AIDS since the early 1980s, but no officials would listen to her.

"One day they'll find me murdered," she shrugged. "It might be pimps, or the sex traffickers, porno guys, drug dealers, cops, johns—any of them. They all know while I'm alive, I'll never quit. Getting the girls off drugs, out of the life. Getting the kids—the ones not even menstruating yet—out of the life, into school. It's hard enough being black, and hard enough being poor, but being black, poor, and a woman—that's a ticket to hell. Sex for sale is mostly where poor black women start out here, and mostly where we end up. If politicians cared, they'd find a way to stop prostitution, all right. But they *want* us where we are. So we try to survive. I get money where I can—some girls give me money to help others, like I helped them. We share. I *don't* take Church donations. The Church is another john—it always wants something for its money. I know safe places in the favelas no guys dare go. The women trust me. That's what matters."

When I offered to help raise money for her work, Maria Alice shook her head. "Look," she smiled, "nobody ever *listens* to what somebody like me says. Most men never listen to what most women say, anyway. And black women who are poor and live on the street—we don't exist, except as a statistic or a blowjob. Sometimes I want to run into the road and scream, '*Look at me! I'm human here inside of me!*' So—if anybody listens to you— *you tell our story*. That's what you can do."

It's a curious way to travel, with the Women's Movement as your guide. When I was seventeen, my mother had sent me briefly to Europe in hopes of ending my adolescent rebellion. She attached me as an informal au pair to one of her stockbroker friends, a wealthy widower who had an eight-year-old girl. I was grateful to go abroad at all, but I disliked the man, couldn't win over his spoiled, twitchy daughter, was mortified by the flashy "ugly American" way they traveled, and in general felt like a character trapped in a Henry James novel as rewritten by Tom Wolfe. I did manage to escape for a day to Stonehenge, all by myself. Fortunately, that was years before it deteriorated into the tourist site it's now become. I arrived in late afternoon, and the fields were totally deserted. I walked around the towering stones for over an hour, then lay down, like Hardy's Tess of the D'Urbervilles, on the altar stone to watch the sun set. It was bliss. There was one other escape—a solo side trip from Florence to Viareggio, to stand on the rocks and fling a rose into the sea where Shelley had drowned. As for the rest of that trip, my poor mother couldn't figure out why I didn't understand this was "the *best* way *any*body could possibly get to see the *world*."

Now I get to see the world very differently, go where I'm needed, learn from the women, share with them, try to be useful, then take what they've taught me and go someplace else, to another country or to my own page, to share it. I've become an itinerant messenger, a town crier, passing it along. Being a poet stands me in good stead here, though poetry and politics are considered inimical in my country—but not in the Arab world, Latin America, or ancient China and Japan with their histories of distinguished poet-politicians. Being a poet has taught me how to listen. The women I meet with are often nonliterate, and they speak in imagery, which is further distilled by the brevity of interpretation. These women *speak* in poetry.

Squatting on the mud floor of a hut in a Philippine rice paddy in the Cordillera Mountains, I talk with a peasant woman about her dreams for a better life. The longing in Gunnawa's voice is clear even before the translation reaches me through another woman. What does she want, more than anything? To learn to read, she says. Not more food, better housing, some easing of her intense labor? No, Gunnawa insists with solemnity: to *read*. "Because," she continues, a shy smile flickering across her weather-beaten face, "though I have never been outside this village, someday I might go somewhere. I know you must walk for half a day until you come to the road. I hear there are signs on the road. *If I could read the signs, I could know where I was going.*"

~ ~ ~

Becoming an internationalist doesn't mean you get to relax in your own country. One day the phone rings and it's Theresa Funiciello, luring me into a project she herself got roped into, because organizers, like misery, love company.

Theresa and I had met in 1979 when she'd phoned *Ms.* to announce that poor women were about to stage a sit-in at the Emergency Assistance Unit of New York City's central welfare office, down at Church Street, to protest demeaning and unconstitutional treatment they'd received at the hands of welfare system bureaucrats. I dropped whatever I was doing and hopped a subway to Church Street. With its three-month lead time, *Ms.* can never cover breaking news, since it hits print too long after the fact, so I wanted to be with these women not to cover the action but simply to support it. To the surprise of both Funiciello and myself, I was apparently the only well-known feminist out of the many they'd called who responded this way, so it would take time and further meetings to convince these activist welfare moms that the feminist movement wasn't all rich, snobby ladies who gave not a damn for their poorer sisters.

I immediately loved Theresa Funiciello. A former welfare mother herself, she's a genius on poverty issues: tactically inventive, a stirring speaker, an indefatigable organizer, and a woman equally unafraid to express anger, humor, and love. Theresa's group at that time, Downtown Welfare Advocate Center (DWAC), was composed of very smart women who mostly had little formal education, and who hotly denied they were feminists while every word issuing from their mouths glowed with incandescent feminist rage. We got on famously once the labels were reexamined, and soon they were claiming (with some justification) that *they* were the only *real* feminists around. I remember one wintery night in early 1980 when Blake, then ten, came with me to a DWAC meeting near Union Square so that he and I could have a snowball fight in the park's fresh powder before it melted to morning grey slush. Everybody still smoked cigarettes furiously back then, and Blake muttered to me as we left, "Great women. Really like Theresa. But you people better not smoke so much if you want to live to win this revolution." A few months later, Theresa and I were together again, this time at a demonstration outside the Grand Hyatt hotel, noting that Donald Trump and other real-estate czars and their companies received increasing city and state subsidies and tax abatements ("corporate welfare") while poor women's and children's stipends didn't even keep up with cost-of-living increases. We belted out our statements on bullhorns to crowds gathered around our makeshift stage, a flatbed truck parked in front of the luxury hotel. (But privately Theresa and I were crestfallen, since we'd been forced to abandon our plot of putting odiferous dead fish into the Grand Hyatt fountain, to be aided by a stink bomb in the ventilating system. This is my kind of woman.)

Now, in 1986, Theresa was hauling me onto the New York State Committee of the Hands Across America (HAA) campaign. HAA was one of those mass do-good/feel-good projects like "We Are the World" rock concerts; in this case, people donated money for the poor here in the United States, and held hands in long lines to demonstrate concern while TV cameras rolled. It was one of those banal charity ideas where the donors get to feel sanctimonious, the money goes to pay office overhead and the high salaries of national honchos, and little if any help ever gets to the folks who need and deserve it.

"Never mind," Theresa said. "This time we can change that. Since each state determines where its share of the money goes, our committee can actually make an impact." The sum allotted to New York was only $839,000—not enough to buy even one meal for every poor person in the state. Consequently, that money had to be used creatively, in order to try to make a lasting difference: to educate, advocate, mobilize. Theresa is an impossible person to say no to, and I somehow wound up being voted in as chair of the New York State HAA Committee. It soon renamed itself the Committee for Justice and Empowerment, *Not* Charity—thus putting the national HAA office on notice: *These are New Yorkers you're dealing with, so goddammit get the hell outta our way.* Other state committees were largely composed of representatives from "poverty establishment" groups—"poverty pimps," as Theresa succinctly terms them. These are the professional experts who never want to address the issue systemically because they *need* the poor to be "always with us," so that they can continue their lucrative careers of providing Band-Aids for temporary solutions. These are the organizations running institutionalized begging sites—shelters, food pantries, soup kitchens—on huge corporate-level budgets while women and kids receive "charity" handouts of stale bread, moldy cheese, and Ronald Reagan's favorite "vegetable," catsup.[5]

Our committee, on the other hand, took the position that people living in the world's richest country had a *right* not to starve to death, freeze, or lack housing. We were the only HAA committee with representatives from all over its state and the only one with a real bloc of *poor* people *on* it, as well as some direct-service providers, civil-rights leaders, lawyers, and activists. We had the strongest representation of black, Latin, and Native American members of any HAA committee, *and* we were 90 percent women—fitting, since "the poor" *are* women: poverty wears a woman's face. We also issued the liveliest statements of any state committee—collaborations reflecting the scrupulous research of Tom Sanzillo (a longtime policy advocate on poverty issues), the fury of Jackie Goeings (a great-grandmother from the welfare rights network), the vision of John Mohawk (a professor of Indian law and activist with the Seventh Generation Fund), Theresa's magnificent fire, and my blue-pencil editing.

Our ideas for ways to use the HAA funds were aimed both at practical solutions and at long-term systemic change. We wanted to put some of the money toward building a statewide campaign to educate people about the need for a children's allowance (the United States is one of last few industrialized nations in the world without one), hoping that eventually New York might lead the way for the rest of the country on this as it had on some other social-justice issues. Second, we wanted to use some of the money to establish a children's survival fund, to be augmented by future

[5] In the 1970s, when state government officials proposed reestablishing soup kitchens and food pantries, which had not existed since the Great Depression, people were appalled, since such institutions were properly regarded as marks of shame against a society that made people choose between feeding their hunger or retaining their dignity. Now, a mere three decades later, the poverty establishment is a veritable growth industry in New York State and around the country—and its propaganda has been so efficient that the public no longer regards the existence of soup kitchens as shameful.

fundraising, in order to give grants to grassroots nonprofit organizations active in advocacy, empowerment, and justice for the poor—so that academic poverty experts weren't always the only ones with platforms from which to speak. Third, we wanted to distribute the balance to direct-service providers who sought directional advice and input *from* poor people and who were committed to legislative and economic change, not to perpetuating the problem.

Seven months of intense work later, we'd been tagged the problem-child committee of HAA, whose national leadership tended toward fancy offices, back-room rule-changing, outright fiat, and the startling overuse of first-class air travel and overnight couriers instead of plain mail. The poverty establishment saw our spunky group as its worst nightmare, and mobilized against us as if we were calling for a storming of the Winter Palace—which I suppose in a way we were. Though we had the strongest statewide backing of any state committee, national HAA threw out every one of our decisions. At last, we countered with the suggestion that the New York money be distributed as cash—literal *cash*—to poor people. At least this way we'd know it would be *getting* to them and would make a difference in their lives, but we suspected that HAA would take out a mob contract on our entire committee rather than let that happen. Indeed, its leaders demanded that we award grants to "established service provider agencies" or they'd fire us. Since we were serving without pay, *that* was a fearsome threat.

We held a press conference at which we resigned en masse and exposed the farce publicly, renaming ourselves the New York Hands Across America Committee in Exile. Marty Rogol, executive director of national HAA, formed a New York scab committee of poverty bigwigs. Less than six months later, HAA went down in the flames of scandal, excoriated in the press for having been somehow "unable"—a full year after the deadline—to distribute the $16 million collected from hand-holding Americans. Whaddya know.

But Theresa would go on to write the most important analysis of women and poverty we yet have,[6] including in it solutions that still give the

---

[6] *Tyranny of Kindness* (Atlantic Monthly Press, 1993).

poverty pimps ulcers—in addition to the indigestion they deserve to get from eating too much.

~ ~ ~

Meeting me at Parliament buildings in Cape Town, South Africa, the Inkatha Freedom Party MP Suzanne Vos is a likable woman, albeit an odd spokesperson for Zulu women: she's a blond "tall poppy"—a transplanted Anglo-Australian former journalist who self-identifies as "a feminist and a fanatical pluralist." But her defensiveness about Inkatha is evident, nowhere more so than in her use of the cultural relativist argument. She claims all Zulu women are strong supporters of traditional Zulu culture, including such practices as mass virginity testing:[7]

"It might appear that the parade of virgins before the king and his men is horridly sexist, but this revival of a puberty custom halted by missionaries is the Zulu way of trying to combat the rise in teenage pregnancies and the soaring HIV/AIDS rate. Once it's publicly known that a girl is a virgin, in Zulu culture she's safe, men honor her. So it's actually a way of *protecting* women!" When I respectfully suggest that, based on thirty years' experience of listening to women at the grassroots, I suspect that the women I am about to meet *in* the villages might tell a different story, Vos asks me to let her know if that's the case. So I am letting her know.

The Midlands Women's Group, whose focus is on rural women in the KwaZulu-Natal province, hosts a meeting to network me with some of these women, and with women from the Association for Rural Advancement (AFRA), Hlomelikusasa, and the Rural Women's Movement.[8] We

---

[7] In early September 1998, in a highly publicized revival and affirmation of traditional Zulu practice, more than seven thousand young women and girls from different areas of KwaZulu-Natal assembled in Bulwer and underwent public testing of the hymen. A Spring Festival Reed Dance involving a march of two thousand virgins, young women in traditional garb—bare breasts and three-inch-wide bead belts with tiny aprons—also took place before Zulu King Goodwill Zwelithini.

[8] These women have courageously been confronting such traditional practices as *lobolo* (bride price, paid by the groom's family to the bride's), *ukuvusa* (in which the family of an "infertile" woman is obliged to provide a "seed-bearer," usually her younger

convene late one afternoon in the sparsely appointed but well-scrubbed
Tembaletu Community Centre, needing to drag more chairs in as more
women than expected—over seventy—arrive. Ten Zulu women have journeyed in the open back of a pickup truck from their villages more than a
day's drive away.

Vuyisile speaks through translation, but her direct gaze never leaves
mine: "I want to tell you about myself. From my earliest memory I was
told, 'You are only a girlchild. Your job is to fetch wood, haul water. You are
the family ox. You must marry and obey your husband and in-laws. He will
pay *lobolo* for you so he owns you. Your money, from marketing what you
grow, is not your money, but his. This is the Zulu way.' I say, this is a bitter
way to live."

Other voices chime in, a chorus filtering through translation:

"They make us marry when we are still little girls."

"Women around here get killed every day!"

"I'm a widow with eight kids. I miss the money my husband made, but
I don't miss *him*. He beat me to stop me going to women's meetings."

"See this scar on my forehead and cheek? The traditional leaders
thought because I was for women I must be ANC,[9] so they slashed me."

"I was called into a chief's court and punished by a fine for talking in a
meeting with men."

"I ran away because I didn't want to be a third wife. But they caught me
and whipped me until I gave in."

"They started calling me a witch, because I said women should have
the right to own land. They still might kill me. Who will hear my screams?"

"By the time I was twenty-five, I had six kids. Our culture says,

sister, to conceive a child for her sister's husband), *ukungena* (in which a widow is
obliged to marry her deceased husband's brother to procreate an heir for her husband's
property), polygyny, primogeniture, corporal punishment of women and children, and
virginity testing. See "The Impact of Customary Law, Legislation, and the Constitution on the Status of Black Women in Rural KwaZulu-Natal," Janine Hicks, LL.B.,
University of Natal, Durban.

[9] African National Congress, the majority and ruling party, which has an adversarial
political history with Inkatha—in part harkening back to ethnic and tribal differences
among the two constituencies.

'Woman, you will sit on the ground while men sit on chairs. You will not speak at meetings. You have no need of education.' I can speak no language but Zulu, so I can't talk directly with any outsiders. But you come from a far distance to hear us, and your eyes fill for us, so to you I can maybe 'speak female.'"

We "speak female." I tell them about my conversation with Suzanne Vos. After the hoots of laughter die down, Zandile, a woman who looks to be in her seventies, responds.

"*Culture*," she murmurs thoughtfully, "*is not a rock. Culture is a river*. It changes. It flows. Streams feed it. As a woman, I was never allowed to feed the culture of my people. Zulu culture is Zulu *men's* culture. Believe no one who tells you otherwise. If it is too late for me, I want my granddaughters to feed the culture, so it flows to the sea for *all* of us."

Sethembile adds a furious coda: "I have four daughters. It angers me that the lady MP says virginity testing and the virgins' parade protect girls. Maybe that was true a hundred years ago. Today it's a lie. The parade is for men's fun. Being known as a virgin does *not* protect a girl—it *endangers* her! *Many* Zulu men believe the superstition that if a man with AIDS sleeps with a virgin, he'll be cured! *So they seek virgins out and rape them.* And this '*protects*' my girls?!"

Vuyisile speaks again. "Tell the lady MP to listen to *us*, not the men who say they speak *for* us. I've been trying to rebel my whole life. Then I met these women here. Now I rebel for other women, too. I've started a water project for my village and surrounding villages. Trying to pipe water in, so women don't have to walk six and half kilometers [four miles] twice a day carrying buckets. Ooooh, am I now unpopular with the chiefs, the traditional leaders! We didn't even ask permission to come here," she says, gesturing at the other rural Zulu women, "because we knew they would want to know why and if we said we were meeting with a woman from far away who writes about women they would never let us come."

I ask what might happen when they return home. There is silence. Then Vuyisile clears her throat and answers, "Some kind of punishment. A fine, probably—some money, maybe a goat. But we won't be stopped. I want *more* meetings like this! I want the whole *world* to ask us what we think and what we want. I will never again sit on the ground and be silent."

When we part, with more embraces, tears, laughter, and fists raised high in the air, it is already dark. The women will stay overnight with others in the group and journey back to their villages the next day. I go on to Durban to meet with women from the Advice Desk—co-founded by my friend Judge Navinathem Pillay—women who work to combat the epidemic of rape and battery that's one of apartheid's legacies in South Africa. It isn't until weeks later that I learn what happened when Vuyisile returned to her village. Her house, and the small caravan she'd used as the office of her water project, had been burned to the ground. She herself wasn't hurt, and other rural activist women have already committed themselves to helping her rebuild, but she's lost her few worldly goods.

Nonetheless, Vuyisile has asked one of the AFRA women to write and let me know, not just about the burning, but that it had actually *strengthened* her—that I should write it down for the world to read:

"Even if I have no ground on which to sit, I will still refuse to sit on the ground and be silent."

Empathy is a profoundly subversive emotion. Once empathy is at work, there's no place to hide. With empathy, you're a refugee in Bosnia, a Tutsi in Rwanda. You don't know where you begin and the suffering of the world ends. (Where empathy *can* backfire is in intimate relationships. I'd ventriloquized myself into Kenneth's needs, desires, and rationales so long that I forgot my own. Later, I would manage to do much the same thing regarding Marilyn. Nevertheless, if I had to choose, I'd err on the side of having too much empathy rather than too little.)

Nor does this have anything to do with fatuous pretensions of self-sacrifice. On the contrary, the rewards of empathy are so great and expansive of the possibilities for the self that it might even be called selfish. For instance, the international Women's Movement has given me a rich cross-cultural nourishment. I've encountered authors too few people ever hear about, like the late Bessie Head, a truly great writer who, had she not been female, black, and Botswanan, might have won the Nobel Prize, and should have. Or Ding Ling, the major Chinese literary figure whose pre-feminist feminism virtually destroyed her literary career. Or the Algerian Assia Djebar, the Pakistani Ismat Chughtai, the Mexican Rosario Castellanos, the Nigerian Buchi Emecheta, the Filipina Ninotchka Rosca, the Moroccan Fatima Mernissi, the Korean Kang Sok-kyong. Those are a few of the *better*-known ones.

I can no longer calculate how this process has influenced my own work. But I can give one example of how it has freed me—quite the opposite of the missionary-type assumption that I'm liberating unfortunate women elsewhere. When I was a young poet, in fear of being regarded as "a lady poet," I stayed far away from flower imagery because that's what nineteenth-century women poets were stereotypically thought to employ. I secretly regretted this proscription of subject matter, because I think there are fascinating aspects to flowers. For one thing, they're a plant's sexual organs (which might make your average florist shop a sort of brothel). For another, horticulture is lavish with metaphor—goodies like the phenomenon called stress-flowering: flowers that normally don't bloom until spring or summer sometimes burst into blossom in the heart of winter *because* of stress. Such gems were, I felt, forbidden subject matter.

Then, some years ago, while traveling in Japan, I learned from the Women's Movement there about an ancient tradition, dating from medieval times, of women who were court poets, bards. We're not just talking about one token Lady Murasaki here. They had many such poets and many levels of bardic accomplishment. As a poet worked her way up through these levels, there were test poems she was assigned to write, on specific subjects. The ultimate test for being recognized as a bard, a fully senior poet, was to write "the peony poem." What a gift. I was freed by foremothers from an entirely different culture to write *my* peony poem.[10]

Why would any of us ever want to settle for monoculturalism when we can celebrate John Donne and peony poems as well? Why would I not have known that, as de Beauvoir scolded, for me art and politics have no fixed border between them? Illiterate women in the world's villages and slums have known that all along.

---

[10] "Peony," originally published in *Death Benefits* (Copper Canyon Press, 1981) and collected in *Upstairs in the Garden*.

~ ~ ~

Her face is hard and lined. She is poor, not young, not highly educated. She works as a doorkeeper at an old house in a sidestreet in Catania, in Sicily. I was there as part of an Italian book tour with Maria Nadotti, the journalist and author who had done a book-length interview with me.[11] As Maria and I rush to the airport, this woman recognizes us from having seen our TV interview on violence against women. She calls out. We stop. Maria translates rapidly.

"Is it true, really true?" the woman asks, clutching Maria with one hand and me with the other. "Is it true what you say, that women in many places are fighting back, against the violence? Against being beaten?"

"Yes," we say, sophisticated journalists trying hard to swallow the emotion rising in our throats. "It's true. Women are fighting back. Many, many places. Far beyond Catania and Sicily. All over the world."

"And one day they will make it stop? The violence, the pain? It will stop? They—we—will make this happen?" Her eyes are shining.

"Yes, yes," we cry, hugging each other and her. "One day. Women everywhere are trying. We *will* make the violence stop. Yes."

She nods, blessing us with a radiant, gap-toothed smile.

"That is very good," she sighs. Then she adds, with quiet dignity, "Because then I am not alone in my fight."

I dedicated the Italian edition of *The Demon Lover* to this woman, whose name is Adriana Costa, and I've told this story in many countries since that day. Hearing it, women spontaneously call out, answering a Sicilian woman they will never meet, "No, you are *not* alone!"

Yet wherever she stands, singular, she re-creates all possibility. She is indeed the Doorkeeper, who opens the portal and shows the way.

[11] This was published as *Cassandra non abita più qui: Maria Nadotti intervista Robin Morgan* (La Tartaruga, 1996). Maria, who became a dear friend, later translated and edited the Italian edition of *The Demon Lover* (*Il demone amante*, La Tartaruga, 1998).

EIGHTEEN

Hot Januaries

> *Leonato: You will never run mad, niece.*
> *Beatrice: No, not till a hot January.*
> —WILLIAM SHAKESPEARE,
> *MUCH ADO ABOUT NOTHING*, ACT I, SCENE 1

Yesterday I read an interview with a deathly serious young man currently considered trendy because he's written a book calling on us all to reject irony. Good god. That's like calling for a rejection of ratiocinative thought. If I were to wake one day into a world devoid of irony, I'd know I was brain-dead or at Oral Roberts University. What would we *do* without irony?

Check out your own daily reliance on it, the foul-weather friend who's there for you when nothing else is. As for me, I'd hardly know where to begin. There's irony in being a writer and a feminist in a world where two-thirds of all illiterates are women. There's irony in writing a prose nonfiction memoir when you've already limned life's starker truths in poetry—and in agreeing to do the former in order to be able to afford to continue doing the latter. There's irony in having resisted writing this memoir and then rambling on so that now, in our penultimate section, we must speed things up to cover sufficient ground or the book will rival the unabridged *OED* in length. There's irony in being a privileged, educated citizen of a superpower while always barely keeping the wolf from the door. There's irony in becoming a radical activist in part because of wanting to abolish money—and then spending obscene amounts of time over the ensuing decades fundraising.

What I most resent about money is the attention it demands when absent. I've never longed to be wealthy, merely solvent. Solvency is freedom from having to *think* about money, just as health is freedom from having to notice pain. Poverty and illness are both horribly preoccupying and time-consuming. In my case, the trick has been to sustain a living from writing, plus such ancillary patchwork pursuits as journalism, editing, lectures, and the occasional grant. Yet even to attempt this way of earning a livelihood is an enormous luxury. Few people get to survive by doing work they love. So I can't complain, although I manage to find ways to do so, particularly on those occasions when friends remind me that I've been working steadily since age one and a half, which tends to tucker a person out. (I did loll around, a lazy slob except for a baby beauty contest or two, for that entire first year). Somehow, I've pulled it off thus far, and even managed to put a kid through private school and college in the process. But I've succeeded unevenly, slipping back into and out of debt with such regularity that by now it's become a familiar, oddly comforting rhythm.

By the end of the 1980s, this cadence was pretty well established. With *The Demon Lover* in production and Blake at college, I spent much of 1988 on the road, coming and going around the schedule of when the copyedited manuscript was due for reading, or when galleys would need to be proofed. My passport for the mid-1980s through the mid-1990s got so crowded the Passport Bureau issued me extra pages, and I'd had so many inoculations for every bug, everywhere, that when I tried to donate blood for a friend, the blood bank attendants laughed and turned me away.

Around the World

There was a September journey to Japan to keynote a conference on international feminism (with a snuck-in side trip to Kyoto, where I crouched for three hours watching how light shifts across the stones of the greatest Zen garden in the world). Other high points were time spent with an old friend, the writer-activist Keiko Higuchi, and our amusement at front-page newspaper articles analyzing what "message" I, as a radical feminist, must have meant to project when I was spied knitting during a panel. (I've knitted during meetings for years, as did Marilyn when she was in Parliament. That way, if things degenerate into blather, when you go home you know you'll have accomplished *some*thing, even if it's only sixty more rows.) Japan was also memorable because the shiny new state-of-the-techno-art Tokyo-Yokohama Women's Conference Center was about to bar entry at the conference to *hibakusha* women—atomic-radiation survivors and their generational descendants—who are still discriminated against in Japan. There was quite a scene and the conference nearly lost its keynote speaker on the spot, but the women were admitted in the end and have been welcome at the center ever since.

A month later, in October, a group of Sisterhood Is Global Institute members—Keiko from Japan, Madhu Kishwar from India, Mahnaz Afkhami from Iran, Marilyn from New Zealand, and myself from the United States—went to the Philippines by invitation of the Philippine Women's Movement to participate in a three-week-long series of meetings, "The Sisterhood Is Global Dialogues in the Philippines," with public and private assemblies throughout Manila, Negros, Mindanao, Olongapo, and the Cordillera region.[1] The Dialogues, expertly organized by the long-time feminist leader Anna Leah Sarabia of the Women's Media Circle in Manila, were with Filipina activists, academics, journalists, and politicians, and focused on topics ranging from reproductive freedom to the sex-tourism industry, from lesbian rights to women's unpaid labor, from nuclear power to religious fundamentalism, and from multinational cor-

---

[1] See *Sisterhood Is Global: Dialogues in the Philippines* (full transcripts, photos, and reports), edited by Rosario Garcellano, Elizabeth Lolarga, and Anna Leah Sarabia (Quezon City, Philippines: Circle Publications, Printworth, Women's Media Foundation, 1992). The Filipinas had requested specific nationalities because of their own priority issues: Keiko regarding Japan's exploitation of Filipinas as mail-order brides and for sex tourism; Madhu for India's regional similarity, solidarity, and democratic structures; Mahnaz because of the rise of Islamic fundamentalism in Mindanao; Marilyn because New Zealand was a Pacific country and a model nuclear-free zone; and me because of my work on global feminism and my opposition to the U.S. military bases in the Philippines.

porate landownership to the (now departed) U.S. military bases. I arrived a week ahead of the group, arranging for Marilyn to be invited early as well, in order to spend time in the north with, among others, indigenous tribeswomen and women of the underground New People's Army. The story of this trip appears as an essay in *The Word of a Woman*.

Those frequent-flier miles were adding up. The following year, 1989, UNRWA would bring me back to the Middle East for a return stay in the refugee camps, this time during the *Intifada*.[2] There would also be a sweep across the United States for *The Demon Lover* book tour, and a three-month stint as guest professor at the University of Canterbury in Christchurch, New Zealand, teaching feminist studies and American literature.

But that was by then my *third* trip to Aotearoa, which was beginning to feel like a second home.

Down on the Farm

It was back in 1988 that I'd visited Marilyn's farm for the first time. She'd then owned Atlantis, as she'd named it, for less than a year, and had poured most of her resources into the land, livestock, and farm buildings rather than the house. Consequently, that first stay of about ten weeks felt a bit like camping out indoors—but roughing it feels smooth enough when the beloved is finally waiting with open arms and a big grin and you're arriving in exultation at *last* into the relationship you feared never would stabilize. It was January, the height of antipodean summer. From that time on, I'd always be aware of the shimmer in time, a palpable shadowing of the seasons with their opposites. The Winter Solstice in New York meant in New Zealand beach picnics, foraging for oysters and mussels along rocky outcroppings, long desultory afternoons, and mornings dozing lightly beaded with fresh sweat from dawn lovemaking. But summer is a labor-intensive season on any farm, and Atlantis was no exception.

I cherished that farm, even when its farmer would drive me batty. Not that there were many problems that first stay. It was an idyll where we

---

[2] See "Women in the *Intifada*," in *The Word of a Woman*.

could enjoy the never-before-experienced luxury of calm days and nights together for weeks on end, broken only by a little socializing: she wanted to show me off to family and friends, and I wanted to win their approval. Mostly, though, we reveled in the seclusion of our own company and in the exclusivity of our passion—that elite dimension reserved for lovers. She kept repeating that being with me this way created "a sense of infinite trust and resurrection," and I felt we'd won through, on a love about which I'd all but given up hope. It was a validation of not having stopped. Shy at first, I soon nested busily in the house, which was large and drafty though brightly painted and glowing with pale wood window sashes, floors, and wainscoting. The kitchen that first year was barely worthy of the name, but eventually Marilyn put in a splendiferous kitchen—"the seductive kitchen," she called it, since she hoped it would be an incentive for me to move full-time to the farm, which was as much a nonoption in my mind as permanently settling in New York was in hers. But in 1988 even the minimalism of the house and its pseudo-kitchen served as a challenge, and I proudly produced some memorable meals from fresh produce plucked twenty steps away: there's nothing like pesto you grind from just-picked basil you've grown yourself.

The gardener in me was ecstatic. I stayed outdoors from early morning until dark, even in the light summer rain, because something always needed tending. There was a row of lush indigo-blue hydrangea bushes, three cutting gardens, and a variety of roses. There was a kitchen garden of herbs and lots of vegetables, including zucchini that endlessly proliferated like the Great God Pan crossed with the sorcerer's apprentice. A sandy asparagus bed produced delicate, crisp shoots. There were passion-fruit vines climbing the garage wall and an orchard—with apple, pear, olive, apricot, and lemon trees—down by the pond, where Canada geese had taken up residence along with visiting ducks and the periodic specter of a white heron. Blackberry bushes ripened around the property, and peppery watercress grew wild along one of the paths. That first stay—and, it must be admitted, every stay thereafter—I spent far too much money buying plants, trees, and bushes as gifts for the farm. It was such glee to roam through garden centers and take advantage of the exchange rate running heavily in my favor, so I became the kid in a candy store: I'll have a golden willow sapling and a claret ash and oh wow look at those mauve prunus trees . . . and then we'd drive home, kiss, and dig them in.

The farm had approximately forty acres of pasture, dotted with out-buildings and sheds. Dwelling thereon were three stately fat black sheep, whom I promptly named Winken, Blinken, and Nod individually, but col-lectively the Shearelles, since they tended to move as one, posture them-selves in a cluster, and then swivel their heads in unison as if on the lookout for a Motown talent scout. There was a henhouse (with a lopsided roost I built in a fit of atrocious carpentry), home to four fussy chickens striped black and white—designer hens—producing fresh eggs each morning. In later years, Marilyn would also pasture cattle for other farm-ers, violating her own rule that she would never raise animals intended for slaughter. But her dream for Atlantis centered on Angora goats: breeding them, providing stud service for other goat farmers, and selling the wool—mohair and cashgora—at market. Since New Zealand is primarily an agrarian country and many of its politicians and writers are also farmers, she saw farming as no contradiction to her now-nonelectoral political activities and the writing she hoped to do, thinking rather it would provide an income to help her pursue her other work. The reverse turned out to be true: she needed to do other work to keep the farm and its three hundred animals in the style to which they were accustomed.

In 1988 she was still learning about farming and goats, and I was meet-ing all this for the first time. Over the years, I became quite a handy goatherd, adept at chasing them, lunging, grasping their horns and wrestling them down for inoculations; at clipping their hooves, and at lur-ing them into zinc-medicated footbaths for the chronic foot-rot to which domesticated goats are prone. I knew how to sort sheared fleece for baling (watching for crimp, texture, and luster); when to apply fly-strike powder, how to rescue a buck who's trapped himself in the brambles, how to mix formula to bottle-feed a kid abandoned by its mother, and a hundred other skills of questionable value in downtown Manhattan.

The goats enchanted me. They get a bad press, so I can set the record straight here: they do *not* smell awful. During "tupping time" (mating), the bucks do give off, well . . . whiffs of raunchiness. But to sniff a doe or a kid is to inhale a milky fragrance accented with sweet clover. The does have enormous golden eyes with long eyelashes in dainty triangular faces that make them all look like Audrey Hepburn. The babies are exquisite: pearl frisks of affection who, once past the rubber-leg wobble stage, bleat demandingly, follow you around, and munch rose petals from your hand; if you obligingly sit down in the paddock, they will flatter you by vaulting onto your shoulders and standing on your head. Goats are quite intelligent; in this they are unlike sheep, who are modest with cause and skittish without it; and very unlike cattle, whose brains, secreted behind those glazed brown eyes moist with sincerity, seem never to have been contaminated by a single thought. Goats, like cats, find ways of going precisely where they shouldn't and of *not* being where anyone dares tell them to be. Fences are studied as provocations, gates as tests of tactical game theory. Pecking orders are won by virtue of intellect and seniority, not size or brawn, and cooperation in problem solving is not uncommon. Furthermore, a sense of humor is truly evident, especially in getting their own back at the taller two-legged goats who can open and close gates and think they own the place, but who at least dutifully deliver hay bales to the paddock in winter or in times of drought, and helpfully turn spigots to fill the water troughs.

When Marilyn began a teaching job at the University of Waikato, in Hamilton, it required her being away for three days and two nights a week, and the truth is I reveled in holding the farm on my own. This wasn't only because I could then write for hours undisturbed or scrub the house from top to bottom or indulge in an orgy of cooking and baking (*some*thing had to be done with all those lewd zucchini). It was also because I didn't have to wait for her proprietary permission to clean rusted junk out of a paddock or hose down the pigsty. Last, it was because I took pride in getting every creature to safe shelter when a cyclone warning was broadcast; in managing to rescue kids from the holes, thickets, and other inaccessible places where they'd wedge themselves; in striding out with a flashlight, slickered and gumbooted, into a windy rainstorm at 3:00 A.M. to find that lost kid I could hear bleating from two paddocks away. I loved the animals, naming many of them as they were born—Sibyl, her daughter Maya, and the twins Lillith and Eve being my special pets—and I relished their acceptance of me. My New York friends were incredulous that their urbanite pal could adapt so well. Unable to picture it, they kept blurring the facts, referring to my stays on a sheep farm in Australia. But I was a happy woman that first hot January—my skin tanned from the sun that had bleached my hair back to near blond, my legs scratched and bruised from butting goat-horns, my muscles aching, my hands scarred from gathering blackberries for jam, my heart at peace.

In February, politics descended on us. Sisterhood Is Global Institute members who currently or previously held public office in Iran, the Philippines, Tanzania, and the United States convened in Auckland for a series Marilyn was producing for New Zealand television called "What If Women Ruled the World?" Bella Abzug had come for the taping, so then we rented a car, took her on a tour of the geothermal area geysers, and brought her back to the farm for a visit. (I enjoyed having the rental car since I couldn't drive the farm truck, and Bella and I toodled around in it when Marilyn was busy. When I drove her to a shearing demonstration at a tourist mecca called Sheep World, I overheard the North American accents of a U.S. or Canadian couple in heated "t'is/t'ain't" argument, until the husband triumphantly demanded, "Then just *tell* me, Hazel, what in *God's* name would Bella Abzug be doing at Sheep World!" We validated Hazel, making her husband look—forgive me—sheepish.) Bella relaxed at the farm, declared she was addicted to my alliterative soup (cold curried cream of carrot), and even helped with the goats; the older does sensed someone of consequence and paid her serious attention. There were long dinnertime conversations and much laughter, and then Marilyn and I would nestle in bed together, giggling and whispering our postmortems about the day.

Life seemed good. Still, there was a hole in my heart from missing Blake. We spoke frequently by phone, and he came and went from college in Boston as usual, having the Village "pad" to himself when in New York, and beginning to assemble his first serious band. He also kept an eye on Bran, who was being fed and cat-sat by kind friends and neighbors on a revolving schedule, and who made his displeasure at my absence known by ignoring me for a full week after my return.

It was a period of discovery with Marilyn. Although ten years my junior, she'd been aged by her three Parliament terms into an intellectually cynical, elderly thirty-six. Both of us were old enough to be refreshed by doing new things, or doing favorite old things but this time together. The cry

"That's a first!" became a refrain, from her try at writing a sonnet to my attempt to back up a tractor, abysmal failures both. She was working at her book on economics and women's unpaid labor, and I was working on it with her, the in-house editor/lover, frequently wrestling with a combination of abstruse economics terminology plus Marilyn's tone, which tended to leak contempt at any reader who might not instantly grasp what she'd intended. Having more experience as a politician than as a writer, Marilyn regarded the act of writing as if it were speech delivery, political platform, or fiat, whereas for me writing has always been an assumed interactive communication, my way of being a social animal. Nevertheless, I'd found her a literary agent, helped her write the proposal, and helped locate a U.S. publisher, so now she had a contract and delivery date.[3] It seemed a satisfactory exchange: my bookish skills for hers in farming, for her expert knowledge of her country, and for her political advice. It felt nice to be useful on subjects I knew well, and nice *not* to have to be the capable one in every other area. In fact, it felt delicious to *follow* directions for a change—up to a point. Aware that we were both irascible, competitive women, I thought we deserved congratulations for equalizing things so well.

There were weeks on end at the farm where we'd joke that nothing happened, meaning nothing dramatic or earthshaking. I would ritually strip off my wristwatch when I arrived, rarely putting it on again until the day I left. My pace altered profoundly. The little datebooks for those months of my farm sojourns—year after year—go blank, except for the occasional notation of a jaunt into Auckland to hear a Kiri Te Kanawa concert or have dinner with friends or catch up on some movies at a film festival. Perhaps happy lovers, like Tolstoy's happy families, are all alike and have no history. Or perhaps, as Tom Stoppard wrote in *The Real Thing*, "Loving and being loved is unliterary. It's happiness expressed in banality and lust." The banality, or blank time, was spent in what I came to call "transparent

---

[3] She'd previously published a short book of essays—*Women, Politics, and Power* (Allen & Unwin, 1985)—in New Zealand and Australia, for which she'd asked me to write the foreword. That foreword, so unambivalently breathless in its praise, is the work of a doting lover who has, for the duration of its penning, ceased exercising what faculties of literary criticism or political analysis she might ever have possessed.

days": morning tea or coffee in bed, collecting the eggs and making breakfast while hearing the radio news, weeding or planting, shearing or baling
or making hay, treading the morning and afternoon rounds to check on the
animals; maybe driving into the one-block town, Wellsford, for a few groceries; picking up the mail, starting dinner, pouring a glass of wine and sitting on the stoop to watch the sun set over the hills while murmuring
about the day; then going inside to eat and bathe, read a bit, drift softly
toward love and then into sleep.

One thing the relationship with Marilyn did was help me play. Playing
was not something I'd done much in my childhood. I still don't play well
or easily. I tend to watch others—Blake when he was little, or adult lovers
who seem adept at having fun—to figure out how they *do* it. The years
with Kenneth weren't what you could call playful, partly because of my
own somberness and partly because of the tenor of the times. Iliana tried
to help me play, and we did have great frolics together; we went ballooning, for instance, and I learned how to dance Latin style—though she tried
in vain to teach me how to ride a bicycle. But the timing went against her,
given *Sisterhood Is Global* and the other crises of that period, and when
she tried to *force* me to play, it backfired. But Marilyn had two elements
on her side: the timing (I was ready for it) and the fact that she herself was
a workaholic, so she understood when and how one could *not* stop and
when and how one could. During the semester I taught at the University
of Canterbury, I'd fly up to the farm most weekends, unless Marilyn was
flying down to Christchurch, in which case we'd drive off to visit the
writer Keri Hulme or explore the South Island's rainforests, to Queens-
town to spy on penguins and seals, to Dunedin to view the nesting royal
albatrosses, to Kaikoura to sail out and gasp reverently at the sperm
whales, blowing and breaching fifty feet away.

Not that I shared all of Marilyn's definitions of fun. New Zealanders are
excessively hearty, athletic types. These are the people who invented
bungee jumping and extreme sports; they probably devised throwing
someone into the water and walking away as a method to teach swimming.
I didn't mind the milder activities, though Marilyn too was unable to teach
me how to ride a bicycle. (Karen had also tried. Apparently this is one of
those things that, once you've not learned it, you never forget how not to

learn it again.) But Marilyn was forever putting me into strenuous physical situations with little or no preparation: skiing, white-water rafting, black-water cave spelunking, hiking up steep mountains, climbing glaciers. I trundled along gamely and sometimes foolishly—despite falling down, spraining, cutting, and fracturing parts of myself, and in general hurting quite a lot. Why not politely decline? Well, the scenery *was* glorious, I was in love, and as usual I confused stopping with acknowledging defeat. It must also be confessed that I was hooked on playing the wide-eyed ingenue, even in my forties.

But the physical danger did frighten me: un-surefooted, I lacked confidence in my balance. I willed myself onward, yet those childhood warnings still commanded my reflexes: *stand back, duck, be careful, watch out; if you get hurt you could be fired and your family will starve!* With less than charitable derision, Marilyn began to consider me a physical coward, a judgment with which I readily concurred. That is, I concurred until Blake, Lois, Karen, and other friends reminded me that going into the refugee camps around Beirut at the height of Lebanon's civil war is not the act of a physical coward. But that had a purpose. Deliberately seeking out physical danger for the so-called thrill of it has always seemed to me at best a mystery and at worst a psychosis. Or perhaps it's the recourse of people who know no other way to experience life intensely—which, for good or ill, has certainly not been my problem.

Oh, the things we do for love. I would perpetuate this commute (twenty-three hours one-way, door to door, New York to Atlantis) through 1994, usually staying at the farm for a three-month period once a year. Marilyn would come to New York for four to six weeks annually, and we'd also meet in some third country where she'd had her way paid to do political consulting or I'd had mine paid for a journalism assignment or a book tour or lecture. Conferences helped, as did frequent-flier mileage. We managed to average half of each year together this way, meeting all over the world: Brazil, the Philippines, Australia, England, Indonesia, Canada, at least fifteen different U.S. cities, and all across New Zealand. I cherished her stays in New York, where my life felt of one piece, since I could be with both Blake *and* my lover in my own Greenwich Village rooftop bower. But I prized the days at Atlantis, felt affectionately adopted by

Marilyn's parents and her brother's family, made friends, picked up a few words of Maori as well as the Kiwi lingo that passes for English, learned the local roads (including how to drive on the left), and sleuthed out where to find decent olive oil and balsamic vinegar in a rural area—no small feat.

I wrote poetry in New Zealand. "Relativity," "The Found Season," and "Arbitrary Bread" (written 1987–88, all in *Upstairs in the Garden,* which I finished while at Christchurch) resonate with contentment. But early drafts of what would become "Country Matters"[4] revealed a darker under-side to Eden, and my own paper trail reminds me that "The Politics of Silence" was written at the farm in July of 1989, reflecting already famil-iar fault lines in the relationship. That essay, in *The Word of a Woman,* is about silence used as *power,* the power of emotional withholding, the power to make the other partner scurry and pursue, second-guess, offer multiple-choice answers, wheedle, cosset, and, in sum, do 90 percent of the work of communication—*except* when the quiet one is angry and then becomes *highly* articulate. You won't be aghast to learn that I—the apos-tate Jewish New Yorker with a romantic temperament and a theatrical past—was the usually communicative one, Marilyn the silent partner. Yet this went deeper than cultural differences. Then again, hadn't I been drawn to her partly for the understatement, her pastel shades so soothing after Iliana's neon colors? Hadn't I been electrified by her rage, righteously expressed against world injustices? Be careful what you wish for? Maybe don't wish at all.

We'd had our share of quarrels and some flat out fights: a screamer in Manila, a storming-out in Jakarta, shouters in London and Montreal, a sulk in Bali, and a whole repertory racked up in Auckland, at Atlantis, and at Perry Street. But we always made up, and I thought it reassuring that we had lovers' quarrels like average couples who lived together, preferring to ignore the fact that we had the *same* quarrel every time. Whatever its topic, its subject was power. "The Politics of Silence"—the essay about which more women have written to me in recognition than perhaps any

---

[4] In *A Hot January: Poems, 1996–1999* (W. W. Norton, 1999).

other I've published—is actually about silence as a conscious or unconscious tactic of control in intimate relationships, in this case same-sex lovers, but not necessarily so.[5] This dynamic has little to do with simplistic butch-femme roles, which didn't apply to us sexually, though certain of my friends (both heterosexual and lesbian) who were critical of Marilyn sometimes wrongly hypothesized the problem that way. This was about extremes of emotional parsimony and emotional extravagance. Now, when I read that essay or early drafts of poems I later unwisely revised into happy endings, I can trace an SOS code being sent to this later me, just as I can read the Mayday messages in poems written early in my marriage. (These days I pay closer attention to what I write at the time I write it.)

But with Marilyn the good times outweighed the bad, in frequency and in intensity. After a while, the bad came to equal, and then outweigh, the good in frequency. But when it *was* there, the good was *so* good that intensity won the day, especially given my romanticism. Marilyn herself confessed she was "clumsy in loving" (by which she decidedly did not mean love*making*), and admitted that she'd never been in a real relationship of any duration before. But I, hubristically, felt as surefooted in knowing how to communicate love as she did in knowing which stone to step on when crossing a brook, so I celebrated the prospect of an exchange. "Here's my hand," I said in effect, "see, put your foot there, now shift your weight here. You can risk it. There's no danger, my darling." I thought, said, and tried to demonstrate how we could work at the relationship, perhaps of necessity harder than most people, given the distance. It was unthinkable we wouldn't be lovers and partners for the rest of our lives, as we'd discussed, many times. Surely we were each arrogant enough to rise to that challenge. But in 1989 the challenges were about to escalate.

---

[5] In most heterosexual relationships, classically, the man is the taciturn one, the woman the one performing "the whole of love," playing "the full dialogue, both parts,"as Rainer Maria Rilke put it in *The Notebooks of Malte Laurids Brigge* (translated by M. D. Herter Norton, W. W. Norton, 1964). Rilke called on men, who had been "spoiled by easy enjoyment" to "learn the work of love, which has always been done for us." In common parlance, this phenomenon could be described as the "Herman? Honey? Is anything wrong? Please? *Talk* to me!" syndrome.

Top of the Masthead

The Demon Lover had come out that spring, as had Marilyn's book, titled, in the United States, *If Women Counted: A New Feminist Economics* (Harper & Row). We were on separate North American book tours at the same time, sometimes merrily overlapping in the same city, which felt glamorous and sexy: "Well, sweetheart, your hotel room or mine?" After the tours were finished, I went to the farm for several months, then Marilyn and I managed a September London rendezvous, since both books came out in the United Kingdom at the same time, too, and we could finesse the timing so our respective promotional appearances were in tandem. Afterward, I returned to the States for an autumn full of talks at colleges and women's centers.

The Demon Lover had helped generate discussion about violence against women, and I seemed in demand as a speaker. Fortunately, it was also a way to promote the Institute, which was engaging that subject constantly via its international Action Alerts. Care and feeding of the Institute, by the way, continued all along, for which read: fundraising. Furthermore, it was now time for the headquarters to move. According to its founding mandate, the Institute would shift locale every five years, so that it would never be under the hegemony of any one country and thus free to criticize all. (This is one of those grandiose feminist notions that in practice constitutes a logistical nightmare. Each subsequent shift has become more cumbersome, as the library and files expand. Recently, the Steering Committee has begun studying the possibility of adopting a different approach, with a permanent headquarters and branches around the world instead of a wandering HQ. At least with the Internet, the Institute can now always be found, wherever its physical location, at its Web site: www.sigi.org.)

In 1989, I'd persuaded Marilyn to host the Institute in New Zealand— such are the vagaries of political pillow talk—so Karen and I packed it up and shipped it there. During the next five years, under Marilyn's guidance, it would pioneer work on women's unpaid labor, among other issues. Still, much of the fundraising of necessity had to be followed up from the New York end. (Work from "the New York end" never quite relents. Following Marilyn's tenure, during the late 1990s the Institute was held metaphorical hostage to a single-issue, single-constituency favoritism approach by its executive director at the time, Mahnaz Afkhami, based in Baltimore, Maryland. This naturally upset many members, who thought "sisterhood" and "global" were words with meaning. I'd been keeping a low profile for fear of falling into what I call "founder's syndrome"—where the founder persists in looming over an institution, trying to control it—but in this case the membership pressure became too strong, forcing me to intervene.[6])

Periodic Institute crises aside, in the fall of 1989 I was in negotiations with the BBC for a never-to-materialize series on terrorism based on *The Demon Lover.* Meanwhile, the United Nations Development Programme (UNDP) and World Health Organization (WHO) had approached me with a proposal for a book they wanted me to compile and edit on women and HIV/AIDS. Sliding toward another financial downswing at the time, I was seriously considering the UNDP/WHO project—but in dread, since working with bureaucracies gives me migraines. Then Gloria and I met for a bite at the Empire Diner on Tenth Avenue, and it turned out to be such a momentous meeting we closed it by throwing discretion out the window and sharing an indecently large piece of Mississippi mud cake.

When Gloria had called, I thought she wanted to meet for another pep talk about the new book she was wrestling with, which would eventually become *Revolution from Within* (Little, Brown, 1992), but which was giving her a hard time in its birthing. Instead, we discussed the magazine, whose perils continued. The sale of *Ms.* two years earlier to the Australian

---

[6] Mahnaz, an elegant woman and devout fundraiser, had been a cabinet minister under the shah of Iran, a connection she unfortunately has not renounced to this day. Awash in sisterly sentiment, I'd chosen her as the Iranian contributor to *Sisterhood Is Global* because she was an exile marked for death by the mullahs who'd seized Iran, and she seemed to be a feminist. I'd defended her to Institute members, even backing her for the post of executive director when the Institute's term in New Zealand ended. So the ensuing debacle was my fault. Mahnaz turned out to have quite conservative politics, to function autocratically in disregard of the Institute's democratic procedures and original vision, and to get highly defensive about the treasurer's regard for fiscal transparency. The moral might be "Once a cabinet minister under a dictator, always a cabinet minister under . . ." or, in my case, "Sisterhood is stupid." But there's good news. In January 2000, the headquarters moved to Montreal—becoming again democratic, inclusive, and multi-issue under the leadership of its new president and chief officer, the distinguished Canadian feminist Greta Hofmann Nemiroff. Its Web site—www.sigi.org—remains the same.

firm Fairfax had devolved into another sale, to Matilda Productions (two women formerly with Fairfax), but their glitzy approach, including recipes, fashion, and movie-star coverage, had driven the loyal readers up a tree and the magazine down a hole. Now it had been sold again, this time to Lang Communications. Dale Lang, the president and CEO, had a stable of *Ms.* imitators (*Working Woman* and *Working Mother*), but now he'd acquired the prototype—which he wanted mostly in order to use its mailing list and subscribers for his *Ms.* clones. Dale had frozen publication but put the staff on hold, saying he might reconstitute *Ms.* as a newsletter, since it probably no longer had a sufficient audience to survive as a magazine. (This was during another of those intervals when the press is re-announcing that feminism surely *is* dead *now;* "post-feminist era" pronouncements were being babbled widely.) Gloria was fighting for the life of her child again. She'd been struggling for the magazine's preservation in one way or another since its founding (at that point for seventeen years)—always insisting to herself and the rest of us that *this* new development would make *all* the difference: surely *this* advertiser, *this* sponsor, *this* investor. It's a lovably irksome tendency of hers, the exuding of deafeningly sentimental optimism—probably a residual survival syndrome from East Toledo. I respect it as her version of refusing to quit. But this time she was tired. Maybe *Ms.* had reached the point of no return? Should she drive a stake in its heart as so many of our mutual friends were counseling? Should she finally just let it go?

Stop? She was asking *me* this question? Do we always seek out the person who will answer us in precisely the way we long to be answered?[7] I told her that, as her friend, I thought she *should* let go, for her health's sake and so that once and for all she could put her writing first and take herself seriously as a writer in ways she'd never permitted herself to do. I added that I thought the magazine had recently become so shallow and boring that I no longer read it, that I wasn't surprised its readership had dropped precipitously, and that were it to continue in the same manner it *would* be better off nonexistent. Then I undid all that good advice by say-

---

[7] Of course we do. Gloria has made it a practice for years to show me raw copy and ask whether I think some phrase or political position is "too radical"—knowing full well I'll answer, "Not by half." This now falls somewhere between a ritual and a running joke.

ing that I also feared if *Ms.* folded the media might misperceive the import
of that and announce it as yet another false proof that the Women's Movement was dead. I added that women I encountered at speeches or meetings across the country were concerned about the magazine's future, that
they wanted it de-glitzed but alive.

She beamed. She said she'd been hearing the same thing. Then she
asked, as if she'd just that minute thought of it, "Why don't you consider
being the editor in chief?"

I burst out laughing and shook my head, reminding her that I knew zero
about editing a magazine. "No problem," she shot back, "you've compiled
and edited two now-classic anthologies. Think of this as a series of temporary anthologies." I laughed again and reminded her that I'd sworn never
to *do* another anthology, that if life were discovered elsewhere in the cos-
mos and turned out to be sexist, somebody else had better do *Sisterhood Is
Galactic*.

"Well then, *don't* think of it as an anthology. But you once were a book
editor. And you've written and edited lots of *Ms.* pieces."

"Editing a book or an individual article is different from editing a magazine. That much I know."

Gloria's genius lies in her persuasiveness, which is why what she calls
the Real Writer in her repeatedly has been sacrificed to the lobbyist/
fundraiser/popular educator/media personality. She abandoned the
anthology simile and segued into two areas where she knew I was highly
susceptible to temptation.

First, she got me talking about what sort of wish list I'd have for the
magazine *if* (hypothetically, you understand) it *could* be saved, how I'd ide-
ally like to see it change. We began to discuss animatedly all the things
we'd wanted to see *Ms.* do over the years, but had been unable for various
reasons to pull off. I said that the magazine I'd like to read would go
against conventional wisdom. It would never have movie-star covers but
would run excellent poetry, first-rate fiction, and the humor some dullards
claim feminists don't have; it would feature major international as well as
national coverage (news *and* analysis); it would unapologetically run feminist theory, not the pedantic kind but the experiential real-life kind that's
always fueled this movement. I said I'd like to see a *Ms.* as striking to look
at in design—with generous amounts of art and photojournalism—as it

would be to read. I said I'd love to see cutting-edge investigative journalism in *Ms.*, but since that often meant confronting the corporate world, it would require freedom from advertisers' subtle or blatant control over editorial content.

Gloria said she thought we might be able to convince Lang of this different vision—including making the magazine reader-supported and free of all advertising. Lang Communications had the resources to make this possible. Then she lodged her second point. It also had the capital, she thought, to pay a decent executive salary, hardly the case in the old days at *Ms.* Good grief. Editorial freedom *and* personal solvency? An effective one-two punch, as my clever friend knew. To make certain, she added the final suave touch, leaning across the table to remind me of the first time I'd ever walked into the *Ms.* offices after their 1972 pilot issue, when I'd warned them to stop taking sexist ads or run the risk of us radical feminists taking over the magazine.

"Here's your chance," she whispered, her eyebrows waggling provocatively in the Groucho Marx imitation she does so well. "We'll stop taking ads, and why don't you take over the magazine?"

I believed not one scintilla of it would happen. But the idea of such a mini-revolution and, yes, the irony inherent in it, called for a celebration—which is where the Mississippi mud cake came in.

Clearly, I was wrong. It happened. There were weeks of meetings, with Ruth Bower, who was then the publisher (frantic, as any publisher would be, at the notion of stepping off the edge and flying ad-free), and with Dale Lang, who refused to be my antagonist no matter how I tried to cast him in the role. To my growing unease, he thought my vision for the magazine was innovative. The man was perhaps getting desperate since he was now being blizzarded by complaint letters from *Ms.* readers demanding their magazine back, plus pressure from his own feminist daughter—and god only knows *what* Gloria was persuading *him* of behind the scenes. Although he exercised final say over his other magazines before they shipped, he even agreed to a total hands-off policy regarding our editorial autonomy. Emboldened yet vigilant, I warned him that betrayal of our agreement would evoke a simple consequence: "Mess with me, and I'll quit and hold a press conference." (There's a peculiar freedom in thinking that something is impossible to attain and that you're not even sure you want it, anyway.) As for corporate bottom lines or management chains of command, I was *so* not impressed: "Dale, let me put it clearly. You: Creon. Me: Antigone. Except I do not intend to wind up walled into a cave." At his dazed look, I snobbishly began to explain who Creon and Antigone were, to have him reply in an injured tone that he'd once taught literature and wasn't a noodlehead.

He wasn't a noodlehead, because "the liberated *Ms.*" soon became the cash cow of Lang Communications, bringing in millions of dollars and keeping his other magazines—reliant on ads at a time when print ads were declining—afloat. But that was farther down the road. At first he said he'd foot the bill only for a make-or-break two issues, after which we had to have achieved a circulation of 75,000 or kaput. We hammered out the details: publication bimonthly instead of monthly, but with a bigger magazine, a "magabook" of one hundred pages per each double issue, those pages all editorial copy, no ads. I told Gloria I couldn't guarantee we'd survive beyond the two trial issues, but I'd guarantee they'd be historic. If we went out, it would be with a bang, not a whimper.

Yet when I realized this was all actually going to happen, in late December of 1989, I cried for three days over the impending loss of personal freedom. I knew myself well enough to realize I would become as obsessively involved with this endeavor as I had with the anthologies, that it would *matter* too much, that I'd care too deeply and work too hard—which would leave little time for my own writing or the more civilized rhythms of the life I'd begun to lead. I also was having panic attacks at the idea of being a boss, and felt like a total imposter in terms of editing a magazine. I called up Suzanne Levine, then editor in chief of *Columbia Journalism Review,* and wailed, "Help! I've made all these nonnegotiable demands, thinking I was perfectly safe—and to my *horror* the man has met them. Oh *Suz.* Now what do I do?"

Her advice was diamond-like: hard, faceted, bright. Insist on an office with a door you can lock. Be sure you have your own assistant, *not* a shared one. Encourage input, but *forget* collectivity. When you must take unpopular measures, do what you have to do, then go walk around the block and *let* the staff talk about you behind your back. The administrative part is always drab, so get to the creative part as fast as possible, and you'll begin to feel your own competence again. Start making assignments: think of pieces you want to publish and writers you want to read. Then put them together and *Go*.

She was right on every count. There were budgetary cutbacks, which meant the ordeal of having to fire some staff, though Gloria and I both took pains to network and recommend people for openings elsewhere. When I then assembled the demoralized remainder (by then they'd been kept dangling about the magazine's fate for months), I tried to infect them with vision and fervor for this new *Ms*. Fortunately, Mary Thom, the executive editor, and Joan Philpott, the copyeditor—both on board since 1972—were still there and could provide expertise and consistency. My other pillar of support was Helen Zia, an astute young Chinese American feminist journalist who'd come to *Ms*. just before the latest sale; she'd already accepted a job elsewhere since rumors were rife about *Ms*.'s demise—but she *got* the vision, taking a risk and even a salary cut to stay on as managing editor and, later, executive editor.

All these formal titles threw me. I'd assumed we'd return to the pre-Australian-era format in which all names on the masthead were listed alphabetically with no titles, and was unprepared for a protest from the market-oriented younger women, who wanted titles they could list on their résumés. Well, the original alphabetical masthead *did* suffer from hypocrisy. Gloria was already nationally known in 1972, and it was disingenuous to think that a famous name listed alphabetically with lessknown ones would be read, regarded, or treated alphabetically. It hurt all concerned. For decades, Gloria has tried to tell the world that she's *never* been the editor of *Ms*., but simply one of its founders, a contributor, and a consulting godmother. She's also been its most consistent protector-defender, having over the years groveled to advertisers, raised funds, corralled investors, done endless publicity and promotion, suggested writers and subjects, and written extensively for the magazine—but editing is *not* her forte. Yet magazines don't just happen. The untitled editor in chief from 1972 to 1987 was, in fact, Suzanne Braun Levine.[8] In my first editorial (July/August 1990), I set the record straight, naming Suzanne editor

---

[8] In her later incarnation as a book author, Suzanne has most recently published *Father Courage: What Happens When Men Put Family First* (Harcourt, 2000).

emerita and noting that for all those years she "steadily performed editorial, administrative, and production miracles with a maximum of grace and a minimum of acknowledgement." The more I tottered along in her footsteps, the more I realized this was an understatement. *She'd* had to deal with *advertising* as well as being "disappeared" into the alphabet.

At the new *Ms.* I'd also hoped to reestablish the more familial tone of the original: the Tot Lot, the friendships, the feminist alternative rituals. But you can't go home again, especially given corporate ownership plus some younger staff members who'd attained maturity during the don't-rock-the-boat Reagan-Bush years. Nevertheless, when I learned that people hated their assigned office cubicles, I urged them to rearrange the space as they wished, even to tearing down the dividers. At first incredulous, they came in the next day with screwdrivers and hammers—and I heard them chattering and laughing. I went into my office (*with* walls and door, per Suzanne's advice) and exhaled. The vitality level was up. The sound of women's laughter was a sign of health.

Things took off from there. The first six months of 1990 were spent on reorganizing, redesign, promotion, and building inventory. Then, that July, our first print run of 60,000 copies sold out within a week, as did the second print run. Before the next issue even came out, we'd not only topped Lang's stipulated circulation goal of 75,000, but were well over 100,000. The numbers would climb from there on in, nearing 250,000 by the time I left, with subscribers in 117 countries, newsstand sales throughout the English-speaking world, and international editions in the planning stages. I'd been told we'd be lucky to sell 5,000 copies on newsstands unless we ran celebrity covers—but within the first year we were selling 50,000 newsstand copies featuring real people's faces and beautiful art. Freedom from advertisers was heady, as Gloria noted in the exposé of advertising censorship she wrote for the first issue. In our "No Comment" section that traditionally lambasted sexist ads sent in by readers, our premiere issue targeted ads that had appeared in the old *Ms.*

Readers loved the magazine's intelligence, the regular diet of fine writing,[9] and especially international feminist coverage they could get

---

[9] I called on old and new friends and brought them into our pages, some returning after years of refusing to publish in *Ms.*, others appearing for the first time. The list includes

nowhere else. My policy was that coverage of other countries would be done by women writers *from* those countries, unless there was some compelling reason otherwise, to avoid insensitive mistakes wrought by outsiders, however well-meaning. I was especially proud of our exclusives, where we made news as well as reported it: the first stories on women in Eastern Europe as the Berlin Wall came down; coverage on the Gulf War from women on the ground in Saudi Arabia, Kuwait, Jordan, Israel, West Bank, and even Iraq; the story of Tiananmen Square told by Chai Ling, its woman student leader; and the story that we broke before anyone else would believe it: the brothel/death camps and ethnic rapes of hundreds of thousands of women in the former Yugoslavia. Prizes began pouring in, from feminist organizations through the American Library Association to five Utne Reader awards in one year, taking special note of our investigative journalism: such cover stories as Helen Zia's piece on women in the Ku Klux Klan, Theresa Funiciello's on welfare and the poverty establishment, and our Special Reports—on young feminists, on violence against women, on sexual abuse, on breast cancer. We did the first national survey on women, race, and racism, and we spent half a year producing the Election Guide to Women Candidates as a supplement to the September/October 1992 issue.[10] I loved affirming feminist classics: the *Our Bodies Ourselves* team—the Boston Women's Health Collective—now wrote our regular health column, and Patricia Ireland, president of the National Organization for Women, delivered her "The State of NOW" address in our pages. But I also liked putting together surprise combinations: a music conversation between K. D. Lang and Lesley Gore, Eleanor Smeal on the need for a new political party, Bella Abzug on widowhood, Sinead O'Connor on motherhood, Alice Walker covering Winnie Mandela's trial.

Margaret Atwood, Sandra Cisneros, Rita Dove, Andrea Dworkin, Louise Erdrich, Marilyn French, Marilyn Hacker, Joy Harjo, Bell Hooks, June Jordan, Maxine Kumin, Ursula K. LeGuin, Audre Lorde, Toni Morrison, Grace Paley, Marge Piercy, Adrienne Rich, Ninotchka Rosca, and Jane Wagner—and that was just in the *first* few issues.

[10] The guide was, as Mary Thom wrote in *Inside Ms.*, "the most comprehensive national survey of female candidates [and their positions on issues] ever compiled, listing nearly twenty-five hundred candidates for Congress, state legislatures, statewide office, or mayor of major cities." Perhaps coincidentally, 1992 was the year that a record number of women won public office in the United States.

We had our detractors. Boycotts were attempted by the Moral Majority and their ilk, protesting our coverage of lesbian women, atheist ethics, old women's sexuality. But this *Ms.* seemed to kindle new feminist fires, emerging as the voice of a revived movement. During the late 1991 Senate confirmation hearings on Clarence Thomas's Supreme Court nomination, when Anita Hill's sexual-harassment testimony galvanized the nation, the press assumed this *Ms.* was "behind it all." Reporters kept phoning me as if we were the war room of a nationwide plot that had prompted the firestorm of letters and faxes raining on the Capitol in support of Hill. In truth, our lead time meant we couldn't cover the subject until three months later, which we then did in-depth, with analyses from the feminist theorists Patricia J. Williams, Eleanor Holmes Norton, Barbara Smith—and Anita herself, choosing to break her media silence in *Ms.*

I drove the staff crazy about language, aiming for the level of scrupulousness we'd employed at *Sisterhood Is Global*. This meant vigilance about unthinking sentences like "You'd have to be blind not to understand the need for affirmative action"—since some of our readers got the magazine on braille. It meant watchfulness about using "riot" in connection with communities of color: the white community riots, too—by moving to the suburbs or cutting back social services. It's not good enough to say or write Native American, African American, and so on, if you don't also use European American instead of "white," which otherwise becomes the generic. It's not accurate to say "working women" because full-time homemakers *work*; for women with paid jobs one can say "employed women" or "women in the labor force." It's not fair to refer, as WHO does, to "maternal" mortality rates instead of "women's" mortality rates when discussing abortion. Language reflects and defines reality. But this sort of effort requires consistent, nagging attention to detail.

I'd told Gloria and Dale that I'd do it for one year: revision and relaunch the magazine, get it on its feet, then move on. But it's hard to argue with success. This time they were *both* persuasive, and the year stretched to two, then three. While extremely proud of our accomplishment (and grateful to be out of debt and have health insurance!), I nonetheless felt the toll the job was taking on me. What I'd feared had come to pass: my workaholism was in full play. There were some issues on which I hands-on line-edited two-thirds of all the copy. I worked an average of seven-day weeks, twelve-to-fourteen hour days—*my choice*, assuredly—but then I would turn grouchy when not all staff members shared that commitment. (Bella reminded me that when she was in Congress and would moan, "Oy, oy! My staff is killing me!" her late husband, Martin, always answered her the same way. "Bella," he'd smile, "your standards are showing.")

I loved hearing from the euphoric readers, and I enjoyed the editing, especially writers' pleasure at encountering a *writers'* editor. I tolerated the press interviews and promotional appearances because they could also be used as forums for political organizing; besides, the four-year-old little girl in me was an old hand at such things. But the administrative problems were incessant. I'm not good at business management and dislike it hugely; in order to perform at all well in this realm I seem to turn into Attila the Hon again. I chafed at spending over two-thirds of my time needing to respond to crises—corporate crises, subscription-fulfillment crises, printer's crises—heading off disaster, being reactive instead of proactive. This focus on averting the negative made me feel like a seventeenth-century weeder woman.[11] Furthermore, since I worked hard to defend the staff, protecting them from corporate ravages in ways they never even knew, I grew as tired of being deplored by them for my standards as I did of being resented by them for depriving them of their complaints. As time went on, I was sinking into a distastefully martyrish attitude.

But here was the true source of woe: although I churned out an editorial every issue and thousands of letters and memos, there was no space for real writing. *Upstairs in the Garden*—in production before I took the *Ms.* job—came out in 1990, poignantly reminding me that I'd once been a poet. *The Mer Child: A Legend for Children and Other Adults* was published in 1991—but I'd actually written it for Blake years earlier. Florence Howe, founder and director of The Feminist Press, wanted to revive its children's series in the Nineties, and thought *The Mer Child* would be the perfect choice for that; since I was earning a salary and could afford to do

---

[11] In seventeenth-century England and much of Europe only men were permitted to be gardeners and planters; women were stuck with the work of weeding. There's an effigy of a weeder woman in the gardens of Woburn Abbey. Although not an old woman, she's bent almost double from her labor.

so, I contributed the book to the press, waiving royalties and giving my literary agent more indigestion.[12] *The Word of a Woman* came out in 1992—but it was a collection of previously written essays, although I did write fresh continuity to contextualize them (the second edition, published in 1994, encompasses later writing, including several of my *Ms.* editorials). All this publishing made it seem as if I was prolific, but the writer in me was wasting away as the administrator-mogulette, my personal Ms. Hyde, took command.

Certainly the daily exercise of power, even in such limited circumstances, was intoxicating. One could enjoy and detest it at the same time—like listening to rumor, which permits you simultaneous curiosity about the rumor and disdain for the person who relays it. But the brand of power in this kind of guilty pleasure ultimately corrodes a creative artist. One begins to identify with one's authority and its product, which produces defensiveness when either is challenged. There's a moral danger in the defensiveness blurring toward feelings of superiority—a danger heightened by the reality that, frankly, in the marketplace one *is* surrounded by blockheads. My characteristic impatience didn't help in all this. When turned against myself, it allowed no leeway for whining. When aimed at others, it revived the efficiency fascist in me. (It's disquieting to realize that being alert to Hannah Arendt's concept of "the Eichmann within" doesn't mean you can stop him from emerging; he must be re-imprisoned again and again.)

So. I was solvent at last. I had the money to buy concert tickets or to go shopping or take vacations. But now I had no time for any of that. Nor was I able to make myself *care* less about the magazine, walk through the paces, regard it as just a job. Back to square one, trying to be anything any-

---

[12] During the 1980s, when Doubleday had been my publisher, there was a plan afoot to publish *The Mer Child* with Judy Chicago as illustrator. Judy and I were enthusiastic at the idea of collaborating, and for a while it looked as if we might pull it off. She wanted to illumine the text rather than simply illustrate it: to draw or etch, then paint, directly onto the plates from which the book pages would be photographed. This meant that each copy of the book would in effect be an original work of art—a lovely idea. Unfortunately, it also meant that each clothbound copy would retail for about $250, and each lowly paperback for a mere $175. Understandably, Judy saw no problem with *The Mer Child* being an art book. Understandably, I wanted to reach average people, who couldn't afford such prices. The deal fell through.

one wants me to be, I'd catch a plane for New Zealand for two weeks, twice a year, trying to morph back into a loving partner. But I'd have to leave right after closing an issue (usually at 1:00 A.M.), and by the time I unwound at the farm I was due back on the plane to New York. What's more, even at Atlantis the faxes and phone calls kept on coming. At the end of each eight-week production cycle, I'd take to the road—if not New Zealand, then Australia or Indonesia to meet Marilyn; or Japan, England, Canada, and around the United States on promotion for Ms. The tension was chronic. I was smoking two and a half packs of cigarettes a day and had chipped a tooth from grinding while asleep. I was becoming a glum, truculent person. But recognizing the pattern made me feel no less help-less to change it.

In 1992 I decided I had to leave, and prepared to turn the reins over to Helen Zia. I thought it well past time that Ms. be edited by a woman of color—and besides, Helen was ready and, I thought, ideal for the job. Then she fell in love and announced she was moving to the West Coast to be near the beloved. Devastated, I tried to convince her of the benefits of long-distance relationships, but she'd made up her mind.[13] Gloria seemed relieved, joking that in twenty years I'd still be saying, "I'm leaving," just as she had, but never managing it, just as she hadn't. Actually, I felt trapped and my resentment was building—but with absolutely no one to reproach for what was externally an ideal situation, and with only myself to blame for my own work patterns. "Bletting" is a wonderful word that gardeners know; it means permitting something to overripen, a form of controlled rotting. I was bletting my resentment.

Even I didn't know how much until, at the close of 1992, I gave a speech and poetry reading at the University of Wisconsin at Madison. Donna Shalala was then chancellor, and Gerda Lerner professor of history. I hadn't seen either one in ages, but they both came to the reading, bless them. Afterward, we had coffee, our conversation centering on hopes for the just-elected Clinton administration and record number of women in the incoming Congress (I remember telling Donna that we would raise hell if she didn't garner a cabinet post; she offered an enigmatic smile and

---

[13] Helen went on to write *Asian American Dreams: The Emergence of an American People* (Farrar, Straus & Giroux, 2000).

demurely waved her hand). Then she dashed off to a late meeting and Gerda drove me back to my hotel, in the process giving me a gift of incalculable value.

She asked what new book I was writing. When I couldn't answer, she demanded in her brusque Teutonic manner when I was leaving *Ms.*, which was "all very important for a magazine of course but really, Robin, that's not who you are." Suddenly it poured out of me, and Gerda listened with empathy but no sympathy—and with stern advice to do what it was time to do. I will always be in her debt, because as I got out of the car, I was already en route to resigning.

Dramatic decisions can take an irritatingly long time to put into effect. It would be seven more months (I gave the longest notice of departure in the history of magazine publishing) until I could step down as editor in chief. First I had to lure Marcia Ann Gillespie, a former *Ms.* editor and for years editor in chief of *Essence*, to come on board as executive editor, learn the ropes of this new ad-free, international *Ms.*, and take over for me. Then we had to fight racism at Lang Communications to ensure "the succession"; they actually expressed fear that Marcia might make the magazine "too black." But it all worked out. At this writing, Marcia is still editor, she and the magazine having survived yet another corporate takeover and, subsequently, a new, independent ownership by all-female investors. (*This* new structure, Gloria notes, will make *all* the difference.)

As for me, I spent those last seven months pushing myself to new depths of overwork with extra lectures, in order to salt away every penny. Then, in the spring of 1993, I bought a co-op, my current apartment, the first turf I've ever owned—though to be honest the bank owns it and I have a small share. When I first saw it, I thought *Be still, my heart*: not far from Perry Street, on a quiet, tree-lined block in the Village, with a working fireplace—and a real earth garden out back. It was a bit seedy (thus affordable), so renovations were necessary, and they began as I camped out in the midst of them. But I didn't mind. I was jubilant, facing a future with the home I wanted, where I wanted it, and time to write ahead of me. I longed to settle in at my desk as soon as renovations were complete. But I'd promised Marilyn I'd come to the farm for a full six months starting that September. I felt I'd neglected her and had to keep my promise. Instead of following my instincts, I followed my heart.

Persephone Redux

Marilyn had begun steady pressure on me to resettle in New Zealand, starting with her blushing "proposal" in a Chicago hotel room during the synchronous book tours in 1989; the proposal was, she said, a first for her. It moved me, but the pressure to resettle disturbed me. On the one hand, the proposal was finally the gesture of authentic full commitment I'd longed for her to make for so many years. On the other hand, the resettlement aspect was unrealistically imbalanced. She'd flatly said she'd never even consider the reverse move to New York, yet she dismissed as inconsequential my concerns: over leaving Blake and friends and my own culture, changing citizenship, having no effective political role as an outsider in New Zealand, and not much means of survival. I thought her increasing pressure on this matter was largely a byproduct of my having been unable to spend the usual time at Atlantis we'd both grown to depend on—so I'd sworn to come for a full half-year stay once I was free of the editorship and the apartment renovations were finished. If that worked well, maybe we could institutionalize it: the Persephone Plan, six months down under together, six up north. (How that particular myth did haunt me!) Now I saw no way to delay that first promised six months without aggravating the situation.

In her own fashion, Marilyn had thoroughly enjoyed my three and a half years as *Ms.* editor in chief. She'd counseled me to take the post and had been supportive at first, though in time she confessed wistfully that she'd "been spoiled by being the center of attention for so long," and missed that. But she was pragmatic and heartily approved the change in my finances. She also liked having articles published in the magazine, and relished coming to New York while her lover was editor and could provide special perks, like press seats to women's tennis finals. Having been famous in varying degrees on and off since the age of four, I was underwhelmed by my revived public status (media-celebrity circuit, markedly different from literary or political circles), but I was amused that it excited her. My darling had never fully owned up to her own ambivalent love of power and fame during her parliamentary days; she functioned from a temperament and culture uninterested in living "the examined life." So she sent myriad double messages she couldn't explain. Buy the apartment, move to New Zealand. Keep the job, quit the job. They seemed to boil

down to her wanting to have all the more to herself someone she perceived the world wanting to have to *itself*. In this equation, the actual *me*
was absent, but I was yet unaware of that.

I was, however, sad at leaving my new home—freshly painted, pristine,
mine. I'd spent the summer working on it and rediscovering life after *Ms.*
with Blake and friends. Marilyn had visited briefly, celebrating and helping me start my own garden. I hadn't begun writing but assumed I would
shortly. Reluctant to leave, I sent two trial balloons over the telephone to
her. Once I hazarded that maybe I should wait a few months and settle in
before coming for the long stay? Her reply was sharp and bitter, so I let the
question drop. Then, a few weeks before leaving for the farm, I felt it only
fair to remind her that I'd just stopped smoking, was still exhausted and
not yet fully detoxed from the magazine stress, and had an even shorter
than usual patience from years of having dealt with corporate dolts. I
warned her that I felt raw, as if I lacked a skin's surface, and that I had less
margin for enduring bouts of the silent treatment. Did she really want me
around in such a state? All the better, she said. It'll be a refreshing switch,
you having tantrums instead of me; I can take care of *you* for a change.
Jump, my love, she said, trust me, I'm here with the net.

I trusted. I jumped. You may be less surprised than I was to learn that I
hit the ground in a thousand pieces. Certainly there had never been a time
in the entire by then fourteen-year stormy relationship totally free of
susurrations intimating it wouldn't work. But if I'd had second sight, I'd
have had it with double vision, needing two different prescriptions, since
love invests everything it perceives with itself. So, for example, in the early
years, Marilyn's impressive enjoyment of grass and wine had seemed to
signify both her spontaneity and her self-discipline, especially since,
unlike me, she could be totally stoned while functioning, driving, giving
interviews, or delivering speeches—and frequently was. But now she was
bombed before noon, and this time the substances helped her hide
behind higher walls of silence instead of letting her break through, as they
sometimes had previously. Fortunately, though I hardly saw it as fortunate
at the time, my own state of weakness strengthened me, in that I was
unable to put up with hurtful behavior of hers that I'd excused in the past.

There's a phenomenon in certain groups where one person can become
what I call the "designated activist" emotionally. Once that person absents

her/himself, the others face a survival test: "Oh dear. We don't have her around to feel/think/do it for us anymore. Does that mean we have to do it for ourselves?" Until that moment she has functioned as the repository, oracle, and articulator of their politics, audacity, passion—all projected on to her. The same is true in some intimate relationships. I'd willingly assumed (possibly grabbed, even hoarded?) the role of designated activist in the partnership with Marilyn, egotistically thinking that my exhibitions of loving—from small gestures to large commitments, from journeying more to her shores than she did to mine, from vulnerably revealing my emotions and thoughts—would inspire hers. Yet now, when I was for the first time too weary to continue as the designated emotional communicator, she was unable to pick up the slack.

How long does it take for a lover to understand that the source wound in the beloved can be healed only by that person her/himself, and *not* by the lover, no matter how hard the lover tries? I had known for years that I was in love with a woman pulsing with conceded need, denied pain, and unacknowledged rage, but I arrogantly thought *I* could heal her. Queen of the codependents, I'd managed to change the sex and gender of the beloved this time, but the plot was dismally familiar.

It was a grim six months. Aware that I'd recently stopped smoking, she defiantly began smoking tobacco as well as grass. When I slipped a lumbar disk doing farm work and could barely sit because of sciatic nerve pain, she swept us off on a motoring vacation that consisted of days sitting in the car. Her verbal sniping could be cruel; she knew my weak spots and took accurate aim. It certainly seemed she was trying to tell me something, in a not very subtle emotionally sadistic manner. But when I said as much, she refused to discuss it and her silent treatment set in. I should have left. Instead, I wondered if my physical pain was making me oversensitive; I told myself she must be acting out her hurt that I wouldn't shift my whole life to New Zealand; I ached for her as I would for a needy child of two, which seemed the level of maturity to which her scarring childhood had stunted her. I did start packing, twice—only to relent after her tearful apologies. Though the prognosis was bad, quitting after so many years and miles of loving seemed an intolerable waste.

But at least this time I watched myself not stop.

In fairness, I believe that over the years Marilyn *tried to try,* that as she herself said, she went further toward feeling and expressing emotion with me than she had done in her whole life. Her tragedy was in lacking the means. She'd joke bitterly that previous lovers had nicknamed her Ice Queen, and confessed she'd never been sexually faithful for so long as in our relationship—not that either of us had expressly required that. She tried to grasp my concern about being stranded at the farm—without a support system of my own or even a vehicle when she'd drive off after a fight—so for a combined Christmas and birthday gift she bought me a sweet little secondhand car. She did *try*, in her way. But what she gave she often qualified, regulated, or rescinded. Poetry notes it more accurately: " . . . you never meant to be ungenerous. This was your way / of giving: partial, controlled, revocable. As if you mistook yourself / for a jealous god . . ."[14] Any critique, no matter how mild, and anything less than effusive gratitude, for even her most minimal effort, made her furious: "Then why bother?"

Given the pattern in my marriage, I thought the substance abuse might be my fault, that I might've enabled it—until her oldest friends sadly told me her pattern predated me by years. Later I would realize my pattern was in being *drawn* to hers. Blake and my other friends had never quite cottoned to her, and some had been openly negative about the relationship, although they hadn't revealed the full extent of their dislike until it was over.[15] In retrospect, I think of Byron's inane lines "Man's love is of man's life a thing apart, / 'Tis woman's whole existence," and I must admit that I let this love become for a while nearly my whole existence. It's maddening that the most sexist relationship I've ever had was with another woman, but I did deliberately lay down my power for the sake of this loving. No one should do that for any lover (as Kenneth should not have for me), since it leads to inevitable combustion. When I began to fight for my sense of self again, the relationship started to dissolve. If I wasn't doing 90 percent of the work to keep us together anymore, that work wouldn't get done.

---

[14] From "The Ghost of a Garden," in *A Hot January: Poems, 1966–1999*.

[15] Gloria and Lois, for example, later said they felt I'd turned into more of a traditional "wife" with Marilyn than I'd ever been in my marriage. They were correct—although they'd stood by me throughout. Gloria had even written, at my request, the introduction to Marilyn's book, loyally hauling in *her* old friend John Kenneth Galbraith to give the book a blurb.

Love takes a long while in its dying. We made it through the six months. I was relieved to return home to friends and laughter: people actually discussed their thoughts and feelings—what a concept! I wrote Marilyn a long letter saying we'd come to an impasse and suggesting she not take her planned spring trip to New York or, if she did, maybe consider not staying with me. She wrote, phoned, and faxed, appealing to come. I relented. She came, careful to be on her best behavior: witty, tender, mostly sober. I fell in love and in hope all over again, never having heard of a pernicious game called First One to Leave Wins.

When I saw her off at the airport in early June of 1994, it would be the last time we would see one another, although I didn't know that then. The definitive break wouldn't happen for another eight months. I went to Nepal for three weeks, did useful political work, felt pleased. Back home, I started on a new novel and cultivated my garden. But for the whole of that summer, fall, and winter, there were torturous phone calls. Marilyn suggested I cancel my September trip to the farm—which was to have been a celebration of our tenth anniversary as lovers—at least for a month or so, while she "processed" how she felt. But, she said, she loved me, and we were still partners, surely. My confusion grew with each call. True forgiveness is an illusion if the forgiven one somehow feels victimized by the forgiver. I believed I harbored no residue from her small cruelties and large detachments, but I was wrong. As for my sin, it was apparently a cornucopian generosity that its recipient found impossible to forgive, no matter how hungrily and deliberately she had invoked and accepted it.

She finally entered therapy. I rejoiced at the possibility of any imminent insight, even if it might widen the gulf between us, though naturally I hoped it wouldn't. I told her that since she'd been alienated from her own feelings for so long, it wouldn't be unusual if she found herself acting out and having an affair, and that I'd understand and stick by her—but I did want the truth. "*Just don't ever lie to me,*" I said. I dived back into therapy sessions myself, as her phone conversations and letters became more bewildering—one day warm and loving, the next day cold and strained.

Of course I was the last to know. She'd begun a flirtation back in June, directly on her return from New York—and with one of her students. It flowered into an affair and then a relationship. All this I learned in retrospect the following January, from one of her friends who assumed I'd known and was horrified to have unwittingly spilled the beans. I then told Marilyn over the phone that I knew, and gently asked why she'd lied to me when I'd been so certain that by now we were way beyond such games. She stammered that she'd been afraid of losing my love and respect.

What a way to try to keep them! Politically courageous but an emotional coward, now this needy child didn't want me but didn't want to let me go either—except that we'd already danced that particular two-step in the beginning, back when *I'd* been the Other Woman.

As it began, so it ended. I got my just karmic deserts—but then isn't karma merely the spiritual version of irony? The denouement was conducted by phone, none of it eye-to-eye, which I found tasteless. I wanted nothing back of what I'd given to her or to the farm, asked her to donate the clothes I kept there to anyone needing them, and to sell my car for me—which became a moot point since she soon totaled it, walking away shaken but unscratched. Still, she begged to remain friends, and still, I was willing. Then, in one conversation she asked if I would read and edit her essays for a new book, as I'd done before—yet when I said I too would like to send her a new poem I'd written, she refused, murmuring it might be too upsetting for her to read. That was a familiar imbalance—old news I didn't want to hear but needed to know. I wished her well and told her not to call me again.

When something is finally over and ends sourly, its having continued for so long becomes a retroactive puzzle. But there are clues. Marilyn—who was at least an equal-opportunity liar in that she also withheld truth from herself—told mutual friends it was the distance that drove us apart. Poor dear, she got it wrong again. It was the distance that kept us going for so long. Had we ever really lived together, we never would've lasted beyond the second year. Lust, lovely lust, helped keep us going, too, and distance fed that lust. I sometimes teased her that she was the greatest lover in the world (another statement to which experience now lends startling perspective). Sex was indeed very good, until those miserable six months, and should not be dismissed lightly. Sometimes, with grief, I think about the millions of female human beings who regard sex as a boring or painful duty owed husbands or lovers, women who maybe once vaguely sensed their own sexual drive—what the late Audre Lorde called "the power of the erotic"—but who've had to trudge through their lives and die without ever experiencing it. Millions of women who've never known sexual pleasure even *once*, not to speak of sexual *joy*—whether with a man or a woman. That calamity has been suffered by most women who ever lived. It should incense us as much as any other kind of starvation.

Whatever held Marilyn and me together for so long, what severed us was the ultimate inaccessibility of her poor, famished heart—plus eight months of ornate, soul-sickening lies. Certainly her affair pained me, but in truth not that much, since I'd expected it and was braced to transcend it (earth-mother style). It was her emotional withholding and her lying that raised fresh blood from my oldest wounds, breaking open scars left by an emotionally cold, inaccessible father—about whom a mother had lied consistently. After I'd managed to transform Kenneth and Iliana into versions of Faith, I'd been so on the alert not to repeat *that* pattern that *this* came in under the radar, recapitulating instead the pattern with Mates. Actually, once Marilyn started lying, she repeated both, a double whammy.

I was not on the alert for that. And the impact almost destroyed me.

Into the Abyss

Insight leaks from memory like light from a late autumn afternoon. If I see patterns in my life or the lives of others, it's because patterns interest me not only in psychological ways, but in aesthetic, archetypal ones.[16] Seeing

---

[16] Maybe I'm just a sucker for the symmetry of form. After all, consider the following. Years after the end of the relationship and the despair in its wake, when passion has withered to pity and finally indifference—late one night, the phone rings. It's the student lover, who's secretly pilfered my number from Marilyn's address book. She's hoping that I, a writer she's read for years, won't hang up on a desperate woman. Their relationship has been a disaster for some time—therapy abandoned, wine, grass, and silence increased, Marilyn claiming such problems are brand-new and the lover's fault, the lover exhausted by attempts to help but unable to breach that emotional citadel. *Is this my doing*, she asks, *am I crazy?* I say *No, you're not crazy, it's not your fault, protect yourself, Marilyn needs help but only she can change her life.* Decades of listening to women and learning from them how to be of use have clicked me onto automatic pilot, and I'm able to be helpful yet not trash my former lover. Moreover, I find I'm actually capable of doing this without relishing the moment. That amazes me. It's one of those rare occasions when validation comes in the form of an opportunity for grace. I am so grateful to existence for its profound wit that I stay awake sipping peppermint tea for hours. Art dare not invent such a pattern. Only life can get away with it. And did.

patterns is like being able to appreciate the black-robed shadows in Bun-raku theater as the figures who really move the puppets, especially since the puppets are all we're meant to notice.

As it gradually bore in on me that this relationship, second in length only to my marriage, was definitively over, I crashed. I descended into a wilderness, a place of loss and chaos, where pride was so lacerated as to become indistinguishable from self-abasement, and where each viciously unforgettable detail of loving intimacy was flipped in an instant, as if in a parallel negative universe, into an artifact livid with grief. I lost all balance. I entered a void where reality flattened to two dimensions, and I felt like a feral child. That bleakness would be my habitat for years, during which time I plodded my hours in a state of nauseous grey despair, longing for each day to wane late enough so I could take a pill and sleep, hopefully not to dream.

I was grieving for the entirety of the past, for my life—not just for the relationship and the violation of trust, not just for the loss of a second country and home and family, animals I missed, gardens I'd nurtured, plans we'd shared. I was grieving all the losses I'd never had time to mourn. But what I knew then was only that this deep depression affected every aspect of my being, and that I might not emerge from it.

Physically, it was intensified by ill-being. With a sense of timing worthy of the Spanish Inquisition, menopause hit full force—taking vengeance on me for all those years when I'd snubbed it as being "socially con-structed," sniffing that if women only had the chance to lead self-fulfilling lives they'd *never* experience empty-nest syndrome *or* menopause. (Tell that to your body when it's betraying you with day flashes, night sweats, and the thousand natural shocks female flesh is specially heir to.) Worse, I was ill. The slipped disk had been misdiagnosed in New Zealand. It turned out I'd been limping around for months with two slipped disks plus a third, ruptured one, hairline fractures, spinal stenosis and growths, and additional medical complications, some of grave concern.

Politically, I paced through months fixated on the question of how women could so betray women. Who *was* this person I had loved so, those many years? How could she—how could anyone—change so drastically? Or had I never really known her? Had she always been the woman of the cruel, final year? If so, how could I have managed to ignore seeing that? Again and again, I circled the question obsessively: if women could so harm women, then who were my people? This was the bitterness of the long-distance runner turned toxic. It would take many months to relearn a politics the other side of that particular despair. Truths I'd known intellectually before would have to be engraved on my flesh this time, like the point of Kafka's story "The Harrow," teaching me a feminism that persists while *truly* understanding what gratuitous cruelties one woman can enact on another—not only because of powerlessness but because of simple human imperfection.

Emotionally, I'd never felt at such a loss. I'd deemed myself a good survivor with the capacity to love life fiercely, and believed experience had trained me for a fairly intelligent willingness to face and grapple with despair. This then was a humbling process, in which certain aspects of my arrogance were finally engaged. The challenge was to relocate energy as separate from that arrogance, because so much of my stamina was braided with the attitude "No matter what it is, I can handle it." Now that certainty was lost. Losing became, in fact, the defining activity of my hours, as if I were an embodiment of Elizabeth Bishop's superb villanelle "One Art." I was learning how to lose: love, pride, sleep, health, weight, hair, bone, time, heart, voice.

Voice was the worst of it. I couldn't write.

In every previous life crisis, I'd survived by writing my way through, around, about it. Now, for the first time: emptiness. I'd left the magazine with the naive assumption that I'd explode with pent-up creativity, as if my voice were a whipped dog that could be starved and ignored but would return whimpering at the first beckon. When that hadn't happened during the six months at the farm, I'd chalked it up to the personal pressures and my physical inability to remain in one position for long without pain. But now, in the safety of my own home, and with proper medical treatment, still no words would come—at least no significant words. I made myself function every day (except for two spent curled fetal-like in bed). I read everything I could find about writer's block. I wrote recommendations for other people's grants and fellowships, forewords and blurbs for other people's books. I wrote *A Woman's Creed*, but had to steal lines from one of my older poems to make it work.[17] The debt skid was gaining momentum, so I hacked some journalism to pay the bills. But poetry lodged in my throat.

The creative impulse bubbled forth everyplace but where I needed it to be. I gardened vociferously, even before my body and doctors would fully allow me to. I baked bread and cooked dinners for friends, pouring myself into satin sauces instead of onto the page. I concocted seven feeders for wild birds, with home-melted suet, peanut butter, and six different kinds of seeds. I confessed to Blake that I was in danger of becoming the Martha Stewart of the Women's Movement and that he had to swear if he saw me start to string necklaces out of Fruit Loops, he'd stop me before they carted me away. But the poems lay strangled.

If I couldn't write poems ever again, I didn't want to take up space on the planet. Prozac worked for a while, but made me sleep fifteen hours a day. While it was nice to be buffered from acute heartache, coma didn't seem the solution. I opted for being awake. Friends were dear. They endured the early months when, still in disbelief, I talked nonstop about the relationship, and they tolerated the later months, when I sleepwalked through social occasions. Blake was the greatest source of love and, when I could manage it, laughter, but even he couldn't always penetrate the

---

[17] A *Woman's Creed* was written for and at the Women's Global Strategy Meeting, sponsored by the Women's Environment and Development Organization (WEDO), November 1994. Bella had organized the meeting and asked me for "a universal, inspirational, visionary" statement women could take to the upcoming UN conference in Beijing. The meeting was attended by 148 women from fifty countries, which is hard enough when hammering out platforms—but as for "inspirational vision," forget it.

My idea of hell is an endless meeting where you have to write collectively. There are two different levels of this hell. One is where the collaborators are all writers; the other is where they're not. Yet a caucus was assembled, and we discussed the subject for hours. Everyone was clear on what we were *against*, but no one could imagine what we'd want to *replace* that with—other than abstractions (peace, justice, equality) and definition by negation (an end to war, an end to violence). Not one woman could tell me what, to her, peace would *taste* like, winning would *sound* like, safety would *smell* like—and if it can't be imagined concretely, how can it be created? Finally, my old friend Perdita Huston, herself a writer, urged everyone to leave me alone, and I stayed up all night and wrote the *Creed*. It has since been reprinted widely around the world and been translated into twelve languages, including Arabic, Chinese, Russian, and Sanskrit, all available from the Sisterhood Is Global Institute.

miasma. (Andrea, with her typical gallows humor, claimed this meant he wasn't doing his part. When I protested, she noted that if only he were robbing banks or sharing needles like a *considerate* son, *those* activities would instantly focus my mind.) I cleaned and recleaned house, walked for hours on end, rented movies. I read, retracing every word of Shakespeare, all of Donne. That was more solace than anything else; it was an astringent consolation to tour the despair of my betters, expressed back when sorrow had stature as a part of existence not to be hurriedly tidied by Zoloft. I sat at my desk doing five-finger exercises, writing maybe a hundred self-pitying, banal sonnets reeking of catharsis. No voice.

I took to the road. I accepted an invitation to speak at a conference in Bologna, and went on from there to Venice—my first visit, walking for days amid the masks and magic. That helped. I went to the 1995 UN Women's World Conference in Beijing, to speak and also cover it for *Ms.* and, at greater length, for *Women's Studies Quarterly*.[18] A year later there was Italy for a book tour, then Spain to promote *Mujeres del Mundo*, the Spanish edition of *Sisterhood Is Global*, and to speak at a Basque women's conference.[19] I went through the motions, but felt I was treading tissue-thin ice and might crash back down—often did—into the icy, inky depths just beneath the surface. Poetry is not just a genre. For a poet, making poems is a way of viewing the world, being in the world, breathing. Without that, I was suffocating.

In a long, thoughtful phone conversation, Adrienne got me to admit that Marilyn, who'd reveled in having love poems written to her, had expressed fear at what poems I might write should we ever "divorce." Was I now letting that fear act as proscription, letting her silences infect me,

---

[18] "The UN Conference: Out of the Holy Brackets and into the Policy Mainstream" and "The NGO Forum: Good News and Bad," both in *Women's Studies Quarterly* 24, nos. 1–2 (Spring–Summer 1996).

[19] One of the unanticipated aspects of attending conferences post-Marilyn was discovering I had so much extra *time*, even during the days. At first I couldn't work out where it was coming from. Then it struck me. I wasn't having to play diplomat and mend her fences, explaining to others that she really hadn't *meant* to be short-tempered, cold, or dismissive, that she was just jet-lagged/having a period/ill with a cold/under the weather, so "please don't take it personally." It was a nose-on-my-face revelation about my previous role as wife-translator-facilitator.

self-censoring? *Write* it, Adrienne chanted, you can revise fairness in later. Get it *down*. Trust your craft.

How to *do* that? I had so lost touch with my own powers that I lacked a sense of hope, which I believed necessary in order to start anything—but I had that backwards. Yet I discovered I was at least curious. All through this sickness of soul, humor never abandoned me, though it turned caustic. Strength never left me, but it was the strength of a dullard: mulish endurance. The first sign of life to return was that intimation of curiosity. Then heightened functioning. Then the supreme comfort of again appreciating art. Then health returned—very slowly, at least in part. Only at the last, shyly, in tiptoed hope. They say what doesn't kill you makes you stronger, and I could almost hear Marilyn claiming credit for having inspired that process.

For financial survival I needed to write prose—journalism, nonfiction. My publishers had patiently waited since 1989 for the memoir they'd signed up then, despite my having warned them I wouldn't be ready to write it for years. Now they were beginning, understandably, to nag a bit. So I tried to start the memoir, dreading the idea of revisiting my life and sarcastically titling it *Ideal American Girl*. I accepted an invitation to be a visiting scholar, the Block Professor at the University of Denver, for three months, and shipped the memoir files out by Federal Express, swearing to write and teach but *not* to get tempted to organize.

Federal Express lost the files. All of them.[20] At first I plummeted again, feeling as if the memoir and I were both hexed. But there's always politics. The Denver women were both inspiring and eager to be inspired, so by the time I left, the campus was organized, with separate groups for women undergrads, graduate students, faculty, clerical/administrative, and even the few women with (relative) power on the board of trustees or in senior positions. But Bran—who'd traveled with me in his cat carrier, frail but game at age twenty-one for a new adventure—succumbed to his kidney condition and died a month into my stay, facing the Rockies at sunset, purring in my arms. A small death, but another loss. At least he hadn't

---

[20] After a year and a lawsuit, some papers were found in a FedEx warehouse and returned, having suffered major water damage.

been left behind, and I was with him at the end. Returning home, the emptiness returned with me.

This time I let it in.

Ancient alchemical texts defined the separation and dissolution of substance as forming the test of alchemy, that moment when base metal would be reduced to chaos so higher energy might melt into it, the precision of that instant when the mind would be forced to free itself from all routine. This phase alchemists called "the ruining of the work" or "the abyss." Only from such ruin, they wrote, comes gold.

The poems—despaired of, financially useless, "unpolitical"—started trickling back. Memoir be damned, practicality be damned, they'd be the first to return. I was afraid of looking too directly at them, as someone who's been in a dark cell winces at the light. To my awe, they emerged simplified, matured, from a craft quietly sure of itself. As they unfolded, I noticed that the incantatory poetry I'd written for years had been conceived in part to be presented at readings, the actor commissioning the poet. Now, though I liked the sound of these new poems aloud, I recognized they issued from a deeper source. They were written for the page, and for some voice other than mine—an older, wiser voice. How strange to discover that *is* my voice now. Once grief was baked in craft's kiln, the unexpected emerged: poems about far more than the death of a relationship. *A Hot January* contains the best work I'd done so far. It's also more descriptive of that period's journey than I could ever approximate in this chapter's prose.

I think the voice will stay. But I'll never again take it for granted.

In the final January of the twentieth century, I turned fifty-eight years old. What new emotional and erotic surprises amused me this past year or so are not for *this* memoir. They need time to mellow into understanding. But I can relate that I retain my (now skeptical) romanticism and that sex, like wine, improves with the vintage. I now *dance* on thin ice, feeling free and hilariously serene.

Actually, to mix my metaphors, it's more like ballooning. Once aloft, you feel no whoosh of speed, because you travel *with* the wind. Everything is absolutely quiet except for the occasional poof of flame from the small oven, to warm the helium. Floating above trees, you see and listen to each distinct bird. Drifting over a town, you hear people talking on the street below, their words curling upward like smoke. What a different way of being on the air! When you descend, you dally down, rocking gently, with no lurching. But not even the balloonist can be certain where you'll land.

I'm ballooning all the time now. It's taken me decades of theatrics to grasp what I suspected right along, that life is a comedy far darker than drama. It just takes time to learn what to smile at.

I should have realized this earlier, because every actor knows that tragedy, being linear and inevitable, is taxing—but comedy, which depends on the element of surprise, is the hardest act of all.

Six Memoirs in Search
of an Author

If I could stand beside my body
and really see the woman I am,
then I would understand at last how envy feels.

— ANNA AKHMATOVA,
"ELEGIES OF THE NORTH," SEC. 3[1]

1. From the Cutting-Room Floor

"Long Shots, Two-shots, Close-ups, and Dissolves."

On safari in South Africa: blessed with sighting a herd of female elephants surrounding a calf less than twenty feet away; their primal, warm, dusky, curry-mustard scent.

The sculptural beauty of Kenneth's forearms in candlelight as we sit reading each other's Tarot cards.

Holding a copy of the first book of mine translated into Chinese.

The Golden Oldies—Bella, Congresswoman Maxine Waters, Gloria—grooving to a performance of Blake's band, and leaving the club owner speechless with bewilderment.

Hiking in the shadow of the Himalayas.

[1] R. M. translation.

Sitting upright on the Dead Sea.

Lying in Marilyn's arms on our hotel-room bed in Canterbury, England, while we listen for hours to the bell ringer at the medieval church across the street make a full-peal attempt.

The twelfth hour of childbirth labor, scraped down to a never-felt energy waiting beneath the exhaustion for precisely this moment.

Sitting up all night arguing with Mary Daly over a bottle of Irish Mist: Mary claims there's no need to read *The Divine Comedy* when Aquinas's theology more purely makes the point; I claim there's no need for any damned theology when the poetry *is* the point.

Spying the first hummingbird to visit the Perry Street roof garden.

The Xhosa activist in Cape Town, South Africa, who points to a wall poster, saying, "I don't know who wrote them, but those words know what's in my heart"; peering closer and realizing it's *A Woman's Creed*.

A naughty afternoon with Iliana on the beach in Miami, making love in the cabana as sun worshipers stroll by beyond the flimsy curtain.

Blake at age seven, sitting by the fire wide-eyed, begging for one more chapter while Kenny and I take turns reading aloud from a prose translation of the Welsh epic poem *The Mabinogion*.

Noticing Friedan across the aisle from me in the audience for a panel at the Beijing conference—asleep, her head lolling on her chest, a tiny drop of spittle drooling from the slack lips—and feeling gratefully betrayed into tenderness for this ill, tired, crochety old adversary who'd denounced me as too radical for so long, never having grasped we were on the same side.

Sneaking into my bookbag the roller skates I'm only supposed to wear indoors and skating the whole five blocks from Miss Wetter's to Aunt Sophie's, all by myself; the sense of speed and balance, the sting of wind-rush in my eyes, the blur of houses passing, one particular gold-leafed October afternoon.

Meeting Iliana at the airport wearing only a raincoat and a chuckle, carrying a paper bag containing an open split of champagne for the taxi ride into Manhattan. Discovering this works so lasciviously well that, shameless, I later repeat it with Marilyn.

Scrawling, "Paid in Protest to a Vicious Monopoly," on the back of checks I write to the phone and utilities companies all through the 1970s.

Swimming with dolphins in the Florida Keys: their warm skin brushing mine; their obvious approval when I hum Bach.

A fireworks burst of happiness inside me at seeing Blake's face, aglow with love, when he gazes at the young woman in his life.

Commiserating with Nawal El Saadawi about writing and husbands as we circle the Great Sphinx in Giza.

Opening a bucketful of just-gathered oysters and a bottle of champagne at Atlantis, in our spontaneous celebration of the news that Toni Morrison has won the Nobel Prize for literature.

Hunched over, learning which is the circuit wire, which is the battery, how to set the timer. Trembling with this knowledge, wanting it, needing it, loathing it.

Standing hand in hand with Blake at my mother's grave, to unveil the pink marble headstone reading simply her name, dates, and the legend "There is nothing you cannot be."

A flight of startled white herons at dawn in the Everglades.

Wolfing down instant noodle soups and cans of Mexicorn with Karen at 5:00 A.M. in our *Sisterhood Is Global* office.

Sharing a carousel horse with Father Joc.

The touch of a newborn kid just rescued from drowning: wet, chilled, shuddering against the warmth of my bare breasts under my shirt.

Eating order-in lobster with black-bean sauce in Lois's kitchen, each of us weepy about respective lovers not appreciating our magnificence.

My end-of-the-day ritual before leaving the office when editing *Ms.*, usually around ten at night: putting my feet up and enjoying the day's reward: mail from readers.

Staying indoors with Marilyn on three different vacations where we sit glued to the TV set, watching the People's Revolution overthrow Marcos in the Philippines, the Tiananmen Square rebellion, and the house arrest of Gorbachev in the former USSR—our contrary sort of vacation.

Walking the beaches of the world—at Big Sur and Staten Island with Kenneth; in Florida, Maine, Crete, and the Hamptons with Iliana; in Bali, Te Henga, Rio, Galveston, San Francisco, and Boracay with Marilyn; alone in more places than I can count, from Dover to the Cape of Good Hope; with Blake when he's six and I wake him, bundle him up, and bring him out to the beach at Amagansett for his very first sunrise.

My mother's face, as she sings Brahms's "Lullaby"—in a soft voice the color of old rose—to me as I drift to sleep.

2. Acting as if It's Worth It

"The Story of an Actor Who Becomes Politically Involved."

(Note: Watch it. The models are an unsavory lot. Eva Peron. Ronald Reagan. Jiang Qing. Sonny Bono.)

When my mother lay dying I thought:

(a) I'll outlive her and be free.

(b) I'll outlive her but never be free.

(c) If it were true or even possible that, as she'd claimed, I'd loved act-ing—*really* loved acting—that would mean her absolution. Her absolution would in turn mean she'd have no need to haunt my consciousness. It might be worth such an admission, which could even be true—after all, look at my life!—if that would buy her freedom from me, and mine from her.

But would it?

Well, if it *weren't* true, couldn't I just pretend it was?

Unforeseen influences: I started working so young that although I could portray mainstream normality, I never believed it existed. That disbelief helped forge a vision for radical change. When you've seen behind the cur-tain where the wizard hides pulling the levers, you learn that no single way of living is foreordained or "natural," and you discover that people are capable of profound metamorphosis, though unfortunately they rarely avail themselves of this genius, force of habit being an even greater enemy of change than cowardice. You also come to recognize how in our most secret hearts we each star in the performance of existence, with everyone else playing supporting roles, character parts, cameos, bits, walk-ons, and extras. There is no girl or boy next door. Each one of us lives in The House; everyone else is relegated to next door.

Unforeseen influences: For me, work has a temporary shape. It arrives in projects, each of which, while part of the consistent vocation, is discrete unto itself: a play, a film, a radio or television one-shot; even a TV series's run is limited. The cast and company become friends, a colleague-family with flirtations, rivalries, enmities, in-jokes, traditions—society in microcosm. This way of working imprinted on me early and deep. Writing each book is such a project, has its own world, is peopled by its own real, fictional, or metaphorical companions as much as each political project is, whether that's organizing a campus or a Dalit group, planning a guerrilla-theater action or helping to draft legislation. Each of the anthologies had its cast of thousands. So did *Ms.* But this was another reason why I couldn't see myself editing the magazine for decades, just as I've always found it preferable to live with financial uncertainty rather than spend years at a steady job. The work itself is too important. It demands and bestows fresh starts with each new effort.

Mine are hardly the only politics influenced by theatrics. *The scene*: Bella's last campaign, to regain a seat in Congress. The first day back on the campaign trail after a month's pause following Martin's sudden death by heart attack and Bella's subsequent collapse. She's finally decided to continue because he would have insisted she do so, because her dear grown daughters, Eve and Liz, will keep her going, and because she can't stomach stopping. We're at a school in Westchester, trailed by press. She slumps into a kiddie seat to rest before her speech on education. She looks old now, and unspeakably weary, but she continues to talk ceaselessly of Martin. We can hear the introduction of her rising to a climax. She looks at me, her eyes glittering with sorrow, and smiles crookedly. "I guess," she sighs, "this is what they mean by being a trouper." Then she heaves her bulk to her feet and walks to the podium—where she comes alive. The audience is on its feet, transfixed, roaring.

All the world's a set. Nowadays audiences join the cast. Scriptwriters strive to forge realistic dialogue imitative of ordinary people, but those people now speak in ways saturated by television, movies, news, popular culture. So there they are on TV, after yet another bombing or school massacre—heaping another memorial with mawkish toys, flowers, prayers, and balloons—local people now using such terms as "seeking closure," "not wanting to speculate," and "constructive dialogue." The egg cackles and lays the chicken.

~   ~   ~

We know the basic political plot, and time is on our side, though exasperatingly slow. The *how* is where suspense, dramatic tension, and comic relief play out. I know it's unfashionable to believe in progress, but I think we *are* evolving. A more humane politics does eventually win out and will continue to do so (barring an ultimate catastrophe born of human stupidity), and historical perspective helps us tolerate the wait. But how tedious to have to wait at all, much less be warned we should consider giving up. (That must be how the blasé tide regards sandbags and dikes.) In 1979, Gloria and I co-wrote an article for *Ms.* on female genital mutilation that most people found shocking;[2] twenty years later, FGM is formally opposed in UN resolutions. The official document of the Year 2000 UN Beijing-Plus-Five Conference affirms the word "herstory," thirty years after I was called silly for having coined it. The senators and congressmen who castigate progressives now are the same breed (in a few cases the same men) who in the 1950s attacked Euripides, Christopher Marlowe, and Mark Twain as communists and in the 1960s predicted racial segregation would endure forever. When table utensils were invented in the 1100s, the Catholic Church condemned them as obscene and heretical, claiming "God gave us fingers with which to eat." And we're supposed to get politically discouraged? Oh please. We're being opposed by people who denounced the fork.

~   ~   ~

[2] "The International Crime of Genital Mutilation," in *The Word of a Woman,* also collected in *Outrageous Acts and Everyday Rebellions,* by Gloria Steinem (Holt, Rinehart and Winston, 1983).

Politics helped me perceive the world, and sent me around it. Acting gave me entree into different roles: organizing, editing, teaching, being a tactician or a spokesperson—what Susan Brownmiller (flatteringly if inaccurately) called being feminism's "most valuable player." But the MVP label has a flip side: virtuosity can be dilettantism—and dangerous for a writer.

"I'm helplessly suspended between the creator in me and the performer in me," groaned Leonard Bernstein. I know what he meant, though in my case the contention certainly has involved less celebrity and less opulence. (I'm not so sure he was being honest about the helplessness, anyway.) I like to think that in my case the creator has prevailed, and has in this memoir even managed to expose the performer, revealing some of what goes on offstage. There's a catch, of course, or there wouldn't be irony. The memoir will require a book tour, TV talk shows, signings, readings. You have to laugh. If you don't, you find yourself back at drama.

This much I know: many skins of the performer—child professional or adult activist—were flayed away during my anointment with solitude that was depression's gift. Apparently, it was necessary to unmake my present self in order to unmake my former selves. I could never become an apolitical nonactivist. But from here on in, for whatever time is left, the words take precedence.

Revision: "The Story of an Actor Who Becomes a Writer."

(Note: Has a *much* a better model Shakespeare.)

3. One Last Late Lifetime

"A Portrait of the Artist as an Old Woman."

It's getting less odd not to be the youngest in a room—often now the oldest, certainly when with friends who are young feminists (and thus, according to the press, nonexistent). But though baby-boomer feminists have been writing about age as if they'd invented it, the subject doesn't carry the same fascination for me. Aging is no distinction. Turtles do it better than anyone. I don't have time for it.

What does give me unease is the slide toward religio-cultural epiphanies many of my contemporaries seem to be suffering. These are women who've led lives of secular integrity and a deliberately chosen non- or multi-ethnic identification summarizable by that defiant cry of Woolf's:

"As a woman my country is the whole world." Yet age seems to have sent more than a few of them into ethnic flounderings and spiritual face-lifts: an almost indiscriminate reaffirmation of the past, with disturbing results that range from a sudden keeping of kosher kitchens to attending mass. Some embark on a key-to-the-universe search (as if the universe were locked), the key revealing itself as a copy of Deepak Chopra's syrupy maxims—this in the hands of women whose tastes previously ran to the vinegar-tart existentialism of de Beauvoir. I do understand that an increasing proximity to history fosters interest in it; people who didn't give a damn about ancestors suddenly care when they realize they're getting closer to becoming ancestors themselves. I also respect the importance of learning about the past—but reenacting it is something else. Most of these retreats and reconversions seem driven by the engines of guilt or fear, and while I want to shrug, "Whatever gets you through the night," this development saddens me. Whatever happened to Elizabeth Cady Stanton's vow that we adopted back in our twenties? *I will not grow conservative with age.*

Granted, such reactions to getting old are typical in the United States where, given the cult of eternal youth, age is ignored unless it can be sentimentalized. Venice reminds us that it's possible to approach age with less compromising clarity. There's a Giorgione in the Galleria dell'Accademia, *La Vecchia* (The Old Woman), which rooted me to the spot while other tourists were agog three feet away over his more famous painting *The Tempest*. The unflinching vision behind *La Vecchia* inspired one of the first poems to break through my personal perdition of silence.[3] The Accademia also is home to Tintoretto's last *Pietà*, which is massive, and so dark that parts are indistinct. Christ, just lowered from the cross, lies contorted in his mother's lap. Her face is a mask of utter despair—hopeless, graceless. Gradually, the viewer notices that off in the lower right-hand corner of the canvas there are paintings stacked against the wall of the tomb—Tintoretto's own works, you can recognize them—earlier depictions of the Crucifixion and the Pietà, each shot through with glorious shafts of light and gleaming with swarms of angels. These are the paintings of youth. Here they lie cast aside in a corner of the scene, while in the center a

[3] "Col Tempo," in *A Hot January*.

shadowed, greasy cross looms over a real death agony—no shafts of light, no angels. This work, completed by the artist in his nineties for his own tomb, is exquisitely devastating.

Maybe it's perverse, but I'm grateful for such examples. My reality is somewhat different from that which mostly surrounds us, and I'm drawn to people whose reality is similarly skewed. Keats described it as "negative capability"—a poet's power to live simultaneously in real and fanciful worlds—and Marianne Moore named this phenomenon when she described poetry's terrain as "imaginary gardens with real toads in them." In that sense, writers really write only for each other. So Keats quotes Shakespeare and I quote Keats . . . we even write for each other across centuries—but perforce only in one direction, futureward.

Thank *god* for the unsentimental Tintorettos, for the maker of Lear and mad old Queen Margaret. Being relatively young at aging, I don't yet know how to carry it off, at least not in the style I prefer. Models in my own culture are rare. I've been fortunate in knowing four: Barbara Macdonald, the brilliant political theorist who, with Cynthia Rich, wrote *Look Me in the Eye: Old Women, Aging, and Ageism* (San Francisco: Spinsters' Ink, 1983), and Simone de Beauvoir, who focused the laser of her intellect as ferociously on age as she had on sex. Then there's Katharine Hepburn. In 1981, when she was seventy-two, I interviewed her for a *Ms.* cover story.[4] Her film *On Golden Pond* had just been released, and she was starring in a new play, *The West Side Waltz*, about to have a Broadway run. As I reread our conversation now, three quotations shine out.

"When you've lived as long as I have, people assume you must be wise. They get very sweet to you, as if you were a monument. I'm just me."

"The humor is important. I mean, you either laugh at it all—or else you blow your brains out."

"Life is very hard, isn't it? It does kill you, after all."

Then, closest of all, there was Bella. At this writing, she's been dead almost two years, yet I feel her loss as sorely as when it happened, though I've mostly recovered from my rage at the vulturous tributes that poured forth from people who, while she was alive, had ignored her once she no

---

[4] "Katherine Hepburn: Getting On With It," *Ms.*, January 1982.

longer held public office. (When *will* the world honor authentic greatness, not just after it's conveniently dead but while it still walks among us?) Bella was only seventy-seven, and in her case the "only" isn't meant facetiously. Her death hit me harder in a way than the loss of my blood mother, because Faith's mind had been gone for so much of the time before her racked body eventually followed, whereas Bella was intensely present up to the moment she was wheeled into the operating room at 6:00 A.M.—sitting up on the gurney and swiveling around to wave back at us, one arm raised in the air with a clenched fist, and a grin on her face as we called out, "Give 'em hell!" Afterward, for weeks, she fought the odds in the intensive-care unit. Standing there talking and singing into her unconsciousness, I'd remember her shrewd aphorisms, the most merciless of which she'd delivered at my home two years earlier, when she'd joined a small group of us as we gathered to watch the 1996 election returns. The Democrats had kept the White House but lost both houses of Congress to ultra-conservative Republicans and suffered major blows in gubernatorial races, including the one in New York. We were nervously eating more and getting gloomier as the night wore on, Blake especially. He'd spent hours of his childhood volunteering in idealistic, losing electoral campaigns (three of which had been Bella's). Now, in his late twenties, he growled, "Goddammit, I want *us* to win for a change. I'm so *tired* of this. It makes you lose hope." To which Bella replied, "Aw no, honey. You gotta live in hope." She paused a beat before landing the punchline, "That's why you die in despair." Then she laughed.

Those are my kind of models.

Suzanne thinks that people read memoirs to find models, hints on how to live their own lives. It would be pretty funny if you, dear reader, had slogged this far in hope of *that*. (Hepburn was right: it's eerie to feel others project wisdom onto one while mournfully aware of one's own inadequacies.) If by chance that *was* your motivation, sorry to have failed you. You should've come around when I was in my twenties, eager to tell *everyone* how to live. These days, I've had a hard enough time battling my own resistances to this book, two in particular.

(1) I feel I'm too young to write a memoir, though others disagree. This could mean I possess a humility I didn't realize I had, or it could mean

they're right and I'm older than I think. Either way, I turn out to be dumb.

(2) I'm preoccupied with what's happening now and what comes next. What's happened—*that's* stuff I already *know*. The future, on the other hand, feels palpable to me. I write for its readers. I feel their age.

Some things I *have* managed to figure out, however.

I do not want to be younger. I want to be exactly who I am now; I like her infinitely better than all the former me's. I admit it would be nice to be who I am *but* with my body the way it was at, say, age thirty-five or even forty—not nubile and ignorant but in its full ripeness, yet free of the current pains and creaks that inspired Bette Davis to snarl, "Old age is not for sissies": while working out at the gym, for instance, it would be nice to bend over and not feel my face slide off my skull. *And* I'd like forty more years to live, be irascible, and write.

There's so much to write about now—especially since penning a memoir effectively cures you of wanting to write about yourself. More levels of my consciousness seem aware of one another, a bonus of aging. I dreamed more when I was younger; my sleeps were deeper. Now I *live* my dreams—which is to say that the state of mind that would have been a dream bestows itself on my waking life. There even are moments of sweet gravity when I notice that if aging is a gradual preparation for dying, then I must say it's quite cleverly devised.

Youth is *not* wasted on the young. I'm discovering youth in ways I never knew back when I was age-deprived. For most of my life, I cared desperately what other people thought. In my forties, I decided "Enough!" and announced to any who would listen that I now felt free of being concerned with what others thought. Then I would sneak peeks at their reactions. Now, soon approaching my sixties, I realize it's not that I no longer care what other people think. I do care, actually. It's simply that I finally care more what *I* think.

Could I have lived my whole life as I now do, at last knowing and saying what I want? I wish I could have, but I think not. It's interesting how many solid brick walls, in retrospect, turn out to have been trompe l'oeil— but only once you've crashed through their papier mâché. Age is something to be earned. I'm earning it still, and would cheerfully break the kneecaps of anyone who tried to steal it from me, or make me settle for the arrested development eternal youth would be.

4. In My Life I've Loved Them All

"Tales of Lovers and Friends."

Luck plays a big part in all this stuff of living, but no one really warns you about that, or teaches you how to recognize luck when it appears, sometimes in questionable guise. From today's perspective, I feel lucky to have been spared the apparent agony of the high-school experience, which left more than a few of my friends scarred. I feel content to have missed siblings (though they get mixed reviews), but the half-brothers situation mitigated that luck. Married for years to a man practicing bisexuality back in the age of innocence when "safe sex" meant solely contraception, I'm profoundly fortunate, as is Kenneth, to be HIV-free.

As for luck in love, some reviewer once said that my literary signature chord was affirmation. There's a refrain in "The Network of the Imaginary Mother"[5] that recurs in two forms: "I affirm all of my transformations" and "I disown none of my transformations." I'll stand by that—at least by the second one. Happily, I no longer feel I have to affirm everybody *else's* transformations. Some I can blithely stomp on. I'm fairly proud that I tried to be as brave as I was capable of being at any given moment, but prouder that I'm no longer so tolerant of cruel or stupid behavior. All that said (and although I'm sure they might disagree) I think I'm still oddly loyal to my former lovers—despite myself.

But beyond lovers, there are friends. It's taken me a long time to admit that I don't like all my feminist colleagues. (Actually, I wouldn't necessarily like all members of any grouping, and why *should* I?) Luckily, many— like Eleanor Smeal (of the Feminist Majority Foundation), who lives in a different state and is in fact more colleague than friend—*feel* like friends, but that's because Ellie and her ilk are generous, warmhearted people; we share a passionate commitment to the same vision even when we may differ on tactics, and we're able to laugh and pick up our conversation like

---

[5] *Lady of the Beasts* and *Upstairs in the Garden*.

old buddies no matter how long it's been since we last spoke. But others—some of whom live in my own city—are full-time feuders, spending all their energy on gossip undercutting women, so I keep my distance from them and their diatribes. Still others—well, I might respect their contributions and be willing to work with them, but that doesn't mean I'd want them for friends. This insight, though banal, is hard-won, since I labored for years under the assumption and hope of a touchy-feely sisterhood. You'd think that would have received its mortal blow somewhere back with the destruction of the Sisterhood Is Powerful Fund, but it kept resurrecting itself.

Sisterhood, then, may be powerful and global, but is not necessarily synonymous with friendship. Friendship is love, without a showy erotic component dominating the discourse, yet it can be just as impassioned and challenging. Friendships require nurturance, and I believe in working at them. I treasure my recently made friends (though, to be honest, I assiduously avoid seeking *out* new ones), but there's a special pride of duration regarding those whose lives have been interwoven with one's own for years; people who've stood as witnesses for each other's tragedies and celebrations. I've known Ned Rorem for almost four decades. Edite Kroll has been my literary agent for twenty years and my friend for over thirty; she was with me in 1968 at the first Miss America protest. Kathleen Barry and I are approaching a thirtieth anniversary as friends. Lois Sasson came into my life in 1974, Lesley Gore not long after, Andrea Dworkin almost the same. "Iliana de Costa," Theresa Funiciello, Karen Berry, and Alida Brill have each put up with me for around twenty years. I've met with a small group of women friends for dinner monthly since 1987; we've known each other since the early 1970s. Such good people have endured my judgmentalism, punctured my pretentiousness, grounded my melodrama, and helped me survive. As I've tried to do for them.

Years ago, some of us came up with the notion of "chosen family," which could be composed of friends, work colleagues, extended family members, or all of the above (not necessarily excluding blood relatives); these were people you could call at three in the morning if you had to, but you'd *picked* them, not merely tolerated them because their noses were shaped like yours. Naturally, given sufficient time, chosen family can be just as irritating as genetic kin, because each grating mannerism becomes as familiar as every endearing trait. Yet if you pay careful enough attention, you notice the lyricism of small, subtle, unique, and lovable details that continually freshen the familiarity.

The aspects I cherish about close friends are distinct from their politics, which are a given. Kathy and I share not only our history but our mutual, ongoing slipped-disk sagas, and I admire the élan with which she periodically reinvents herself, of late becoming a fine photographer. Theresa and I can talk for hours—about stuffed-artichoke recipes and psychology as well as patriarchal economics—and I treasure her fiery sense of outrage. Andrea and I meet regularly for dinner, *not* necessarily to confer about strategies for combatting pornography or prostitution but to talk about literature; she's one of the few activists with whom I can discuss Kafka at length, or Seamus Heaney's poems, or Kobo Abe's fiction— and we also share the guilty pleasure of being hooked on a spooky TV series modeled on the film *La Femme Nikita*. What I most value about Gloria is the diametric opposite of her glamorous persona: it's the deadline procrastinator, the chocoholic, the shaggy-dog-storyteller, the rabid movie-goer; we once went to see *Superman II* at midnight in Times Square, another time stood in line for Kenneth Branagh's *Hamlet* for over an hour, and we share a devotion to an early Marcello Mastroianni film, *The Organizer*, which I finally found on video and gave her for one of her birthdays. Alida has a ravishing wit; to talk or correspond with her makes me feel as if my head's been spinning in a pencil sharpener and has now been honed to a respectable point. Karen's long-lost Kentucky drawl resurrects itself if she's stressed or tired. Suzanne's face acquires a luminous quality when she registers a new idea or insight that she likes: "*Ohhh*," she'll say, every feature lighting up, "oh, *that's* interesting!"

Frail, human, imperfect, these idiosyncrasies form the minutiae of familiarity. But they charm the soul almost as much as the laughter that peals from such friendships—and the sometime tears. These are people who understand how to take themselves seriously but not pompously, and who know humor is as integral to love as to sanity.

For better or worse, in sickness and in health. Pronounced friends.

5. Blood Ties

"A Tale of Generation."

It has not escaped me that the two most significant relationships in my life revolved around having a mother and being one.

Blake's presence has been from the first for me a benevolence, opportunity, lesson, and joy. For one thing, though I'd somehow assumed I'd have a daughter, his being a son turned out to be a blessing, in that it's kept me honest.[6] On days when I've been tempted toward thinking Men Bad, Women Good, or when certain sexist atrocities have provoked fantasies of androcide, his existence has helped me remember that male human beings are *not* born inherently destructive, cruel, or stupid—no, not just his existence, but *his* existence: the person he is, his quick intelligence, intensity, moral courage, sense of self (and of humor), honesty, and talent. The person he's always been has helped me grow into the kind of mother I wish I'd had, feared I never could be, and now think with pride I pretty much managed to become. The freedom I watched him enjoy in his childhood has helped heal the lack of it in my own.

The only place where my usually boomeranging, self-punishing honesty has wholly succeeded is here, and I believe that Blake is partly the person he is because I never lied to him, and tried to stop anyone else from doing so. Certain hurts are *not* inevitable, need not be passed on, generation after generation.

There's a distinct prejudice regarding mothers and sons. If such a pair demonstrates authentic intimacy and understanding, that elicits raised eyebrows implying depravity, while the same judgment isn't inflicted on a close father-daughter relationship. I believe there's a subtle homophobia inherent in this reaction, as if every mother-son relationship reflected Violet and Sebastian in Tennessee Williams's *Suddenly Last Summer*—that is, when it's not reflecting direct Oedipal incest. After conversations with other close and affectionate mothers and sons, I realize the prejudice is also rooted in plain sexist fear—of a woman in touch with her own mature power, and a man who was once dependent on her yet who remains, even

---

[6] Besides, it seems I may have wound up having hundreds of daughters.

as an adult, unafraid to love her. Cleansing this relationship from its nay-saying bigots is another item on my Yet To Do list.

Bless him, Blake's never bored me. To this day, even arguing with him can be fun. Meeting the great pianist Artur Rubinstein when he was in his eighties and Blake was perhaps five, my son looked down at the astound-ingly long fingers wrapping themselves around his little paw in their hand-shake, then looked up at the maestro and announced, "I've admired your work for a very long time." The poet and novelist Jay Parini still recalls the story of coming to visit and telling Blake, then all of six, that he was a pro-fessor—to have the child reply with interest, "Really? And what do you profess?" And when he was about eight or nine, the feminist writer Louise Bernikow asked him if he thought she would make a good mother: "That," he answered gravely, "would depend on the child." Before he started touring with his own bands in the United States and abroad, his seventeenth-birthday present was accompanying me to Germany (for a conference speech), and thence to London for a holiday, where we indulged our Anglophilia unabashedly, and where he became fixated with awe at the tomb of Henry V—"Hal's actually *in* there!" When I was fin-ishing *Dry Your Smile*, I expressed concern about the quasi-autobio-graphical protagonist's love relationship with another woman, thinking the book's publication just as he started college might make life awkward for him among new friends. His immediate reply: "If anybody's going to be put off by *that*, I'd rather find out sooner than later, so I don't have to bother knowing them at all."

As an infant, he'd innocently taught me an unthreatening, tender, free sensuality I'd never before known, which I now realize reflects the experi-ence of many mothers. When he was about three or four—that age when children are diminutive Zen masters—we began a personal game that per-sisted throughout his childhood, one we still refer to today with a knowing glance. Some would call it a form of meditation, and it does have a qual-ity Buddhists might term "mindfulness." To us it was just something fasci-nating and precious to do (not overdo) now and then. It involves looking—really *looking*, carefully, keenly—at some object: wood grain, an apple slice, or the palm of your own hand, until the sight begins to res-onate with its own acute reality. Blake would thrill to it, whispering, "This is it, Rob. It's really *happening*. It's *now*. I'm truly *alive*."

Me too, now, every day, in part thanks to him. It's something he, my beloved friend, understands: this fleeting fastidiousness of spirit.

6. In the Now

"A Mystery Story."

It's a cold January afternoon, but the garden is alive with traffic at the feeders: slate-grey juncos, song sparrows, black-capped chickadees, weaver finches, ruby-breasted house finches, tufted titmouses, downy woodpeckers, and the flamboyance of bluejays and cardinals. There are mourning doves, too, and ubiquitous city pigeons (it's impossible to feed only the birds you prefer without also serving up survival to pigeons—an elementary political lesson). Sea gulls sometimes drop by after a storm, a duck once landed and looked around, and twice a red-tailed hawk has appeared from nowhere to snap up a pigeon, midair, for lunch (another political lesson, but let's not go there). Since Bran's death, no cat lives here, no dog. I miss that presence, but am not yet ready for another such companion, and may never be. For now, I seem to prefer my pets wild. Having often used others—Kenneth, Iliana, Marilyn, Blake—as an excuse to create living spaces of comfort and beauty yet not feel selfish for doing that, now I can celebrate what sweetness I've created for myself and share it with these creatures. I love coming home to this place, kicking the door shut behind me, dropping my keys, shuffling the mail, drifting through the rooms, undressing, fixing a bite to eat. . . .

In the garden, the witch hazel is already in bud and the lenten rose unfurling. Soon crocuses will rear their gallant lavender heads, and winter aconite, and nodding snowdrops. Before this page reaches your hands and these words light on your retina, the daffodils and creamy poets' narcissus will have trumpeted and gone, as well as the stately, claret-black Negrita tulips and milky drifts of azalea. The lilacs will have exhaled and brittled, the magnolia flared and dropped, the Cardinal de Richelieu and Peace roses blown to full riot. In summer jewel-spangled dragonflies will swoop above lilies of the valley that grow along the little waterfall and pond I built from old slate and stones. By the time page proofs have been corrected, the tomato plants will be higher than my head and in flower, the herb bed a cacophony of fragrances when you brush its leaves, the grapevine heavy with sweet green fruit. When bound books finally arrive, it will be harvest—time to dry the herbs, eat the grapes and tomatoes, churn the latest batch of compost back into the earth for overwintering.

I love the sensuality of soil on my fingers. It's alive—not only with red wrigglers and nematodes and microscopic beings—the soil itself is alive. Did you know that if you strike an ordinary lump of clay with a hammer, it blows ultraviolet energy for a month? Though I've never grasped the concept of owning land or, in truth, owning anything, I comprehend the *borrowing* of things, the *using* of things, and in turn the *being* useful. That, it seems to me, is the most we can manage in the brevity of our days, and is all the more reason we ought to leave what we use in decent shape for those to come. Native Americans urge that, in everything we do, we consider the impact it will have in seven generations, a mind-stretching exercise.

When I was perhaps twelve, I had a glimpse of it, the Mystery—from the distant firmaments to the grain of tweed in the coat lapel of a man on the street corner—and it was so vast it was unbearable. Yet that glimpse has remained lodged in the corner of my eye every day for almost half a century. I think of a fresh-faced young woman in some Polish-Russian border village, her eyes agleam with excitement when the marriage broker returns, announcing that the young rabbinical student *is* interested. I can see in her something indomitable that years and circumstances might coarsen and corrupt, but never kill. And I see Blake, a man now, her genetic mitochondria alive in him.

Looking along time like this, I notice that my self-consciousness has drained away—the consummation I so longed for back when I was young and beautiful and unaware of being either. Always too outer-directed—relationships, actions, impressions—maybe I've earned the right to be, in Cervantes's words, "the joyful solitary person I am," attuned to the inner (as uninterruptedly as possible, that is). Now I can let others decide whether I'm working or playing, since I know I'm continually doing both, another reason to be grateful for the gift that work is.

As for what's to come, like the lacy leaves of the Japanese maple, I plan to crisp bright red and gold before I die. If it turns out there is an afterlife, and even a Deity, then I'd like Her to greet me saying, "It's all right, sister. I know, I *know*. I'm an atheist, too."

~ ~ ~

Things I'd like to do before croaking:

Dare write the poetry I was born to write.

Finish at least fifteen more books.

Tour a grandly mysterious archaeological site: perhaps the Plain of Jars in Laos.

Visit a society of extremely old people—maybe somewhere near Bhutan—and ask them about life. (Cancel that: I wouldn't want to find out they're as clueless as the rest of us.)

Visit a polygynous society—and try to find a polyandrous one. (Cancel *that*: the first would make me crazy since it would be one big harem. The second would make me crazy because one woman would have to please multiple men.)

Get my Himalayan blue poppy seeds to *grow*.

Visit a nudist camp. (But go clothed? Wouldn't work.)

Start playing the piano again. Learn the harmonica. Build a harpsichord and play it.

Angkor Wat, yes. The Galápagos Islands, yes. Actually *be* there when ice breaks on the Neva. Machu Picchu—or is that too high, dangerous, uncomfortable? Iceland   oh *yes*!—for the geothermal region and especially to see the Northern Lights.

Peer into an active volcano, preferably not when it's erupting.

Scuba dive in the Great Barrier Reef.

Get to watch Blake's face when he first sees Venice.

Ride naked, bareback, on a fine horse along a beach at sunrise.

Things it's highly unlikely I'll ever do now but would have liked to:

Learn to sail a boat.

Go snowboarding.

Speak Spanish fluently. Get my French and German back. Learn to read Greek.

Ride a goddamned bicycle.

~ ~ ~

Things I definitely will never do now:
    Hang-glide.
    Conduct an orchestra.
    Learn to fly a plane.
    Have a second child (whew).
    Marry again or share living space with a lover (*whew*).

~ ~ ~

Yeats wrote, "All life weighed in the scales of my own life seems to me a preparation for something that never happens." Oh dear, he got it wrong. It *is* happening, right now, a marvel of details, a mystery in perpetual motion.

Each summer, fireflies sneak in through the screen door to the garden; at night I lie in total darkness and watch them winking on and off in my own bedroom. Each winter, after the smaller potted plants have been shifted indoors and the garden sleeps a foot deep in snow, the white night-blooming jasmine flowers again. Isn't this miracle, in one's own bedroom to breathe jasmine flowers in winter and watch fireflies dance in summer?

For the entirety of my life, every moment except the one I was actually living seemed real. Now, every moment preceding this one, as well as those still to come, feel imagined.

Only Now is utterly alive.

So it is possible, after all, to have a happy ending.

It just depends on knowing when to stop.

PHOTOGRAPH CREDITS

With Frederick Franklin and Alexandra Danilova: Globe Photos

With Bill "Bojangles" Robinson: Lou Layne

With Steve Allen: CBS Photo Archive

With Rosalind Russell: Empire Photographs

Age six, with the R.M. doll: Jerry Saltsberg & Associates

The *Mama* show and Hanson family photographs: CBS Photo Archive

Kenneth and Blake: © 1973 Eva Rubinstein

Blake Morgan, 1997 *Anger's Candy* album photo: Frank W. Ockenfels III

Women Against Pornography March: Jim Anderson/Black Star

Sisterhood Is Global contributors: Robin Platzer, Twin Images

The 1990 *Mother Jones* cover: *Mother Jones* magazine (Nov/Dec 1990)

Incidental snapshots: Private collection of the Author

Index